bohemian:
a person, typically one with artistic
or intellectual aspirations,
who lives an unconventional life.

Artful Lives

Edward Weston, Margrethe Mather,
and the Bohemians of Los Angeles

BETH GATES WARREN

THE J. PAUL GETTY MUSEUM
LOS ANGELES

Published by the J. Paul Getty Museum, Los Angeles
Getty Publications
1200 Getty Center Drive, Suite 500
Los Angeles, California 90049-1682
www.gettypublications.org

Dinah Berland, *Editor*
Jim Drobka, *Designer*
Anita Keys, *Production Coordinator*

Printed in China

Library of Congress Cataloging-in-Publication Data

Warren, Beth Gates.
  Artful lives : Edward Weston, Margrethe Mather,
and the Bohemians of Los Angeles / Beth Gates
Warren.
    p. cm.
  Includes bibliographical references and index.
  ISBN 978-1-60606-070-4 (hardcover)
  1. Weston, Edward, 1886-1958. 2. Mather,
Margrethe. 3. Weston, Edward, 1886-1958—Friends
and associates. 4. Photographers—United States—
Biography. 5. Los Angeles (Calif.)—Intellectual
life—20th century. I. Title. II. Title: Edward Weston,
Margrethe Mather, and the Bohemians of Los Angeles.
  TR139.W365 2011
  779'.9979494—dc22
                        2010051328

Front jacket: Edward Weston (American, 1886-1958),
  Epilogue (Margrethe Mather) (detail, fig. 49), 1919
Back jacket: Margrethe Mather (American
  1886-1952), Edward Weston (detail, fig. 68), 1921
Frontispiece: Imogen Cunningham (American,
  1883-1976), *Edward and Margrethe 3*, 1922.
  Gelatin silver print. Image courtesy of the
  Imogen Cunningham Trust © 1922, 2010 Imogen
  Cunningham Trust. www.ImogenCunningham.com

Contents

Preface

In writing about an artist's career many biographers choose to concentrate on that period of time when the artist's work reaches an apogee of maturity and sophistication. However, the exploratory phase of an artist's life, as he or she attempts to establish an identity and define a future direction, is often just as important and, in many ways, more interesting. That is what inspired me to begin my study of Edward Weston's years in Los Angeles, the city where the noted photographer lived from 1906 until 1923 and where he launched his career.

The seminal imagery Weston produced during those years has long been overlooked, even dismissed—perhaps most emphatically by the photographer himself. As a result, most of the critical appreciation of his work has been focused on the iconic photographs he made between 1924 and the early 1940s, while he was living in Mexico and Carmel-by-the-Sea in Northern California. Of course, those images could not have been created without what had come before.

Soon after beginning my research, I discovered that surprisingly little primary documentation from Edward Weston's Los Angeles years still exists. To my dismay, I learned that in the mid-1920s he had destroyed most of his correspondence and diary entries from the first decade of his career. Strangely though, after intentionally jettisoning so much of his early history, Weston took great pains to save comparable documents from the rest of his career. That fact piqued my curiosity, leading me to wonder what had motivated him to ruthlessly delete part of his past but then carefully preserve the rest. As I began to review the photographs he had created in his Southern California studio, I decided they were the clues that might allow me to unwind the shroud of opacity he had so tenaciously and effectively wrapped around his early career.

Each image became a rebus in a jumbled and perplexing pictorial puzzle, attesting to various personal contacts, implying a myriad of deeper connections, provoking a flood of questions, suggesting that the story could, in fact, be told. I convinced myself that all I had to do was devote enough time and energy to order the photographs in some logical fashion, flesh out the personalities involved, and place that information into the appropriate historical context. Challenging but not impossible. Then, before I knew it, an entire decade flew by as I assimilated and expanded on the information gleaned from those photographs.

Very early on I realized that wherever Edward Weston was during his early Los Angeles years, Margrethe Mather was also, and frequently she was leading the way. Known primarily as a model in many of Weston's early images, she was also a photographer. However—aside from a smattering of comments in Weston's later journals, a few insightful paragraphs authored by photography historian Nancy Newhall, an abbreviated memoir by one of Mather's close friends, and a brief essay describing some of her accomplishments—almost nothing had been written about her. I soon understood why.

Her life and career proved to be much more of a mystery than Weston's, and uncovering her past, a far greater challenge to my skills as an art historian. Except for a handful of notes sent by Mather to Weston, there were no primary documents at all. As I continued my search, however, a few nuggets of information began to surface, and the more I learned about Mather, the more impossible it became to separate her from Weston, either personally or professionally. I discovered that Mather had been extraordinarily talented, and that her life and activities had coincided with Weston's for an entire decade. I came to believe that during the years of their association, their influence and contributions had been more or less equal. Thus, this book necessarily became *their* story.

Then, as I studied the photographs Weston and Mather had created, I began to understand that many of their portrait subjects had played vital roles in their lives. A deeper knowledge of this motley assortment of people became critical, because often it was their correspondence and journals and memoirs that filled in the blanks between Weston's and Mather's images. Quite unexpectedly I found myself learning about anarchists and hobos, silent movie actors and muckrakers, but in the process of educating myself about Weston's and Mather's friends, much valuable and previously unknown information about the two photographers' interests and activities came to light. Perhaps most important, my research led me to conclude that Weston and Mather had not worked in isolation, as many historians had previously thought. Rather they were part of a circle of avant-garde personalities who sought each other out for companionship and encouragement, and whose sphere of influence encompassed such far-flung locales as New York City's Greenwich Village, Cape Cod's Provincetown, and Chicago's Hyde Park, as well as the small but vigorous artistic community that existed in Los Angeles.

Finally, as I attempted to contextualize this unruly group of bohemians, the City of the Angels (as it was then called) loomed large, an amorphous but all-encompassing presence demanding its fair share of attention and recognition. I realized that the exhilaratingly beautiful backdrop of early twentieth-century Los Angeles, with its incomparably sunny weather, nefariously corrupt politics, and exuberant embrace of eccentricity, had provided a totally unique environment in which Weston, Mather, and their friends were both nurtured and challenged as they struggled to make their mark and develop their artistic identities. And even though a majority of the photographs Weston and Mather had created in that upstart of a city were portraits made inside a studio, those images were inextricably linked to a very specific sense of place that required further investigation and explanation.

In 2001 I curated and wrote the companion essay for a traveling exhibition of Weston and Mather photographs organized by Karen Sinsheimer, Curator of Photography at the Santa Barbara Museum of Art. As a result of that exhibition and its accompanying publication, interest in Weston and Mather's collaboration grew and more of their early photographs surfaced, adding to a continuously expanding accumulation of information. The next few years were devoted to distilling and interpreting that information until, bit by tantalizing bit, the story of Edward Weston's "lost years" and his interactions with Margrethe Mather began to unfold.

It is my hope that readers of this book will come away enlightened about the evolution of Weston and Mather's personal relationship and professional partnership, and with a far better understanding of the milieu in which the two photographers worked and the impact their fascinating circle of acquaintances had on their lives. I would also like to think that devotees of photography will be prompted to ponder just how much of the relatively short, but surprisingly labyrinthine, history of the medium has been forgotten, or intentionally obscured. B.G.W.

Note to the Reader
Margrethe Mather's name was frequently misspelled by her friends and acquaintances. Variant spellings of her name have been reproduced here exactly as they appear in the original documents.

Prologue

He was going to be famous. Of that Edward Weston was unshakably confident. As he stood on the platform in Chicago's Union Station, waiting to board the westbound train that would take him to Los Angeles, the shriek of metal on metal and the shower of burning embers that accompanied the steam engine's approach would have surely brought to mind newspaper accounts of the horrific earthquake and fire that had leveled San Francisco a few weeks earlier. Most people would have been reluctant to set out for California on the heels of such a devastating disaster, but Weston was undeterred.

The year was 1906, and he had only recently celebrated his twentieth birthday. His face was still quite boyish, and he stood a scant five feet four inches tall. He possessed a powerful physique, however, with broad shoulders and well-muscled arms and legs, due to countless hours spent training his body to excel at competitive sports. His ginger-colored hair was closely trimmed and smartly slicked back, leaving little camouflage for a prematurely receding hairline. Coffee-colored eyes were Weston's most arresting feature. Wide-set and warmly expressive, they glowed with an intensity that diverted attention away from an insubstantial chin. His mouth, shaped like a classic cupid's bow, was also compelling, because it curved upward at the corners into a parenthetical half-smile that gave him a permanently pleasant, slightly amused expression.

Desperate for a change after two decades spent in the same city, Weston had no regrets about abandoning his promising job as a salesman at a local department store. His older sister, who had moved to Southern California two years earlier, had long been urging him to put aside a portion of his paychecks in order to afford the train fare to Los Angeles. Her breezy letters had filled his head with visions of fragrant orange blossoms, succulent strawberries, pristine beaches, and snowcapped mountains, so he was fully primed to shed his old life and assume the configuration of a new one. Now that the moment had arrived to follow Horace Greeley's sage advice, "Go west, young man," Weston was filled with the bravado that comes of a sheltered youth, and as he departed his hometown he was convinced that someday people would know the name Edward Weston.

Not long after Weston left Chicago, Margrethe Mather purchased a rail ticket in Salt Lake City. Her upbringing had been far less conventional than his, and her exit from Utah, both hasty and necessary. At least that was how she later described the circumstances of her departure to a close friend. Although her confidant knew she was prone to invention and often exhibited an undeniable flair for the dramatic, he believed every word she said, because her anecdotes contained just enough sordid detail to lend them credibility. She undoubtedly felt justified in exercising a certain amount of poetic license by the time she spun her tales. After all, like so many others, she had headed west to reinvent herself, so why let the mundane dreariness of her childhood years obscure the person she had since become?

It was Mather's good fortune to possess a delicate beauty, a ferocious intelligence, and an innate drive for perfection, all of which allowed her to fend off her personal demons and acquire the lofty aspirations that eventually led her down an auspicious, if unconventional, path. Certainly no one could have predicted that Margrethe Mather would become an accomplished photographer; as her confidant later dryly observed, "Many artists, in a sense, become prostitutes. For a prostitute to become an artist is, I believe, much rarer."[1]

When Edward Weston and Margrethe Mather first encountered each other in 1913 neither foresaw that their pairing, both as colleagues and as lovers, would make photographic history, or that the wide array of talented people they were about to befriend and photograph would one day be remembered as vivid, archetypal characters in the history of early twentieth-century America. Even though their feelings for each other ran deep, their relationship was undermined by the multiple burdens of obligation, guilt, poverty, ambition, and jealousy, and when their collaboration finally came to an end, the result was bitterness and disappointment on both sides.

In fact, it was very soon after the dissolution of their business arrangement that Weston purposefully deleted much of his early history, and with it, virtually every trace of Mather's presence in his life. It was a hasty decision Weston came to regret, and many years later, as he readied his journals for publication, he attempted to make amends by recalling Mather as "the first important person" in his life.[2] But it was much too little and far too late.

Over the past half-century Mather's reputation has faded completely away, while Weston's has grown exponentially. Today he is rightly remembered as one of the most accomplished and influential photographers of the twentieth century, and she is all but forgotten. Since Weston's death in 1958, photography historians, prompted by Mather's appearance in so many of his early photographs, have occasionally speculated about her origins and the role she played in Weston's life, but because so little written documentation remained as evidence, the details of their relationship were generally believed to be irretrievable.

Fortunately that assumption proved to be incorrect, although piecing together the facts has required several years of research. Using newspaper archives, articles and reviews from long-defunct photography periodicals, census and military records, city directories, birth and death certificates, immigration and naturalization documents, correspondence among Weston's and Mather's friends and colleagues, interviews with various family members, and, of course, the existing photographs as sources of previously undiscovered information, the framework of Weston and Mather's years together gradually began to take shape. The history of their shared endeavors and intertwined friendships, played out against the dynamic backdrop of the City of the Angels during the early decades of the last century, has now been reconstructed, and their story can be told at last.

Edward Weston— A Midwestern Upbringing, 1886–1905

The photographer Edward Henry Weston was born into a world awash in sunlight on March 24, 1886, in the small town of Highland Park, Illinois, on the shores of Lake Michigan, about two dozen miles north of Chicago.[1] He was the third generation of Westons to call Illinois his home. His grandfather, Edward Payson Weston,[2] had arrived there from Maine in 1869 to become the first principal of Ferry Hall, a female seminary in a tiny settlement called Lake Forest, which bordered Highland Park on the north.[3] He had been recruited for the position by Reverend James Taylor, Lake Forest's Presbyterian minister, whose sisters had attended a school under Weston's direction.[4] A graduate of Bowdoin College and a well respected educator, Professor Weston was a former editor of the *Portland Transcript*, as well as an ex-superintendent of the Common Schools of Maine. He had been twice married, but his three children were all by his deceased first wife, Mary E. Burbank.[5]

After his arrival in Lake Forest, Professor Weston lost no time in instituting a rigorous course of study at Ferry Hall, organizing a curriculum that included classical history, trigonometry, and art appreciation.[6] His intention was to make the school a place where adolescent girls would be educated, as well as "finished." His first class consisted of sixty-six students, including a young lady named Alice Jeannette Brett of Farmington, Maine, who would one day become his daughter-in-law.[7] Weston soon became known as a liberal educator who took a surprisingly permissive view toward the transgressions of his young pupils. He was highly regarded within the Lake Forest community, even though an 1894 article recounting Ferry Hall's history noted:

> He [Weston] was an educator of great ability, and from this point of view the school was highly successful....[However] then even more than now the principal, to be highly successful, needed to be a good business man....Prof. Weston was not a financier. The work he found here was a burden instead of a pleasure, and in '76 he withdrew.[8]

In spite of Professor Weston's apparent lack of business acumen, he left Ferry Hall to become Superintendent of Highland Hall, another female academy, operating out of a refurbished Victorian-era resort hotel in neighboring Highland Park.[9] That same year, his only son, Dr. Edward Burbank Weston, a gynecologist and obstetrician, joined his father on the Highland

Hall board of directors.[10] Young Dr. Weston had married his father's former pupil, Alice Brett, in 1874, after completing his medical training at Rush Medical College in Chicago and his residency requirements at Long Island College Hospital in Brooklyn, New York.[11] A few months later the couple had returned to Illinois so that Dr. Weston could open his medical practice in Highland Park, and it was there, on March 18, 1877, that Alice bore their first child, a daughter named Mary Jeannette (nicknamed May or Mazie).

In October 1879 Professor Weston died quite unexpectedly, at the age of 60, from typhoid-related pneumonia,[12] leaving behind considerable confusion and financial complications due to his partial ownership interest in Highland Hall. Foreclosure proceedings were initiated against his estate, and much of his personal property was sold to repay debts.[13] Once those unpleasant money matters were resolved, however, Highland Hall continued under new management, and young Dr. Weston and his wife remained in their handsome, three-story, gabled house at 286 Laurel Avenue for another seven years.[14] In March 1886 they celebrated the arrival of their second child.

The baby—Edward Henry Weston—was delivered by his own father in the house on Laurel Avenue.[15] By the time his son arrived, Dr. Weston's medical practice had been established for a decade, and he was well known locally, not only as a physician but also as an archery enthusiast, an officer in the local Masonic Lodge,[16] and a breeder of prize-winning poultry.[17] The Weston family enjoyed a comfortable life in Highland Park, but with fewer than a thousand residents, the town offered limited career opportunities, so a few months after his son's birth Dr. Weston packed up his wife and children and relocated them to 3225 Vernon Avenue, in the residential area known as Douglas, on Chicago's South Side.[18]

Dr. Weston's career flourished, and by 1891 the Westons could afford a move further south to 3975 Drexel Boulevard, a wide, impressive thoroughfare lined with gracious homes in the fashionable neighborhood of Oakland.[19] There the family lived in upper-middle-class comfort while Dr. Weston made the daily commute, via the Cottage Grove cable car, to his office at 65 Randolph Street, on the periphery of the downtown business district encircled by elevated train tracks known as the Loop. The Westons' new home was situated only twenty blocks north of Jackson Park, where construction of the White City, as the 1893 Columbian Exposition complex would come to be known, had just gotten under way. The family quickly settled into the upwardly mobile lifestyle of typical South Side Chicagoans, but it was only a few short months before their lives were turned upside down.

In July 1891 Alice gave birth to a third child who died almost immediately.[20] The following winter, as a relentless cold snap held Chicago in its frozen grasp, Alice fell victim to the pneumonia epidemic that was raging through the city. After two weeks of fighting for her life, she took her last, labored breath on January 25, 1892.[21] Edward later recalled the trauma: "My mother died when I was five and all that returns to me of her are a pair of black piercing eyes—burning eyes—maybe burning with fever."[22]

FIGURE 1. Chester P. Rice (American, act. late 19th century), *Edward Weston with Sunflower*, ca. 1892. Gelatin silver print, 12.5 × 9.6 cm (4⅞ × 3¾ in.). Collection of the author

At the time of Mrs. Weston's death, May Weston was fourteen, nine years older than her little brother. Because of the age difference between the two siblings, May was quick to assume the maternal role in Edward's life, establishing a steadfast, lifelong bond of loyalty between them. She later teased her brother about his mischievous behavior. "Do you remember how you used to sit on the curb in front of our house on Drexel Boulevard, having put a good-sized rat under your cap," she wrote, "and the passers-by would look with the greatest astonishment at your cap to see it moving about on your head. You never cracked a smile."[23]

In the fall of 1892 Edward entered Oakland Grammar School, a block away from his home, and gradually a sense of well-being returned to the devastated Weston family (see fig. 1). However, this quietude lasted only until the spring of 1895, when Dr. Weston remarried. His new wife, Minnie D. Randolph, was a widow with an elderly mother and a son four years older than Edward, and all three step-relatives moved into the Weston household.[24] These additions to the family greatly discomfited Edward and May, who sought refuge from the unwelcome intruders by withdrawing to the second floor of their spacious home.[25] In this way they endured the situation for several months, but when May married John Hancock Seaman on November 27, 1897,[26] and left her childhood behind, eleven-year-old Edward was forced to cope with his unwanted step-relatives all by himself.

To add to the tension resulting from the merger of the two families, between 1897 and 1900 the Westons relocated four more times within the immediate neighborhood, finally settling at 3847 Langley Avenue.[27] Edward's life was considerably disrupted during this period, and his growing disdain for formal schooling may have been a result of his tumultuous, unhappy home environment.

SALVATION During the summer of 1902, Dr. Weston sent a gift to his sixteen-year-old son, then on holiday with relatives in Michigan. It was a camera—a Kodak Bulls-Eye #2—which produced negatives 3½ inches square, together with an instruction booklet. An enthusiastic Edward immediately wrote an endearing letter of thanks:

> Dear papa,
> Received camera in good shape. It's a dandy....Took a snap at the chickens. I think it's a good one as I was right near them....It makes me feel bad to think of the fine snaps I could have taken if I had had the Kodak the other day. I was within six feet of two swallows perched on a wire fence. It would have made the prettiest imaginable picture.... I suppose I'll have plenty of chances and I'm going to wait for good subjects.[28]

Photography turned out to be Edward's salvation. The lonely teenager detested school so vehemently he often refused to go. In a snapshot Edward made of the front facade of his former grammar school, a nearby billboard, presumably advertising Bull Durham Tobacco, is cropped so as to reveal only the word "*Bull.*"[29] This juxtaposition reveals much about Edward's cynical opinion of traditional education. He later confessed:

> Schools, I only remember as dreary wastelands. I cannot believe that I learned anything of value in school, unless it be the will to rebel, to "play hookey" which I have done on numerous occasions since those first days with my camera in the snow-covered Chicago parks: "played hookey" from my first job, from my own business, from my family life—not without some sense of responsibility, but never with after-regrets.[30]

Instead of concentrating on his studies, Edward found solace in his pursuit of "good subjects" for the camera he kept always close at hand. He trekked through the neighborhoods near his home and rode the streetcar to the outskirts of the city, braving the frigid temperatures of the Chicago winters to record the subtle textures of the frosty prairies and celebrating the return of spring in tender, lyrical woodland scenes. He attended his first photography salon exhibition at the Art Institute of Chicago, where he admired the work of Rudolf Eickemeyer and Louis Fleckenstein.[31]

He also honed his athletic prowess, developing enough strength and stamina to excel at sprinting and boxing, and under his father's tutelage he took up archery.[32] Compulsively neat and organized, Edward already exhibited the self-discipline and willingness to sacrifice that would stand him in good stead in later years. Then, around 1903, his world was again disrupted when his sister and her husband announced they were moving to California. Although May corresponded frequently with her little brother in cheerfully affectionate letters, she missed him terribly and agonized over his dissatisfaction with life in Chicago. She wanted her sibling to come west for a visit as soon as possible, and she tried her best to convince him that he, too, should settle in California:

> Save up your pennies—spring is here and you must be thinking about your vacation in California. Never mind what you wear, grease your pants and slide here if you have to....The ocean is waiting to be bathed in....The mountains are waiting to be climbed—strawberries are in bloom....
>
> This is the place for you without an atom of a doubt. Every year you spend back east is so much lost to you. This is the country you have been longing for.[33]

Soon after May's departure, a rebellious Edward dropped out of high school and went to live with his mother's brother, Theodore, and his wife, Emma. Theodore (Uncle Teddy) Brett was employed at Chicago's premiere department store, Marshall Field and Company, as a manager in the dry goods department, and it was through Brett's connections that his seventeen-year-old nephew was hired, first as a "rabbit," or errand boy,[34] and then as a salesman earning about ten dollars a week. Edward's department store stint lasted almost three years and held substantial promise, but in spite of his mother's dying wish that he become a businessman like her brother, he was determined not to pursue a career in retail sales. Around the middle of 1905, Edward decided it was time to make his move. Spurred on by words of encouragement from his sister, he began putting aside small sums of money from his paltry weekly paychecks in order to purchase a train ticket to California.

Weston Takes On Tropico, 1906–1912

Unfazed by the devastating earthquake that destroyed San Francisco on April 18, 1906, Edward departed Chicago the following month, arriving in Los Angeles on May 29.[1] He stayed with May and John Seaman (see fig. 2) in the small, rustic bungalow they had built in rural Tropico, a few miles north of the city, and almost immediately Edward made the decision not to return to the Midwest. Through his brother-in-law, an electrical engineer, he obtained a job as a surveyor with the San Pedro, Los Angeles, and Salt Lake Railroad, and during the summer of 1907, while traveling for the railroad, he continued his hobby of photography, carrying a $3^{1}/_{4} \times 5^{1}/_{2}$ inch Kodak so he could snap a few photographs along the way.[2]

The physical hardships of the surveyor's life held no attraction for Edward, however, and within a few months he was back in Tropico, living with his sister and her family while he attempted to support himself as an itinerant photographer. He purchased a used postcard camera and canvassed for clients door-to-door, "photographing brides, pets, everything from the newborn in its cradle to the corpse in its coffin."[3] May and John Seaman introduced him to a number of their friends, and Edward discovered he especially enjoyed the company of one of his sister's closest chums, Flora Chandler.

Like Edward, Flora was descended from New England stock by way of Chicago. Her father was Cornelius C. Chandler, originally of Concord, New Hampshire.[4] As a young man, Cornelius had established himself in the contracting and building business, first in Syracuse, New York, and then in Chicago, where he prospered during the post–Civil War boom years and especially after the great Chicago conflagration of 1871. In 1899 Cornelius and his wife, the former Ann Elizabeth Denick, moved to California, and Cornelius opened a real estate business in Tropico, a tiny settlement full of citrus groves ripe with development opportunities. The Chandlers were civic-minded property owners, so when a new tile factory was promoted in town, they purchased a twenty-acre parcel along the Southern Pacific Railroad tracks, which they proceeded to donate to the Pacific Tile and Terra Cotta Company as a building site. This magnanimous gesture firmly established the family as generous benefactors of the local community.

By the time Edward Weston arrived in Los Angeles, the Chandler name was already closely linked to Southern California real estate development, due in large part to the actions of Harry Chandler, one of the most prominent men in early twentieth-century Los Angeles.

FIGURE 2. Unidentified photographer, *Edward Weston with Mary (May) Weston Seaman on His Shoulder*, ca. 1906. Gelatin silver print, 9.5 × 6.9 cm (3³/₄ × 2³/₄ in.). Dayton, Ohio, Dayton Art Institute, 1994.29

Undoubtedly because of their shared surname, it has often been assumed that Harry and Cornelius Chandler were cousins; that was not the case, however.

By 1906 Harry Chandler, editor of the *Los Angeles Times* and son-in-law of *Times* publisher, Colonel Harrison Gray Otis, had already been instrumental in shepherding through many pieces of legislation that would have a dramatic impact on the future of his chosen city. Chandler and his father-in-law were currently engaged in a vicious and effective battle against organized labor in Southern California, and Chandler was actively involved in real estate development. In fact, over the past decade he had accrued a well-deserved reputation as one of the most cunning and ruthless businessmen in the country, bent on building himself an empire by uniting raw acreage, one of the most abundant natural resources in Southern California, with potable water, one of the scarcest.[5]

FIGURE 3. Unidentified photographer, Edward Weston and Flora Chandler, early July 1907. Gelatin silver print, 8.1 × 11.6 cm (3³/₁₆ × 4⁹/₁₆ in.). Los Angeles, J. Paul Getty Museum, 86.XA.716.8

But despite Harry Chandler's New Hampshire origins and his real estate interests, the only male ancestor he and Cornelius shared in common had lived two hundred years and ten generations before either man was born.[6] Perhaps the myth that has since grown up around Harry's and Cornelius's close kinship was first nurtured by Cornelius himself. His real estate business was a highly successful but much smaller enterprise than Harry's, so he might have thought that implying a blood bond between them would bolster his own prestige and clout within the Los Angeles community, or perhaps referring to Harry Chandler as a cousin simply began as a family joke that, with the passage of time, became accepted as fact.

Flora, the youngest of Cornelius's six children, had accompanied her parents on their move to Tropico, and soon after May Weston Seaman's arrival there, the two women became acquainted. Even before Edward left Chicago, his sister was praising Flora in her letters to him, calling her "one of the finest girls I ever saw"[7] and declaring, "Flora Chandler and I are getting to be great friends."[8] The moment her little brother arrived in California, May saw to it that he and Flora were introduced. At the time of their first meeting, Edward was twenty and Flora was seven years his senior. Generously proportioned, standing almost a head taller than Edward, and endowed with a theatrical temperament, Flora was an attractively statuesque, tempestuous young woman (see fig. 3). But even more important, she had been vetted by the most influential person in Edward's life—his beloved sister.

FIGURE 4. Unidentified photographer, Retouching Studio of Photographer A. Louis Mojonier, Los Angeles, showing Edward Weston seated on left, ca. 1910. Platinum print, 9.5 × 14.3 cm (3¾ × 5⅝ in.). Los Angeles, J. Paul Getty Museum, 86.XA.715.184

SETTLING DOWN   By the autumn of 1907 Weston was already contemplating marriage to Flora and a career as a photographer. However, there was no professional photography school west of the Mississippi River, so in early 1908 Edward returned to his home state to attend the Illinois College of Photography in Effingham, a small town in southeastern Illinois.[9] The school, which unhesitatingly promoted itself in the photography trade publications as "the leading institution of its kind in the world,"[10] was run by Lewis Horace Bissell, an old friend of Weston's father.[11] Edward tore through the nine-month course of study in only six months, but when Bissell insisted he pay tuition for the full term, Weston indignantly refused.[12] He had no intention of succumbing to Bissell's demands, which he considered grossly unfair, and he returned to California sans diploma.[13]

Even though he lacked an official document attesting to his skills, by the end of 1908 Weston had found employment with George Steckel, a well-known photographer who specialized in portraits of children, with a studio at 336½ South Broadway in downtown Los Angeles.[14] Weston and Steckel did not see eye to eye, however, so a few months later Weston left Steckel's employ for an opportunity at the rival Hemenway Studio. That job lasted exactly one day.[15] Finally Edward settled into a position with A. Louis Mojonier, another long-established portrait photographer, who had recently opened a new studio in the Auditorium Building at the northeast corner of Fifth and Olive (see fig. 4), overlooking downtown's Central Park (later

FIGURE 5. Edward Weston (American, 1886–1958), *Home of Edward and Flora Weston, Tropico,* ca. 1908. Gelatin silver print, 10.5 × 16.2 cm (4¹/₈ × 6³/₈ in.). Los Angeles, J. Paul Getty Museum, 86.XA.714.23

renamed Pershing Square).[16] Weston chose his three employers judiciously, for they were the most prominent photographers in Los Angeles. Steckel, Hemenway, and Mojonier portraits dominated the *Los Angeles Times* society and entertainment pages, and Weston must have realized that an affiliation with their studios would enhance his professional credentials and provide him with many useful contacts.

On January 30, 1909, Edward Weston and Flora Chandler were married in Tropico,[17] where he had recently finished constructing a small bungalow on land owned by Flora's parents (see fig. 5). The property bordered the acreage the Chandlers had donated to the tile factory, and it sat adjacent to a dirt lane the young couple jokingly dubbed Weston Avenue.[18] Fifteen months later, on April 26, 1910, Flora gave birth to their first child, Edward Chandler Weston (whom they would call Chandler).[19] Weston proudly took dozens of photographs of his wife and baby, including his first female nude, an image of Flora, made when she was about four months pregnant with Chandler.[20]

A second son, Theodore Brett Weston (whom they would call Brett) was born December 16, 1911.[21] The young couple devoted much attention to their two cherubic children, preserving Edward's charming portraits of his tiny sons in albums lovingly arranged and captioned by Flora.[22] Weston's family time was already becoming quite limited, however; a few months before his second son's birth he had decided to leave behind the world of steady paychecks and commuting to downtown Los Angeles in order to open his own photography studio.

THE TROPICO STUDIO   At 113 North Brand Boulevard,[23] a few blocks away from his Tropico home, Weston erected another modest, Craftsman-style bungalow, romantic and picturesque in the style of the period. In its earliest days the studio had various names, including the Little Studio[24] and the Bungalow Studio,[25] but within a few months it became known as the Weston Studio. Edward reluctantly installed one of the newfangled telephone devices, a modern convenience he begrudged because it interrupted his concentration, and advised potential customers that he could be reached at "Sunset Phones: Studio 11-J; Residence 25-J."[26]

The studio, which was built on another piece of property belonging to Flora's parents, was situated very near the street, on a lot 65 feet wide by 160 feet deep, located approximately 100 feet from the northwest corner of Brand Boulevard and Tropico Avenue.[27] The building's footprint occupied a rectangle roughly 20 feet wide by 15 feet deep,[28] and its board and batten exterior was saturated with a dark brown stain. Across the rear Weston constructed a porch covered by a fanciful overhang supported on rough-hewn tree branches. A dovecote built into the eaves was an artistically rustic touch.

During the first rainy season, visitors had to slog through ankle-deep mud to reach the front door, but Weston soon began making improvements to the property. He paved a walkway to the boulevard, planted acacia trees and floral borders of daisies and nicotiana, installed an ivy-festooned arbor around the front door, and cultivated a grassy lawn. Very quickly the building nestled into its surroundings (see fig. 6). To promote his portrait business, Weston used the studio's bucolic setting as a selling point. One early advertisement read, "Make an appointment NOW with the WESTON STUDIO—a quiet retreat, away from the noise and confusion of the city," and he reassured potential clients that "Camera Portraits by Weston Are Chemically Tested for Absolute Permanence."[29]

The interior of Weston's studio consisted of one room separated into three areas by freestanding partitions. Upon entering the front door, visitors found themselves in a four-by-six-foot reception area which opened into a much larger, L-shaped studio space.[30] The floor was covered by lengths of stained pine boards, and the crudely finished walls were disguised by a series of panels upholstered in gray, burlap-like fabric. Concealed behind one section of panels were the darkroom and storage areas. At the back of the room, opposite the front entrance, was a pair of large, multipaned French doors that faced west to the rear garden. The ceiling of the studio stretched all the way to the peaked roofline, where an eyebrow window served as a skylight, bathing the interior space with a soft wash of illumination. Decorative props included a curvilinear, horsehair settee; a side chair or two; a chest of drawers; an arched mirror; a few framed artworks; and a variety of small trunks and vases.[31]

A few yards from the studio's front door, the Pacific Electric commuter train bisected Brand Boulevard and made the six-mile trip to downtown Los Angeles in approximately twenty minutes for a fare of fifteen cents.[32] This proximity to convenient public transportation ensured that an ever-changing audience would see the Craftsman-style sign, "EDWARD HENRY

FIGURE 6. Edward Weston, Edward Weston's Studio, Tropico (rear view), ca. 1915. Gelatin silver print, 11.9 × 20.3 cm (4 11/16 × 8 in.). Los Angeles, J. Paul Getty Museum, 86.XM.719.27

FIGURE 7. Edward Weston, Edward Weston's Studio, Tropico (front view), ca. 1920. Gelatin silver print, 18.7 × 23.8 cm (7 3/8 × 9 3/8 in.). Los Angeles, J. Paul Getty Museum, 84.XM.229.30

WESTON PHOTOGRAPHS," hanging over the ivy-draped entrance (see fig. 7). There was one drawback, however. In 1911 Tropico was a small burg of only fifteen hundred people, quite removed from the hustle and bustle of the city. Weston's sister had serious misgivings about his choice of location, which she later recalled in a letter to her brother. "When you had left Mojonier and decided to open a studio for yourself, I asked you [why] in such a small town? Why not in Los Angeles? And you replied, 'Sis, I'm going to make my name so famous that it won't matter where I live.'"[33] Weston obviously remained convinced that he could realize his ambition, even as a twenty-five-year-old with a wife and two small children to support.

TRANSITIONS   Within months of opening his studio, the world outside Weston's front door began to undergo a dramatic shift. Since his arrival in California, Tropico had almost tripled in size, and housing lots were selling for six hundred and fifty dollars.[34] Brand Boulevard was fast evolving into the main north–south traffic corridor linking Los Angeles to Tropico, Glendale, and other communities of the San Gabriel and San Fernando Valleys. Dusty, unpaved Tropico Avenue was being transformed into an extension of Los Feliz Boulevard, an important east–west artery that provided ready access to the bean fields and orange groves of Hollywood, the hills of Beverly, the canyons and palisades of Santa Monica, and the beaches along the Pacific Ocean.

In 1913 the village of Tropico began construction on a handsome, new City Hall, located one block south of Weston's studio, and almost before he knew it, he found himself in the midst of a thriving business district, at the crossroads of two major thoroughfares. Although these alterations were a boon to his business, Weston was not pleased about the growing congestion and noise that accompanied Tropico's urbanization. He was even more dubious about the usefulness of the automobile, and he resolutely refused to drive one.

Change was in the air, however, and gradually Weston responded by making modifications in his equipment and printing methods, which inevitably led to alterations in the physical appearance of his photographs. His earliest images, taken with a $6\frac{1}{2} \times 8\frac{1}{2}$ inch Seneca camera, fitted out with a Voightlaender & Sons Collinear lens,[35] had been sharply focused and printed in a 5×7 inch format on hard-surfaced, silver-sensitized paper, replicating the method of presentation he had learned at Mojonier's. Many of these early prints were brown-toned, and he often signed them by scratching "WESTON" in large, block letters into the emulsion of the glass plate negative, or by inscribing "Edward Henry Weston" or "E. H. Weston" in a taut, vertical script along the lower right edge of the print or its mount.[36]

But around 1911 he acquired an 11×14 inch view camera fitted with an 18 inch Wollensak Verito,[37] a diffusing lens that allowed him to achieve soft-focus images, accented with chiaroscuro-like highlights, then considered the ultimate in artistic photography. He also began using an elongated, exaggerated calligraphy to carefully draw his signature in the lower right corner of each print. Occasionally he even returned to his earlier habit of photographing out of doors rather than in his studio, using local parks or other scenic spots as backdrops.

FIGURE 8. Edward Weston, *Self-Portrait*, 1911. Gelatin silver print, 22.9 × 17.7 cm (9 × 7 in.). The Audrey and Sydney Irmas Collection, Los Angeles County Museum of Art, AC1992.197.135.

This transition in his work can be seen in a self-portrait in which Weston wears a loose-fitting smock and a neckkerchief as he turns away from the camera to render his profile on film (fig. 8). The image is soft and romanticized in conception and presentation, and it garnered much praise and won first prize in an outdoor portraiture competition in October 1912. Applauded for its "attitude, illumination and modeling," the photograph was described as having been "taken on the top of Mt. Wilson, California, February, 10 A.M.; R. R. Lens; 8-inch; U. S. 16; 2 seconds; Orthonon; pyro-soda; 10 × 12 Royal Bromide; sulphide toned; enlarged about seven diameters from an unretouched negative; shaded during the enlarging. Exposure made with the aid of a ten-yard bulb and tubing."[38] In this self-portrait Weston was not only employing the latest photographic techniques, he was trying out an entirely new persona.

In the meantime, he continued to earn a living from commercial portraiture, specializing in images of children.[39] To achieve the degree of flexibility he needed to successfully photograph active, mobile toddlers, he acquired a $3^{1}/_{4} \times 4^{1}/_{4}$ inch Graflex camera. He also began to produce

FIGURE 9. Edward Weston, *Tropico* (looking west toward the Griffith Park hills, with Pacific Ocean visible on horizon), 1910. Gelatin silver print, 8.7 × 13.8 cm (3 7/16 × 5 7/16 in.). Los Angeles, J. Paul Getty Museum, 86.XM.719.26

highly contrived genre scenes with overtly sentimental, narrative titles typical of the period. One titled *Let's Play Hookey*,[40] which depicts a boy with a fishing pole slung over his shoulder tempting a young scholar away from his studies, recalled his own prodigal youth, while another, *The Far-Away, Dreamy Gaze into Some Distant Fairyland*,[41] features a fetching, two-year-old girl with a charmingly wistful expression.

When he was not making portraits or genre scenes Weston tried his hand at still life and landscape compositions. Usually these images were made for his own enjoyment, although one of his early commercial projects was a series of views produced for a brochure sponsored by the local chapter of the Knights of Pythias—a popular fraternal organization—to promote the pleasures and advantages of living in the small town of Tropico (see figs. 9, 10).[42]

From the moment he became a professional photographer Weston was unabashedly ambitious and willing to work hard for his success. Even before leaving Chicago, he had doggedly submitted his amateur photographs for publication in national camera magazines, but now that he had a reputation and a business to build, he redoubled his efforts to get his photographs published. Between early 1910 and the end of 1912, examples of his work appeared on at least twenty-five occasions in three of the most influential photography periodicals of the period— *The Camera*, originating out of Philadelphia; *Photo-Era*, based in Boston; and *American Photography*, the publishing arm of the New York Camera Club.

FIGURE 10. Unidentified photographer, Edward Weston on Horseback, ca. 1910. Gelatin silver print, 7.9 × 10.2 cm (3 1/8 × 4 in.). Collection of the author

He also contributed an occasional "advice" article in which he gave practical hints to other photographers, both amateur and professional.[43] In one of these articles he recommended that all students of photography should read Professor Arthur Wesley Dow's book, *Composition: A Series of Exercises in Art Structure for the Use of Students and Teachers*. Dow was an influential instructor at Columbia Teacher's College in New York City, and his book was required reading in art classes all across the country.[44] Weston was already quite familiar with Dow's aesthetic theories, which included the Japanese concept of *notan*, or the asymmetrical arrangement of dark and light areas within a composition. This idea of balancing positive and negative space without relying on classical symmetry was one that Weston thought every photographer should understand and employ.

Surprisingly though, even as Weston was busily advising other photographers and promoting himself in the photographic periodicals, he remained aloof from the local photography scene, which consisted chiefly of the Los Angeles Camera Club. Instead he focused his energies on acquiring a national reputation, and with very little time to socialize, he chose to work alone in his small studio for the first two years of its existence, industriously making pictures and writing articles, all the while perfecting his craft. As he struggled to be a responsible breadwinner and, at the same time, achieve recognition as a photographer, he was blissfully unaware that a maelstrom was about to whirl through his life in the person of Margrethe Mather.

Margrethe Mather—
An Inauspicious Start,
1886–1912

argrethe Mather was one of the most controversial and provocative individuals Weston would ever meet, and one of the least transparent. Throughout their association much of her personal history would remain a mystery to him, primarily because she wanted it that way. Margrethe possessed a well-developed talent for obfuscation and a desire to hide her true feelings from those around her, so when she did finally share a few anecdotes of her misspent adolescence with a confidant, she did not allow her imagination to be constrained by fact.

Margrethe's embellished version of her past, as she related it to the artist and writer William (Billy) Justema,[1] was that she had been born in Salt Lake City where, after being left parentless at an early age, she had spent most of her youth in an orphanage. Her most vivid memory from those days was of the scarlet underclothes she had been forced to wear to identify her status as a waif. She was subsequently adopted and raised by a mathematics professor named Mather and his common-law wife, whom she referred to only as Aunt Minnie.

Margrethe told Justema that Professor Mather's ancestors were the famous Puritans Increase and Cotton Mather, the illustrious father and son clergymen who had so zealously instigated and presided over the Salem witch trials in seventeenth-century Massachusetts. Their descendant was himself a severe taskmaster who had little patience with Minnie or her small charge, and the two females lived in a constant state of apprehension, totally dependent on Professor Mather for their livelihood and entirely subject to his erratic disposition. Although Aunt Minnie accepted this unpleasant situation as her lot in life, Margrethe vowed to extricate herself as soon as possible.

As she approached puberty, Margrethe gradually became aware of the power she wielded over the opposite sex. However, those who sought her company were not boys of her own age but a group of married Salt Lake City businessmen who made a habit of teaching adolescent girls to accommodate them sexually in ways that would not technically violate the girls' virginal status. The girls were reimbursed for these services with dollar bills, and were encouraged to promptly spend their fortune on sweets and toys so as to eliminate all incriminating evidence. Taking her cue from Aunt Minnie, who surreptitiously hoarded a few dollars from the grocery money each week to supplement a growing nest egg, Margrethe opted to let her funds accumulate.

After a year or two of pleasuring the local businessmen, Margrethe had saved enough money to buy a train ticket to some faraway destination where, she must have imagined, she would one day create a splendid new life for herself. She continued to add to her cache, carefully hidden inside the china cupboard, until Aunt Minnie discovered the money during a frenzy of spring cleaning. Forced to improvise a hasty explanation, Margrethe threw the wad of bills into the cook stove, declaring it to be worthless play money. When the businessmen learned of the girl's misfortune, and realized their clandestine activities had only narrowly escaped detection, they took up a collection just generous enough to cover a one-way train ticket to California and prevailed upon her to use it. One admirer, in particular, even promised to visit her there. Realizing the time had come to jettison her life in Salt Lake City, Margrethe boarded a train and headed west, looking only toward the future.

Margrethe's first stop was San Francisco, where she rented a room and cast about for employment. Her youthful appearance continued to make her attractive to men who fancied a certain type of liaison, so for a time she was able to support herself on the lustful yearnings of strangers. Confident there were more lucrative opportunities awaiting her elsewhere, however, she soon migrated southward to a nondescript boarding house on a hillside overlooking the heart of downtown Los Angeles. There she established herself on a circuit that revolved around two of the city's most exclusive hotels—the Lankershim, at the southeast corner of Seventh Street and Broadway, and the Alexandria, at the southwest corner of Fifth and Spring streets.[2]

The Alexandria, which had opened its doors in 1905, was the most luxurious hotel in the city. Every prominent person who came to Los Angeles stayed there, and the society pages of local newspapers were bursting with accounts of tea parties and social events held in its plush meeting rooms. Margrethe's strategy was to position herself in the Alexandria's Palm Court, the most fashionable place in town to be seen, where she would sit, demurely dressed in a wide-brimmed straw hat and proper white gloves, and exchange pleasantries with respectable-looking gentlemen, all the while sipping endless glasses of lemonade. Once a suitable prospect had initiated a conversation, she, with a masterful show of feigned innocence, would exert her flirtatious charms, and he, not believing his good fortune at having discovered such a delightfully refined companion, would become yet another conquest in her long list of seductions.

For a few months after her arrival in Los Angeles, Margrethe's favorite Salt Lake City patron continued to supplement her income, but when he finally came west for a reunion he was disappointed to find that the precocious young girl he had known in Utah was now a striking young woman. Although an entirely predictable development, her maturation was not to his liking, and he perfunctorily ended their relationship. From that moment forward, she was on her own, and she spent her time perfecting her ingenue guise and admiring her reflection in the finest shop windows.

At least that was what Margrethe told her friend Billy Justema, and he eagerly absorbed every scandalous word. However, many years later, recounting her confidences in his memoir, he was careful to note that his attempts to substantiate the details of her early years had gone unrewarded.[3] The reasons for his failure were twofold: Margrethe Mather was not her real name and she had been selective—creative even—in sharing her past with him.

Although careful to weave strands of truth into the tales she related to Justema, she had freely sifted through her memories, discarding those that displeased her and inventing new ones that appealed. A few of her embellishments were undoubtedly concocted for dramatic effect, to shock or impress her much younger friend, who was still a teenager when she confided in him. Others were elements in a carefully rehearsed scenario of half-truths, part of a calculated subterfuge she relied on to ameliorate the bitter and painful experiences in her past and disguise the tendency toward recklessness that had so often put her in harm's way.

THE "REAL" MARGRETHE MATHER Margrethe Mather's name was actually Emma Caroline Youngren.[4] She had been born on March 4, 1886, in Salt Lake City,[5] to Gabriel Lundberg Youngren and his wife, Ane Sofie Laurentzen, two young Danish emigrés converted to the Mormon faith by an evangelist sent to Denmark around 1880.[6] During the late nineteenth century the Mormons, also known as Latter-day Saints, enjoyed considerable success proselytizing to Scandinavians, especially those weary of the harsh conditions of a rural existence in an inhospitable climate. The Saints promised prosperity, creature comforts, and salvation to anyone willing to embark on a pilgrimage to America, and many careworn Scandinavians were eager to listen and believe.

Both of Emma Caroline's parents came from Lolland, an island in the southeastern portion of Denmark. Gabriel Youngren, born in 1856 to a Swedish father and a Danish mother, was a seasoned sailor and adventurer who had already crossed the Atlantic nine times before embracing his newfound religion.[7] In 1881 he made one last sea voyage so that he might begin an entirely different kind of life in the Mormons' landlocked, holy city. His future bride, born in 1860, arrived in Utah at approximately the same time.

The two young Danes were married in Logan, Utah, on March 8, 1883, and during the next four years they produced three children—Annie C. (b. August 21, 1884); Emma Caroline (b. March 4, 1886); and James (b. May 2, 1887).[8] The difficult conditions in the rugged frontier town exacted a terrible toll on them when Annie, the firstborn, became ill and died in November 1886. The Youngrens dutifully struggled on until tragedy struck again in March 1889. That month Ane Sofie passed away, one week after giving birth to her fourth child, Peter Alfred,[9] leaving her husband a widower with three young children to raise.

Gabriel Youngren frantically appealed to his mother, who had accompanied her son as far west as Ohio, for assistance in caring for his young family. She agreed to help but only if he would renounce the Mormon religion and rejoin her and other family members in Cleveland. He adamantly refused to accept her ultimatum, but his decision had bitter consequences when his infant son passed away the following July.[10] A few months later Youngren married another young Danish convert to Mormonism named Maren Sophie Kragh. They kept his surviving son, James, with them but at some point during the 1890s they sent his only remaining daughter, Emma Caroline (known as Emmy to her family and friends) to live with her maternal aunt, Rasmine Laurentzen, also a resident of Salt Lake City.

Rasmine Laurentzen had come to Utah after enduring great personal suffering herself. As a young woman she had been impregnated by a wealthy landowner who owned the farm her parents worked in Denmark, and her daughter had grown up under the stigma of illegitimacy.[11] Many years later, in 1881, the landowner had finally agreed to sponsor Laurentzen, her daughter, and her elderly, widowed mother, so they could join the large contingent of Danish Mormons immigrating to America. Following their arrival in Utah, Laurentzen managed to support her daughter and mother by selling newspapers at the Zion's Cooperative Mercantile Institution (ZCMI), the large, Mormon-run general store in the heart of downtown Salt Lake City. It was not until the late 1880s or early 1890s that Laurentzen seized an opportunity to better her circumstances by becoming the live-in housekeeper for a man named Joseph Cole Mather.

Working for Joseph Mather brought Laurentzen trials of a different sort, however, for he was a stern, embittered man. Born in 1824 in Elbridge, New York, Joseph was the son of Judge Hiram Foote Mather and Mary Parsons Cole.[12] Judge Mather, a graduate of Yale College, had served as a New York State Senator before he and his wife and their eight children moved to Niles, Michigan, in 1844, and it was there, in 1856, that their son Joseph married an Englishwoman named Clarissa Lewis.[13] The following year Joseph Mather and his bride relocated to Chicago where their only child, a daughter, was born.[14]

After Judge Mather's wife died in 1858, he followed his son to Chicago, where his reputation for fairness preceded him. As a result, he was soon recruited by a group of prominent Chicago businessmen to act as an arbiter in the planning of a new summer community along the shores of Lake Michigan, north of Chicago.[15] (Thus, in a rather remarkable coincidence, Judge Mather became the person chiefly responsible for the design and incorporation of Lake Forest,[16] the same small town where, eleven years later, Edward Weston's grandfather would preside over Ferry Hall.)

In spite of the Chicago business community's esteem for Judge Mather, and the opportunities that might have come to his son as a result, Joseph Mather decided to leave Illinois in 1864. He and his wife and daughter lived for a time in Nevada, Kansas, Missouri, and Nebraska before finally settling in Salt Lake City in the early 1870s.[17] There Joseph found employment with the Omaha Smelting and Refining Company, but not long after their arrival in Utah his wife, Clarissa, died.[18] Eight years later his daughter also perished.[19]

Approaching the age of sixty, robbed of his loved ones, and dwelling in the midst of a religious community where daily rhythms revolved around very different belief systems than his own, Mather began to feel isolated and angry at the world. Although Emma Caroline would later describe Joseph Mather as a mathematics professor,[20] his real occupation, as characterized in various historical documents, was "metallurgy,"[21] "smelting,"[22] or "mining."[23] But whatever

FIGURE 11. Charles R. Savage (English, 1832–1909), *Emma Caroline Youngren (Margrethe Mather)*, Salt Lake City, ca. 1896. Gelatin silver print on cabinet card mount, 13.9 × 9.8 cm (5¹/₂ × 3⁷/₈ in.). Collection of the author

the exact scope of his professional skills, his expertise would have been in great demand in the mineral-rich frontier town of Salt Lake City, a nexus for dozens of mining operations. As a busy workingman and widower, Joseph Mather needed someone to manage his household, and he turned to Rasmine Laurentzen (called Minnie by her family and friends) to provide that service.

Sometime during the 1890s, Emma Caroline Youngren joined her Aunt Minnie in Joseph Mather's home. Minnie's only daughter, Jensigne, was already married and living elsewhere by the time Emma Caroline was born, so Minnie might have taken in her niece immediately after her sister's untimely death as a welcome replacement for her own absent daughter. Or possibly Emma Caroline remained with her father and stepmother until the latter part of the decade, when Gabriel Youngren lost his job as the manager of a Salt Lake City lumberyard and moved to a small farm a few miles south of town.[24] Whichever household Emma Caroline resided in during her early childhood years, she appears healthy and well-dressed in a photograph taken when she was approximately ten years old (fig. 11).

This portrait, the first known image of Emma Caroline, coincidentally documents one of the most unexpected encounters in American photographic history, because Emma Caroline's likeness was taken by none other than C. R. Savage, the most venerable photographer in Utah. Savage's fame had come approximately twenty-five years earlier, in 1869, when he documented the driving of the Golden Spike at Promontory Point, the ceremony that marked the completion of the first cross-country train route in America. By the time Emma Caroline sat for her portrait in the mid-1890s, Savage was still operating his photography studio, in partnership with his son. Located at 12 and 14 Main Street, the Savage establishment stood directly across the street from the ZCMI store where Minnie Laurentzen had once sold newspapers, and less than a dozen blocks away from both the Mather and Youngren households.[25]

In Savage's portrait Emma Caroline wears a frilly white organdy frock. A few locks of hair curl about her face, while the rest is pulled back and neatly plaited. The little girl appears composed but melancholy as she looks intently at the photographer, her frontal pose softened by the downward tilt of her head and the upward gaze of her eyes. Even at her tender age Emma Caroline had already allied herself with the camera.

TAKEN IN Many discrepancies exist between Emma Caroline's tales of her early life, as related to her friend Billy Justema, and historical fact. For instance, no evidence exists to indicate that she was ever adopted by Joseph Mather, and prevailing customs would suggest she was not. Utah was still a territory in 1889 when Emma Caroline's mother died, and legal adoptions were very rare, even in the more civilized courts of the eastern states, but especially under the territorial governments, which were not bound to uphold the same laws that existed within the ratified states. Furthermore, adoptions occurred only if there was a substantial estate with property to be distributed. Under normal circumstances, an orphaned child would simply be taken in by a relative.

More to the point, however, Emma Caroline was not an orphan. Whether she lived with her father or not, he was very much alive while she was in Salt Lake City, and she was fully aware of his identity. Even though Emma Caroline would later tell Justema that she had spent her early childhood years in an orphanage, if she did it was most likely immediately following her mother's death, as an interim measure until her father could make other arrangements. If she did not, it may have been that adding such an embellishment to her story simply made it more dramatic in the telling.

Additionally, even if Joseph Mather had been legally free to adopt Emma Caroline, there is no reason to think he would have done so. He was a cold, strict, perhaps even abusive, man who did not relish having children in his home.[26] Moreover, Minnie and Emma Caroline were Mormons, and Danish Mormons at that. Although certainly in the majority in Salt Lake City, Mormons had long borne the brunt of discrimination when they had attempted to settle in other parts of the country, primarily because of their belief in polygamy, but Danish Mormons were unwelcome even among fellow Latter-day Saints.

As newly arrived immigrants who had not yet mastered the English language, Danish Mormons tended to keep to themselves within enclaves of their own countrymen, and they became easy targets for those quick to label them ignorant and brutish. Undoubtedly Joseph Mather would have viewed Minnie and her niece as social inferiors, and although Minnie did cohabit Joseph Mather's small home—and perhaps his bed—during the time Emma Caroline lived with them, theirs was not a legally sanctioned union.

One of Emma Caroline's statements to Justema was true, however. Ironically, it was a statement Justema doubted, because he later insinuated that Joseph Mather's claim to famous New England forebears had been based purely on a coincidence of surname. In fact, Joseph did belong to the same family tree that had produced the fire and brimstone duo, Increase and Cotton Mather.[27] Joseph was a sixth-generation descendant from Timothy Mather, Increase's brother and Cotton's uncle, and he might well have inherited some of the same Puritanical zeal that had so effectively motivated his tyrannical relatives in their persecution of the Salem "witches."

Justema also theorized that Emma Caroline must have felt rejected by her father. Although that assumption was probably accurate, it was quite common in the nineteenth century for the female children of a widower to be sent away to boarding schools, or convents, or their maternal relatives, while their father worked, remarried, and produced another family. And Gabriel Youngren did precisely that, eventually siring six more children with his second wife.[28]

Whatever emotional baggage Emma Caroline brought to the unlikely, makeshift family of three, she did reside with Joseph Mather and Rasmine (Minnie) Laurentzen from at least 1900 through mid-1906 in a cramped, four-room, brick "shotgun" house at 844 South West Temple Street.[29] The streetcar line that ran in front of their home provided easy access to the all-important Mormon Temple eight blocks to the north and to nearby Salt Lake High School where Emma Caroline was enrolled from 1900 to 1903. Predictably, her academic record was painfully undistinguished. She was a below-average student who received poor, even failing, marks in some subjects and only mediocre grades in others,[30] and although she attended high school through the spring of her seventeenth year, she never completed the requirements necessary to graduate.[31]

A NEW IDENTITY   From the time her name was first recorded in the 1900 Salt Lake City directory, and continuing through 1903, Emma Caroline Youngren was consistently described as a "student" and "boarder" in Joseph Mather's household. Then, in the 1904, 1905, and 1906 directories, the teenager was inexplicably identified as Emma Mather.[32] The 1905 volume also documented her status as an assistant in the office of Dr. W. H. Hanchett, a physician in the McCornick Building, where Joseph Mather's employer was headquartered.[33] The reasons behind Emma's decision to change her surname remain unknown, but very probably her appropriation of the Mather name, at the same time she was coming of age and striking out on her own, simply reflected her awareness of the advantages to claiming an Anglo-Saxon heritage instead of a Danish one.

By the time the 1907 Salt Lake City directory was published, Emma Caroline Youngren/ Mather's name had disappeared from the rolls,[34] a likely indication that her journey west had begun. However, the circumstances behind her departure from Utah may not have been as colorful as she later led Justema to believe. It could have been her employer's high-mindedness that prompted her migration to California.

Immediately following the 1906 San Francisco earthquake, an urgent call for assistance had gone out to physicians in the western half of the United States,[35] so perhaps it was a mission of mercy that caused Emma Caroline's employer, Dr. Hanchett, to leave Salt Lake City that same year, bound for Oakland,[36] the robust town on the opposite side of San Francisco Bay where most of the refugees had sought temporary shelter.[37] And it seems plausible that Emma Caroline, weary of her familiar surroundings and eager to see California, might have taken the opportunity to accompany him west as his assistant.

However, even though Emma Caroline's departure does not appear to have been abrupt or under duress, as she later maintained, there may have been some truth to her far more salacious version of events, which had her leaving Utah to escape the consequences of an episode of sexual misconduct. Perhaps her misadventure involved her employer, Dr. Hanchett, as the prominent, married businessman, bewitched by his beautiful, young assistant, who abandoned his family and medical practice to follow her west, only to realize that she was no longer the nubile teenager he had dallied with in Salt Lake City.

But both of these scenarios are purely speculative. From the historical record, we know only that Emma Caroline departed Salt Lake City in 1906, not as a sexually precocious adolescent, but as a twenty-year-old office worker with modest ambitions. We know, too, that she had time to anticipate her exit, because shortly before leaving town she sat for another portrait, this one taken by twenty-seven-year-old Charles Monroe, who had opened a photography studio in Salt Lake City earlier that same year.[38] In Monroe's portrait (fig. 12), Emma Caroline wears a formfitting suit adorned by a demure, tatted collar. Her hair is arranged in a soft pompadour, and she holds a single, long-stemmed rose. The only hint of excesses to come is her exuberant felt hat with its cascading ostrich plume. Presumably, Emma Caroline presented Monroe's photograph to her Aunt Minnie as a farewell memento and then promptly vanished.

No evidence has been found to place Emma Caroline in San Francisco or Oakland, or any other Bay Area community, from early 1907 through the end of 1909, leaving her whereabouts during those years undetermined. Her disappearance is understandable, however, especially when one considers that Emma Caroline was reinventing herself long before she ever left Salt Lake City and, for any number of reasons, might have found it desirable to drop out of sight for a time. Her temporary vanishing act only adds a fittingly cryptic flourish to the initial chapter in a life full of shadowy assignations and clandestine rendezvous.

Three years after leaving Salt Lake City Emma Caroline resurfaced, but in the interim she had assumed a wholly new identity, prefacing her borrowed Mather surname with the given

FIGURE 12. Charles Monroe (American, act. ca. 1906–10), Emma Caroline Youngren/Mather (Margrethe Mather), Salt Lake City, ca. 1906. Gelatin silver print (vignetted), 10.2 × 6.4 cm (4 × 2 1/2 in.). Collection of the author

name of her deceased maternal grandmother, Margrethe Pedersen Laurentzen.[39] In this way, the person who had been Emma Caroline Youngren gradually faded away, and Margrethe Mather took her place.[40] She never shared the whole truth about her transformation with even her closest California friends, and certainly not with her extended Utah family, who later recalled her only as "Emmy Youngren, a distant relative who moved to California and became a photographer."[41]

LOFTY PERSPECTIVES   It was in the late spring of 1910 that the newly invented persona of Margrethe Mather made her first public appearance in the historical record. By then she was living in San Francisco, in a small apartment building at 1291 Pine Street inhabited by two men and four other women.[42] When a federal census taker interviewed her on April 22, she demonstrated an indifference to the facts of her life by telling the truth about the place of her birth but professing ignorance about the nationalities of her parents. She also coyly shaved three years off her actual age of twenty-four, and she claimed to be making her living as a "manicurist," a common euphemism for a much older, and far less respectable, profession.[43]

Mather's lodging house was located near the southeast corner of Pine and Hyde streets on the southwestern slope of Nob Hill, in an area that had suffered total destruction during the

1906 earthquake. One block north and six blocks east, at the very summit of the hill, the stone walls of the Fairmont Hotel and the James Flood mansion had been the only Nob Hill structures to survive the violent jolting of the earth and the gas-fed inferno that had followed. The neighboring Victorian and Italianate palaces built by Collis P. Huntington, Leland Stanford, Charles Crocker, and Mark Hopkins, the multimillionaire industrialists known as the Big Four, had been completely incinerated.[44]

The city was quick to rebuild itself, however, and by 1908 the St. Anna Apartments, where Mather would make her San Francisco home, was already rising from the rubble.[45] The building was four stories tall, with a symmetrical facade and six bay windows, an architectural style echoed in hundreds of small apartment houses erected at the time.[46] The St. Anna stood only a few steps east of the intersection of the California and Hyde Street cable car line, which provided easy access in all directions—to Russian Hill and North Beach, framed by the redwood-studded hills of Marin County across San Francisco Bay; to Union Square in the heart of downtown; to the vice-ridden Barbary Coast near the docks; to the Western Addition and the U.S. Army base known as the Presidio, which stretched all the way to the Pacific Ocean. Nevertheless, in spite of her convenient location, a distinct advantage for a working girl like Mather, she stayed in San Francisco only a short while.

Sometime after the census taker knocked on her door in the spring of 1910, and prior to the middle of 1912, Mather moved south to Los Angeles. Perhaps she decided to leave San Francisco because of the tremors that rocked the city in July 1911.[47] Those relatively modest shakes caused only minor damage but sent panicky residents scrambling into the streets, their memories of the 1906 devastation all too readily recalled. A large number of citizens, convinced that the San Francisco peninsula was destined to shake itself into the Pacific Ocean, hastily departed the city, and Mather may have been among them. But whether it was a natural cataclysm, potential business opportunities, or some entirely different reason that convinced Mather to leave San Francisco, by the summer of 1912 she was living in the very heart of downtown Los Angeles, high atop the promontory known as Bunker Hill.[48]

Mather's first Los Angeles residence was a bleak, sunless room at the Chadakoin,[49] an unprepossessing boarding house located at 306 South Clay Street, a narrow two-block-long passageway carved into the eastern flank of Bunker Hill, one block north of downtown's Central Park. Clay Street was a nondescript byway, more an alley than a street, named for the clay deposits that had once been excavated there and molded into bricks for many of the city's nineteenth-century buildings.[50] The Chadakoin stood only two doors south of the funicular known as Angels Flight, which vaulted over Clay Street on an elevated wooden trestle before climbing up a steep incline to its terminus on Olive Street, adjacent to a tiny public park known as Angels Rest (see fig. 13).

Just down the hill from the park, and directly above the man-made cavern where Third Street tunneled under Bunker Hill, stood an observation tower, and inside the tower was a large camera obscura.[51] From that vantage point one could observe the entire panorama of the City of

FIGURE 13. Van Ornum Colorprint Co., Angels Flight and Third St. Tunnel, Los Angeles, ca. 1912. Color postcard, 9 × 14 cm (3¹/₂ × 5¹/₂ in.). Collection of the author

the Angels spread out below, and the novelty of the view, projected through a double-convex lens onto a ground-glass screen, made the local landmark the busiest, most popular destination on the hill.

The Angels Flight railway was operated by cables that pulled its two cream-colored cars, named after the Biblical peaks of Sinai and Olivet, along a pair of parallel wooden tracks. The cars made approximately four hundred trips a day, and each time the cycle was about to begin, a Klaxon horn would blare to warn passengers of their imminent journey up or down the incline,[52] a routine that would have made Mather's Clay Street apartment a very convenient, but altogether deafening, place to live. In spite of the pervasive ambient noise, however, she remained there for several months, having successfully completed her supernal transit from the place of her birth—the City of the Saints—to the place she would call her home for the next forty years—the City of the Angels.

The City of the Angels, 1850–1913

By 1912, the year Margrethe Mather arrived in Los Angeles, the city was already well on its way to becoming a bustling metropolis with a terribly congested downtown and a rapidly burgeoning crime rate. Its growth was accelerating at an unprecedented pace, encouraged by prominent men who had personal motives for allowing expansion to proceed unchecked. But the same population explosion that was lining the pockets of the city's power brokers was now threatening to undermine the very reasons Los Angeles had gained a reputation as such a desirable place to be.

At the halfway point of the previous century, the promontory located southwest of the city's birthplace—the eighteenth-century plaza known as El Pueblo de Los Angeles—had stood barren and uninhabited. But by the 1880s the rugged outcropping had been christened Bunker Hill in honor of the nation's recent centennial, and thanks to the completion of railroad lines connecting Los Angeles to the rest of the country and the tremendous real estate boom that followed,[1] Bunker Hill had become the most desirable residential district in Los Angeles.[2]

The city's wealthiest citizens built fanciful Victorian houses within the Hill's boundaries, a twenty-four block area roughly defined by Temple Street on the north, Fifth Street on the south, Flower Street on the west, and Hill Street on the east. From their spacious verandas and lofty towers, the privileged of Bunker Hill could survey the dusty, raucous city from a comfortable distance (see fig. 14). With its gingerbread architecture and undulating streets, Bunker Hill most closely resembled the Pacific Heights neighborhood of San Francisco, while the downtown business district, built on flat terrain, looked very much like the urban centers of Chicago or Kansas City.

By 1900 the city of Los Angeles, with a population of 102,479, was the thirty-sixth largest metropolis in the United States—smaller than Toledo, Newark, Rochester, Indianapolis, and Denver; on a par with Memphis, Syracuse, and Omaha;[3] and barely one-third larger than Margrethe Mather's hometown of Salt Lake City (pop. 77,725).[4] Los Angeles still lagged far behind San Francisco (pop. 342,782),[5] and its growth potential seemed destined to be irreversibly stunted by an excessively arid climate. Within the next decade, however, remedies to this shortcoming would be sought by those most likely to prosper from unfettered growth.

FIGURE 14. Unidentified photographer, Panoramic View of Hill Street and Third Street Looking West, Los Angeles, ca. 1900. In 1901 Angels Flight was erected on the hillside just to the right of the Crocker Mansion, the large Victorian house shown in the upper right corner of the photograph. Los Angeles, USC Libraries Special Collections, Doheny Memorial Library, The University of Southern California, call no. CHS-6715

In 1901 the Angels Flight funicular was erected to connect the heights of Bunker Hill with the rest of downtown Los Angeles, making the steep incline more accessible, and as a result, less exclusive. In search of more private havens, the wealthy began to flee the Hill and seek refuge in the Westlake Park district, the orange groves of Hollywood, the grazing lands of Rancho Los Feliz, and the deep, wooded ravine known as the Arroyo Seco, which slashed diagonally through the hills across the northern fringes of the city.

As the second decade of the new century began, the city was expanding in all directions, and thousands of homes were being built to accommodate the influx of new residents. The 1910 census figures revealed that Los Angeles had tripled in size since 1900, and with its current population of 319,198, the city was fast catching up to San Francisco (pop. 416,912).[6] Tract developments were proliferating and being heavily promoted in the newspapers. Percy H. Clark was advertising a new development in the "hills of Beverly," where "some very sightly and magnificent acre pieces suitable for villa sites and country seats" could be had at prices "cheaper than any other similar property...in Southern California." The advertisements also promised that "those who buy now are bound to make money on their investment."[7]

Proposals to tame rugged Griffith Park[8] and reconfigure downtown's verdant Central Park[9] were controversial topics of discussion. In an effort to attract more vacationers to the Southland, architectural drawings of palatial, soon-to-be-built tourist hotels were allocated generous spreads in all the local newspapers,[10] and the *Times* announced plans for a graceful, new automobile bridge that would span the Arroyo Seco, linking downtown Los Angeles to the towns of Garvanza, South Pasadena, and Pasadena.[11]

A CULTURAL HAVEN   Eager to keep up with its East Coast counterparts, Los Angeles was playing host to the latest terpsichorean and vaudevillian sensations. Dancer Maud Allan, a native of San Francisco, was the toast of the town, appearing at the Auditorium Theatre after a successful run in New York City.[12] The exotic Russian actress Alla Nazimova was starring in a repertoire of sophisticated Henrik Ibsen dramas,[13] and famed dancer Ruth St. Denis was making her Los Angeles debut in a series of programs based on "Hindu" and Egyptian themes.[14] The Great Selig Polyscope Company, recently relocated from Chicago, was presenting an elaborate, live action drama based on the life of the pirate known as Blackbeard. Staged on the sands of Redondo Beach, the spectacle utilized a real sailing ship as the backdrop for an onboard battle between pirates and crew, and spectators seated along the shore were advised to bring "opera glasses to get the smaller details of the tragic play."[15]

A growing number of musicians were finding gainful employment as audiences responded enthusiastically to performances by the Los Angeles Symphony under the management of impresario Lynden E. Behymer.[16] On a more populist musical note, the California School of Artistic Whistling was offering classes in the Blanchard Building at 233 South Broadway.[17] This multi-purpose hall, whimsically decorated with potted tropical trees and an aviary filled with dozens of colorful songbirds, met a wide array of civic needs by providing conference rooms, offices, and studios, as well as the largest, most desirable art exhibition space in town.

Women's suffrage was an urgent matter of great concern, particularly to the businessmen of Southern California, who formed the Committee of Fifty in September 1911 to fight the pending ratification of the state amendment that would grant women the right to vote.[18] On Tuesday, October 10, the day of the referendum, the *Los Angeles Times* editorial page declared that "Women's suffrage should be defeated because it tends to unsex society and destroy the home and puts a burden on women which most of them do not want."[19] The following day, as the ballot count was just getting under way, a front-page banner headline gleefully predicted "SUFFRAGE APPEARS LOST."[20] But two days later, after all the votes from across the state had been tallied, the *Times* begrudgingly announced, "WOMAN'S SUFFRAGE PROBABLY WINS, AFTER ALL,"[21] and the females of California celebrated their victory.

Fashion was quick to reflect the newly acquired power and status of the feminine half of the population. Cumbersome bustles were discarded in favor of man-tailored suits and no-nonsense shoes. Bucking the trend toward simplicity, however, were the broad-brimmed, lavishly trimmed chapeaus that sat atop every fashionable female head, a fad that forced the owners of Cawston Ostrich Farm on the outskirts of Pasadena to step up their harvest of luxuriant plumage to meet the demand.

AN ARTISTIC REFUGE   In the years immediately following the 1906 San Francisco earthquake, the pine groves and craggy coastline of Carmel-by-the-Sea had provided a picturesque place of refuge for the artists of California,[22] but by the second decade of the century the canyons of Topanga and Santa Monica to the west of Los Angeles, the hills and beaches of nearby Santa Barbara, the mountains of the Sierra Madre to the northeast, and the sea cliffs of La Jolla near San Diego were attracting plein-air painters from all over the world.[23]

The Los Angeles-based California Arts Club, founded as a social and exhibiting organization, could now count among its members many recent transplants from the East Coast, Chicago, and even Europe, and the Art Students League, a cousin to the New York City organization of the same name, was rapidly expanding its exhibition schedule.[24] Advanced drawing and painting classes were being offered at the Los Angeles School of Art and Design near Westlake Park, the College of Fine Arts in Garvanza, Throop Polytechnic in Pasadena, and the State Normal School on Bunker Hill,[25] while adolescents were learning the basics at Polytechnic High School and the recently opened Manual Arts High School.

Painter Detlef Sammann was working on a series of eight panels of Western scenes for the Indian Room in the Chester Place mansion of oil magnate Edward L. Doheny.[26] The most popular artist in Los Angeles was Paul DeLongpre, famed for his floral still lifes.[27] Japanese prints were being displayed and discussed in intellectual circles, and the venerable Dawson's Book Shop was introducing fine art etchings to a fledgling audience.[28] Most critical to the future of the city's cultural scene, however, was the new Los Angeles Museum of History, Science, and Art, the area's first such institution, which was being constructed in Agricultural Park, near the campus of the University of Southern California (USC) on the city's southern fringes. Sculptress Julia Bracken Wendt had been commissioned to create a monumental bronze for the museum's impressive rotunda. Comprising three colossal female figures bearing an inspirational stained-glass torch, the sculpture symbolized "history, science, and art" triumphantly bringing enlightenment to Southern California.[29]

Willard Huntington Wright was the youthful literary critic of the *Los Angeles Times*, while his brother, Stanton MacDonald Wright, was studying painting in Paris,[30] with the intention of bringing back firsthand knowledge of the European avant-garde to American art students. Norwegian-born Antony E. Anderson was the *Times* art critic. He reported regularly on the local painters and sculptors, and during the slow weeks when nothing much was happening in Southern California, he would flesh out his column with commentaries on the national and international art scene.

Anderson, a former painting student at the Art Students League in Manhattan and the Art Institute of Chicago, was very familiar with New York City's art world.[31] He especially revered Alfred Stieglitz and his 291 gallery, so when Anderson heard that Stieglitz's young colleague, photographer Alvin Langdon Coburn, was coming to Los Angeles he could scarcely contain his excitement. Well aware of Coburn's international reputation, Anderson enthusiastically described him as "one of the most famous exponents of his art in the world."[32]

Set to join Coburn on his visit west was Arthur Wesley Dow, the renowned Orientalist, author, and professor at New York City's Columbia Teachers College, whose book, *Composition*, was so highly regarded by Edward Weston. Anderson was positively exhilarated that two such illustrious artists would be taking up temporary residence in Los Angeles. His subsequent reviews of Coburn's two local exhibitions were the first indications that Anderson was harboring a keen interest in photography.[33]

THE BLAST THAT ROCKED LOS ANGELES By contrast, even as the cultural life of Los Angeles was growing richer and more catholic, the city was being racked by an evolving political controversy fomented, in no small part, by the *Los Angeles Times*. During the first decade of the century, the *Times* had begun publishing article after article about the robust local economy and the tremendous potential of the city. Los Angeles had been promoted as a place that automatically conveyed prosperity and good health upon its inhabitants.[34] But that impression was based, in large part, on decrees issued by the aforementioned *Los Angeles Times* publisher, Colonel Harrison Gray Otis, and his son-in-law, Harry Chandler, who, together with various business and political cronies, controlled a substantial share of the local real estate market. Shrewd to a fault, these entrepreneurs were determined to drive up property values by making the Southland fantasy they continually promulgated in the pages of the *Times* a reality.

Colonel Otis, a veteran of both the Civil and Spanish–American Wars, was a hard-boiled, militaristic businessman. Famous for lashing a canon to the running board of his car during times of labor unrest, he even went so far as to name his spacious Wilshire Boulevard residence The Bivouac.[35] Equally aggressive when it came to promoting the city of Los Angeles, Otis's unrestrained public relations barrage had come to be known as *boosterism*, and its proponents as the Boosters. Throughout the Midwest and the East Coast, the Boosters waged their campaign, but they achieved their greatest success in Illinois, and particularly in Chicago, where the extremes of weather made the delightful Southern California climate an easy sell.[36]

By 1910, even as the Boosters were advocating Los Angeles as an idyllic destination, Otis and Chandler, together with a group of powerful colleagues known as the Merchants and Manufacturers Association (the M & M), were lobbying against the unionization of the city. Los Angeles was still a "free shop" town, where labor was cheap and plentiful and unions were not welcome, and the Los Angeles Chamber of Commerce and the M & M were determined to keep it that way.[37] At that very moment the shallow waters of the small port at San Pedro were being dredged so that large cargo ships could be anchored there. The deepening of the harbor was a critical improvement if Los Angeles was to compete with San Francisco as a trade center, and labor leaders decided it was the perfect time to flex their muscles and eliminate the vise grip of big business interests on the labor pool once and for all.

While Otis and Chandler railed against unionization in the pages of the *Times* and the situation grew increasingly adversarial, the steelworkers' union began to position itself as the *Times*'s number one enemy. These two opposing forces collided, with fatal consequences, on October 1, 1910, when a tremendous explosion tore apart the *Los Angeles Times* Building at the northeast corner of First and Broadway, killing twenty-one employees.[38] Within hours of the event Colonel Otis pronounced the tragedy the result of a "unionist bomb."[39]

Otis's proclamation provoked a vitriolic and enduring schism between management and labor that had ramifications on a nationwide level. Otis and Chandler immediately declared an out-and-out war against the unions and vowed to track down the perpetrators. Tensions ran high and death threats were made against the *Times*'s management and other movers and shakers in Los Angeles. When several undetonated explosive devices, including one at Otis's home, were discovered a few days later, the *Times* again pointed an accusing finger at labor.[40] Union leadership countered that Otis himself had planted the bombs in a Machiavellian attempt to gain sympathy and support from the general populace. Then, on Christmas Day, a second explosion occurred at the Llewellyn Iron Works, a non-union factory on North Main Street, and the *Times* had further cause to ratchet up its campaign to discredit the labor movement. By the end of 1910 Los Angeles had responded to the onslaught of inflammatory articles by becoming a place of paranoia and barely contained rage.

For the next six months the *Times* management placed every available resource behind the search for the perpetrators. In April 1911 the *Times* was finally able to announce the capture of one Ortie McManigal, a member of the International Association of Bridge and Structural Iron Workers. In exchange for a guarantee of leniency, McManigal confessed to a role in the *Los Angeles Times* bombing and agreed to cooperate in the apprehension of the remaining fugitives.[41] On the basis of McManigal's sworn statement, two brothers, James B. and John J. McNamara, also members of the Iron Workers union, were captured, charged with the bombing of the *Times*, and speedily brought to trial. Their case became a *cause célèbre* for the entire labor movement. Famed Chicago attorney Clarence Darrow was retained for the defense, but to the considerable consternation and disappointment of organized labor—whose leaders assumed the McNamaras were being framed—the brothers unexpectedly agreed to a plea bargain. In return for their admission of guilt, they managed to escape the death penalty, although James McNamara received a life sentence and John McNamara, fifteen years, in San Quentin.

The McNamaras' sudden about-face had negative repercussions for all associated with the defense. Darrow's reputation was sullied at both ends of the political spectrum, and later that year he found himself on trial for jury tampering in the case. Conservatives reviled him for having agreed to defend the brothers, while labor leaders believed Darrow had talked the McNamaras into entering guilty pleas by convincing them it was the only way they could avoid execution. But the most devastating effect of the McNamaras' confessions of guilt was the continued erosion of public support for the national labor movement.

Meanwhile, others implicated in the crime remained at large, in spite of the relentless pursuit of Detective William Burns, who had been handed the difficult assignment of rounding up every last one of the suspects. It was an extraordinary challenge for the Burns Detective Agency, because within days of the explosion many of the suspects had slipped through the cracks and gone underground. Some had headed for the remote islands of Puget Sound in Washington State, others had hidden themselves among the congested tenements of New York City, and a few had fled the country entirely. But the boldest had done the unexpected and settled directly under Burns's nose, a few blocks away from the bombing site. As Burns and his agents doggedly continued their manhunt, the city of Los Angeles suffered sorely from its loss of innocence and lack of responsible journalism.

A MYRIAD OF PROBLEMS As the months passed, a steady stream of bombing-related articles appeared in the *Times*, but finally even that publication was forced to turn away from local conflicts to concentrate on the international scene. By early 1912 Los Angeles newspapers were regularly reporting on European skirmishes involving territorial disputes and political oppression, and the *Times* was reserving its front-page headlines for daily updates. These events were unfolding half a world away, however, and most ordinary Angelenos remained far more concerned about the troubles percolating in Mexico, a mere hundred miles to the south, as well as the more mundane problems of overpopulation in their own backyard.

Local citizens were painfully aware that their city was rapidly outgrowing all aspects of its infrastructure. City leaders had already begun scouting for properties where large-scale municipal buildings could be erected. Among the most pressing dilemmas was the need for a new library facility. One potential location being discussed was the recently vacated campus of the State Normal School at Fifth Street between Olive and Flower streets, a property that straddled the southernmost ridge of Bunker Hill.[42] Former *Los Angeles Times* City Editor and erstwhile photographer Charles Fletcher Lummis was quick to voice serious objections to the site, declaring the hillock too far from the business district and too steep a climb for the general public. Added to this indictment was his stern admonition, "[It is] bad public policy to place the conduct of the library in the hands of State politicians."[43]

The future of Bunker Hill in its entirety was a topic that supplied plenty of opportunities for contentious public debate. The Hill's very presence was perceived by many as an obstacle to urban expansion, and the fate of the problematic outcropping repeatedly provoked fractious citywide disputes.[44] Certain segments of the public favored the extraction of a large chunk of the promontory in order to give access to the valuable business district in the northwestern part of the city, an approach that would eliminate the steepest grades and the need for additional tunnels. Others lobbied for the use of brutal hydraulic mining techniques to forcefully erode deep trenches through the hillside large enough to accommodate vehicular traffic. Still others advocated lopping off the bothersome mass of earth entirely and disposing of the extraneous soil in the swales of nearby Elysian Park. It was the beginning of a forty year tug-of-war that would undermine the prosperity and stability of the residential district on Bunker Hill as surely and systematically as any bulldozer.

In April 1912 news of the tragic sinking of the Titanic dominated the front pages of the nation's newspapers, but the *Times* once again got the headline wrong, announcing that Mrs. J. J. (Molly) Brown, a well-known Denver socialite, had met her death in the icy waters off Newfoundland.[45] It was soon learned that, in fact, Molly Brown was unsinkable. In May, labor activist and anarchist Emma Goldman and her business manager/lover, Dr. Ben Reitman, visited San Diego. In that supposedly progressive community, Reitman was kidnapped, stripped, tarred, feathered, and branded by local vigilantes, who then abandoned him in a remote desert area east of the city where he was forced to find his own way back to safety.[46] On the heels of this ignominious behavior on their back doorstep, Angelenos loftily compared their own domain to ancient Athens by describing the proposed Southwest Museum, which was to be built in the hills above the Arroyo Seco, as a "splendid acropolis to house treasure."[47]

By 1913 the streets of downtown Los Angeles were completely overrun with automobiles, and there was no end in sight.[48] The *Times*, safely ensconced in its newly built "earthquake-proof and dynamite-proof"[49] headquarters, began to devote an entire section of its newspaper to the concerns of motorists. In an effort to provide additional public transportation, a second streetcar line connecting Glendale and Tropico to the newly built station at Fourth Street and Glendale Boulevard doubled its service to those suburbs, guaranteeing their rural charm would soon be a thing of the past.[50]

HYPERBOLE AND CONFLICT   In spite of ballooning congestion everywhere, new building projects were being announced weekly in response to a seemingly unending demand. Multistory office buildings were proliferating downtown, especially along the major thoroughfares of Main Street, Spring Street, and Broadway. Luxurious homes west of downtown were selling briskly for $17,000,[51] and movie companies, recently transplanted from the East Coast, were snapping up undeveloped parcels of land to use as back lots. The environs of Los Angeles were fast becoming known as "Bungalow-land,"[52] as row upon row of the low-slung homes with their widespread eaves, fieldstone fireplaces, and spacious porches replaced uprooted orange groves almost overnight. Meanwhile, the elaborate Victorian manses erected on Bunker Hill thirty years earlier were already being demoted to rooming houses.

As the city continued to expand at an alarming rate, some inhabitants sought refuge in the rural areas that still encircled the densely populated urban center. The newly built Beverly

Hills Hotel, located "midway between Los Angeles and the sea," began to advertise itself as the "ideal winter resort" for wealthy Easterners and Midwesterners,[53] and a coastal road was under construction that would link Los Angeles to the seaside health spas of Santa Barbara ninety miles to the northwest.[54] Although building such a thoroughfare along the Pacific Ocean posed many legal and geographical challenges, it was viewed as a necessary improvement that would eliminate the need to traverse the hazardous Lake Casitas Pass.

Wealthy developers, such as Henry E. Huntington, began to purchase large tracts of land and subdivide them.[55] Huntington had already inherited one fortune from his uncle, Collis P. Huntington, founder of the Southern Pacific Railroad, and he was in the process of accumulating another from his real estate investments and his ownership of the Pacific Electric Railway, better known to Angelenos as the Red Cars. Huntington was also remodeling an existing hotel in the Oak Knoll section of Pasadena into another lavish tourist destination. After hiring the well-known local architect Myron Hunt to oversee the makeover, Huntington announced that, for the enjoyment of his guests, his refurbished establishment would feature a novel "moving picture machine,"[56] an idea that proved to be a remarkably prescient indicator of things to come. No one—not even Colonel Otis—was more prone to enthusiastic hyperbole about Los Angeles than Huntington, who proclaimed:

> I am a foresighted man, and I believe that Los Angeles is destined to become the most important city in this country, if not in the world. It can extend in any direction as far as you like. Its front door opens on the Pacific, the ocean of the future. Europe can supply her own wants; we shall supply the wants of Asia. There is nothing that cannot be made and few things that will not grow in Southern California.[57]

Wealthy businessmen were not alone in envisioning a dazzlingly bright future for the city; more esoteric groups were also convinced it would come to pass. A branch of the Theosophists established their Krotona Institute on a fifteen-acre tract off Vista Del Mar in the hills above Hollywood, where they prophesied a "new and superior race"[58] would soon prosper and an important religious leader would miraculously appear and be nurtured. The United Ancient Order of Druids announced the formation of a new "grove" in Los Angeles, as well as plans for the construction of a temple, just as soon as the ranks of their acolytes numbered two thousand.[59]

In the spring of 1913, as artists from other parts of the world were exhibiting their latest work at the Sixty-Ninth Regiment Armory on East Twenty-Fifth Street in Manhattan, eliciting reactions of shock and scorn from all but the most sophisticated New Yorkers, the artists of Los Angeles remained staunchly conservative. Critic Antony Anderson reported that San Francisco painter Maynard Dixon had recently rented a temporary studio in the Copp Building at 431 South Hill Street, where he was completing a comprehensive scheme of wall paintings based on Western subjects.[60] The murals had been commissioned by Anita Baldwin McClaughry, daughter of the notoriously ill-behaved millionaire and rakish founder of the Santa Anita racetrack, Elias Jackson (Lucky) Baldwin. The wall paintings were destined for McClaughry's new home, Anoakia, which was under construction on one corner of her father's vast rancho property in Arcadia, at the base of the Sierra Madre foothills.[61]

The conflicts that had long been simmering in Mexico exploded into full-blown warfare in November 1913 when rebel Mexican leader Francisco (Pancho) Villa won critical victories at Chihuahua and Juarez, a grassroots legacy that would ensure him a permanent place in the labyrinthine history of the Mexican Revolution.[62] Villa, who stood for drastic agrarian reform through revolution, was viewed as a dangerous but romantic underdog in the complicated power struggle, and a good many Americans entertained at least a mild fascination for the outlaw and his legendary escapades.

Angelenos, however, held much stronger, albeit mixed, opinions. Mexico was too close by, and her natural resources far too tempting, to allow for nonchalance. While the man-in-the-street empathized with the plight of the poverty-stricken peasants, businessmen like Harry Chandler and Edward Doheny saw the profit potential in private land ownership and the development of Mexican oil fields. It was a classic clash between opposing political and economic interests that would flare repeatedly over the coming years. What most Los Angeles residents failed to realize was that Chandler and his increasingly senile father-in-law, Colonel Otis, were cunningly bankrolling several rival protagonists in the epic Mexican drama, expressly to ensure that whoever ultimately prevailed would be in their debt.[63]

As the citizenry of Los Angeles kept a wary eye on developments unfolding to the south, they were momentarily distracted when a spate of quarreling broke out over San Francisco's upcoming Panama-Pacific International Exposition. After a *Times* article stated that fair officials did not intend to allow Los Angeles and surrounding Southern California communities to participate in the festivities, irate Angelenos responded with indignation at the slight.[64]

WATER AND POWER Adding injury to insult, the *Times* reported that the city's water supply was dwindling and what little drinking water remained was tainted. In fact, the problem was so severe that hundreds of citizens had already fallen ill from the contamination. According to the *Times* editorial page, this situation further justified the construction of the new Owens River aqueduct, which was then nearing completion.[65] Secure in the knowledge that the aqueduct would soon be finished, Angelenos remained smug in spite of their tribulations, confident that their half of California, i.e. the portion south of the Tehachapi Mountain range, would ultimately be proven superior to the half occupied by their exclusionist neighbors to the north.

Indeed, as far as Angelenos were concerned, the completion of the aqueduct was the most eagerly anticipated event of the decade. When those promised gallons of diverted river water finally spewed forth to irrigate the sandy soil of Southern California, Los Angeles would turn into a tropical paradise. So said Harry Chandler in the pages of the *Times*,[66] and he was in a position to know; it was his land holdings, and those of his real estate syndicate, that were about to skyrocket in value as a result.

After months of preparation, the momentous occasion finally arrived on November 6, 1913, when forty thousand people watched excitedly as the sluice gates were raised to bring a torrent of water crashing through the aqueduct at the head of the San Fernando Valley.[67] It was a triumphant day for Los Angeles, Colonel Otis, Harry Chandler, and, particularly, for the aqueduct's chief engineer, William Mulholland, director of the Department of Water and Power, the city agency destined to have more influence over the future of Los Angeles than any other.

The following day a celebration took place in Agricultural Park, recently (and prematurely) renamed Exposition Park, and the Los Angeles County Museum of History, Science, and Art opened its doors to the public for the first time. The highlights of the museum's debut exhibition were two oil paintings—one depicting the aqueduct; the other, William Mulholland.[68] Already the juxtaposition of water and power had come to symbolize the very essence of the city.

To commemorate the opening of the aqueduct and the "greening" of Los Angeles that would surely follow, one citizen proposed the creation of an "aqueduct fountain."[69] His prospectus called for a five-hundred-foot-high waterfall to pour forth hundreds of gallons of precious, imported river water every fifteen minutes, while a powerful searchlight—mounted above the surging cascade—oscillated across the Los Angeles basin and alternating displays of red, white, and blue electric lights glowed patriotically through the mist. No scheme was too grandiose or outrageous to receive due consideration as life in Los Angeles grew more complex by the minute. A pervasive atmosphere of expectation and unrealized potential made the city quite unlike any other in America. Some believed it was the seductive scent of California poppies mingling with the pungent odor of opportunity that gave the air such an intoxicating quality.

Getting Established, Early 1913

I n the midst of the rapidly evolving milieu that was 1913 Los Angeles, Edward Weston was well on his way to establishing a solid national reputation. His work was appearing regularly in several of the most important photography publications, and he was systematically sending prints to competitions and exhibitions, especially if there was a cash prize at stake. Several of his most popular images were genre scenes, many of them featuring local Tropico children. One example depicted two of Flora Weston's nieces, dressed in eighteenth-century garb, seated on a high-backed oak settle.[1] Another bore the overwrought title *We Die! We Die! There Is No Hope!*[2] A few featured attractive young women like Helen Cole, a sweet-faced schoolteacher who lived nearby.[3]

Weston had also recently published an article in *American Photography* titled "Shall I Turn Professional?" in which he offered pointers to amateur photographers who were considering photography as a career. He urged "every amateur determined to become a professional to get a job in some studio" in order to learn how to "turn out work in quantities and in a uniform, systematic manner." He counseled his readers that they must know how to "do every little step of the business from operating to mounting" because "only a thorough knowledge of all details will enable you to impart your ideas to your assistants, or to tell whether they are competent or a useless expenditure." He also warned of the difficulties in photographing homely sitters who, nevertheless, expected to look attractive in their portraits, and he sternly admonished prospective photographers:

> Don't cut prices. You hurt your competitor…but you hurt yourself infinitely more.… And, besides being a disgrace and a detriment to the profession, the public will soon turn to your neighbor whose drawing card is the continual betterment of his work, and you, unable to crawl out of the hole you have dug for yourself, will sink into oblivion, where you justly belong.[4]

SWITCHING CAREERS While Weston was busy building his reputation and handing out tips to fellow photographers, Mather was on the verge of a career change. After her arrival in Los Angeles the previous year, and once her erstwhile Salt Lake City admirer had come and gone, she had taken stock of her options. Not surprisingly, she had found them limited. Now in her mid-twenties, she was uneducated, unskilled, and without funds. She had little choice but to return to what she knew best. As the months passed, however, Mather's career as a courtesan began to exact a toll on her peace of mind, especially after an aging client died of a heart attack in the midst of a particularly vigorous liaison.[5] While the elderly gentleman's body was being quietly spirited out of his hotel room to a more suitable location, a disconcerted Mather discreetly vanished through a rear entrance, all the while vowing to find another occupation.

Although that unnerving experience may have been what prompted Mather's initial investigations into photography, she would later maintain, with characteristic flippancy, that she had picked up her first camera purely on a whim, more out of boredom than any compelling interest.[6] Her companion on that fortuitous occasion was a friend named Elmer Ellsworth, a laconic jack-of-all-trades, who also hailed from Salt Lake City. Ellsworth, whose interests were varied and legion, joined the Los Angeles Camera Club (LACC) sometime in 1912, and he persuaded Mather to do the same.[7] The club, in the midst of a membership drive at the time, was offering the added incentive of discounted rates, a bargain the two friends were unable to resist.

The LACC had suffered through a beleaguered existence ever since its founding in 1899.[8] Despite a successful debut, the Club had been forced to disband in 1905 due to waning membership. A second incarnation held out renewed promise, but in 1910 another enervating lull occurred. Only by promoting their activities in conjunction with specialized local events, such as the Pasadena Tournament of Roses, did the LACC manage to attract a flurry of new members, and it was around this time that Mather and Ellsworth joined their ranks.

The LACC was headquartered at 321 Hill Street, on the top floor of the three-story Wright-Callender (Real Estate) Building.[9] The rooms had been specially designed a few years earlier under the supervision of the building's owner, Mr. C. J. Fox, who was also an avid amateur photographer and club member.[10] The layout included offices, a spacious meeting room, a studio with north-facing skylights, a darkroom, various developing and toning rooms, an assortment of dressing rooms and lockers, and a rooftop area where exposures on printing-out paper could be left outside to develop slowly under the cloudless California skies. The facility was as complete and up-to-date as any in the country, and it offered the additional benefit of providing a respectable social environment where those with common interests could mingle. Perhaps that was what Mather was really seeking when she joined the club—a touch of respectability.

Although most members bicycled to and from club meetings, Mather was close enough to walk. The Wright-Callender Building was located just down the hill from Clay Street and almost back-to-back with her Bunker Hill boarding house, and that proximity, even more than Ellsworth's prodding, may have been what finally convinced her to join. By the time entries were solicited for the annual American Salon, the most important photography exhibition venue in the country, with a submissions deadline of October 1, 1912, Mather was already an LACC member, because one of her photographs was selected to represent the club in that prestigious competition.

Mather's entry, titled *Maid of Arcady* (fig. 15), is her earliest known photograph. The image depicts a young woman posing in the nude, a subject considered quite risqué at the time. Indeed, it might have been the shocking subject matter, coupled with the rather sensational fact that the photograph had been taken by a woman, that prompted the editor of *American Photography* to reproduce it in the January 1913 issue.[11]

FIGURE 15. Margrethe Mather (American, 1886–1952), *Maid of Arcady*, 1912. Reproduction courtesy of the George Eastman House, International Museum of Photography and Film, Rochester, N.Y.

The title Mather bestowed on her photograph reflected her awareness of the currency of classical themes within artistic and academic circles. Arcady (or Arcadia) was a reference to a region in Greece where the inhabitants were known for their pastoral innocence, and as a setting with paradisiacal connotations, it was invoked frequently in the visual arts and literature of the period. In 1889 William Butler Yeats, the legendary leader of the Irish literary renaissance and friend to William Morris, founder of the English Arts and Crafts movement, had published a famous poem containing the stanza:

> The woods of Arcady are dead,
> And over is their antique joy;
> Of old the world on dreaming fed;
> Gray Truth is now her painted toy.[12]

Artists and writers, sympathetic to the nostalgic yearning in Yeats's poem, sought to express their own longings to return to a bucolic past, and thus "looking backward" became a popular theme in *fin de siècle* America.[13] *Maid of Arcady*, like many works of art from the early years of the twentieth century, symbolically depicted the self-consciously romantic notion of a paradise lost. In Mather's allegorical study, the nude figure, untainted by worldly corruption and concerns, peers into a wooded bower as she stands with her back to the viewer, her derriere modestly hidden behind a leafy branch. Considering the difficulty in finding females willing to pose nude for the camera, and based on the body type of the model, it is entirely possible that Mather herself was playing the part of the innocent maiden, a role she had already perfected in real life.

The Ninth American Salon exhibition opened at the Carnegie Institute in Pittsburgh in November 1912 and traveled on to the Portland Art Museum in Portland, Maine, and the Toledo Museum of Art the following spring.[14] The acceptance of Mather's *Maid of Arcady* into the competition was her first noteworthy success in the photography world. Later that year she also achieved a small degree of international exposure when the same image was included in the Salon International d'Art Photographique held by the Association Belge de Photographie in the Palais des Beaux-Arts in Ghent, Belgium.[15]

RESTLESS ELMER   Elmer Ellsworth not only introduced Margrethe Mather to photography, he also brought her into contact with a wide array of new acquaintances, many of whom would become lifelong friends. Ellsworth was himself a collegial chum and a memorable character (see fig. 16). Born in 1867 in Portage, Wisconsin, he had spent most of his youth in Salt Lake City, where his stepfather ran a successful livery business and Ellsworth served as the firm's bookkeeper.[16] In 1892, at the age of 25, he proposed marriage to Lucile Gilmer, the daughter of a wealthy Salt Lake City businessman. Possibly because Ellsworth did not travel in the same social circles as Gilmer, his proposal was not well received; indeed, quite the opposite. Lucile's

FIGURE 16. Unidentified photographer, Elmer Ellsworth, Los Angeles, ca. 1913. Gelatin silver print, 7.5 × 12.7 cm (3 × 5 in.). Palo Alto, Calif., Collection of Jenifer Williams Angel

father, then on his deathbed, issued strict orders that Lucile was not to marry Elmer under any circumstances.[17]

Thwarted in his pursuit of love, Ellsworth turned to an unlikely alternative—show business. He and a partner leased the Lyceum Theatre in downtown Salt Lake City as a vaudeville venue,[18] and around 1900 Ellsworth expanded his theatrical career to become a "traveling amusements" agent,[19] dividing his time between Utah and California. Then, ten years after his proposal of marriage to Lucile, he decided to make a bid for the economic prosperity that might finally convince her now-widowed mother of his sincerity and worthiness. In 1902, at the age of thirty-five, he headed east to New York City to seek his fortune in the stock market.[20]

Settling on the Upper West Side of Manhattan, near the newly erected City College campus,[21] Ellsworth used his savings to purchase a seat on the Consolidated Stock (and Petroleum) Exchange (CSE), which was fast becoming a serious rival to its big brother, the larger and more prestigious New York Stock Exchange (NYSE).[22] However, the NYSE fought back, and a series of governmental investigations was initiated to look into accusations of faulty business practices at the CSE. Unfortunately for Ellsworth, those investigations began in 1903, the same year he plunked down his savings to acquire a seat on the doomed exchange. Under the government's watchful eye, the CSE's power and influence steadily declined, and Ellsworth's prospects for wealth dwindled proportionately. In 1909 he departed New York City in financial ruin, his hopes of winning Lucile once again dashed.

Ellsworth was not one to concede failure so easily, however. In 1910 he returned to Los Angeles to dabble in the real estate loan business,[23] but by 1913 the restless entrepreneur was already considering other career opportunities, such as civil engineering, architecture, and photography. As Mather would later explain, "For Elmer, activity was the need."[24] In the course of his travels, and perhaps due to his dismal failure as a capitalist, Ellsworth also developed an avid interest in socialist causes. While living in New York City, he had written political satire for the national humor magazine, *Judge*,[25] so it was no doubt a combination of Ellsworth's finely tuned cynicism and deeply ingrained disillusionment with government bureaucracy that prompted his admiration for that infamous heroine of the American working class, the Russian-born, Rochester-raised Emma Goldman.

RED EMMA   Emma Goldman had immigrated to America in 1886 at the age of seventeen.[26] By the time Ellsworth made her acquaintance, the woman known to her enemies as Red Emma had already spent more than twenty years fighting for the rights of the common man and woman, defying the federal authorities on countless occasions, and repeatedly defending people accused of crimes ranging from the dissemination of birth control information (Margaret Sanger, the founder of Planned Parenthood) to assassination (Alexander Berkman, Goldman's former lover, who served fourteen years in prison for the attempted murder of industrialist Henry Clay Frick, Chairman of the Carnegie Steel Corporation).

Goldman also made regular cross-country lecture tours, stopping in the major cities en route and shuttling up and down the West Coast, all the while loudly and proudly declaring herself an anarchist as she lobbied for the rights of workers and stirred up controversy wherever she went. In anticipation of her arrival, factory owners and police departments would brace themselves for the bouts of labor unrest that would inevitably follow.

Elmer Ellsworth still had many contacts on the vaudeville circuit, and he soon became one of Goldman's most valuable associates in California due to his ability to secure venues for her West Coast lectures, not an easy task given the powerful forces that opposed her public appearances. But some of Goldman's Los Angeles supporters were prominent, wealthy citizens, with a great deal of influence themselves, and they wholeheartedly believed it was their civic and moral duty to back Goldman in her defense of the poor and disenfranchised. Around 1913 Ellsworth brought Mather into Goldman's circle of like-minded Angelenos, whereupon she, too, began to fight behind the scenes on behalf of the anarchist's many causes.[27]

LEFT-WING ANGELENOS　　Most prominent among Goldman's Los Angeles comrades were Gaylord and Mary Wilshire, an eccentric, fascinating couple. Born into a wealthy Cincinnati family in 1861, Gaylord Wilshire was a millionaire socialist, politician, world traveler, inventor, publisher, entrepreneur, and real estate mogul (see fig. 17).[28] As this array of designations would imply, he was also a complicated, contradictory, and controversial man. In his manner of dress, Wilshire was a sartorial Beau Brummell, whose trademark Van Dyke beard and moustache and fancy waistcoats made him hard to forget. His relentlessly creative attempts at self-promotion prompted one contemporary to dub him "the P. T. Barnum of American Socialism."[29]

In the 1890s Wilshire's Los Angeles real estate holdings included a thirty-five-acre barley field due west of the city center that he soon developed into a residential area. Aptly known as the Wilshire District, it was bisected by an eponymous east–west boulevard that would

FIGURE 17. Attributed to Russell Coryell (American, 1891–1941), *Gaylord Wilshire*, ca. 1912. Gelatin silver print, 9 × 6.5 cm (3 ¹/₂ × 2 ¹/₂ in.). Cold Spring Harbor, N.Y., Collection of Bea Coryell

eventually be extended all the way to the Pacific Ocean, sixteen miles away. After twice running unsuccessfully for a California congressional seat and founding the *Challenge*, a socialist newspaper, Wilshire moved to New York City in 1901, and then on to Toronto, where he renamed his newspaper *Wilshire's Magazine*. By the time he brought his publication back to Manhattan in 1904, it was considered "the most influential socialist journal"[30] circulated in the United States.

In February of that year, in Saint Bartholomew's Church on Park Avenue, Wilshire married Mary McReynolds, a young Illinoisian twelve years his junior, who had trained as a social worker.[31] After the birth of their son, Logan, in 1906, the couple decided to adopt London's Hampstead Heath neighborhood as a home base while they made forays throughout Europe. During their travels they befriended such notables as George Bernard Shaw, H. G. Wells, Edwin Markham, Prince Peter Kropotkin, and Edward Carpenter. While in Zurich, Switzerland, Mary began studying with psychologist Carl Gustav Jung and, inspired by his teachings, she decided to pursue a career as a psychoanalyst, hoping to rid deeply disturbed people of their neuroses by interpreting their dreams.

Around 1914, with hostilities threatening in Europe and Wilshire's fortune almost depleted, the couple fled to Los Angeles, where they rented a modest residence near the Arroyo Seco, the deep ravine noted for its scenic beauty and the artistic types it attracted to its leafy slopes.[32] A few months later they purchased a house and eight acres of citrus trees on Elizabeth Street in Pasadena, and Wilshire began to focus his attentions on a gold mine near Bishop, from which he hoped to extract his next fortune.[33]

Because of their erudition and worldliness, the Wilshires quickly became key members of a group of idiosyncratic, independent thinkers who supported left-wing causes, but even though Wilshire's interest in Emma Goldman was a natural extension of his own political beliefs, his allegiance to her was not without reservations. A few years earlier she had published an article in her magazine, *Mother Earth*,[34] which was mildly critical of him and his maverick brand of socialism, so his regard for her was somewhat tempered by his memory of that slight.

One of Wilshire's close associates, Dr. Theodore Perceval Gerson, was another of Goldman's allies. A native of Philadelphia, educated at the University of Pennsylvania and Johns Hopkins University, Dr. Gerson had come to Los Angeles in 1903 to accept a position as an associate of Dr. John Randolph Haynes, the most prominent and forward thinking physician in Los Angeles.[35] In short order Dr. Gerson established his reputation as a skillful surgeon, an empathetic doctor, a charmingly modest man, and an avid promoter of cultural activities.

In 1906 Haynes invited Gerson to join the Severance Club, self-described as a "cultural conversation group," founded in honor of esteemed Los Angeles resident and social reformer Madame Caroline Severance. Gerson was soon elected Secretary, and then President, of the organization, and with these offices as his mandate, he set about promoting free thought and an open, uncensored exchange of ideas. Whenever a nationally renowned figure announced an upcoming trip to Los Angeles, Gerson would invite them to appear at the Severance Club, and it was in this capacity that the good doctor first came in contact with Emma Goldman.[36]

Although Gerson did not agree with many of Goldman's public declarations, he staunchly defended her right to make them, and beginning around 1913 and continuing through 1916 he played an important role, along with Ellsworth, in organizing Goldman's public appearances in Los Angeles, even underwriting some of them himself and lobbying prominent friends to do the same.[37] His enthusiastic endorsement of Goldman put his reputation within the local community at some risk, but Gerson, never one to be cowed by public opinion, persisted in supporting Goldman's efforts, and the two became close personal friends as a result.

The fourth member of the Los Angeles left-wing contingent was a domineering pacifist named Kate Crane Gartz.[38] Born in Chicago, she was the eldest daughter of millionaire Richard Teller Crane, an iron and steel industrialist who had been the primary financier behind Hull House, Jane Addams's famous settlement house for the poor of Chicago. In 1888 Kate Crane married Adolph F. Gartz of New York City, a businessman of German extraction. The couple produced five children, but after two of their daughters perished in Chicago's deadly Iroquois Theatre fire in 1903, the Gartzes had sought solace in Altadena, California, where they built a large residence in the San Gabriel foothills called the Cloister and became active in supporting local causes. Mrs. Gartz, who was determined to carry on her father's legacy of socially conscious philanthropy, enjoyed hosting salons in her home, and the Wilshires and Dr. Gerson were often among her guests.

This left-leaning coterie of prominent local citizens took great pains to invite their politically active, working-class compatriots to their social gatherings, and very soon their guest list expanded to include Elmer Ellsworth and Margrethe Mather. The people who attended these functions were a diverse lot, ranging from disillusioned descendants of the Mayflower Pilgrims, to members of the artistic avant-garde, to Russian- and Eastern European–born political refugees. Most were "parlor radicals" or "philosophical anarchists," people who believed in thoughtful discussion and nonviolent protest against the status quo as the most productive way to draw attention to a needy cause. Others were rebels who simply aspired to be different. But a few were genuine provocateurs who adamantly advocated premeditated violence as the only effective way to gain fair treatment for the masses.

Margrethe Mather moved fluidly among all three factions. Her predilection for even the most violent among them came naturally to her, for her hometown of Salt Lake City had long been central to the struggles of the American labor movement. During the late 1890s, while Mather was still a child, William Dudley (Big Bill) Haywood, a Utah-born, rough-and-tumble bear of a man, had become active in the Western Federation of Miners, and under his leadership the miners of Salt Lake City had subsequently fought many bloody battles as they protested against thirteen-hour work shifts, hazardous working conditions, and low wages.[39] They had even taken on the industrial titans of the period, including Meyer Guggenheim and his

American Smelting and Refining Company and John D. Rockefeller and his Standard Oil trust, using strikes, intimidation, and occasionally dynamite, to shut down production lines. Having witnessed firsthand the dangers and hardships that plagued the miners' everyday lives, Mather was predisposed to supporting those who fearlessly championed the miners' cause.

At social functions sponsored by the Wilshires, Dr. Gerson, and Kate Crane Gartz, Mather contributed not only beauty and wit to the gatherings but also a deep-seated desire to right the social injustices perpetrated by those who had accumulated their fortunes on the backs of the poor, and no one understood better than Mather what it was to be socially and economically disadvantaged, and completely self-reliant.

A ONE-MAN OPERATION Edward Weston was also experiencing the struggles that came with being self-reliant. In March 1913 he published another article in *American Photography* in which he weighed the advantages of operating an independent, one-man studio against the burden of having to attend to every detail oneself. While he strongly favored "the little fellow" over the large "picture factories," because an operator working alone could provide more individualized attention to his clients, he also acknowledged the interruptions and frustrations that often arose when a photographer had to act as his own proprietor, developer, printer, retoucher, and mounter. He recommended the use of "any labor-saving device of merit" that would give the photographer "more time for the study of art and technique." And he ended his article with a plug for the publisher:

> I am a great believer in the value of competitions and exhibitions, both as an education and as a business getter.... Not all of us are blessed with the opportunity of seeing salons, and we must derive our inspirations from the splendid halftone illustrations of works by the masters of our art published monthly in leading photographic periodicals. Those who do not read and subscribe to these magazines and patronize their advertisers unwittingly deal a blow at the advancement of pictorial photography; those who do, reap the benefit of knowledge imparted by those who know, and also avoid the necessity of digging out perplexing elementary problems in both art and technique.[40]

A real-life dilemma apparently informed his musings because later that year Weston hired his first assistant. She was Rae Davis, a young woman whose family lived a few blocks away from Weston's home. Davis, who aspired to become a photographer herself, would serve as Weston's receptionist, darkroom assistant, and model for the next three years.

Indeed, one of Weston's most popular photographs of the period, *Summer Sunshine*,[41] was an image of Davis, posing under the brilliance of the Tropico sun, holding a basket of roses. Although the photograph appears saccharine to modern eyes, it was entirely typical of the period and generally regarded as highly artistic. Davis was grateful to Weston for hiring her, and for the rest of her life she remained deferential to him, addressing him in letters as "Dear

Boss" or "Dear Mr. Weston." When he wrote to her years later, asking to borrow some of the photographs he had given her so he could include them in an upcoming exhibition, she immediately responded:

> I shall be most happy to loan these to you....The packing & shipping expenses will gladly be paid—and forgotten—it is little enough for the pleasure I have had from them these many years—and the memories of our association & the "glimpse" into the world of this type of art—which I would never have had had it not been for those three years with you.[42]

While Weston's relationship with Davis remained strictly professional, he would not be capable of observing such proprieties with Margrethe Mather.

TRANSPLANTED REBELS   As Weston struggled with the problems of enlarging his business, while at the same time maintaining a personalized approach to his photography, Mather was becoming better acquainted with many of the people who regularly attended the salons sponsored by the Wilshires, Dr. Gerson, and Kate Crane Gartz. The people she met in this context provided her with companionship and meaningful intellectual stimulation, and it was not long before three of her new acquaintances became close friends. Just like Mather, they were all from somewhere else.

Mollie Price was in her mid-twenties and recently divorced when she and her two small children arrived in Southern California in early 1913. Price hailed from Chicago where her father, Dr. James Russell Price, was a physician, a well-known freethinker, and a supporter of left-wing causes.[43] Mollie Price aspired to be a journalist and social reformer, and around 1906, after meeting Emma Goldman and Alexander Berkman, she followed them to New York City where she worked for several months on the staff of Goldman's newly founded magazine, *Mother Earth*.[44]

Price then returned to the Midwest to pursue a career as a newspaper journalist. There she encountered a ruggedly handsome, intense young man with Thoreau-like instincts and a patrician pedigree named George Cram (Jig) Cook.[45] Cook had grown up in Davenport, Iowa, but contrary to his rough-hewn appearance, he was a Harvard- and Heidelberg-educated intellectual who had already achieved limited fame as a novelist. Cook was determined to sustain his promising literary career, even from his remote Iowa location, and he was greatly aided in this ambition by his many ties to a group of talented people then in residence in Chicago.

This convergence of extraordinary personalities, a cultural phenomenon now known as the Chicago Renaissance, included then-fledgling authors Ben Hecht, Sherwood Anderson, Theodore Dreiser, Floyd Dell, Vachel Lindsay, and Carl Sandburg, as well as Harriet Monroe, editor of *Poetry* magazine, and Margaret Anderson, the soon-to-be editor and publisher of *The Little Review*.[46] These literary lions conducted lively soirees all over town but especially in the coldwater flat of Floyd Dell and his wife, Marjorie Currey, located near the University of Chicago in Hyde Park.

During Price's second pregnancy, Jig Cook (already once divorced) was again tempted away from the precarious state of marital bliss by author Susan Glaspell. He soon abandoned Price and moved with Glaspell to Chicago where he replaced his friend, Floyd Dell, as editor of the *Chicago Evening Post's* venerable *Friday Literary Review*. Much to her credit, the fiercely independent Price did not remain despondent over her husband's desertion for long. Just before Dell left the Midwest to take up residence in Greenwich Village, he and Price indulged in a brief but long anticipated coupling, and a short time later she left for California with her two toddlers in tow.[47]

After renting a house near downtown Los Angeles, Price decided to open the city's first nursery school based on the innovative teaching techniques of Maria Montessori, the Italian educator.[48] In addition to running her school, which she called The Children's House, Price began taking classes in psychology, and she often consulted with her new friend and mentor, Mary Wilshire, now a practicing Jungian analyst, about her work with disturbed children and her intentions to author innovative children's textbooks.[49] With all of these responsibilities and aspirations to juggle, Price needed assistance, both at her nursery school and with her own two children, Nilla and Harl, so she turned to a young woman, recently arrived from Texas, for help in both areas of her life.

Maud Emily Taylor was still a teenager when she left her mother and siblings behind in Dallas and moved to Los Angeles to continue her schooling. An extraordinarily bright and capable girl, she was determined to become either an actress or a writer. Born in 1895 in Atlanta, Georgia,[50] Taylor had received her early education at the Salem Female Academy (now Salem Academy) in Winston-Salem, North Carolina.[51] Her family had subsequently moved to Texas, but her father, an engineer and inventor of sorts, deserted his wife and children soon after their arrival there. Taylor dreamed of attending college, but she lacked money for tuition, so she gladly accepted Price's offer of employment even though, as far as Taylor was concerned, laundry, cooking, and entertaining someone else's mischievous children were little more than time-consuming obstacles that had to be endured and overcome.

Price often regaled her young helper with tales of the literati she had known in Chicago and New York City, and she promised Taylor that when Ellen Katherine Cook, her former mother-in-law, arrived in Los Angeles to help care for Nilla and Harl, Taylor would have more time to concentrate on her own writing career. Meanwhile, between Taylor's obligations at the nursery school and her two lively charges, she toiled long hours each day. In spare moments, however, she still found time to enjoy the new friends she was making in her adopted city. Price introduced her to the Wilshires, Dr. Gerson, and Kate Crane Gartz, and Taylor's name quickly became a permanent addition to their guest lists.[52] In this context, she and Price met Margrethe Mather, and the young women struck up a close, three-way friendship. Price also introduced Taylor and Mather to a charming young man named Russell Coryell, who had recently moved to Los Angeles from the East Coast.

Coryell was a college dropout who believed he could learn far more about life by traveling the world than by cloistering himself within the ivory towers of an Ivy League university.[53] A native of New York and Maine, Coryell had attended Harvard University during the 1911–1912 academic year, but having descended from a long line of unconventional derring-doers, he had found the academic life pretentious and uninspiring. In the summer of 1912 he decided to set out for the Wild West with his parents' blessing.

Russell's father, John R. Coryell, was a highly successful writer whose fame was derived chiefly from a series of lively adventure stories for young boys, featuring an adolescent protagonist named Nick Carter, and a string of romance novels intended for consumption by prepubescent girls, which Coryell published under the pseudonym, Bertha M. Clay.[54] These dime-novel serials were so popular that Coryell eventually hired ghostwriters to churn out sequels on his behalf, creating an income stream that gave the Coryell family a comfortable lifestyle and enough financial freedom to enable John R. to pursue his real interests—politics and education.

John R. and his wife, Abby Hedge Coryell, were both loyal friends of Emma Goldman, and they lent their support to several of her pet projects, including *Mother Earth*, Goldman's magazine.[55] Mollie Price became acquainted with the Coryells during her stint at *Mother Earth*, and she was well aware that, when Emma Goldman had opened a day school in association with her Francisco Ferrer Center, a social and educational gathering place for politically radical adults on St. Mark's Place in lower Manhattan, she had chosen the Coryells to run it.[56] In fact, Price was now modeling certain aspects of her own nursery school on the alternative teaching methods pioneered by the Coryells and their successors, Will and Ariel Durant, at Goldman's Modern School. Since leaving New York City, Price had kept in touch with the Coryells, so when their youngest son arrived in Southern California, Price was quick to offer guidance and make introductions.

After settling into the Alta Vista boarding house on Bunker Hill,[57] Coryell embarked on a series of rather unusual employment opportunities.[58] For a few weeks he assisted in the training of boxer Freddie Welsh, who would soon become lightweight champion of the world; then he donned an advertising sandwich board and skimmed along on water skis behind a small boat that motored back and forth to Catalina Island; and when he had the time and inclination, he made a little money posing nude for local artists. Coryell, a born athlete with a well-developed musculature, was an avid believer in physical culture and the inherent beauty of the human body, so he considered nude modeling a perfectly natural and respectable pastime.

Coryell's parents were great admirers of Alfred Stieglitz and frequenters of his 291 gallery, and they had instilled in their son an appreciation for the art of photography. Consequently, the moment Coryell arrived in California he began to document his experiences in a series of photographically illustrated scrapbooks.[59] For a time the young man's life seemed to echo that of the thrill-seeking protagonist in his father's rollicking adventure novels, but Coryell's California idyll was suddenly cut short when, only a few months after his arrival, he suffered a throbbing toothache. After receiving treatment from a local dentist, he developed an infection that caused serious damage to his heart valves, rendering him weak and infirm almost overnight. Nevertheless, Coryell, who intensely enjoyed his active, vigorous lifestyle, was determined not to let his misfortune turn him into an invalid. In a heroic effort to recover his strength, he decided to relocate to the recuperative environment of Santa Barbara, where an acquaintance of his parents had recently offered him a position at an innovative boys' school. Coryell left Los Angeles in the autumn of 1913,[60] but he remained in close touch with Price, Taylor, and Mather, and he often visited them for brief interludes of gaiety and high jinks, which greatly bolstered his sagging spirits. Very soon, however, Margrethe Mather found another young man to occupy her time.

Getting Acquainted, Late 1913 to 1914

Just as Russell Coryell was departing Los Angeles for Santa Barbara, Margrethe Mather and Edward Weston came face to face for the first time. Once again Elmer Ellsworth was responsible for the introduction. On a Sunday afternoon in October 1913 Mather and Ellsworth attended a Los Angeles Camera Club outing designed to provide social as well as photographic opportunities for Club members.[1] On this particular occasion the setting happened to be Griffith Park, the vast expanse of rugged terrain that encompasses the eastern portion of the Hollywood Hills.

Bored with their rather mundane companions and activities, Ellsworth suggested to Mather that they pay a visit to a nearby neighborhood where he had recently noticed the studio of a photographer he thought they should meet. They telephoned to see if the proprietor was in, and when he issued a cordial invitation to drop by, the two friends began walking east along Los Feliz Boulevard. After crossing the long wooden trestle bridge that spanned the unpredictable Los Angeles River and detouring through a field of withered grapevines to steal handfuls of dusty raisins, they made their way into Tropico. As they approached Brand Boulevard, Edward Weston's small, ivy-draped studio came into view. Weston welcomed them, invited them in for a tour of his modest workplace, and their friendship was launched.[2]

Weston would later recall that at first sight he had not been particularly impressed with Mather, but a second look had held him captive. Since her arrival in California, Mather had blossomed into a lovely, fine-featured woman with startlingly direct blue-gray eyes, high Scandinavian cheekbones, an ivory complexion punctuated by a smattering of freckles, and a cloud of flyaway, blondish brown hair. Her one physical flaw was an off-kilter nose that slightly diminished her delicate, understated beauty. She spoke only infrequently, in a low, pleasantly modulated voice,[3] but when she chose to express herself she did so in a charmingly lyrical, deftly original way that left little doubt as to her intelligence. A few days after meeting Weston, she returned to Tropico to pose for him.

In Weston's first portrait of Mather (fig. 18), she bears an uncanny resemblance to the courtesan Billy Justema would later describe in his memoir. Dressed fashionably in a primly tailored suit, she still manages to appear disarmingly disheveled in a soft white blouse with an asymmetrical, crimped ruffle at the neck. Sitting ramrod straight, she looks down her crooked, upturned nose at Weston with an engagingly piquant expression. Her hair is tucked up under

FIGURE 18. Edward Weston, *Margrethe Mather*, ca. 1913. Platinum print, 16.3 × 10.9 cm (6³/₈ × 4³/₈ in.). Tucson, Center for Creative Photography, University of Arizona, 78:151:1

a gently crumpled, broad-brimmed hat, and a cameo brooch tugs the eye slightly to the right of her throat. Balancing the visual drama of the organdy ruffle escaping from her lapel is a lustrous, blown-glass bottle containing a cluster of hydrangeas, perfectly placed to anchor the composition and add dimensional and decorative interest. Her hands lie casually crossed in her lap with the fingers of one hand curved in an expressive crescent.

The right half of the background is densely shadowed while the left side is flatly and brilliantly lit. The image divides vertically along the left side of Mather's face just before the illumination skims down her lapel and zigzags sharply to the left to outline the knife-pleat of her skirt. The highlights reflected from the glass bottle and her simple bangle bracelet, together with the lighter tonalities of blossoms and blouse, create a formal rhythm of lights and darks that is at once stimulating and pleasing to the eye. Mather proves herself to be a very appealing model, and although she poses in a rather static, old-fashioned way, the resulting portrait is surprisingly candid and fresh. It is particularly remarkable when compared to Weston's other studio portraits from the same period, which are much more conventional and formal in their arrangement. Apparently Mather was already having an effect on Weston's creative process, even though they were not yet intimately acquainted.

AN AFFAIR TO REMEMBER   Very soon, however, Mather became a regular visitor to Weston's studio, and within a matter of weeks their attraction evolved into a full-blown love affair. Around this time she sent a note to Weston in which she included a floral tribute:

> narcissi   tulips   cyclamen
> daffodils and   marguerites
> for you
> and the child's garden of verses[4]

Accompanying her note was a copy of Robert Louis Stevenson's popular classic, *A Child's Garden of Verses*. This well-known children's book, first published almost thirty years earlier, must have been particularly meaningful to their relationship, because Weston reciprocated by presenting Mather with a copy of the same volume.[5] Perhaps, their exchange was a symbolic gesture, made in an effort to replace the dismal memories of their own, abbreviated childhoods with more agreeable fantasies.

In another of her love letters, Mather, consciously or not, echoes the words of William Mulholland, the hard-driving engineer behind the Owens River aqueduct project. On November 13, 1913, just as Mulholland gave the signal to open the floodgates so the first rush of confiscated river water could come surging into the Los Angeles basin, he uttered one of the most succinct and prophetic sound bites in American history. "There it is. Take it," he growled to the huge crowd of onlookers.[6] His eminently quotable directive was repeated again and again in the local press until it was etched into the public psyche, and Angelenos were quick to heed his advice.

Although Mather's romantic prose poem borrows its rhythms from the *au courant* Imagist poets and the man who inspired them, the eighth-century Chinese poet Li Po, its final line paraphrases Mulholland's terse dictate:

> branches of wild roses!
> A child's face mirrored on the water—and pink petals drifting
> into the tiny shore-waves—and
> humming-birds' nests among the thorns—this—on a June
> morning so far away
> did it come again—now?
> Perhaps—because I seem to have caught a few of the petals
> here—take them[7]

FIGURE 19. Edward Weston, *Portrait of Margrethe in Garden*, ca. 1918. Platinum or palladium print, 18.8 × 23.5 cm (7³/₈ × 8¹/₄ in.). Tucson, Center for Creative Photography, University of Arizona, 81.207.21

Both of Mather's missives are written in a carefully precise, calligraphic backhand, on expensive, deckle-edged, laid papers. Adorned with sprigs of pressed flowers and encrustations of cinnabar- or amber-hued sealing wax, they are precious, elaborately prepared offerings, conceived and presented by a woman in love. Unquestionably Mather was smitten with Weston, and he with her. She was unlike any woman he had ever known, and he was challenged by her intelligence, baffled by her elusiveness, and stimulated by the things she made him see clearly for the first time (see fig. 19).

A few brief sentences, written in the early 1950s by photography historian Nancy Newhall and based on her firsthand conversations with Weston, recall his initial meeting with Mather, their subsequent relationship, and the emotional impact it had on him:

> One day there burst into his studio a little woman and a huge man, come expressly to tell him what his work meant to them....The woman was Margrethe Mather, at first sight no more interesting than a wren. If you looked again you saw she was exquisite. Then you could not take your eyes from her. Afterwards, you could not forget her; behind your eyes she moved, haunting, elusive, delicate. Where she came from, how she lived,

Edward, though he loved her many years, never really knew.... You opened the door—on the sill lay a drift of jonquils or a spray of acacia, or leaves half silver, half brown, and a note on grey green paper sealed in brown wax....

M. was an aesthete; nothing less than the perfect would do.... She was maddening to the eye, the heart, and whatever might be left of reason. Edward tried to pin her down, keep her close to him; took her as pupil, made her his assistant in studio and darkroom—anything, everything. She was still elusive. She was incorrigibly late—he called her "the late Miss Mather." But when she came she came laden. She brought him a world he did not know and made it visible and audible and tangible.... The woman was distinctly marvelous and infuriatingly an individual. But the new world, as it was so often to do for Edward, came in her shape.[8]

As Weston's attraction to Mather grew, he became quite perplexed about his personal predicament, because, of course, he was still very much a married man. Even though he endeavored to convince himself that his family was the most important thing in his life, he was unable to ignore the feelings he had for Mather, but no matter how intensely he and Mather were drawn to each other, their hours together were necessarily limited by other obligations, and they were forced to spend a good deal of time apart during the first few months of their relationship. That changed, however, when Mather came to Weston with a proposal that would bring them together with much greater frequency—all in the name of photography.

FOUNDING THE CAMERA PICTORIALISTS   Mather had decided it was time to form a camera club that would concentrate more on aesthetics and less on group activities, and she wanted Weston to join her in that endeavor.[9] She had already enlisted the help of Elmer Ellsworth and her Clay Street neighbor, Arthur S. Little, a draftsman for the Los Angeles Railway system, who also yearned to become a serious artistic photographer. Her vision for the new club was that it should remain small and select, with a minimum of bureaucracy and an overriding emphasis on creativity. The genesis of Mather's concept came as the result of three separate conflicts that were then ongoing. One had just surfaced among her Los Angeles photographer colleagues; another was erupting in San Francisco; and a third involved broader-based issues that were being hotly debated within the national photography community.

The dissension closest at hand was taking place within the ranks of the still-troubled Los Angeles Camera Club. Louis Fleckenstein, the elder statesman among California photographers, much respected because of the role he had played in organizing the Salon Club of America, had recently resigned as president of the LACC after a terribly disruptive, internal political squabble.[10] That struggle was one Mather had witnessed, and possibly even instigated, and now she hoped to convince Fleckenstein to direct her new organization, knowing his name would immediately bestow credibility on the endeavor.

Mather was also keenly aware of the ongoing battle between America's photographers and the management of the Pan-Pacific International Exposition, scheduled to open in San Francisco in early 1915. The fair's organizers had already announced that photographs would not be hung in the Fine Arts Building with paintings and other art works, but rather would be displayed in the Liberal Arts Building alongside commercial photographic equipment and supplies.[11] That decision had prompted a round of articles and protest letters in the San Francisco–based periodical, *Camera Craft*, and many photographers were now considering a boycott of the exhibition.[12] Those who wanted to be taken seriously as artists were wounded by the dismissive attitude of the fair's organizers and galvanized by the realization that, if they were going to change the public's perception about the artistic merits of photography, they would have to begin presenting their work in a more appropriate and dignified context. Mather was determined that her new club would address precisely that issue.

The third dispute involved a number of accomplished photographers who wished to carve out a legitimate niche for themselves somewhere between the autocratic Alfred Stieglitz and his exclusive, handpicked stable of photographers—a group he dubbed the Photo-Secessionists for their subjective, aesthetic vision that went beyond the purely documentary use of the medium—and the throngs of casual camera practitioners who swarmed from beauty spot to beauty spot, producing thousands of predictably prosaic photographs each year. A few of America's most renowned photographers were now vying for the privilege of putting Stieglitz in his place, and Clarence White had recently emerged as the most likely candidate to challenge the all-powerful, always irascible Stieglitz.

In response to this goal, the first issue of *Platinum Print* was published in October 1913. Edited by Edward R. Dickson and Charles Barnard, with substantive, behind-the-scenes, editorial input from Clarence White, the mission of the new journal, as described in the November 1913 issue of *Camera Craft*, was "to serve the needs of men and women whose delight is in the use of the camera as a personal expression."[13] The journal's prospectus explained that *Platinum Print* aimed to bridge the wide chasm between Stieglitz's exquisitely produced *Camera Work* and the plethora of cheaply produced camera magazines that specialized in giving instructional pointers to a mass audience.

Mather heard about the new journal almost immediately, and her enthusiasm for it undoubtedly played a critical role in the formulation of her own plans; in *Platinum Print*'s second issue, published in December 1913, there appeared an abbreviated letter to the editor. It read, "Platinum Print sounds most interesting. Enclosed find thirty cents for two copies," and it was signed by Margrethe Mather.[14]

By the early spring of 1914 Mather's concept for a new Los Angeles camera club had been realized. A dozen photographers were already on board, and the organization was ready to go public. A formal announcement was sent to all the major camera magazines in May:

Feeling the need of competent criticism and association, a number of the pictorially ambitious have formed the "Camera Pictorialists of Los Angeles." The membership is composed of Messrs. [Fred] Archer, [Elmer] Ellsworth, [Louis] Fleckenstein, [A. R.] Lindstedt, [Arthur S.] Little, [F. E.] Monteverde, [Charles E.] Smith, [J. Wiley] Wallace, [Edward] Weston, [Ernst] Williams, and Mrs. C. D. [Marie E.] Allen and Miss Margarethe Mather. Nothing but strictly pictorial work will be done and they hope to add their small mite towards the advancement of pictorial photography.[15]

Within a few weeks of the announcement, Fleckenstein agreed to assume the role of director, and membership quickly grew to the club's stated maximum capacity of fifteen.[16] Members dined together at a Quaker cafeteria before their informal monthly gatherings in the Blanchard Building. Eschewing bureaucracy as much as possible, the club had no bylaws or membership dues. The only requirement was that each member had to bring at least one new photograph to every meeting. Soon after the club's inception, the Camera Pictorialists began to discuss the possibility of sponsoring an annual, by-invitation-only salon.

WESTON RECEIVES ACCLAIM   The year 1914 turned out to be an extremely important one for Weston. Not only did he join Mather in taking a stand for the advancement of photography as a fine art, he also began to receive widespread national and international acclaim. By the end of that year he had become a highly regarded mainstay on the salon circuit, exhibiting a wide array of images in most of the major national and international salon competitions.

The photograph that brought him the greatest success was a genre portrait titled *Carlota* (fig. 20), in which Margrethe Mather portrays Empress Carlota, widow of Ferdinand Maximilian Joseph, Archduke of Austria, also known as Emperor Maximilian of Mexico. The Archduke had been named Emperor of Mexico by Napoleon III, only to be court-martialed and shot to death in 1867 after the French monarch abruptly withdrew his occupying forces. The unfortunate emperor had been much adored by his Belgian-born wife, Carlota, and following her husband's violent demise, the distraught widow had lost her hold on reality. Declared insane by her own brother, Carlota was packed up and sent back to Belgium, where she had been confined to a chateau in the countryside ever since.

Weston's decision to depict the romantically tragic figure of Carlota may have been suggested by Mather. Mollie Price's ex-husband, Jig Cook, had published a historical novel titled *Roderico Taliaferro: A Story of Maximilian's Empire* in 1903,[17] and although the book had been only a modest commercial success, Mather's familiarity with it might have prompted her to propose the grief-stricken Carlota as a compelling subject for Weston's camera. Depicting the ill-fated Empress of Mexico was, in fact, a particularly astute choice at a time when the citizens of Los Angeles were becoming increasingly aware of Mexican politics due to the ongoing battles between rivals Pancho Villa and Venustiano Carranza. Their aggressions were threatening to

FIGURE 20. Edward Weston, *Carlota*, 1914. Platinum print, 23.5 × 15.8 cm (9¼ × 6¼ in.). Philadelphia, Penn., Collection of John Medveckis

encroach on American soil at any moment and bring the still unresolved Mexican Revolution to the front doorstep of fearful Angelenos.

Weston created *Carlota* in January 1914,[18] and when he showed it later that year it became the first of his exhibited images to feature Mather as model. Almost immediately their pairing as artist and muse brought him good fortune. With *Carlota* prominent among his entries, Weston won a bronze medal and two honorable mentions at the Toronto Camera Club Salon;[19] a first place prize at the annual Photographers' Association of America convention in Atlanta;[20] and the Grand Prize for the best group of photographs submitted to the Northwest Photographers' Convention in Saint Paul, Minnesota.[21] However, his most significant success came at the London Salon of Photography, which was generally regarded as the most prestigious and competitive photography salon in the world.

Mr. Bertram Park, secretary of the London Salon, waxed lyrical over the American newcomer, and declared Weston's five photographs the best group of pictures submitted:

> Mr. Weston is evidently a man of original ideas, sound technic [sic], a refined artistic perception, and sense for decoration. I cannot remember having ever seen any of his work before, and it is a very great pleasure to welcome a newcomer whose pictures show such a distinctive personality....
>
> [In] "Carlota,"...the model...is lit from top and from the rear, so that her face is mostly in shadow with a halo of light illuminating her profile. There is a charming softness about the work, a softness which is so different from fuzziness, and an atmosphere of refinement and mystery which is exceedingly attractive.[22]

Another of Weston's photographs taken in 1914 was an image of his four-year-old son, Chandler, titled *I Do Believe in Fairies*,[23] in which the chubby little boy stands naked in a garden, his back to the camera as he searches for imaginary pixies. A composition remarkably similar to Mather's *Maid of Arcady* made two years earlier, it was the first of Weston's images to depict an allegorical subject, taken out of doors in a romanticized, "high-key" landscape, a pictorial device that would soon become a characteristic feature of his photographs.

Weston's portrait of his assistant, Rae Davis, posing in dappled sunlight, was yet another example of this trend in his work. Exhibited under a variety of titles it was selected for inclusion in the 1914 volume of the prestigious British annual, *Photograms of the Year*.[24] As a result of Weston's national and international successes, a local newspaper featured a glowing write-up about the young photographer and the work he was so determinedly sending out into the world from his modest studio in tiny Tropico:

> Mr. Edward H. Weston, who conducts the bungalow studio at 113 North Brand boulevard, Tropico, has an international reputation as an artist of ability in his profession, that of photographer....

Mr. Weston has to his credit nearly half a hundred prizes won at exhibits everywhere. Honors won in the past few months will serve to prove the excellence of his work....

Just recently, however, Mr. Weston has been enjoying the greatest distinction of any that has yet come to him. He sent six prints to the International Salon of Photography held at the galleries of the Royal Society of Painters in water colors, 5A Pall Mall East, London, England. He received a letter stating that of the six photographs submitted five were being hung. This is the leading exhibition of the photographic world....To have five out of six prints hung is indeed true recognition of merit.[25]

This article must have captured the attention of Mrs. Randall (Helen) Hutchinson of Pasadena, the Art Chairwoman of the Friday Morning Club (FMC), an influential women's organization headquartered in downtown Los Angeles, because soon after it appeared she contacted Weston and invited him to exhibit his work at the club.

CIVIC MATTERS   Founded in 1891 and housed in its own building at 940 South Figueroa, the FMC had recently played an instrumental role in the fight for women's suffrage, thanks to the considerable power its all-female membership wielded within the local community.[26] Many club members were married to men who made up the financial, industrial, and political backbone of the city, and the women did not hesitate to parlay their husbands' clout, as well as their own, to make their influence widely felt.

An invitation to speak or exhibit at the FMC indicated a certain degree of social acceptance and conferred a large dose of cultural prestige on its recipient. Knowing this, Weston must have eagerly agreed to display a dozen and a half of his photographs, including the five he had just shown to such acclaim in the London Salon, at the FMC's clubhouse during November 1914.[27] He also attended one of the club's luncheon meetings as guest of honor. As a result of this event, Weston finally received his first, albeit perfunctory, notices in the *Los Angeles Times*, that newspaper being far too concerned with civic matters and society fetes to pay much attention to photography.[28]

Freelance journalist Homer Croy, in the midst of a round-the-world tour for *Leslie's Weekly*, had recently stopped over in Los Angeles long enough to make a few acerbic observations about the place. In his commentary he poked fun at the pronunciation guide, printed each morning on the *Times's* editorial page, reminding citizens to enunciate their fair city's name as "Loce Ahng'-hayl-ais," and he mocked the local fascination with cafeterias, describing how Angelenos "get a plate of soup here, run over to Hollywood for asparagus, then trot back to town for a plate of prunes."[29] He also feigned amazement over the typical Los Angeles apartment, declaring that it consisted solely of a room with a telephone, a gas burner, and a bathtub that folded up into the wall. The *Times* excerpted his amusing essay but quickly moved on to more pressing matters.

What should most concern the city's residents, lectured the *Times* editorial page, were the mysterious foreign forces conspiring to undermine the good life of Angelenos who were not vigilant. Opium ships were regularly landing near Ensenada, Mexico, the *Times* reported, where a "well-known Chinese firm"[30] waited to take possession of the drug and schemed for its illegal distribution among Californians. Following this revelation, articles decrying the crimes and depravities of the Chinese began to appear in the *Times*. At the same time, a proposal for a new civic center, to be sited where Chinatown currently stood, was put forth. The *Times* also let it be known that "local reds" were arming themselves with rifles following a series of demonstrations by the unemployed in New York City and a spate of violent strikes in the mining camps of the western states.[31] Dire warnings were issued to anyone who dared disturb the peace in Los Angeles.

Even this sinister cloud of implied evil hanging over the city did nothing to put a damper on urban expansion, however. The largest excavation in the city's history was in progress along Seventh Street between Grand and Hope streets, where the flagship J. W. Robinson Department Store would soon tower above its neighbors.[32] Further proposals regarding the redevelopment of Bunker Hill were also under consideration. This time around, the plans called for an open cut through the hill to widen Fifth Street between Grand and Olive streets, along with the incorporation of a tunnel that would extend Fifth Street beneath the southern end of the old State Normal School campus and allow automobile access between Olive and Flower streets.[33] At the top of the hill, directly above the proposed tunnel, a fine new municipal arts center would be erected. This revised scheme was applauded by all those with an interest in the cultural life of the city, particularly the members of the Friday Morning Club.

MATHER AND THE MOVIES   Meanwhile, aside from her portrayal of Empress Carlota and her incipient role in the founding of the Camera Pictorialists, Margrethe Mather's name was nowhere to be found in the newspaper columns, photography journals, or salon exhibitions of 1914. Her absence was very likely due to yet another introduction provided by her friend Elmer Ellsworth who had just become acquainted with a brilliant, twenty-five-year-old Englishman named Charles Spencer Chaplin. Chaplin had only recently left the vaudeville circuit to begin working at Mack Sennett's Keystone Studio in the rural district of Edendale, halfway between downtown Los Angeles and Tropico. Although the Cockney comedian was just beginning to adapt his skills to Sennett's particular brand of slapstick comedy, his raw talent was overwhelmingly obvious to both Ellsworth and Mather.

The desultory Ellsworth, known for his short attention span, was famous as an inveterate practical jokester, so he was naturally drawn to Chaplin's subtle but fast-paced antics. Ellsworth stood over six feet tall and sported a rather flaccid, pear-shaped silhouette, topped off by a lopsided face, a physique that only complemented his own comedic proclivities (see fig. 16). He loved nothing more than conceiving and carrying out complicated pranks, and his droll sense of humor, coupled with a feigned, bumbling naïveté, usually had those around him convulsed in hysterics.[34] He was also notorious for inveigling his many friends into helping him perpetrate his elaborate schemes.

In one such episode, Ellsworth and an entourage of conspirators boarded a Pacific Electric Red Car for an excursion from downtown Los Angeles to the Santa Monica beachfront.[35] As Ellsworth's friends climbed aboard the streetcar, one by one, he made a great show of ceremoniously ticking their names off a list. There ensued a riotous ride to the seashore, but just as they arrived at their destination, the rowdy passengers suddenly ordered themselves and filed, military fashion, down the steps. As the last rider disembarked, Ellsworth abruptly leapt off the streetcar, turned on his heel, and tipped his hat to the bewildered conductor, at which point the entire group took off running down the street, leaving their fares unpaid and the flustered conductor angrily shaking his fist after them.

If such conduct was reminiscent of a caper from a silent comedy short it was for good reason. One of Ellsworth's closest friends was Ford Sterling, then starring as Chief Teeheezel in Mack Sennett's Keystone Kops films,[36] and the pranksters on board the Red Car were Kops in street clothes, perfecting a routine at the unsuspecting conductor's expense. Fittingly, Ellsworth was about to find his true calling as a gag writer for some of the best-known comedy actors of the silent film era.

THE LITTLE TRAMP   Indeed, Ellsworth had already been dabbling in this vocation when he accompanied Mather to Weston's studio, and it was not long after their meeting that his interest in still photography evolved into an obsession with images that danced and flickered across a silver screen. Ellsworth's conversion to "moving pictures" came about, in large part, because of his friendship with Chaplin. It was Ford Sterling who had initially brought the two men together, and Chaplin, still ill-at-ease with his brash American colleagues, later recalled his first edgy encounter with Ellsworth in his autobiography:

> Ford...would console me, and after work he would occasionally give me a lift downtown, where we would stop in at the Alexandria Bar for a drink and meet several of his friends. One of them, a Mr. Elmer Ellsworth, whom I disliked at first and thought rather crass, would jokingly taunt me....
>
> He was a big, cumbersome man...with a melancholy, hangdog expression, hairless face, sad eyes, a loose mouth and a smile that showed two missing front teeth. Ford whispered impressively that he was a great authority on literature, finance and politics, one of the best-informed men in the country, and that he had a great sense of humor. However, I did not appreciate it and decided I would try to avoid him.[37]

Then one night at the Alexandria Bar, on the heels of yet another tart exchange, Ellsworth offered to buy Chaplin a drink, and the two men put aside their misgivings long enough to get acquainted. One of Chaplin's biographers later described Ellsworth as "a socialist, with a fund of stories about the glory days of the IWW (Industrial Workers of the World, also known as the Wobblies), [who] soon began inviting Charlie to his house...and introduced him to his socialist friends."[38] Two of those friends were Margrethe Mather and Edward Weston.

Charlie Chaplin had arrived in California in 1913, weary from the rigors of the vaudeville circuit and eager to launch a movie career. His first Los Angeles residence was a threadbare room at the Hotel Northern[39] on Second Street between Hill and Olive streets, just one block from Mather's quarters at the Chadakoin. Infamous among his actor colleagues for neglecting the niceties of personal hygiene, Chaplin often betrayed his seedy living accommodations and general disinterest in tidiness by showing up for work with frayed collars and food-stained lapels.

Even his new boss, the notoriously coarse Mack Sennett, decided that if Chaplin was going to become a movie star he would have to start looking like one, so in mid-1914 Sennett secured an apartment for the rumpled comedian at his own club, the Los Angeles Athletic Club (LAAC) at Seventh and Olive streets, where Chaplin would have the services of a valet to monitor his wardrobe and grooming, as well as an opportunity to mingle socially with the power brokers of the film industry.[40] He would also have access to the club's physical fitness facilities, a perquisite even more critical to the comedian's future success. Chaplin, whose slight build belied his prowess as an accomplished athlete, already embodied the LAAC's motto, "Health, Recreation, Grace, and Vigor," but in the club's gymnasium he would be able to maintain a disciplined program of exercise that would further develop his acrobatic skills and hone his split-second timing.

While he was employed by Sennett, Chaplin worked furiously to churn out thirty-five of the short films known as two-reelers. In addition to Ford Sterling, Chaplin's Keystone colleagues included Roscoe (Fatty) Arbuckle and Mabel Normand, comedians already well established in their careers and generously compensated for their efforts. Chaplin, who was determined to become just as popular with audiences and even more successful financially, began to experiment with various costumes and props in an effort to invent his own signature character. By the end of 1914 he had combined a pair of oversized shoes—originally belonging to Ford Sterling—with an ensemble consisting of baggy pants, a bowler hat, and an abbreviated, bristling moustache to create the on-screen persona that would soon become known around the world as the Little Tramp.

Chaplin's provocative shenanigans, together with his disarmingly irreverent attitude, toothy grin, and death-defying pratfalls, made him an instant hit with moviegoers, and as his fame grew, so did his circle of friends and admirers. Ellsworth and Mather became two of his most trusted companions, and Chaplin soon persuaded Ellsworth to leave his current job at Universal Studios and begin writing comedy scenarios for him. Using the streets and parks of downtown Los Angeles as backdrops, Ellsworth strung together story lines while Chaplin waddled and skipped his way into American hearts, providing much needed comic relief from the worries and struggles of everyday life.

As Ellsworth and Mather became an integral part of Chaplin's ever-expanding orbit, they were introduced to a number of the talented and fascinating people who were beginning to converge on Hollywood from all parts of the world. As a result Mather allowed her photography career to lapse for a few months while she and Ellsworth immersed themselves in Chaplin's celebrity. Movies were fast becoming a glamorous business, and the two friends had plenty of opportunities to observe at close range the ambitious individuals who unhesitatingly pursued fame and fortune at breakneck speeds. Those months were heady ones for Mather, who was free to join the fun-loving, high-living movie crowd, while Weston went home to his wife and children every night.

MATHER TURNS ANARCHIST   Paradoxically, at the same time Mather and Ellsworth were lightheartedly frolicking with Chaplin they were also becoming more deeply enmeshed in the anarchist movement. From 1910 through 1914 Emma Goldman had continued her annual visits to California—showing support for the McNamara brothers in the autumn of 1911, while they stood trial and were found guilty of the *Los Angeles Times* bombing; fighting for the right of free speech in San Diego in May 1912; and decrying the unfair treatment of Mexican freedom fighters in the spring of 1913.[41] After each visit Goldman would publish the names of those who had been most helpful to her cause, and beginning in 1912 Elmer Ellsworth regularly appeared on that list.[42] Others named were Dr. James Russell Price (Mollie Price's father); Dr. and Mrs. Perceval Gerson; Enrique and Ricardo Magon, publishers and editors of a Spanish-language, pro-revolution newspaper in Los Angeles; and Moses Lerner,[43] a Russian-born street peddler recently arrived in California from Toronto.

In the early spring of 1914, just as Goldman was making final preparations for her next cross-country tour, the unemployed workers of New York City waged a series of protest meetings in Cooper Union and Union Square that provoked violent responses from the police.[44] Although Goldman was incensed by the ruthless brutality unleashed on the protestors, she was forced to depart on her lecture tour in spite of the emotions running high in New York City. Before leaving she entrusted the *Mother Earth* offices to her colleague, Alexander Berkman. Goldman interrupted her journey west to give many speeches along the way, including an extended series of lectures in Chicago, before arriving in Los Angeles on May 15 for a three-week stay. During her prolonged absence, *Mother Earth* took on a much more incendiary tone as Berkman, who had no patience for compromise, exercised his newly assumed editorial powers.

On July 4, while Goldman was visiting San Francisco, an anarchist bomb, supposedly intended for the much-reviled industrialist John D. Rockefeller, then in residence at Kykuit, his summer home near Tarrytown, New York, accidentally exploded prematurely, demolishing an apartment building at 1626 Lexington Avenue in New York City.[45] Three of the bomb makers were blown to bits, and Berkman organized a funeral demonstration for his fallen colleagues in Union Square.

Following the event, an elaborate funerary urn containing the ashes of the cremated anarchists went on display at the *Mother Earth* offices.[46] The urn had been crafted by the sculptor/poet Adolf Wolff, a close friend of two other Goldman followers—Joseph Ely O'Carroll, a fiery Dublin-born Irishman who had been badly beaten by the police during the demonstrations of the unemployed earlier in the year, and Emmanuel Radnitsky, a young artist from Brooklyn and a frequenter of Goldman's Ferrer Center, who had recently wed Wolff's ex-wife, the Belgian poetess, Adon Lacroix.

Although Goldman was most anxious to return to New York City, she remained in California long enough to fulfill her speaking commitments. As she was making her way back across the country, she sent Berkman a handwritten report on her West Coast experiences, a communiqué that, as usual, included a list of people who had been helpful during her stay. Forced to interpret Goldman's often illegible scrawl, Berkman offered thanks in the August 1914 issue of *Mother Earth* to Mollie Price, Elmer Ellsworth, and "Margaret Mato" for their active support during Goldman's recent Los Angeles visits.[47] Featured on the magazine's cover was a drawing that depicted the double-headed dragon of "Capitalism" and "Government" devouring a helpless figure labeled "Humanity." This grim political cartoon was the work of Emmanuel Radnitsky, the artist from the Ferrer Center, who had only recently shortened his multisyllabic name to Man Ray.

Recognition from Goldman was much appreciated by her acolytes, but after their names appeared in her magazine they often found themselves operating under the watchful eye of law enforcement. Predictably, Price, Ellsworth, Mather, and by association, Chaplin, were soon added to the list of Los Angeles troublemakers and subjected to the unflinching gaze of local police. Also taking an interest in their activities was the Bureau of Investigation, a division of the United States Department of Justice and the predecessor to what would soon become the Federal Bureau of Investigation (FBI).

By the time Goldman returned to the helm of *Mother Earth* many of her anarchist colleagues had scattered. Adolf Wolff was serving out a jail sentence on Blackwell's Island for his subversive political activities;[48] Joseph O'Carroll, now known to the police by the sobriquet Wild Joe because of his fearless belligerence during the Union Square riots, was nursing his wounds amidst the sand dunes of Cape Cod;[49] and Man Ray and Adon Lacroix were living in a small cabin in Ridgefield, New Jersey, where they had spent a good part of the previous year collaborating with poet Alfred Kreymborg on a small literary journal called the *Glebe*. Featured in the journal's inaugural issue was Wolff's poetic ode to anarchism, titled "Songs, Sighs, and Curses."[50]

CHOOSING SIDES　A roiling undercurrent of dissatisfaction was now spreading across America. This general feeling of unrest stemmed primarily from the federal government's unfair labor policies and management's refusal to improve deplorable working conditions. But critical as these issues were, domestic woes soon took a back seat to more significant international events.

Just days before the botched attempt on Rockefeller's life, a successful assassination had occurred in Sarajevo, the capital of Bosnia.

On June 28, 1914, Archduke Franz Ferdinand of the Austro-Hungarian Empire had been gunned down by a Serbian suicide terrorist. Austria's reaction was swift and unmitigated, and one month later, assured of Germany's full support, Austria-Hungary declared war on Serbia. Germany, under the leadership of Kaiser Wilhelm II, wasted no time making good on its promise to Austria, and in early August 1914 the German Kaiser also formalized hostilities against Russia and its ruler, Czar Nicholas II, who happened to be the German Kaiser's first cousin. When Germany subsequently launched invasions of Luxembourg and Belgium, the King of England, George V (also a cousin to both the kaiser and the czar), went on the offensive and declared war against the Germans.

As the trio of royal cousins feuded, and European countries lined up like dominoes behind them, Americans were stunned to find the world inexorably sliding toward an unprecedented apocalypse. Although President Woodrow Wilson reiterated his election campaign promise to keep the United States isolated from conflicts in other parts of the world, America's usual smugness and apathy toward international affairs began to dissolve as the Great War spread into the Alsace-Lorraine region of France, along the border with Germany.

While the French stood their ground in the horrific Battle of the Marne and Americans began to grasp the enormity of the situation, Edward Weston was preoccupied on the domestic front. Weston and Mather had now known each other for just over a year, but their ongoing love affair remained a well-kept secret, and Weston was not about to confess his illicit behavior to his wife. Flora offered him a conventional home filled to overflowing with the boundless energy of his two young sons, and he took considerable comfort there in spite of his growing disillusionment with the obligations of married life (see fig. 21). In another of Nancy Newhall's insightful profiles, written around 1951, she vividly described Weston's stubbornly loyal but exasperating spouse:

> And then there was always Flora... too vital, too generous, too noble, too emotional, always throwing herself before events as though they were juggernauts, rising to any illness of the children as though it were the Black Death and she alone could save civilization;... her very passage through a room disrupting conversation, even thought, her presence "like an electric fan nobody remembers to turn off"... Flora who would give you her blood when all you wanted was coffee.[51]

Nevertheless, Weston fully recognized the strengths, along with the many shortcomings, of the woman he had chosen to be his wife and the mother of his children, so he remained with Flora even though their relationship was becoming more strained with each passing day. Of course, he was also painfully aware of his financial indebtedness to his wife's family. Having built both his home and studio on his in-laws' property, so he could live and work rent free, and thus

FIGURE 21. Unidentified photographer, Flora Weston, Brett Weston, Edward Weston, and Chandler Weston, 1914. Gelatin silver print, 11.3 × 16 cm (4⁷/₁₆ × 6⁵/₁₆ in.). Los Angeles, J. Paul Getty Museum, 86.xm.719.5

support his household and business on a very modest income, Weston was now growing increasingly uncomfortable with this arrangement. What had once seemed like a shrewd business decision was fast turning into a stifling form of entrapment, and he began to regard his economic tethers with mounting resentment.

In spite of these distracting complications at home, Weston continued to be mesmerized by Mather and her sophistication in matters of love. He found their surreptitious liaisons particularly exciting, because Mather's approach to lovemaking was creative, and the inexperienced Weston had never before strayed beyond the conventional. Although in later years some of Weston's acquaintances would claim that his relationship with Mather had been purely platonic, this confusion over their status as lovers was probably a question of semantics, stemming from misleading comments made by Weston himself. It seems his definition of a sexual relationship was quite narrowly drawn, leaving little room for nuance. As far as Edward was concerned, sex meant intercourse. Anything short of the act itself simply did not count.[52]

Challenges, 1915

As Charlie Chaplin's popularity grew under Mack Sennett's tutelage, his star became an impressive comet cutting a brilliant swath through the skies above Hollywood. The numerous two-reelers Chaplin churned out during those months at Keystone Studio secured his reputation as a box-office draw, but when his contract with Keystone came to an end, Chaplin allowed himself to be wooed away by an offer from one of Keystone's closest competitors, Essanay Studios.[1]

Unfortunately for the comedian, however, his new employers were headquartered in Chicago, so in January 1915 Chaplin bundled himself into a heavy overcoat and headed for the snow-covered shores of Lake Michigan. It only took a few frosty weeks in the Windy City for Chaplin to decide he had endured enough. He insisted on returning to California where he could fulfill the balance of his contractual obligations in warmer climes, at the studio's back lot, located on a parcel of ranchland near San Francisco. It may have been Chaplin's prolonged absence from Los Angeles that precipitated Mather's reemergence on the photography scene in early 1915.

Although Mather and Weston had founded the Camera Pictorialists in the spring of 1914, she apparently retained her membership in the rival Los Angeles Camera Club until at least February 1915, for she participated in the club's fifth annual exhibition held that month at the LACC's headquarters on Hill Street. Her submissions brought her to the attention of local newspapers for the first time:

> Five of the twenty-three exhibitors are women. They are Mrs. Hattie Buskirk, Mrs. Gertrude M. Dodds, Miss Margrethe Mather, Mrs. B. Gray Shirley and Mrs. D. E. Spencer. As might be expected, they lean towards the home for subjects, though they vie and in some cases surpass the male exhibitors in the catching of the vital beauty of Southland scenes.[2]

In spite of this rather patronizing review, which evaluated the women's contributions based solely on gender, Mather must have been thrilled to have her efforts publicly recognized.

The LACC exhibition was probably the occasion documented in two photographs taken by Russell Coryell in 1915 and preserved in one of his California scrapbooks. They show Mather perched on a stool in front of a wall hung with photographs (fig. 22). Her hair is carelessly gathered into a frowsy bun and she wears a work smock over her dress, as though she had just

FIGURE 22. Attributed to Russell Coryell (American, 1891–1941), Margrethe Mather at Photography Exhibition, ca. 1915. Gelatin silver print, 9 × 6.5 cm (3 ½ × 2 ½ in.). Cold Spring Harbor, New York, Collection of Bea Coryell

emerged from long hours in the darkroom. Across her lap lies a precariously balanced portfolio case of the type used to transport and store photographs. Coryell's portraits of Mather reveal a serious, determined young woman, quite unlike the serenely disarming coquette depicted in Weston's portrait from the previous year. Instead Coryell's snapshots provide a fascinating, first glimpse of Margrethe Mather, fine art photographer.

BOYLAND   By the spring of 1915, Russell Coryell had been living in Santa Barbara for a year and a half. He was now teaching at Boyland, an experimental boarding school that based its instructional methods on those introduced by Coryell's parents at Emma Goldman's Modern School. The founder of Boyland, a young man named Prince Hopkins, was, like Mollie Price, an admirer of Goldman's educational philosophy and a friend of the Coryell family.

Hopkins had been born in Oakland, California, in 1885, but in the 1890s his parents had moved to Santa Barbara, where they built a gracious home called El Nido at the corner of Garden and Pedregosa streets.[3] Hopkins attended the Thacher School in nearby Ojai, the Chateau de Lancy near Geneva, Switzerland, and the esteemed Hill School in Pennsylvania, before graduating from Yale University in 1906. He then went on to enroll in an assortment of classes at Massachusetts Institute of Technology, Stanford University, and Columbia University.

Rebelling against his privileged upbringing, Hopkins veered sharply to the left in his interests while he was living in New York City. On a lark he attended the Anarchists' Ball, an annual fund-raising event, where he first encountered Emma Goldman and her colleagues. He came to admire the fiery, fearless Goldman, and soon he began contributing part of his generous allowance to her many causes. Most assuredly it did not please Hopkins's conservative father when he learned that his son was one of the principal benefactors of Goldman's Modern School.[4]

Around 1911 Prince Hopkins was diagnosed with tuberculosis, so he returned to California to recuperate at the acclaimed Pottenger Clinic in Monrovia, where his brief association with Goldman inspired him to immerse himself in the literature and politics of Russia during his confinement.[5] His intensive course of study resulted in his further alignment with leftist causes and a complete estrangement from his father. Nevertheless, upon the elder Hopkins's death in 1913, the family fortune, derived from an inheritance of stock in the Singer (Sewing Machine) Manufacturing Company, passed from father to son. It was with a portion of these funds, reportedly amounting to some $3.5 million,[6] that Prince Hopkins opened Boyland, his Santa Barbara boarding school loosely modeled on Goldman's Modern School prototype.

Boyland was located on fourteen acres adjoining Mountain Drive in the hilly terrain known as Santa Barbara's Riviera.[7] Like its French namesake, the area offered a glorious view of the city and the sea in one direction and a ridge of rugged mountains in the other. The school's main building featured broad porches where the children could gather to attend classes in the out of doors.[8] Hopkins's plan was to teach the boys about agriculture, engineering, and geography by encouraging them to plant vegetable gardens, build structures of their own design, and lay out a map of the world on the school's playground.

Hopkins embraced a practical but progressive approach to learning, and Russell Coryell, with his rather unusual upbringing and immense curiosity, was the perfect person to carry out his employer's unstructured but ambitious educational program. Coryell enthusiastically agreed with Hopkins's philosophy of "educating by doing," and as much as Coryell's weakened physical condition would allow, he threw himself wholeheartedly into his teaching experience, regarding it as one more facet of his own academic enlightenment. He also found time to correspond regularly with his Los Angeles friends, particularly Maud Emily Taylor, of whom he was especially fond.

In one of her responses, Taylor included a few snapshots of herself and Mollie Price (possibly made by Margrethe Mather), which Coryell pasted in his scrapbook alongside his candids of Mather at her 1915 exhibition.[9] A few pages further along in his album he inserted two formal portraits of himself taken by Mather,[10] in which he poses in a white sailor shirt and soft felt hat. His handsome face is somber, an uncharacteristic expression for the normally ebullient Coryell.

Two of Coryell's favorite students at Boyland were Leicester and Thornton Wagner, the sons of another of Margrethe Mather's friends, writer and portrait painter Rob Wagner. Wagner's life experiences were varied enough that his mind was open to many possibilities, and he fully appreciated what Hopkins was trying to accomplish at his school. Wagner hailed originally from Detroit, where he had begun his career as an illustrator for the *Detroit Free Press*.[11] He went on to produce artwork for *Chap-Book*,[12] a magazine headquartered in Chicago, and *Criterion*,[13] a periodical published in Manhattan. He then traveled to London and Paris where he studied painting.

Eventually Wagner returned to New York City, married, and sired two sons, but in 1905, when his young wife was taken seriously ill, the Wagners headed west in search of a gentler climate. They decided to settle in Santa Barbara where, a few months later, Wagner's wife died.[14] He spent the next four years raising his two boys and building his reputation as a portrait painter, while sharing a State Street studio with fellow artist John M. Gamble.[15]

Around 1909 Wagner remarried and moved to Los Angeles. There he began to achieve recognition in Southland artistic circles. His accomplishments were frequently chronicled in the local press, along with those of other noteworthy artists, such as Elmer and Marion Kavanaugh Wachtel, William and Julia Bracken Wendt, Carl Oscar Borg, Hanson Puthoff, Charles A. Rogers, Detlef Sammann, Charles Percy Austin, Helena Dunlap, Jean Mannheim, Mabel Alvarez, Granville Redmond, Joseph Greenbaum, and Nellie Huntington Gere. Wagner also tried his hand at writing, and one of his screenplays, *The Artist's Sons*, was made into a movie in 1911.[16] Perhaps Wagner's most admiring supporter was *Times* critic Antony Anderson who had a keen appreciation for the artist's talent, cordiality, and wit.[17]

The moment Prince Hopkins opened Boyland, Wagner enrolled his children there. He was hopeful that Hopkins's avant-garde approach to education would benefit his two boys, who still sorely missed their mother. If Russell Coryell's scrapbooks are any indication, then Wagner's hopes were realized, because the albums contain many candids of Wagner's towheaded sons, cheerfully absorbed in various activities at Boyland. While it was their mutual interest in progressive social and educational causes that first drew Wagner to Hopkins, it was probably Rob Wagner's brother, James R. H. Wagner, who was responsible for introducing him to Margrethe Mather and Edward Weston.

James Wagner followed his brother from Santa Barbara to Los Angeles, where he then embarked on a prosperous career in real estate.[18] He also played a role in the management of the annual Pasadena Tournament of Roses celebration,[19] and he pursued an interest in photography by joining the Los Angeles Camera Club. Like Mather, James Wagner was a participant in the 1915 LACC salon, and his photographs were cited as one of the "most pleasing contributions"[20] to that exhibition in the same newspaper review that praised Mather's work. The Wagner brothers inevitably crossed paths with Mather and Weston, and in turn, Charlie Chaplin. Rob Wagner and Chaplin discovered they were especially compatible, and the two became fast friends, forging what would turn out to be a beneficial but highly controversial relationship for both men.

Later that summer Maud Emily Taylor informed Coryell and Mather that Mollie Price's former mother-in-law, Ellen Katherine Cook, would soon be arriving from Iowa for a visit. Known as Ma-Mie[21] to her friends, Ellen Cook was a recently widowed, diminutive, sixty-year-old who was just beginning to emerge from her previous life as the very conventional wife of a prominent judge of the Superior Court of Iowa.[22] Having finally discovered the pleasures of eccentricity, she was now seeking out stimulating and unusual experiences of all kinds, and she arrived in Los Angeles fresh from a holiday spent on Cape Cod, where she had visited her son, Jig Cook, in Provincetown and socialized with many of his artistic, literary, and political friends from Greenwich Village, including Max Eastman, Floyd Dell, Eugene O'Neill, and Hutchins Hapgood.[23]

Now determined to seize the moment in all matters, shortly after her arrival in Los Angeles Cook suddenly announced that she would be taking her grandchildren, her former daughter-in-law, and Maud Emily Taylor to the Bay Area for the rest of the summer. There was good reason to go north, for at that particular moment San Francisco was the most exciting place in America to be.

THE PAN-PACIFIC INTERNATIONAL EXPOSITION   Indeed, all eyes were now turned toward San Francisco. The long-anticipated Pan-Pacific International Exposition (PPIE) had opened its doors the previous February, and the event was attracting tourists from all over the world.[24] Celebrating the opening of the Panama Canal and the commercial opportunities the waterway represented for America, the Exposition emphasized the increased facility of access the canal would bring to cargo ships crisscrossing the Pacific Ocean. The underlying purpose of the Exposition was to position San Francisco as the ideal gateway through which all incoming and outgoing merchandise could pass easily and efficiently. The result was a sudden burst of interest in the aesthetics of the Orient as San Franciscans began to realize that their city's fortunes were destined to be closely linked with those of their Asian neighbors.

Laid out on a flat stretch of landfill adjacent to San Francisco Bay, the fairgrounds blazed with lights for ten straight months. The entryway was highlighted by the Fountain of Energy, designed by the sculptor Alexander Stirling Calder, and a glittering architectural folly known as the Tower of Jewels (a clever play on words by the tower's designer, Jules Guerin). The fair complex was divided into three majestic courtyards—the Court of Abundance, the Court of the Universe, and the Court of Nations. It was an unforgettable spectacle—the most important in California's history thus far—and it was not to be missed under any circumstances.

Not everyone was delighted with the Exposition, however. For two years prior to the fair's opening, the photographers of America had continued to begrudge the fact that their work would be displayed in the Palace of Liberal Arts rather than in the much grander Palace of Fine Arts, and many potential contributors had decided to make good on their threat to ignore the competition altogether. Nevertheless, the exhibition went forward as planned, and in the end 148 photographs were hung, including three by Edward Weston.[25]

Once again Weston chose to exhibit *Carlota*, undoubtedly hoping to repeat his successes of the previous year. This time, however, the grand prize went to San Francisco photographer

Anne Brigman.[26] Two gold and four silver medals were also awarded to others, while Weston had to settle for bronze medal honors along with Francis Bruguière of San Francisco and Karl Struss of New York City. On this occasion, Weston's medal winner was not *Carlota*, but *Child Study in Gray*,[27] a portrait of Tropico's own Miss Marjorie Green, a winsome little tyke sporting carefully crafted sausage curls.

Weston paid a visit to the Exposition and later discussed his experience in an address given before the Los Angeles College Women's Club. He was indignant at the way photography had been so summarily treated:

> We will start today with this premise, that pictorial photography is, or at least can be, one of the Fine Arts, basing our assumption on its acceptance in that classification by such institutions as Carnegie Institute, Chicago Art Institute, Albright Art Gallery and others. On the contrary California, usually progressive, relegated pictorial photography to the Liberal Arts building at the Exposition where it reposed in a delightful "atmosphere" with telescopes, talking machines, butter churns and patent nursing bottles!
>
> I suppose the exposition authorities were imbued with the old idea that photographs are simply mechanical products because [they are] made with a machine—the camera. To be sure most of them are; however, may I offer this suggestion, that a painter if he uses only his hand and brush is a mere draughtsman, but, if he uses his brain to make the brush—and hand—create an idea and express his personality, then and then only is he an artist. Why not apply the same reasoning to a photographer?...
>
> ...Refering [sic] again to the Exposition, that little room, which contained pictorial photographs, lost in one corner of the Liberal Arts Building among the wilderness of mechanical devices, contained many a gem, that would put to shame some of the paintings in the Fine Arts Building....I felt a wave of indignation come over me as I...thought of the exquisite prints by Clarence H. White, Karl Struss, Anne Brigman, and others, hidden away in the Liberal Arts Building. Many leading workers in modern photography would not exhibit on account of this classification, hence the exhibit was not at all representative of the best that can be done in this country.
>
> Those of you who have not followed the progress of photography will, I hope, not be misled into believing that pictures which are sometimes displayed with great assumption as having won awards in this and that salon, are examples of what our leading workers are doing. Many a so called photographic salon is entirely undeserving of such a title and the standard in them is so low that an award means next to nothing....
>
> ...To my mind, it is a faint way of damning a photograph to say it looks like a drawing or etching—for to have any art value Photography must stand on its own base, must offer some inherent quality not obtainable in the other arts....I have no use...for the photographer who with malice aforethought, deliberately apes the technique of a painting or drawing.[28]

Weston went on to describe the factors that went into making a good photograph, citing selection of exposure time, dry plate, printing stock, lens, and lighting as elements of utmost importance, but he was careful to add that the most critical difference between a mediocre photograph and a masterful one was the photographer's "artistic ability." He also displayed several examples of his own work, describing them as "straight photographs, without handwork, shading, or manipulation of any kind."[29]

The message contained in his lecture indicates that his attitude toward photography had changed dramatically from his position a few months earlier, when he had presented himself as a simple craftsman offering practical tips to amateur enthusiasts. Now he was holding himself up as an artist and championing photography as an aesthetic medium with unique characteristics that offered distinct advantages to both the artist and the viewer. As the most significant influence on Weston during this period, Mather was undoubtedly the catalyst behind his newly impassioned stance as a public advocate for the artistic merits of photography.

WAR AND ESCAPISM   While the Exposition attracted throngs of tourists to San Francisco, the *Los Angeles Times* began to feature maps of battlefields and chronologies of the hostilities in Europe.[30] The *Times* reported that the Turks, now allied with the Germans, were using the war as an excuse to slaughter Armenians who, the Turks claimed, were plotting with the Allies to overthrow the Ottoman government. As thousands of Christian Armenians fled Muslim Turkey in a massive diaspora, Middle East relief efforts became a compelling cause for concerned Americans who wanted to ease the suffering generated by the ongoing genocide.

On May 7, 1915, the country awoke to news of the sinking of the Lusitania. The British luxury liner had been torpedoed by a German submarine off the southern coast of Ireland, and more than a thousand people had died, including 128 Americans. A few voices called for immediate revenge, but President Wilson was not yet ready to forfeit his position on American neutrality, undoubtedly because the vast majority of citizens were far more upset by the shortages of certain coveted items, caused by interrupted trade routes and the reallocation of resources in Europe, than by the European conflict itself.

Perhaps of greatest concern to Angelenos was the scarcity of cyanide, normally imported from Germany and critical to the process of refining gold ore.[31] There had recently been a surge of interest in reactivating some of the long-abandoned gold mines of California, and the steadily shrinking supply of imported cyanide was threatening to put an end to the newly revived industry. Dedicated drinkers bemoaned the disappearance of absinthe, the anise-flavored aperitif made in France, where production of the potent green spirit had now been outlawed,[32] and photographers were growing increasingly anxious about the scarcity of platinum ore coming out of Russia, a shortage that would soon impede the production of their beloved platinum printing papers, manufactured in England and distributed in America by the Philadelphia firm of Willis & Clement.[33]

Weston and Mather were among those most dismayed by this last development because platinum papers were a vital element in achieving the subtle range of tones they sought in their work. Willis & Clement had recently invented a paper sensitized with a combination of silver, platinum, and ferrous oxalate that they claimed would replicate the quality of pure platinum papers,[34] but many photographers were dubious. They had no desire to compromise the quality of their prints but feared they would have little choice.

Ignoring the tumult abroad, the city of Los Angeles continued to promote itself as the "Globe's Moving Picture Center."[35] The Jesse L. Lasky Feature Play Company sported an unbeatable cast with Lasky as President, Samuel Goldfish (who would soon change his surname to Goldwyn) as Treasurer and General Manager, and Cecil B. DeMille as Director General.[36] Mack Sennett's Keystone Studio was still thriving,[37] even without Chaplin, and Thomas Ince was about to turn his Santa Monica ranch/studio into an incorporated town called Inceville.[38] On the north side of the Hollywood Hills, Universal City was under construction,[39] and W. N. Selig of the Selig Polyscope Company, formerly of Chicago, was adding an elaborate zoo to his new studio complex near Eastlake Park.[40] Another Chicagoan, the popular children's book author, L. Frank Baum, had also left behind the vagaries of Midwestern weather to settle in Southern California.[41] He was now producing films based on his famous *Land of Oz* books, having just completed the construction of Ozcot, his fairy-tale bungalow situated in the midst of downtown Hollywood.

A number of new movie stars had been added to the popular lexicon, with Mae Marsh, Blanche Sweet, William Desmond Taylor, Douglas Fairbanks, Mary Pickford, Dorothy and Lillian Gish, and Alla Nazimova joining Chaplin, Mabel Normand, and Roscoe (Fatty) Arbuckle as household names. As more actors gained fame and wealth, real estate developers competed for their attention by building bigger, grander estates. An area adjacent to Los Feliz Boulevard in northeastern Hollywood was being promoted as "home to the movie stars." This private enclave, called Laughlin Park, was being offered by Homer Laughlin and Beverly Hills developer John R. Powers, who boasted that it was "the last word in residential masterpieces."[42] Laughlin Park's sylvan hillsides and picturesque lanes would soon attract the likes of Cecil B. DeMille and Chaplin to its elite confines.

A little further to the southeast the gigantic sets constructed for the filming of David Wark (D. W.) Griffith's *Intolerance* towered three hundred feet above the triangular wedge of land formed by the intersection of Prospect Boulevard (soon to be renamed Hollywood Boulevard) and Sunset Boulevard, on the eastern side of Vermont Avenue. Built on a massive scale to a Hollywood set designer's fanciful specifications, the make-believe Babylonian ziggurats, with their stone walls and massive columns, remained intact, even though filming on D. W. Griffith's movie had recently been completed. Griffith had run out of money, and the cost of demolishing the elaborate backdrops was far greater than the value of the real estate on which they stood.[43]

Angelenos, still stinging from San Francisco's rescinded invitation to participate in the Pan-Pacific International Exposition, decided to follow their rival's lead and embrace all things Oriental. The new San Pedro Harbor, now nearing completion, promised to make Los Angeles an even more attractive port of call than San Francisco, and Angelenos wanted to be strategically positioned to take their revenge when the opportune moment arrived.

While local architects and builders incorporated Japanese and Chinese motifs into their designs, and wealthy businessmen competed to see which one could acquire the finest Asian furniture and objets d'art, the *Times* ran an illustrated article about the trend. Featured was the newly completed residence belonging to two bachelor brothers, Adolph and Eugene Bernheimer, cotton importers from New York City. The Bernheimers' Yama Shira was an exact replica of a palace near Kyoto. It crowned a hill overlooking downtown Hollywood, and was described in the *Times* as a veritable "shogun's castle."[44] Along the base of Yama Shira's hill ran a narrow dirt road that would soon be paved and named Franklin Avenue.

Keenly aware that dozens of young women and men, physically beautiful but lacking in grace and poise, were descending on Los Angeles, famed dancer Ruth St. Denis and her new husband, Ted Shawn, opened their Denishawn Dance Studio near Westlake Park. In addition to organizing a troupe of dancers to tour vaudeville venues across the country, St. Denis and Shawn were planning to offer a multitude of classes specially geared to the unique aspirations of their ambitious Los Angeles pupils. Included would be instruction in the proper way to move across a stage, as well as advice on how to seek out the most flattering camera angles. Actresses Mabel Normand, Ina Claire, the Gish Sisters, Colleen Moore, Myrna Loy, and aspiring dancer Martha Graham would soon sign on as Denishawn students.

IMAGES OF THE DANCE   It was around this time that St. Denis, Shawn, and several other Los Angeles dancers became an important source of inspiration for Weston, who photographed them, to the exclusion of most other subjects, for the next several months. The first public manifestation of Weston's budding interest in dance subjects came in October 1915, when he mounted an exhibition of forty-two photographs at the State Normal School, recently relocated from its former Bunker Hill campus to a new site at Vermont and Heliotrope on the eastern edge of Hollywood.

The display elicited another review of Weston's work from Antony Anderson of the *Los Angeles Times*. This time he wrote about photography as an art form, and referred to Weston as an acknowledged master of his medium. Many of Weston's images featured well-known dancers currently living or appearing in Los Angeles. Anderson heaped mounds of praise on Weston:

> In the present exhibition he shows one decorative study, a few landscapes, and many portrait and character studies. Each is truly a work of art for each has been touched with the artist's imagination ... so that their subtle chemistry seems to have obliterated almost

every sign of the chemistry of the camera.... The proprieties of photography are observed by Mr. Weston in every picture he makes, and this is why, he being a genuine artist from his soul to his fingertips, his work is always true art.[45]

Singled out for special mention was a portrait of Mather, "a very strong head...held high and thrown back, showing the lines of the throat" and *Carlota*, "a Carmen type." Anderson's article also featured *Toxophilus*,[46] a study of a faunlike archer; *Valley of the Long Wind*,[47] one of Weston's rare landscapes from the period; *Summer Sunshine*, the sun-dappled figure study of Rae Davis; *Dolores*, a romantic genre portrait; and several studies of dancers Maud Allan, Ruth St. Denis, and Ted Shawn. Anderson particularly responded to Weston's depictions of the dancers, commenting that they "fell into the intent of the artist with a grace and abandon impossible to the ordinary mortal."[48]

Although Weston was an enthusiastic amateur dancer himself, it was probably Mather's numerous connections to the movie business that first brought him into contact with the professional terpsichoreans he now photographed with regularity. Chaplin, whose balletic style reflected an intense interest in modern dance, was a close acquaintance of the set and costume designer George Hopkins.[49] Weston had made Hopkins's portrait earlier in the year,[50] just as Hopkins was beginning his career at the Lasky Studio, where his first assignment was a series of set designs for William Desmond Taylor, then in the midst of directing films with actresses Mabel Normand and Mary Miles Minter. Taylor and Hopkins were also friendly with directors Marshall Neilan and James Kirkwood, and all four men had recently joined Chaplin as members of the Los Angeles Athletic Club. Their escapades were well known to the Hollywood crowd, and there were rumors of homosexual relationships, particularly between Taylor and Hopkins.

Soon after sitting for his portrait, Hopkins hired Weston to photograph a number of his realized costume designs modeled by dancers Yvonne Sinnard,[51] Katharane Edson, and Margaret Loomis, all pupils of Ruth St. Denis and Ted Shawn. Around that same time Weston also met and photographed Maud Allan, the former San Franciscan who was now an internationally known performer,[52] and Violet Romer, a Pasadena girl who regularly entertained local audiences. Both of these dancers posed for his camera wearing elaborate gowns, probably created by Hopkins.

Several of Weston's dance studies were taken on the grounds of Anoakia, the estate owned by heiress Anita Baldwin McClaughry, where construction of her imposing, fifty-room home—built on nineteen acres of ranchland formerly belonging to her father, E. J. (Lucky) Baldwin—had now been completed.[53] McClaughry had recently announced plans to breed prize-winning livestock, Percheron stallions, and Russian wolfhounds on the grounds of her estate, which she was determined to turn into a Southern California showplace. Maynard Dixon's American Indian murals had already been installed, and a number of other artists were currently assisting with various aspects of the interior decoration.

FIGURE 23. Edward Weston, *Violet Romer (as a Peacock by a Pool)*, ca. 1916. Platinum print, 24.1 × 17.1 cm (9½ × 6¾ in.). Photographed at Anoakia, Anita Baldwin McClaughry's estate in Arcadia, California. San Marino, Calif., The Huntington Library, Art Collections, and Botanical Gardens, 000.111.505

As one of the favored few allowed access to the magnificent property, Weston took the opportunity to make several fanciful pictures, including a series of Violet Romer dancing in the gardens and posing near an outdoor reflecting pool.[54] In one image (fig. 23) Romer wears a gown lavishly adorned with white peacock plumes, a reference to the peacock motif that appeared throughout McClaughry's new home.[55]

Over the next year and a half, Weston would exhibit or publish at least seven portraits of St. Denis and eleven of Shawn striking poses borrowed from their current dance repertoire. His photographs of Violet Romer and Katharane Edson would also meet with considerable success, and his images of Romer would twice serve as cover illustrations for the *Camera*,[56] while other variants were exhibited in a number of photography salons.

It was also during this period that Weston published his second photograph of Mather. In this full-length nude study, her body is turned away from the camera and her face is concealed in dark shadows (fig. 24). Above her head she brandishes a shawl, pulled taut at the

FIGURE 24. Edward Weston, *Nude with Black Shawl* (Margrethe Mather), 1915. Platinum print, 15.6 × 7.6 cm (6¹/₈ × 3 in.). Scarsdale, N.Y., Collection of Michael Mattis and Judith Hochberg

corners to form a dark, triangular backdrop, which contrasts effectively with the pale skin of her exposed torso. Startlingly decadent for its time, the image was exhibited widely, and it became Weston's second photograph selected for inclusion in the prestigious British annual *Photograms of the Year*.[57]

MOUNTING A DEFENSE   Despite the excitement being generated by the Pan-Pacific International Exposition and the aura of glamour beginning to emanate from Hollywood, the tense situation that existed between labor and management in Los Angeles reached a new level of palpability in the autumn of 1915. Earlier in the year, at almost the same moment the San Francisco fair had opened, Detective William Burns had finally succeeded in capturing Matthew Schmidt[58] and David Caplan,[59] thought to be the last of the alleged conspirators in the 1910 *Los Angeles Times* bombing.

Schmidt's trial was set to begin on October 4. Several of his anarchist friends, including Emma Goldman and Alexander Berkman, were coming to Los Angeles to testify on his behalf. Also making an appearance for the defense would be an attractive young woman named Marie Latter, who was known to have socialized with Schmidt during his earlier years in Chicago and subsequently in San Francisco, just prior to the *Times* explosion.[60] Angelenos watched with rapt attention as the trial unfolded.

The anarchists' collective testimony fell on deaf ears, however, and on December 31, 1915, Schmidt was found guilty of murder in the first degree.[61] Declared a martyr of the labor movement by his compatriots, Schmidt was sentenced to life imprisonment and packed off to join the McNamara brothers in San Quentin. His conviction did not bode well for his friend and fellow anarchist, David Caplan, whose trial was due to begin the following month. As the year came to a tumultuous end, angry labor leaders muttered diabolical threats about a "ten-year war" against the captains of industry in Los Angeles if Caplan, too, was convicted.

Outside Influences, 1916

Shortly after Schmidt's sentence was announced, unrest in Mexico reached a crisis point when Pancho Villa—recently relegated to a position of diminished importance following the rise to power of his foe, Carranza—took revenge on the Americans who had sided against him. On January 10, 1916, Villa and his men attacked and killed a group of seventeen American engineers en route to a mine near Chihuahua, Mexico.[1] While debate ensued as to how America should respond to the outrage, Villa crossed the border and invaded the town of Columbus, New Mexico, where he and his men opened fire on its citizenry, leaving another fifteen Americans dead.

President Wilson immediately ordered the Spanish-American War veteran, Brigadier General John Joseph Pershing, and six thousand American troops into Mexico to apprehend Villa and his renegades. (Even though the highly esteemed soldier failed to capture Villa, he would soon go on to become an American war hero, and the City of Los Angeles would subsequently honor his extraordinary leadership by renaming Central Park, in the heart of downtown, Pershing Square.[2])

Most Americans believed President Wilson had no choice but to put a stop to the violence being wrought by Villa. However, political radicals, who revered Villa as a defender of the rights of the common man, saw his violent rampage as the inevitable, frustrated response of Mexico's peasants to America's overwhelming capitalist greed. When the two Magon brothers—publishers of *El Regeneracion*, a Spanish-language revolutionary newspaper originating out of Los Angeles—were identified as incendiaries in the conflict, many Angelenos, and especially the freethinkers of the Severance Club, became concerned that an overzealous American government was trampling on the right of free speech. That sentiment took root and spread.

Even the Friday Morning Club, under Mrs. Seward Simon's leadership, promoted a surprisingly radical agenda in 1916. One of the Club's featured lecturers was Dhan Gopal Mukerji, a Stanford graduate who had recently spent time living among the anarchists of San Francisco—a motley group that included a man named Terry Carlin, who was a known associate of several of the *Los Angeles Times* bombing suspects.[3] Another guest speaker was author Max Eastman—editor of the socialist periodical *The Masses*—who addressed the Club on "What Socialism Really Is."[4]

Also appearing at the FMC that year were the muckraking author, Upton Sinclair, who had recently moved to Pasadena; the controversial birth control advocate, Margaret Sanger;[5] the Bengali poet and mystic, Rabindranath Tagore;[6] and a literature professor from the University of California, Berkeley, named Paul Jordan-Smith, who gave a lecture titled "The Message of the Radical Women." Jordan-Smith, in particular, shocked the more conservative club ladies with his admonition that women must follow "love's spontaneous choice" and his declaration that "Puritanism is paralysis." He also predicted that "one of the first steps the radical woman will take will be to hang the yellow journalists."[7] His dire forecast did not sit well with some of those present, especially William Randolph Hearst's *Los Angeles Examiner* reporter, who later lambasted Jordan-Smith in the pages of his employer's newspaper.[8]

As the trial of bombing suspect David Caplan unfolded during the spring of 1916, America's anarchists again gathered in Los Angeles to rally for the defense. Taking the witness stand in a repeat performance was Marie Latter, the same young woman who had appeared on Matthew Schmidt's behalf a few months earlier.[9] However, this time she was identified in the trial transcripts as Mrs. Mary Lipton, although she was not actually married to her companion, George Lipton. Both Latter and Lipton were avowed anarchists, longtime associates of Emma Goldman, and outspoken advocates of left-wing activities. Margrethe Mather took a special interest in this portion of the trial proceedings, because Latter and Lipton were already well known to her, and she was about to become a frequent guest in their home.

AN ANARCHIST COUPLE   Mather might have learned of Marie Latter as early as 1906, the year Latter's name first appeared in the pages of Emma Goldman's *Mother Earth*, alongside that of her then-lover, Terry Carlin, after the pair disrupted a Chicago political rally while Goldman looked on in amusement.[10] In 1909 their names again appeared in print when a journalist named Hutchins Hapgood, writing about the seamier side of Chicago's anarchist community, chronicled their lives in a book titled *An Anarchist Woman*.[11]

In recounting his story, Hapgood describes in great detail how two anarchists named Marie and Terry take turns supporting themselves as menial laborers, flouting convention, suffering the gross indignities of poverty, and abusing drugs, alcohol, and tobacco until their health is broken. The book ends with the unhappy dissolution of their relationship and Marie's departure to a commune somewhere on the West Coast.

In real life their relationship did not end there, however. Terry Carlin followed Marie Latter on her flight west, and the two eventually made their way to San Francisco, where Latter worked for a time as a "nurse-girl" to a wealthy family and Carlin regularly mounted a soapbox to harangue passersby for spare change. In San Francisco the couple reconnected with a group of Chicago anarchist friends who had recently come west, and two of those Chicago acquaintances were Matthew Schmidt and David Caplan.

Although, in her testimony at Schmidt's trial, Latter had maintained that she and Carlin were only casual observers at an anarchists' dinner they had attended at Chute's Café in San Francisco on September 25, 1910—six days before the *Times* explosion—they were hardly innocents in the matter. Latter and Carlin had once shared Schmidt's San Francisco apartment, where the dynamite used in the blast was temporarily stored, and Latter had witnessed David Caplan and Terry Carlin leave Chute's Café together, so they could catch a late train bound for Los Angeles.[12] Within days of the *Times* blast on October 1, the West Coast anarchists had scattered. Matthew Schmidt and Terry Carlin had departed California, intending to flee to London, but only Carlin had actually succeeded in leaving the country. For the next several months Carlin had remained abroad, but gradually he became more daring, and eventually he sailed for New York City, convinced that Burns's manhunt had been effectively foiled. Meanwhile, Matthew Schmidt had gone underground, donning disguises, assuming false names, and roaming from state to state. But while Marie Latter's colleagues were resorting to elaborate precautionary maneuvers, she had defiantly remained in California, hiding in plain sight.

Following Schmidt's arrest in New York City, several anarchists, including Emma Goldman, came to believe that Terry Carlin had somehow played a role in Schmidt's capture, despite Carlin's vehement protestations to the contrary.[13] Carlin was devastated by his compatriots' accusations, and as a result he lost all faith in the anarchist cause, a disillusionment that caused him to withdraw to the solace of a notorious Irish bar in Greenwich Village, where he drunkenly poured out the story of the *Times* bombing and its various protagonists to a young man, also of Irish descent, named Eugene O'Neill.[14] O'Neill would eventually pay homage to Carlin by basing the character, Larry Slade, in his play, *The Iceman Cometh*, on his anarchist friend. Woven into the complex plot of O'Neill's play would be the thinly disguised story of the *Times* bombing and the many personalities O'Neill had come to know through Carlin's eyes.

While Terry Carlin was schooling young O'Neill in the politics of anarchism, Carlin's former lover, Marie Latter, was beginning to achieve a modest amount of fame as the underground heroine of Hutchins Hapgood's novel. After Carlin's departure from California, Latter had begun living with another anarchist acquaintance named George Liberman.[15] A Lithuanian immigrant, Liberman had come to San Francisco shortly after the 1906 earthquake, and a few months later he opened an upholstery business on Presidio Avenue in Pacific Heights, an area of the city that had only narrowly escaped destruction.

Soon after joining forces with Latter, however, Liberman decided to relocate to Los Angeles, where he opened another upholstery shop on South Vermont Avenue, very near the campus of the University of Southern California.[16] Like Mather, Liberman and Latter might have been motivated to leave the Bay Area by the 1911 tremors that shook the city, or more likely, they were seeking relief from the probing questions of Detective Burns and his team of investigators, who were then scouring San Francisco in pursuit of the *Times* bombing suspects. As a man of radical sympathies and actions, George Liberman's decision to change his surname to Lipton before opening his Los Angeles shop had been a carefully considered, if ultimately unsuccessful, evasive tactic.[17]

Latter and Lipton took great pleasure in throwing parties in their apartment behind Lipton's upholstery shop. Necessarily financed on a miniscule budget, the gatherings were, nevertheless, raucous, bawdy events orchestrated to provoke outrageous behavior on the part of the attendees. In a letter written to a close friend, Latter included a glowingly vivid description of her preparations for one such evening, explaining that it would be a "rather Bacchanalian" event, where "lots of terribly naughty things" would be discussed, and those invited would be "people who have no morals."[18] Two of those amoral invitees were Margrethe Mather and Elmer Ellsworth.[19]

A RUSTIC LIFE In contrast to Mather's exploits with these extreme characters, who often led her into dangerous territory, Weston was living the life of a recluse, or so it seemed when he gave an interview to a journalist who dropped by his Tropico studio. The writer described Weston as enjoying a modest, rustic life in the country, surrounded by simple pleasures. He even compared Weston to David Grayson, the pen name of Ray Stannard Baker, a popular author who had written a pseudoautobiographical book published in 1907 titled *Adventure in Contentment*:

> Out in the town of Tropico, a beautiful suburb of Los Angeles, stands a shack studio of rough boarding that is so full of art that its range of influence reaches to the ends of the earth.
>
> In that studio, which cost perhaps six hundred dollars to build, dreams and works Edward H. Weston, "photographer," as the simple mission-style, brown-stained sign hanging in front of the door announces.
>
> …Weston had a way of taking photographs for customers that seems to stamp him as a genius at once. Coming into the four-by-six reception room of the shack studio, the customer prepares his features and necktie in the arrangement that he fancies he wishes them to be in the reproduction.
>
> He is engaged in conversation by Weston; and before the visitor is aware, he is sitting in the skylit room in a big chair, answering Weston's questions as to his likes and dislikes. He talks carelessly and entirely at ease, waiting, as he believes, for Weston to finish preparing the big camera, around which he hovers.
>
> When the sitter has begun to get nervous again, thinking that it is time to arrange his necktie and features once more, Weston quietly asks him to move his chair over a bit, into the ray of sunlight. He is not quite satisfied with the first six plates he has taken. Then the visitor realizes that, instead of hovering over the camera, Weston has been caressing it and coaxing from it the highest form of picture art.…

Much like Grayson, Weston was shut up in the city for several years in an [sic] huge studio, where he did nothing but print from plates all day long, a cog in the machine. It was not until he tore himself free from the city and built his shack in the country that he began to develop his individuality and widen his artistic horizon to the ends of the earth.[20]

Indeed, Weston's daily existence was the complete antithesis of Mather's, but it was precisely her freewheeling attitude, daring liaisons, and surreptitious activities that continued to make her so provocatively attractive to him. In spite of their widely divergent lifestyles during this period, the two photographers still managed to keep up their clandestine love affair, even as they collaborated professionally on an important event that would realize a dream they had shared for the past year and a half.

A MUSEUM VENUE   That dream reached fruition in February 1916, when the Camera Pictorialists held their first photography salon. The committee in charge, which consisted of Mather, Weston, Louis Fleckenstein, and Ernst Williams, knew that the success of their inaugural exhibition would determine whether an annual event was viable. Organized as part of the First Annual Arts and Crafts Salon, the photography display was held in the Gallery of Fine and Applied Arts at the new Museum of History, Science, and Art in Exposition Park (see fig. 25).[21] Because there were no museums in Los Angeles prior to the autumn of 1913, photographers had previously been limited to displaying their work in rented rooms at the Blanchard

FIGURE 25. California Postcard Co., Museum of History, Science, and Art, [Exposition] Park, Los Angeles, ca. 1916. Color postcard, 9 × 14 cm (3 1/2 × 5 1/2 in.). Collection of the author

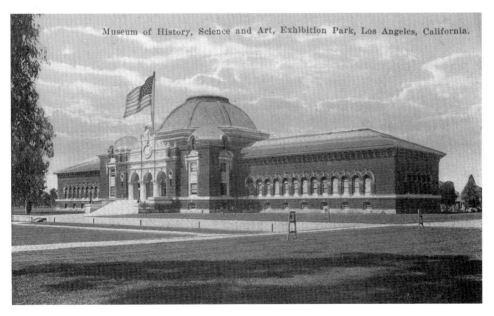

Building, or on the walls of various private social clubs, or at the Los Angeles Camera Club. For this reason, the Camera Pictorialists' participation in the Arts and Crafts Salon was a particularly momentous occasion, because it marked the first time photographs were exhibited in a museum setting in Los Angeles.

In an effort to encourage contributions from other parts of the country, each of the fifteen members of the Camera Pictorialists had agreed to exhibit only one photograph, allowing the majority of the exhibition space to be filled by guest participants. Invitations had been issued to thirty photographers around the country, including New Yorkers Karl Struss, Clarence White, Gertrude Kasebier, Arnold Genthe, Alice Boughton, Rudolf Eickemeyer, and Dr. D. J. Ruzicka, as well as Anne Brigman from Oakland, Imogen Cunningham from Seattle, Jane Reece from Dayton, and a young portrait photographer from Chicago named Eugene Hutchinson.[22] The overwhelmingly positive response was most gratifying.

Although the Art and Crafts Salon emphasized mainly decorative objects, including ceramics, pottery, jewelry, prints, bookbindings, and tiles from the kilns of Ernst Batchelder of Pasadena, the photographers were allotted the entire south wall of the museum's main gallery, as well as several standing screens, on which to display their work.[23] Thousands visited the museum that month, and a good many came expressly to see the photographs. The *Los Angeles Graphic* covered the exhibition and singled out Weston, Ellsworth, and particularly Mather, calling her work "subtle and shadowy."[24]

Antony Anderson of the *Times* reviewed all the exhibits, but devoted a third of his column to the photography display. Curiously, he identified Weston as the leader of the group, even though Louis Fleckenstein was still president of the club:

> The exhibition of the Camera Pictorialists, the local society of artistic photographers with Edward Henry Weston at its head, occupies one long wall and many screens, though each of the fifteen members is represented by only one picture. All the others are by outsiders from every part of the country, many of whom show as many as half a dozen prints. This generosity on the part of the pictorialists, like that of the other craftsmen of Los Angeles, was done that the annual salon might become a power, with contributors from everywhere.[25]

Once again the photograph Weston chose to represent his work was *Carlota*, made two years earlier. Mather's selection was a photograph titled *The Stairway* (fig. 26),[26] an image that reveals a great deal about her development as a camera artist. It is far more accomplished than her 1912 *Maid of Arcady*, or her 1915 portraits of Russell Coryell, or her other known pre-1916 images. *The Stairway* depicts a woman (very likely Maud Emily Taylor) holding a parasol as she stands at the top of a darkened staircase, a subject quite typical for the day. However, Mather's picture differs from those being produced by most of her contemporaries due to the unusual, starkly formal, compositional devices she employed.

FIGURE 26. Margrethe Mather, *The Stairway*, ca. 1915. Reproduction courtesy of the George Eastman House, International Museum of Photography and Film, Rochester, N.Y.

The image is virtually slashed in half along a diagonal, with the left foreground enveloped in shadow. The lone figure stands at the top and center of the image, with the geometry of her open parasol and the horizontal edges of the stair treads reflecting the light in a rhythmical pattern of illumination. The amount of information in the image is greatly reduced; the dense shadows produce a negative syncopation critical to the success of the composition; and the precise arrangement of elements, even down to the backlit parasol, suggests the stylized angularity and asymmetry of a Japanese woodblock print. By carving the picture into geometrical planes, and using the darkness of the foreground for emphasis, Mather creates an image that is both romantic and bold. It is particularly instructive to compare this photograph with examples of Weston's images from 1915 and early 1916, all of which demonstrate a far less daring approach.

In March 1916 Weston and Mather both celebrated their thirtieth birthdays. They had now known each other for two and a half years, but Mather was still an enigma to Weston. Although the two photographers regularly labored together in the Tropico studio, she would sometimes disappear for extended periods of time and, upon her return, give evasive answers as to her whereabouts. Her emotional state was often erratic, and she occasionally claimed to be experiencing strange physical symptoms that left her too exhausted to work.

Weston, who prided himself on his unfailingly workmanlike, professional attitude, could not understand Mather's lackadaisical manner. His patience was severely tried at times, and he attributed much of her behavior to an overly sensitive, artistic temperament, privately labeling her a *neurasthenic*, a catchall, pseudomedical term commonly applied to someone whose actions cannot otherwise be explained. Nevertheless, he was still thoroughly enamored with Mather, and he enjoyed her company and respected her innate talent. No doubt he also recognized that her artistic standards were even more rigorous, and her vision more refined, than his own, although he could certainly match her, measure for measure, in his determination to achieve perfection.

THE NEED TO MOVE ON   The June 1916 issue of the *Camera* featured an unusually comprehensive visual summary of Weston's recent accomplishments. Seven images received full-page illustrations, including two of dancer Violet Romer[27] and one each of dancers Ted Shawn[28] and Maud Allan.[29] A fifth portrayed Weston's loyal assistant, Rae Davis,[30] who had recently left Weston's employ to marry, while the remaining two were portraits of the woman who had replaced her, Enrica (or Enrique) Jackson.[31]

A former colleague from Weston's Mojonier Studio days, Jackson was an attractive, dark-haired woman with a flair for modeling. Weston enjoyed having a beautiful new assistant, and he proceeded to make a number of portraits of her, many of which he sent to publications and salons. Several of Weston's published portraits of Jackson, which began appearing in various camera magazines in mid-1916, are very similar to photographs he took of Margrethe Mather during that same time period. A portrait of Mather that appeared in the July 1916 issue of the *Camera*,[32] in which she stands, hands on hips, head cocked to one side, is almost identical to one of Jackson reproduced in the same publication a month earlier.

Oddly, Jackson would later claim to have no memory of Margrethe Mather.[33] While it seems almost impossible that the two women could have remained strangers, given that Mather was very much a part of Weston's life, and in and out of his studio with regularity during the months Jackson worked for him, Weston would prove remarkably successful at compartmentalizing his personal relationships, especially those he enjoyed with the opposite sex. Perhaps he feared he might reveal too much about his feelings for Mather in Jackson's presence, and, if so, Jackson's failure to recall Mather may have been due to Weston's concerted efforts to keep them apart.

In the summer of 1916 Antony Anderson unexpectedly devoted an entire column to a description of his recent visit to one of the Camera Pictorialists' monthly meetings. Anderson's article offered insight into the group's workings and explained his growing interest in their cause. Once again Anderson mistakenly identified Weston as the organization's leader:

> For years it has been my endeavor...to keep this column far removed from the field of photography. I felt that I had no business there, and so did my managing editor. We argued that art was art, and photography was photography....
>
> My conversion [to an appreciation of photography] has been gradual. The exhibition of prints by the pictorial photographers of America, recently held in Exposition Park, did a great deal to open my eyes. I studied it with much care and increasing delight, and soon saw that I must perforce treat the prints as pictures. Before that, however, I had gone to the exhibition held by Edward Henry Weston in the Normal School, and what I felt and wrote about it pleased him and the other pictorialists so much that they recently asked me to attend a meeting of the Camera Pictorialists of Los Angeles, a club of fifteen men and women who meet once a month, and whose president is Mr. Weston himself. New work is shown at these meetings, for suggestions and criticisms....
>
> I was in for it. The dreaded room proved to be brilliantly illuminated, and the fifteen held no inquisitorial frowns for me. They were, in fact, amiably smiling, quite as if they were glad to have me there. They asked me to criticise their work precisely from the painter's point of view, urging me to forget entirely "the limitations of their medium."...
>
> ...I saw...that [the photographs] had every good thing but color, and even color was often cunningly suggested. There was a portrait of a girl in white that might have been painted by Alexander, a twilight landscape that reminded me of a Corot, a head with the distinction of a Cabanel, a decorative scheme as simple and exquisite as a Japanese print in grays—and everywhere the evidence of a sincere search below externals to inner meaning. In short, the camera pictorialists are worthy of being called artists.[34]

Although Anderson's comparison of photographs to paintings represented an outmoded approach to photography criticism, at least he was paying attention to the club and its aspirations. His article might have encouraged Weston to broaden his horizons, or it could have been photographer Arnold Genthe's *Book of the Dance*, published in the spring of 1916, that convinced Weston it was time to seek out more varied subject matter.[35]

Featuring over seventy pictures of Maud Allan, Isadora Duncan, Ruth St. Denis, the Marion Morgan Dancers, and other famous performers of the era, Genthe's volume firmly established his reputation as the premiere dance photographer in the country, a development that caused Weston considerable consternation, because he had entertained thoughts of claiming such a distinction for himself.[36] However, any attempt to do so now would inevitably be viewed as derivative, so Weston decided he must explore new territory. Before the end of the year he moved on, and once again it was Margrethe Mather who showed him the way.

MATHER'S FOURTH STREET STUDIO   Mather's life had recently taken a dramatically different turn. She had just moved into the carriage house behind a Queen Anne–style, Victorian-era house (see fig. 27), on the opposite side of Bunker Hill from her former Clay Street apartment.[37] The house had originally been built, undoubtedly to Mather's amusement, as a rectory for Reverend Edwin Hildreth,[38] a minister affiliated with a nearby Congregationalist Church.[39] An architecturally distinguished structure, unique because of its ornate brickwork and intricately patterned shingles, the house was the work of the most famous architect of Victorian Los Angeles, Joseph Cather Newsom.[40] Erected in the late 1880s, at the very end of the real estate boom that had created the prosperous neighborhood on Bunker Hill, Newsom's beautifully executed design was a superb example of the elaborately embellished "painted ladies" that had once been the pride of Los Angeles.

Around 1905, however, the Hill had begun to change as word spread that the fast-expanding State Normal School, which had long anchored the neighborhood, was considering a move to a larger site. With plans already in the works to rearrange Bunker Hill's topography, the glory days of the Hill and its ornate houses had soon come to an end. In January 1907 Reverend Hildreth passed away, and by 1910 his once elegant residence had been converted to a boarding house occupied by seventeen people from six states and five countries.[41]

Over the next half-dozen years the Hildreth house became increasingly isolated from the rest of the city, due in large part to its rather unfortunate location near a dead-end street.[42] The house and the small, pitched-roof carriage house behind it stood on the northwest corner of the intersection of Fourth and Hope streets where, just a few yards further west, Fourth Street was abruptly interrupted by a sheer precipice before continuing its journey at Flower Street some fifty feet below. Access between Hope and Flower was denied to all but the few pedestrians who were adventurous enough to make their way up or down the zigzagging wooden staircase that clung to the face of the steep bluff separating the two streets.

FIGURE 27. Unidentified photographer, Rev. E. T. Hildreth House, 357 S. Hope Street at West Fourth Street, Los Angeles, ca. 1920s. Gelatin silver print, 17.7 × 22.6 cm (7 × 8⅞ in.). Mather's studio sat a few yards behind and down the hill from the Hildreth house. Security Pacific National Bank Photo Collection, Los Angeles Public Library, s-000-109

By the time Mather made her move to that part of the hill, the neighborhood was already beginning to attract bohemian types drawn to its atmosphere of benign neglect. Scattered among the older Victorian structures, tucked into the crevices of the hillside, were a few recently constructed apartment buildings, and this combination of old and new made for a wide array of inexpensive accommodations, perfectly suited to the needs of the many budding writers, directors, and thespians who were flocking to the city in search of movie work and a cheap place to live. Of course, the Hill's low-budget lodgings inevitably attracted a number of unsavory characters, and as the caliber of tenants declined, so went the neighborhood.

Nevertheless, Mather's new home was a significant improvement over her bleak quarters at the Chadakoin, and the relative quiet of its out-of-the-way location came as a welcome alternative to the hubbub that prevailed near Angels Flight. The carriage house also commanded an enviable view (see fig. 28). While the east wall of the building was terraced into the slope behind the Hildreth house, on the west side the hillside dropped vertiginously away, affording Mather an unimpeded vantage point from which to survey the city, spread out below. On a clear day, she could even catch a glimpse of the Pacific Ocean shimmering on the distant horizon.[43]

FIGURE 28. Dick Meier, Works Progress Administration (WPA) Artists' Scale-Model of Bunker Hill, late 1930s. The Hildreth house (see fig. 27) and Mather's carriage-house studio at 715 West Fourth Street are visible in the center of the photograph (see arrow). The Castle Tower Apartments is the building with three corner towers, across West Fourth Street and down the hill from Mather's studio. Flower Street (below arrow) runs diagonally across the lower part of the picture. This model of Bunker Hill is in the California History Hall at the Los Angeles County Museum of Natural History. Gelatin silver print, 19 × 19 cm (7 1/2 × 7 1/2 in.). History Collections, Seaver Center for Western History Research, Los Angeles County Museum of Natural History

The address of the Hildreth house was 357 South Hope Street, but the small carriage house behind it opened onto the intersecting street, and by the time Mather made her move there, the small building had acquired its own address—715 West Fourth Street. Mather finally had a place that was entirely her own, and this exciting development prompted her to list herself, for the first time, on the roster of professional photographers featured in the 1916 Los Angeles City Business Directory.[44]

Mather proceeded to remake the interior of the carriage house into a pristinely modern space that would serve as both home and studio. Her friend Billy Justema later described it:

> On Bunker Hill…just four blocks from the Philharmonic [then headquartered in the Auditorium Building at 5th and Olive], Margaret remodeled the carriage house of a late Victorian mansion into what was to become the most elegantly simple studio in the city. Although an uncluttered Japanese atmosphere was generally favored in current avant-garde circles, the opulent austerity at 715 West Fourth Street would still have been startling, with its rough, white plaster walls, its pale amethyst-colored wall-to-wall carpeting, and the huge French doors that opened on a high wooden deck that overlooked a terraced garden down which lavender mesembryantheum flowed from a group of three conical cypress trees until, at the lowest terrace, the vivid ground-cover reached a long row of dwarf bamboo that led the eye to the ruins of a fanciful summerhouse. There were no pictures, hardly any furniture.…the first impression a visitor received was that the occupant was either moving in or moving out. Margaret's flat bed disappeared into a recess behind low doors set flush with the wall and all one saw on entering was a large, faintly opalescent V-shaped room (made so by a closed-off kitchen and bath occupying the nearest corner at the left side) with a pair of those chests of drawers the Japanese call tansu, a tall teak-framed mirror above a severely delicate side-table of teak and, a concession to comfort, several split-bamboo chairs and hour-glass stools in the room's center.[45]

Indeed, the interior of Mather's studio was extraordinary in its minimalism (see fig. 29). Her developing eye for extravagant simplicity and elegant composition seems to have first manifested itself in her new space. It was as though, by meticulously editing her personal environment, she gained the courage and confidence to further distill and refine her photographic vision. The result was the spare but sensual style that would soon become her trademark. Her new home, with its wide moldings, hand-troweled stucco walls, carpeted floor, and massive doors, became a laboratory for experimentation, and certain of these elements began to appear in Mather's photographs, setting apart the images made in her studio from those made in Weston's. The most distinctive of these features was the pair of oversized French doors later recalled by Justema. Divided into glass panels suggestive of a Japanese *shoji* screen, they became an attractive backdrop in many of her photographs.

FIGURE 29. Attributed to Margrethe Mather, Untitled (Interior of Margrethe Mather's Studio, 715 West Fourth Street, Los Angeles), n.d. Gelatin silver print, 7 × 12.2 cm (2³/₄ × 4³/₄ in.). Tucson, Center for Creative Photography, University of Arizona, 79:13:35

How Mather was suddenly able to afford this dramatic change in her lifestyle remains something of a mystery. There is a remote possibility that she may have come into a small inheritance because two people from her past died in 1916. The first was Joseph Mather,[46] who had legally become her uncle five years earlier after finally marrying Minnie Laurentzen.[47] Theirs was a union based entirely on mutual necessity, however.[48] As Joseph Mather had grown increasingly infirm, he realized he would need someone to care for him in his dotage, and Minnie had recognized that, once her employer was gone, she would be without a roof over her head. The two had come to an understanding: Joseph Mather would wed Minnie and leave his home and personal belongings to her if she would agree to nurse him until his death. Both parties kept their word, but by the time Joseph died, his assets were so depleted it seems doubtful that Margrethe Mather could have profited in any way from his demise.

Then, a few weeks after Joseph Mather's death, Margrethe's only surviving sibling, twenty-eight-year-old James Youngren, also passed away after being stricken by pneumonia while working in the mountainous mining region near Hunter, Utah.[49] Like Joseph Mather, James was a smelter, and the illness that caused his death was a common malady among those forced to spend many hours each day in the unhealthy, oxygen-starved atmosphere far below the surface of the earth. Perhaps her brother left some small inheritance for Margrethe, but almost certainly it was not a substantial enough sum to cover the leasing and renovation of her carriage house. More likely her sudden prosperity in 1916 came from an entirely different source.

MATHER'S BEAU   Even Billy Justema, who later spent many hours in her West Fourth Street studio, never understood how her sudden change of lifestyle, or her extraordinarily refined taste, came into being. He did have a theory, however:

> I was of course not around during this early crucial period in Margaret's life but, by asking her the right questions at the right time, I could have cleared up much of the mystery regarding how she acquired her stringent taste—a matter still unexplained and of the greatest importance not only to her own photography but for the effect her obsession with perfection had on Edward Weston. . . .
>
> During this period, a lesbian by the name of Beau became Margaret's intellectual guide and, in the old-fashioned sense, her protector. Theirs was anything but a domestic relationship. Margaret never happened to tell me how they met but it was assuredly not in a hotel lobby. Beau had money, breeding, education, and the well-heeled lesbian's firm grasp of style. . . . Her mission, or their affair, completed, Beau seems to have departed as quietly as she came and Margaret had nothing but grateful memories.[50]

Either Justema did not know the real name of Margrethe Mather's mysterious mentor, or he chose not to reveal it when he wrote his memoir, because he never made a definitive statement about her identity. However, a variety of circumstantial evidence suggests that Mather's protector was Florence Reynolds, a woman from Chicago, who often visited Salt Lake City during Mather's adolescent years, and who made frequent visits to Los Angeles between 1915 and 1918.

Although Justema refers to Mather's mentor only as Beau, he apparently misremembered her nickname or intentionally altered it to obscure her identity, for Reynolds was known to her family and friends as Ho, not Beau.[51] Perhaps Justema chose his double entendre as an intentionally oblique way of characterizing Reynolds's role in her relationship with Mather. It is also possible that Justema knew Emma Goldman affectionately referred to her business manager/lover, Dr. Ben Reitman, as Hobo,[52] and therefore he assumed Mather had borrowed (and then truncated) the same term of endearment for Florence Reynolds. In any case, Ho/bo would have been a very appropriate nickname for Florence Reynolds, who manifested vagabond propensities throughout her life.

Most certainly Mather and Reynolds had several friends in common. In a letter written in January 1916, Ma-Mie Cook informed her son, Jig Cook, that she and his ex-wife, Mollie Price, and his two children were now back in Southern California after their extended visit to the San Francisco Exposition.[53] She also mentioned that she was currently enjoying the company of four women, including former Chicagoan Esther Mabel Crawford, an artist friend of Mather, who taught in the art department of the State Normal School.[54] Enclosed in her letter was a snapshot of Jig's son, Harl, and an explanation as to why there was no complementary photograph of his little daughter. "We have had an appointment to take Nilla to Margaret Mather, an artistic woman photographer, for days, but it rains and is cloudy every day," she told her son.[55] At the time she wrote her letter, Ma-Mie Cook was residing in the Sierra Madre foothills in a cabin belonging to Florence Reynolds.

TINY HEART Reynolds had been born in Chicago in 1879. Although her father was a successful insurance company executive, and the Reynolds family lived in comfortable circumstances in that city's Lakeview neighborhood, even they could not escape the ravages of tuberculosis, a disease more commonly associated with less prosperous households and less desirable living conditions. While she was pregnant with Florence, Mrs. Reynolds was diagnosed with the dreaded disease, and shortly after giving birth she died.[56] Perhaps as a consequence of Florence's prenatal exposure, she suffered from a variety of maladies throughout her life.

The most obvious manifestation of these physiological abnormalities was her small stature (see fig. 30). Although her frame was perfectly formed, an aberration in body chemistry had

FIGURE 30. Unidentified photographer, Florence Reynolds, ca. 1920. Gelatin silver print, 10 × 7.2 cm (4¼ × 2⅝ in.). Newark, Del., Florence Reynolds Collection, related to Jane Heap and *The Little Review*, Special Collections, University of Delaware Library, MSS 258

FIGURE 31. E. O. Hoppé (German, 1878–1972), *Jane Heap*, ca. 1916. Gelatin silver print, 22.5 × 14.9 cm (8⅞ × 5⅞ in.). Little Review Records, UWM Manuscript Collection 1, Archives Department, University of Wisconsin–Milwaukee Libraries, box 10, folder 17

caused Florence Reynolds to cease growing when she was only four feet and a few inches tall.[57] The diminutive young woman was extraordinarily intelligent, however, and she possessed a remarkable gift for languages, excelling in high school and at Northwestern University, where she graduated with honors in 1901.[58] By then Reynolds's older sister, Hattie, was married to Dr. William F. Mack, a dentist with an established practice in Salt Lake City,[59] and between 1900 and 1906 Reynolds often visited her sister and brother-in-law in Utah.[60] This fact suggests the possibility that Reynolds might have encountered the adolescent Emma Youngren/Margrethe Mather long before she ever left Salt Lake City.

During her own adolescence, Reynolds had discovered that, in addition to her petite size, she was different in other ways as well. While visiting her sister and brother-in-law, Reynolds corresponded regularly with a Chicago woman with whom she was emotionally involved. Reynolds's lover, a young art teacher named Jane Heap, was also a talented writer, and her daily letters to Reynolds were lyrical, obsessive valentines.[61] Heap invented several affectionate nicknames for Reynolds, but most often referred to her as Tiny Heart.[62]

The two women were physical and temperamental opposites. While Reynolds was delicate, reserved, and charming, Heap was a manic Amazon who could turn boisterous one minute and brooding the next (see fig. 31). In spite of these differences—indeed, perhaps because of them—their relationship lasted eight years. It finally reached an end when Heap came under the spell of Margaret Anderson, the flamboyant publisher/editor of *The Little Review*, the literary journal she had recently founded in Chicago.[63] Anderson and Heap then embarked on what would become an intense and sometimes destructive thirteen-year partnership as coeditors of that landmark publication.

Somewhat surprisingly, Florence Reynolds remained on good terms with both women and often came to their aid when money was in short supply. Reynolds's one stipulation was that she wanted her contributions to remain anonymous, so very few people were aware she was supplying *The Little Review* with financial aid in times of need. The monetary cushion Reynolds provided was critical, however, especially after *The Little Review* came under intense scrutiny by the federal government because of the magazine's sudden and unexpected alignment with anarchist Emma Goldman.

THE LITTLE REVIEW MEETS MOTHER EARTH   Goldman had first encountered Anderson when she swept through Chicago in the spring of 1914 on her annual lecture tour.[64] The anarchist had happened upon a copy of one of the early issues of *The Little Review* and was quite impressed by it. Arrangements were made for Goldman and Anderson to meet, and one day Anderson simply materialized at Goldman's hotel room door. Although Goldman was initially disappointed when she saw the "chic society girl" with the "butterfly appearance,"[65] it did not take long for the effusive editor to win over the recalcitrant anarchist, and Goldman soon abandoned her hotel room in favor of the apartment overlooking Lake Michigan where Anderson lived with her then-lover, Harriet Dean, who also worked at *The Little Review*.

Goldman thoroughly enjoyed her visit with Anderson and Dean, marveling at the two women who, like Reynolds and Heap, were antithetical personalities. She recalled Dean as "athletic, masculine-looking, reserved, and self-conscious," while Anderson was "feminine in the extreme, constantly bubbling over with enthusiasm" (see fig. 32). Goldman was impressed with the two young women because, as she would later explain, they "had broken the shackles of their middle-class homes to find release from family bondage and bourgeois tradition. I regretted their lack of social consciousness, but as rebels for their own liberation Margaret Anderson and Harriet Dean strengthened my faith in the possibilities of my adopted country."[66]

Goldman began to promote Anderson and Dean in the pages of *Mother Earth* while they, in turn, attempted to advance Goldman and her anarchist causes.[67] Not surprisingly, by the spring of 1915 *The Little Review* was beginning to experience financial difficulties due to its rather abrupt editorial swing to the left, a disconcerting move that startled many of the

FIGURE 32. Eugene Hutchinson (American, 1880–1957), Margaret Anderson, ca. 1916. Gelatin silver print, 24.1 × 19 cm (9¹/₂ × 7¹/₂ in.). Little Review Records, UWM Manuscript Collection 1, Archives Department, University of Wisconsin–Milwaukee Libraries, box 10, folder 1

magazine's former supporters into canceling their subscriptions and advertising contracts. It was during this period of financial crisis that Anderson and Goldman first encountered Jane Heap and Florence Reynolds.

Heap, a graduate of Chicago's School of the Art Institute, was then employed as an art teacher, but in her free time she designed jewelry, sketched, and acted in productions at Maurice Browne's newly founded Little Theatre in the Fine Arts Building on Michigan Avenue.[68] The Fine Arts Building was the fulcrum around which Chicago's artistic, literary, and music worlds revolved, and it was also headquarters for *The Little Review*.

When Anderson and Heap crossed paths at the Fine Arts Building in early 1915, the two women took to each other immediately. It was not long before Anderson convinced Heap to join the *Little Review* staff,[69] and soon after that the two became lovers. In spite of Florence Reynolds's waning romantic relationship with Heap, she volunteered her secretarial and translating skills at the *Little Review* offices, where she, too, met Emma Goldman. Reynolds may have even assisted Emma Goldman during her lecture tours to the West Coast, because it was around 1915 that Reynolds began to regularly travel back and forth to Los Angeles, the city where her sister and brother-in-law, Hattie and William Mack, had recently relocated.[70]

The petite young woman rapidly developed an affinity for the climate and flora of Los Angeles and for the comfortable guestroom in the Macks' modest bungalow at 1523 Curson Street on the western fringes of Hollywood.[71] Reynolds's brother-in-law, a specialist in dental radiology with offices in downtown Los Angeles,[72] was fascinated by photography, and sometime around 1916 he joined the Los Angeles Camera Club (LACC).[73] It remains an open question as to whether Mack's interest in photography and the LACC might have begun as a result of his sister-in-law's friendship with Mather, or whether he joined the club purely on his own volition.

NINETEEN MILLIONS By June 1916 *The Little Review*'s coffers were completely empty, so Margaret Anderson decided, with characteristic aplomb, that she and Jane Heap should temporarily move the magazine to California. The idea came to her because of an invitation extended by Aline Barnsdall, an oil heiress and drama enthusiast who owned a home near Mill Valley, north of San Francisco.[74] A few months earlier Barnsdall had been on the verge of founding her own theatrical company in Los Angeles, and she had stopped by the Fine Arts Building in Chicago to meet with architect Frank Lloyd Wright, whose business offices were located there, so they could discuss the theater she wanted him to design for her in California. It was during her visit with Wright that Barnsdall was introduced to Anderson and Heap.[75]

After hearing of *The Little Review*'s financial predicament, Barnsdall offered her home to Anderson for the summer. However, her invitation did not include Jane Heap, whom she intensely disliked. Anderson unwisely chose to ignore that fact, and she and Heap headed for Mill Valley. In her autobiography, Anderson never cites Barnsdall by name but rather refers to her only by the size of her bank account:[76]

Nineteen Millions asked me to visit her in Mill Valley, . . . California, a small town in the mountains surrounding San Francisco. . . . [Jane Heap and I] would rent some sort of mountain cabin to live (talk) in, we could conduct the Little Review from San Francisco, and I could see Nineteen Millions at intervals. There may be millionaires with whom one is willing to spend more than intervals. I have never seen one. . . .

California plans progressed. We put a sign on the studio door announcing our departure for the beginning of June. . . . We were going tourist, on the Canadian Pacific. As to our living in California, we would have a subscription boom for the magazine which would help both it and us. And as to getting back, we would stop in Los Angeles and Denver (where we already had faithful followers) and collect enough subscriptions for the return fares.[77]

Predictably to everyone but Anderson, Barnsdall did not greet the two women with open arms, and the weary travelers were forced to find other accommodations after Barnsdall and Anderson calmly engaged in a fierce argument. Anderson recalled, "Neither of us raised her voice. We contrasted our opposing points of view for half an hour, exchanged insults and regrets, and said good-by amicably."[78]

It was a rocky beginning to an often testy friendship between the two strong-willed women, but Barnsdall was endowed with a deep-rooted streak of generosity, which she would soon extend to Anderson, Emma Goldman, Florence Reynolds, and, in later years, to Mather. As Mather became more fully integrated into *The Little Review* circle, she shared her new social contacts and awakening zeal for the avant-garde with Edward Weston. He, in turn, became interested in her friends and their activities, and this development inevitably led to the expansion of his literary horizons, an enrichment that had ramifications within the visual realm as well. For the next several months, Mather acted as a conduit of culture (and potential sitters), as she delivered a veritable who's who of literary and political personalities to Weston's doorstep.

PREPAREDNESS Just as Anderson and Heap were settling into a rented ranch house near Muir Woods for the summer, Emma Goldman and Alexander Berkman arrived in Los Angeles to show support for accused bombing suspect David Caplan, now in the midst of his second trial. (Surprisingly, the jury in Caplan's first trial had been unable to reach a verdict,[79] an unexpected event that had come as a tremendous shock to the increasingly senile Colonel Otis, aged publisher of the *Los Angeles Times*, who made sure the case was immediately retried on appeal.)[80]

Goldman was also going to give a speech in San Francisco arguing against America's entry into the war in Europe. Alexander Berkman was now making his home in San Francisco, where he had been publishing his own anarchist periodical, the *Blast*, since the previous January,[81] and he had carefully scheduled Goldman's lecture to counter the effects of the city's Preparedness Day Parade (an event intended to galvanize San Franciscans into supporting the war effort) which was to take place on July 22, 1916. Other plans were afoot, however.

On the morning of the parade a bomb exploded at Steuart and Market streets, killing six and injuring many others.[82] Goldman and Berkman, knowing they would likely be blamed as instigators, hastily retreated to Anderson's and Heap's rented abode near Mill Valley.[83] Goldman was also scheduled to give a lecture arranged by Mollie Price, now a student at the University of California, Berkeley,[84] but when Goldman and Berkman confirmed that the authorities were indeed searching for them, they abruptly left for Portland and Seattle before heading back to the East Coast. It was the last time either one would see California.

WESTON CHANGES COURSE   On the day the San Francisco bombing occurred, Weston was on his way to Cleveland, Ohio. Because of his growing reputation, he had been asked to exhibit his work and demonstrate his printing techniques at the annual convention of the Photographer's Association of America.[85] Flattered by the invitation to participate, Weston had happily undertaken the long journey east, and in spite of a full slate of activities, he stole time to telegraph word of his success at the Cleveland convention to his colleagues in Los Angeles. The *Times* reported:

> Telegrams received here yesterday announce that Mr. Weston for the third time has been one of the fifteen photographers whose work has been selected for place [sic] in a permanent salon in the East by the Photographers' Association of America. He was the only photographer in Southern California to receive this honor. There were 800 photographers competing....
>
> Mr. Weston was invited to visit the convention of photographers, which met this week in Cleveland, in order to demonstrate his new impressionistic work, the secret of which is the soft-focus effect.[86]

On his way back to Los Angeles, Weston stopped off in Chicago to visit his aging father and his Uncle Teddy and Aunt Emma Brett. During his stay there he called on Eugene Hutchinson, another portrait photographer who was beginning to build a national reputation. It was probably because of Mather's *Little Review* connections that Hutchinson had been invited to show his work at the Los Angeles Camera Pictorialists's salon the previous February, and it may well have been at her urging that Weston met with Hutchinson at his studio, also located in the Fine Arts Building.

Hutchinson was highly regarded by Margaret Anderson and Emma Goldman, both of whom had already posed for his camera.[87] In the summer of 1915, shortly after twenty-eight-year-old Rupert Brooke, the much-lionized English poet, had perished in the Dardanelles, Anderson published a memorial tribute in *The Little Review* and illustrated it with Hutchinson's portrait of the ethereally beautiful young man.[88] It was the first time a photograph had appeared in *The Little Review*, and Weston and Mather would certainly have taken note of it.

FIGURE 33. Edward Weston, *Eugene Hutchinson*, 1916. Reproduction courtesy of the George Eastman House, International Museum of Photography and Film, Rochester, N.Y.

While Weston and Hutchinson talked photography, Weston made a portrait of his colleague with entirely surprising results. Realized in a dramatically different style from anything he had previously attempted, Weston's image of Hutchinson moves away from the sentimentality of the work he had recently shown to such acclaim at the Cleveland convention. In this far more cerebral composition (fig. 33), Hutchinson strikes a theatrically mannered pose, his figure lit from the side, so that the dark, distorted shadow on the wall behind him becomes the primary design element.[89] Weston must have been influenced by some of the work he had recently viewed in Cleveland, because he had never before emphasized shadows in his photographs. In the months that followed, however, Weston's portrait of Hutchinson would become a departure point for his experimentation with a newly sophisticated visual vocabulary.

Upon his return to Los Angeles, Weston made a portrait of Anita Baldwin McClaughry's daughter, Dextra, at the entrance to Anoakia.[90] His use of bands of filtered light to balance the asymmetrical placement of his subject adds visual drama to an otherwise unremarkable portrait. In this photograph, which recalls the syncopated rhythms of Mather's *The Stairway*, created the previous year, Weston is reinterpreting certain formal elements and refinements of composition already employed by Mather.

COOL MORNING EYES   In the autumn of 1916, probably at Florence Reynolds's suggestion, Margrethe Mather hosted a fund-raiser for Margaret Anderson and Jane Heap in her recently remodeled West Fourth Street studio.[91] This event generated enough support that Anderson and Heap were able to purchase train tickets to Chicago and add a number of new names to their subscription list. Their goal was to keep *The Little Review* afloat until they could regroup in New York City; Anderson had decided Manhattan would be a more advantageous place for their publishing endeavors to flourish.

While Anderson and Heap headed east, Anderson's former lover and colleague, Harriet Dean, recognizing that her *Little Review* days were over, stayed behind in San Francisco where she became a regular at Coppa's, an eating establishment and gathering place for San Francisco's bohemian crowd.[92] It was during this time, and undoubtedly because of their mutual ties to *The Little Review*, that Margrethe Mather was called upon to make a handsome portrait of the stately, aquiline Dean.[93]

Another *Little Review* associate who entered Mather's life during this period was the Chicago-based artist and poet, William Saphier.[94] The Romanian-born Saphier was a contributor to *The Little Review* and a close friend of fellow poet, Alfred Kreymborg.[95] Saphier and Mather trysted sometime around the end of 1916, and the following spring she exhibited a portrait of the stocky man with the twinkling eyes alongside her portrait of Harriet Dean.[96]

Saphier must have spent many intimate hours with Mather, because he understood her well enough to compose a poetic profile, later published by Kreymborg in an anthology of avant-garde poetry, in which he demonstrated remarkable insight into Mather's personality and an empathetic acceptance of her checkered past:

Margrethe

You are an ice covered twig
with a quiet, smiling sap.
The spring winds of life
have tested your steel-blade soul
and the harsh breath of men
covered you with a frigid shell.
But under the transparent ice

I have seen your warm hand
ready to tear the shell
and grasp the love-sun's heat,
and your cool morning eyes
look clear and calm into the day.[97]

At the end of the summer Weston wrote an article for *American Photography* titled "Notes on High Key Portraiture."[98] It was illustrated with more photographs of dancers Ted Shawn[99] and Maud Allan,[100] as well as a study of a young child named Bobbie,[101] and a portrait of his wife's attractive young niece, Emily Ellias.[102] In November the same periodical published Weston's old standby, *Carlota*, accompanied by notes detailing his technique, as follows: "8" × 10" studio camera, 18" focal length Verito lens, January 10 a.m. by light of Window and door, 3 seconds at: 5.6 on a Hammer Red Label plate, pyro-metol developer, print on E. B. platinum."[103]

Also illustrated was Mather's *The Stairway*.[104] It was the first time one of her photographs had been reproduced in a national periodical since *Maid of Arcady* had appeared three and a half years earlier, and it marked her reemergence as a figure of note on the national photography scene.

THE TRAMP STRIKES IT RICH   While Mather and Weston were surrounding themselves with people from the *Little Review* circle and attempting to keep their names before the public, their friend the Little Tramp was enjoying an immensely successful year. A few months earlier Chaplin had traveled by train to New York City to meet with the directors of the Mutual Film Company.[105] His contractual obligations to Essanay Studios had finally been fulfilled, and he was a free agent again. Much time had passed since Chaplin's last visit to the East Coast, and he was amazed to find adoring fans awaiting his arrival at each stop along the way.

The arduous trip turned out to be well worth the effort. Mutual made Chaplin an unprecedented salary offer—$670,000 for one year's work. They also agreed to form a subsidiary production company solely for Chaplin's benefit, appropriately called the Lone Star Studio.[106] Chaplin was to have his own facility on Lillian Way in Hollywood and the power to assemble whichever actors and production people he wanted. Triumphantly, Chaplin returned to Los Angeles with an annual income higher than that of the President of the United States and complete artistic control over his own films.[107] In a matter of months he had gone from being a poverty-stricken ex-vaudevillian to the hottest property in Hollywood. Unfettered and fully financed, Chaplin immediately set about making an inspired series of highly original films: *The Floorwalker*, *The Vagabond*, *The Pawnshop*, *The Rink*, *Easy Street*, *The Cure*, and *The Immigrant*.

He also hired an entourage of employees, including a valet, a chauffeur, and a diction coach[108] to help him smooth the rough edges of his Cockney accent into the clipped, cultured tones of an Etonian Englishman. Chaplin then engaged his friend, the charming painter-cum-writer, Rob Wagner, as a part-time secretary.[109] Intimidated by the crowds that inevitably gathered around him, Chaplin no longer ventured out by himself, so he often asked Wagner, whose sons were still attending Boyland in Santa Barbara, to be his companion on spur-of-the-moment fishing trips to Catalina Island and late-night jaunts to boxing matches in the working-class neighborhood of Vernon.

As a result of his deepening friendship with Wagner, an avowed socialist, and because of his own painful childhood experiences in poorhouses and orphanages, Chaplin began to express an interest in various social causes. He often accompanied Wagner—a member of the Severance Club since 1914[110]—to club meetings, where conversations were now centered around the war in Europe and America's response to it, in both political and moral terms.

WORLD AFFAIRS   Throughout 1916, even as the *Los Angeles Times* concentrated on extensive coverage of the devastating, ten-month Battle of Verdun, one of the bloodiest and most brutal chapters of the Great War, the newspaper also reported on a variety of local entertainment events organized to help ordinary citizens temporarily forget the world's conflicts. Several of these activities were cultural in nature, inspired by historical events and exotic places. Others offered more immediate, banal distractions.

Perhaps the most lavish of these events was a true Hollywood extravaganza conceived as an homage to the greatest bard of Elizabethan drama. To celebrate the tercentenary of William Shakespeare's birthday, an open-air production of *Julius Caesar* was staged in the natural amphitheater at the head of Beachwood Canyon.[111] The backdrop consisted of a 360-acre swath of land in the heart of the Hollywood Hills, cleared of sagebrush and chaparral and decorated with columns and archways constructed in the Classical style. A cast of 5,000 actors wearing togas and sandals performed before an audience of 40,000, while ushers dressed as Roman gladiators escorted attendees to their seats.[112] The event was a huge success, but it was never again repeated. Apparently it was too much spectacle, even for Angelenos.

The influence of Asia had now thoroughly permeated Southern California, as evidenced by the 300-image exhibition of Japanese woodblock prints, including examples by Ando Hiroshige and Kitagawa Utamaro, which opened at the Los Angeles Museum of History, Science, and Art.[113] In another manifestation of the widespread public interest in all things Japanese, the Palette Club, a local organization of artists, invited a young man named Clarence McGehee to give a demonstration of Japanese classical dance and deliver a lecture on Japanese folklore.[114] McGehee had recently returned from an extended stay in the Orient, and his lectures on Asian subjects were in great demand.[115]

The city's social calendar was filled with notable dramatic and musical performers. Terese Van Grove, eleven-year-old child prodigy and pupil of Ruth St. Denis, was touted as the next Sarah Bernhardt.[116] Pianist Ruth Deardorff-Shaw gave a recital "quite as modern as the neo-impressionistic or futurist painting, and quite as much unappreciated by the public at large,"[117] and another pianist, Leo Ornstein, "a boy of about 20 years and a Russian Jew,"[118] made his second visit to Los Angeles. This time he was characterized in a *Times* headline as "The Boy Who Bangs the Piano with His Doubled Fist,"[119] and critics declared that Ornstein's atonal compositions perfectly expressed the mood of a country on the verge of war. (Weston would soon photograph all three performers.)

Indeed, the war effort was beginning to take center stage for all patriotic Angelenos. Los Angeles sponsored its own Preparedness Day Parade to drum up support for the troops, but unlike San Francisco's ill-fated event, the Los Angeles demonstration proceeded peacefully. The only incident of violence involved a drunken lout who attacked a policeman on Main Street. The ruffian was wrestled to the ground by Charles Fletcher Lummis, former City Editor of the *Times* (and erstwhile photographer), who became indignant at the apathy of the observers gathered round to watch the fisticuffs. Berating the onlookers for shirking their civic responsibilities, Lummis yelled, "You make me laugh. Seventy thousand of you march for preparedness and then mostly stand around and gawp while a policeman gets beaten up. How in the name of the yellow monkey is a nation ever going to be prepared whose men can't see their little duty in the street?"[120]

It was also in 1916 that the Rindge family of Malibu began their fight against the seizure of a portion of their 45,000-acre rancho by the County of Los Angeles.[121] The Rindge's seaside property, originally a Spanish land grant known as the Rancho Topanga Malibu Simi Sequit, had been purchased in 1891 for $32,000 by Frederick Rindge, founder of Union Oil (and, a few years later, Southern California Edison). His private ownership of the land remained the last major obstacle to the construction of a continuous coastal highway that would extend from the northern end of California all the way south to the Mexican border. Until the County's battle with Rindge could be won, however, the fastest way to travel from Los Angeles to San Francisco was still the overnight car ferry.[122] Run by the Yale and Harvard Steamship Line, the ferry made the roundtrip journey four times a week for a fare of $10.70 per passenger.[123]

During the summer of 1916, after the *Times* published proposed plans for a new train station to be built opposite the eighteenth-century El Pueblo de Los Angeles, a development that would require the total destruction of Chinatown, local businessmen applauded the news.[124] Soon stories began to appear in the *Times* about the popular craze for opium. Opium smokers, reportedly running rampant in the hills surrounding Topanga Canyon, were taking automobile "joy-rides" so they could partake of the illegal drug in secret, without fear of apprehension by the police.[125]

When one group was caught with "opium tools" in a café near the pier in Ocean Park, they were accused of using "the Malibu district, north of Santa Monica, as a place to bring opium into the country."[126] However, the *Times* was quick to point out that the drug was being funneled into Southern California by the corrupt tongs of Chinatown. In the rush to accuse, Angelenos seemed not to recall that the Chinese had waged their Opium Wars of the previous century expressly to prevent the importation of opium into China by British and American businessmen, who stood to profit handsomely from sales of the highly addictive substance.

All of Los Angeles was thrilled with the October debut of the Little Theatre, the experimental ensemble founded and run by Aline (Nineteen Millions) Barnsdall.[127] Barnsdall had imported Polish dramatist Richard Ordynsky to direct her company, and he promised to bring an international cast and a new standard of excellence to Los Angeles audiences.[128] Barnsdall and the debonair Ordynsky were frequently seen together at dinner parties celebrating the success of their joint venture.[129]

Rarely united about anything, Southern and Northern Californians alike grieved when Jack London, the state's most famous novelist, died at his ranch in Glen Ellen north of San Francisco.[130] It was rumored that London, unable to endure the pain caused by advanced kidney disease, had committed suicide by ingesting a lethal dose of the morphine he kept in his nightstand for just such a purpose.[131]

As the 1916 holiday season approached, the *Times* reported that local fashion designers were busily creating gowns in the style of costume designer Leon Bakst, who would be accompanying Serge Diaghilev's Ballet Russe to California for their Los Angeles debut at the end of the year.[132] The featured performer would be the incomparable Vaslav Nijinsky, re-creating his role in *L'Apres-midi d'un faune*, a lascivious bit of choreography that had scandalized even the unshockable Parisians. Balletomanes queued up for hours to purchase tickets.

Following the much-anticipated Ballet Russe performances, however, a reviewer for the *Times* concluded that Angelenos had not been terribly impressed by the Russians. Southland audiences had failed to appreciate the ensemble nature of the company and wished only to witness Nijinsky leaping to record heights.[133] *L'Apres-midi d'un faune*, inspired by Debussy's symphonic poem, had not been beautiful or rhythmic enough to suit, and while Nijinsky's climactic performance had titillated elsewhere, Angelenos voiced disappointment that, all in all, the Russian had not been half as wicked as they had hoped.

Charlie Chaplin, however, had found the Ballet Russe delightful and Nijinsky's dancing "hypnotic, godlike."[134] One journalist speculated that, because Chaplin had been such "a regular and attentive attendant upon the performances," he must be about to open "the Chaplin Ballet school" or produce "a screaming screen parody of the great pantomime dance affair."[135] Indeed, Chaplin could not get enough of the fabled Russian dancer. Before Nijinsky departed Los Angeles, Chaplin invited the dancer to the set of his latest movie for a behind-the-scenes tour. Hoping to impress and amuse the Russian, Chaplin leapt and whirled like a dervish, but he was greatly unnerved when Nijinsky, already sinking into the mire of depression and madness that would ultimately kill him, failed to respond to the comedian's frenzied antics.[136]

In spite of Nijinsky's glassy-eyed stoicism, however, he apparently enjoyed the experience, because he returned to the set three days in a row, and it was during one of those visits that Margrethe Mather photographed the legendary dancer and his colleague, Leon Bakst.[137]

Surprisingly, Weston did not join her, but perhaps his assistance was needed at home. Three weeks earlier, on December 6, 1916, Flora had presented him with a third son, Lawrence Neil Weston (whom they would call Neil).[138]

Immediately following Nijinsky's exit from Los Angeles, Mather's friend Elmer Ellsworth consummated a long-awaited personal triumph. Twenty-five years after his first proposal of marriage to Lucile Gilmer, Ellsworth and Gilmer were wed in Salt Lake City on Lucile's forty-seventh birthday.[139] Attending the couple was the bride's mother who had apparently decided, in light of Ellsworth's persistence and growing prosperity, to ignore her husband's deathbed decree. The newlyweds returned to Los Angeles, where they planned to make their home in the affluent West Adams District, a few doors away from actor Roscoe (Fatty) Arbuckle.[140]

The Tide Turns, 1917

I n early January 1917 Weston photographed art critic Antony Anderson, looking every bit the scholar and pedant.[1] Cultivating a relationship with Anderson had been one of Weston's smartest career moves. Since Anderson's earliest reports on the Camera Pictorialists, a collegial friendship had blossomed between the two men, and Weston realized that Anderson's continued support would be invaluable to his and Mather's professional reputations. Anderson had a deep regard for the painter James Abbott McNeill Whistler, and he often referenced the popular artist in his columns. By making Weston and Mather more aware and appreciative of Whistler's artistry, Anderson brought his own influence to bear on their work, and soon both photographers began to create Whistler-style compositions, undoubtedly hoping to elicit further critical praise from Anderson.

That spring Weston's elderly father arrived in California for a visit, and Weston made two photographs of him. One image is a conventional portrait of Dr. Weston posing with Edward and his sister, May Seaman, who was about to move with her family to Ohio.[2] The other depicts Dr. Weston seated in profile, bundled in a dark coat and silhouetted against a brightly lit backdrop (fig. 34).[3] Compositionally, the latter image is very reminiscent of Whistler's iconic painting of his aging mother. It is also one of Weston's first attempts at a more simplified form of portraiture. All extraneous details are eliminated and the geometrical massing of Dr. Weston's seated form dominates the picture, resulting in a bold image that emphasizes the sitter's strength of character.

At nearly the same moment, Mather created an ode to another facet of Whistler's genius in a portrait of her friend Maud Emily Taylor, taken in Mather's West Fourth Street studio.[4] This image (fig. 35) demonstrates that Mather's abilities behind the camera and in the darkroom had progressed markedly. The photograph is a technical tour de force, indicating just how accomplished a photographer she had become. The image is diffused and bathed in a soft, otherworldly illumination, with the compositional elements reduced to the essential. The appeal of the photograph is largely due to the deceptively casual positioning of the sitter and the subtle differentiation of white-on-white tonalities, achievable only with platinum papers. Although similar in composition to Weston's photograph, Mather's image is a celebration of light and atmosphere, whereas his is an exercise in contrast and volume. *Miss Maud Emily* would soon become one of Mather's most widely known and acclaimed photographs.

FIGURE 34. Edward Weston, *Portrait of My Father*, 1917. Reproduction courtesy of the George Eastman House, International Museum of Photography and Film, Rochester, N.Y.

In March 1917 a controversial exhibition destined to alter the course of American photography took place in Philadelphia. It was the annual salon sponsored by the John Wanamaker Department Store. For the first time the Wanamaker event threatened to eclipse the Carnegie Institute's salon, running concurrently in Pittsburgh, as the most important photography exhibition venue in America. Although no one disputed the excellence of the work submitted to the Wanamaker exhibition, when the judges elected to display only fifty-five of the eleven hundred photographs submitted to the competition, they provoked intense criticism from their audience.[5] The most prominent members of the judging panel were Alfred Stieglitz and his young colleague, Eduard Steichen, and as usual, Stieglitz's vision had prevailed.

The editor of *American Photography* commented:

> The exhibits were pleasingly hung under glass, and the greater space allotted each print as compared with that available in past years did much to give each study an opportunity to display its particular merit to best advantage.[6]

FIGURE 35. Margrethe Mather, *Lady in White* (or *Miss Maud Emily* [Taylor]), 1917. Platinum print, 24.5 × 18.8 cm (9 5/16 × 7 3/8 in.). San Francisco Museum of Modern Art, 78.78

But, overtly critical of what he felt was yet another outrageous example of Stieglitz's elitist cronyism, he added:

> Whereas the Wanamaker exhibitions have done much in times past to encourage and stimulate progress in the growth of pictorial photography, and should be heartily supported by all sincere workers, it is to be regretted that the judges did not view the exhibition on a broader plane. . . . it is time for the old school to give way to the new and broader endeavors of those who are not restricting themselves to a system of mechanics that introduces very obvious limitations. The result of judging an exhibition from the standpoint of a purist is a monotony that cannot fail to be felt by an impartial critic who views the selections thus made.[7]

When the Wanamaker prizewinners were announced, no one was surprised to learn that Stieglitz's friend and protégé, Paul Strand, had been singled out to receive the one-hundred-dollar First Place award. Strand's winning photograph, titled *Wall Street*, depicts a powerfully evocative urban scene of ordinary humans dwarfed by the imposing fenestration of the J. P. Morgan Bank at the corner of Wall and Broad streets, in the heart of New York City's financial district.[8] Strand's image of plodding figures, seemingly subject to forces beyond their control, perfectly captured the mood of a country about to join an international cataclysm, but even Stieglitz could not have foreseen that Strand's photograph would become both a potent visual metaphor for America's disenfranchised and an icon in the history of photography.

Weston was disappointed when he learned that his entries had garnered only two Honorable Mentions, worth five dollars each, awarded to his portraits of Eugene Hutchinson and Dextra Baldwin, taken several months earlier.[9] Once again he had recycled his previous successes, but this time they were no match for Strand's *Wall Street*.

Fortunately, however, Weston enjoyed a much more positive response at the 1917 Pittsburgh Salon, where six of his pictures were selected for display. One reviewer wrote:

> Edward Henry Weston's reputation as an artist-photographer is not dependent on his success at the present Salon, where he made his first appearance this year. Magazine publishers long ago recognized the value of the work that came from his studio at Tropico, Cal., and gave him space accordingly. His group of prints at the Salon are characteristic, and, whether it be landscape, portraiture, or figure compositions, there is ever present the unmistakable quality that, once known, requires no appended signature to establish identification.[10]

Mather was represented in the Pittsburgh Salon by two pictures—*The Stairway* from 1916 and a new image titled simply *A Lady*.[11] The latter, a portrait of an elegant woman in a striking black gown, was selected as the frontispiece for the May issue of the *Photographic Journal of America*, prefacing photographer William H. Porterfield's review of the exhibition.

A LITERARY LIFE   Later that spring, when Weston mounted his second display at the Friday Morning Club,[12] he learned that the Welsh-born author John Cowper Powys would soon be lecturing at the Club.[13] Powys was a frequent contributor to the *Little Review*, so it may have been Mather who obtained an invitation for Weston to photograph the writer. At the time Powys sat for Weston's camera, he was staying at the home of Paul Jordan-Smith, the University of California professor who had shocked the ladies of the Friday Morning Club a few months earlier, and it was likely on this occasion that Jordan-Smith and Weston first became acquainted.[14]

Jordan-Smith and his wife, Sarah Bixby Smith, were recent arrivals in Claremont, a college town located about thirty miles east of Los Angeles, where he was fast gaining a reputation as a scholar and lecturer on a wide variety of literary and political subjects.[15] Born in Virginia and raised in Chattanooga, Tennessee, Paul Smith, as he was then known, had graduated from Ryder Divinity School in Galesburg, Illinois. His first posting as the minister of a Universalist Church in Unionville, Missouri, led to a similar appointment in Chicago, frequent engagements on the Chautauqua lecture circuit as a speaker on religious topics, and a position as the manager of a local lyceum bureau.

While enrolled in graduate level classes at the University of Chicago, Smith was introduced to Clarence Darrow, Floyd Dell, Emma Goldman, Maurice Browne, and Margaret Anderson, as well as to Powys, who was then temporarily residing in Chicago. Through faculty friends, Smith was soon offered a teaching position at the University of California, Berkeley, and because he was in the midst of a rather scandalous divorce (his second), he gladly seized the opportunity to escape.

In due course, however, Smith's personal conduct once again provoked the public's ire. This time it was because of an affair he was conducting with the wife of the minister in whose Berkeley pulpit he had been substitute preaching. Smith, who indignantly maintained that the whole incident was a case of mistaken identity, took the opportunity to hyphenate his name (so he would be harder to find in the telephone directory, he later claimed). However, the administrators at the University, unconvinced of his moral rectitude, insisted he forfeit his career as an academic. Jordan-Smith reluctantly complied, and as soon as his latest lover could obtain a divorce, the couple married and moved south to Claremont.

Jordan-Smith's union with Sarah Bixby Smith (coincidentally, her first husband shared the same common surname as her second) was quite a fortuitous match for him, because his bride was from one of the most prominent and wealthy families in Southern California. The newlyweds moved into a neglected, fourteen-room manse in Claremont and lovingly restored the stone structure, which they named Erewhon after the book by Samuel Butler, Jordan-Smith's favorite author.

As a man of newly acquired means, Jordan-Smith took up the intellectual life in earnest. With the time and wherewithal to indulge his interests, he became an avid bibliophile and novelist, and whenever he was not playing father to the eight children he and Sarah Bixby had accumulated from their assorted marriages, he sought out stimulating companionship among the members of the Severance Club.

Jordan-Smith's adulterous past apparently forgiven, or at least partially forgotten, it was not long before he was invited to teach extension courses in Los Angeles, under the auspices of the University of California, Berkeley, and by the time he met Weston he was already well known as a lecturer in English and American literature (see fig. 36). Occasionally, however, Jordan-Smith's speeches took on a more provocative, political tone, especially when he addressed such topics as "The Literature of Individual Revolt."[16]

Attending one of Jordan-Smith's lectures that spring was another former Chicagoan, the aforementioned Altadena philanthropist, Kate Crane Gartz.[17] She and some of her like-minded friends were members of The People's Council of America for Peace and Democracy, a national pacifist organization that vigorously opposed America's entry into the war. The organization's membership, drawn from all segments of the political and social spectrum, included Max Eastman, editor of *The Masses*, a socialist magazine based in New York City; Robert Whittaker, the powerful, ultraconservative clergyman from Los Gatos, California; Eugene V. Debs, the soon-to-be socialist candidate for President; and Dr. David Starr Jordan, president of Stanford University. It was a remarkably diverse group, united only by their common belief that America should remain isolated from the war in Europe.

After hearing Jordan-Smith lecture, Gartz asked him to organize and lead the Southern California chapter of the People's Council. He rose to the occasion and accepted Gartz's challenge. Jordan-Smith then recruited a young Pasadena woman, B. Marie Gage, as his chief assistant and began a tour throughout Southern California to solicit new members. However, even as the antiwar movement was growing ever more vocal, so was its opposition, and there were many charged and ugly confrontations between the new organization and those who believed America had no choice but to join in the conflict. Jordan-Smith's life was threatened a number of times during the spring of 1917, and he once escaped only by brandishing a loaded pistol over the heads of an angry mob bent on doing him physical harm.

Momentum had been gathering for America's participation in the war on Germany since the beginning of 1917 when the German ambassador had declared that, as of February 1, his country's submarines would no longer recognize the neutrality of American ships, but instead regard them as fair targets.[18] President Wilson's response was to sever all diplomatic relations with Germany. Talk of imminent engagement was on everyone's lips, so when Wilson addressed a special session of Congress on April 2, 1917, his formal call to arms came as no surprise. The United States government could no longer ignore what was happening in Europe, and the world shrank overnight as America prepared to do battle.

Wilson's declaration of war prompted the federal government to take drastic protectionist measures, and on June 15, 1917, Congress passed the Espionage Act. As a result America became a place where free speech and diverse opinions could no longer coexist with patriotism.

FIGURE 36. Edward Weston, *Paul Jordan-Smith*, 1918. Platinum print, 24.1 × 19.4 cm (9¹/₂ × 7⁵/₈ in.).
Los Angeles, J. Paul Getty Museum, 86.xm.745

The Department of Justice immediately began surveillance of those citizens deemed to be the greatest security threats, and Jordan-Smith and his pacifist friends were among them.[19] It was during the tense months that followed that Jordan-Smith's friendships with Weston, Elmer Ellsworth, and Charlie Chaplin were forged and solidified.[20]

ON THE HOME FRONT In spite of the unprecedented turmoil on the international front, Weston was keeping up a relentless round of activities at home. In May 1917, after winning a bronze medal at the Toronto Camera Club Salon for his portrait of Dextra Baldwin, which Weston exhibited alongside a group of other portraits employing "unusual lighting effects,"[21] he was asked to shoulder an important responsibility in the local photography community.

Soon after holding its 1915 salon the Los Angeles Camera Club had disbanded for the second time. Several of its members had then joined forces to form another organization, the Southern California Camera Club (SCCC), with clubrooms on the fourth floor of the Lyceum Theatre building. The SCCC's inaugural exhibition, held in the summer of 1916, had been a hastily assembled selection of amateurish work, supplemented by complementary exhibits borrowed from four of the better-known local photographers—Fred Archer, W. C. Sawyer, D. Doerr, and Weston.[22] But club members aspired to make the May 1917 exhibition a much more ambitious, juried event, and they tapped Weston to serve as one of the judges.

After the SCCC salon opened, Antony Anderson enthusiastically reported that the 1917 exhibition was "undoubtedly the best show ever held by the Camera Club [apparently inclusive of those sponsored by the LACC, the SCCC's predecessor], as every picture not pictorial in quality was rigorously excluded." He then conscientiously added a disclosure stating that the jury had been "composed of one pictorial photographer, Edward Henry Weston; one painter, J. Duncan Gleason; and one art reviewer, Antony Anderson."[23] Because Weston wore a judge's badge he could not compete for salon prizes, although he did hang a selection of his work drawn, in large part, from his recent showing at the Friday Morning Club. Mather's contributions received positive reviews from Anderson, who wrote, "Margrethe Mather's 'Poster Portrait' is very charming, absolutely correct in placing."[24] He also praised her portraits of Harriet Dean and William Saphier, her friends from the staff of *The Little Review*, taken a few months earlier.

Just as the salon came to a close, Saphier's colleague, poet Alfred Kreymborg, arrived in Los Angeles, where he was scheduled to read a selection of his latest poems and discuss his recently launched literary journal, *Others*, at the Friday Morning Club.[25] His collaboration with Man Ray and Adon Lacroix on the *Glebe* had ended unsatisfactorily a few months earlier with the dissolution of that publication, and Kreymborg was now in the midst of his second publishing venture. This time his success was virtually assured, because he had gained access to the well-lined pockets of the New York City art collector and fellow chess enthusiast, Walter Arensberg. Saphier had encouraged Kreymborg to make the trip west,[26] and it was likely at his

FIGURE 37. Margrethe Mather, *Alfred Kreymborg*, 1917. Platinum print, 16.5 × 11.6 cm (6¹/₂ × 4⁹/₁₆ in.).
Los Angeles, J. Paul Getty Museum, 86.xm.721.1

suggestion that Kreymborg now made his way to Mather's studio. In her portrait of the poet
(fig. 37), Mather imagines his shadow as a dark, ghostly doppelgänger, suggesting a potent inner
spirit driving the shy, introspective young man.

As the summer of 1917 approached, Weston and Mather began to prepare their entries
for the London Salon of Photography, still regarded as the most important photography exhibition in the world, which was scheduled to open in mid-September. Weston submitted seven
pictures and Mather sent three.[27] Amazingly, even though shipping lanes across the Atlantic
Ocean were blockaded, their photographs arrived safely in England. Weston's entries particularly impressed the judges, and as a result he was elected to membership in the London Salon.[28]

It was the first time a Californian had been honored by that prestigious organization, and the Los Angeles photography community received the news of Weston's elevated stature with great enthusiasm.

In September *Camera Craft* published an article about the Platinotype Company, which had recently begun to produce a new photographic paper called Palladiotype.[29] The paper was sensitized with palladium, rather than platinum, which was now being diverted to munitions plants for use in the war effort. The journal went on to describe the technical aspects and appearance of the finished palladium print and rated the results equal to those achieved by the platinum process.

Weston and Mather must have read the article with great interest, relieved at the prospect of having a viable alternative to the platinum papers on which they had become so reliant, and very soon after palladium paper became available they began to experiment with it. Palladiotype paper was produced in two colors—white and buff—but Weston and Mather found the buff background preferable, especially when mated with the warm brown tones produced by the palladium salts.[30]

By this time many of Mather's and Weston's friends and acquaintances were being featured prominently on the entertainment pages of local newspapers. Articles about actors/directors James Kirkwood, William Desmond Taylor, Marshall Neilan, and, of course, Chaplin, appeared regularly in the *Times*. Another new theatrical venture, the Community Theatre of Hollywood, had just opened on Ivar Street, with oil heiress Aline Barnsdall among its benefactors.[31] One of the Community Theatre's first productions was a play titled *Suppressed Desires*. The play had been authored by Jig Cook and Susan Glaspell, who had recently founded their own theatrical company on Cape Cod called the Provincetown Players.

Talented dramatists were suddenly in great demand. Hollywood movie producers were seeking writers who could transform popular books into successful screenplays. Harry Leon Wilson, former editor of the New York City–based humor magazine *Puck*, was engaged in just such an endeavor.[32] His recently published, highly acclaimed *Ruggles of Red Gap* had made him a much-sought-after commodity in Hollywood, and he was presently in the midst of adapting his novel into a screenplay. Even though he had long since retired from his editorial duties and was now residing in Carmel with his much younger wife, Helen Cooke, and their two small children, he was temporarily staying in Los Angeles until he could complete his adaptation.

To help promote interest in the forthcoming movie, a studio publicity photograph of Wilson's two toddlers, Leon and Helen, sporting identical Dutch-boy bobs, appeared in the *Times*.[33] Young Helen, who would later drop her first name in favor of her second (Charis) was only three years old when her likeness was published. If Edward Weston happened to notice the little girl's picture, he would never have guessed, given their twenty-eight-year age difference, that he and Helen Charis Wilson would one day marry.

THE CASTLE CROWD   Frayne Williams, an old friend of Charlie Chaplin, became Margrethe Mather's Hope Street neighbor around the end of 1917 (see fig. 58). A Welshman by birth, Williams had endured an impoverished childhood very similar to Chaplin's.[34] The two actors became acquainted when both were performing in the theaters of London's Piccadilly Circus, but while Williams established his reputation by taking on roles in Shakespearean dramas and the raw, earthy fare popularized by John Millington Synge and Lady Augusta Gregory, cofounders of the Irish Players, Chaplin made his name in the boisterous, physical comedies of vaudeville.

Williams came to Los Angeles with Richard Ordynsky, the suave Polish director hired by Aline Barnsdall to oversee her fledgling Little Theatre. In the autumn of 1916 Williams directed and assumed the starring role in Barnsdall's production of Arthur Schnitzler's *Anatole*.[35] But even though his Los Angeles stage career held much promise, his success was cut short when his friend Ordynsky became embroiled in an affair with Barnsdall that ended just as impulsively as it had begun. A few weeks after their breakup, Barnsdall learned she was pregnant.[36] Angry and disillusioned, she abruptly paid off her company of actors, closed down her theater, and went into seclusion to await the birth of her child. Due to this unexpected turn of events, Williams suddenly found himself among the ranks of the unemployed.

He need not have worried though. His vast stage experience and remarkable versatility counted for much in Hollywood, where few actors were as well trained as he. Thanks to his old friend, Chaplin, and his new friend, Elmer Ellsworth, it was not long before Williams found work at Universal Studios, where dozens of short features were being produced each year.[37] However, despite his gratitude for the steady income, Williams soon realized that minor roles in Universal's second-tier productions were a waste of his prolific talents, and he began to hatch plans for his own theatrical company.

A few months later Williams left his rundown Hope Street boarding house and took up residence at the Castle Tower Apartments (see fig. 28), a large, turreted apartment building perched on the edge of the steep bluff where West Fourth Street dead-ended, directly across the street from Mather's carriage-house studio.[38] Popularly known as the Castle, it served as an inexpensive stopping-off place for bohemian and theatrical types until they could afford better accommodations.

Williams and Mather soon became friends, and she photographed him on a number of occasions, usually in character, portraying one of his better-known stage roles. Williams utilized several of these portraits on promotional brochures to publicize his fledgling theatrical endeavors, as well as the dramatic interpretation classes he had begun teaching through the University of California, Berkeley.[39] It was thanks to his university connections that Williams met Paul Jordan-Smith, who would later refer to the actor as "one of my best friends of the past forty years."[40] Williams was a gentle, jovial man, with a keen eye for the ladies, and he was highly regarded by Mather and Weston for his intelligent, entertaining conversation.

Coincidentally, at the same time Williams moved to the Castle, Mather's friend Maud Emily Taylor was also in residence there. Taylor had entered the University of California, Berkeley, in the autumn of 1916, but a few weeks into her first term, she had fractured her arm in an equestrian accident.[41] Forced to drop out of school, the disappointed young lady had returned home to Texas to recuperate from her injury, but by the spring of 1917 she was back in Los Angeles, renting a room at the Castle. It was there that she received a long letter from her old friend Russell Coryell.[42]

Coryell had abandoned his position at Boyland a few months earlier, after Prince Hopkins had tried to put him in charge of the school. Alarmed at the thought of assuming cumbersome administrative duties and yearning for more exotic scenery, Coryell instead decided to tender his resignation. Still determined to realize one of his fondest fantasies, Coryell then signed on as a ship's chandler, and in spite of closed shipping lanes, lurking German submarines, and his own precarious health, he managed to make his way safely to Genoa, Italy, where he found a job as an English tutor and occasionally served as a war correspondent for the *Los Angeles Times*.[43]

In his letter to Taylor, Coryell sounded homesick for his California friends. He was more serious and reflective than in his earlier communications, and he once again urged Taylor to reconsider her own future and examine her feelings for him:

> If I came as close to your rusty old heart as you came to mine, then it's only a question of
> months before you pack a couple of suitcases...take a last look at your little, crooked old
> room which overlooks the little old provincial city of Los Angeles, say good bye to the
> fair Margrethe and sail for here...Love to Mary & Gay [Wilshire] & Mollie [Price Cook]
> & Margrethe. I won't offer any to you. It's for you to take yourself....Russ.[44]

Taylor was mightily tempted to join Coryell, but instead she made the decision to stay in California and return to her studies at Berkeley in the autumn. Her youngest brother, Jack, was about to arrive in Los Angeles, and she wanted him to take her place at the Castle, where she knew he would have a ready-made set of congenial friends to look after him in her absence.[45]

Although Jack Taylor was only eighteen years old when he moved into his sister's apartment later that summer, he already knew he wanted to become an artist. In spite of his youthfulness, the shy, lean Texan got along well with Mather and Weston, and they were protective of their friend's naive little brother. Soon after his arrival, the young man took a job as an advertising salesman for the *Los Angeles Times*[46] so he could save enough money to pay for painting classes when the right opportunity presented itself.

While visiting with Frayne Williams and Jack Taylor, Mather became friendly with several other residents of the Castle. One was an Irish-born actor named Thomas Gerald Joseph Mary MacMurrough Kavanagh who, for brevity's sake, was known in Hollywood as Douglas Gerrard.[47] He and his younger brother, Charles Christopher MacMurrough Kavanagh (aka Charles Gerrard),[48] claimed as their grandfather the Right Honorable Arthur MacMurrough

Kavanagh of County Carlow, an extraordinary man descended from one of the kings of ancient Ireland.[49] Their grandfather had been born without arms or legs, but he had overcome his physical deficiencies to become an intrepid world traveler and a member of the British Parliament. The Gerrard brothers demonstrated a similar resolve.

Both young men had begun their acting careers on the stages of Dublin and London. In 1907 Douglas had traveled to New York City as a member of the Charles Frohmann Theatrical Company,[50] but in 1913 he moved west to Hollywood just in time to appear opposite the much-revered ballerina, Anna Pavlova, in her first and only film role. With that stellar credit on his resumé, he successfully continued his movie career and occasionally had the opportunity to direct. His sibling, Charles, had recently followed him to Los Angeles, and Mather photographed the younger Gerrard as a debonair bon vivant, impeccably dressed, moustache waxed to perfection.[51]

In the autumn of 1917, while Douglas Gerrard was directing a picture at Universal Studios, he encountered a handsome Italian-born dancer in need of a place to live. Fascinated by the attractively beefy young man, Gerrard befriended him and brought him home to meet his brother and the other residents of the Castle. Rodolpho Guglielmi, a native of Castellaneta, Italy, was a newcomer to California. A few months earlier, Guglielmi had been the toast of Manhattan cabarets, performing a sensuous new ballroom dance, known as the tango, with his partner, Joan Sawyer.[52] He had been forced to leave the East Coast rather suddenly, however, due to his involvement in a scandalous love triangle and blackmail plot.

This complicated situation had culminated in the shooting death of real estate magnate and playboy, Jack de Saulles, at the hands of his wife, the Chilean-born heiress, Bianca Errazuriz, who was reportedly in love with Guglielmi. After testifying at her murder trial, Guglielmi had fled to San Francisco in an attempt to forestall any further encounters with the New York City Police Department and put the unsavory episode as far behind him as possible.

While he waited for the scandal to subside, Guglielmi moved south to Los Angeles, where he supported himself with his dancing skills and studied to improve his English. As a street-smart young man, he instinctively knew that many opportunities awaited him in Hollywood, if he was properly prepared to take advantage of them. Determined to enhance his chance for success, he dutifully enrolled in acting classes, but it was only after Guglielmi's agent persuaded him to change his name to Rudolph Valentino that his career as a silent-screen heartthrob began to take shape. Frayne Williams, Jack Taylor, the Gerrard brothers, and Valentino often dropped in on Mather, who gladly offered up her studio as a welcoming and convenient location for their boisterous social gatherings.

Just as Maud Emily Taylor was returning to Berkeley in the autumn of 1917, her friend Mollie Price was departing that city. After accruing a few credits at the University of California, Price was on her way to Santa Barbara, where she was about to assume the role her friend Russell Coryell had rejected—that of Superintendent of Boyland, which was now in its second incarnation. Hopkins's first school had enjoyed such a warm reception that he had recently built another, much larger facility near Oak Park on the western fringes of Santa Barbara, and he had spared no expense in realizing his new endeavor.[53] His goal was to make his school the finest facility of its kind on the West Coast.

The new campus now encompassed thirty acres and was expansive enough to accommodate a day school for children of both sexes, as well as a boarding school for boys under the age of ten. The school's elaborate design, inspired by the architecture of Persia, incorporated ogee arches, formal gardens, picturesque fountains, and grand vistas. Included in the scheme were an administration building; a large gymnasium; an aboveground, glass-sided swimming pool; and the very latest in kitchen and pantry facilities.

Constructed inside a central courtyard was a map of the world, just as in the first rendition of Boyland, but this one was much more elaborate than its predecessor, with meticulously detailed, three-dimensional continents surrounded by water-filled oceans. Complete with volcanoes that belched real steam, this scale model, known in contemporary educational circles as a Phillips projection, was specially designed to teach the children about geography and geology. Under Mollie Price's supervision, Hopkins's lavish new school began to receive a great deal of positive publicity in Southern California newspapers. However, world events would soon spell disaster for Hopkins and everyone associated with Boyland.

THE WOBBLIES With the passage of the Espionage Act the previous June, the Justice Department had begun formal surveillance of many American citizens. Paul Jordan-Smith was among them, and he was already feeling the effects of being subjected to their stony gaze. In September 1917 he returned from a speaking tour to find federal agents raiding his Los Angeles office and rifling through his files.[54] Jordan-Smith hurriedly retreated to his home in Claremont, where his actions were kept under constant scrutiny and his household staff was quizzed repeatedly about whether the Jordan-Smiths were entertaining Germans at Erewhon.

Although he had already registered for the draft, Jordan-Smith's loyalty remained in question because he had actively spoken out against America's entry into the Great War and had continued to lobby for peace and a democratic approach to foreign policy, even after President Wilson's formal declaration of hostilities. Jordan-Smith was badly shaken by his encounters with the Justice Department, although based on his personal experiences with some of the more radical antiwar organizations, he could understand why such drastic measures might be necessary.

Much of his disillusionment stemmed from his interactions with the International Workers of the World (IWW), a labor group formed in 1905 in Chicago.[55] Jordan-Smith regarded them as "fanatics"; in later years he would disparagingly refer to their membership as "the dregs of the world."[56] The IWW, popularly known as the Wobblies, was a group of primarily American-born members. The Wobblies, whose objectives were well intentioned but often confused, took great pride in public displays of bombastic behavior. Heading their organization was William (Big Bill) Haywood, the same burly ex-miner and union organizer who had made a name for himself in Salt Lake City as the leader of labor's epic struggle against the large mining trusts.[57]

The Wobblies could claim only a few hundred members, but they were a demonstrative lot, and as such, the group managed to have a disproportionately significant impact on the labor movement. Their opinions and methods were the most extreme of any left-wing organization and their collective voices the loudest expression of outrage in America. Two of their loyal members in Los Angeles were Mather's anarchist friends George Lipton and Marie Latter, who both felt entirely at ease within the unpredictable and often violent ranks of the Wobblies.[58]

THE CHAMELEON   During these uncertain times Marie Latter was communicating regularly with another loyal member of the IWW, a woman named Betty Katz, who had come to Los Angeles after spending several years in New York City.[59] Born in Romania, Katz had immigrated to Manhattan's Lower East Side around 1905 with her mother, two sisters, and a brother. After her brother was killed in a streetcar accident, Katz was forced to go to work in a succession of sweatshops to help support her family.

She eventually took a job at the Triangle Shirtwaist Company on Washington Square and was employed there when, on March 25, 1911, a deadly fire engulfed the top three floors of the ten-story building. The conflagration killed 146 garment workers, as many as 90 of whom jumped from the windows rather than succumb to the flames when they discovered that the exit doors to the stairwells were locked.[60] Purely by chance Katz had been assigned to work a different shift, and she realized she had only narrowly escaped a horrible death. The tragedy radicalized her and inspired her to join the IWW in their fight against unfair and unsafe labor practices.

While living in New York City, Katz made a number of friends who, like herself, were from Eastern European or Russian backgrounds. For a time she was romantically involved with a young man named Isadore (Fleggie) Kaufman, and through him she became acquainted with George Liberman/Lipton and Isidore (Roy) Rosen. All three men would eventually make their way to California.[61]

In the months that followed the Triangle Shirtwaist Company fire, Betty Katz proved herself to be an effective public advocate on behalf of women employed in the needle trades, so when she was diagnosed with tuberculosis in 1915, union leaders sent Katz to California to recuperate and, at the same time, continue organizing workers in the fast-growing garment industry in Los Angeles. Together with her mother and two sisters, Dora and Pauline, Katz settled in the Boyle Heights district, a bustling neighborhood east of downtown Los Angeles that was fast filling up with an influx of recent immigrants.[62]

Shortly after her arrival in Los Angeles, Betty Katz's tuberculosis worsened, and her kidneys began to fail. Doctors advised her to relocate to the desert, where the arid climate would help heal her body, so she rented a small cottage near Palm Springs, and as her strength allowed,

FIGURE 38. Margrethe Mather, *Betty Katz*, ca. 1916. Palladium print, 24.1 × 19.4 cm (9 1/2 × 7 5/8 in.). Los Angeles, J. Paul Getty Museum, 85.XP.249.1

she periodically shuttled back and forth between Los Angeles and her desert retreat. Around 1916, during one of her Los Angeles visits, Katz met Margrethe Mather, and the two women were instantly drawn to each other. Katz was a striking presence with her dark, luxuriant hair, expressive brow, and commanding demeanor. Mather photographed Katz in profile, standing in front of a Roman window shade, holding a single, long-stemmed rose (fig. 38). A few days later she sent a set of prints to Katz, along with a wistfully romantic note:

> Betty-girl—
> here they are—at last! I wish I had much better to offer you—you and your rose deserved it—Someday—again—?
> My evening with you was sweet—only I so regretted sending you home alone. I had a white little bed at home.—you should have had that—and I could have the floor—Really I mean it—Forgive my thoughtlessness—
> I'm sorry you are going—I so want to know more of you—
> I like you—
> This note—should be a poem—I feel like one—
> but———
> Margrethe[63]

Katz was a complicated woman who harbored many secrets. She relished subterfuge, and never hesitated to concoct spur-of-the-moment anecdotes or rewrite her personal history if it suited her needs. In one demonstration of her resourcefulness, she cleverly obtained an American birth certificate under the name Betty Kopelanon by claiming she had been born in San Francisco, knowing full well that no one could challenge her statement because most of the city's vital records had been destroyed in the 1906 earthquake.[64] Katz was colorful, formidable, and unforgettable, and Mather was transfixed by her. Indeed, with their shared fondness for bold prevarication and their mutual interest in political rabble-rousing, the two women had much in common.

THE HOBO   It was through Betty Katz that Mather met Isidore (Roy) Rosen.[65] Like Katz, Rosen was of Romanian extraction.[66] Born in 1893 to an Orthodox Jewish family in New York City, he had received his early education at a rabbinical school, but when he reached adolescence he decided to turn his back on Orthodoxy and explore America by hitching a ride on the nearest freight train. His aim was to find excitement and occasional employment, while experiencing all the country had to offer.

Rosen's chosen lifestyle, known as hoboing or vagabonding, had become a necessity for some and an amusement for others by the end of the first decade of the twentieth century. Inspired by Jack London's popular novel *The Road*, published in 1907,[67] and spurred on by difficult economic conditions, three million young men had "hit the road" or "flipped the freights" by 1910.[68] At that time, the term *hobo* had a very specific meaning, as compared to *tramp* or *bum*, and it was Emma Goldman's business manager and lover, Dr. Ben Reitman, known as "king of the hobos," who elucidated the differences. "The hobo wanders and works," he wrote. "The tramp wanders but does not work and the bum neither wanders [n]or works."[69]

Rosen considered himself a member of the first group, and his conversation was liberally peppered with snatches of colorful hobo jargon. During his travels he also became a philosophical anarchist and a member of the Wobblies, although his greatest satisfaction was derived not through political activities, but from his adventures as a "bindle stiff," the term applied to a wanderer who carried his possessions tied in a bundle slung over his shoulder on a stick. Rosen loved the freedom and exhilaration he felt while being constantly on the move, living life moment to moment.

The migratory existence was perilous, however, and like so many who lived it, Rosen suffered from a myriad of injuries and illnesses as a result of his vagabonding. In 1910 he was diagnosed with tuberculosis, which forced him to endure several months of confinement in a Colorado sanitarium, the first in a series of prolonged stays at similar institutions.[70] Nevertheless, whenever his illness went into remission he would return to the road or the rails, eager to strike out for unfamiliar destinations.

Around 1916 Rosen's meanderings took him all the way to Southern California, where he found the climate agreeable enough to settle down for a time. During one of his earlier jaunts on the Southern Pacific Railroad he had encountered a sympathetic train conductor from Los Angeles who had offered to rent Rosen a room in the attic of an ornate, if somewhat dilapidated, Victorian-era house, known to Angelenos as the Hancock Banning House.[71] Located at 416 North Broadway the house stood high atop Fort Moore Hill, overlooking Old Chinatown and the eighteenth-century El Pueblo de Los Angeles, where the city of Los Angeles had been born.

Whenever Rosen's tuberculosis symptoms recurred he would enter Barlow's Sanitarium, a clinic for indigent tuberculars on the edge of Elysian Park, where he would often remain for months at a time.[72] During these prolonged absences his friend, Betty Katz, would take over his attic apartment on North Broadway, provided she felt strong enough to be away from her beloved desert.[73] After Rosen was introduced to Margrethe Mather she agreed to store some of his possessions, including his treasured travel journals, in the small crawl space beneath her carriage-house studio. He was grateful for her kindness, and that simple gesture sealed their friendship.

While living in New York City, Rosen had often attended exhibitions at Stieglitz's 291 gallery, so he had already acquired a passing interest in photography. As he watched Mather work, however, he quickly became even more appreciative of photography's artistic potential. It was not long before Mather took him to meet Weston, and Rosen developed a deep respect for her colleague's abilities.[74] Soon Rosen was spending long hours regaling the two photographers with stories of his travels on "the tops of trains on summer nights,"[75] while they labored in the darkroom. He also commiserated with their lack of steady incomes, and whenever Rosen obtained a temporary job, he would offer monetary assistance to his two friends.[76]

Rosen and Mather became so close she even attempted to loan her Graflex camera to him, thinking he might want to take some photographs himself, but he was intimidated at the thought of revealing his limited skills to his supremely talented friend, and so declined her offer.[77] Instead Mather gave him several prints of her photographs that he especially admired, including her portraits of Vaslav Nijinsky and Leon Bakst, actresses Lillian and Dorothy Gish, and oil heiress Aline Barnsdall.[78] Impressed and touched by her generosity, Rosen became her staunch advocate.

In later years Rosen fretted that Billy Justema's comments about Mather's days as a prostitute might besmirch her reputation and malign her character unfairly. Rosen described Mather as having the "elegance of a high-born lady," and he fiercely defended her honor, but in doing so provided evidence that Mather occasionally returned to her former ways, even after she became a photographer:

> This prostitute business at the hotel at Hill St. and 3rd where the cog railway went to the top of Bunker Hill I think is just nonsense. So Margrethe went out and needed paper, needed negatives, needed photographic materials, and went to bed with somebody for the money....So what? There was a dealer on South Olive Street that ran a Kodak shop, and he would come to see her for a full afternoon or an evening. And once I said to her jocularly, "Does he pay you the union rate?" which threw her into transports. She said, "Don't worry, Roy, about me. I manage."[79]

There were also times when Rosen did not approve of Weston's treatment of Mather, even though he was awed by Weston's consummate talent. On several occasions Rosen was present when portrait sittings that had been secured by Mather were commandeered by Weston. One such incident involved a set of portraits commissioned by William A. Clark, a flamboyant bibliophile and founder of the Los Angeles Philharmonic Orchestra. The job had come through Mather's literary contacts, but Weston ultimately claimed the prize and the $2,400 fee that went along with it.[80] It was a record order for Weston, and presumably he shared some portion of the proceeds with Mather, but Rosen believed the spoils should have been hers alone. Although Mather rarely displayed displeasure with Weston, this event and others witnessed by Rosen were among the earliest manifestations of growing tension and competitiveness between the two photographers.

SADAKICHI Whenever Betty Katz was forced to retreat to the healing warmth of Palm Springs she would look forward to receiving letters from Marie Latter telling of the latest radical get-togethers, their immediate aftermath, and the personalities who had attended them. One such letter described a particularly successful bacchanal at which their mutual friend, Sadakichi

Hartmann, who visited Los Angeles in September and October 1917, was the guest of honor. As a young girl in Chicago, Latter had once had an affair with the much older Hartmann, and the two had stayed in touch over the intervening years.

Latter's gossipy, detailed description of the evening conveys the bonhomie of the uninhibited crowd, whose preoccupations—namely free love and its accompanying vices—were typically bohemian:

> I had the party in the 2 rear rooms, the walls of which are a neutral shade of green and lent themselves beautifully to my decorative scheme, which consisted of tacking up pictures and picture postcards of the so-called "art" specimens, over all the grease spots and torn places, the Bakst pictures of the Russian dancers covering the greatest sins & the postcards the lesser. On the floor I placed all my little rugs and several old pieces of tapestry & velvets and all the "rags" I could find in Georgie's store, then I had several long cushions also covered with these "rags" and I made about thirty pillows in futurist colours, black & white checks, yellow, black, red, green, every colour I could find and over the three lights I placed crepe paper of a vivid rose hue....
>
> Not all the people I expected came, & some unexpected ones did. [Sadakichi] Hartmann, of course, was the "celebrity," and read [to] us from his "memoirs" choosing his first adventures in the realm of love for our delection!...
>
> Of course, there were intermissions during which we drank and ate sandwiches, and talked and laughed. Hartmann had very carefully barricaded the whiskey bottle in the pantry, he remembered too well his disastrous experiences...the day you and Joe [O'] Carroll were there and Joe drank up all the whiskey. And he gave me strict orders not to invite Joe, for he had committed the one great unforgivable sin, not to share the drink with a comrade-in-arms....
>
> ...But, oh Betty, you should have seen my beautiful Oriental room the next day. Oh ashes of love, ashes of joy, and ashes, ashes everywhere.... And so my party ended.[81]

Born around 1867 on an island near Nagasaki, Japan, Sadakichi Hartmann was the son of a German businessman and a Japanese mother who reportedly died when he was just a boy.[82] After his mother's death, he was sent to live with a wealthy uncle in Hamburg, Germany, where he received an excellent education. A few years later Hartmann's authoritarian father returned to Germany, remarried, and attempted to install his son in a German naval academy, but the rebellious adolescent bolted, resolutely refusing to pursue a military career. His dismayed father subsequently packed off the obstreperous youth to relatives in Philadelphia, where he struggled to adulthood and eventually became a self-taught writer, critic, philosopher, and performance artist.

In his prime, Hartmann had been widely recognized as an unusually brilliant, erudite man who wrote intelligently and insightfully about a wide range of subjects, one of which was photography. But by 1917, when Hartmann visited Los Angeles and entertained at Latter's party, he had become an alcoholic, and his unusual, wizened appearance made him appear much older than his fifty years. Although Hartmann could still be a charmingly witty conversationalist when sober, as soon as his alcohol consumption got the better of him he would invariably turn boorish and rude. He was notorious for his arrogant attitude that the world owed him a living, and his incessant wheedling for "donations" was not always well tolerated, even by the bohemian crowd whose ranks were more sympathetic than most.

While Hartmann was in town, Edward Weston photographed his exotic Eurasian features as he struck various poses for the camera (see fig. 39). Weston had long wanted to meet Hartmann, because the critic had authored an enthusiastic analysis of *Carlota* for the *Bulletin*

FIGURE 39. Edward Weston, *Sadakichi Hartmann*, 1917. Gelatin silver print, autographed in ink by the sitter, 24.1 × 19.2 cm (9^1/$_2$ × 7^9/$_{16}$ in.). Los Angeles, J. Paul Getty Museum, 85.xm.170.5

of Photography the previous year,[83] and Weston was hopeful that Hartmann might continue to write about his photographs in the many art magazines to which Hartmann was still a regular contributor, usually under the *nom de plume*, Sidney Allan.

In one of Weston's portraits, Hartmann wears a kimono over his emaciated frame as he emerges from the right edge of the picture plane, looking as though he had accidentally walked in front of the camera just as the shutter clicked.[84] His casual pose creates an impression of movement within the composition, an element previously missing in Weston's work. With a lingering nod to Whistler, an artist much revered by Hartmann,[85] Weston signed his photographs of Hartmann with a spidery, stylized flourish, which may have been his attempt to imitate the butterfly-like monogram Whistler often applied to his paintings and etchings.

Hartmann also posed for Mather during his 1917 Los Angeles visit, and was reportedly dismayed to learn that a woman of her beauty and artistic talent would have to resort to prostitution as a means of support. Whether Hartmann knew about that aspect of her life from rumor, observation, or firsthand experience he did not reveal.[86]

A few days after Latter's party, Hartmann appeared at the Friday Morning Club, where he happened to share the podium with a congressman from California who was there to discuss the ongoing war with Germany. The congressman quoted Kaiser Wilhelm extensively, citing example after example of Germany's belligerent intentions toward the United States. Hartmann, who still considered Germany his intellectual home, apparently felt ill at ease while listening to the congressman's address, because when a reporter from the *Times* queried him about his background, he responded that he had been born to "a Japanese mamma and an American papa."[87]

WAR CASUALTIES   Within weeks of Hartmann's Los Angeles appearances, while the Allied Forces were intently focused on bringing the war with Germany to a close, the Bolsheviks of Russia culminated their October Revolution in "ten days that shook the world."[88] The anarchists of America, many of them Russian immigrants, were galvanized by the news, and a few even returned to their homeland to help move the process along. Radical organizations, particularly the IWW, took up the revolutionary cry with characteristic fervor, provoking the Justice Department to raid their offices, confiscate their records, and imprison three hundred of their members.

Meanwhile, average Americans were being called upon to prove their patriotism by participating in the war effort in any way possible. Photographers were encouraged to apply for positions in the Aviation Corps, where skillful aerial photography and rapid developing techniques could greatly enhance America's effectiveness in battle.[89] Late in the year a significant American war casualty was mourned by Antony Anderson in the *Times*:

> Perhaps the most unfortunate result of the war on art life of New York was the closing of "291." The Photo Secession Gallery at No. 291 Fifth Avenue has for many years been the center of all the radical strivings of the newer American painters, and has been the most

potent force in the encouragement of this country's modern experimentation. It was at "291" that the first Rodins, the first Cezannes, the first Matisses and the first Picassos ever exhibited in America were shown, and every season it has held a series of exhibitions of the earnest younger men who were denied the more conservative galleries. The organ of "291"—Camera Work—has long been recognized as the finest art publication of its kind in English. Alfred Stieglitz, the guiding spirit of "291," has devoted his life to the task of helping and stimulating all the deserving young artists who are seriously struggling toward a high and serious ideal; and the closing of his gallery will be a genuine loss to modern American painting.[90]

Anderson's tribute, which failed to emphasize the important role Stieglitz's 291 gallery had played within the photography community, recalled the January 1915 issue of *Camera Work*, in which Stieglitz had published sixty-eight responses to his question, "What does '291' mean to you?"[91] Included were comments from Abby Hedge Coryell (Russell Coryell's mother), Hutchins Hapgood (author of *An Anarchist Woman*), poet Alfred Kreymborg, artist Emmanuel Radnitsky (already signing his name Man Ray), and anarchist/sculptor/poet Adolf Wolff (writing from the prison cell on Blackwell's Island where he was then incarcerated).

Stieglitz was from a German-Jewish background himself, and when he posed his query almost three years earlier, he could not have foreseen what havoc the European war would bring to American shores, or how much disruption it would cause in the lives of his fellow German-Americans. Nor could he have known that the comments he chose to publish, culled from a plethora of laudatory responses, would become his gallery's most eloquent epitaph.

Around that same time, the Weston family faced a very profound, personal loss when Cornelius Chandler, Flora's father, died at the age of eighty.[92] With his death, the land on which Edward Weston had built his home and studio passed to Flora's mother, Ann Elizabeth. This sad event only served to remind Weston that any future success he might have in Tropico would necessarily be tied to Flora and her family.

As 1917 came to a close Antony Anderson reviewed an exhibition of paintings and political cartoons by the Mexican-born artist Gerardo Murillo, who claimed to be descended from the Spanish Old Master painter, Bartolomé Esteban Murillo.[93] However, Gerardo Murillo chose to paint under the name Dr. Atl, a word borrowed from the Nahuatl language of the ancient Aztecs meaning "water." Anderson preferred Atl's caricatures over his paintings, and he especially appreciated those with pointed political overtones:

His cartoons are astonishingly vivid and original. . . . he makes use of symbolism, and, of course, with absolute sanction, for the good cartoon is always a symbol. His cartoon of the Kaiser as superman is the revealment of a grewsome [sic] and repulsive being, half man and half beast.[94]

The Germans, or Huns, as they were regularly described, were now being vilified every day throughout America. Organizations or individuals who did not fully support the war effort were derided as Hun-loving and regarded as potential spies. Preposterous rumors reflecting anti-German sentiments were circulated daily. The *Los Angeles Times* even took the opportunity on several occasions to aggressively attack their archrival, San Francisco newspaper publisher William Randolph Hearst, dubbing him "Herr Hearst" and declaring him "a threat to the nation," along with the IWW, the socialists, and the pacifists.[95] The German language was banned in the Los Angeles school system, German books were interned in a special room at the public library, and anyone of German nativity or descent was suspect.[96]

The political climate had been gradually worsening since the previous spring, causing a rapid decline in thoughtful discourse and responsible behavior that not even the July death of pugnacious *Los Angeles Times* publisher Colonel Otis could halt. The steady disintegration of reliable standards of journalism and the growing disregard for due process were now conspiring to undermine whatever common sense remained in Southern California. Paranoia had reached dangerous proportions.

War and Pestilence, 1918

B y the beginning of 1918 the war had disrupted the normal rhythms of life for virtually
all Americans. Even Californians, at the greatest geographical and psychological remove
from the conflict, were forced to fix their undivided attention on Europe. Artistic pursuits
ground to a halt as America waged an all-out military campaign against its enemies. Along with
the rest of the nation's artists, America's photographers fell into a creative lull, and their collective state of ennui was evident when the First International Photographic Salon—sponsored by
the Camera Pictorialists, with Louis Fleckenstein still at the helm—opened its doors in January.

The event attracted a record 60,000 people to the Los Angeles Museum, but popular
appeal was not enough to satisfy Antony Anderson, who gave the salon a negative review.[1] He
found the overall quality of the prints disappointing, and he was especially critical of the presentation and hanging of the photographs. Very likely, Mather and Weston influenced Anderson's
blunt assessment. Having grown increasingly disillusioned with the Camera Pictorialists, they
had recently resigned from the club, opting out of the event they had helped conceive two
years earlier.

On February 8, 1918, a tall, handsome stranger knocked on the door of Weston's studio.
He had come at the suggestion of friends in San Francisco. The stranger was blond, musta-
chioed, and dramatically garbed in a voluminous black cloak (see fig. 40). He spoke with a
thick foreign accent, and in a small pocket diary he recorded his visit to the studio in bursts of
rudimentary English. He noted, "a perfect day—met Miss Mather at Mr. Weston's."[2] The following day he added, "to Tropico again—decided to study with Weston."[3] It had taken only
two encounters for the stranger to recognize the diminutive, bespectacled photographer as a
kindred spirit.

Born in Amsterdam on June 1, 1884, Johan Hagemeyer was one of five children in a
middle-class Dutch family.[4] A rebellious adolescent like Weston and Mather, he had dropped
out of school while still a teenager. After working for a short time in an insurance brokerage
and fulfilling an eighteen-month obligatory term in the Dutch army, he decided to prepare for a
career as a horticulturist, an ambition that eventually led him to study pomology, the science of
fruit growing. Somewhere along the road to maturity, Hagemeyer also became a philosophical
anarchist and an avid amateur photographer.

FIGURE 40. Edward Weston, *Jean-Christophe* (Johan Hagemeyer), ca. 1920. Platinum or palladium print, 19 × 24.2 cm (7¹/₂ × 9¹/₂ in.). Tucson, Arizona, Center for Creative Photography, University of Arizona, 76:5:9

In 1910 two of Hagemeyer's brothers, Hendrik and Herman, immigrated to America. Their intention was to eventually make their way to California where they hoped to establish a dwarf fruit tree nursery. The following spring, Johan, age twenty-six, decided to join his siblings in their proposed venture. He arrived at Ellis Island aboard the SS *Nieuw Amsterdam* on May 1, 1911,[5] and after spending the summer working on a farm in Riverton, New Jersey, Johan and one of his brothers continued on to the West Coast, where they secured jobs at Congressman Everis A. Hayes's ranch near Edenvale in the Santa Clara Valley. In spite of his fractured English, Johan subsequently found employment at the botanical gardens of the University of California, Berkeley, but a few months later he moved south to work for members of the Popenoe family, who were engaged in cultivating avocados and dates on extensive acreage in Altadena and the Imperial Valley.

Impressed with Hagemeyer's propagating skills, the Popenoes sent him for further training to the Department of Agriculture in Washington, D.C. It was there, while recuperating from a bout of pneumonia, that he spent long hours in the Library of Congress, perusing a run of

Alfred Stieglitz's *Camera Work*. Duly impressed with what he saw, Hagemeyer traveled to New York City in late 1916 to meet Stieglitz in person. His encounter with the godhead of American photography was an epiphany for Hagemeyer, and a few days later he departed for California with the messianic zeal of a fledgling convert.

Hagemeyer arrived back in the Bay Area on January 15, 1917, an inscribed issue of *Camera Work* in his suitcase, determined to make contact with the most accomplished of California's photographers. His goal was to immerse himself in their world in order to learn as much as possible about the art of photography. The first person he called on was Anne Brigman, the only Californian in Stieglitz's stable of Photo-Secession photographers. A few days later Hagemeyer took a job developing and printing film at Martin's Camera Shop in San Francisco, but soon after attending a lecture by Francis Bruguière at the San Francisco Camera Club, he began an apprenticeship in the Berkeley studio of portrait photographer Edwin J. McCullagh.[6] All the while he was pursuing his interest in photography, he was supporting himself as a gardener and dishwasher.

This burst of frenetic activity continued for almost a year, but in December 1917 Hagemeyer finally decided to move south to Pasadena, where his brother Herman was then living. Although the two Hagemeyer brothers had always been close, Johan had another reason for moving to Southern California. On an earlier visit to Pasadena he had become infatuated with a woman named Lula Boyd Stephens. His attraction to her had since flamed into an all-consuming passion that was threatening to displace photography as the motivating force in his life, but geographical distance was not the only obstacle to his romantic yearnings. Lula Boyd Stephens was already a married woman.

Hagemeyer was far too besotted to think clearly about the ramifications of such an entanglement, however, and he proceeded to muddle through the early months of 1918 in a feverish emotional state, existing only for the brief interludes when he and Stephens could steal away together. That spring the calmest moments of his otherwise turbulent life were those he spent with Weston and Mather. The three photographers had much to share, being of like minds on many subjects. Weston was impressed with Hagemeyer's worldliness and his extensive knowledge of music and literature. Hagemeyer admired Weston's highly developed artistic eye and technical prowess. When it came to politics, Hagemeyer and Mather were sympathetically aligned; whenever romance and its complications became the topic of conversation, Hagemeyer and Weston could commiserate.

In mid-March Hagemeyer moved into Weston's "shack," as he called it, under the terms of a reciprocity agreement. Hagemeyer later reminisced:

> I…clicked with [Weston] right away.…He was known locally as a very outstanding portrait photographer. I never had done much portraiture, but he had, and I liked his work very much. I liked his setting.…

He liked me because I had something else. I was one of those European "Dagos," travelers. I brought things to him. He already had a family and I had never had a family. I was free and I could move around....[7]

...He asked me to come and live with him and I did some cleaning of the studio, housekeeping at the house, and they fed me. At the same time I just played around and worked some with him in the studio, mostly making trouble....

We had very much in common.[8]

In spite of his desire to learn as much as possible from Weston, Hagemeyer spent a good portion of the next few weeks in bed, suffering from painful dental abscesses and a seemingly endless array of other, possibly imagined, ailments. In April Hagemeyer noted in his diary, "feel bum all day—Mrs. W. did my housework."[9] After several days of accommodating Hagemeyer's numerous infirmities and caring for three young children, Flora Weston was understandably disillusioned. She demanded an alternate solution, and her husband complied by asking Hagemeyer to move out. However, Weston then followed up his request with an apologetic letter written on May 12:

I am very, very busy or would have written sooner.

I must tell you the new arrangements—which as I understand will be in force indefinitely—Flora is going to work in the studio as receptionist—and incidentally I shall teach her all branches of the work—

She has engaged help to do the housework—I think we will all be better satisfied with the arrangement—You and I might have "batched" it together and made a go of it—but a woman must have a woman to do her work to be happy I guess.

Now—all this will not affect in any way the studio. I still want you to make the studio headquarters—to feel it is *your* workshop as well as mine—I do want to help you—*if* I can—to advance in your chosen art....I think now that Flora will be at the studio—we will have all the more time to study and think. She will take so much of the writing and reception-room work *off* my hands—and now we can each have someone to use as a model while the other looks on.[10]

Surely Weston was not surprised that both Hagemeyer and Mather were missing from Flora's latest scheme, in which she envisioned herself playing a more active role in her husband's photography business.

Hagemeyer then returned to his brother's home in Pasadena, and to provide himself with a steady income, he obtained a job working for George Steckel, Weston's former employer. Although Hagemeyer's apprenticeship with Weston had lasted only two months, out of that brief association would grow a friendship of many years' duration. For the time being, however, Weston maintained a studied distance from his new colleague, and Hagemeyer later offered a very different explanation for his sudden departure from Weston's home, "At one stage of the game, during the war, Weston asked me as a friend to leave his house. He said, 'I have a family.' He didn't want to be involved, for fear they might pick me up."[11]

As Weston had become better acquainted with Hagemeyer, he had begun to worry that his new friend's radical views might compromise the safety of his family. Hagemeyer was an outspoken critic of the war, and by 1918 there were extremely serious consequences for any individual—especially someone foreign-born—who dared to oppose America's involvement in the war effort. As one historian of the period put it,

> Bitten by the dog of war, America had gone mad. The reasons were as complex as the result was simple. A historic anxiety over national identity, and long-running trends of nativism, individualism, capitalism, and antiradicalism, issued in the demand for total conformity and one-hundred-percent Americanism.[12]

On April 18, 1918, a few days before Weston asked Hagemeyer to leave his home, Congress had passed the Sedition Act,[13] further strengthening the Espionage Act of 1917. The combination of these two laws made it a crime to obstruct the war effort, or even to speak out against the conflict. Anyone convicted of such an offense was subject to a twenty-year prison sentence. In addition, an Enemy Alien Act (on the books since 1798 but rarely enforced) was revived, forcing those who had been born elsewhere to register with the federal government. It also allowed for the incarceration and deportation of any foreign-born resident who showed even the slightest degree of disloyalty to America. Diligently overseeing the Enemy Alien Registration Section of the Justice Department was an extraordinarily ambitious young man, a twenty-two-year-old recent law school graduate named J. Edgar Hoover.[14]

It was the Enemy Alien Act that made Hagemeyer especially vulnerable. He enjoyed close friendships with several well-known, foreign-born anarchists and labor activists in the San Francisco Bay Area, and he was quite vocal about his personal opposition to the war. Hagemeyer later explained his dilemma:

> It was during the war years. . . . there's where the trouble came in for me, really, because I was a pacifist. . . .
>
> The government followed me up. They wondered who I was. They must have noticed, or heard, or were told. . . . The government was after certain people and I knew those people. They were I.W.W. members. I never was, but they were poets and I like poets. . . .
>
> I knew Emma Goldman very well. A wonderful woman. She knew all about drama, in which I was also very interested.
>
> I knew many of the people she was with. Bill Haywood. He was, of course, a so-called "bomb-throwing" anarchist. . . .

I associated with them because they had something to say. And somehow I feel it is good, like Gide writes, to disturb, to arouse....

Of course, I didn't want to go to jail. Many of my friends went to jail who weren't as radical as I was; they were just pacifists....

Although I was against the war, I had enough sense not to call myself a pacifist. Actually I didn't believe completely in pacifism. I believe there must be a constant stirring.[15]

INTIMIDATION TACTICS   Hagemeyer was not the only one of Mather's and Weston's many radical friends who were at risk; in fact, several had already been arrested. In June 1917, almost a year after fleeing San Francisco and the aftermath of the Preparedness Day parade bombing, Emma Goldman and Alexander Berkman had been taken bodily from the *Mother Earth* offices in New York City and charged with "conspiracy against the draft."[16]

The following month they stood trial in a sweltering Manhattan courtroom with Jane Heap and Margaret Anderson at their sides.[17] In the midst of the proceedings, Heap wrote Florence Reynolds that she was disappointed in their mutual friend, Harriet Dean, then visiting in New York City, because she had chosen to absent herself from the trial. Heap commented that Dean had become uncharacteristically cautious almost overnight.[18] When the jury found Goldman and Berkman guilty, they were briefly incarcerated and then released on bail so they could prepare their appeals. In January 1918 their appeals were denied, and by the following spring, during the weeks that Hagemeyer was living in Weston's studio, Goldman and Berkman were both in the midst of serving out eighteen-month prison sentences.

In the meantime, the left-wing American press had completely vanished. With the passage of the Espionage Act the previous summer, the Postmaster General had been empowered to halt the circulation of antiwar propaganda by revoking mail permits issued to any organizations or periodicals that dared question American foreign policy. Within six months most of the nation's leftist journals had been suppressed, including Goldman's *Mother Earth*, Anderson's and Heap's *Little Review*, and Max Eastman's *The Masses*.

But worse assaults on the Constitution were yet to come. In April 1918 Prince Hopkins appeared as the featured speaker at an antiwar gathering in downtown Los Angeles. At its conclusion Hopkins was chased through the streets by police and thrown in jail.[19] Within hours arrests were also made in Santa Barbara. Boyland's loyal superintendent, Mollie Price, was taken into custody, along with several of Hopkins's pacifist friends.[20] When the group was brought to trial a few weeks later, all of them pled guilty to the charge of having interfered with the recruitment efforts of the military, which as Hopkins later admitted, "was no more than the truth."[21]

Fortunately, Hopkins could afford to pay his own $25,000 fine, and he and Gaylord Wilshire jointly covered the $10,000 price tag attached to Price's freedom, but because of this highly unpleasant episode, Hopkins became deeply disillusioned with the American government's strong-arm tactics. He closed down Boyland at the end of the 1918 spring term, departed Santa Barbara, and sought an intellectual diversion by enrolling in psychology and creative writing courses at Harvard University.[22] Even the normally resolute Mollie Price gathered up her two children and fled California, returning to her hometown of Chicago.[23]

When federal authorities quizzed Rob Wagner about Prince Hopkins's politics and sexual orientation, he came to Hopkins's defense. In a letter to the Justice Department, Wagner fearlessly championed the motives and educational philosophy of the man to whom he had entrusted his own two sons:

> Prince started out in life with a silver spoon, a million dollars and a chance to dedicate his life to polo and highballs, but as a mere youngster surprised and shocked his friends by showing an amazing intellectual appetite. Yes, Prince is a "nut," according to country club standards, but it always seemed to me he was simply a good healthy protest against his own bunch....
>
> When I was in Santa Barbara last, everybody was telling me that they were going to "get" Prince, and they all seemed most happy about it. They whispered about mysterious doings at Boyland, sex degeneracies, and whatnot! It was dear old sex-sick Santa Barbara. I lived there six years and I know how the idle parasites love to play in the mud. But my answer to all that stuff is that I sent my own two boys to Boyland and I regard Prince Hopkins as one of the finest influences that ever came into their lives. And so well were they trained that they entered the Los Angeles High Schools at twelve years of age. If Prince holds any "liberal" sex ideas, they are purely intellectual; his own life has been as disciplined as a monk's. Furthermore, you can't fool children on that stuff, and every kid that's been to Boyland regards Prince as a real prince.[24]

Wagner soon paid a stiff penalty for his loyalty to Hopkins when he was forced to resign his part-time teaching position at Manual Arts High School, but luckily Charlie Chaplin's need for companionship and conversation was expansive, and Wagner soon began spending the majority of his time as the comedian's confidant.

Chaplin was particularly sympathetic to Wagner's plight because he was fending off criticism himself.[25] Eligible to serve in either England's or America's armed forces, Chaplin had shown no inclination to defend either country, and the draft boards of both nations were now eyeing him with intense interest. The Lone Star publicity department had issued a press release in June 1917 declaring that, although Chaplin had registered for the U.S. draft, he had not passed the physical, because at five feet four inches and 129 pounds, he was too short and underweight to qualify.[26] However, this statement had only succeeded in eliciting skepticism from the American public, and Chaplin was now beginning to find himself the butt of sarcastic slacker jokes.

Even though Chaplin's antiwar sentiments were not widely known, some of his ill-considered words and actions had provoked the ire of the wrong people at an especially sensitive time, and he now turned to Rob Wagner to help staunch the flood of negative publicity that was beginning to rise to the surface. Wagner, no doubt also hoping to deflect further criticism of his own situation, responded by orchestrating a series of public events where he and Chaplin could be seen actively supporting the war effort.

Remarkably, even as his patriotism was being questioned, Chaplin was able to negotiate a lucrative new contract for himself, this time with the First National Film Corporation. In spite of the federal government's problems with Chaplin, his movies were still generating record-breaking figures at the box office, and several major film companies were keen to sign him. At the end of a protracted, convoluted negotiation Chaplin triumphantly walked away with a contract worth $1,250,000.[27]

With a continued source of revenue assured, Chaplin purchased a large plot of land south of Sunset Boulevard and east of La Brea Avenue, where he set about building his own movie studio. Rows of mock-Tudor bungalow offices and dressing rooms were constructed, bracketing the entrance to a large, open-air film stage where scenes could be shot under natural light, virtually year round.

Chaplin's first production at his new studio, titled *A Dog's Life*, included scenes of Rob Wagner making his acting debut as a barroom patron. The moment the film was completed, Chaplin and Wagner joined their friends Douglas Fairbanks and Mary Pickford on a Liberty Bond tour to raise money for the war effort. Knowing that the Justice Department was assiduously watching his every move, Chaplin hoped that his participation in the tour would demonstrate his support for America and Great Britain and effectively silence his critics. After three and a half weeks of nonstop travel, however, an exhausted Chaplin lost all enthusiasm for the endeavor, and he began to cancel his speaking appearances.

Nevertheless, by the end of the tour Chaplin and his colleagues had succeeded in raising several million dollars, including a $350,000 cash pledge from Chaplin himself. As soon as he and Wagner returned to Los Angeles, Chaplin immediately launched into the production of another film, aptly titled *Camouflage*, a word that quite accurately described his recent Liberty Bond tour activities, which had been carefully designed to disguise his antiwar, antinationalist tendencies.

WILD JOE   Chaplin's decision to publicly support the war effort, despite his private opposition to it, was regarded as nothing less than spineless capitulation by another of Margrethe Mather's friends. This man, whom Johan Hagemeyer would later describe as an IWW poet,[28] was Joseph Ely O'Carroll, the same querulous fellow who, after leading the protests of the unemployed in New York City in the spring of 1914, had spent the following summer on Cape Cod recovering from his beating at the hands of the New York City Police Department and frolicking with the likes of Hutchins Hapgood, Susan Glaspell, and Jig Cook.[29]

O'Carroll was now living in Los Angeles, where he was continuing his activities as a labor organizer and socializing with the IWW crowd who regularly convened in the home of Marie

Latter and George Lipton. Hagemeyer found O'Carroll to be good company because, unlike some of the ruffians within the ranks of the Wobblies, O'Carroll was an articulate, literate fellow. These attributes, coupled with an extremely volatile temperament, made him a natural leader of the Wobblies' often contentious demonstrations. Unlike Chaplin, O'Carroll never compromised, and he was always prepared to take the consequences of his actions, on the chin if need be.

O'Carroll had been born in 1888 in Dublin, Ireland, the first child in a large, prosperous, Catholic family.[30] His father, Dr. Joseph Francis O'Carroll, was one of the most prominent physicians in all of Ireland, greatly admired as both an inspirational professor at University College, Dublin, and an empathetic practitioner who made time for even the weakest and poorest of his many impoverished patients.[31] Within his own family, however, Dr. O'Carroll was regarded as a stern and unforgiving father with the touchy temperament and unrealistic expectations of a martinet.[32] Seeking to escape the unavoidable pressures of being the formidable Dr. O'Carroll's eldest son (and perhaps attempting to assuage a guilty conscience stemming from the drowning death of his youngest brother),[33] a rebellious, alienated Joseph O'Carroll fled Ireland, bound for America, when he was still a teenager. Upon arriving in his adopted country, he immersed himself in the labor movement, a natural outlet for his pent-up adolescent anger and resentment.

In 1908 O'Carroll joined the recently formed IWW during their third annual convention in Chicago, and by 1911 he was publishing poetry in *Solidarity*, the IWW newspaper.[34] Three years after that O'Carroll made the front page of the *New York Times* as the ringleader in a succession of protests by unemployed workers, culminating in the demonstration that earned him the nickname Wild Joe.[35] Widely known as a scrappy, fearless fighter for the anarchist cause, O'Carroll won his place in the vanguard of the American left the hard way—by repeatedly thrusting himself forward to man the front lines of their battles. Following one of his encounters with New York City's police force, whose ranks included a good many of his own countrymen, a reporter asked the bludgeoned, bleeding O'Carroll where he lived. The belligerent Irishman responded by bellowing out Emma Goldman's address.

O'Carroll and his reputation for ferocity were well known to Hagemeyer, Marie Latter, George Lipton, and Betty Katz. In one of her letters to Katz, Latter wrote at length about O'Carroll, and coincidentally recorded the occasion of his first meeting with Margrethe Mather. Latter was skeptical of Mather's motivations but intrigued by her "originality":

> Now Betty, if you ever tell this to Joe he is liable to dynamite, burn down the house, and then shoot! So if you love me, don't. I haven't the slightest thing against Joe, in fact [I] rather like him but as you say he should be taken in very small doses. And of course I feel sorry for him having to work. I don't like to work myself, nobody does, but he isn't clever enough, or entertaining enough, or he hasn't enough of that indefinable quality, personality, or magnetism or whatever one may call it, that makes people so interesting and

absorbing that one is only faintly conscious of the process of their moochings! Like Terry Carlin, for instance, who never, never whined or begged. One actually had to sometimes force money on him!…

I don't mean to insinuate I hate Joe, he will no doubt perfect his methods, he's young yet. Yes, he and Margaret were evidently much smitten with each other, but Margaret is not the type that will take care of a man, she's too preoccupied looking about for men to take care of her. She's a queer girl, very interesting and I would like to know her. Gertrude [Barrett, a neighbor of Mather's] has told me a lot of things about her—you know in these days one must be "different" and "original" so no doubt a lot of this stuff is put on but I am so old fashioned that unless the "put on" is done very very cleverly I prefer the real.[36]

FIGURE 41. Margrethe Mather, *Joseph (Wild Joe) Ely O'Carroll*, ca. 1918. Platinum or palladium print, 23.5 × 18.7 cm (9 1/4 × 7 3/8 in.). Collection of the author

After being introduced at Latter's party, Mather and O'Carroll began a relationship that would last for several months. Mather chose to look beyond O'Carroll's bellicose swaggerings, because she had high regard for his intellectual capacity and a genuine appreciation for his poetic nature, an Irish national trait with which he was thoroughly imbued. Surely Marie Latter underestimated O'Carroll's appeal, because in the photograph Mather made of him around this time (fig. 41) the strength of his personality and the intensity of his animal magnetism are abundantly obvious. Clearly Latter also misjudged Mather, whose originality was very real indeed.

THE CHINESE POET   In the summer of 1918 Margrethe Mather began working on a series of portraits of another fascinating young man, a Chinese scholar/poet who called himself Moon Kwan.[37] Born in a village near Shanghai, Kwan came from a well-respected, prosperous family. Shortly after his 1914 arrival in San Francisco he enrolled at the University of California, Berkeley. Possessing a remarkable facility for languages, Kwan rapidly became adept at speaking and writing in English, but when a family member died very unexpectedly he was forced to leave his university studies behind.

Kwan then moved to Los Angeles, where he gradually became integrated into the local arts community. At the time Mather photographed him, the twenty-one-year-old was living at 342 North Main Street, in a nineteenth-century building converted to artists' studios (known as the Baker Block), where he was acting as a "cultural consultant" to D. W. Griffith, then in the midst of filming *Broken Blossoms*, a film set in London's squalid Chinatown.[38]

The first of Mather's portraits of Kwan is an image titled *The Chinese Flute*[39] in which Kwan stands in profile at the viewer's left, his shadow forming a dense, distorted figure in the middle of the picture frame. Two other images depict Moon Kwan holding a *yit-kim*, a mandolin-like, stringed instrument. In one he appears in the lower left corner of the image, his body visible only from the waist up.[40] A pictographic scroll hangs from the upper right edge of the picture to balance the composition. In the other, the young man is positioned in the center of the picture, with his own shadow acting as counterpoint to the hanging scroll at the right edge of the image.[41]

A fourth photograph (fig. 42) is the most daring of the series. Moon Kwan is placed in the lower right corner, his body truncated at the shoulders so that his head and upper chest form a solid, triangular mass.[42] In the upper left corner hangs a Chinese figural scroll, cropped so as to give the impression that the painted figures are on the verge of exiting the picture plane. An oblique light source creates a dense vertical shadow along the edge of the scroll, bisecting the composition and providing an illusion of depth. In the upper right corner, another area of deep shadow acts as a visual anchor.

This last composition is particularly successful in the way it combines stasis with movement, two-dimensional design with spatial ambiguity, and restrained elegance with sensual texture. It clearly demonstrates Mather's growing command of her medium, as well as the

FIGURE 42. Margrethe Mather, *Portrait of Moon Kwan*, 1918. Reproduction courtesy of the George Eastman House, International Museum of Photography and Film, Rochester, N.Y.

confidence and vigor with which she was pushing the aesthetic boundaries of photography. When the picture was exhibited the following year, one critic confessed his failure to fully comprehend her accomplishment, while expressing an intuitive understanding of her abilities:

> "Portrait of Moon Kwan," by Margrethe Mather, is an experiment in composition which is probably based on some Oriental model. The balance between the three dark spots seems to be carefully worked out, and undoubtedly has a sound logical basis. The appreciation of this form of composition however, is at present with the writer purely an intellectual one, like that of some of the newer forms in music and painting. Presumably the next generation will accept arrangements like this instinctively. Such is the way in which art grows.[43]

The Moon Kwan series was an impressive leap forward for Mather. With the creation of these photographs she outdistanced her critics and surged ahead of Weston. She not only rendered her sitter with originality and respect, portraying him as an individual rather than as the stereotypical, inscrutable Chinaman so commonly depicted, she set new aesthetic standards for herself and her colleagues in the process. The sensitivity and sophistication of her approach, and the disciplined rigor of her vision, had very few precedents or parallels within the medium of photography.

While Mather concentrated on developing her artistry, Weston continued to work at keeping his professional profile as high as possible. In March he hung another group of photographs at the State Normal School in eastern Hollywood,[44] and in June the *Los Angeles Times* reproduced seven of his photographs in a full page spread.[45] The July issue of *American Photography* featured one of Weston's portraits of dancer Violet Romer, displaying her peacock feather plumage at Anoakia,[46] and in September the *Camera* printed his photograph of an unidentified, sad-faced woman wearing a broad-brimmed hat.[47] Once again Sadakichi Hartmann did the critiquing, but this time he found fault with the photograph on technical grounds.[48] Weston was incensed when he read the negative review, and from that moment forward Weston had little use for Hartmann as a critic or a human being.

The paper shortages caused by the war necessitated the postponement and consolidation of the 1917 and 1918 *Photograms of the Year* into a single volume, but when the British publication finally appeared, Mather and Weston were both represented—Mather by *Miss Maud Emily*,[49] her white-on-white, Whistlerian confection, and Weston by *Miss Dextra Baldwin*,[50] with its striated lighting effects. Only two years had passed since the creation of those photographs, but in the interim the world had become a vastly different place.

UNEXPECTED INSPIRATION   During the summer of 1918 young Jack Taylor, still residing at the Castle, heard about the imminent return to California of artist Stanton MacDonald Wright. Wright and another expatriot, Morgan Russell, had spent the early months of the Great War in France and England, where they had founded a painting movement called Synchromism, based on the use of color as the primary expressive element.[51] But in 1916 the

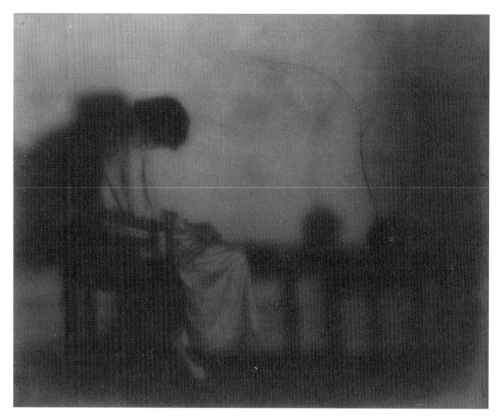

FIGURE 43. Margrethe Mather, *Maud Emily Taylor in Chinese Chair*, ca. 1918. Platinum or palladium print, 19.3 × 25.1 cm (7³/₄ × 9⁷/₈ in.). Private collection

deteriorating European situation had forced Wright to flee to New York City, and a few months after his arrival there Alfred Stieglitz honored Wright with an exhibition at his 291 gallery.[52]

Now the painter would soon be returning to his home state to bring a breath of the Parisian avant-garde to Southern California art students. This was the opportunity Jack Taylor had been waiting to seize. As soon as Wright arrived in Los Angeles Taylor signed up to become one of his first pupils, and in exchange for tuition, which he was still hard pressed to afford, Taylor agreed to clean and maintain the studio space where Wright would be teaching his classes.[53]

Taylor's sister, Maud Emily, had recently left her studies and married a designer named Ray Glass, and she was now awaiting the birth of her first child. She returned to Los Angeles for a visit with her brother and posed for several photographs by Mather. In one she stares solemnly at the camera, wearing a dark dress adorned only by an impressive Navajo squash-blossom necklace.[54] In another (fig. 43) she sits in profile in a Chinese chair, wearing a white, embroidered tunic. Her head is bowed, and on the small table in front of her sits a simple black pottery vase containing a single bare branch. The composition is restrained, and the mood is contemplative.

It was around this same time that Mather's mysterious Beau discreetly disappeared from her life, but before departing she presented Mather with an invaluable farewell gift—a lifetime lease to her Bunker Hill carriage-house studio.[55] Surely it was no coincidence that Florence Reynolds left Los Angeles late that summer and returned to Chicago for a few months, prior to accepting a permanent administrative position at a private girls' boarding school in Manhattan.[56]

That autumn Marie Latter and George Lipton also traveled to New York City for a long-postponed visit with his family. Latter soon found a job at a millinery factory and, with a steady source of income established, Lipton and Latter decided to extend their stay from a few days to several months.[57] During the first few weeks of Marie Latter's New York City sojourn, she became friendly with Christine Ell, a flamboyant redhead who had just opened a self-named restaurant above Jig Cook's Provincetown Playhouse theater, recently relocated from Cape Cod to 133 MacDougal Street in Greenwich Village.[58]

Ell had formerly been a prostitute, but she had left that chapter of her life behind after hearing Emma Goldman speak about the obligation society has toward women who are forced by circumstance to choose between a life of poverty and one of degradation. While Latter was spending time with Ell in Greenwich Village she had the opportunity to meet Eugene O'Neill, whose play *Moon of the Carribees* was in the midst of rehearsals at the Provincetown Playhouse one floor below.[59]

It was now Latter's turn to be scrutinized by O'Neill, just as her former lover, Terry Carlin, had been two years earlier, and during the months that Latter lived in New York City, O'Neill began drafting the play that would eventually become *Anna Christie*, his tale of a young Midwestern "nurse-girl" turned prostitute. The similarities between O'Neill's character and the real-life Marie are unquestionably striking. Anna Christie's personal history closely replicates Marie Latter's, and her speech patterns eerily echo the cadence and phrasing found in Latter's correspondence.[60]

QUARANTINE   That September, while Marie Latter was steeping herself in the bohemian atmosphere of Greenwich Village, unaware that she was about to be immortalized by one of America's greatest playwrights, the city of Los Angeles was gearing up for yet another celebration. The Liberty Fair, planned as a massive fund-raiser for the war effort, was to include all manner of parades and entertainment, as well as displays of the finest specimens of plump California poultry, elaborate arrangements of succulent citrus fruit, and the latest in fine art photography.[61]

The photographic portion of the exhibition was scheduled to be on view from September 23 through October 26 at two successive venues—first at the Brack Shops at Seventh Street and Grand Avenue, and subsequently at the Pavilion of Fine Arts in Exposition Park.[62] The selection committee, which included Mather's friend Rob Wagner, sculptress Julia Bracken Wendt, and painter/photographer Oscar Maurer,[63] had already culled an overwhelming 338 photographs from the many hundreds entered in the competition.

Shortly before the fair was to open the judges surveyed their selections and awarded First Prize honors to Weston, Mather, and Louis Fleckenstein in the portrait category and an honorable mention to Mather in the genre category.[64] One of Mather's prizewinning pictures was *The Chinese Flute*,[65] her portrait of Moon Kwan. Also recognized for his efforts was Dr. William Mack, Florence Reynolds's brother-in-law, who received a Third Place ribbon in the landscape category.

To Weston, these small triumphs must have come as a much-needed bit of cheer in an otherwise gloomy month. He had recently received word of the death of his seventy-two-year-old father on September 14.[66] Weston was furious when he learned that his stepmother had committed the failing Dr. Weston to Chicago's Hospital for Incurables, where the elderly gentleman had been forced to spend his final days.[67] Even though Weston's relationship with his father had often been an uneasy one, he felt genuine, filial affection for the man who had given him his first camera, and deep sadness at his passing.

Just as final preparations for the opening of the Liberty Fair were taking place, the specter of the deadly Spanish influenza, which had been relentlessly spreading across the country since the early summer, suddenly hovered over Los Angeles.[68] Caused by one of the most lethal viral strains ever to surface in America, the influenza outbreak had already been responsible for tens of thousands of deaths, primarily in the urban centers of Boston, New York City, and Philadelphia. The pandemic was now snaking its way west along the rail lines, and public health officials were desperate to prevent a disaster of similar proportions on the West Coast.

Because the potentially lethal virus was airborne, public health officials decided that the most effective way to halt its spread would be to ban public gatherings altogether, so the Liberty Fair celebration was put on hold while the city reluctantly endured a strict quarantine for the next several weeks.[69] The bored citizenry, forbidden to gather in public places and with very few amusements to distract them, had little to divert their attention when rumors of Charlie Chaplin's marriage began to surface.

After days of speculation and denials, it was finally confirmed that Chaplin, who had parted company with his former girlfriend and leading lady, Edna Purviance, earlier in the year, had quietly married a sixteen-year-old actress named Mildred Harris on October 23 in a private ceremony.[70] Shortly after Chaplin's return from the Liberty Bonds tour, he had been introduced to Harris, whereupon he had become obsessed with the delicate, underage beauty.[71] But in early October Harris had confounded the comedian by announcing that she was pregnant, and his predilection for her childish charms had instantly vanished when he found himself in the untenable position of having to marry her.

Highly resentful of this unwelcome development and suspicious of Harris's motives, Chaplin perfunctorily deposited his young bride at the house he had rented in the recently established enclave of Laughlin Park, while he fled to Porter Ranch north of the city, where he was about to begin shooting his next film, *Sunnyside*. As his latest movie scenario took shape, Chaplin wove into its improvised plot a strange hodgepodge of dream sequences in which his character cavorts in the woods with a bevy of nymphs, à la Nijinsky in *L'Apres-midi d'un faune*, and then inexplicably commits suicide. This bleak attempt at cinematic farce was painfully indicative of his glum state of mind.

Two and a half weeks after Chaplin's nuptials, on November 11, 1918, America awoke to the news that an armistice had been signed. The country went wild with relief and elation. The dreaded Huns had finally gotten their comeuppance, and Americans congratulated themselves on having been instrumental in handing them a sound defeat. Of course, all the backslapping and celebrating was necessarily tempered by the horrible casualties that had been suffered by American soldiers on the battlefields of Europe and by the aftermath of the influenza epidemic, which had killed an astonishing 675,000 people on the home front during the previous ten months.[72] Even so, when the influenza quarantine was finally lifted later that month, the Liberty Fair, conceived as a wartime fund-raiser, became a jubilant victory party instead.[73]

Just as the armistice celebration began, the city of Tropico ceased to exist. After seven years of public wrangling, Tropicans passed a referendum calling for a large portion of their town to be officially annexed to the city of Glendale, their neighbor to the north, while a much smaller section on Tropico's west side would become an addendum to the Atwater district of Los Angeles.[74] This blending of Tropico into the surrounding communities necessitated the renaming and renumbering of dozens of streets. As a result Edward Weston's studio address was changed to "1315 South Brand Boulevard, Glendale,"[75] while his home address became "4102 Verdant Street, Los Angeles." For the first time since his arrival in California a dozen years earlier, Weston was officially an Angeleno.

Exhilaration, 1919

T he exuberance that accompanied the war's conclusion brought with it a wave of unprecedented activity that coincided with the beginning of the new year. Like the all-engulfing force of a tsunami, this surge of long-pent-up energy swept over America almost as rapidly as the recent flu epidemic. As communications resumed with Europe, and Americans began to venture across the Atlantic again, it became evident that the world was forever altered. Gone was the lingering romanticism and slow, measured pace of the nineteenth century. The globe was suddenly spinning at a faster tempo and the future was all that mattered. This truth gradually manifested itself in the glint of sun on sleek, steel skyscrapers and the growing din of industry reawakening.

Artists were among the first to notice the changes, and Mather and Weston responded in a rush of intense creativity that lasted for several months. However, they continued to absent themselves from the Camera Pictorialists' activities, even after Antony Anderson pronounced the January 1919 salon "the most notable photography show ever held in Los Angeles."[1] Nine hundred entries had been received, of which two hundred were chosen for display. Prominent among the exhibitors was Mather's Keystone Kop friend, Ford Sterling, who had recently joined the club.

A few days after the salon closed, on January 30, 1919, Flora Weston gave birth to a fourth son. Unlike his three older brothers, who had each been welcomed into the world with carefully preselected names that proudly reflected their joint Weston-Chandler heritage, this infant was identified on his birth certificate only by the surname Weston.[2] Such inattention to detail may have been a result of Flora's grief over the death of her mother, who had passed away two weeks earlier.[3] Mrs. Chandler's demise meant an imminent distribution of her real estate holdings, and Flora and her sister, Elizabeth Ellias, had been named as coinheritors of several parcels of land, including the South Brand Boulevard studio property and the Westons' Verdant Street lot.[4]

It is also possible that the Westons' failure to give their new baby a proper name occurred because they were in the throes of yet another tumultuous crisis in their increasingly dysfunctional marriage. Whatever the explanation, when a degree of calm finally returned to the Weston household, they named their infant son Frayne, in honor of Weston's actor friend, Frayne Williams.[5] However, several months later, for reasons unknown, they would change their youngest son's name to Cole.[6]

Weston's relationship with his children was a complicated one. He enjoyed parenting, but in small doses. He dearly loved his sons, but he preferred to be around them one at a time and only when they were well-behaved. He routinely read bedtime stories to them, and he made many charming portraits of his boys, but he left the day-to-day childcare responsibilities to his wife. Unfortunately, his lack of affection for Flora caused him to severely limit the time he spent at home, and he often used his work as an excuse to absent himself from the family circle.

That February, while Flora was trying to cope with her mother's death, care for her newborn, and oversee the activities of three exuberant children, her husband frequently extricated himself from the melee at home so he could enjoy several social outings with Mather and Hagemeyer. Hagemeyer had recently moved downtown to 414 South Grand Street to be near the Steckel Studio where he was still employed, and he made his usual diary notes about their activities:

[February 7]
"Bohemian Day" w/LL [an abbreviation for Lady L, his nickname for his girlfriend, Lula Boyd Stephens] to Weston (left P[asadena] 9:30) lunch at Miss Mather['s]—exhibits, symphony event, Café du Paris, [Geraldine] Farrar in "Hell Catt" home 11:30—perfect day—perfect end.

[February 21]
Exposition Park Gallery (2–2:30 Lirber Landsen). To Chinatown with Margrett, Clara, Joe O'Carroll, Weston—afterward to Harold's (Mr. Miles) studio until 1:30. Weston stayed for the night in my room.

[February 26]
Saw Carmen—afternoon Max Eastman at night (with Weston, Margrethe, Helene [Cole], Miss [Enid] Ross, Joe [O'Carroll], and Jack [Taylor]).[7]

Socialist Max Eastman was in town to talk about America's proposed intervention into the politics of postrevolutionary Russia.[8] Eastman was opposed to any such meddling, and instead urged Angelenos to support the Russian peasants as they attempted to seize control of their own destinies. His audience included Rob Wagner, already an acquaintance of Eastman through socialist circles, and Charlie Chaplin. Following Eastman's lecture, he dined with the two men, and before they parted company Chaplin invited Eastman to visit his La Brea Avenue studio. Eastman was mightily impressed by Chaplin's celebrity, and he later proudly recalled the circumstances of their first meeting:

In the Los Angeles Opera House, a square-shouldered, businesslike, energetic member of the audience came up after my speech with congratulations and a genial handshake. It was Rob Wagner, author of Filmfolk and editor of a little local semisocialistic paper. He greeted me with the startling news: "Charlie Chaplin is in the wings and would like to meet you."

It was a breath-taking announcement. Charlie Chaplin was then the most famous man in the world, not excepting President Wilson, Lloyd George, General Foch, not excepting anybody—the most famous and the most mysteriously inaccessible. I remember his exact words in praise of my speech . . . "You have what I consider the essence of all art—even of mine, if I may call myself an artist—restraint."[9]

THE BYRON OF THE LEFT   Restraint was not really one of Eastman's strong points, however. Characterized by his biographer as "the Byron of the left"[10] because of his dashing good looks and indefatigable charm, Eastman was known throughout America as a controversial and inflammatory public speaker. Like his colleague Emma Goldman, Eastman's cross-country lectures were frequently attended by squads of local police, as well as unpredictable vigilante groups who were not in the least sympathetic to his leftist views. Although Eastman was an accomplished lecturer, he sometimes suffered from panic attacks before his public appearances, an understandable malady considering he was often forced to leave the lectern at gunpoint after a particularly rousing address.

Following the forced closure of Eastman's magazine, *The Masses*, by the Postmaster General in November 1917, he and former Chicagoan Floyd Dell (who had become Eastman's assistant editor shortly after his arrival in New York City four years earlier) had been accused of sedition. The two men had stood trial in the spring of 1918, and, thanks to an eloquent defense argued by the well-known socialist attorney Morris Hillquit, and Eastman's lawyer friend Dudley Field Malone, the proceedings had ended in a hung jury.[11] A retrial was held with similar results, and a few weeks prior to Eastman's departure for Los Angeles the charges against him and Dell had finally been dropped.[12] Although Eastman immediately launched a second publication, he lacked the funds to keep it going, so in addition to addressing Los Angeles audiences about the possibilities for Russia's future, he was now actively seeking backers for his latest venture, the *Liberator*.

Eastman hoped he could convince Chaplin to supply a portion of the capital needed to keep the new magazine afloat, and he was delighted when, in face-to-face conversation, Chaplin professed an avid interest. But then Rob Wagner quietly took Eastman aside and warned him about Chaplin's notoriously short-lived enthusiasms. Although Eastman was disappointed to learn of the comedian's fickle ways, he nevertheless found himself drawn to Chaplin's clever mind and his intuitive understanding of the nature of humor. Eastman was in the midst of writing a book about the human capacity for laughter,[13] and even though he regretted that he could not count on Chaplin to underwrite his politically controversial magazine, Eastman could not resist the temptation to befriend the little man widely regarded as the world's funniest human being.

Physically and temperamentally, Chaplin and Eastman were as different as two men could be. Chaplin was short, dark, and exotic in appearance, having inherited his looks from an assortment of Romany ancestors. His compact body was astoundingly well-toned and unusually strong for its modest size, but his quick and agile mind was untutored and lacking in focus. His formal education had consisted entirely of lessons learned in the hardscrabble workhouses of London's unforgiving East End.

By contrast Eastman was tall, blond, and elegantly handsome. He had been born in 1883, in Canandaigua, New York, to parents who were both accomplished orators and highly respected Congregationalist ministers, but their sterling accomplishments had only served to burden Eastman with a debilitating inferiority complex, an unhealthy obsession with perfection, and an assortment of phobias.[14] He possessed an extraordinary intellect, however, and a highly literate passion for socialism and poetry. After graduating from Williams College in Massachusetts, he went on to enroll at Columbia University, where he shouldered an intense course of study under the aegis of prominent liberal educator John Dewey, persevering until he was only a dissertation away from a Ph.D.

As an adult Eastman managed to meld the erudition of a serious scholar with the fresh-scrubbed ingenuousness of a prep school Adonis and the simmering passions of a repressed ascetic. Simply put, Chaplin and Eastman each recognized in the other qualities he longed to possess. No doubt it was Chaplin who encouraged the photogenic Eastman to visit Margrethe Mather's studio, where he posed for several camera studies, including one he would later fondly refer to as his "laughing portrait."[15]

During his stay in Los Angeles, Eastman was corresponding regularly with his lover in New York City, a beautiful young actress and model named Florence Deshon, with whom he had been involved for the past several months after leaving his wife and son to pursue a relationship with her.[16] Deshon had begun her acting career on the stage, but in 1916 she had appeared in her first movie, a Vitagraph production titled *Jaffery*, inspired by a best-selling book.[17] The film had brought her to the attention of executives at the Coca-Cola Company, who wanted to use her likeness in their advertising campaigns, and she was subsequently offered a supporting role in another Vitagraph picture, *The Auction Block*, based on a lurid Rex Beach novel. It seemed inevitable that more movie opportunities would follow.

However, at an event promoting *Jaffery*—which had taken place during Eastman's first sedition trial—Deshon had refused to stand for the national anthem as a demonstration of her anger at the state of American politics, and her protest had not sat well with Vitagraph.[18] Since then her overnight success in the movie business had been gradually evaporating. In addition, her relationship with Eastman was beginning to sour to the point that, when Eastman departed for California, he did not know whether his prolonged absence would revitalize or put an end to their love affair, and he was uncertain which outcome he would prefer.[19] But now that he had experienced the siren call of Hollywood, Eastman was contemplating how a relationship with a beautiful film star might enhance the possibilities for his own future. With his interest in Deshon and her career thus revived, Eastman began to formulate a plan, and he returned to New York City having already enlisted Chaplin's complicity in the matter.

WESTON STRUGGLES ON   In early March 1919 Johan Hagemeyer joined Mather and Weston at the Glendale studio for a lengthy portrait session.[20] Weston and Hagemeyer took turns posing in Hagemeyer's flowing black cape, a garment that automatically bestowed an aura of drama and mystery upon its wearer (see fig. 44). The three friends knew they might not meet again for some time, because Hagemeyer was due to return to Northern California the following week. Although he had been living in Los Angeles for the past fifteen months, his relationship with Lula Boyd Stephens remained equivocal. Nevertheless, the Dutchman was still hopeful that she would eventually divorce her husband and join him in San Francisco.

The following month Weston received a wan letter from the beleaguered Hagemeyer, and he answered with a long wail of his own. Weston and his wife had been living apart since the birth of their fourth son two months earlier, but they were now back together, and Weston conveyed his dissatisfaction with the current situation by confiding, "I am living at home now and am some depressed!"[21] In spite of his negative state of mind, however, he was comforted by the prospect of adding new classical recordings to his growing collection, and he solicited Hagemeyer's advice about which ones he should acquire.

Weston also informed Hagemeyer that a painter/photographer friend of his, newly released from McNeil Island, the federal prison in the middle of Puget Sound where many of America's political prisoners had been detained during the war, was on his way to San Francisco. He knew Hagemeyer would be sympathetic:

> He [Louis Legendre] has just received his "pardon" after serving eight months at McNeil's [sic] Island for saying less than I have said on many an occassion [sic]. This alone should be sufficient introduction.... He knows a good deal about you from what I have told him.... I took a liberty perhaps—I told him I had never had a friend of my own sex that I liked as well. I hope this does not sound affected.... I have had so few friends in my life—Margrethe—yourself—Enid Ross—Helen Cole—I do not know why I name them—I just am thinking and writing at the same time![22]

For most of his life Weston would be a self-declared loner who considered himself temperamentally unsuited for group activities, but in April 1919 he made an uncharacteristic move when he decided to join his friends Elmer Ellsworth, Paul Jordan-Smith, Dr. Perceval Gerson, and Rob Wagner as a member of the Severance Club.[23] After attending a few of their meetings as both guest and lecturer, he found himself so powerfully drawn to the atmosphere at the club that not even the two-dollar annual membership fee could deter him from joining, in spite of the burden it placed on his already precariously balanced budget.

Of course, the Severance Club was unlike any other organization in the city. It was the most intellectual, literate, and liberal private club in Los Angeles, and its members included men (and even a few women) from all sorts of backgrounds and occupations.[24] The group met more or less regularly and conversed freely on any and all subjects. Club members were particularly

FIGURE 44. Margrethe Mather, *Edward Weston*, 1921. Palladium print, 24.1 × 15.6 cm (9¹/₂ × 6¹/₈ in.).
Los Angeles, J. Paul Getty Museum, 86.XM.721.4

opposed to the idea of governmental censorship of the private press and dedicated to advancing worthwhile social causes. Their discussions were often erudite but never dry, and members were encouraged to invite guests who could contribute to the content and complexity of the discourse. Frequently in attendance, sponsored by either Ellsworth or Wagner, were Charlie Chaplin and his friend Douglas Fairbanks.

Although Weston undoubtedly joined the Severance Club because of the companionship and intellectual stimulation it offered, his commitment to such a politically charged organization, particularly at a time when it was extremely risky to declare such allegiances, is surprising. He had already demonstrated his concern about openly associating with those likely to attract the unwanted attention of the Justice Department, and most certainly many of the Severance Club members fell squarely into that category.

In early May, Weston wrote to Hagemeyer again. This time he addressed his letter to "Jean Christophe Hagemeyer,"[25] a reference to a character in a popular series of novels by the French author Romain Rolland, who had won the Nobel Prize for Literature three years earlier.[26] The protagonist in Rolland's novels, Jean-Christophe, is a peace-loving, vagabond musician who enjoys the kind of adventurous life Weston was longing to lead. To Weston, increasingly burdened by his growing family, numerous financial obligations, and other people's expectations, the picaresque Hagemeyer seemed like the very personification of Jean-Christophe's carefree, romantic spirit. Weston informed Hagemeyer, "I printed one of your negatives yesterday—'Air for the G String' [27]—others soon and will send on to you.... Will send cape very soon—Margrethe wants to make another sitting but has been ill!" He closed his letter by signing only his first and last names, and then casually added the postscript, "have dropped Henry."[28]

Until that moment Weston had followed his family's custom of using their full given names, and he never offered any explanation as to why he suddenly decided to abbreviate his signature. Perhaps he thought that using all three names sounded pretentious or old-fashioned, or he may have wanted to shorten his name for aesthetic purposes, so it would be less obtrusive when he signed his photographs. Whatever prompted his decision, from that moment on he became simply Edward Weston.

Later in the month Weston hung simultaneous exhibitions at the Friday Morning Club and the Long Beach Public Library. Once again Antony Anderson reviewed his work and drew parallels between his photographer friend and Whistler. This time, however, Anderson focused on the aesthetics of Japanese art as having inspired both artists:

> Weston has studied the canvases of the masters in portrait painting, as all pictorial photographers should, and he has learned much from them. Undoubtedly Whistler has influenced him greatly in both tonal quality and composition....

But the Japanese cartoonists of everyday life, the makers of color prints, have exerted even greater power over him—and it was the same compelling power that Whistler felt and yielded to so completely. Temperamentally these two men have much in common. They are twin brothers in art, so to speak, though the one worked over a canvas, the other is working on sensitive films.

Anderson also praised Weston's portraits of Paul Jordan-Smith, John Cowper Powys, and Spencer Kellogg Jr., a pictorialist photographer from Buffalo, New York, who had recently visited Weston's studio. And Anderson found an image titled *Margrethe and Plum Blossoms* to be "full of distinction in spacing, a poem without words."[29]

FORBIDDEN PLEASURES   In June 1919 Mather took the overnight car ferry up the coast to San Francisco where Hagemeyer joined her for a social evening at the home of one of her women friends. Joe O'Carroll was also in the Bay Area, and as usual he was short on cash, so Hagemeyer loaned him money on at least two occasions. Although Mather was still involved with O'Carroll, when she wrote to Hagemeyer shortly after her return to Los Angeles she seemed anxious that he not share the contents of her letter with their blustery Irish friend. Her urgent message, accompanied by a shopping list, was sent special delivery:

Johann [*sic*] Hagemeyer—

Keep this communication to yourself—(J. O'Carroll—don't let him in on it)—I am anxious to get some liquor. Had expected some one else in S.F. to manage it—but so far have had no word.... purchase ... what you can—and at the best possible price....

Would hate to duplicate—as I am stretching a point in buying this stuff—but I'm going to need in the future.... About getting here—more later—unless store will guarantee packing & delivery—But I think that risky at this late hour...You get it wrapped & locked up in your trunk—one of my friends one of these days will bring it down. If you want to telegraph I will stand expense—Enclosed find cheque—you fill out for the amount needed....

2 bottles whiskey—as old as possible—good whiskey must be old—if old any brand is ok.
2 bottles of good gin
1 bottle apricot brandy
1 bottle Jamaica rum
a brand suitable to use—with tea.

I figure this lot should not come much over $15—however if you can get good stuff don't let a dollar or so stand in the way.... If you cannot fill this order complete—do the best you can.[30]

Although this puzzling communication contrasts sharply with the brief, lyrical notes Mather often penned to Weston, the letter's date—June 27, 1919—provides the explanation. Prohibition was about to go into effect in California, and Mather was hastily preparing for a long dry spell. As was her habit, she had procrastinated until the last minute, and she was now in a frenzy to stock her liquor cabinet before it was too late. A few days later, Hagemeyer recorded in his diary that he, Joe O'Carroll, Sadakichi Hartmann, and the aging author George Sterling had enjoyed a "regular bacchanal"[31] on what would turn out to be the last legally "wet" night in California for more than a decade.

RAMIEL   In early July Weston attended a dance performance by Clarence McGehee, the young man who was often called upon to share his knowledge of the arts and culture of Asia with local organizations. Weston immediately decided to photograph McGehee in costume, striking the prescribed postures of the classical Japanese dances he had recently demonstrated, and he wrote to McGehee, who lived several miles away in Redondo Beach, inviting him to the Glendale studio for a portrait session:

> Clarence B. McGehee—
>
> Greetings!
>
> Would Sunday—July 20—be a satisfactory time for you and Mr. XXXXX (you see my memory!) to visit us?
>
> Plan to spend the night if you can stand our poor accommodations. . . . I should very much like to make a few negatives of you in costume Monday morning. We will endeavor to get a piano over here—and it will be a great delight to us if you can give a few numbers as you suggested. I got such a genuine thrill—I am hungry for more! We will have just a few friends out—I do not like large gatherings.[32]

Clarence Blocker McGehee was known as Ramiel (pronounced Rä-meel') to his friends.[33] Born in Texas in 1882, he had moved to Los Angeles with his mother, sister, and brother shortly after the turn of the century.[34] While in his early twenties, McGehee made an extended trip to China. He later told his friends that his adventure had been underwritten by a wealthy widow who enjoyed his company and attentions. One confidant described Ramiel as a "sensitive fellow" who enjoyed

> all the subtleties of Chinese civilization when it was in a sort of noble decay. He was a gourmet and found the Chinese food a great and never-ending adventure. He had Chinese women, he walked with the Chinese intellectuals in the evening, each carrying a cage containing fireflies, and he talked with all the philosophers, artists and those in the twilight zone of every conceivable sensual, artistic and inventive persuasion.[35]

FIGURE 45. Edward Weston, *Blind* (Ramiel McGehee), 1922. Gelatin silver print, 24.3 × 19 cm (9 5/8 × 7 1/2 in.). Tucson, Center for Creative Photography, University of Arizona, 81:276:3

McGehee then escorted his wealthy patroness on a tour of Japan, where he developed a keen interest in Zen Buddhism. A few months later he returned there to spend a year living in a Buddhist monastery. During his second visit McGehee tutored the future Emperor Hirohito in English and befriended the widow of Japanophile author Lafcadio Hearn. He also acquired a fine collection of Asian art objects, which he brought home to California and gradually sold off to collectors.[36]

In addition to lecturing and performing, around 1916 McGehee began directing a theatrical troupe, known as the Cherry Blossom Players. The Players' repertoire, as described in the *Los Angeles Times*, included a series of "ritualistic and religious dances interpreting legend and myths, and done with the use of masks."[37] Complementing the highly skilled Japanese actors were stage settings designed by architect Frank Lloyd Wright, himself a devotee of Japanese art.

McGehee's expertise in Japanese dance forms greatly influenced Ruth St. Denis, whose innovative choreography already owed much to her interest in foreign cultures. St. Denis would later credit McGehee with introducing her to the refined stylizations of Japanese choreography:

> I...became almost as engrossed in Japan as I had in India and Egypt. Japan represented a blossoming of all my deepest aesthetic sense.... At this time I met a young man named Clarence McGhee [sic] who shone very brightly in my life because he had lived and studied in Japan. He guided many of my first wanderings in the maze of Japanese culture, and the idea of a dance-drama began to take shape.[38]

Considering McGehee's close ties to St. Denis and Weston's sustained interest in photographing her and the Denishawn Dancers during 1916 and 1917, it is rather surprising that McGehee and Weston did not cross paths before 1919. Once acquainted, however, they became steady companions.

McGehee was a ruggedly handsome man who moved through space with a surprisingly lissome grace in spite of his stocky, muscular build. His most memorable physical feature was a glass eye, which he would casually pop out of its socket at odd moments, provoking groans of dismay from squeamish onlookers.[39] He was intelligent, well-read, and inquisitive, and he devoted much of his free time to the study of Eastern religion and philosophy (see fig. 45).

FIGURE 46. Unidentified photographer, Betty Katz, Ramiel McGehee, and Unidentified Man in Japanese-Style Garden, ca. 1919. Gelatin silver print, 8.7 × 11 cm (3 1/2 × 4 3/8 in.). Breckenridge, Col., Collection of Martin Lessow

Within weeks of meeting Weston, McGehee joined the tight circle of friends that now included Mather, Johan Hagemeyer, Betty Katz, and Jack Taylor. Together they enjoyed all aspects of a bohemian existence, from exploring the city's increasingly sophisticated nightlife to discussing contemporary aesthetic movements. McGehee's many associations within the Japanese quarter also provided Weston and his friends with an entrée into a community previously closed to them (see fig. 46). With McGehee as his guide, Weston began to learn about Noh, the classic drama form of Japan, which employs highly conventionalized and thematic routines, as well as distinctively stylized costumes and masks.

For some brief period of time Weston and McGehee even became lovers.[40] Although in later years Weston would dismiss the importance of this homosexual episode in his life, maintaining that it had been nothing more than an experiment, undertaken at McGehee's urging and in spite of his own misgivings, the two men remained extremely close. Most of Weston and McGehee's correspondence has long since been destroyed, but the few letters that still exist suggest a touching intimacy and deep mutual affection between the two men.

THE BLACK PANTHER   Long after Max Eastman had resumed his editorial chores in New York City, his thoughts kept returning to Hollywood and his contacts there. Since Eastman's return to the East Coast, Florence Deshon's acting career had gone dormant, and in spite of his ambivalence about making a long-term commitment to Deshon, he was guilt-ridden because he believed her loyalty to him and his politics was undermining her ambitions.

However, political protest was nothing new to Deshon. She came to it as a birthright. She had been born on July 19, 1893, in Tacoma, Washington, to a Welshman named Samuel Danks, who was a musician and union organizer, and an Austro-Hungarian pianist named Caroline Spatzer.[41] Around 1900 the Danks family moved to New York City where Florence's parents continued their musical careers. According to Eastman, Florence's father was an emotionally distant man, who abruptly packed his bags one day and moved out,

> leaving his beautiful daughter and ineffectual child of a wife to get along in a dingy flat on the poor side of Second Avenue without his company. Instead of continuing her education as she would have loved to, Florence had to leave high school and support her mother. Her clearly delineated beauty made the task rather easy.... From photographer's model to chorus girl was a short step, and from there to acting a bit part on the stage or in the movies was another.... To make the ascent easier, Florence invented the name Deshon, which she accented on the last syllable, thinking it sounded rather French. At least it sounded better than her patronymic name, Danks.[42]

Deshon was a strikingly lovely twenty-three-year-old when Eastman first encountered her. Blessed with a rich mane of dark chestnut hair, a glowing complexion, a modest acting talent, an abundance of ambition, and a natural but uneducated intelligence, Deshon exuded a blend of waiflike innocence and sensual appeal that perfectly embodied popular ideals of beauty and desirability. Eastman was mesmerized from the first moment he glimpsed her at a fund-raising dance at New York City's Tammany Hall, and Deshon responded to his attentions in kind. Eastman later insisted it was not stardom or social status that Deshon wanted, but rather membership in what he called "the natural aristocracy, the people who love ideas with an intellectual passion, and love life, and live it in a restlessly aspiring, rather than a carefully conforming way."[43]

Although Deshon was, to all appearances, a cheerful, vivacious young woman, beneath her seemingly carefree facade was a highly complex and emotional person who regularly experienced periods of great darkness. Her mood swings were intense and unpredictable, a condition that put a tremendous strain on her relationship with Eastman. Painfully aware that her actions were often overwrought and inappropriate, Deshon tried to suppress her outbursts, but frequently she was unable to control herself. Whenever these states of depression and anger surfaced, Deshon and Eastman would refer to them as the return of the "black panther,"[44] and it was this disconcerting aspect of her personality that made Eastman wary of an unequivocal commitment.

While Eastman was in California, Deshon appeared in a variety of David Belasco stage productions and took on modeling assignments for photographers Arnold Genthe and Baron Adolph De Meyer.[45] She was also featured in an article in *Photoplay*, a pulp publication for star-struck movie fans, in which she conducted the magazine's readers on a tour of her favorite haunts in Greenwich Village.[46] But by the late spring of 1919 Deshon's theatrical and modeling prospects had dwindled, and she was at loose ends.

Then, at the beginning of the summer, seemingly out of nowhere, came a personal summons from Samuel Goldwyn, ordering her to report to his studio in Culver City "not later than August first, 1919...to begin work not later than August 8th 1919."[47] In early July Deshon excitedly boarded a train headed for Hollywood. She was accompanied by her mother, who was afraid of being left alone in New York City. The two women arrived in Los Angeles on July 13 and took rooms at the Alexandria Hotel until Deshon could find a suitable place for them to live. Unbeknownst to her, it was very likely Eastman's meeting with Charlie Chaplin a few months earlier that had brought about Goldwyn's offer.

But in spite of the perquisites and favors that Goldwyn bestowed upon her, Deshon's enthusiasm soon began to ebb. She was homesick and constantly irritated by her mother's presence, and she expressed her discontent in daily letters to Eastman. He urged her to persevere, knowing that as soon as she began working on a movie she would become more optimistic about her new venture. At the end of July he reassured her that he had written to Rob Wagner, Joe O'Carroll, Kate Crane Gartz, and B. Marie Gage (who had recently returned to Los Angeles from New York City, where she had become romantically involved with Floyd Dell), and they were all looking forward to meeting her. He also wrote:

After three visits to Lumiere I managed to see proofs of your pictures. In many of them you would have been perfect if you hadn't felt so mad and sad about the dress. As it is I'm not satisfied with any of them, and I don't think Goldwyn took the best sitting.... You might go to my friend Margarethe Mather, 715 West 4th St., studio. I wish you would go and get the plate of the laughing picture of me which she endlessly postpones sending.[48]

A few days later Deshon called on Mather, and she told Eastman, "I saw Margaret Mathers also this week[.] She gave me a lovely print of you. She said Charlie [Chaplin] had asked for one."[49] During that first meeting Mather and Deshon struck up a cordial acquaintance that led them to spend time together on several occasions while Deshon waited for her work call from Goldwyn's studio (see fig. 47). Eastman was pleased that Deshon had made a friend, and he later recorded his insightful impressions of Mather:

FIGURE 47. Margrethe Mather, *Florence Deshon*, ca. 1919. Platinum or palladium print, 22 × 17.3 cm (8³/₄ × 6⁷/₈ in.). Collection of the author

Goldwyn, alas, had not yet thought of anything for Florence to do in a picture. But that would soon be coming, and meanwhile...she had made, as always, a circle of admiring friends, and I was able, reviving the contacts of the previous winter, to widen the circle. Among her friends, the dearest was Margarethe Mather, a slim, quietly magnetic girl, snub-nosed, gray-eyed, with this-way and that-way floating ash-blond hair. She was a devotee of photography, a close friend and co-worker of Edward Weston, who was then already becoming famous in this field. Only a something too gentle in her nature, something suggested by that softened ending of her name, prevented Margarethe, I used to think, from getting her share of that fame.[50]

With so many acquaintances in common, and considering Eastman's carefully laid plans for Deshon's future, it was inevitable that sooner or later she would encounter Charlie Chaplin. That moment came when they both attended a dinner party at the home of Rob Wagner. Deshon reported to Eastman, "The girl who photographed you [Mather] sent Charlie Chaplin one of your pictures.... He said he thinks it is beautiful, he thinks it is such a good picture of you."[51]

A HARBINGER   That summer Mather and Weston had an opportunity to attend a lecture given by Columbia University professor Arthur Wesley Dow, who had returned to Los Angeles to speak at the State Normal School where several of his former pupils, including Mather's painter friend, Esther Mabel Crawford, were art instructors.[52] Dow also exhibited a few of his own woodblock prints, providing firsthand examples of his design philosophy, based on the Japanese principle of *notan*.

Soon after Dow's visit, Weston began working on an elegiac series of male nudes, posing languidly around a large, indoor swimming pool (see fig. 48). Although the resulting images are softly focused, with an ethereal, dreamlike sensuality, the angles of the rectangular pool and the repetition of real and reflected architectural elements combine to create a number of highly effective and deliberate compositions. Asymmetrically balanced, Weston's photographs rely entirely on the precise arrangement of figures against an array of geometrical shapes rendered in varying intensities of gray, almost as though he had set out to create his own illustrative examples of the venerable Professor Dow's design principles.

Weston also took time out from his routine portrait sittings that summer to produce an extraordinary image titled *Epilogue* (fig. 49).[53] His first serious foray into the world of stylized abstraction, the photograph owed a great deal to the Japanese Noh dramas that Weston had recently been introduced to by Ramiel McGehee. Decorative, haunting, and altogether puzzling, the photograph depicts Margrethe Mather positioned in the lower right corner of the image, her body encased in a dark, cowl-collared garment that distorts her torso into a peculiarly hunched silhouette. In her left hand she holds an unfurled paper fan. Her face is whitened and her features highlighted, so that her facial contours disappear and her countenance becomes

FIGURE 48. Edward Weston, *Bathers*, 1919. Platinum print, 24.1 × 19.2 cm (9½ × 7⁹/₁₆ in.). Los Angeles, J. Paul Getty Museum, 85.XM.257.1

FIGURE 49. Edward Weston, *Epilogue* (Margrethe Mather), 1919. Palladium print, 24.5 × 18.7 cm (9 5/8 × 7 1/4 in.). Tucson, Arizona, Center for Creative Photography, University of Arizona, 76:5:20

flattened and frozen into an expressionless, ovoid mask. Filling the left half of the picture is an enlarged, multilayered shadow of a vase containing a spiky arrangement of agapanthus and iris.

Particularly unsettling is the overpowering scale of the vase and the table on which it sits, in relation to the eerie otherworldliness of Mather's small, one-dimensional figure. Only her left arm appears in naturalistic detail, while the rest of the image is rendered in broad, bold strokes and simplified geometrical shapes. The ambiguous, distorted perspective and the looming shadows create a sense of mystery and an air of foreboding, while the composition is very much akin to that seen in Japanese woodblock prints.

But if the aesthetics of Japanese art and drama inspired Weston to create *Epilogue*, it was Mather's Moon Kwan pictures that challenged him to attempt such a remarkable image. In its overtly asymmetrical composition, compressed perspective, and brazen use of empty space, Weston's photograph was unlike anything he had previously created but quite reminiscent of Mather's work from the previous year. She had laid down the gauntlet with her Moon Kwan images (see fig. 42), and Weston had responded. By creating *Epilogue* when he did, he irrefutably acknowledged Mather as teacher and rival, as well as muse and collaborator.

Weston further explored his growing interest in stylized simplification by making another arresting image, this one a close-up of Mather taken on the same day as *Epilogue*, in which the fabric of her garment sculpts the pale flesh of her neck and face into a foreshortened orb hovering above her torso, and her hands gleam like disembodied entities against her dark gown.[54] He also made a second series of portraits of art director George Hopkins, aptly titling one of them *Sun Mask*.[55] Undoubtedly because of his own interest in design, Hopkins was more receptive to an interpretive rendering than most sitters would have been, a predisposition that allowed Weston the freedom to record Hopkins's facial features in an unusual, and to most eyes, unflattering way.

During the summer of 1919, Weston's series of mask-inspired portraits was his preoccupation, and as the most fully realized example of these explorations, *Epilogue* stands as a harbinger of the transition that was about to occur in Weston's work, a transmutation in which he would combine the soft-focused romanticism of his shadow pictures with the angularity and stylization of the newly emerging Art Deco aesthetic. *Epilogue*, in its melding of the two sensibilities, provides an important visual link between Weston's conventional portraiture done between 1915 and 1919, and the innovative series he would undertake in the months to come.

DISTRACTIONS   The early autumn of 1919 brought several visitors to the Glendale studio. The Los Angeles Museum and the Los Angeles Public Library hosted displays of photographs by Jane Reece, a Pictorialist from Dayton, Ohio,[56] and while Reece was in town to attend her openings she called on Weston and Mather at the Glendale studio. Appearing at the Friday Morning Club was Eugenia Buyko, a young friend of Mather, whose parents were two of Emma Goldman's loyal Los Angeles supporters. Buyko presented a dance interpretation of the Old Russia bursting her manacles to seek freedom for the New Russia, and the clubwomen declared her presentation "authoritative" and "very valuable in the understanding of modern style in all the arts."[57] Both Mather and Weston photographed the dancer, dressed as she had appeared before the club ladies, in the garb of a Russian peasant.

Around that same time Weston played host to his sister who was visiting from Ohio. Because May had been a close friend of Flora's, and the person responsible for introducing her to Edward, she must have been saddened to learn that Edward and Flora's marriage was foundering. May's arrival prompted Hagemeyer to travel down the coast expressly to meet his friend's sibling for the first time. Just as Hagemeyer was departing San Francisco, the museum known as the Palace of Fine Arts, housed in a much-beloved architectural remnant left over from the 1915 Pan-Pacific Exposition, announced the formation of an Oriental Department by unveiling fourteen galleries, newly installed with Asian works of art on loan from six private collections.[58]

Not to be outdone by its northern rival, a few weeks later the Los Angeles Museum opened an exhibition of Chinese paintings and Japanese prints from the collection of T. R. Fleming of Long Beach.[59] Containing over four hundred objects representing all aspects of Asian art—from the sophisticated, monochromatic scroll paintings of the Chinese scholar-aristocrats to the colorful Ukiyo-Ye prints of Japanese popular culture—the exhibition made a lasting impression on the artists of Los Angeles.

THE KID Ever since her arrival in Los Angeles, Florence Deshon had been urging Max Eastman to come west for a visit, but he had obligations in New York City that he could not easily abandon. In the early autumn Eastman was finally able to temporarily shift his editorial responsibilities at the *Liberator* to Floyd Dell, and by mid-September 1919 he was on his way to Los Angeles. In anticipation of Eastman's arrival, Deshon went looking for an apartment they could share. The one she selected was located in the heart of downtown Hollywood, at 6220 DeLongpre Avenue. Eastman later recalled their hideaway in lyrical prose:

> We found a long-shaped cool clean white-walled apartment two flights up on DeLongpre Avenue—"Long Meadow Avenue"—and though it was only one block from the studio traffic of the town, there was in fact a meadow running beside it back to the next street…Remember…Hollywood was then a small town, quiet though excited. Just across our meadow, and across one more open lot, was a movie studio where they were using a troop of lions in a picture. The dreamlike romance of the place came vividly to mind in the mornings when we would be wakened by lions and meadow larks roaring and singing. The two months we spent there were altogether sweet and gay; they were a second blossom-time of our love. No cloud ever passed over us, no thin veil of mist between us.[60]

It was a period of great contentment for them both, and as they relaxed and rejoiced in each other's company, their activities often included evenings spent with Mather and Chaplin.

Chaplin had recently formed a film distribution company called United Artists, together with his friends Douglas Fairbanks, Mary Pickford, and D. W. Griffith.[61] Their partnership would allow them to compete with the major studios by controlling the bookings, and hence the financial success, of films in which they starred and, in some cases, films they had produced and/or directed. However, Chaplin was obliged to fulfill the remainder of his contract with First National before he could begin to release his own pictures through United Artists, and by the late spring of 1919 he had made only three of the eight movies he was legally bound to complete.[62]

Chaplin blamed his lack of enthusiasm and energy on his disastrous marriage to Mildred Harris. Following their forced nuptials, Harris had informed Chaplin that her pregnancy was a false alarm. Then, after confessing that disconcerting bit of news, Harris had discovered she really was pregnant, so the couple was forced to keep up their ruse of marital harmony by appearing in public together, even though they lived apart during most of Harris's pregnancy. When their son, Norman Spencer Chaplin, arrived on July 7, 1919, he was suffering from a fatal congenital birth defect.[63] The deformed infant survived only two days, and while Chaplin had deeply resented the idea of his child's pending arrival, he was surprisingly saddened by his son's unexpected death.

Chaplin's response was a characteristic one; he used the tragic event as the inspiration for his next movie scenario. Within two weeks of his son's burial, he began work on a film titled *The Kid*, in which his Little Tramp character adopts an abandoned child and cares for him with fatherly devotion. This method of allowing painful memories and emotions to spark his creativity was an approach Chaplin would rely on again and again. Equally susceptible to his scrutiny, however, were the lives of others, and it was not uncommon for one of Chaplin's friends to attend a screening of the comedian's latest movie, only to recognize some deeply personal dilemma re-created on the silver screen in excruciating detail for all to see.

PARLOR GAMES   As soon as Chaplin's six-month lease on the Laughlin Park house expired, he purchased a large home at 674 South Oxford Drive, in the Wilshire district west of downtown, and Eastman and Deshon called on him there a few weeks after his infant son's death. It was not long before they began spending a great deal of time together. Eastman later reminisced about their association:

> We soon were . . . as intimate as one can be with Charlie, who carries a remoteness with him however close he comes. We formed almost a nightly habit of coming together, Charlie and Margarethe and some friends from the movie colony, to play charades and other dramatic games. I remember those nights' entertainments as the gayest and most enjoyable social experiences of my life.[64]

The house itself was ideally suited for their purposes. A large archway separated the dining room from the living room, and on either side of this makeshift proscenium were draperies that could be drawn shut to create an impromptu stage. Guests would be asked to write down a topic on a slip of paper and drop it into a hat. Each person would then select one of the folded papers, mount the "stage," and invent a one-minute speech on whatever topic they had drawn. As Eastman noted, it was an extremely effective way to find out how long a minute is, and an "unfailing means of limbering people up to the point of playing charades. After they have suffered through one of those lonely minutes, they are ready for anything that is done in company."[65]

Chaplin's early two-reelers had been produced by much the same methods, so spontaneous, on-the-spot performances came easily to him, and he often made good use of the characters he invented during these evenings by re-creating some of them on film. As the weeks passed,

FIGURE 50. Unidentified photographer, Jack Taylor, Edward Weston, Tina Modotti (her mouth covered by an ink blot), Margrethe Mather in Studio of Japanese Photographer Where Many Parties Were Held, ca. 1922. Gelatin silver print, 15.5 × 12 cm (6¹⁄₈ × 4³⁄₄ in.). Rochester, N.Y., George Eastman House, International Museum of Photography and Film, 1974:0061:0093

Chaplin's parlor games became more and more complex, and as Eastman explained, what had begun as hastily thrown together skits now evolved into "elaborately worked-out dramas and scenic spectacles, in the preparation of which all human experience and the entire contents of Charlie's house would be commandeered."[66] Mather, Weston, Rob Wagner, Jack Taylor, the Gerrard brothers, Ramiel McGehee, Frayne Williams, and Elmer Ellsworth were frequent participants, and over the next few months they would occasionally invent their own dress-up games when Chaplin was too busy to join them (see fig. 50).

In addition to these group activities, Eastman, Deshon, and Chaplin also spent many hours together as a trio, and Eastman later recalled warmly, if rather condescendingly, their relationship during this period:

> Although few then realized it, Charlie was capable of loyal, everyday, untumultuous, faithful and friendly affection. His tastes on the whole were rather quiet. And I must add that he was as much entranced by Florence's quick mind and radiant beauty as I was. He was not, I think, in love with her; he merely loved to be with us both. At least, our three-cornered friendship was free from any hint of rivalry. Indeed, I experienced sometimes almost a parental feeling toward the two of them, their interest in Hollywood's affairs being so much more vivacious than mine, and they liked so much better than I did to sit and talk.[67]

Eastman remained in Los Angeles for about ten weeks. During the daylight hours he worked on various articles for the *Liberator*, including a reply to a letter from Romain Rolland, the French novelist lauded for his Jean-Christophe character. In his letter to Eastman, Rolland had called for the renewal of a brotherly union among the intellectuals of the world following the devastation and deaths that had recently occurred in Europe. However, Eastman considered Rolland's proposal naively simplistic and no longer feasible in a world forever altered by the cruel and violent realities of modern warfare. Eastman's usual charm was absent in his scathing response, which clearly demonstrated the zeal with which he could skewer the clouded logic of his political opponents on the deadly blade of his own keen intellect.

ROMANCE AND INTRIGUE   In early December 1919, Mather became preoccupied with a friend's marriage gone awry. Her neighbor, Rudolph Valentino, had wed actress Jean Acker on November 6, and their union was speedily disintegrating into an unmitigated disaster.[68] Still an unknown relegated to minor parts in low-budget films, Valentino was sometimes reduced to sustaining himself on the complimentary hors d'oeuvres served at the Alexandria Hotel bar, so he had jumped at the opportunity to accompany his friend Douglas Gerrard to an autumn dinner party hosted by Alla Nazimova at a Santa Monica café. Jean Acker was also in attendance, and soon after she and Valentino were introduced they had embarked on a whirlwind courtship that ended in marriage a few days later.

To Valentino's chagrin, no sooner had the wedding vows been exchanged, than Acker declared it all a huge mistake. She even refused to admit her groom to their honeymoon suite, causing an acutely embarrassing scene. Some believed that Acker had entered into the marriage as a practical joke, a prank instigated by Nazimova and her women cohorts and carried to a cruel extreme. Valentino's friends were concerned about his future, now that he had allowed himself to become mired down in such unpleasant matters. They did not suspect that he was about to take his revenge by becoming a much bigger star than his reluctant bride could ever have imagined.

That same month, Mather's work was featured in a one-woman exhibition—her first—at the Boston Young Men's Christian Union (YMCU) Camera Club on Boylston Street in Boston's blue-blooded Back Bay.[69] Through camera club channels, several Californians had been invited by the Boston YMCU to display their work. Weston had already been honored there the previous May,[70] and actor Ford Sterling was to be similarly feted the following spring.[71] Although Mather was undoubtedly excited by the attention her work was receiving, she was even more delighted at the prospect of having Florence Deshon all to herself, now that Max Eastman was about to return to New York City.

Before heading east, however, Eastman planned to visit friends in San Francisco. Set to accompany him on the initial leg of his rail journey was his rabble-rousing comrade, Joe O'Carroll, who would soon be off to seek employment and stir up labor unrest in the oil fields around Bakersfield.[72] The thought of O'Carroll's pending exit from Los Angeles was painful for Mather, but his imminent departure came as a great relief to Weston, who was thoroughly disenchanted with the unpredictable Irishman and his penchant for provocative behavior. Weston was baffled by Mather's affection for O'Carroll and dismayed that she could admire such a pugnacious character.

Just before Eastman and O'Carroll left town, Weston sent a cryptic message to Hagemeyer, frantically stressing the need for secrecy:

> Jean Christophe—addressing you with affection—and great haste (Xmas rush)
>
> I beg a great favor—a certain party has been down here (J. O'C.) incognito—if he sees you—do not tell him you were here at all.
>
> I told him I had not seen you.... So you can know nothing safely.... All this very mysterious but necessary.[73]

And a few days later:

> Only a word again—If "Joe" tells you that I said I had not seen you—would you mind saying that "you were down here 'incognito,' which probably accounts for my falsification"—I simply do not wish to be caught in a misstatement by Joe—

The fact is the less you know or I know about anyone or anything so far as Joe is concerned the better—especially in relation to M. [Margrethe].

I will tell you more when I see you—Joe is a dangerous person—practically unbalanced just now. Max E. has no direct connection as far as I can relate or know just now though he got him out of town—the saints be praised—but do not discuss Joe with Eastman, or vice-versa. I guess you will think I am the one "unbalanced"!...

... Please destroy this immediately. This whole affair may result most seriously for me and others down here.[74]

But in spite of his apparent anxiety over O'Carroll and Eastman and their political activities, Weston seemed to be enjoying the intrigue.

As Deshon and Eastman were saying their emotional good-byes just before he boarded his San Francisco–bound train, he absentmindedly pocketed her car keys, leaving her stranded in downtown Los Angeles. Mather came to her rescue, and Deshon was grateful to her new friend. She told Eastman, "I was mad but I controlled myself, and hired a taxi, met Margaret.... [She] is so lovely. She was just as patient through the whole thing tho she was very tired and hungry."[75]

With Eastman out of the picture, Mather seized the opportunity to move into Deshon's DeLongpre Avenue apartment. The Jordan-Smiths had invited Deshon to spend Christmas Day at their home in Claremont, but she told Eastman that instead, "Margaret and I are going to the beach."[76] On December 26 she casually informed him that she had spent Christmas Eve with Charlie Chaplin, who had presented her with the very proper gift of hand-embroidered handkerchiefs. She added, "He told Elmer he got more kick out of the presents he bought for me and Margaret and one little girl in the office, wasn't that nice.... Margaret is still here, but I feel every day that she will fly. She is very unsettled."[77]

Eastman responded:

How glad I am that you have Margaret with you. "She seems to me like a god" [his parody of a phrase often uttered by Chaplin]. Give my love to Charlie, and try to keep my memory green—or at least not too red—among the child-millionaires of Hollywood. Try not to be afraid when the lions roar. I will be back before they ever catch you. And don't love Margaret too much, for I have no other home but where you are—Max[78]

While messages flew back and forth between Deshon and Eastman, Mather was receiving periodic communications from Joe O'Carroll. His letters put her in a restive state of mind, and Deshon wrote to Eastman, expressing her dismay over her new friend's behavior:

Margaret is a strange girl, you wouldn't like her if you knew her. I don't mean like. I mean you couldn't be in love with her. I think she would remind you of Ida [Rauh, Eastman's ex-wife]. She never accomplishes anything and has excuse after excuse. I like her so much and wish I could help her but it's no use. She is very stubborn.[79]

The year 1919 ended on a melancholy note for longtime admirers of Emma Goldman. She and Alexander Berkman had been released from prison in the late autumn, only to learn that they were about to face immediate deportation hearings. While waiting to learn their fate Goldman received a visit from her old friend Aline Barnsdall. Barnsdall's generous streak came to the fore when she handed Goldman a check for five thousand dollars, a gift that would allow Goldman to remain financially independent, even if she was forced to leave the country.[80]

Predictably, the court's decision went against Goldman and Berkman, and on December 21 they were placed in the hold of the SS *Buford*, bound for Russia.[81] Their ship sailed from Ellis Island in the early hours of the morning, before they could wish even their closest friends a sad farewell. The Justice Department had waited a long time to rid America of Red Emma and her disruptive influence, and federal authorities were determined to expel her from the country before the new decade could begin. During her journey Goldman wrote a despondent letter to a colleague confessing that, while she had always dreamed of escaping on a long sea voyage, a ship was now her prison.[82] Goldman had just turned fifty. Fifteen years would pass before she would be allowed to set foot on American soil again.

Seeking Acclaim, 1920

S oon after the decade turned, Weston made a photograph of his sons Chandler and Brett posing against a wood-shingled shed (fig. 51). He also created another image of Mather, called *Prologue to a Sad Spring* (fig. 52), in which she stands in front of a whitewashed barn with the expressionistic shadow of a leafless, gnarled tree falling across the rough-hewn facade behind her. The two Weston boys, placed in opposition to each other, confront the viewer directly, but in *Prologue to a Sad Spring*, Mather poses in profile, cocooned inside a shawl, her soft, immutable features barely visible under her broad-brimmed hat. In both of these photographs, Weston was experimenting with unusual arrangements and cropping, although neither image is as radically innovative as *Epilogue* (see fig. 49).

The contrast between the two photographs of Mather is especially striking, with *Prologue to a Sad Spring* representing Weston's temporary retreat back to the lyrical romanticism of the late 1910s and *Epilogue* exemplifying his first bold attempt to portray the mannered stylizations that would become prevalent during the 1920s. The marked shift in taste that was occurring as one aesthetic approach gave way to another was perfectly perceived and expressed in these two photographs. Apparently Weston agreed with that assessment, because he exhibited them as complementary images later in the year.[1] He instinctively knew, however, that to continue along the path to modernity would test the allegiances of an audience he had spent the past decade courting. Indeed, one well-respected critic had already responded, "I cannot understand it [*Epilogue*]. Is it modern art expressing disdain of naturalism?"[2] Wounded and unsure of his next move, Weston teetered on the brink of abstraction for several more months.

Although Weston never explained what sorrow or disappointment inspired *Prologue to a Sad Spring*, the photograph bore that title when he first exhibited it in March 1920. It may have been a reference to the crumbling state of his marriage and the conflicting emotions that were tormenting him. He had not corresponded with Hagemeyer in several weeks, but in mid-April he finally resumed communications:

> J. H. Dear Friend—
> yes—I often think of you! my silence means simply a condition of mind not conducive to writing. I should be tempted to come up if a certain party were not there [Joe

FIGURE 51. Edward Weston. *Chandler and Brett Weston*, 1920. Palladium print, 19.1 × 22.9 cm (7 1/2 × 9 in.). Los Angeles, J. Paul Getty Museum, 86.XM.710.11

FIGURE 52. Edward Weston, *Prologue to a Sad Spring* (Margrethe Mather), 1920. Platinum or palladium print, 23.8 × 18.7 cm (9⅝ × 7¾ in.). Tucson, Arizona, Center for Creative Photography, University of Arizona, 76:5:24

O'Carroll]—and at this point let me repeat—please—never a word about me nor about "M[argrethe]"— you never hear from me! I hope a crisis will come soon—

I should like to see you very much—Have two cots at studio and plenty of blankets another step in my emancipation! Also have a phonograph of my own at studio! You are always welcome—I need not say—surely—and can now put you up quite comfortably...

Do let me hear from you—even a pessimistic letter would cheer me up—who am in the depths![3]

Weston was obviously preparing for a drastic change in his living situation, and he was still very much concerned about Joe O'Carroll's presence.

Some of his anxiety and depression may have also stemmed from the disturbingly repressive policies of the federal government following the First World War. Even though the war had now been over for six months, the Justice Department's Bureau of Investigation, overseen by Attorney General A. Mitchell Palmer, remained intent on rounding up those perceived to be labor agitators and political troublemakers. This witch hunt, which would later be dubbed the Red Scare, was in full swing during the spring of 1920, and a series of raids, conducted under the direct supervision of Palmer himself, had been ongoing since January.[4] Aiding Palmer in his quest to find and capture America's radicals was rising star J. Edgar Hoover, who had recently been appointed head of the Bureau's General Intelligence Division (also known as the anti-radical division), with the authority to investigate all questionable individuals and organizations.[5]

Hagemeyer, aware that he was under constant scrutiny, began to rent and vacate a progression of apartments in an attempt to lose himself amidst the anonymous, cold-water flats of San Francisco, and Weston and Mather became fearful that they, too, might soon be subjected to harassment. In spite of the risks involved, however, Mather remained in close touch with O'Carroll, even though he was high on the Justice Department's list of undesirables. Deshon was baffled by Mather's loyalty to her Irish friend, and she expressed her sentiments to Eastman:

Margaret is not much with me. I like it better alone. It was a little depressing her never accomplishing anything and her relation with Joe [O'Carroll] is amazing. She answers every letter religiously and at great length. I feel that is one reason nobody helps her.[6]

It suddenly occurred to Eastman that Mather might be about to borrow a page from O'Carroll's book, especially when it came to financial matters. His response was cautionary and cynically pragmatic:

I want to warn you, dear, also not to think it is necessary for you to help Margaret. Just don't let such an idea ever come up. You owe it to yourself to have and keep what you earn, and she can exist upon somebody that is rich and to whom she gives in return.[7]

PHOTOGRAPHY, THE ONLY ART   Despite Deshon's frustration with Mather, however, she was thoroughly enjoying her California life. She had been rehearsing for a stage production of *Othello*, in which she and Paul Jordan-Smith were to appear, along with a handsome young actor named Reginald Pole. She was secretly delighted that both Chaplin and Pole were now actively pursuing her, and she coyly mentioned their interest in a letter to Eastman.[8] He responded by peckishly critiquing Deshon's lackadaisical approach to punctuation and lecturing her about her careless, spendthrift habits.

Four days later Deshon informed Eastman that Mather's poet friend Moon Kwan was organizing an expedition to China that Deshon longed to join. Her comments indicate the actress already felt quite comfortable among her California friends:

> Margarethe is still getting around to printing your pictures and from what I know of her it would be best for you never to expect them and some day they will drop from the sky to your waiting hands. The people here are so kind to me. Mr. Weston is going to give me a lovely portfolio and some exceedingly fine prints, and Mr. McGehee is giving me three presents, a Japanese book with a lovely tapestry binding and a Japanese print and a Weston picture of himself in Japanese costume.... Margarethe has given me a lovely old Chinese fan.[9]

But even as Deshon was expressing appreciation for the gifts her new acquaintances were bestowing upon her, she was growing disillusioned with the pretensions and commercialism of Hollywood. The dedication and devotion displayed by her photographer friends contrasted sharply with the attitudes of her more materialistic actor colleagues, who seemed eternally preoccupied with discussions of money. She told Eastman, "I must say that as far as I'm concerned, all this talk about a new art being born is untrue, it's simply a new business. Its name gives it away. Moving pictures. That's all they are and the only art is that of photography."[10]

INDISCRETIONS   By the end of January 1920, Deshon was seeing Chaplin on a regular basis and paying frequent visits to his studio where he was in the midst of assembling a rough cut of *The Kid*. In her letters to Eastman, Deshon described Chaplin's film as "the most exciting thing"[11] she had ever seen. Eastman, who was beginning to feel increasingly uneasy and abandoned, retaliated by growing cooler in his attitude toward Deshon. He requested photographs of her, implying that his memories of her were fading. He also suggested that Deshon should have her publicity photographs taken by someone other than Mather, because Mather's approach was artistic rather than commercial:

> Another very important thing. I need some pictures of you. I only have those two reproachful ones that Margaret took. They are very sweet while I'm with you, but when I'm away they're altogether too sad....

…I don't believe [her] pictures are much good for publicity purposes. Some of them are, but she is more interested in line than in personality, and movie fans are not![12]

Another month passed as Deshon's and Eastman's correspondence became increasingly guarded and churlish. Although both parties continued to assert their belief in free love without stifling, monogamous commitments, their emotions were not wholly compliant with their intellectual stance, and they now fell prey to the tortures of in absentia jealousy. Infidelity became an unwritten but implied leitmotif in their correspondence. The truth was, however, that after parting the previous December, neither had wasted any time in taking substitute lovers.

Eastman was currently infatuated with Lisa Duncan, a beautiful dancer who performed under the surname of her mentor, the famed Isadora. Deshon's platonic friendship with Chaplin had now become a full-blown romance, and following their Christmas Eve dinner together, their relationship had become physical. After receiving a letter from Deshon, liberally peppered with anecdotes about Chaplin, Eastman countered with pointedly sarcastic reminders about Chaplin's inability to linger on any one subject for very long.

This jab-and-parry exchange continued until Deshon unexpectedly received devastating news. Goldwyn Studios was reshuffling their handpicked deck of players, and Deshon was slated for the discard pile. In a panic she telegraphed Eastman for advice. Momentarily putting aside his preoccupation with Lisa Duncan, he immediately responded, offering the counsel of his attorney friend, Dudley Field Malone. After it appeared that Deshon might be gaining the upper hand in the legal maneuvering that ensued, she grew calmer, and her letters gradually became more upbeat as she began to explore other options. "I am working on a scenario for Mabel Normand [Chaplin's first leading lady at Keystone Studio]," she told Eastman, "and she is very excited about it."[13]

Deshon's optimism abruptly vanished in March, however, when she heard rumors of Eastman's love affair with Duncan. She fired off an angry telegram to Eastman, who sheepishly confessed his infidelities by return post. Despite her own indiscretions, Deshon was crushed by his admission. In despair she gave up her battle with the studio, allowed her contract to be bought out at a ridiculously low figure, and cut off all correspondence with Eastman. Even though he sent her letter after letter, brimming with self-loathing over his duplicitous conduct and begging for forgiveness, she did not relent.[14] Instead Deshon's anger drove her to an even deeper involvement with Chaplin, and in April she wrote a perfunctory note to Eastman, coldly informing him that she was in love with someone else.[15] She did not name names, however, so Eastman could only assume that her lover was Chaplin.

All the while these stressful events were battering the emotionally fragile Deshon, Mather remained her stalwart ally, loyally offering moral support and companionship. Considering Deshon's deprecating comments about Mather's lack of direction, she must have felt some remorse over her remarks when she learned that her friend's professional reputation was continuing to expand and solidify.

MATHER MAKES HER MARK   A few weeks earlier the annual Pittsburgh Salon had opened at the Carnegie Institute. The Pittsburgh Salon, initiated in 1914, was now the most highly regarded American exhibition venue for photography, and 1920 proved to be Mather's year for special recognition. An article about the Salon in the March issue of *Camera Craft* pointed out the significant contribution made by the photographers of Los Angeles:

> [The Pittsburgh Salon,]…the most important photographic event of the year, is well under way with the catalogue out and in the hands of the more than one hundred exhibitors. Nearly thirty per cent of the pictures were from Pacific Coast workers who represented over twenty-five percent of the total contributors, Los Angeles coming in for the lion's share of the representation.[16]

One reviewer singled out Mather and Weston for praise:

> Margrethe Mather essays two charmingly decorative bits of still-life, "Black Acacia" and "Pointed Pines,"[17] and two figure-studies, "Claire" and "Eugenia Buyko," all of which are in her usual splendid vein.…Edward Weston's interesting pictures, "Silhouette" and "Margrethe Mather" are typically Weston.[18]

Actor Ford Sterling's showing also elicited a positive response from the same critic, who wrote, "Ford Sterling continues to demonstrate genius and growth in his six prints."[19] As a result of his and Mather's demonstrated commitment to artistic quality, they were both selected to join Weston on the Pittsburgh Salon's roster of Contributing Members "in recognition of their consistently high grade of pictorial work."[20] This honor was the most highly coveted award handed out in an American salon competition, and Mather was one of the few women ever to receive it.

PIERROT   Invigorated by her triumph in Pittsburgh, Mather soon set to work on a new series of portraits featuring another actor friend, Otto Matiesen. Born in Denmark in 1889, Matiesen had begun his acting career in Copenhagen.[21] He went on to work with theatrical impresarios Max Reinhardt in Berlin and Sir Herbert Beerbohm Tree in London, and he arrived in Hollywood in 1919, hoping to transform his Shakespearean roles and Ibsen characterizations into a lucrative screen career. Like Florence Deshon, Matiesen initially found employment as a contract player at Goldwyn Studios, and not long after his arrival he rented an apartment at the Castle.[22] Perhaps, it was their mutual Danish heritage that prompted Matiesen and Mather to become fast friends.

Matiesen, who would later become renowned in Hollywood circles as a skilled character actor and consummate makeup artist, displays these talents in Mather's photographs, as he portrays the role of the mournful French mime, Pierrot, in tulle neck ruff and velvet skullcap, his face whitened and features heightened with tinted powders and pigments. In one of these compelling portraits (fig. 53), Matiesen's body is truncated at chest level, and the triangular mass

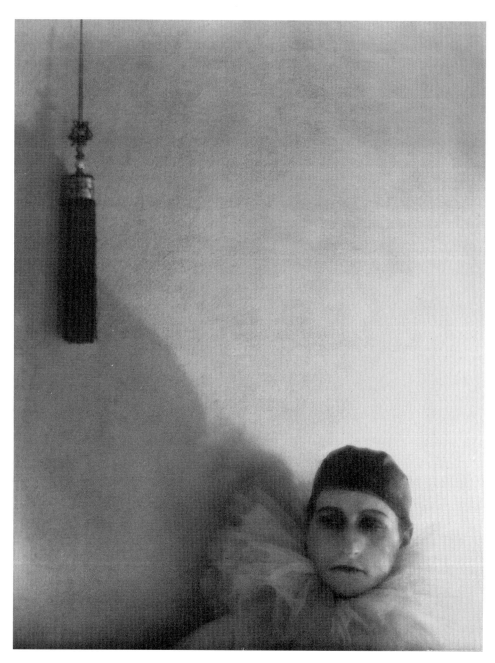

FIGURE 53. Margrethe Mather, *Pierrot* (Otto Matiesen), 1920. Palladium print, 24.4 × 19.1 cm (9⅝ × 7½ in.). San Francisco Museum of Modern Art, 76.111

formed by his head and the slope of his shoulders is asymmetrically balanced by a large, silken tassel hanging from the top left corner.

In another variant all extraneous elements are eliminated so as to focus the viewer's attention entirely on Matiesen's downcast expression, while the rough plaster wall and vertical section of a door frame serve as a subtle, textural backdrop, across which highlights and shadows flicker in a carefully considered interplay of tonalities.[23] In this second version, Mather fearlessly relies on the visual weight of empty space to achieve equilibrium.

It is through these two timeless images that Mather's deft editorial eye is best revealed. Her ruthlessly reductive approach—honing and refining from one image to the next—was the most impressive of her many talents, and Mather's riveting Pierrot pictures exemplify that moment when she propelled herself into the ranks of the world's most accomplished photographers.

THEOSOPHICAL MEANDERINGS   While Mather continued to experiment with placement and emphasis, Weston hung another display at the State Normal School. Once again his old friend Antony Anderson came through with an admiring review:

> Edward Weston, over forty of whose recent compositions are now showing at the State Normal School, is one of the Southern California pictorial photographers whose art is on a par with his manipulative dexterity in films, and, perhaps, beyond it. He understands the way and the value of the chemical bath, but he seems to know even more of the subtleties of the bath of light—his finished plate is always a picture, and almost always a beautiful one....
>
> ...Often, in his portraits, Mr. Weston suggests much more than he tells. By cunning manipulation of lights and shadows, as well as by the postures of his models, he hints at subtleties of character that he never actually reveals....
>
> Among the notable pictures in a collection that holds no print lacking in originality and distinction, are..."Margrethe and Plum Blossoms," beautifully spaced and placed,...the even lovelier "Prologue to a Sad Spring"—Mr. Weston has a genius for titles—and that perfect pictorial arrangement known as "Sybil [sic] Brainerd."[24]

Brainerd was a young, aspiring musician when Weston first photographed her, but she would become one of his lifelong friends. Born Marie Augusta Phillipson in Chicago in 1896, she and her younger sister, Belle, had been raised by their maternal grandparents, Wesley and Marie Brainerd, following their mother's untimely death in 1905.[25]

A few months later the Brainerds, who were drawn to spiritualism as a way of coping with their daughter's unexpected demise, moved with their granddaughters to Lomaland, California, a Theosophical community established by Madame Katherine Tingley on Point Loma, the peninsula that guards the northwestern end of San Diego Bay.[26] Since its founding in 1900, Lomaland had become a well-established institution. The campus, which covered an impressive

500-acre site overlooking the Pacific Ocean, featured fanciful glass-domed buildings and a Grecian-style, open-air theater (the first of its kind in California and the prototype for several more that would be erected across the state in years to come). The Lomaland community also included Madame Tingley's Theosophical Institute, a school offering a curriculum based on the principles of a religious discipline known as Raja Yoga,[27] which the Phillipson girls attended.

Marie Brainerd died in 1908, and after her husband passed away in 1910, their adolescent granddaughters were placed in the care of Marie Brainerd's brother, Lyman Judson Gage.[28] Gage, an illustrious Chicagoan and former Secretary of the United States Treasury Department, had caused a minor scandal in 1906 when he had announced that he, too, was planning a move to Lomaland.[29] Under Gage's close supervision, his two young charges continued their schooling at Madame Tingley's, and both began to show an aptitude for music. By the time Marie Phillipson sat for Weston she had become a serious student of the violin, but she was no longer living at Lomaland and she had changed her name, in honor of her deceased grandparents, to Sibyl Brainerd.[30]

Brainerd was just one of many Theosophists who would weave in and out of Weston's life. By 1920 there were three communities of Theosophists based in California—Lomaland, near San Diego;[31] Krotona, in the Hollywood Hills;[32] and Halcyon, adjacent to the towering sand dunes of Oceano along the Central Coast.[33] Each faction had its own leader and doctrine, but all three groups practiced a hybrid brand of religion that, with varying degrees of emphasis, combined the trappings of secret, Masonic-like rituals with an esoteric vocabulary borrowed from Far Eastern philosophies and a mysticism based on strong undercurrents of the occult.

Weston's introduction to Theosophy may have come through Helen Hutchinson (the person responsible for giving Weston his first Los Angeles exhibition at the Friday Morning Club), who was loosely affiliated with Krotona.[34] Although Weston did not take Theosophy, or any religion, very seriously he maintained several close friendships with those who did.

CURRENT EVENTS　　In the late spring of 1920 Weston selected a few examples of his work to display at the Los Angeles Museum, but this time Antony Anderson failed to review his exhibition, giving it only a brief mention.[35] Another article in the *Times* must have caught Weston's attention, however. It discussed the increase in thefts of platinum ore, which was now selling for one hundred dollars an ounce, or five times the current value of gold.[36] As a result, supplies used in jewelry making and dentistry were being pilfered and sold on the black market. The article noted that the cost of platinum had increased fivefold since the beginning of the Great War, an unfortunate fact that was now forcing Weston and Mather to rely almost exclusively on the less costly palladium papers, while they carefully hoarded their dwindling supply of platinum papers and hoped that prices would someday return to affordable levels.[37]

There were also accounts in the *Times* of a film currently under production at Metro Pictures. *The Four Horsemen of the Apocalypse*, based on the book of the same name, was being directed by the talented, Irish-born Rex Ingram, recently married to actress Alice Terry, who was playing the female lead.[38] Appearing opposite Terry was Rudolph Valentino in his first starring role. Valentino's chance for fame and fortune was upon him, and he did not disappoint. One enthusiastic critic, invited to preview the film, gushed that in his portrayal Valentino had

> the reverence of Dante who would worship; the vitality of Don Juan who would woo; the extravagance of Don Quixote who would exaggerate; the courage of D'Artagnan who would dare;…the desire of D'Annunzio who would achieve; the strength of Vulcan who would excel; and the philosophy of Omar whose "yesterday is dead and tomorrow never comes."[39]

When Valentino read the review, he had no notion of what these literary allusions implied. He only knew he had come a long way from his humble beginnings in rural Italy and his life as a petty con artist working the nightclub circuit in New York City.

NETWORKING   In the late spring of 1920 Weston was saddened to learn that Johan Hagemeyer would soon be making an extended trip to Europe. However, Weston realized that his friend's departure was a necessary precaution. Several San Francisco Bay Area anarchists had recently been apprehended by federal agents, and Hagemeyer had reached the conclusion that it was time for him to leave the country. Upon hearing of Hagemeyer's plans, Weston responded immediately:

> Jean C.
> I am very sad to know you are going—selfish of course—for I know—it will be fine for you.…
>
> J. O. [Joe O'Carroll] is down here now—Has he "talked" any in S.F. He has peddled a lot of "scandal" which has reached my ears—If possible I would come north before you leave.[40]

On June 4 Weston traveled to San Francisco for a final visit with Hagemeyer, and the following day the two friends attended a party at the studio of Dorothea Lange, a young photographer from New Jersey who had just begun to establish herself in the Bay Area. Weston also met photographers Anne Brigman, Helen MacGregor, Imogen Cunningham and her artist husband, Roi Partridge, as well as the renowned painter, Maynard Dixon, who had married the much younger Lange in March.

This convivial group convened several times over the next ten days,[41] and Weston shared a sampling of his latest work with his new acquaintances and made portraits of Lange[42] and Brigman.[43] His trip north was fruitful and invigorating. It placed him within a much broader social and professional context, and put him in direct contact with the most accomplished photographers on the West Coast, colleagues with whom Weston had much in common. His friendship with Imogen Cunningham would prove particularly meaningful.

Hagemeyer and Weston greatly enjoyed their San Francisco spree, and when Weston's visit came to an end, Hagemeyer decided to accompany him back to Los Angeles. They then continued their round of socializing for two more weeks, and Hagemeyer posed for a portrait wearing his black cape while glowering menacingly at Weston's camera (see fig. 40). The two friends also traveled to Redondo Beach to spend time with Ramiel McGehee. In McGehee's rented rooms Weston made the first in an innovative series of images that would become known as his "attic pictures."

THE REDONDO BEACH GARRET   McGehee was now living on the top floor of a large private home at the southeast corner of Esplanade and Avenue B in Redondo Beach.[44] Directly across Esplanade from the house was a high sea bluff that overlooked the Pacific Ocean and a pristine white sand beach one hundred feet below. The building's unobstructed western exposure inspired Weston to photograph McGehee against the acute angles of the dormer window in his attic room, as planes of brilliant light and impenetrable shadow slithered slowly across the peaked ceiling, following the sun's protracted journey through the midsummer sky.

Although McGehee's face is clearly discernible in the photograph titled *Ramiel in His Attic* (fig. 54), the resulting image is not really a portrait at all. Instead, McGehee's features and personality are subordinate to the overall design scheme as he sits in profile, surrounded by receding and advancing parallelograms of light. Weston's attic study is a dramatic departure from the soft, dreamy romanticism of his earlier photographs but quite closely related to *Epilogue*.

Ramiel in His Attic was the first in a series of photographs that, in their angularity and stylized starkness, flirt with cubism and abstraction, but in their dramatic lighting effects and geometrical backdrops, are more akin to the filmic conventions of early twentieth-century German cinema. Indeed, Weston might have been inspired to make these pictures by the groundbreaking German Expressionist film *The Cabinet of Dr. Caligari*, directed by Robert Wiene, which had been released in Europe the previous year.[45] Even though *Caligari* had not yet debuted in Los Angeles when Weston made his first attic pictures, he could have seen publicity stills from the film as early as mid-1920, either reproduced in publications or through the Gerrard brothers, Frayne Williams, or Otto Matiesen, all of whom had close ties to Berlin's theatrical world. Whatever influences inspired Weston to make *Ramiel in His Attic*, he was undoubtedly pleased with the image, because he included it in at least five exhibitions in 1921.[46]

MISCONCEPTIONS   While Weston and Hagemeyer were enjoying their seaside holiday, Chaplin's divorce negotiations with Mildred Harris were reaching a crisis point. Unbeknownst to Florence Deshon and Margrethe Mather, Chaplin had recently handed over $300,000 in cash to Elmer Ellsworth, asking Ellsworth to hide it for him until his divorce was finalized, and in return for this favor, Chaplin had promised Ellsworth a $10,000 bonus if he successfully carried out his surreptitious mission.[47] Then, in an about-face typical of the comedian, Chaplin became

FIGURE 54. Edward Weston, *Ramiel in His Attic*, July 1920. Platinum or palladium print, 24.2 × 19.1 cm (9 1/2 × 7 1/2 in.). Washington, D.C., Photographic History Collection, National Museum of American History, Smithsonian Institution, 3611

paranoid about his decision and obsessed with worry that Ellsworth might not return the money. Chaplin hated direct confrontation, so he manifested his concern by snubbing his old friend, and Ellsworth, wounded at Chaplin's peculiar behavior, responded in anger. As a result of this impasse, a highly charged tension developed between the two men.

Florence Deshon perceived that something was amiss, but she did not suspect the real reason behind the friction. Several months had now passed since her contretemps with Eastman, and she had recently begun writing him again, in a casually friendly way, with news of their mutual friends:

> Elmer is still with him [Chaplin], though he is going through [a] terrible reaction against him [Elmer], but of course Charlie would keep him there forever rather than go through the agony of telling him. Elmer's personality has changed a lot. He had all his teeth pulled out and his false teeth are so noticeable.[48]

Deshon's assumption was incorrect, of course. Chaplin was not repelled by Ellsworth's flawed physical appearance but instead doubted his colleague's trustworthiness. The rift between the two men forced their mutual friends to take sides and puzzle over the reasons behind the break. Unfortunately, Ellsworth's difficulties with Chaplin were minor compared to the problems Deshon was about to face. She and Mather attended the National Women's Party political convention in San Francisco in July, and during their stay Deshon fell ill.[49] After her return to Los Angeles, Deshon was placed under the care of a private nurse, presumably paid for by Chaplin. Instead of regaining her strength, however, Deshon grew steadily weaker. Mather was especially attentive during her friend's ordeal, and consequently was absent for prolonged periods from the Glendale studio. However, she did take time out from her vigil to help Weston prepare a package for shipment to the San Francisco Bay Area.

CRAVING RAW PLATINUM   Inspired by Hagemeyer's example, Weston now had a bad case of wanderlust himself. During his recent visit to San Francisco, he had begun to dream about leaving Los Angeles, or at least joining Hagemeyer for an extended stay in some faraway city, and he had confided his desire to Imogen Cunningham. In mid-July, just as Hagemeyer was finalizing his European travel plans, he received a package of photographs from Weston and Mather, together with a note asking him to deliver the parcel to Imogen Cunningham and Roi Partridge. Inside was a selection of prints—some by Weston, some by Mather—carefully chosen to please the most discerning eyes.

Cunningham immediately responded with a heartfelt, four-page letter praising their work. She seemed particularly impressed by Mather's skill as a printer, and she also commented on Weston's prospective journey, wrongly assuming he intended to make it a family affair. Her resentment at the role that she, as a woman, was expected to play, both professionally and within her marriage, was plainly evident:

July 27th, 1920—

Dear Edward Weston,

Do you know that from a very indefinite and uncertain personality you emerged into a very vivid one for us up here…I never make up my mind very definitely about people, whose work I like, beyond feeling that if I like their work there must be something to like about them also…This recalls your latest effort brought to us by Mr. Hagemeyer. I think so many things about this "Ramiel in his attic" that I can't say them all at once as I felt them and should like to say them. Of course it is clever, you know that, but it is much more.…

It is literal in a most beautiful and intellectual way. It is such a contrast to your "Prologue to a sad Spring" which is so poetic.… The "Prologue" is full of dreams. The "Epilogue"…is to me more of the intellectual type.…

Also the prints that Mr. H. brought of Margarethe Mather, gave us great pleasure. She expresses a charming self in her work and a niceness in printing which just makes me grieve that I cannot have a piece of raw platinum in my hand.… Since seeing the work of you two I feel, when I let myself think about it, as if I had a stone in my stomach and my hands tied behind my back.…

Any way I hope you will come along with your plans as you want to. I didn't get a very definite idea from Mr. H. but presume he is going to look out for a suitable location while he is abroad this trip. It seems like a great adventure, especially when you consider taking a whole family and making a go of it for them, but it will doubtless be good for you all.…

Roi will expect me, after using up so much paper, to have put in his appreciation of the print you sent him and his most personal thanks.… I am supposed to act as his go between a good deal but it isn't often I permit myself the luxury of an obliging letter for my husband when I cannot do the ones I want for myself. I hope you will be frightfully busy this whole winter and be frightfully opulent afterward. We shan't expect to hear from you, but of course shall be very glad to, especially if you are in flight.[50]

The photographs Weston sent to Cunningham—*Ramiel in His Attic* (see fig. 54), *Prologue to a Sad Spring* (see fig. 52), *Epilogue* (see fig. 49), and *Sun Mask*—succinctly summed up his most important artistic accomplishments of the previous few months, and although it is unclear which photographs Mather elected to include in the package, their impact on Cunningham was enduring.[51]

Immediately prior to Hagemeyer's planned departure at the end of July, Weston mailed off a flurry of last-minute communiqués, as well as a new camera lens he had purchased in Los Angeles on his friend's behalf.[52] In one note Weston offhandedly announced his decision to change the spelling of his name to "Eduard," apparently in imitation of the Luxembourg-born

Eduard Steichen, who had not yet Americanized the spelling of his first name. It was an affectation Weston would use for several months as he continued to experiment with his signature. He also happened to mention that the poet Alfred Kreymborg, a "fine fellow," was "coming out Tuesday" for a portrait sitting.[53]

BALLOON FANTASY   Kreymborg was then in the midst of his second extended lecture tour in California. He had already been making the rounds in Los Angeles for almost three months. On April 12 he had lectured at the Ebell Club, and on May 7 he had appeared with the bombastic Illinois poet, Vachel Lindsay, at the Friday Morning Club, presenting a program titled *The Mandolute and the Marionette, Rhythm in Poetry and the Drama*.[54] The marionettes, based on traditional Italian *burattini*, were constructed and operated by Kreymborg and his new bride, Dorothy Bloom.

On August 3, the day Kreymborg arrived at the Glendale studio, Mather was absent, presumably preoccupied with Florence Deshon's health problems, so Weston was left to his own devices. He chose to depict the poet playing his *mandolute* (a bespoke instrument that combined the attributes of mandolin and lute) under a cloud of balloons floating overhead. Titled *Balloon Fantasy*,[55] the image is a surprising bit of whimsy, especially when compared to the sophistication of *Ramiel in His Attic*, taken in Redondo Beach only two weeks earlier, but Weston took his cue from one of Kreymborg's most popular poems, "In A Dream," which begins:

> Oh, what delirious fun this is,
> this juggling of crazy balloons!
> Up with the crimson one;
> down comes the blue;
> up with the copper one;
> down comes the gold;
> up with the cinnamon—
> up with them, each of them, all of them here:
> the evening star and Venus and Mars,
> the morning star and the whole milky way!
> I am tossing and catching them, catching and tossing them,
> hundreds of worlds at one time.[56]

Before Kreymborg left the Southland he was introduced to Ruth St. Denis and Ted Shawn, who were so enchanted with his marionette performances they engaged him to choreograph a program of pantomimes in which he introduced his diminutive players into the live action movements of the Denishawn dance troupe. Kreymborg later described his efforts:

In order to disclose a variety of dramatic dynamics,…[I] added the static play, Manikin And Minikin, and the puppets, playing from the hands of Dorothy.…Rehearsals proceeded daily for five or six weeks, and along with the earth and the flower, the owls and the daisies that…[I] had introduced…a bird, a tree, and a stream, a willow, a sprite, and a shadow, a juggler of balloons and stars and other dancing things were incorporated.…A cordial audience attended.[57]

It must have been during rehearsals for this performance that Mather made a delightful portrait of one of Kreymborg's marionettes (fig. 55). While the poet's miniature "juggler of balloons" performed his antics for Mather's camera, she skillfully captured the jolly, beguiling marionette, with only a web of strings, one deft hand, and a few shadowy traces of a human figure testifying

FIGURE 55. Margrethe Mather, *Marionette*, ca. 1920. Platinum print, 23 × 29.1 cm (9 × 7 1/2 in.). Kansas City, Mo., Nelson-Atkins Museum of Art, 2005.27.4261

to the clown's manipulated status. Productions featuring marionettes or puppets were a widely popular form of entertainment at the time, and although Mather may have photographed the little clown simply because she found him endearing, no doubt she was fully aware of the dramatic import of puppet theater and its ability to communicate on many levels.

Due to the success of his Denishawn performances, Kreymborg was asked to create a similar program for a different dance troupe, this one directed by Norma Gould. Among her acolytes were Ruth Wilton, Bertha Wardell, and Dorothy Lyndall. Very likely Weston attended the performance, because it was around this time that he, too, became acquainted with Gould and her three dancers, all of whom he would eventually photograph.

In addition to hosting Kreymborg and Vachel Lindsay, the Friday Morning Club (FMC) heard from a number of illustrious specialists in 1920. Irishman William Butler Yeats, the premiere poet of the mauve decade and cofounder of Dublin's Abbey Theatre, whose poem about an idyllic Arcady had inspired Mather's first published photograph, urged the club ladies to take up the cause of a "people's theater."[58] A few weeks later Frayne Williams, who would soon heed Yeats's call by founding the Literary Theatre of Los Angeles, lectured on the life and works of Irish playwright St. John Ervine.[59] On other occasions Ruth St. Denis and her pupils Claire Niles and Doris Humphrey presented a program of interpretative dance,[60] and a classical pianist named Richard Buhlig launched a series of informative, preconcert lectures sponsored by the Friday Morning Club, which he delivered prior to each of the Los Angeles Philharmonic's performances in the Auditorium Building.[61]

As one more aspect of their mission to support the arts, FMC members were busily organizing themselves to obstruct the city fathers' latest plans for Bunker Hill, which now included a scheme to lop off the Hill's southern slope entirely. The clubwomen were vehemently opposed to such an undertaking because it would eliminate the site for the long proposed and eagerly awaited municipal arts center, which they staunchly supported.[62] The FMC's membership had now grown to 2,100, making it the largest, most influential organization in Los Angeles, and a force to be reckoned with as the battle over Bunker Hill's future waged on.[63]

ON BOARD THE *METAGAMA*   In late July Hagemeyer made his way to Vancouver, British Columbia, where he was scheduled to board a ship bound for Europe in early August. His plans were thwarted, however, when he met with unanticipated resistance from the Canadian authorities, who temporarily denied him permission to leave the country. On July 30 Weston sent one last message to his friend:

> Splendid Japanese evening at their temple—the Japs I mean—music—sword dancing—tonight—the Japanese give us a party—McGehee—Margrethe—Betty Katz—Jack Taylor and myself—very private and very secret! Geisha girls—music—mysterious dishes and drinks!—and so I wish for you—[64]

FIGURE 56. Johan Hagemeyer (Dutch, 1884–1962), *Foreboding*, 1920. Palladium print, 18.2 × 24.1 cm (7¹/₈ × 9¹/₂ in.). Tucson, Arizona, Center for Creative Photography, University of Arizona, 81:111:93

Weston had already confided to Hagemeyer his own desire to depart Los Angeles, and had even suggested that after he made his exit, perhaps in the spring, Hagemeyer might step in and take over the Glendale studio. Now Weston expressed second thoughts about the feasibility of such a plan, and he cautioned Hagemeyer, "Do not return too quickly on my account or the studio's account—for something might happen to prevent my going in the spring and I should regret bringing you back."[65]

Several more days passed before Hagemeyer was finally cleared to leave Canada, but by mid-August he was crossing the Atlantic on board the SS *Metagama*. His primary destination was his hometown of Amsterdam, but he intended to visit other Northern European cities as well, and he went prepared with several notes of introduction from Otto Matiesen, addressed to the actor's friends in Copenhagen. Written in Swedish on the back of Matiesen's calling cards, all the notes read more or less the same: "Mr. Johan Hagemeyer brings you a personal greeting from me. Mr. Hagemeyer is a good friend of one of my artist friends here. Please extend courtesy to him."[66]

During his voyage, Hagemeyer passed time aboard the ship by making a few pictures. One of the photographs he took en route depicts clusters of passengers standing on the deck of the ship. Titled *Immigrants*,[67] the image was undoubtedly inspired by Alfred Stieglitz's *Steerage*. In a second picture, titled *Foreboding* (fig. 56), he places his own silhouette in juxtaposition to the unusual, flared shape of one of the steamship's exhaust funnels, and in two others, both titled *On Deck of the "Metagama,"*[68] he poses against the riveted geometry of the ship's hull.

Hagemeyer's imaginative compositions reflect the shift toward industrial subject matter that was just beginning to occur in photography, and the images he created on board the *Metagama* are particularly impressive in their depiction of line and volume. It was as if Hagemeyer, at a remove from his California colleagues and without the distractions of his painfully protracted love affairs and convoluted political intrigues, was suddenly able to express much of what he had been absorbing about photography in these meticulously seen images.

COVER GIRL   Just as Hagemeyer's ship was approaching European shores, Weston received considerable attention from the American photography community when *Epilogue* was reproduced on the cover of the August 1920 issue of *Photo-Era* (see fig. 49). It was only the third time one of Weston's photographs had achieved cover status, but on this occasion the recognition brought him little satisfaction. Even though *Epilogue* made an arresting cover, the critical response was, at best, tepid. *Photo-Era's* Wilfred French was at a loss:

> The beholder who would decide for himself the significance of the episode expressed by Edward Weston in his capricious design, "Epilogue," needs the gift of a fertile imagination. It is, perhaps, idle to speculate as to artist's intent, which may have none other than to create something strikingly unconventional, based upon a plausible theory of design. There seems to be a logical connection between the well-placed aesthetic figure, which monopolizes the center of interest, and the decorative vases—but let those that study this arrangement on the front cover and repeated on the frontispiece—amid the cooling breezes of the seashore or the mountains, form their own conclusion. The reviewer, confined to his sun-baked office, is content to relinquish this pleasure to others.[69]

The public was a bit more generous, with one reader even composing a painfully trite poem inspired by Weston's "picture-fantasy,"[70] but for the most part *Epilogue* went unlauded. The majority of photographers, and those who critiqued their work, simply did not understand its significance. They did not appreciate the simplified forms, the unusual flattened perspective, the out-of-kilter relationship of the figure to the vase of flowers, the grotesquely stylized appearance of the model, or the exaggerated lighting. The image was not allegorical or romantic or pretty. In short, it did not look like an Edward Weston photograph.

By the time Weston read Wilfred French's baffled assessment, he had already exhibited *Epilogue* in the autumn 1919 London Salon,[71] the spring 1920 Wanamaker salon,[72] and a late summer 1920 salon in Copenhagen that coincided with the photograph's appearance on the cover of *Photo-Era*.[73] Following that, however, Weston seems to have tucked the controversial photograph into a drawer and left it there. He was humiliated and angry that his recent effort had once again been subjected to ridicule by such an uninformed and, to his mind, undeserving audience.

In late August Weston wrote to Hagemeyer in Europe. This time he was forced to dash Hagemeyer's hopes (and his own) and face up to the fact that he would not be leaving Los Angeles anytime soon:

> I have not written before for I have been utterly hopeless about a trip to Europe—I can't write details—and perhaps I should not write this way to possibly cast a shadow on any part of your trip—perhaps when I get with you again my mood will change!
>
> …What a terrible mess you had getting away.
>
> You have the "news"—so even a line will be appreciated.…do not shorten your trip to get back here—please—[74]

As it turned out, Hagemeyer had departed America just in the nick of time. On September 16, 1920, precisely as the clock in the Trinity Church tower in lower Manhattan was striking twelve noon, a bomb hidden on a horse-drawn cart exploded in front of J. P. Morgan's bank at 23 Wall Street.[75] Thirty-three pedestrians were killed by the blast, another two hundred were injured, and the seemingly impervious facade of the House of Morgan, so ominously depicted three years earlier in Paul Strand's *Wall Street*, was pitifully defaced by the force of the explosion, becoming a pockmarked reminder that even the mighty have vulnerabilities. America's anarchists were accused of having perpetrated the violence, and efforts were renewed to ferret out those foreigners who had slipped through the Justice Department's net during the Palmer Raids earlier in the year. Meanwhile Hagemeyer was safely on the other side of the Atlantic.

MÉNAGE À TROIS   That same month, a frail and pallid Florence Deshon followed Charlie Chaplin to Salt Lake City, where he had fled to assemble a rough cut of *The Kid*, far away from his wife's divorce attorneys.[76] Mildred Harris's lawyers had recently joined forces with First National's executives, who were petitioning the California courts to attach the comedian's assets because he had failed to meet the conditions of his contractual obligations to the studio. Chaplin planned to personally hand his finished film to First National executives in New York City, in hopes that they would recognize *The Kid* as a potentially colossal hit and drop their lawsuit against him.

Chaplin had cloistered himself at the Hotel Utah under the pseudonym, Charles Hill,[77] and even after Deshon arrived in Salt Lake City, he was so completely absorbed in his editing chores and legal woes that he was oblivious to her precipitous physical decline. Several days passed and her condition worsened. In growing desperation, she decided to travel on to New York City alone. She contacted Eastman, telling him of her plight,[78] and he anxiously responded by telegram, assuring her that he would be at the station to meet her.[79]

The moment Deshon stepped off the train Eastman rushed her to Dr. Herman Lorber, a trusted physician friend in Greenwich Village, who diagnosed her illness as blood poisoning from a botched abortion.[80] Lorber urged an immediate operation, and Deshon underwent emergency surgery. During the next few days Deshon was watched over by a concerned and attentive Eastman. When Chaplin finally arrived in Manhattan, the completed version of *The Kid* in hand, and attempted to make amends, Deshon was reluctant to accept his contrition. For several weeks she volleyed back and forth, staying first with Eastman at his cottage in Croton-on-Hudson and then with Chaplin in his suite at the Ritz-Carlton Hotel in Manhattan.

This long-distance ménage à trois lasted for more than a month, and by the time Deshon was finally well enough to return to California, her feelings toward Eastman and Chaplin had waxed and waned through several cycles of renewal and decay. In early October, just before Deshon departed for the West Coast, she told Eastman that she could not commit herself to either man because there was "real ambition burning fitfully in [her] heart for personal achievement."[81] Once she was back in California, her relationships with both Chaplin and Eastman gradually ebbed into little more than strained friendships.

In early November, Deshon struck up an acquaintance with author Theodore Dreiser, whom she had met through Eastman four years earlier in Greenwich Village. In keeping with his unpredictable, idiosyncratic ways, Dreiser had simply vanished from Manhattan without telling anyone, least of all his editors, that he was leaving, where he was going, or when he might return. He even refused to reveal his Los Angeles address, supplying only a post office box number to those with whom he wished to stay in touch.[82]

Deshon wrote at least two letters to Dreiser, inviting him to the homes of some of her Hollywood acquaintances, but Dreiser demurred. He bluntly informed her that he was not interested in pursuing celebrities, but if she was "singly and frankly seeking to know,"[83] he would be happy to "walk or dine"[84] with her. When Deshon called on Dreiser in person, however, he found his meeting with her memorable. He was then in the midst of working on a series of novelized, biographical sketches of intriguing females he had encountered, and when his book *A Gallery of Women* finally appeared in bookshops eight years later it included a chapter loosely based on Deshon's life.[85]

Dreiser was just one of several famous people Deshon contacted as she struggled to find her niche in the cruel, callous world of Hollywood. With her resources rapidly dwindling, she began to write magazine articles for some of the popular fan magazines as a way of supplementing her income until she could secure another movie role. She soon sent a telegram to Eastman, telling him, "Margaret took some lovely pictures of me. I will send you a set."[86]

After receiving one of the promised portraits, he responded with little appreciation for Mather's efforts. The photograph still did not meet his expectations. "I forgot to thank you for the picture," he wrote. "It is a beautiful picture but still no picture of your beauty. I begin to think Margaret doesn't know what you are. Remember you promised me a set of the pictures she took recently—if ever a set is done! I mean that Margaret doesn't take pictures of the Life that shines in you."[87] Meanwhile, another wire arrived from Deshon. "Am going to pose [for Margrethe] again Friday," she informed him. "Then she will select the best ones and send them to you."[88]

Several weeks later, when a package of Mather's photographs finally materialized in Eastman's mailbox, he was forced to concede her success (see fig. 57). This time he responded

FIGURE 57. Margrethe Mather, *Florence Deshon*, 1921. Palladium print, 24.2 × 19 cm (9 1/2 × 7 1/2 in.). Los Angeles, J. Paul Getty Museum, 86.xm.721.2

FIGURE 58. Margrethe Mather, *Frayne Williams* (as "Anatol"), 1920. Palladium print, 24.1 × 18.7 cm (9 1/2 × 7 3/8 in.). Los Angeles, J. Paul Getty Museum, 86.XM.721.3

enthusiastically. "The pictures have come. They are perfect and they are you," he wrote. "I have never possessed anything that I loved so much."[89]

Mather also found time that autumn to make another portrait of Frayne Williams (fig. 58), dressed as the title character in Arthur Schnitzler's controversial drama *Anatol*. Wearing an overcoat and fedora, walking stick in hand, Williams poses in front of the rough plaster backdrop of Mather's studio wall, while a trio of shadowy parallelograms—reflections cast by the glass panes of her French doors—define the space and create an illusion of depth behind him. When the image was reproduced in *Photo-Era* a few months later,[90] an accompanying caption provided insight into the technical aspects of Mather's creative process:

> Studio; October [1920], 3 p.m., north light, 8 × 10 Seneca View-Camera; 14½ inch Wollensak Verito; stop ⅝; 3 seconds; Eastman Portrait Film; Metol-Hydrokinone; Palladiotype.[91]

ATTIC INTERLUDE   The Christmas rush started in early October that year, so when Weston sent a note to Hagemeyer in Europe, it was necessarily brief: "Busy with holiday work—Margrethe helping—raised prices to [$]15 per—Eduard—"[92]

However, even in the midst of his preholiday labors, Weston found himself distracted by a new love interest. During the evenings he had recently spent cavorting with his friends in the Japanese quarter, he had gotten much better acquainted with Betty Katz, who was once again residing in Los Angeles. By late October Weston's commissions had dwindled just in time for his affair with Katz to consume most of his attention. He indirectly mentioned his latest amour in a letter to Hagemeyer:

> I have much to talk of—a great deal unwritable—it will be saved for our next all night session!
>
> I have had some thrilling adventures! And done some new "attic prints" from new negatives made in "Betty's" attic—you will like them I think.
>
> Work has been *very very* slow—and I have been blue as the result and in no mood to write and spoil some pleasant afternoon of yours—but things seem better now.
>
> I wonder when you are returning or what you think of conditions by this time—I have never given up entirely the idea of Europe—if not this year why next—I will try and write you more interestingly soon—but this will let you know I think of you— Good luck.[93]

With her masses of ink-black hair and dark, expressive eyebrows, Betty Katz made an indelible impression on Weston. She was then staying in Roy Rosen's attic crow's nest in the Hancock Banning House on North Broadway, high above the streets of downtown Los Angeles (see fig. 59), and it was there that she and Weston conducted their clandestine affair.

FIGURE 59. Al Greene & Associates, The Hancock Banning House on Fort Moore Hill, 416 N. Broadway, ca. 1900. Gelatin silver print, 23.3 × 15.8 cm (9 1/8 × 6 3/8 in.). Seaver Center for Western History Research, Los Angeles County Museum of Natural History, neg. no. H100 8481

FIGURE 60. Edward Weston, *Betty Katz* (on balcony of Hancock Banning House), Los Angeles, 1920. Palladium print, 16.5 × 17 cm (6 1/2 × 6 11/16 in.). Los Angeles, J. Paul Getty Museum, 85.XM.170.11

Although Weston kept his romance with Katz a carefully guarded secret, he could not resist commemorating their *pas de deux* in a series of images destined to take their place among his most important photographs of the period. He first photographed Katz lounging on the attic balcony of the Hancock Banning House, veiled like some twentieth-century Scheherazade spinning Arabian Nights tales. Then he positioned her in juxtaposition to the balcony's Moorish-style arches and the tower and turrets of the city's fanciful 1891 sandstone courthouse in the distance (fig. 60).

In other photographs Katz poses against the spare angles of her attic room, in various states of undress and with an assortment of props. In one she wears only a lacy shawl as she exposes her right breast;[94] in another she sits on the floor, fully clothed, casually smoking a cigarette; and in a third she appears to be moving a fabric-covered panel.[95] Weston's affair with Katz continued for several weeks, and he sent her a series of highly passionate letters as a paean to their electric embraces. Each of the following excerpts is from a different undated letter written between October and December 1920:

> Ever vivid and reoccuring [sic] comes the remembrance of a lithe brown body—pretending at being hidden by—or let us say—more subtly than by mere nudity—displaying it's loveliness under the white shawl—I come again Tuesday—
>
> . . .
>
> Our friendship has been a series of sharp vivid flashes—with a climax of unusual intenseness. How fortunate we have such lovely records of our "secret"—Your face beside me here with its unfathomable expression—lips delicately passionate—eyes to carry one into a dream-world—hair, brows, chin—all!
>
> . . .
>
> How beautiful the evening was—We (or should I say "I"?) seem to be favored by the constellations in every step— . . . think of having missed those moments on your balcony!—to have never known that starlit hour of ecstasy—
>
> . . .
>
> Moszkowski's Bolero!
> I found and played it just now—I was swept away from the present—carried back in a surge of desire to those moments when you danced to its impassioned rhythms—I heard again the swish of your white kimono—and I saw again the gleam of its brilliant textures—gliding—shifting—swirling—against the soft—golden gloom of my half lit walls—and finally playing the March of the Sirdar I sank once more with the beat of the drums into that rapture of the final abandonment—my loved one—these have been wonderful hours to me![96]

Weston was deeply grateful for the time they spent together, and he continued to press Katz for further liaisons. Within weeks of their first tryst, however, Katz was forced to return to Palm Springs after symptoms of her tubercular condition began to recur. Upon learning of her imminent departure, Weston wrote a farewell letter in which he seemed to breathe an almost audible sigh of relief that their affair was coming to an end. He may have realized that Katz was too vivid a presence, and very possibly too demanding a consort, to fit inconspicuously into his carefully compartmentalized life:

> If this be the end—the last episode—farewell sweetheart of the shadowed attic—I am sad—perhaps my eyes are moist—but I think the Gods are good to force an ending by sending you away before even one little cloud has passed over the intriguing glamour of our many nights—
>
> Neither by spoken nor written word will I be able to tell you how beautiful these weeks have been to me—but when you look at the attic pictures they will tell you—for in them I poured all my affection for you and used all the stimulus your association has given to me—At least one of them will always live among the few "best things" I have ever done—[97]

PURE CUSSEDNESS   In the months that followed, Weston entered a photograph titled *Betty in Her Attic* (fig. 61) in several salons, where it received much attention. The image was not universally appreciated, however, and the negative comments he received from some quarters became yet another factor in his mounting dissatisfaction with the state of photography criticism in America and England. When *Betty in Her Attic* appeared in *Photograms of the Year*,[98] along with Mather's *Pierrot*,[99] reviewer F. C. Tilney demonstrated just how unreceptive the critics could be when faced with the unfamiliar. This time Mather shared in the rebuke:

> I fear some such notion of "pure cussedness" prompted the idea in M. Mather's "Pierrot" (XXVIII), whilst queerness for its own sake must have obsessed Edward Weston when he recorded the stiff and angular lines in "Betty in Her Attic" (XXIX), although there is no denying the truth and beauty too of tones of the floor and wall. But the position of the girl!—is there not a touch of pure cussedness in that?[100]

Understandably, Weston and Mather grew increasingly frustrated with the salon establishment. Weston angrily expressed his disillusionment to Betty Katz. "I have learned a lesson," he wrote. "I am through with these contests—usually judged by men of inferior intellect who would likely only wonder what it was all about when viewing the attic prints! Of course I knew this before sending—but "hope springs eternal."[101]

Even though Weston was convinced that his affair with Katz had been discreetly executed, those closest to him could discern the meaning behind his attic pictures more clearly than he had anticipated. He soon wrote to Katz again, this time in a much more despondent frame of mind:

FIGURE 61. Edward Weston, *Betty in Her Attic*, 1920. Palladium print, 23.2 × 19.2 cm (9¹⁄₈ × 7⁹⁄₁₆ in.).
Los Angeles, J. Paul Getty Museum, 85.xm.170.9

I am alone—have been all day—that is except my clientele—my sittings—someone is going through a devastating crisis of some kind—I am almost undone with various worries—you—are you all right? It has been so long since I have heard—just a word would mean much....

M.[argrethe] said Otto [Matiesen] had been in Palm Springs and you might go to Calexico [Mexico]—tell me more....

...what memories and beauty return—I was going over some prints—preparing an exhibit—M. suddenly said "Edward, that is the loveliest thing you ever made"—it was "Betty in her Attic"—Please—this must be burned—[102]

Shortly before Christmas, Hagemeyer returned from Europe to spend the holidays in Pasadena with his brother's family. In one of his first diary entries, dated December 20, he noted, "Glendale—Margr. & Edward very busy—general talk—stayed."[103] Hagemeyer was delighted to be reunited with his two photographer friends, and they saw each other as often as possible over the next few days, perhaps sensing that their three-way friendship was about to be dramatically altered.

Fame and Angst, 1921

I n early January 1921 Max Eastman was in the midst of planning another visit to California when Florence Deshon sent word that she had bobbed her glorious chestnut tresses. He responded with details of his departure plans, and then added a teasing proviso, "I am so happy. I am starting in about a week. I wish you could find me a lovely room or a house to work in. I would pay a good deal for it. If I don't like your hair I am going right on to Japan."[1] Florence retorted, "Must I pay the price Samson paid?"[2]

Mather also cut her hair around this same time, and it is easy to imagine the two women visiting the hairdresser together and giddily admiring each other's shorn locks. Much more than a simple fashion statement, cropped hair was visual proof that a rite of passage had occurred. The boyish bob signaled female emancipation from all manner of old-fashioned constraints, and American women lined up in hair salons across the country, eager to tout their modernity.

A swelling cacophony of female voices also began to proclaim a preference for sleek lines, hard edges, concentric curves, and repetitive angles, and in response, silhouettes grew longer and leaner, waistlines plunged to encircle the hips, generous bosoms were tightly bound, and skirts were shortened to display the knees. The result was a physical transformation every bit as startling as the contrast between the two aesthetic approaches personified by Mather in *Epilogue* (see fig. 49) and *Prologue to a Sad Spring* (see fig. 52).

As the twenties came roaring in, the sentimental strains of wartime ballads and the jaunty syncopations of ragtime were drowned out by the sinful wail of saxophones and the unpredictable riffs of free-form jazz. Anxious to fulfill their destiny as trendsetters, the Hollywood crowd rushed to be at the forefront of the cultural and social metamorphosis that was taking place all across America.

AN ART PARTNERSHIP   In the midst of this ongoing revolution, Mather's relationship with Weston underwent a profound readjustment, resulting in a renegotiated professional arrangement between them. Perhaps, like Florence Deshon, Mather was determined to become a more independent, responsible person, a decision that precipitated the need to forge a new understanding with Weston. Although there remains no record of Weston's thoughts on the matter, a change had definitely taken place by early February 1921, when Weston and Mather began cosigning their studio work and publicly billing themselves as partners. In retrospect this was an extraordinary development, because it was the only time in Weston's career that he shared creative credit with another photographer.

Reviewing their first dual exhibition, held at the Friday Morning Club that same month, Anderson made reference to their newly altered relationship:

> Another art partnership at the Friday Morning Club this month is the exhibition of photographs from the cameras—or is it lenses? of Edward Weston and Margarethe Mather.
>
> Cameras? Lenses? Say, rather, souls, for if ever photographs were "artistic expressions" we have them here. These two photographers...took as much thought, exercised as much care, gave as much feeling to the production of one of the photographs on the walls as ever [a] painter thought, cared or felt for his picture.... At all events, you will admit that if photography may be called at any time one of the "fine arts," it is here....
>
> You will like (I am sure) Edward Weston's "Polly," for its distinction and beauty; his fine "Ramiel in His Attic," with its cubistic composition; his lovely "Prologue to a Sad Spring;" his "Alfred Kreymborg," "Portrait of Mrs. Charles L. Lewin," "The Donaldsons at Home." And you will like Margrethe Mather's "Moon Quan, Chinese Poet," the "Gray Vase," "Edward Weston," "Eugenia Buyko," "Claire,"—for all are exceptionally beautiful.
>
> A photograph may be a "poem in print," you will discover.[3]

The spring of 1921 was one of the busiest periods Weston and Mather had yet experienced. No sooner had they finished hanging their joint FMC exhibition, than they found themselves preparing for four competitive salons, all scheduled to open before the end of March. Weston wrote to Betty Katz, telling her of his hectic life:

> I am frightfully busy—getting off four exhibits—sent "Betty in Her Attic" to Boston and Philadelphia and "Attic Arrangement" to Kansas City—all [$]100.00 first prizes—Opened at Friday Morning Club joint exhibit with M—yesterday—all your attic things away—that is the good ones so not showing any—would like to show best one if I could borrow your copy—is any one coming to town?
>
> ...Miss Lerner coming here Saturday to see me—or rather I should say—my work—much more important—please get well—cut out one cig a day—it is distressing that you should have had another hemmorhage [sic]—dear girl—you do not take care of yourself—[4]

Katz immediately responded to his suggestion that she mail him one of her photographs from the attic series, and a few days later Weston wrote to thank her:

The print arrived safely—Betty dear—I will try and get it up this week so it will at least have a couple of weeks showing—I did have a very nice visit from Miriam Lerner—I found her very lovely and with taste and discrimination.

In Philadelphia I am showing—that is if they hang anything—at the John Wana-maker Store—March 7 to 26—I feel very sure of at least getting hung and even quite confident of pulling down a prize—

I am distressed to hear of your sickness again—you have had your share— please— please get well! I have had a strenuous winter so far with sickness on all sides of me—plus a very hard economic fight—to raise an unexpected amount on short notice to clear our property—

Do tell me you are better—you and your desert—[5]

DIVIDED LOYALTIES   Weston's mention of Miriam Lerner, Katz's close friend, marked his initial meeting with that young woman. Lerner was an employee of businessman Edward L. Doheny, a former miner from Colorado who, in November 1892, had been extracting chunks of *brea*, or pitch, from a swamp near Glendale Boulevard in Echo Park when he decided to speed up the collection process by bringing in a drill to enlarge and deepen the hole he had been excavat-ing manually. A few weeks later, when the drill bit was withdrawn from the void it had created deep beneath the earth, a dark, viscous liquid came bubbling to the surface.[6] The substance, quickly identified as crude oil, caused the whole city to go berserk with excitement. Doheny's unexpected oil strike set off the state's second round of extracting vast deposits of valuable natu-ral resources from beneath the California soil, and the resulting boom led to the drilling of thou-sands of oil wells throughout the Los Angeles basin. Thirty years had now passed since Doheny's extraordinary find. In the interim he had become one of the wealthiest men in California, and at his right hand sat young Miriam Lerner, his trusted personal secretary.[7]

However, if Doheny had been aware of Lerner's family history, he might not have been so trusting. In fact, he would have had good reason to be downright wary, for Miriam was the daughter of Moses and Sophia Lerner, Russian-born Jews who were devoted disciples of Emma Goldman and diametrically opposed to Doheny's capitalist enterprises. Between 1910 and 1914, when Goldman was raising money on behalf of the Mexican peasants and the insurgent Magon brothers, she had also taken a determined stance against foreign (i.e., American) ownership of Mexico's natural resources.[8] Chief among her targets was Doheny's Mexican Petroleum Com-pany, and one of the Angelenos who staunchly supported Goldman and her many causes was Moses Lerner, Miriam's father.[9]

The fact that Miriam Lerner was now an employee of the same American capitalist who had inspired Goldman's rage—with access to much inside information about Doheny's busi-ness dealings—would have been of great interest to her left-wing compatriots. Although one of Lerner's friends would later maintain that her loyalty to Doheny had been unwavering,[10] condoning her employer's capitalist activities would have been completely antithetical to her nature and upbringing. Raised among political radicals who desired nothing more than to topple Doheny and his oil-based empire, Lerner was in a uniquely advantageous position to help them accomplish that goal.

Whether Lerner chose to use that inside knowledge against her employer remains an open question, but it is a fact that several months after leaving Doheny's employ Miriam Lerner began working as an assistant to Emma Goldman in Saint-Tropez, France, where the exiled anarchist was in the midst of writing her autobiography.[11] This otherwise inexplicable shift in Lerner's allegiances suggests that political historians might someday discover information linking Lerner to Edward Doheny's precipitous tumble from grace, which began a few months after Lerner's first meeting with Weston.

(On June 5, 1924, Doheny and fellow oilman Harry Sinclair would be indicted on bribery and conspiracy charges brought against them by the U.S. government. Federal prosecutors would maintain that in late November 1921 Doheny had made a $100,000 payment to Albert Fall, Secretary of the Interior under President Warren G. Harding, in exchange for the right to extract oil from beneath a vast expanse of government-owned land in Wyoming.[12] At the heart of the conspiracy was an important reservoir of oil contained within a massive underground cavity, known to geologists as a "dome," which was marked aboveground by an unusual rock formation.[13] After much legal maneuvering, Doheny would be acquitted, but his reputation would never recover from what came to be known as the Teapot Dome Scandal.)

Miriam Lerner was only twenty-four years old when she arrived on Weston's doorstep.[14] She was an extraordinarily bright and talented person, and undoubtedly quite interesting to Weston, but he apparently did not suggest a portrait session, his usual modus operandi upon meeting an attractive female.

When the awards for the spring salons were announced, Weston wrote to Katz in disgust:

> I had hoped to have interesting news to write you with the coming of news from various exhibits—but alas—Betty and Ramiel in their respective attics are out of the running—In the Wanamaker exhibit which I had counted on so very much with either Ramiel or you—I received seventh prize for a new picture just made—a nude called "Fantastique"—of course seventh in an exhibit usually having some fifteen hundred entries is not being entirely left behind—but I needed the money! In "American Photography" Margrethe and I both received minor prizes unworthy of mention—At Kansas City I only got a "Special Mention"—while M—received 6th prize—some 748 prints entered—So you see—excepting at Carnegie Institute (no money prizes only honor counts!) where I had six hung out of six sent—I had a bad year.... Well I shall send Betty and Ramiel to London this summer and see how they are received over there—But I spent so much time and effort—I'm a little blue—[15]

He went on to describe the more prosaic activities that had been consuming his free time of late. His bungalow studio, now ten years old, was in desperate need of repair, and the surrounding yard and garden areas had become overgrown with dense vegetation. He and Flora were temporarily on good terms again, perhaps because her sister, Elizabeth Ellias, had recently agreed to sell them her half of the studio property, and Weston, exhilarated at the thought that the studio lot might finally be his, had embarked on a beautification project:

> [I] have been expending tremendous effort over the place which I attempted to fix up a little and had to finish! All the chicken houses and fences have been moved in the back—all the trees dug out around the place excepting two oranges and the acacia—my ceiling painted twice—and my front parkway planted—this with pruning fruit trees at home and catching spring gophers has kept me out of mischief.[16]

But those last few words were far from the truth.

A LITERARY CELEBRITY In March 1921 the Illinois poet Carl Sandburg arrived in California for a lecture tour. Sandburg was already a literary celebrity, with three widely popular books of poetry, *Chicago Poems* (1915), *Cornhuskers* (1918), and *Smoke and Steel* (1920).[17] His personal appearances were often multimedia events that combined poetry recitations with guitar strumming and folk singing. Born in 1878 in Galesburg, Illinois, Sandburg was from a working-class background. Involved with socialist causes since his youth, he had been unsuccessful in his own political ambitions, and so, had instead turned to writing as an expressive outlet for his opinions.

Sandburg launched his writing career by covering labor issues for a variety of publications in Chicago, and around 1913, at roughly the same time that Jig Cook and Floyd Dell were employed by the *Chicago Evening Post's Friday Literary Review*, Sandburg began working as a staff writer for an innovative tabloid newspaper called the *Day Book*. The publication "ranged freely over international, national and Chicago concerns, expressing fervent, often audacious views, most of them liberal if not socialist,"[18] and it accepted no advertising, claiming to print nothing but the truth. Sandburg enjoyed his stint at the *Day Book* because he was free to write whatever he pleased about the city's political and social issues, but when wartime economic pressures and governmental censorship caused the paper to close its doors, he was forced to become a freelance writer to support his family.

Sandburg then began to develop an interest in moving pictures. During the period when Essanay Studios (Chaplin's former employer) was headquartered in Chicago, Colonel Robert McCormick, editor and publisher of the *Chicago Tribune*, had touted his city as "the cinematic culture center of the world."[19] Although McCormick's claim was wildly overstated, it inspired Sandburg to take a serious look at the medium, and in doing so, he was seduced by the visual magic movies had to offer. He came to regard movies as a uniquely democratic form of communication and entertainment, easily accessed and appreciated by viewers in all social and economic strata.

In 1920 Sandburg made a fateful change of direction in his writing career when he agreed to substitute for a vacationing movie critic at the *Chicago Daily News*, and subsequently replaced him as a regular columnist. Charlie Chaplin was one of Sandburg's greatest cinematic heroes, and after previewing *The Kid* in early 1921, Sandburg became even more convinced of Chaplin's genius. He was particularly moved by the silent but universally understood language Chaplin had invented. "He [Chaplin] speaks to all the peoples of the earth," Sandburg wrote. "As an artist he is more consequential in extent of audience than any speaking, singing, writing or painting artist today."[20]

When Sandburg decided to visit California on a lecture tour, his first objective was to secure an interview with Chaplin. The two men met at Chaplin's apartment on the premises of his La Brea Avenue studio. When Sandburg arrived for the interview, Chaplin was just slipping out of his clothes to take a bath, so their initial meeting provided the Chicago poet with a much more intimate view of his idol than he had expected:

> Before starting for his bath the naked, sinewy, frank, unaffected Charlie Chaplin paused for a short interchange of thought about climate, a war day's work, and how they had done the same thing over and over fifty times that afternoon. Whether his clothes are on or off, the impression is definite that Chaplin is clean physically and has a body that he can make obedient to many kinds of service."[21]

Chaplin then took Sandburg for a drive through Hollywood in his Locomobile limousine, and Sandburg later recalled his host's low-pitched, melodic voice and tentative conversational style, his words coming "sometimes with terrible rapidity and then again slow and stuttering."[22] Sandburg stayed in Los Angeles for almost a month, and during that time he made a number of public appearances. On March 11 he entertained the ladies of the Friday Morning Club with poetry readings and lively renditions of American folk tunes. Following Sandburg's performance, a reporter for the *Los Angeles Record* enthused, "If America has an authentic spokesman today, Sandburg is that voice. If tomorrow has her [Walt] Whitman it looks as if his name would begin with 'S.'"[23]

Chaplin also invited Sandburg to one of his famous charades parties, and it was probably there that the poet was introduced to Weston and Mather. The two photographers would have wanted to meet Sandburg for a variety of reasons, not the least of which was his marriage to Clara Steichen, Eduard Steichen's younger sister. They would surely have been curious to hear about Sandburg's famous brother-in-law, previously Alfred Stieglitz's closest ally, who was now making a name for himself (under the new spelling of *Edward* Steichen) in the world of fashion photography.

Before Sandburg departed Los Angeles he traveled to Glendale for a portrait sitting. Instead of posing the celebrated poet inside their studio, however, Weston and Mather led him

FIGURE 62. Edward Weston and Margrethe Mather, *Carl Sandburg*, 1921. Platinum or palladium print, 19.7 × 23.5 cm (7³/₈ × 9¹/₄ in.). New York, JGS Collection, 001206

to the nearby banks of the Los Angeles River, to the site where the Pacific Electric train traversed the riverbed, carrying passengers from downtown Los Angeles to various stops in Glendale and beyond. Even though Mather was ill and it was pouring rain that day, the two photographers were determined to succeed, and their efforts were rewarded with excellent results.

As soon as the portrait session was over, the threesome returned to the Glendale studio where they passed several pleasant hours engrossed in conversation, imbibing illegal Japanese rice wine. At some earlier date, Mather and Chaplin had amused themselves by collaboratively sketching a drawing which Mather now presented to Sandburg. He, in turn, promised to reciprocate by inscribing a poem on their joint creation and mailing it back to them as a memento. The poet also made some critical observations about Weston's library. A few weeks after Sandburg's visit Weston wrote:

Dear Sandburg—
Margrethe and I are sending on (soon) a couple of prints—on the bridge and by the embankment—They will serve as "souvenirs" of your trip—if nothing else!

I thought of you especially today because of the pouring rain—remembering a similar afternoon when we drank "saki" and talked and looked at prints—Rainy afternoons have been more delightful ever since—if I may say so without being accused of sentimentalism! You see I do not forget your remark about my library—

If you send on that sketch or rather the poem on the sketch that Margrethe and Charlie did—do not forget me!

Margrethe is better—she was so miserable when you were here. Good luck to you—Edward Weston 5-21-21

Damn it—I might as well say it despite the possible accusation—that the few hours spent with you made me sorry I cannot know you better—E.W.[24]

Weston did eventually send Sandburg two photographs, just as he had promised. In one, Sandburg stands next to a massive, rocky outcropping along the riverbank.[25] In the other (fig. 62) he poses on the Monte Sano bridge (popularly known as the Glendale Boulevard bridge),[26] bundled in a heavy woolen overcoat and billed cap, jaw jutting, as he leans heavily on the railing to his left. Behind him the curved roadbed of the intricately designed, timber trestle bridge creates an opposing arc that vanishes into the distant Verdugo hills above the Silver Lake reservoir. Sandburg looks more like a pugilist than a poet in this powerful portrait, which successfully utilizes the structural elements of the wooden bridge to create a tightly compressed perspective. The composition funnels the viewer's eye past the commanding figure of Sandburg in the foreground and into the sweeping vista beyond, a spatial convention commonly seen in Japanese woodblock prints.

A JAUNT TO THE BEACH   In March, just as Sandburg was bidding farewell to his new California friends, Max Eastman returned to Los Angeles and Florence Deshon, and a few days later he also posed for a series of portraits. In several of these images, taken at the beach in the midst of softly rippling sand dunes, Eastman is an anonymous figure whipped and buffeted by the forces of nature.[27] In one image, however, his handsome features and cerebral nature are plainly evident as he stares out to sea from his perch atop a rustic wooden fence that stretches diagonally away from the viewer and disappears into the drifting sand (fig. 63).

As another exercise in forced perspective, this image may have been composed as a companion piece to the portrait of Sandburg on the bridge, for that is how it was exhibited on at least two occasions later in the year.[28] These photographs of Eastman, emphasizing the undulating rhythms of sand and sea, were among the earliest visual manifestations of a subject Weston would develop into a sublimely abstract theme some fifteen years later.

Curiously, even though the portraits of Sandburg bear both Weston's and Mather's signatures, Eastman later recalled that Weston had been absent the day they were taken. It was Mather, working alone, who had made them. Eastman remembered the occasion clearly and perceptively:

[Margrethe impressed me]…by finding some kinship between me and the vast far-reaching dunelands out south of the city. (They're not dunelands any more, but a sea of hot-dog stands leading to a forest of oil wells.) Margarethe drove me out there and took some Westonlike pictures in which I was supposed to blend with the infinity…of that mysterious landscape. The pictures were Westonlike enough so that Weston himself signed his name beside hers, and I might lay claim to the glamour now possessed by those whom he chose to immortalize in those old-fashionedly significant poses.[29]

Eastman's recollections are a revelation, as well as a confirmation of the altered professional relationship that now existed between Weston and Mather. Not only were the two photographers acting as equal partners in the day-to-day operations of the Glendale studio, but Weston was occasionally signing his name to photographs taken by Mather, a sure indication that he approved of the quality of her work enough to claim it as his own. Even the calligraphic signatures on Eastman's portraits appear stylistically similar, as if Weston and Mather were intentionally trying to blur the lines between their individual efforts, with the goal of attaining complete professional synchronization.

FIGURE 63. Edward Weston and Margrethe Mather, *Max Eastman*, April 1921. Palladium print, 19.2 × 23.8 cm (7 1/2 × 9 3/8 in.). New York, Museum of Modern Art, D00098179

MERGING SENSIBILITIES   This collaborative approach continued for several months. Among the images produced during this period was a series of the Marion Morgan Dancers taken in a garden setting,[30] possibly at Anita Baldwin's Anoakia estate. Morgan, who had begun her career as an instructor at Los Angeles's Manual Arts High School, had since nationalized her reputation by opening a dance school in New York City.[31] Her troupe was widely known, and her dancers had already been immortalized by many of the country's best photographers, including Arnold Genthe. The Morgan Dancers often traveled to the West Coast on the vaudeville circuit, regularly appearing at the Orpheum Theatre when they were in Los Angeles. A firm believer in the desirability of the California lifestyle, Morgan declared, "From California will come the great dancers of the future…for our climate, our traditions, our wholesomeness and vitality, our freedom of thought and openness to new ideas all point in that direction."[32]

Although Weston and Mather's photographs of Morgan's troupe hearken back to his dance images from 1916, these collaborative images are more skillfully composed and far less idealized. Undoubtedly inspired by Morgan's own choreography, which incorporated antique Greco-Roman themes, the dancers are posed out of doors, in the nude, in theatrical tableaus framed by classically inspired architectural elements. Because the images clearly reveal the bodies of the dancers, the photographs were somewhat controversial, which probably explains why Weston and Mather never exhibited them locally. However, certain images from the series were reproduced in dance magazines of the period, and one appeared in a 1921 issue of *Vogue*.[33]

The two photographers also made a series of portraits of the artist Gjura Stojana, who was honored with an exhibition at the Los Angeles Museum of History, Science, and Art during the summer of 1921.[34] Born in France to a French mother and a Russian father,[35] Stojana (who also went by the Anglicized name of George Stanson) had just returned from a year in the Hawaiian Islands, where he had gone to absorb the native culture and colors of the tropics. As a result of his Gauguin-inspired journey, he was now painting mosaic-like abstractions in bright jewel tones, which he surrounded with vividly colored frames of his own making. In one of Weston's and Mather's portraits, the artist stands before a large-scale canvas, dressed in shirt, slacks, and sandals.[36] In another he goes native, sporting the rather incongruous combination of a Panama hat and a batik loincloth.[37]

Only a dozen or so examples of these jointly signed photographs exist, but Weston's and Mather's attempt to meld their individual artistic sensibilities is especially meaningful and poignant in retrospect, because it came at a time when their personal lives were diverging in a painful and irrevocable way.

TINA AND ROBO   True to form, in the spring of 1921, at the same time Weston was assuring Betty Katz of his mischief-free existence, he was already involved in another affair. This time, however, the object of his affection would turn out to be much more than a passing fancy. His new love interest was the sultry young actress Tina Modotti de Richey, star of the 1920 film adaptation of the misogynist novel, *The Tiger's Coat*.[38] The film's plot, which revolves around the classic premise of mistaken identity, relates the story of a handsome hero who falls in love with a woman he believes to be a wealthy heiress, but who is actually the heiress's Mexican servant. Modotti, with her long dark hair and flashing eyes, plays the stereotypical, hot-blooded Latina role with smoldering gusto, and in spite of the film's many shortcomings, she demonstrates her capacity for drama in the exaggerated style typical of the day.

Modotti had come to Hollywood two years earlier, accompanied by an artist who called himself Robo l'Abrie de Richey.[39] Born in 1890 and raised on his family's farm near Portland, Oregon, the young man's real name was Ruby Richey, but he aspired to grander origins, and so had embellished his name and concocted a fanciful autobiography to achieve the desired effect.[40] Although de Richey claimed that he and Modotti had met at the 1915 Pan-Pacific International Exposition, while he was employed in the Palace of Fine Arts as an exhibition guard, they were actually introduced by de Richey's sister sometime in late 1917.

An announcement that de Richey and Modotti had wed in Santa Barbara appeared in San Francisco's *l'Italia* newspaper on October 16, 1918, but that, too, was a fabrication because de Richey was not yet divorced from the teenage bride he had acquired in 1914.[41] Modotti and de Richey apparently decided to circulate the apocryphal story of their nuptials for the sake of propriety and Modotti's budding acting career. She was already known locally as an actress in the *Teatro d'italiano* of San Francisco's North Beach, so it was important that their relationship be condoned by the large numbers of devout Italian Catholics who followed Modotti's every word and gesture with great interest.

Tina Modotti had been born Assunta Adelaide Luigia Modotti in Udine, Italy, on August 16, 1896, the third of six children. Affectionately addressed by the diminutive, Assuntina, the little girl soon became known simply as Tina. Her birthplace was the capital city of Friuli–Venezia Giulia, an agricultural district located in the northeastern corner of the country, on the border with Austria. About a year after Modotti's birth, the family moved north across the Alps to the small Austrian village of Saint Ruprecht, where her father, Giuseppe Modotti, a machinist and engineer of sorts, found employment as a mill worker. Seven and a half years later the family returned to Italy, and by then Tina had become fluent in both Italian and German.

In August 1905 Giuseppe Modotti immigrated to New York City but two years later he traveled west, choosing San Francisco, with its large Italian community, as his adopted home. Like so many immigrants, his goal was to save enough money to bring over the rest of his family, one child at a time. His oldest daughter, Yolanda, made the voyage in 1911, and in 1913 seventeen-year-old Tina joined her father and sister in their apartment at 1952 Taylor Street,[42] on the steep slope of Russian Hill, overlooking the North Beach district known as Little Italy.

Although Giuseppe Modotti began his San Francisco life with ambitions of becoming a photographer like his brother, Pietro, who operated a profitable photography studio in Italy,

Giuseppe's photography business at 1865 Powell Street (in partnership with a friend named Augustino Zante) survived for only one year. He subsequently opened a machine shop on Montgomery Street where he repaired, and sometimes invented, mechanical gadgets.[43] Tina helped put bread on the family table by working in the needle trades—first in a shirt factory, then alongside her sister as a seamstress at I. Magnin's department store, and finally as a salesgirl at DuBarry Hats, a millinery shop owned by Alice Rohrer, a stylishly imposing woman who specialized in creating custom-made hats to reflect her clients' personalities.

Despite Modotti's busy workdays, by 1917 she was regularly appearing in local Italian theatrical productions, where her great beauty and exaggerated displays of emotion garnered accolades and she was hailed as a minor celebrity. It was around this time that Marionne Richey introduced Modotti to her artistically inclined brother, who had just returned from a stint at the Art Students League in New York City. By then de Richey was separated from his child bride, and he began to aggressively pursue the beautiful actress, whose performances were being described in the local press as "all fire, vivacity, and seduction."[44]

Shortly after the announcement of their supposed wedding in the autumn of 1918, Tina Modotti and Robo de Richey moved to Los Angeles so she could pursue a movie career. Their arrival in Hollywood was well-timed. The war had just ended and the deadly flu epidemic was on the wane. For several weeks they lived with de Richey's sister and mother, Marionne and Vocio Richey, who had preceded them to Los Angeles, but eventually the couple moved into the Bryson, an apartment building across the street from Lafayette Park. Advertised as the largest and finest apartment house on the Pacific Coast, the Bryson was fitted out expressly to meet the needs of the many silent movie players who lived there. Modotti and de Richey undoubtedly chose their new home because they thought it would be conducive to the kind of lives they were longing to lead, but in reality it was way beyond their means.

While Modotti concentrated on her acting career, de Richey occupied himself by making drawings in the style of his artistic hero, Aubrey Beardsley, and supplying political cartoons to the radical English-language monthly *Gale's Magazine*, published in Mexico City.[45] At the same time de Richey was pursuing his artistic career, he also held down a job as an attendant in the cloakroom of a Hollywood cabaret, and in his spare moments he created luxurious batik fabrics, based on ancient Javanese design techniques, from which Modotti fashioned gowns and tunics for wealthy clients.

In spite of the couple's efforts to make ends meet, however, within a year of their arrival they were forced to give up their pricey apartment at the Bryson, as well as the spartan simplicity of the studio space they briefly shared in the Baker Block at 342 North Main Street, the same building where Mather's friend and model Moon Kwan was then residing while he advised D. W. Griffith on the finer points of Chinese dress and customs. After reluctantly relinquishing the lifestyle to which they both aspired, Modotti and de Richey rejoined his mother and sister, who had recently moved to a modest cottage at 313 South Lake Street.[46] There, in a large,

FIGURE 64. Walter Frederick Seely (American, ca. 1886–1959), *Tina Modotti and Robo Roubaix de l'Abrie Richey* [de Richey], ca. 1921. Gelatin silver print, 18.2 × 23.5 cm ($7^{1}/_{8}$ × $9^{1}/_{4}$ in.). The Lane Collection, Museum of Fine Arts, Boston

vine-covered shed behind the Richey house, the couple created a retreat filled with rustic furnishings, an oversized worktable, and Robo's batik wall hangings. In this secluded environment, reminiscent of a medieval artisan's workshop, they spent many hours in companionable collaboration (see fig. 64).

A LOVELY ITALIAN GIRL　Although there is no record of Modotti's first meeting with Weston, perhaps they were introduced by their mutual acquaintance, Moon Kwan, as early as 1919 or 1920. Most certainly Weston and Modotti were well known to each other by April 18, 1921, when Weston wrote to Hagemeyer, boasting of his latest amorous adventure: "Life has been very full for me—perhaps too full for my good—I not only have done some of the best things yet—but also have had an exquisite affair. . . . the pictures I believe to be especially good are of one Tina de Richey—a lovely Italian girl."[47]

Since 1917 Weston had been committing his innermost thoughts to paper. He would later refer to this accumulation of miscellaneous pages—initially intended for his eyes only—as his *Daybooks* (no doubt recalling the defunct Chicago newspaper that had claimed to tell the truth in all matters). It was here that he preserved a passage copied from one of Modotti's first love letters.

From Tina: "Once more I have been reading your letter and as at every other time my eyes are full of tears—I never realized before that a letter—a mere sheet of paper could be such a spiritual thing—could emanate so much feeling—you gave a soul to it! Oh! If I could be with you now at this hour I love so much, I would try to tell you how much beauty has been added to my life lately! When may I come over? I am waiting for your call."—this was our start![48]

Weston was so captivated by his new lover that Mather must have quickly sensed a sea change in their own relationship. The two photographers were now thirty-five years old, and the intense physical attraction and emotional attachment that had once existed between them had gradually subsided into reciprocal feelings of friendship and professional admiration. Both had enjoyed dalliances with other people that, for the most part, they had not kept hidden from each other, and mores in the bohemian world they inhabited would have discouraged any bourgeois inclinations to possessiveness. But surely Mather was not entirely impervious to jealousy as she watched Weston become completely and totally absorbed in Modotti. Perhaps that was the real reason behind the revised partnership arrangement Mather and Weston entered into in the early spring of 1921, just as his love affair with Modotti was in its first flush, and it was becoming apparent to Mather that Weston's interests and allegiances were realigning.

From the moment Weston and Modotti acted on their feelings for each other, he began to capture their intimate moments on film, and it was not long before Modotti replaced Mather in Weston's photographs (see figs. 65, 66), as well as his affections. During 1921 he produced at least ten images of Modotti, each one more erotic than the last. She was completely uninhibited and natural in front of the camera, and Weston's photographs of her expressive face and shapely body clearly reflect the highly tempestuous nature of their relationship.

The impresario and book publisher Merle Armitage, who would become one of Weston's closest friends, later re-created his first conversation with Weston, in which Weston supposedly described Modotti as a voluptuous temptress under the spell of a Svengali-like mentor:

Tina it seemed, was a girl that had been the protégé of a character in San Francisco, an Oscar Wilde type aesthete, with the notable exception that he liked women. He had made it his profession to educate a number of women. [This] education consisted of buying them chic and expensive clothes, rare perfumes, teaching them the art of make-up, languages, poise, and in fact the kind of discipline administered to the geisha girls, but his great gift was teaching them all the arts and subtleties of making love. In fact he instilled a love of sensuality on a delicate basis, in every department. They became fastidious about their person, in their knowledge of food, in grooming, and particularly in the art of making physical love.[49]

FIGURE 65. Edward Weston, *Tina Modotti*, 1921. Palladium print, 24.2 × 19 cm (9$^{1}/_{2}$ × 7$^{1}/_{2}$ in.). Los Angeles, J. Paul Getty Museum, 85.XM.170.7

FIGURE 66. Edward Weston, *The White Iris* (Tina Modotti), 1921. Platinum or palladium print, 20.6 × 18.8 cm (8¹/₂ × 7³/₈ in.). Private collection

Although these recollections were exaggerations filtered through Armitage's notoriously overactive, priapic imagination, Weston's portraits of Modotti offer ample proof that her reputation as a femme fatale was justified.

Later that spring, even as Weston's attention remained ardently fixed on Modotti, he managed to concentrate on photography long enough to complete a third group of attic pictures. This time he solidified the Euclidean geometry of McGehee's garret into sharply delineated planes and depicted his sitters in starkly silhouetted isolation against them. Three memorable pictures came out of these investigations.

FIGURE 67. Edward Weston, *Sunny Corner in an Attic*, 1921. Platinum or palladium print, 19 × 24 cm (7½ × 9½ in.). Tucson, Center for Creative Photography, University of Arizona, 76:5:14

In the photograph *Sunny Corner in an Attic* (fig. 67) Hagemeyer poses in hat and cape, pipe firmly clenched between his teeth, as he leans against the obtuse angle formed by the dormer window behind him.[50] All extraneous details of the room's features are eliminated as the sun stakes out a stark parallelogram on the white plaster wall behind him. This brilliance is repeated in the flat wash of illumination that falls across Hagemeyer's features like a pale mask, as well as in the white-hot flash of ambient light that ricochets off his pipe, creating an abrupt check mark of punctuation against the dense black quadrilateral threatening to engulf him.

In two other images, a female model (probably Tina Modotti or Betty Katz), shrouded in a cloak with her back to the camera, occupies the same attic space. In *Grey Attic*[51] the model is placed at the lower right edge of the image, in contrast to the abstract design created by the intersection of walls and ceiling behind her. In *Ascent of Attic Angles*[52] she leans slightly forward, arms wrapped tightly around her torso, as planes of light and dark zigzag back and forth in the space above her head. In these three photographs, Weston's vision crystallizes into a sublimely focused, multifaceted world of sunlight and shadow, angle and interstice.

ENTIRELY FLORENCE   Long before Max Eastman's March 1921 arrival in Los Angeles, he and Florence Deshon had agreed they should live apart so that Eastman could have a private space in which to work on his book, *The Sense of Humor*. But very soon he and Deshon began reviving their love affair and revisiting their friendship with Chaplin, and before long the three had resumed their old habits and pastimes. Eastman recalled:

> We renewed all the old exciting ways of life, the privacies and the associations. We played charades and our great oratorical and impromptu drama games with Charlie and his friends and ours. Charlie knew nothing—or was deft enough to pretend he knew nothing—of the fluctuations in my relation with Florence. The fact that we had both loved her made us better friends, but not more confidential....
>
> ...Charlie's motherly valet and factotum, Tom Harrington, a genius of his kind, had helped Florence secure a new Buick car at the price of a second-hand one, and we took long drives in the country together. The drive from Hollywood down to Santa Monica through orange and avocado groves and black-earth vegetable gardens, and spaces of land with weeds and wild flowers growing on them, would seem a dream of heaven to anyone visiting Los Angeles today.[53]

In April the local newspapers printed breathless accounts of the unprecedented success of *The Four Horsemen of the Apocalypse*. The movie had recently opened in New York City to splendid reviews, and almost overnight Rudolph Valentino had been catapulted to fame as America's sexiest romantic idol. The same newspapers revealed that Charlie Chaplin had just become engaged to his new secretary, May Collins.

This announcement had a disastrous effect on Deshon's career. No longer linked romantically to Chaplin, she ceased to be of interest to the power brokers of Hollywood. Instead of being offered desirable film roles, she now had to settle for parts in local stage productions, a development that filled her with mounting anger as she watched her coveted movie career dissolve into the ether. Deshon vented her frustration on Eastman, who was often too absorbed in his own work to pay much attention to her need for reassurance, and even though Deshon continued to insist that she did not wish to marry anyone, Eastman's refusal to be possessed by his feelings for her led to frequent, and increasingly physical, scenes between them.[54]

In early June Eastman completed his book and, as he was making preparations to return to the East Coast, he and Deshon engaged in one last, devastating argument. They parted in anger, but as had happened so many times in the past, distance gradually softened their outlook, they relented and regretted, and soon they were making overtures to repair the damage. Eastman later received an apologetic letter from Deshon, in which she enclosed a lovely portrait of the two of them taken by Margrethe Mather.[55] She ended her note by asking, "Do you miss me, dear? Do you think tenderly of me? There is no Black Panther. I'm all Florence."[56]

REFRESHINGLY ORIGINAL   During the early summer of 1921, a review of the recent Pittsburgh Salon exhibition appeared in *Photo-Era*. It was written by photographer John Paul Edwards of Sacramento, a colleague who could fully appreciate just how innovative Mather's and Weston's contributions had been:

> The pictures of Margrethe Mather of Los Angeles are, first of all, refreshingly original. One seeks her work at the salons with anticipations of rare pleasure, and one always finds in her pictures much that is new and interesting.... Edward Weston of Glendale, California, is a master of aesthetic design in portraiture.... No two of his portraits are alike, all interesting—sometimes startling in their originality. His "Ramiel in His Attic" is a gem of cleverness. It should fairly startle the conventional portraitist and leave him gasping.[57]

That July Weston and Mather's collaborative work was featured in a joint exhibition at the California Camera Club in San Francisco. One reviewer was wildly enthusiastic:

> Probably no photographic exhibit in recent years has excited so much comment as that of Edward Weston and Margarethe Mather....
>
> Portraits of men and women famed in art or letters, figure studies, symbolic and allegorical compositions make up the exhibit which is strikingly original. In some instances only a portion of the face is shown in a portrait; again the figure of some noted man, like Max Eastman or Carl Sandburg, is portrayed against an overwhelming background of massive rocks, sand dunes or stormy sky.
>
> Not many years ago Weston was an [*sic*] humble assistant printer in a Los Angeles photographer's finishing room. He opened a little bungalow gallery in Tropico and rose almost immediately to national fame. Miss Mather, who is also a vivid figure in Southern California art realms, and who for a time maintained a studio in an abandoned barn, has joined Mr. Weston in the task of depicting celebrities with the camera.[58]

Around this same time Mather made several photographs of Weston, one of which is arguably the finest portrait of Weston that exists (fig. 68), thanks to Mather's ability to capture her colleague's sensitivity and forthrightness, coupled with a touch of arrogance. Then she turned her camera on Weston and Hagemeyer simultaneously. In this photograph (fig. 69), Hagemeyer's face protrudes abruptly into the picture plane on the left, his features dramatically cropped and sharply etched beneath a jaunty billed cap, his lips firmly pursed around the stem of his ever-present pipe. Weston stands slightly further away from the camera, on the right, his countenance fully revealed but softly rendered. Separating the two friends, and at the same time uniting them, is a dark, impenetrable void of emptiness.

The solidity of this dense negative space between them defines each man as an individual, even as it conveys the deep mutual affection that binds them together, but it also suggests the

FIGURE 68. Margrethe Mather, *Edward Weston*, 1921. Platinum or palladium print, 24.3 × 18.7 cm (9 × 7 3/8 in.). Carmel, Calif., Collection of Margaret Weston

FIGURE 69. Margrethe Mather, *Johan Hagemeyer and Edward Weston*, 1921. Platinum print, 19.2 × 18.4 cm (7 1/2 × 7 1/4 in.). Tucson, Center for Creative Photography, University of Arizona, 76.5.54

uneasiness that occasionally loomed like an unbridgeable chasm between their competitive, intransigent personalities. Only Mather, with her deeply intuitive understanding of both men's strengths and shortcomings, could have captured the complexities of their relationship so successfully. Her stunning dual portrait is surely one of the most revealing and intimate artistic portrayals of the convoluted intricacies of male bonding.

That year, for the first time, Hagemeyer joined Weston and Mather in the pursuit of salon recognition and prize money. In addition to their participation in the 1921 San Francisco Camera Club Salon, Weston and Mather also sent work to the Pittsburgh Salon at the Carnegie Institute, the Royal Photographic Society Exhibition in London, and *American Photography's* First Annual Competition, while Weston and Hagemeyer both had pictures hung at the Wanamaker competition. All three artists were represented in the newly established exhibition sponsored by the Frederick & Nelson Department Store in Seattle, as well as in the annual Oakland Museum Salon and the Kansas City Photo Supply Company exhibition. Some of Hagemeyer's submissions included *Immigrants*,[59] the image he had made during his *Metagama* voyage; *Pedestrians*,[60] taken while he was in Europe; *The Jaw*[61] and *Work*,[62] two industrial studies; and *Portrait of My Brother*,[63] a close-up of Hendrik Hagemeyer. This last image recalls Weston's *Sunny Corner in an Attic*, right down to the punctuation mark of the pipe and the strong geometrical passages of light and dark behind the sitter.

Although Hagemeyer's participation in the national and international photography salons was a sure sign of his growing confidence as an artist, Weston made no mention of his friend's successes. Instead his letters to Hagemeyer were filled with prosaic discussions related to the never-ending saga of the Dutchman's love life. Hagemeyer's infatuation with Lula Boyd Stephens had now cooled, and he had recently begun a liaison with Alma Tucker, another married woman in the Los Angeles area. Complicating matters further was the fact that Tucker and Stephens were friends.

Weston had recently begun acting as a courier for the messages Hagemeyer was surreptitiously sending to his new lover, and it was a role he did not relish. Even though Weston had little room to criticize, he felt obliged to scold his friend for allowing such complicated machinations to distract him from his higher calling:

> May I give you some [advice]—I do not often do it—please—please do not let this trouble weaken you—and allow your work to suffer—
>
> You have shown what you can do—and you must feel that it is worthwhile—may I ask you not to let pity pull you under—if it does perhaps something very valuable to many people will be lost because of your regard for one—[64]

In spite of Weston's impatience with his friend's entanglements, when Hagemeyer wrote again, this time in anguish over some communication gone astray, Weston responded empathetically but laid the blame squarely at Mather's feet:

You know I would not fail you! Certainly nothing could be too much bother when you are distressed!…I never received your letter—sent through M—She has been staying with Florence [Deshon] though I saw her yesterday and expect to today.…If you do not here [sic] from me by return mail I have never received your letter.[65]

HARD TIMES   Although Mather had assisted Hagemeyer with his lovelorn shenanigans in the past, she was distracted from his current plight because she had been helping Florence Deshon move from her spacious apartment on DeLongpre Avenue into a much smaller one a few blocks away. Following Eastman's departure in June, Deshon's financial situation had become so precarious she had been forced to drastically reduce her expenditures. Not only was her career in shambles because her romantic relationship with Chaplin was over, but a strike in the film industry had recently caused the suspension of all productions. A subsequent lockout at the studios had resulted in immediate job losses among those who worked in front of, as well as behind, the cameras, and no one could predict how long the situation would last.[66] Chaplin had already come to Deshon's rescue by assuming the unpaid balance on her car and purchasing an insurance policy on her behalf, but even so, the Buick convertible was an extravagance Deshon could no longer afford.[67]

It also was very likely Chaplin who covered the first month's rent on Deshon's new living quarters at 1743 Cherokee Avenue, one block north of Hollywood Boulevard and only a few doors away from Ozcot, where Chaplin's Los Angeles Athletic Club colleague, author L. Frank Baum—the wizard behind the Oz books—had died a few months earlier.[68] At the time of his demise, Baum was in the midst of writing *Glinda in the Land of Oz*, the story of a beautiful, beneficent "white witch" who casts her spells over the inhabitants of Emerald City and makes all their wishes come true. From Deshon's disillusioned perspective, Baum's vision of goodness triumphant in the land of emeralds and poppies must have seemed like a far-fetched fairy tale indeed.

Deshon wrote Eastman that she was preparing for a role at the Pasadena Playhouse and still harboring hopes that an attractive movie offer might materialize. She had just returned from Santa Barbara, where she had stayed at the Samarkand, the newly opened, Persian-themed hotel that now inhabited the former administration building and dormitories of Prince Hopkins's Boyland.[69] During the 1918 influenza pandemic Hopkins had agreed that his school might be used as a makeshift, emergency hospital, but once the danger was past he had turned his property over to a hotel management team, and they had just finished recasting Boyland as a luxurious resort, catering to the Hollywood crowd.

As a postscript, presumably on Mather's behalf, Deshon inquired whether Eastman had seen "the Steiglitz [sic] exhibition of photographs,"[70] referring to Alfred Stieglitz's showing at the Anderson Galleries in New York City, which had opened earlier in the year. Included in the exhibition of 146 photographs were forty-five images of Stieglitz's lover and protégé, painter

Georgia O'Keeffe. Taken over a period of two years, during the early months of their love affair, Stieglitz's photographic essay had scandalized many viewers because of its intimate nature and frankly sexual subject matter, and his ode to womanhood, and to O'Keeffe in particular, remained the talk of the New York City art world.

Although Charlie Chaplin displayed considerable generosity in his dealings with Deshon, he was not so magnanimous with many of his friends. After finally reaching a financial settlement with his ex-wife, Chaplin now decided it would be safe to retrieve the $300,000 he had placed on temporary deposit with Elmer Ellsworth. When he requested the return of his money, however, Ellsworth responded by producing a check for $290,000.[71] Pretending to be puzzled by the missing $10,000, Chaplin inquired as to its whereabouts, and Ellsworth, still stinging from their misunderstanding of the previous year, pointedly reminded the comedian of the bonus he had been promised for successfully hiding the funds. That Ellsworth actually intended to collect for his services infuriated the parsimonious Chaplin, and he abruptly fired his old friend, an act that greatly distressed Mather and Deshon.

At the end of July 1921 Eastman and Deshon had another long-distance misunderstanding. In a rage, Deshon declared, "I am not going to write to [you] anymore.... Your neurotic selfishness has wiped any memory of you from my mind. It is [as] though I had never known you."[72]

This time, genuinely baffled by Deshon's anger, Eastman refused to beg for forgiveness as he had on previous occasions. He was weary of Deshon's hysterical outbursts, and he had finally come to the bitter conclusion that the only way he could ever achieve peace of mind was to allow their relationship to founder.

DRIFTING AWAY   Like so many of his friends that summer, Weston was also suffering through a series of emotional and financial crises. His family was away on holiday in Redondo Beach, and he was grateful for the calm and quiet their absence afforded him. However, he was unable to take full advantage of this rare stretch of freedom because he was struggling even more than usual to make ends meet. He wrote Hagemeyer, "I am having a 'fine time' away from Redondo—that is I'm working hard. 'Business' poor—I'm retouching for Ellias! At a dollar a negative! Overdrew on the bank ninety dollars—and am sure in a mess!"[73]

Retouching another photographer's prints was the worst sort of indignity for Weston, especially when the photographer in question was Edward Ellias, his wife's sister's husband and a man of very modest talents who, after learning the rudiments of photographic technique from Weston, had recently opened a competing portrait business in Glendale. Nevertheless, Weston had many bills to pay, so he forced himself to endure the humiliation.

Weston was also concerned that Hagemeyer's complicated romantic attachments were continuing to interfere with his friend's artistic productivity, and he was melancholy about his own love life:

Well, first of all—you may well guess that I protest against fate or life or what you will have it—which once more destroys your working capacity—To me you have potentialities as a creative artist which must not be dragged down....I can't tell you—in a letter—what a depressing period I have been going through with—all my dreams drifting away—with the one big love of my life drifting away—both of us absolutely broke—bitter—hopeless—and yet—so strong is the creative urge in me that last week I made pictures at least as good as my best—[74]

Weston's "one big love" who was "drifting away" could have been either Mather or Modotti. Mather was now spending most of her time looking after Florence Deshon, who was terribly depressed about her flagging career, and during the past few months, as Mather had watched Weston's infatuation with Modotti turn into an even deeper attraction, the emotional breach between Mather and Weston had grown even wider.

Modotti, too, was beginning to distance herself from Weston, a withdrawal likely caused by a guilty conscience. Robo de Richey had recently announced his intention to make an extended, exploratory expedition to Mexico City, and Modotti realized she would soon have to choose between departing for Mexico with de Richey and staying in Los Angeles with Weston. Meanwhile, the seemingly guileless de Richey was encouraging Weston to join him and Modotti in Mexico. He had even offered to look for a studio space that the three of them could share.

The notion of Mexico as an attractive refuge for artists and writers was now pervasive throughout America but especially so in Los Angeles. In spite of Mexico's recent turbulence, a new government headed by President Alvaro Obregon, who had taken office in November 1920, was now firmly in place. Obregon placed considerable value on the contributions made by artists to society, and his administration was exerting every effort to preserve the indigenous crafts unique to each region of Mexico.

Weston viewed the idea of moving to Mexico as a thrilling adventure and an appealing alternative to remaining in humdrum Glendale, a town that, to his mind, had become unbearably conservative and narrow-minded. However, Weston was also beginning to sense Modotti's reluctance to commit unreservedly to him, and her ambivalence made him doubt whether their plans for a future together would ever come to pass.

With his family away at the beach, Weston would ordinarily have relished having so much time to himself, especially with Modotti nearby, but she was about to leave for San Francisco and a visit with her family. Weston wrote Hagemeyer that, against his better judgment, he had given Modotti the Dutchman's address. "I shipped six prints to the L.[ondon] Salon[75] and four to Royal [Photographic Society]—Tina leaves tonight for San Francisco—She has your address—which I was kind enough to give her—knowing your favor in the eyes of the ladies! Alas! It is with mixed emotions that I see her go!"[76]

Modotti did contact Hagemeyer before she returned south. As Weston had anticipated, the two got along famously and were enormously attracted to each other. Hagemeyer's brooding good looks and uncompromisingly spontaneous approach to life set him apart from more ordinary men, and Modotti was understandably susceptible to his charms. They spent a seductive afternoon together, listening to classical music and discussing poetry.

Modotti particularly responded to Hagemeyer's recording of Giovanni Battista Pergolesi's *Nina*, in which a young man beseeches a beautiful young girl to awaken to his amorous attentions. Modotti recalled the hours she and Hagemeyer had spent together in a letter sent to Hagemeyer shortly after her departure:

> I have written you about a dozen letters in my mind but never have I been able to put them into written form.... here I am now making a brave effort to express all I feel full well knowing it is futile—for not even to myself can I clearly answer why I suppressed the great desire I had to call on you once more. Was it power or will? or was it cowardice? Maybe the same spirit moved me then, what moved Oscar Wilde to write this paradox, "There are only two tragedies in this world: one consists in not obtaining that which you desire; the other consists in obtaining it. The last one is the worst—the last is a real tragedy." And so I left without satisfying my desire of listening once more to Pergolesi's "Nina" in your company. Since then I have played it twice... I must be alone when I listen to it—all alone—in order to give myself the illusion that I am not alone, nor here, but in 2616 Webster Street [Hagemeyer's address]. Whether I will ever see you again or not, the brief but rich hours spent with you are most precious to me and I will live them over with the same beauty and sadness of that day.[77]

She also hinted that her relationship with Weston might be coming to an end, and she confirmed that she would soon be departing for Mexico. "I have not seen your friend Edward since I returned," she told Hagemeyer, "but he asked me to pose once more for him before leaving for Mexico."[78]

Not long after Modotti arrived back in Los Angeles she contacted Weston by mail, giving him an edited version of her meeting with Hagemeyer, and Weston, in turn, wrote to Hagemeyer, telling him how much Modotti had enjoyed their afternoon together:

> Soon I will see you—then we can talk—and talk! I have my Aunt here now on top of all my worry!...Tina goes to Mexico shortly—she wrote me and said—"I realized then how deep the friendship between J. H. and you must be—for in him there was so much that made me think of you—and again you remind me much of him." "Thanking him for the precious afternoon is not enough—I must also tell you how much I appreciated his cordial kindness and sympathetic company"—[79]

While Modotti was away in San Francisco, two notable American authors had visited Weston's studio. Floyd Dell and his new wife, B. Marie Gage, Paul Jordan-Smith's former assistant, had arrived in California following a grueling cross-country trip to visit Dell's parents on their farm near Barry, Illinois, and Gage's family at their home in Pasadena. Because the Dells shared so many friends in common with Weston and Mather, it was a foregone conclusion that Floyd would stop in Glendale to have his portrait made. On August 6 Weston noted, "M and I photographed Floyd Dell—last week interesting subject—fair results."[80] Misanthropic Theodore Dreiser, still living as a recluse in Los Angeles, had also emerged from hiding long enough to make several jaunts to the Glendale studio, perhaps hoping to catch a glimpse of the lovely Florence Deshon.[81]

A LOTUS IN THE MUD POND   In October 1921 Weston traveled north to serve as one of the judges at the Annual Salon of Photography at the Oakland Municipal Art Gallery.[82] Joining him on the judging committee were William H. Clapp, director of the Oakland Municipal Art Gallery; John Paul Edwards, the Sacramento photographer; J. Nilsen Laurvik, director of the San Francisco Palace of Fine Arts; and Roi Partridge, now an art instructor at Mills College. Aside from the complementary exhibitions contributed by Weston and Edwards, those competing for salon honors included Mather, Hagemeyer, Imogen Cunningham, Dorothea Lange, Anne Brigman, Helen MacGregor, Karl Struss, Clarence White, and Jane Reece.

Mather exhibited *Portrait of Judith*;[83] *Robo de Richey, Painter*; and *Hands of Robelo*. In the first of these images, an elegant woman sits with her back to the camera, the pale flesh of her neck and shoulders exposed by a low-cut gown and her hair arranged in an intricate chignon. On the wall behind her hangs a framed photograph. In this taut and accomplished composition, Mather pivots the model away from the camera as a way of creating interest in the picture's formal elements rather than in the sitter's identity.

Weston took the opportunity to display *Ramiel in His Attic* (see fig. 54), as well as several other recent works, including *Fragment of a Nude*[84] (Anne Brigman); *The Batik Gown*,[85] identified in the exhibition catalogue as "*Tina Modello*"; *Robo—a Portrait of the Artist at Work*; and *Sr. Lic. Ricardo Gómez Robelo*. Señor Robelo, the gentleman portrayed by both Mather and Weston (fig. 70), had only recently become a friend of theirs.[86]

At the time of their first meeting, Robelo had been living as a political exile in Los Angeles. He had once served as Attorney General of Mexico before the revolution had left him without position or power. An aficionado of nineteenth-century literature, Robelo often translated the stories of Edgar Allan Poe and Oscar Wilde into Spanish for publication in Mexico, and in 1920 he had produced a book of his own poetry, illustrated with drawings by his friend, Robo de Richey.

While biding his time in Los Angeles, Robelo had eked out a living as a newspaper correspondent, but he remained in close touch with many powerful people in Mexico and hoped

FIGURE 70. Edward Weston, *Ricardo Gómez Robelo*, 1921. Platinum or palladium print, 19.2 × 24.3 cm (7⅝ × 9⅝ in.). Tucson, Center for Creative Photography, University of Arizona, 81:276:2

to return there as soon as it was politically expedient to do so. That moment arrived in the late spring of 1921, a few months after President Obregon took office, when Robelo was called back to Mexico to accept a position as Director of the Department of Fine Arts at the Ministry of Education in Mexico City.

In June he wrote to thank Weston and Mather for the photographs they had given him as a farewell gift. It was Robelo's intention to mount a public display of Weston's and Mather's work in Mexico City, and in his letter he mentioned that he had recently shown some of their photographs to a select circle of people in order to generate interest:

> Oh, dear Edward!... you are the best giver of surprises! Not only because of your wonderful letter, but for everything you remember and furthermore, [for] that splendid gift of the prints you have given to Mrs. Robelo!
>
> Long life to you! Viva!... never before have I had such an intense, dreamy and vibrant life as in Los Angeles.... It was so great! Yes, the day by the river, and the parties.... Miss Mather is the most terrible spiritual genius!...

The exhibit has been a private one only, for some artists and newspapermen…in the meantime the public is growing more and more interested in it….I am happy to tell you that your prints and those of Miss Mather have made the greater impression. My portraits, made by you and that wonder artist, Margreth, and Tina's portraits, have proven to be the best liked, and I am teased to death….

Please present some [of the enclosed clippings] to Miss Mather, with my best regards and compliments, and tell her that every time I sip my old cognac, I can't help but to sigh for my very dear, my most wonderful friends there, whom I passionately love and for whom I am longing, and for the parties at Weston's, and at Robo's, with the magic of art, of congenial exquisite friends, and saké![87]

Robelo's growing influence in Mexico City's cultural scene and his wide circle of acquaintances would soon prove invaluable to his Los Angeles friends.

A few days after Weston returned from his judging responsibilities in Oakland, Ramiel McGehee paid him a visit. McGehee then wrote to Betty Katz in Palm Springs to bring her up to date on their mutual friends. He seemed especially concerned about Mather:

Autumn Breeze from the Desert!…

My trip to town—barren as a Pentecostal spinster—and yet, this would not be quite true, for there were moments with Edward in which there was something fine and stimulating. Especially, his contacts in San Francisco. His walk there and back, and the encouragement he recieved [sic] from the northern artists and critics.

I try not to remember the sordidness of his home life—but to carry away preciously the tonality of Edward—the knowing of the other—the destructive forces constantly surrounding him—I reach out my hands to protect him—a vague insidious void!…

Mrs. Weston was away for the evening. We supped with the children, and afterwards talked until she came home. I had two short glimpses of Margarethe. Margarethe, the unchanging. I have done all I can—nothing further to offer, one way or another. She must work out her destiny quite alone—no one can help her. A lotus in the mud-pond[88] near an old, deserted temple.

Florence [Deshon] was to leave soon for New York—had given up stage work, and was to return east, planning hopefully to enter Columbia University. Feels that she lacks training for any special work, may take a literary course, and later try to write. She needs self-discipline most of all.

And Jack [Taylor] is finding himself—I am really proud of him. Long had I urged him to get away from the others, and seek self-expression. He is living as cloistered as a monk, interested only in his work…Now and then he runs down to see me for a week-end. He seems quite cleansed of that hideous, hectic life of the hill. I am happy for him. He has real talent.[89]

HOLLYWOOD ENDINGS   Unbeknownst to Jack Taylor's friends, however, at that moment his mind was not on artistic endeavors. Instead the retiring young man was steeling himself for the supporting role he was about to play in Guglielmi vs. Guglielmi, a trial that would soon get under way in Los Angeles. Rudolph Valentino had recently filed for a divorce from his runaway bride, Jean Acker, and Taylor and Douglas Gerrard were due to appear in court on their friend's behalf.[90] As the proceedings unfolded, the two men took the stand to verify that Acker still continued to shun her husband. The judge, apparently impressed by their testimony, granted Valentino his freedom a few weeks later on the grounds of desertion.

While the Valentino marriage was coming to its inevitable conclusion, having amounted to little more than a Hollywood farce, another scandal was deteriorating into a gut-wrenching, Hollywood tragedy. In the early autumn the American public had been shocked to learn that Roscoe (Fatty) Arbuckle, Chaplin's rotund comedian friend from his Keystone Studio days, had been arrested and accused of the rape and possible murder of an actress named Virginia Rappe.[91] Her death had taken place in a suite on the twelfth floor of the St. Francis Hotel in San Francisco, during an orgiastic Labor Day weekend party replete with alcohol and drugs, and as the sordid story unfolded Los Angeles gossip columnists obligingly supplied their readers with a surfeit of lurid details. Arbuckle, who was eventually charged with manslaughter rather than murder, would suffer through two mistrials before finally being acquitted, but his acting career was already over, due to the nature of the allegations and the lingering doubts about his innocence.

The Arbuckle affair, which held the moviegoing public's attention for many weeks, was the first warning sign of serious trouble brewing in paradise. The carefree spirit and ribald frivolity that had accompanied the end of the Great War were now manifesting themselves in a seemingly unquenchable thirst for excess and decadence. Nowhere was this more evident than in Hollywood where relaxed morals, an abundance of money, and a plentiful supply of opium and bootleg liquor threatened to undermine the lives of those who succumbed to temptation. Many had already ventured far beyond the boundaries of acceptable behavior, and for them the Arbuckle trial was a wake-up call, an opportunity to retreat from moral turpitude before it was too late.

A few weeks after Arbuckle's Labor Day weekend debauch, Mather and Weston bore witness to another, far less public, Hollywood denouement, when a dispirited Florence Deshon finally abandoned the ambitions that had brought her to California two and a half years earlier. At the end of August Chaplin had embarked on an extended European voyage after perfunctorily calling off his brief engagement to May Collins and ending his long-standing friendship with Elmer Ellsworth. His abrupt departure had left Deshon short on rent money, and she had finally come to the realization that she could no longer survive in California on her own.

In October, with her fiercely proud spirit severely battered, Deshon said farewell to Mather and her other Los Angeles friends and took the train back to New York City, where she temporarily assuaged her despair by setting her sights on a return to Broadway and a reprise of the success she had enjoyed there five years earlier.[92] After she had achieved financial security, she assured her friends, she would study to become a journalist, an occupation that had already brought her some small degree of recognition. Somewhere in the back of her mind she also entertained the notion that, once she was established in Manhattan, she would be able to resuscitate her love affair with Max Eastman.

Deshon initially stayed with her friend, feminist author Marie Howe, in an apartment on West Twelfth Street.[93] A few days later she took a small room at the Algonquin Hotel, where she hoped to make valuable contacts among the authors and publishers who regularly convened for lunch and conversation around a large, circular table in that establishment's dining room. Even though Deshon was ill-equipped to secure a place at the Algonquin's famed Round Table, she kept up the pretense for several days and was still in residence there when Eastman had a copy of his newly published book, *The Sense of Humor*, sent to her room. As she perused the volume, Deshon was thrilled to find her own name on the dedication page. Touched by Eastman's tribute, she instantly responded, "Nothing ever made me so deeply happy as my name in your book."[94]

But as far as Eastman was concerned, the publication of the book he had labored on during those months in California marked the conclusion of that chapter in his life. He realized that his on-again, off-again relationship with Deshon was much too destructive and painful to continue, and although he hoped to remain on friendly terms with his former lover, he had no intentions of resuming their affair. Instead he was thinking of abandoning his publishing career and sailing for Russia, where he wanted to write eyewitness accounts of the political situation unfolding there.

In early December Eastman informed Deshon of his plans. His blunt words dealt the deathblow to their love affair, and although Deshon attempted to resign herself to the conditions Eastman had imposed, her mood swings became so pronounced she began seeing a psychoanalyst. A short time later Deshon moved from the Algonquin to a friend's Greenwich Village apartment, where she hoped to husband her meager resources until she could return to the lights of Broadway, replenish her bank account, and recover her self-respect.

DRUNK WITH DESIRES   Back in Los Angeles Robo de Richey continued to prepare for his trip to Mexico. His friend, Robelo, had recently offered him a studio and a teaching position if he would permanently relocate. Robelo also wanted de Richey to organize and mount the pending exhibition of Mather's and Weston's photographs, as well as a display of his own batik wall hangings, and to ease de Richey's concerns about leaving his mother and sister behind, Robelo had even suggested they should accompany him to Mexico.

In the meantime, Modotti accepted roles in two more movies—a Western melodrama, *Riding with Death*, and a heavy-handed romance, *I Can Explain*—in which she again portrayed fiery Mexican beauties. Impatient with Modotti's busy work schedule and anxious to begin his journey, de Richey set a departure date of December 6. However, Modotti's professional obligations, passport complications, and an upcoming, monthlong visit from her sixteen-year-old brother, Beppo, gave her convenient excuses to linger in Los Angeles, and a disappointed de Richey finally left for Mexico without her.[95]

Modotti received her first letter from de Richey on Christmas Eve as she opened gifts with his mother and sister, Vocio and Marionne Richey. As soon as the holidays were over Vocio wrote to her son, telling him that she and Marionne had decided to forgo the expense of a trip to Mexico in favor of purchasing a home in Los Angeles, and de Richey, who had heard only infrequently from Modotti since his departure, began to fret that she, too, was losing interest in sharing his adventure.[96]

ENDORSEMENTS   While Modotti was preoccupied with holiday festivities and entertaining her brother, Weston served as a judge for the Camera Pictorialists' Fifth International Salon, which had opened on December 13.[97] Also judging the competition were the artist Dana Bartlett and the New York City photographer Karl Struss, who had arrived in California a few months earlier to try his hand at cinematography. Mather had contributed portraits of Weston and Robo de Richey and a study of Robelo's hands, and Weston, who could not compete because of his

FIGURE 71. Edward Weston, *The Source* (or *The Breast*), 1922. Platinum or palladium print, 19.1 × 24.3 cm (7 1/2 × 9 1/2 in.). Washington, D.C., Photographic History Collection, National Museum of American History, Smithsonian Institution, 3615

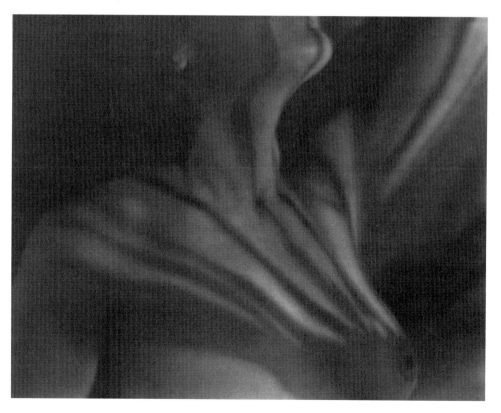

judging responsibilities, had hung a sampling of his own work. It was the first time since 1916 that he and Mather had participated in one of the Camera Pictorialists' salons. Just as the exhibition came to a close, Weston excitedly wrote Hagemeyer with the news that his photograph *The Breast* (fig. 71),[98] a lush image of shadows falling in abstract patterns across a female bosom, had been purchased by a collector during the exhibition.[99]

Both Weston and Mather were now using palladium paper almost exclusively, and in late December Weston received a letter of thanks for a recent endorsement he had sent to his paper supplier, Willis & Clements of Philadelphia:

> I must thank you ever so much for your words of appreciation. I quite agree with you in all you say. Palladiotype suits me better even than Platinotype. Singularly enough a letter from Clarence White came in the same mail as yours in which amongst other things he said "I use Palladiotype for all my work." In his school he teaches it as well as Platinotype and many of his pupils who have "launched out," mostly use one of these two papers.
>
> My eldest son, Willis, is now in England at the factory, endeavoring to thresh out better price conditions without I fear being able to accomplish much in that direction,

FIGURE 72. Edward Weston, *Japanese Fighting (or Fencing) Mask*, 1921. Platinum or palladium print, 19.1 × 24.3 cm (7¹/₂ × 9¹/₂ in.). Wilson Centre for Photography, Collection of Michael and Jane Wilson

as the fad for Pt. [platinum] & Pd. [palladium] jewelery still continues and this keeps up prices.

Won't you please thank Miss Mather for me, for her interest in the paper? I shall use both your names, as well as Mr. White's in my little letter to the trade… A. Clements[100]

It was also around this time that Weston revisited his preoccupations of the past in a remarkable series of photographs of an unidentified person[101] wearing a Japanese fencing mask, an object so unfamiliar to Western eyes that it must have been virtually unrecognizable to Weston's audience. In these images, the mask and its shadow transmogrify into a menacing alien creature with an exoskeleton both elegant and fearsome. Weston's initial approach to his subject was similar to the one he had used a few years earlier in his shadow pictures, but in this instance his explorations went much further.

Using the same reductive method that Mather had employed in her Pierrot pictures, Weston made at least three versions of the fencing mask, moving his camera closer with each exposure. In the final variant (fig. 72), background details have been eliminated and all contextual clues are gone, forcing the viewer to examine the image purely in terms of form and line. The imposing mask becomes an abstraction as it almost fills the picture frame, radiating an ominously threatening power that conveys the original intent behind the mask's creation far more effectively than a more literal rendering could have. For the first time in Weston's career, he delves below the surface of the depicted object to summon forth its very essence, as he leaves behind the world of representation and enters the realm of symbols and nightmares.

Tragedies and Triumphs, 1922

It turned out that Robo de Richey had every reason to worry about Tina Modotti's apparent disinterest in making the trip to Mexico; while he was writing passionately tender love letters to her, she was slipping away to Glendale for a few stolen hours of pleasure with Weston. In January 1922 Modotti sent Weston a letter containing the sentiments de Richey had been longing to hear:

> Edward: with tenderness I repeat your name over and over to myself—in a way that brings you nearer to me tonight as I sit here alone remembering—
>
> Last night—at this hour you were reading to me from an exquisite volume—or were we sipping wine and smoking?—or had darkness enveloped us and were you—oh, the memory of this thrills me to the point of swooning!—tell me; were you at this hour—kissing my left breast?
>
> …to be drunk with desires to crave their attainment—and yet to fear it—to delay it—that is the supreme form of love.
>
> It is very late now—and I am exhausted from the intensity of my feelings—My eyelids are heavy with sleep but in my heart there is a hidden joy for the hours that will still be ours—[1]

Edward Weston was unquestionably the real reason behind Modotti's reluctance to leave Los Angeles. De Richey's absence had finally allowed her the freedom to discover just how all-consuming her attraction to Weston could be, and although she did not wish to wound her partner of three years, she had no intentions of depriving herself of such a scintillating, amorous interlude.

That same month, Mather and Weston attended a showing of the film *The Cabinet of Dr. Caligari*, first released in Europe in 1919, but only now making its debut in Los Angeles. It did not live up to Weston's expectations, however, and he wrote Hagemeyer, "Perhaps, I had hoped for too much—always dangerous—or more likely—the surroundings—presentation—music—spoiled it.…this is only because I had expected to be swept off my feet! We had to leave a little before it was over but I go again tonight—Hope I am not becoming blasé." He also passed along alarming news about his Glendale environs. "A Standard Oil Station is going up on the corner," he wrote. "I'm afraid the little studio shack is doomed."[2]

After viewing *Caligari* for the second time, Weston spent a passionate night with an unidentified lover (probably Modotti) in the tiny studio where Ramiel McGehee now lived, behind his sister's residence at 206 South Broadway in Redondo Beach. Before hurriedly setting out the following morning, Weston scribbled a brief note:

Key enclosed—also thank[s] offering! a small token of appreciation—

I left several dirty dishes and the bed was hurriedly made—having to catch an early car—left a taste in the bottle—butter and cheese—caught a mouse—think this all the news.... many thanks—for untold beauty you have enabled me to possess.[3]

MURDER AND MAYHEM   On February 3, 1922, America awoke to headlines trumpeting yet another Hollywood scandal, this one involving several figures well known to Weston, Mather, and Florence Deshon. On the morning of the previous day, Charlie Chaplin's Athletic Club colleague, director William Desmond Taylor, had been found shot to death in the living room of his bungalow court apartment at 404 South Alvarado Street, near downtown Los Angeles.[4]

Two of Chaplin's former leading ladies, Mabel Normand and Edna Purviance, were among the suspects, as was the ingenue actress Mary Miles Minter, who was reportedly involved in a May/December romance with Taylor; also suspect was Minter's mother, who had been overheard warning Taylor to stay away from her daughter. The art director George Hopkins, long rumored to be another of Taylor's lovers, had arrived at the murder scene just in time to witness public relations people from Famous Players–Lasky Studios (Taylor's employer at the time) frantically closing ranks as they attempted to spin their way around an out-and-out calamity. Hollywood insiders knew, however, that there were complicated subplots of cocaine abuse and homosexual affairs lurking behind the scenes, and they were well aware that, even though charges had not yet been filed, suspicion alone would be enough to destroy several Hollywood careers.

The following day, on the opposite side of the country, Florence Deshon happened to bump into Max Eastman as they simultaneously emerged from the subway station at Broadway and Forty-Second Street.[5] They walked uptown together, no doubt discussing the Taylor murder and all of its implications, until Eastman abruptly turned away at Forty-Eighth Street. Although he offered no explanation to Deshon for his brusque behavior, he was on his way to meet Maxwell Perkins, his editor at Scribner's, where he was to pick up a copy of *The Sense of Humor* that he had arranged to have specially bound as a surprise gift for Deshon.

That evening Eastman was attending a play in the theater district when a stranger suddenly approached him with the urgent message that Deshon had been taken to the hospital. A neighbor had discovered her lying across the bed in her borrowed apartment, unconscious, with the gas jets turned on. Eastman rushed to Saint Vincent's Hospital where he watched as "friendly" blood from his veins was transfused into Deshon's, but in spite of all efforts to save her, in the early morning hours of February 4, 1922, Deshon succumbed to the carbon monoxide poisoning that had caused irreparable damage to her internal organs.[6]

The following Monday, Weston and Mather learned the details of the shocking tragedy from a lengthy article that appeared on the front page of the local news section of the *Los Angeles Times*:

CLEWS SOUGHT IN DEATH CASE
Actress's Passing Caused Police Investigation
Florence Deshon Victim of Gas; Once Lived Here
Link Names of Chaplin and Eastman in Romance

Baffled by the strange circumstances which led to the death of Florence Deshon, well-known local film actress, after she was found unconscious in a gas-filled apartment in Greenwich Village....

Miss Deshon died in a New York hospital late Saturday night. Police say her case was not brought to their attention until ten hours after she had been removed to the hospital.

According to reports from New York, the young woman was found lying on the floor of her room. The chamber was filled with gas. One window was partly raised which is a point that leads the police to believe that her death may have been the result of an accident.

...A dispatch from New York last night said that the breaking off of a love affair which had lasted several years was recalled in the gossip concerning her death...The girl was taken to St. Vincent's Friday night after she had been found unconscious. On Saturday morning Max Eastman, writer, submitted to blood transfusion in an effort to save her. Mr. Eastman, when asked about the asserted love affair, refused to comment, but gave out the following statement:

"Miss Deshon was a dear friend. I am sure her death was accidental. I do not know the slightest reason why she should commit suicide. I was about to start for Europe to attend the Genoa conference and had expected to sail next week. I am perfectly sure, as are her friends, that her death was accidental."

Friends of the couple insist the friendship between Eastman and Miss Deshon was rudely broken recently. Persons living at 120 West Eleventh street tell of a recent scene between them when Eastman called at the apartment....

...It was also said the first breach between Eastman and Miss Deshon took place after the screen actress met Charlie Chaplin...gossip on the coast had it that the comedian had asked Miss Deshon to marry him. (Mr. Chaplin could not be reached last night.)...

...Miss Deshon admitted to friends here that she was deeply in love with an author in the East, but said she did not intend to marry him, as he was too jealous and she felt that her life with him would be miserable....

…Miss Deshon had an unhappy life from childhood. She was known to be of a very moody disposition and, though witty and possessed of a tremendous sense of humor, when the black moods assailed her she kept to herself for days.

One obsession she had was that she would die young…she was 28 years old.[7]

Services were held at the prestigious Frank E. Campbell Funeral Church at Sixty-Sixth Street and Broadway, but Eastman was too distraught to attend. Deshon's bewildered mother arranged for her daughter's remains to be interred at Mount Zion Cemetery in Maspeth, Queens, where many of New York City's labor activists, as well as the victims of the 1911 Triangle Shirt-waist Company fire, had been laid to rest a decade earlier. Even in death, Deshon's rebellious spirit would be in like company.

Deshon's friend Marie Howe wrote a lengthy condolence letter to Eastman, telling him that she believed Deshon had committed suicide, not because she had lost his love, but because she had failed in her career ambitions. "No love affair could ever kill our beautiful proud Florence. You know and I know that she could always rise above her emotions. They never conquered her, she conquered them—But with pride lost, she could not face the world."[8]

A few of Deshon's acquaintances treated her passing, and the success she had so fleetingly enjoyed, as one of life's random events. Betty Katz was especially cavalier in her own assessment. "Florence Deshon did not commit suicide," she wrote. "It was an accident like everything else which came to her."[9] However, there were those who believed Deshon's death had everything to do with Eastman and his coldness toward her, and Eastman, the only person who knew what had really transpired between them, was certain of it.

Although Weston was deeply distressed by the news of Deshon's demise, Mather was inconsolable. During Deshon's two and a half years in Hollywood, the two women had worked together, played together, and fallen in love with each other. Deshon had served as Mather's model on many occasions, and although Mather had shared her portraits of Deshon with Eastman and Chaplin, she had never exhibited any of them, signaling that her own admiration for Deshon was far too private and special to be displayed to casual observers. Even Eastman had sensed the attraction between the two women when he cautioned Deshon, "Don't love Margaret too much."[10] For many months—long after Eastman had sailed for Russia and Chaplin had gone on to his next film—Mather remained in mourning.

DEATH IN MEXICO   Unfortunately, Deshon's tragic death was only the first in a series of sobering events. Just as the initial shock of her suicide was subsiding, Weston and Mather received word that on February 9 Robo de Richey had died in Mexico City from a highly virulent infection.

Since his arrival there seven weeks earlier, de Richey had thoroughly explored the city and its environs. He was delighted with the tantalizing atmosphere and sensibilities of the place and wildly enthusiastic about the beauty of the country and its potential to inspire artists.

Shortly before Christmas he had written Weston a letter crammed full of picturesque descriptions of the many locales he had visited and the people he was meeting. He was trying his best to convince Weston that he must experience Mexico for himself:

> I must say that for subject matter it is the artists' paradise. The place drips with colour and overflows with character and "life."...
>
> ...There is for me more poetry in one lone zerape [*sic*] enshrouded figure leaning in the door of the pulque shop at twilight or a bronzed daughter of the Aztecs nursing her child in the church than could be found in L.A. in the next ten years....
>
> There is a great turning backward to original sources here—They have grown tired of trying to imitate foreign art and are now seeking to find themselves in themselves.[11]

He continued in his letter to relate news of their mutual friend, Robelo, and his prestigious governmental post, and to reassure Weston that their own friendship was still intact:

> Robelo is now Chief of the Dept. of Fine Arts. He has not yet given the talked of exhibition but will do so in January. I will help him. He is having prepared a three story colonial bldg. facing the "Zocolo" and near the palace.... He says to tell you he is sorry for the delay but that it could not be avoided. I shall post notices saying that if a sufficient number will order your photos you will come and make them here. What do you say? Please send me your prices....
>
> ...Robelo sends you his very best—You can imagine how busy he is. Remember me to the family—Also to Miss Mather—write me about your pictures and if you will come. Believe me to be as ever, your friend, "Robo"[12]

Ironically, less than a week before de Richey's death, Modotti had finally decided to join him in Mexico. Although Weston intended to follow her there, de Richey was apparently unaware of their plans; in anticipation of Modotti's arrival, he had renovated a one-room hideaway on the upper floor of his friend Robelo's home, painstakingly fitted out to suit her needs, with a dressing table, *petates* (floor mats woven from palm fronds), and a spacious closet.

On February 3, the same day that word of William Desmond Taylor's murder spread across the country and Florence Deshon could no longer shrug off life's disappointments, Modotti had boarded a train to Mexico City.[13] She carried with her several additional photographs by Weston and Mather for the exhibition de Richey was planning to mount at the Academia de Bellas Artes. As she departed, she was unaware of de Richey's developing illness, but soon after leaving Los Angeles two telegrams were delivered to her on the train, one informing her that de Richey was suffering from a case of smallpox and a second warning her not to continue her trip. Filled with foreboding, Modotti pressed on.

She arrived in Mexico City on the evening of February 7, only to discover that de Richey had been confined to an isolation ward in the British Cowdray Hospital. Due to the highly contagious nature of his disease, she was not allowed to see him. Instead of bringing comfort to de Richey, as she so desperately wanted to do, she was forced to stand by helplessly while he slipped into a coma and died. A dazed and grief-stricken Modotti suddenly found herself making arrangements for de Richey's burial at the American Cemetery.[14]

Following de Richey's passing, Modotti was too upset to contact Weston directly, or perhaps she feared someone might intercept her communication. Instead, under the pretext of notifying Weston that his exhibition would have to be postponed because of de Richey's death, she asked her mother-in-law to call him with the dreadful news. On February 13 Weston wrote to Hagemeyer, "Robo died from small-pox in Mexico City—and I almost had started when Tina went! I of course am terribly depressed with this and Florence's death—have done no work this year—but will—I hope you have and believe Hendrik [Hagemeyer's brother] so suggested. Do send proofs to cheer me up"[15]

A HERITAGE TO UPHOLD   Ten days passed before Weston wrote again. This time his letter to Hagemeyer was philosophical and introspective:

> You have come to me so poignantly just now—reading for the first time the Stieglitz article by Rosenfeld—and in the margin someone has taken exception to a remark of Rosenfeld's—a sentence which reads—"And yet, with the exception of Stieglitz not a one of the photographers has used the camera to do what alone the photographer can do," disagreeing—someone has written—"Yes—one—Edward Weston"—and I am moved—unsentimental pretenses are swept aside—and I have tears to brush away—for how much I love my medium and those who think and express themselves with it's [sic] same beauty—only you and a few others can realize.
>
> —And what a heritage we have to carry on—from Stieglitz and his group—you and I and M—and a mere handful of sophisticated minds who are "willing to accept fully the pain of existence"—...
>
> ...I have been dormant of late—that inaction which nature imposes at times in order that we may gain new strength and vision—
>
> —but now I awake—awake to the inscrutable trees and the fresh glow of light ahead—
>
> —much affection to you dear friend—[16]

Strangely, Hagemeyer's response failed to acknowledge the recent tragedies, and instead focused on his own problems. After apologizing for his long silence Hagemeyer continued:

> I've done some work but not much....Am mostly interested...in earning some money...and since I cannot make my camera do that for me I have to resort to other means and methods....conditions with me are not quite conducive to much accomplishment in

the photographic direction—I hope this is reversed with you—and what I learned from your fine letter of the other day I am certain that you are doing some big things again....

My success at exhibits is rapidly waning...in Buffalo they hung one of my things while the Am. Photography didn't deem a single one worthwhile mentioning—I am discouraged, despondent, disheartened, disillusioned....Above all thoroughly disgusted...with the Pictorial Photographic Salons or Contests in general....You know, Edward, I am not saying this because I am jealous—(I wish I could be—I mean that the pictures hung would justify envy)....but where is this Pictorial business coming to...or rather [this] salon business—I am afraid it is getting like everything else here...too democratic—everything leveled down to commonplaceness—mediocrity—not to say downright stupidity—ass-dom—

Tell me—did you send to American Photography?—or Pittsburgh—Will you ever sent [sic] to any again?—That is: where they go through a jury one doesn't know (and usually an incompetent one)—?

Which reminds me: I wrote you some time ago that I tried to interest people in Holland (Amsterdam) to hold an exhibit of prints by Margrethe, you and myself—Just a few days ago I received a letter from one of the people there, saying that they would consider it an honor to have us send them a number of prints (i.e. about 30) for their annual National Exhibit to be held in the Municipal Museum in Amsterdam—(by the way one of the finest Art Galleries we have in Holland.) from June 8 to 18 coming—for which purpose they sent "personal invitations to Margrethe Mather, Edward Weston and myself."...since they are jury-free—I hope you and Margrethe still feel like sending—I think is it [sic] well worthwhile...We ought to give them a good show....

Remember me to Margrethe—Hope she is well!

To you a good old handshake—and "au revoir" Edward—[17]

MEMENTO MORI   Soon after de Richey's funeral, Modotti set about organizing the exhibition he had intended to oversee. When the display opened on March 9 at the National School of Fine Arts, it served as a tender *memento mori* to her late partner. Included was an extensive selection of his drawings and batiks, together with a large group of photographs by Weston and Mather, as well as a few contributions by Jane Reece, Arnold Schroeder, and Walter Frederick Seely. Also displayed were pastels and oil paintings by two of de Richey's artist friends, Mahlon Blaine and J. W. Horwitz. A florid review of the photographs appeared in El *Universal Graphico*, alongside images by Weston:

Edward Weston and Margrethe Walther [sic], two formidable artists from Glendale, California, are the most splendid organizers of linear and chiaroscuro harmony, which they have interpreted knowingly in these compositions. These artists already are known throughout almost the entire world for their original compositions and for the prizes, medals, and diplomas—which they deserved—conferred on them in different international exhibitions....

Gómez Robelo said to me: "And this distinguished work that you see is not merely the product of someone who is concerned with developing or printing well; no, it is not the craft of photographic technique that produces this. It is that and something more, much more; it is artistic culture which they have; it is that supreme refinement produced by good living: private libraries, fine music, museum visits, and the cultivation of taste, far from all vulgar banality."[18]

Once the exhibition was on the walls Modotti was tireless in her dedication to its success. She staffed the exhibition desk herself, greeted visitors with charm and cordiality, and discussed the works of art on display with potential buyers. She even found time to write Weston, telling him that she had sold a few of his photographs and reassuring him that his display was receiving lavish praise from many admirers.

Modotti's stay in Mexico lasted approximately six weeks, and as Robelo spent long hours in her company his infatuation with her grew. He took great pleasure in introducing his beautiful friend to his political and social cronies and escorting her through the thriving arts scene that now existed in the city center, near the National Palace. It was a cultural renaissance he had been instrumental in nurturing, and he was proud to parade his accomplishments before her. Newly estranged from his wife, Robelo tried to convince Modotti that she should remain in Mexico with him.

TOO MANY MEMORIES   Modotti had no choice but to return to California, however, when on March 17 she learned that her father, ailing for several months, had finally lost his battle with stomach cancer.[19] Although Modotti yearned to leave immediately to join her bereaved family, she forced herself to remain in Mexico City until the exhibition closed on March 23. Ricocheting from one tragedy to another, she gathered together de Richey's unsold artworks, packed them in a trunk, and boarded a train to California. Pausing briefly in Los Angeles to comfort her grieving mother-in-law and relinquish de Richey's precious trunk, she then continued on to San Francisco.

Shortly after her arrival there she spent several days in bed recovering from a severe case of influenza, but as soon as she had recuperated she resumed the responsibility of tending to her mother's needs. Only two years had passed since Assunta Modotti's arrival in America, but already she was a widow, living in a strange city, with no source of income. As Modotti consoled her mother, she found herself longing for an escape from the many burdens that were suddenly raining down on her shoulders. She wrote to Hagemeyer, hoping a visit with him would distract her from her immediate predicament:

I hesitated long whether to get in touch with you or not for I had made it my programme before coming here not to see anyone outside of my family.

But the other day—finding myself alone—an uncontrollable desire came upon me to hear "Nina" again...as I listened the agitated life of these past few months became dimer & dimer [sic], while the memory of a certain afternoon came back to me with all the illusion of reality....

And because of all this I feel the desire to spend another afternoon with you—can the first ever be duplicated? I fear not—but "Nina" at least—will be the same—

Can you drop me a card & let me know when I can call?

I will remain here until Easter—fond as I am of this place—yet I am anxious to leave it—it holds too many memories for me—here I live constantly in the past...For me life is always sad—for even in the present moment I feel the past—...

...I wonder how you feel about all this—perhaps we can talk it over—[20]

If Modotti and Hagemeyer had their "talk," no mention of such a meeting appeared in Weston's or Hagemeyer's correspondence. Instead there was much discussion of an upcoming exhibition at San Francisco's Palace of Fine Arts, as well as the showing in Amsterdam that Hagemeyer was attempting to organize. Once again Weston was cynical about the quality of American photography salons when he queried Hagemeyer about the San Francisco event. "Have you any idea who the S.F. judges are to be?" he asked. "I do not wish to waste time on the usual camera club juries."[21]

In March Weston opened an exhibition of forty photographs at the MacDowell Club in the Tajo Building in downtown Los Angeles. Mather was still too distraught over Deshon's death to participate. In fact, her low spirits may have brought about the dissolution of her partnership agreement with Weston, because by the time the MacDowell Club exhibition took place they were no longer cosigning photographs, and even though several of the pictures on display were joint efforts from the previous year, Mather received no credit. Instead, the *Times* reporter mentioned only Weston, calling his work superior to that of the other six artists represented:

The real show of the month is that of Mr. Weston's photographs. Mr. Weston is an artist to his finger-tips, and his pictures have all the qualities of painting except color. His compositions are strikingly original, yet they are never forced and he poses his figures with an unerring instinct for line and balance. And how fascinating his lighting often is!

Could portraiture be more revealing, and at the same time beautiful, than that which we find in "Floyd Dell, Novelist," "Carl Sandberg [sic]," "W. A. Clark Jr.," "Ruth Deardorff Shaw," "George Stojana," "Profile of J. J. K." and "Gengo Rigos—"

And what loveliness of lighting, what strength of modeling, we note in "Japanese Actor," "The Breast," "Fragment of Nude," "The Lacquer Chest" and "Sybil" [sic].[22]

On April 14, 1922, Weston's exhibition at the MacDowell Club was taken down, and a display of Robo de Richey's work took its place. Weston had cut short his own exhibit to make room for de Richey's. Organized by Modotti, who had just returned from San Francisco, the one-man showing of de Richey's batiks and drawings was mounted as a second homage to her late partner.[23] The occasion also provided an opportunity for Modotti to raise some much-needed cash. The *Los Angeles Record* covered the event in an article titled "Art, Love And Death, Widow Must Sell Batiks." The interviewer described Modotti as manifesting "a momentary quiver of the lids and a quick little paroxysm of the throat" when she announced her intention to part with de Richey's creations. "They will do no good here or locked up in trunks," she told the reporter.[24]

Soon after the memorial exhibition ended Modotti prepared a selection of de Richey's drawings for publication. Titled *The Book of Robo*, the thin volume included an introduction by John Cowper Powys and a highly inventive biographical sketch of Robo de Richey's life written by Modotti. With her moral obligation to honor her deceased lover's memory thus fulfilled, and her guilt in some measure assuaged, Modotti began to consider how she was going to support herself and also assist with her mother's finances. For the moment Modotti put all thoughts of returning to Mexico aside.

Weston, however, was now eager to open a studio in Mexico, especially since his photographs had been so well received there. Nevertheless, his familial, financial, and professional obligations continued to weigh on him. He was not yet emotionally capable of making a wholehearted commitment to such a momentous change in his life, and he endlessly debated the pros and cons with his friends.

In fact, it may have been Weston's indecision about his future that inspired the ending of Charlie Chaplin's film *The Pilgrim*, shot between April and July 1922. In the movie's final scene, the Little Tramp waddles away from the camera, straddling the border between Mexico and the United States, with one foot in each country, as he tries to choose between "the land of anarchy and that of Puritanism."[25]

AN INFLUX OF ARTISTIC TYPES   During the summer of 1922, as Weston and Modotti continued to sort out exactly what they meant to each other and whether they might have a future together after all, a handsome, intellectual couple who had recently arrived from the Midwest paid a visit to the Glendale studio. The man was an architect, trained in Vienna and Chicago; the woman, a teacher in an alternative elementary school.

Rudolph Michael Schindler had left Austria for Chicago in 1914[26] to work for the architectural firm of Ottenheimer, Stern and Reichart. However, after his three-year employment contract with that firm ended, he had transferred his allegiances to another well-respected Chicago architect, Frank Lloyd Wright.[27] Sophie Pauline Gibling, a recent Smith College graduate, had just returned to her hometown to begin a teaching career when she encountered Schindler at a Sergei Prokofiev concert in 1919. The two married the following August, and immediately the young couple immersed themselves in the stimulating atmosphere that surrounded Wright, both at his Chicago office and at his residence and studio, Taliesen, in Spring Green, Wisconsin.

One of Schindler's first responsibilities was to assist Wright with the engineering and drawings for an extremely important and prestigious commission—the Imperial Hotel in Tokyo, Japan. Wright was also in the midst of designing and constructing a large house in Los Angeles for Aline Barnsdall. Thwarted in her earlier plans to build a theater because of her disastrous love affair with Richard Ordynsky and the subsequent birth of their love child, Barnsdall had instead hired Wright to design a large residence for herself and her infant daughter. Her long-range plan, however, was to make her home the hub of a much larger cultural center, which would eventually include a theater, a director's residence, living quarters for actors and artists, and a plaza of small shops.

The site Barnsdall had selected for her new home was a thirty-six-acre parcel of land—located on the west side of Vermont Avenue between Hollywood and Sunset boulevards—that included the promontory known as Olive Hill. While the plans for Barnsdall's house were being drawn up, the Babylonian-style sets erected five years earlier for D. W. Griffith's *Intolerance* still stood near the eastern flank of Olive Hill, and it may have been the stepped geometry of those crumbling faux ziggurats that suggested the stylized design motif Wright proceeded to incorporate into every aspect of his renderings for Barnsdall's house (although he and Barnsdall would later maintain that his ornamentation had been inspired by the profusion of wild hollyhocks that grew on the property).[28]

Barnsdall, who expected Wright to complete her Hollyhock House in a timely, responsible manner, grew increasingly impatient as he instead focused his energy on his commitments in Japan, to the virtual exclusion of everything else.[29] An exasperated Barnsdall began excoriating her architect friend, and in an effort to calm her and put an end to the untenable situation, Wright sent Rudolph Schindler to Los Angeles to oversee the completion of Barnsdall's home, and the erection of the satellite buildings around it, thus fulfilling Wright's contractual obligations to the oil heiress.

The Schindlers arrived in Los Angeles on December 3, 1920. Pauline was an extremely bright, temperamental woman, a "genteel rebel... high-minded and ambitious and at the same time self-defeating in her activities."[30] Although she approached life with a sense of entitlement and enjoyed playing hostess at frequent social gatherings, Pauline was a serious, politically aware woman who, prior to her marriage, had spent many hours teaching underprivileged children in the slums of Boston and at Jane Addams's Hull House in Chicago. Like Mollie Price and Prince Hopkins before her, she was an advocate of progressive education and a proselytizer on behalf of the Modern School movement, the educational progeny of Emma Goldman's prototype elementary school in New York City.

Rudolph Michael (R. M.) Schindler was far more enigmatic and aloof than his gregarious, articulate wife. Often uncommunicative, gruff, and irritatingly distant, he nevertheless possessed an infectious laugh and the ability to instill confidence in his clients. Although Schindler's design sensibilities were greatly influenced by the refined geometry of the Vienna Secession, he had also been taught by his first mentor, Adolf Loos, to admire the handcrafted surfaces of primitive architecture. As soon as Schindler became accustomed to his new environs, he decided he would express the Southern California lifestyle utilizing a completely different vernacular than that articulated in the earth-toned, redwood bungalows so ubiquitous throughout Los Angeles.

The Schindlers resided in assorted hotel rooms and rented apartments until Barnsdall's house was finally completed in the autumn of 1921. They then set out to locate a suitable piece of property on which they could build a two-family home for themselves and their friends Clyde and Marian Chace. After much searching, the foursome purchased a lot in the middle of a lima bean field on the western fringes of Hollywood. Ground was broken in February 1922, and by the time the Schindlers met Weston they were already occupying their new home, even though Pauline likened their early living circumstances, sans electricity and gas, to camping out.

The walls of the Schindlers' house were constructed of concrete poured into molds to form slabs that were then tilted into place, an innovative building technique borrowed from Clyde Chace's employer, architect Irving Gill. However, unlike Gill's more restrained approach, Schindler melded the cool, mottled surfaces of hand-buffed cement floors and walls with the warm glow of copper-hooded, open-hearthed fireplaces to create a sensual, tactile environment. He also incorporated outdoor sleeping porches into his design, and surrounded the house with extensive gardens, blurring the distinction between interior and exterior living spaces to create a dwelling quite unlike anything previously seen in California.

Because the Schindlers' political sympathies leaned far to the left of center, they naturally gravitated toward a group of like-minded individuals in Los Angeles. In fact, one of the first social events they attended was a tea party at the home of Gaylord and Mary Wilshire. As they began to establish the flow of their Los Angeles lives, the Schindlers became active in several local organizations. One was the Workers' Defense League, an organization that fought for the release of imprisoned labor activists, including many IWW members who had been rounded up during the Red Scare. Another was the Hollywood Art Association, where Rudolph Schindler quickly became a driving force. A third was the Walt Whitman School at 517 South Boyle Avenue in Boyle Heights, a day school for the children of political radicals that described itself as "the first proletarian school in the West."[31]

The Walt Whitman School had opened in 1919 under the umbrella of the Modern School movement, and for a few months Pauline Schindler taught English there, and both she and her husband served on the school's board of directors. It was very likely at the Walt

Whitman School that the Schindlers first encountered Edward Weston, because the Westons' sons Chandler and Brett were enrolled at the school, under the progressive tutelage of William Thurston Brown, one of Emma Goldman's Modern School disciples.[32] Perhaps the Westons had decided to send their two eldest sons to the Walt Whitman School because of Edward's friendship with Paul Jordan-Smith, who served as the school's educational director, or because they respected the academic philosophy of Prince Hopkins, who had donated what was left of Boyland's science books and equipment to the school.

Not long after the Schindlers became acquainted with Weston, Pauline wrote a letter to her parents, telling them about an evening she and her husband had recently spent at Weston's studio:

> On Sunday we stole time for a lark,—and went off to call on Mr. Weston, an artist of whom we had heard much, and whose personality we liked through having heard him lecture, and seen his work. He was exceedingly interesting—showed us his things, responded, of course, to R.M.S.—and when the evening was ripe, took us over to the house of a brilliant pianist, who happened to be among his guests. Jolly, the way we all drifted over to her studio from his, and all sat on her floor to listen. She really was very brilliant,—said to be the finest player of modern French literature upon the Pacific coast . . . and to out-Ornstein Ornstein. Shortly before midnight I suggested that we all motor over to our house, to try our Steinway. . . . Mr. Weston of course very much excited about the house, and wanting to see it by daylight. All of it a fearfully stimulating evening . . . R.M.S. and I couldn't sleep, with the stimulus of the music, and Mr. Weston's pictures.[33]

As one of the earliest visitors to the Schindlers' home, Weston was understandably impressed by the artistic couple and the unique environment they had created for themselves. The friendships that resulted would be long-standing, particularly between Weston and Pauline Schindler.

The "brilliant pianist" mentioned in Pauline's letter was Ruth Deardorff-Shaw, the same woman whose portrait Weston had exhibited at the MacDowell Club a few weeks earlier. She had given several public recitals in recent months, but her performances were not well understood by Los Angeles audiences, who found her selection of music unappealing, even distressing.[34] Deardorff-Shaw was, in Weston's opinion, a strident and disagreeable individual, and he perfectly captures her discordant personality in a portrait full of sharp edges and jagged angles (fig. 73).

Although Deardorff-Shaw poses in profile, her face is cropped so as to reveal only her wedge-shaped bangs, the exaggerated sliver of one eyebrow, and the razor-sharp ridge of her prominent nose. A stark backdrop of strongly contrasting passages of black and white, which Weston created by angling a photographic exhibition mat against a dark ground, adds visual

FIGURE 73. Edward Weston, *Ruth* [Deardorff-] *Shaw—A Portrait*, 1922. Palladium print, 19 × 24.4 cm (7 1/2 × 9 9/16 in.). The Lane Collection, Museum of Fine Arts, Boston

drama and produces an uneasy tension in the image. Perhaps he was already sensing the disruption the acid-tongued pianist would soon cause in his own life.

Late in the summer of 1922 Weston befriended Peter and Rose Krasnow, who arrived on his doorstep following a long and harrowing cross-country drive.[35] Peter Krasnow, born in 1890, was from the Ukraine, where he had learned to crush and combine brightly colored pigments while working with his painter/interior decorator father. At the age of seventeen, fleeing the persecution of the Russian pogroms, Krasnow came to America where he began to study painting, first in Boston and then at the Art Institute of Chicago, all the while supporting himself as a manual laborer. It was in the second city that he met Rose Blum, a social worker and teacher, who became his wife in 1920.

The couple then moved to New York City, where Krasnow's reputation grew and several of his paintings were shown at the Whitney Studio Club.[36] After one reviewer, impressed by Krasnow's distinctive painting style, commented that the artist's depiction of trees reminded him of the eucalypti of Southern California, Krasnow became intrigued by the notion that somehow he had intuitively painted a landscape he had not yet experienced. Embracing the coincidence as an omen, Krasnow and his wife set out for the West Coast the following summer.

Like the Schindlers, the Krasnows hoped to purchase a plot of land and build a home, and after meeting Flora and Edward Weston, they decided to acquire one of the lots Flora and her sister had inherited. Located near the banks of the Los Angeles River and in the shelter of the Griffith Park hills, the property was just a few steps north of the Weston's small bungalow. There, at what would become 4323 Perlita Avenue, the Krasnows constructed a home / studio out of redwood and surrounded it with a garden full of exotic succulents and specimen trees. Peter Krasnow, in his dual role as neighbor and fellow artist, soon became one of Weston's closest male friends.

A WELCOME CHANGE OF PACE   In July Weston wrote to Hagemeyer:

> I remember distinctly—I promised weekly notes—but you will forgive me for this delay—when I explain that I have been doing some really creative work—and several very good things—one both R[amiel]- and M[argrethe]- think the biggest thing I've done—
>
> —and too life has been one grand whirl—need I say more?
>
> —the "Partridges" are evidently on their way—and I may come back with them and then "walk" home…one way looms as enough "beating it"—can you return?…
>
> —write me one line to start an argument—or at least a trend of thought…my mind seems very clear—I believe this will be my best year—may it be yours too—[37]

After Imogen Cunningham and Roi Partridge arrived in Los Angeles, they stayed in Weston's home for several days.[38] Partridge was in town to finalize arrangements for a showing of forty of his etchings that was scheduled to open in September at the Los Angeles Museum of History, Science, and Art[39] and in October at the Los Angeles Public Library.[40] While Partridge tended to the business of planning his exhibitions, his wife spent several hours at the Glendale studio where she took more than a dozen photographs of Weston and Mather.

The two photographers must have greatly enjoyed the novelty of being in front of the camera for a change, because they patiently donned an array of costumes and struck an assortment of poses for Cunningham. The result was a series of memorable dual portraits. Cunningham was especially pleased with one variant in which Mather leans her head against Weston's shoulder in a gesture of tender intimacy. Cunningham would later single out this image as the one that most successfully conveys the intense emotional connection between her two colleagues.[41] In another image from the series (see frontispiece), Weston and Mather pose side by side but divert their eyes away from each other, as though they are about to head off in opposite directions. It was as though Cunningham had somehow divined the future and conjured up a portent of things to come.

Weston reciprocated by making an impressionistic portrait of Cunningham (fig. 74), strategically lighting her face so that much of it remains in shadow. His approach skillfully draws attention away from Cunningham's plain features, and instead emphasizes the graceful gesture of one hand and the lovely silhouette of her head, with its braided coil of russet hair wound tightly over one ear.

Weston also made a study of Roi Partridge standing in front of an ancient adobe near Pasadena.[42] This photograph was part of a series of portraits of contemporary artists who all had exhibitions in Los Angeles that autumn. Included were images of Ralph Pearson,[43] an etcher who had recently opened a studio in Taos, New Mexico; Arthur Millier,[44] an Englishman who had just won the California Society of Etchers' prize; and Franz (Frank) Geritz,[45] a Hungarian-born printmaker who taught art classes at various schools in and around Los Angeles. Geritz's exhibition consisted of woodblock portraits depicting several local personalities, and among them were renderings of Weston, Mather, and an attractive young man named Billy Justema.[46]

FIGURE 74. Edward Weston, *Imogen Cunningham*, 1922. Palladium print, 24.3 × 19.1 cm (9⁹/₁₆ × 7¹/₂ in.). Los Angeles, J. Paul Getty Museum, 84.XM.896.3

REBEL WITH A CAUSE   William (Billy) Justema had dropped into Weston's and Mather's lives quite unexpectedly earlier in the year.[47] On a day when Weston was absent and Mather was occupied in the darkroom, a pimply-faced, sixteen-year-old boy had suddenly appeared at the front door of the Glendale studio. The gangly teenager explained that he was an artist and a student of Xavier Martinez, a well-known Mexican-Indian painter who lived and taught in the Piedmont hills above San Francisco's East Bay. Mather was very well acquainted with Martinez. She had met him several years earlier through her friend Harriet Dean, formerly of *The Little Review*, who was now living with Martinez's ex-wife, Elsie Whitaker,[48] and it was Mather who had introduced Martinez to Weston.[49]

As soon as Martinez learned that Justema was from Glendale, he urged his pupil to make a pilgrimage to Weston's studio, so Justema arrived expecting to have a high-minded discussion about aesthetics with Weston. He soon discovered, however, that Mather's company was every bit as stimulating. As the two of them became better acquainted, it became obvious to Mather that Justema was harboring a deep-running contrarian streak. Rebelliousness was a personality trait she understood all too well, and she decided it was time to take Justema into protective custody. Years later, recalling the early days of their friendship, Justema explained, "[Margrethe Mather] would nurture and shield me, thoroughly if unwittingly corrupt me, and yet, above all else, would casually set up standards of ethical behavior and artistic excellence from which I have benefitted for over half a century."[50]

Born in Chicago in December 1905, Justema was almost twenty years Mather's junior.[51] When he was still a child, his parents had moved to Glendale,[52] where they proceeded to lead lives that were, to Justema's youthful eyes, stultifyingly boring. Long before he reached adolescence, Justema realized he was not cut out for such a banal existence. Instead he was destined to be a nonconformist whose sexual preferences ran to other attractive young men struggling to reach a place, or a state of mind, where they could lead free and uninhibited lives. Justema found Mather to be a nonjudgmental, even conspiratorial, companion who was more than willing to provide a safe harbor, and as a result they became intimate confidants.

Still recovering from Deshon's suicide and feeling bewildered that her relationship with Weston had deteriorated so dramatically, Mather was searching for her own emotional sanctuary when Justema arrived on the scene. Within weeks of their first meeting she began inviting the teenager to spend time at her Bunker Hill studio. Soon Mather and Justema were freely exchanging ideas and discussing the latest avant-garde literature and art, and before long they began to pose for each other (see fig. 75).[53] Mather photographed Justema's boyish torso against a cloudless sky,[54] and he made pencil sketches of her face and hands.[55]

The moment Justema could extricate himself from the restrictive confines of his Glendale family he rented a room on New High Street, atop a knoll that overlooked Chinatown and the Pueblo de Los Angeles. From there he could easily make daily pilgrimages to Mather's Bunker Hill studio, or she could travel to his rooftop to set up her camera. They were good for

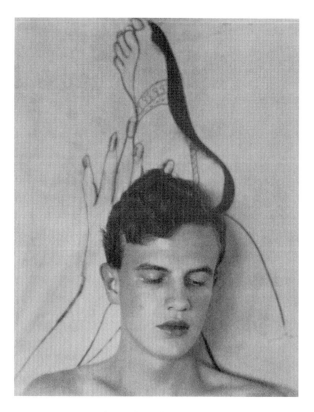

FIGURE 75. Margrethe Mather, *Billy Justema*, 1924, showing subject posing in front of one of his own drawings of Mather's hands and feet. Reproduction courtesy of Dennis Reed, Glendale, Calif.

each other. Justema supplied youthful vitality and inspiration to Mather, and she offered him the encouragement and acceptance he was unable to find elsewhere. As Weston's role in Mather's life diminished, she took great comfort in Justema's presence, and soon she began to confide anecdotal fragments of her past, embellished to suit her finest dramatic instincts, to her young and impressionable colleague.

MUSICAL GIFTS Justema soon introduced Mather to his other artistically inclined friends, and they brought much variety and interest to her everyday routine. Prominent among them were two musicians, Richard Buhlig and Henry Cowell, both of whom had begun playing the piano at an early age.

Buhlig, born in Chicago in 1880, had trained in Vienna with the legendary Theodor Leschetizky from 1897 to 1900.[56] At the age of twenty-one Buhlig made his musical debut in Berlin, followed by a series of concerts in London and New York City, but even though his career was off to a promising start, greatness somehow eluded him. In 1918 he joined the staff of the Institute of Musical Arts in Manhattan, and when the Great War finally ended he briefly returned to Europe before moving to Southern California in 1920. In Los Angeles he soon became known for his informative, preconcert lectures, delivered to Philharmonic audiences under the auspices of the Friday Morning Club,[57] and for his formidable talents as a music instructor. One of Buhlig's most promising young protégés was Henry Cowell, an extraordinarily gifted pianist and composer from Northern California.

Cowell had been born in 1897 in Menlo Park to supremely unconventional parents.[58] Harry Cowell and Clarissa Dixon Cowell were intellectuals who considered themselves philosophical anarchists, and they refused to rely on conventional schooling methods for their son's education. They also saw to it that, by the age of five, their precocious little boy had his own violin.

When young Henry's parents divorced in 1903 he remained in San Francisco with his mother, but following the 1906 San Francisco earthquake, mother and son moved back to her hometown in the Midwest where they boarded with relatives. Thus, it was in Kansas that young Henry first began to play the piano. After Clarissa Cowell was diagnosed with cancer in 1910, she and Henry returned to Northern California, and Henry became the breadwinner, "working variously as a janitor, cowherd and wildflower collector."[59]

By 1913 Cowell had so impressed professors at nearby Stanford University with his musical and conversational abilities that one of them established a fund for his support. Cowell made his formal debut as a composer/pianist at the age of seventeen, and later that same year he enrolled at the University of California, Berkeley, where he began to study with musician Charles Seeger. After Cowell's mother died in 1916, he elected to continue his musical education in Northern California, with the exception of a brief period of study at the Institute of Musical Arts in New York City, where Cowell met and was influenced by the iconoclastic pianist Leo Ornstein.

Cowell's closest associate during this period of his life was John O. Varian, an Irish-born poet who lived as a recluse at Halcyon, one of California's three Theosophist communities, located near the vast sand dunes of Oceano on California's Central Coast. Cowell spent many days at Halcyon, where he passed the time by setting a selection of Varian's eccentric texts to music.

By 1920 Cowell was already becoming known for his unusual approach to harmony, which he manifested by striking multiple piano keys with his fists and forearms to create chords he referred to as "tone clusters." Further experimentation led him to alter the sounds of the piano by plucking the strings internally or by placing various objects on top of the strings to muffle or distort the tones they produced. These techniques, which often resulted in rather startling dissonances, caused some critics to classify Cowell's innovations as the product of a disturbed mind. When musician friends introduced Cowell to Richard Buhlig he decided he would move to Los Angeles to begin studies in composition and performance with the older musician. Both men traveled in homosexual circles, so it was not long before they also became lovers.

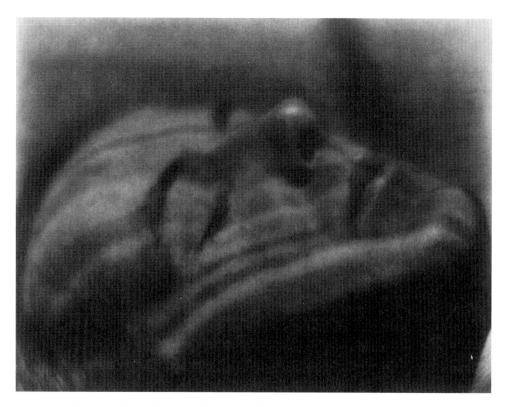

FIGURE 76. Margrethe Mather, *Henry Cowell*, ca. 1922. Platinum print, 18.5 × 27 cm (7¼ × 9⅜ in.). Scarsdale, N.Y., Collection of Michael Mattis and Judith Hochberg

Soon after Justema brought his two musician friends to meet Mather she photographed them. She first portrayed Cowell in a conventional pose, as the boyishly handsome celebrity he was about to become.[60] Then Mather did something quite extraordinary. She photographed Cowell's head positioned horizontally as though disembodied, resting on a flat surface (fig. 76), creating an image that immediately brings to mind Constantin Brancusi's abstract sculpture *Sleeping Muse*, of the previous decade.

Mather chose to render Buhlig in a tight, moody close-up (fig. 77), treating his face as a psychological map, allowing its contours, modeled by dense, somber shadows, to reveal the topography of his more mature and complex personality. At first glance Buhlig's portrait can be read as a double exposure, with his features depicted from two points of view—head-on and in three-quarter profile—an approach that can only be characterized as cubistic.

As the autumn of 1922 approached, and Mather and Weston drifted further apart, Justema became Mather's constant companion in all sorts of activities. Preoccupied with her young friend and his fascinating circle of acquaintances, Mather took it in stride when Weston announced he was going on an extended journey.

FIGURE 77. Margrethe Mather, *Richard Buhlig*, 1922. Platinum or palladium print, 24.2 × 19.1 cm (9½ × 7½ in.). Washington, D.C., Photographic History Collection, National Museum of American History, Smithsonian Institution, 3623

OUT FOR BLOOD   Ever since the beginning of the summer, Weston had been longing for a break from his everyday routine. He was in the midst of planning another trip to see Hagemeyer in San Francisco when he received a letter from his sister, offering to pay for a train ticket if he would visit her in Ohio. He happily agreed. May Seaman soon delivered on her promise, and on October 7 Weston wrote a brief note to Hagemeyer, informing him of his unexpected good fortune and advising Hagemeyer to be on the lookout for the repayment of a loan he had extended to Weston. "[This letter] written on the train for Chicago—will no doubt surprise you!" Weston jubilantly announced, "and also account for the check which Flora sent yesterday— ... wish me luck dear Johan for I am out for blood—to conquer the east!"[61]

Weston's relationship with Modotti was still going through a fallow period. After de Richey's death and her return from Mexico the previous spring, Modotti had been uncertain about whether their paths should coincide in the future. Now, as Weston was making his way east, Modotti was on her way to San Francisco to spend time with her family (and perhaps Hagemeyer). Shortly after boarding a northbound train, Modotti composed a letter that read like a tentative preamble to a more permanent farewell:

FIGURE 78. Edward Weston, *ARMCO Steel*, 1922. Palladium print, 24.4 × 19.4 cm (9⁵/₈ × 7⁵/₈ in.). Los Angeles, J. Paul Getty Museum, 86.XM.710.7

I looked out at the black night—at the houses lit from within—at the trees shadowy and mysterious—I thought of you—of your trip—of your dear letters to me and the desire to draw near you was so intense—I suffered—the best in me goes out to you my dear one. Good-bye—good-bye Edward—may you attain all you deserve—but is that possible—you give so much—how can "Life" ever pay you back? I can only send a few rose petals and a kiss—[62]

Weston thoroughly enjoyed his reunion with May and John Seaman.[63] They took him for long drives through the surrounding Ohio countryside, brilliant with intensely saturated autumn hues. He called on photographer Jane Reece and made numerous forays to photograph nearby sites of interest. One of his most memorable and productive days included an excursion to the American Rolling Mills Steel Factory, better known as ARMCO, where he shot a series of remarkable industrial studies (see fig. 78).

On this occasion, deliriously free from the confines of his portrait studio and the mundane tribulations of his domestic life, he sought out and photographed the robust geometry of the steel mill's smokestacks, depicting them as a rhythmical pattern of metallic cylinders etched against the sky. Taking his cue from Hagemeyer's *Metagama* photographs, Weston chose this moment to stake his own claim to industrial subject matter. He knew he had made an artistic breakthrough with his ARMCO pictures even before he developed the negatives, because suddenly he was seeing the world through changed eyes.

CONQUERING MANHATTAN Much to his astonishment, just as his three-week stay in Ohio was nearing an end, John and May Seaman suggested he continue his journey east, at their expense, all the way to New York City. Modotti, who was now friendly with Miriam Lerner and Betty Katz, informed Lerner of Weston's extended trip, and Lerner passed along the news to Katz:

[Edward went] to see his sister, and while there, so he wrote Tina, he got an opportunity to run over to N.Y. where he said he would stay as long as his money lasted I was very glad to hear that he had the chance to go, as N.Y. is humming now. I have that kindly feeling towards him, so that to hear of his good fortune was a pleasure. I expect he will be returning here very soon, however.[64]

Never one to miss an opportunity, Weston managed to arrange an illicit rendezvous in New York City even before he crossed the Hudson River. Meeting him at the train station was a young woman with whom he had enjoyed a brief dalliance earlier in the year. Hazel Jo Kellogg, a former pupil at the Denishawn Dance Studio, had recently come to New York City for further training, and she now welcomed Weston to her rented room in a Brooklyn brownstone at 104 Columbia Heights, directly across the East River from lower Manhattan,[65] and only a few short blocks from 56 Joralemon Street, where Weston's physician father had resided back in 1873 while he was fulfilling his medical residency requirements.[66]

Weston awoke the next morning to find the mighty cityscape of downtown Gotham laid out before him. On his right hovered the magnificent span of the Brooklyn Bridge, and across the East River a quartet of buildings dominated the horizon. The Singer Tower, the Woolworth Building, and the Equitable Building stood in a cluster along lower Broadway, near the southern tip of Manhattan Island, while the Metropolitan Life Building soared in splendid isolation at Twenty-Fourth Street and Madison Avenue, dwarfing the much smaller but oft-photographed Flatiron Building one block away. Each of the four buildings exceeded five hundred feet in height,[67] making them the tallest manmade structures in America. Weston was completely awed by New York City's scale and complexity. Los Angeles was a backwater by comparison.

Like so many tourists before and since, Weston and Jo Kellogg visited the Metropolitan Museum of Art and the Brooklyn Museum, hiked across the Manhattan Bridge, and enjoyed a hansom cab ride through Central Park at sunset, but very soon Weston got down to the business of seeking out the city's best-known photographers. He particularly enjoyed meeting Gertrude Kasebier, "a remarkable old woman" and a "brilliant" conversationalist with a "delicious" sense of humor. At the end of his visit with Kasebier he made a portrait of her, and they "parted with a fine and understanding interchange of personalities."[68] He was also favorably impressed with John Tennant, the editor of *American Photography*, especially after Tennant placed an order for one of Weston's photographs and insisted on receiving a bill.

Weston then spent an afternoon with Clarence White at 460 West 144th Street, the four-story brownstone in the Hamilton Heights neighborhood near Columbia University where White had recently relocated his school. Weston found White to be "an unusual character," and pronounced his work "disappointing" and lacking in vitality. He believed that White overemphasized design, with a resulting loss of spontaneity, and he noted that, while White was "a great admirer of the Japanese print," the inclusion of Japanese-inspired elements in his photographs often resulted in messy over-elaboration, rather than refined simplification. Weston was even less impressed with an evening spent at Nickolas Muray's Greenwich Village apartment, and he declared Muray's work "way overrated."[69]

In the midst of this whirl of activity, Weston briefly took time out to pen a breathless letter to Hagemeyer:

> By this post-mark you will know that I am—
> —two days later—you will see how hectic my life is by the above uncompleted sentence—I shall finish it now by adding "in New York"!
> This no doubt surprises you?—well it does me too!...
> I am living within a couple of minutes walk from Brooklyn bridge—across the street from Joseph Pennell—and just think Johan a room for [$]4.50 a week in New York!

I am writing especially to you at this certain moment because Clarence White told me that if he had had his way you should have had first prize in the Shadowland contest—I think you got second?—and that he was very much interested in your work which he had seen—that you seemed lacking technically but had fine vision....So did your ears burn?...

Monday night I go to a supper in honor of Gertrude Kasebier—as a guest of Clarence White—too I have hopes of finding Stieglitz—

Well Johan—no more till I reach home! I can only wish that we might be here together[70]

AN AUDIENCE WITH THE MASTER   As much as Weston was enjoying his New York City social spree, he was only biding his time until he could achieve the one goal he had so casually mentioned in his communication to Hagemeyer. He was determined to have an audience with Alfred Stieglitz. After hearing so much about Hagemeyer's encounter with Stieglitz and absorbing every issue of *Camera Work* cover to cover, Weston was not about to leave New York City without meeting the great man himself. Shortly after his arrival, Weston had telephoned Stieglitz's apartment, only to learn that his mother, Hedwig, already partially paralyzed by a stroke, was dying and Stieglitz was unavailable for appointments.

Disappointed but undeterred, Weston wrote to Stieglitz on November 8:

Greetings—
—and regrets that I should have called you at such an unopportune time—

My excuse for phoning you once more—even with the knowledge of your trouble—shall be that this chance may never come to me again—Since I leave for Mexico City in the Spring—

This is my first visit to N.Y. and I looked forward to a possible meeting with Alfred Stieglitz—indeed I might say more—that this contact I desired more than any other single event—[71]

Stieglitz replied, "Dear Mr. Weston: Thanks for your kind greetings. I shall arrange most positively to see you.—I'll let you know shortly. My mother is sinking slowly but positively.—She is unconscious."[72] His brief note was written on stationery bearing the address of his childhood home at 14 East Sixtieth Street, where he was keeping a deathwatch over his failing mother.

Four more days went by without further communication, and by November 13 Weston was beginning to lose hope. He decided to make one more attempt:

Thank you for writing me at such a distressing time—I was only hopeful of finding you in New York—not at all sure—

I am going to be perfectly frank with you—and then you can use your judgement. I am only staying on in the hope of meeting you—perhaps if I tell you that fortunately I have a room at $4.50 a week—you will understand me without further elaboration I hope I have not said this crudely—it distresses me to bother you in the face of your trouble—but you are the one person in this whole country (and photographically this surely means the world) with whom I wish a contact at this important time of my life—

If I may come I should like to bring with me a girl friend—a dancer—just starting in life—who has shared much with me—and now I would share with her—But this latter request—please use your own desire in answering.[73]

Stieglitz must have sensed Weston's desperation, because in spite of his mother's deteriorating condition he sent word that he would meet Weston and Kellogg at 60 East Sixty-Fifth Street, where he and Georgia O'Keeffe were living on the top two floors of a spacious brownstone leased by Leopold Stieglitz, Alfred's physician brother.

In a letter written to Hagemeyer on November 18, Weston triumphantly informed his colleague that at last he had succeeded in his quest:

"A maximum of detail with a maximum of simplification"—with these words as a basis for his attitude towards photography—I talked with Alfred Stieglitz for four hours—

Brilliantly—convincingly he spoke—with all the idealism and fervor of a visionary—

I saw a few of his prints too though most of them were in storage—I can only say in this brief note—they were the greatest photographs I have ever seen—And they were photographs—nothing else—And I was proud of my medium!

Steiglitz [sic] has not changed me only intensified me—Technically I was tending more and more to sharpness—any indefinite wavering line or portion distressing me greatly—So when I found he used a 13 inch anastigmat lens on an 8 × 10 plate stopped down to f.45 (not 4.5) or more—that he used a head rest! To enable him to give exposures of 3 or 4 minutes—I rejoiced in the possibilities of entirely new experimentation.... This message I send for you to ponder over till we meet![74]

A day or two later Weston jotted down a second, more complete account of his audience with the most famous photographer in America. By this time, however, his awe and excitement had subsided somewhat and his reactions to the momentous event were more measured:

[Stieglitz's] attitude towards life presented no revolutionary premise to distress me—though it was all fascinating conversation—but my work he irrefutably laid open to attack. And I am happy! I saw print after print go into the discard—prints I loved—yet I am happy! For I have gained a new foothold—a new strength—a new vision—I knew when I went there something would happen to me—I was already changing—yes changed—I had lugged these pictures of mine around New York and been showered with praise—all the time knowing them to be part of my past—indeed not hardly enthusiastic enough to put on an exhibit—I seemed to sense just what Stieglitz would say about each print—So instead of destroying or disillusioning me—he has given me more confidence and sureness—and finer aesthetic understanding of my medium—Stieglitz is absolutely uncompromising in his idealism and that I feel has been my weakness....On the other hand I feel that I was well received by Stieglitz—it was obvious that he was interested and the praise he interjected was sufficient to please me—for I know his reputation as an egoist and his rightfully intolerant attitude towards most photographic salons.[75]

CONSTRUCTIVE CRITICISM   After Hedwig Stieglitz passed away on November 21, Weston returned to Stieglitz's apartment for one last discussion about their mutual passion. This time O'Keeffe joined them, as did author and critic Herbert Seligmann. Weston had again brought along several of his photographs to show Stieglitz, and he later pondered the older photographer's comments and, in turn, his own response:

> I am still reflecting—perhaps more deliberately—on the afternoon with Stieglitz—I am not extravagant when I say it was one of the important days of my life and memories of it are burned into my heart and brain forever....if it had not been for his photographs and his conversation—I could have spent much pleasurable time in [the consideration of Georgia O'Keeffe's paintings]...they were remarkable—her lone green apple on a black tray will be as vivid ten years hence as it is today—I met her just as we were leaving and can well see how she and Stieglitz could mean so much to each other—and how he has been able to express so much through photographing her.

And then, even though he took issue with some of Stieglitz's comments, Weston acknowledged that the older man had presented him with a challenge he was determined to meet:

> Without wishing to minimize the praise I have bestowed on his work—I think Stieglitz over exaggerates the importance of several of his portraits—feeling quite sure that a number of mine are just as vital in their own way—and I believe that I prefer in some instances my own rendering of flesh and textures over the almost too revealing and inquisitive feeling that he releases—But Stieglitz gets a depth and resulting solidity and clean outline which I may miss at times...Now I have a problem to work out—to retain my own quality and rendering of values and yet achieve a more desirable depth.[76]

After seeing Weston's ARMCO photographs, Stieglitz had murmured, "You should see Sheeler's work," but then in the same breath, "No, it is not necessary." Nevertheless, Weston decided he would make the effort to meet Charles Sheeler, and in doing so, felt amply rewarded for his trouble. Afterward he declared Sheeler's images of Manhattan "the finest architectural photographs I have seen." Paul Strand happened to call on Sheeler while Weston was there, and their chance encounter led to a viewing of his photographs as well. Although Weston pronounced Strand's work "splendid," he qualified his praise by noting that Strand was "very much under the influence" of his mentor, Stieglitz.[77]

Weston's encounters with Stieglitz stimulated his creative processes and reinvigorated his determination to achieve greatness. Never before had he received such intelligent criticism and advice, and although he found fault with many of Stieglitz's observations, he was forced to reassess his work and demand more from himself as an artist. Weston left Manhattan immediately following his encounters with Sheeler and Strand, and during the train ride back to the Midwest, he memorialized his New York City adventures in several pages of hastily scribbled notes.

In Chicago he spent a few days visiting his aging Aunt Emma and Uncle Theodore Brett in their home at 2213 Washington Boulevard, where he had once sought refuge from his despised stepmother. He also reacquainted himself with photographer Eugene Hutchinson and attended a "tiresome party" with Carl Sandburg, who "apologized profusely" for the inane company.[78] Awaiting Weston's arrival in Chicago was a note from Hazel Jo Kellogg. She had experienced a very different kind of revelation as a result of his recent visit. "When you read this," she wrote, "your stay will have ended—you off to your work and I off to mine....as in L.A. you were the first to awaken me—again it has been you to continue the awakening, and some day the complete awakening will come thru you....It has been the big event of my stay here to have this visit from you...I love you, Edward dear. Jo"[79]

Weston arrived home in early December, still so dazzled by his New York City experience that he was unable to adequately express his feelings, even to Mather and Hagemeyer. He sent only a perfunctory greeting to Hagemeyer, but enclosed the pages of reminiscences he had composed during his railway journey back to Los Angeles:

> What shall I say!—except that I am home—and would see you and talk long into the night hours!—that being (perhaps) impossible I enclose the notes I made on Alfred Stieglitz—O what a trip I have had dear Johan—I can never be the same!—but have no regrets—not even asking back "my yesterday."
>
> Strange—though I have more to say to you than anyone—I can write less—it is futile—so farewell—and my love—[80]

HOME FOR THE HOLIDAYS A few days later Weston attended an exhibition of Mexican art and handicrafts that had opened in Los Angeles while he was away.[81] Overseen by Xavier Guerrero, one of Mexico's best-known artists, the display was being sponsored by the Mexican government in an effort to forge better relations with their neighbor to the north. Weston had almost postponed his visit to Ohio because he had not wanted to miss the opportunity to see the show, originally scheduled to open in October, but he had ultimately chosen the trip over the exhibition. However, when the train carrying the artworks arrived at the U.S. border, customs agents detained it because certain requisite paperwork was lacking, and for many days boxcars full of paintings and artifacts sat stranded on a rail siding until the impasse could be resolved. Weston had departed for the East, unaware that the dates of the exhibition would be extended because of this bureaucratic snarl, so he was surprised and delighted to find the exhibit still on view when he returned.

During Weston's absence, Tina Modotti had become acquainted with Guerrero, probably through Roberto Turnbull, an old friend of Robo de Richey, who had shepherded the exhibition on its journey to Los Angeles. Guerrero invited Modotti to assist him in his administrative duties before, during, and after the exhibition opening on November 10,[82] and as the two worked side by side, an attraction grew between them. It was probably only Weston's return to Los Angeles that prevented their relationship from developing further. The Mexican display was well received by the public and critics alike, and the positive publicity it generated helped ease the way for an even more important exhibition, organized by the Society of Independent Artists of Mexico under the direction of muralist Diego Rivera, which would go on display at the Waldorf-Astoria Hotel in Manhattan in February 1923.[83]

Weston had also missed the opening of the Camera Pictorialists' exhibition on November 20. Mather had contributed three photographs and, once again, her work was well received. The reviewer for *Saturday Night* magazine wrote, "Maragarethe Mather's 'Water Lily' [fig. 79] for sheer loveliness, stands alone in the collection. Sunlight, like an evanescent ray of beauty, catches the gleam of itself in the white of the lily, the glass bowl, the clear water and melts away in the silvered glow of the bowl beneath."[84]

With the holidays fast approaching, Weston found himself in no mood for the usual festive rituals. He lacked pocket money for frivolous Christmas expenditures, and he was growing more and more disillusioned with the increasingly restrictive atmosphere in Los Angeles. An ultraconservative organization, the Better America Federation (BAF)[85]—led by businessman Harry Haldeman[86] and bolstered by editorials in Harry Chandler's *Los Angeles Times*—was still trying to stem the rising tide of unionization. The same group was actively engaged in "red-baiting" in an attempt to discredit social reformers of all stripes, including educators, religious leaders, and members of the newly organized American Civil Liberties Union (which Prince Hopkins had helped to found, alongside his friend Roger Baldwin).[87]

Adding to this unsavory turn of events was the alarming fact that Los Angeles, formerly a city with a thriving downtown, was fast becoming decentralized into many disparate districts surrounded by blocks of residential sprawl. Although decentralization had initially been touted by city planners as the solution to freeing up the bottlenecks of congestion that hampered movement in the downtown business district, this new pattern of development had, in fact, produced even more traffic problems throughout the Los Angeles basin. Automobiles were now

FIGURE 79. Margrethe Mather, *Water Lily*, 1922. Platinum or palladium print, 18.7 × 23.8 cm (7³/₈ × 9³/₈ in.). The Lane Collection, Museum of Fine Arts, Boston

clogging virtually every transportation artery, making travel from one area to another a time-consuming and frustrating chore.[88] Amplifying this problem was the city's unprecedented population growth. Since 1920 more than 100,000 newcomers had been arriving every year, eager to become Angelenos. The city of Los Angeles was no longer the paradise Colonel Otis and Harry Chandler had so enthusiastically and successfully promoted two decades earlier.[89]

On top of Weston's disgruntlement over the general state of affairs in Los Angeles, his personal life was now in a state of complete disarray. His conflicts with Flora had been exacerbated by his recent absence and Flora's understandable insecurities. It was perhaps inevitable that the year 1922 would end in a cataclysmic scene between Weston and his wife. After receiving a holiday greeting from Ramiel McGehee, Weston wrote a tormented response:

> Dear—dear Ramiel how beautiful your letter was!—what would I do without you and Tina these days—I fear the whirlwind is upon me—and perhaps if it comes too near engulfing me I shall call for you in my distress—for I have fought so long—I am weary—so tired—O why all this—when beauty is everywhere—to those who are not blinded—know that I have seldom loved as I love you—Edward—Dec—28—1922[90]

FIGURE 80. Edward Weston, *Flora Weston*, 1918. Gelatin silver print, 24.1 × 18.6 cm (9 1/2 × 7 5/16 in.). Los Angeles, J. Paul Getty Museum, 86.xm.719.12

The Weston marriage was finally, after fourteen years, coming apart at the seams. In trying to provide a stable home for her boys, Flora Weston (see fig. 80) had long ignored pointed comments from friends and family regarding her husband's wandering eye, but she was now beginning to face the fact that her marriage was a sham. There were even times when she blamed herself, using Mather as an unlikely sounding board. Mather later recalled Flora's confidences in a note to Ramiel McGehee:

> She [Flora] wept around here one a.m. after Edward's first Stieglitz letter—blaming herself for holding Edward back—I told her—in front of Tina—that she was responsible for Edward's success—without the balance of her and the children—the forced responsibility—Edward would have been like the rest of us—dreaming—living in attics—living a free life (O God!) etc. etc. not growing and producing as he had. Opinions to the contrary Edward is as gregarious as anyone I know—Flora seemed grateful for my words but soon forgot them.[91]

By the end of the year Weston had reached the conclusion that it was time to take his leave from Flora, the children, and Los Angeles. Mather was not convinced he was making a wise decision. She blamed Modotti for putting the idea of Mexico into Weston's head and encouraging him to abandon the responsibilities of home and family.

Of course, Edward had never admitted to his wife that any sort of romantic entanglement existed between him and Modotti. Instead he continued to assure the gullible Flora that Modotti was merely accompanying him to Mexico as his apprentice, and that he had agreed to take her along so he could teach her about the technical aspects of photography and thus enable her to become self-sufficient. Maintaining that his own reasons for leaving Los Angeles were purely professional, he argued that Mexico would provide fresh artistic inspiration and an opportunity for unprecedented economic success, a conclusion he supported by pointing to the sales that had been generated by his 1922 exhibition in Mexico City.

Mather, however, was painfully aware of the true nature of Weston's and Modotti's relationship, and she could anticipate rough times ahead for Weston. She must have foreseen that he was setting himself up to experience the same extremes of emotion he had so often provoked in her, and Mather knew that those feelings of jealousy and betrayal would only result in misery and regret.

Endings and Beginnings, 1923

B y the time Weston wrote to Hagemeyer in mid-January, a crisis had been reached:

> I send you more notes which for obvious reasons please destroy—but send on the Stieglitz notes to Roi [Partridge] and Imogen [Cunningham]. Many things have happened to me too. I am living at the studio—a definite break having come at last—and Ruth [Deardorff-] Shaw who caused the trouble is living with Flora!
>
> We leave for Mexico in March. Tina—Chandler—and I—this seems quite definite at this writing—
>
> I am working desparately [sic] in order to "burn my bridges" behind me. Shall we meet again? I hope in some far off country—perhaps sooner?[1]

Weston now began in earnest to lay the groundwork for his departure, but his efforts were Sisyphean. No sooner had he ventured one step forward, than he was forced to take two in the opposite direction. On February 7 he sent McGehee a fragment of a letter from his sister in which she had referred to Ramiel as a "dear boy,"[2] prompting Weston to comment:

> Yes—you are a "dear boy"—and don't think I have not thought of you—but God! How swiftly do events move on—Ruth [Deardorff-Shaw] and family have left—!!? Brett is going to Ohio—Cole and Neil have the measles. Margrethe has been very sick—Tina and I go to Claremont Sunday—I have not been able to get in to tell Jack [Taylor] your trouble—will today—Love—love—Edward[3]

Busy as he was, Weston knew he must attend to several personal and professional obligations before he could leave the country with a clear conscience. One involved a commitment he had made a year and a half earlier after receiving a letter from A. J. Olmstead, who had described himself as the "custodian" of the Photography Section of the United States National Museum, a division of the Smithsonian Institution in Washington, D.C. Olmstead had written requesting a representative sampling of Weston's photographs for inclusion in the Smithsonian's collection, which Olmstead was attempting to build into a meaningful survey of nineteenth- and early twentieth-century photography. Surprised and delighted by Olmstead's interest, Weston had immediately responded:

I shall be glad to send a collection of my work to the Institute as you suggest. Photography as one of the most vital means of expressing this strenuous age in which we live should have some recognition at the hands of the government—May I ask a few questions—Is the collection to be a permanent one? About how many prints from one individual do you wish?

My own idea would be to send on a print or so (after the first set were submitted) every time I made something I considered worth preserving—...

May I suggest that the work of Margrethe Mather—715 West Fourth Los Angeles—is worth your consideration—In fact she is one of the best pictorialists of the day—[4]

Weston had inexplicably failed to act on the Smithsonian's request, however, and he had recently received a follow-up inquiry. This time Weston replied:

I have not forgotten our correspondence—but the exigencies—even trivialities of life—have so far intervened!...

I would suggest the name of Johan Hagemeyer...as worthy of your attention.[5]

A few days later Weston sent off a package containing fourteen photographs. Nine of the images were his: *Ramiel in His Attic*, *Epilogue*, *Fragment of a Nude* (Anne Brigman),[6] *Girl in Canton Chair* (Tina Modotti),[7] *The Source* (aka *The Breast*) (Tina Modotti),[8] *Roubaix de l'Abrie Richey*, *Head of an Italian Girl* (Tina Modotti),[9] *The Ascent of Attic Angles*, and *Prologue to a Sad Spring* (Margrethe Mather). Five were Mather's: *Dr. William F. Mack, Roentgenologist*,[10] *Roentgenologist* (another portrait of Mack), *Pierrot* (Otto Matiesen), *Richard Buhlig — Pianist*, and *Portrait of a Lady* (aka *Portrait of Judith*).

In early February Olmstead acknowledged receipt of the package, "Your and Miss Mather['']s pictures came this morning and I wish to thank you for them they will make a material addition to our exhibit and are an addition of a forward looking type of the pictorial that we did not have."[11] As a result of Olmstead's persistence and foresight, the Smithsonian became the first museum in America to acquire Weston and Mather photographs for its permanent collection.

A FRANK APPRAISAL   With that important task accomplished, Weston tackled the rest of his outstanding correspondence. One of his letters conveyed long overdue words of gratitude to Alfred Stieglitz:

Because I have not told you so before must not lessen the intensity of a message I now send—that my brief contact with you was the most vitally important of my life—and my appreciation of the time and energy you gave so freely—is none the less sincere because of my long silence....

I often ponder over just what it was you gave to me—those several short hours in New York—Your attitude towards life presented no revolutionary premise to distress me—nor did your criticism of my work annoy me—for I seemed to sense and accept—at least most always—just what you had to say—I was already changing—yes changed—for the work I did on the way to N.Y. indicates a quite different mental attitude from that which I showed to you—What I wish you to feel and what I believe you would be glad to know—is—that you have intensified me in my own direction—given me more sureness and confidence—and finer aesthetic understanding of my medium—What I felt in you—was the fervor and idealism of a visionary—and the great love of the craftsman I have dreamed and loved—but compromised—sold myself to the public—and to lens concerns—not absolutely—but enough to keep food in the bellies of four boys—and shoes on their feet—As I look back—perhaps I could not have done otherwise—you see I make excuses! Well the future will tell—I leave for Mexico City in late March to start life anew—why—I hardly know myself—but I go—

I shall always work—seek—experiment—I prey [*sic*] never to become formulated—I shall have to make money—but somewhere within there will always be that flame of desire which has never been smothered—and which you fanned once more into a fiercer glow—

I turn alternately hot and cold—remembering some of your photographs—those based on the mons veneris—the breasts—the hands sewing—and Georgia O'Keefe's [*sic*] paintings too—her lone green apple on a black tray—how vividly it still remains!

Please remember me to her and to Mr. Seligmann—also to Paul Strand and Charles Sheeler—whose very very excellent work I was forced to view so hurriedly on my last afternoon in N.Y. I saw in the Chicago Art Institute a drawing by Mr. Sheeler which gave me as pure joy as anything I viewed in the building—

Enclosed find two dollars for a few of the "Manuscripts"—I should like them from the start if possible, especially No. 2—with the article by Strand—I shall subscribe further from Mexico—when I am definitely established—[12]

However, Weston was forced to delay his departure. In mid-March Hagemeyer wrote to say he was coming to Los Angeles for one last visit, and Weston eagerly responded:

I too have been wondering—was I to see you again! So your note thrilled me strangely. Do come—I feel we must meet again before the expedition leaves!—which will be about one month away—

I too have much work ahead—should like most of it out of the way before your arrival—How about two weeks or so from now? But suit your own time and come—no matter when![13]

THE PALM SPRINGS DIVA AND HER BABYLON   While he waited for Hagemeyer's arrival, Weston busied himself with several lucrative portrait commissions. One of his most important new clients, Lois Kellogg, came to his studio at the behest of Betty Katz. Kellogg was Katz's ersatz employer in Palm Springs, although their relationship amounted to much more than a business arrangement.

Kellogg hailed from Chicago where her birth had been the result of a merger between two of the city's most prominent families.[14] Her maternal grandfather, Charles P. Kellogg, had founded a wholesale clothing business that placed him solidly within the ranks of Chicago's most successful entrepreneurs. In the 1880s Charles Kellogg had built a lavish home on Prairie Avenue, a South Side thoroughfare then generally considered the "most expensive street in America west of Fifth Avenue."[15] His next-door neighbors were Marshall Field Sr., founder of the eponymous department store, and his playboy son, Marshall Jr. Down the block lived Philip Danforth Armour, the meatpacking magnate, and George Mortimer Pullman, manufacturer of state-of-the-art railroad cars.[16] Charles Kellogg fathered three children, but only one, a daughter named Emma Lois, survived childhood. She went on to marry the son of another of Chicago's most illustrious citizens, Edward Swift Isham.

Edward Isham, a graduate of Williams College, had enjoyed a career as a respected lawyer and member of the Illinois State Legislature prior to becoming the law partner of Robert Todd Lincoln, eldest son of the slain American President, in 1872. Edward Isham's son, Pierrepont, joined his father's illustrious law firm after graduating from West Point Military Academy and serving a term in the United States Army. Pierrepont Isham and Lois Kellogg were wed in 1893, and in September 1894 they became the parents of a daughter, named after her mother. The Ishams' marriage was troubled, however. Pierrepont was a heavy drinker, and in 1899 Lois Isham filed for a divorce.[17] She subsequently renounced her married surname, and she and her daughter became known as Lois Kellogg Sr. and Jr.

Around 1913 Lois Sr. was diagnosed with tuberculosis, so she and her daughter headed west to seek out the sea air and health resorts of Santa Barbara. The arid climate of the California desert proved more agreeable, however, and they soon relocated to the tiny, remote village of Palm Springs in the Coachella Valley, a vast expanse of mostly uninhabited land east of Los Angeles. To pass the time while her mother rested, Lois Jr., already an accomplished equestrienne, began taking daily rides through the desert, and it was on one of these excursions that she first encountered Betty Katz. The two women struck up a friendship, and it was not long before Lois Jr. engaged Katz to be her companion/secretary, a convenient camouflage for their much more intimate status as lovers.[18]

In spite of the dry Palm Springs climate, Lois Sr. was unable to fight off her lung-ravaging disease, and when she finally succumbed in June 1918,[19] twenty-three-year-old Lois Jr. (fig. 81) became the sole beneficiary of her mother's share of the Kellogg family fortune. The beautiful young heiress then proceeded to immerse herself in the social whirl demanded by her position

FIGURE 81. Unidentified photographer, Lois Kellogg, ca. 1923. Gelatin silver print, 10.2 × 15.3 cm (4 × 6 in.). Breckenridge, Col., Collection of Martin Lessow

in life, flitting from city to city and country to country, with Betty Katz accompanying her as often as her own health would permit. Between journeys, as a respite from their peripatetic lives, the two women always returned to Palm Springs, eager to spend time in their desert hideaway.

Kellogg's Palm Springs retreat consisted of three very modest buildings strung along Main Street (later renamed Palm Canyon Drive), near Tahquitz Canyon. Surprisingly primitive, these structures were intended as purely temporary accommodations, because Kellogg's ultimate goal was to erect a much larger, infinitely grander manse on her property. She envisioned her new home as an exotic haven, complete with intricately patterned Moroccan and Persian tile, highly polished wood floors, elaborately carved doors, and a sixty-five-foot swimming pool, and she had already named her imaginary desert oasis after the ancient Mesopotamian city of Babylon.[20]

Architect Harold Bryant Cody, who had designed Kellogg's three temporary dwellings, was also in charge of executing the renderings for Babylon.[21] He had been introduced to Kellogg and Katz by his wife, Harriet Dowie, who ran a stable across the street from Kellogg's property. Cody, trained as an architect at the University of Pennsylvania, had come to Los Angeles around 1910 to join the firm of John Parkinson and Edwin Bergstrom, the well-known architects of the Alexandria Hotel and the Los Angeles Athletic Club.

Around 1912 Cody left their firm to begin working for architect Myron Hunt, who had only recently completed the Beverly Hills Hotel, and who would later become famous for his reinterpretation and popularization of the Spanish Mission vernacular throughout Southern

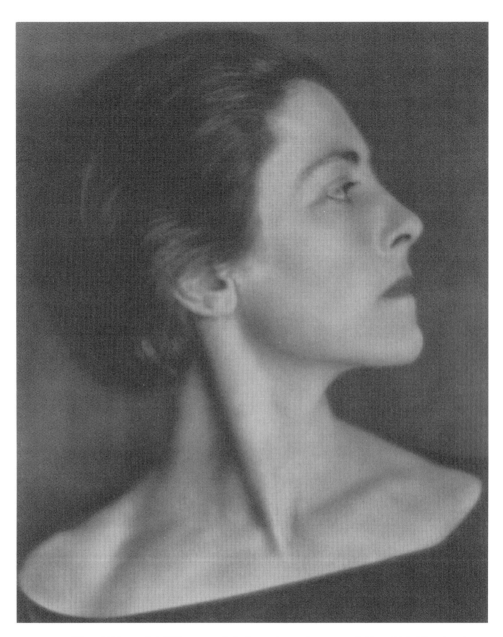

FIGURE 82. Edward Weston, *Lois Kellogg*, 1923. Palladium print, 23.8 × 19.1 cm (9 3/8 × 7 1/2 in.). Los Angeles, J. Paul Getty Museum, 85.XM.250.1

California, and particularly in Santa Barbara. Cody assisted Hunt on many important commissions, including the makeover of Henry Huntington's hotel in Pasadena, but after four years in Hunt's office, the ambitious Cody moved on to found his own firm, in partnership with another young architect, Lester H. Hibbard.

Cody and Hibbard opened their practice with a flourish by winning the commission to design two of the earliest buildings at the University of California's Citrus Experimental Station in Riverside, but Cody was soon forced to quell his ambitions when he developed breathing difficulties, which subsequently led to a diagnosis of tuberculosis. As his lung capacity deteriorated, Cody and his wife were forced to seek out a more hospitable climate, and around 1920 they, too, settled in Palm Springs, where Harriet Cody opened her riding stable as a means of supporting her ailing husband and their young daughter. The Codys soon became acquainted with their neighbors, Kellogg and Katz, and it was likely Katz who provided them with introductions to Weston, Mather, Ramiel McGehee, and Tina Modotti.

In the spring of 1923, when Lois Kellogg came to Weston's studio to be photographed, she was twenty-eight years old, svelte, and self-assured. Back in her hometown of Chicago, Kellogg had been considered one of the city's best-dressed debutantes, but in the relaxed atmosphere of rural Palm Springs she was free to adapt her apparel to meet her immediate needs. Depending on her activities, her attire might include dungarees, spurs, and a cowboy hat one day and a Worth gown the next.

Kellogg also cultivated a diverse group of friends who broadened her interests and sharpened her wit. Her hospitality was legendary, as was the celebrity of her guests—Alla Nazimova and Rudolph Valentino were reportedly frequent visitors—and Kellogg went to great trouble and expense to supply her friends with all the comforts, luxuries, and forbidden delicacies large amounts of money could buy. Motoring around the dusty dirt roads of Palm Springs in her imported Hispano-Suiza sedan, Kellogg cut quite a swashbuckling figure, but in Weston's portraits she assumes the role of the haughty, imperious socialite she had been brought up to be (see fig. 82), rather than the roguish, idiosyncratic adventuress she had since become.

TOO GERMANIC   That spring Weston also made a number of portraits of Karl Struss, the renowned photographer who was already well on his way to becoming an even more famous cinematographer.[22] Beginning in 1908, Struss had enrolled in several of Clarence White's photography courses, and from there he went on to enjoy a highly successful photography career in New York City, where his activities included an editorship on the influential but short-lived journal *Platinum Print*, alongside his former instructor, White.

However, Struss's career came to an abrupt standstill following the outbreak of the Great War. Although his father was an American of German heritage, his mother had been born in Germany, and in 1909 Struss had spent ten weeks traveling with his family through his mother's homeland and other European countries. Quite naturally the tour had left him with feelings of loyalty toward his ancestral land, and he was devastated when America declared war on Kaiser Wilhelm and his territorial aggressions. Nevertheless, in spite of his feelings of loyalty toward Germany, as soon as America formally entered the fray Struss enlisted and was immediately put to work teaching photography skills to new recruits.

At the end of his first month in the Army, Struss was made a sergeant and appointed an instructor at the newly opened School of Military Aeronautics at Cornell University. His budding military career was cut short, however, when one of Struss's acquaintances sent a memo to the Department of Justice hinting that Struss should be carefully investigated because of his pro-German sentiments. The memo also pointed out that he was in a particularly strategic position to aid the enemy if he chose to do so. Shortly thereafter, government agents began to interrogate Struss's friends.

Interviews with his former colleagues Edward R. Dickson and Clarence White provided confirmation that Struss had, indeed, publicly expressed strong pro-German opinions. Within weeks Struss was relieved of his duties at Cornell and taken into custody. Curiously though, instead of being jailed as a suspected spy, Struss was assigned to the Vocational Training Department of the federal prison at Fort Leavenworth, Kansas, the Midwestern counterpart to the prison on McNeil Island in Puget Sound, where a large number of IWW members and conscientious objectors were being detained.[23] Nevertheless, rumors persisted within the photography community that Struss himself was incarcerated.

The ultimate insult to Struss came in May 1918 when the Pictorial Photographers of America, an organization he had founded along with White and Dickson, formally requested his resignation. Devastated that his colleagues would turn on him with such finality, Struss distracted himself from his unpleasant predicament by attending movies, carefully analyzing the effectiveness of each camera angle and the placement of every light source. At war's end Struss was given an honorable discharge, even though the accusations of his former colleagues were never expunged from his records. Wishing to leave the military and his turncoat friends in New York City as far behind as possible, Struss immediately boarded a train headed for California, where he had decided he was going to pursue a career in the movie business.

Only three weeks after his arrival in Hollywood, Struss was successful in landing a job as a still photographer at Famous Players–Lasky Studios, working with their most important director, Cecil B. DeMille. Unbeknownst to Struss, during the war DeMille had been a clandestine informer on behalf of the Justice Department, using his studio ties to provide information about individuals he employed or casual acquaintances he met at Hollywood social functions. It was, therefore, particularly ironic that Struss's initial success in Hollywood was achieved while working on one of DeMille's pictures.

On Valentine's Day 1920, almost exactly one year after his arrival in California, Struss was introduced to a young woman named Ethel Wall. The two were married in early 1921, just as he was beginning to parlay his career as a still photographer into a position as a fledgling

FIGURE 83. Edward Weston, *Karl and Ethel Struss*, 1923. Palladium print, 24 × 18.7 cm (9⁷/₁₆ × 7³/₈ in.). Los Angeles, J. Paul Getty Museum, 85.xm.257.4

cinematographer, and by the time Struss posed for Weston he was already well on his way to accruing an enviable reputation as a master of both mediums. In one of Weston's photographs of the multitalented Struss, he utilized a movie camera as the principal design element.[24] In another he created a tenderly romantic dual portrait of Struss and his wife (fig. 83). It was probably around this same time that Margrethe Mather wrote a brief note to Struss, congratulating him on his recent accomplishments as a cinematographer:

> Karl Struss—
> Will you accept my compliments upon your fine photography in the film at the Rialto?
> it was truly a delight!
> Some
> bits *perfection*—Margrethe Mather

Weston also spent time on several occasions that spring photographing his son Neil in the nude.[25] These bold images were the first in a series of nude studies that would command Weston's attention over the next several weeks.

A KIND OF FAREWELL   As March merged into April, Weston still had not heard from Hagemeyer regarding the dates of his upcoming Los Angeles visit. Weston was anticipating a short trip of his own, and he did not want to be absent when his friend arrived:

> If possible let me know when you expect to leave—so that I may plan ahead. I am going on a little adventure the latter part of this week—to be away for two or three days—and do not want to miss you. However if you arrive when I am gone—make your self at home as usual! Tina will have care of the studio I think—so you will not be without company!
>
> This trip just mentioned is a kind of farewell—so you will understand.
>   I await with great happiness your arrival![26]

The farewell mentioned by Weston may have been the occasion of his final tryst with Margrethe Mather. It was likely during those stolen days they spent together that she posed for two separate series of nude studies. In the first group of images, Mather stands or sits in front of a paneled screen, employing various props, including an assortment of vases, a small trunk, a pair of embroidered Chinese slippers, and a feathered fan, to add visual interest.[27] When viewed as a sequence these images become an exercise in rhythm and light, with Mather's figure acting as the focal point around which the compositions revolve. The most extraordinary element in all of the pictures, however, is the silvery luminescence emanating from the paneled screen behind her. One variant (fig. 84) is especially reminiscent of Mather's portrait of Maud Emily Taylor seated in a Chinese chair (see fig. 43), taken some five years earlier. It is one more instance in which Weston, deliberately or not, references Mather's work in his own.

FIGURE 84. Edward Weston, *Nude* (Margrethe Mather), 1923. Gelatin silver print, 15.4 × 21 cm (6¹/₁₆ × 8¹/₄ in.). Los Angeles, J. Paul Getty Museum, 85.XM.257.2

The second series of images, a sequence of tight close-ups of Mather's nude torso (see fig. 85), is unabashedly voyeuristic. As Mather reclines on the sands of Redondo Beach, bathed in blazing sunlight and framed against the spiny whorl of a paper parasol, one can imagine Weston hovering above her, crouching beneath the black drape covering his camera lens, ravishing her body, picking out its most intimate details, and preserving them for all the world to see.

Although Mather's torso is carefully cropped at the neck and thighs, so as to preserve her anonymity, Weston's images are neither discreet nor coy. Rather they are sharply focused and daringly seen, with each pore and hair and every crystalline grain of sand recorded on the ground glass with spectacular clarity. Although Weston was undoubtedly inspired by Stieglitz's frank studies of Georgia O'Keeffe, which he had viewed a few months earlier, his nudes of Mather are much more shockingly realistic. With Mather as his malleable and willing subject, Weston took another important stride down the path toward modernity in these images.

In a handful of contact proofs from their session on the beach, Mather is outstretched on the sand, basking in the sun. In one she lies facedown and tucks her head into the crook of one arm;[28] in another she props herself up on her elbows as she tilts her head sharply backward.[29] In still another, a fully clothed Ramiel McGehee, sheltered from the glaring sun by an unfurled,

FIGURE 85. Edward Weston, *Nude* (Margrethe Mather), 1923. Gelatin silver print, 18.9 × 23.5 cm (7³/₈ × 9¹/₄ in.). Tucson, Center for Creative Photography, University of Arizona, 81:151:31

black umbrella, sits next to Mather as she reclines, nude and completely exposed to the elements.[30] Although Mather is seemingly oblivious to the photographer and the shrouded tripod beside her, McGehee stares directly at the camera lens in an amusing, if unwitting, twist on Edouard Manet's famously scandalous painting, *Le Déjeuner sur l'herbe*. (Thirteen years later these images of Mather would serve as the prototypes for another, far more famous series of nudes of Charis Wilson reclining amidst the wind-sculpted sand dunes of Oceano, adjacent to the Theosophist community of Halcyon.)[31]

Weston and Mather's Redondo Beach assignation was a memorable episode, which he would later fondly recall as "that last terrific week with her, before leaving for Mexico."[32] It was as if Mather, suddenly registering the import of Weston's pending departure, was finally offering herself fully and unreservedly to him. Possibly she was trying to convince him to stay, or more likely she was simply seizing the opportunity to collaborate with him one last time. Even though the flame of their physical attraction was briefly reignited during their seaside rendezvous, it was too late for Weston to change course.

VIVID HOURS   Hagemeyer's long anticipated arrival came on April 11. Weston met him at the train station, and the two friends stayed awake half the night talking. Delighted to see each other again, they passed much of the next ten days together. According to Hagemeyer's diary, he also spent a significant amount of time with Modotti, and his cryptic notes seem to indicate that his trip south had as much to do with seeing her again as with bidding Weston farewell:

> [Thursday, April 12]—supper at Edward's house back to studio at night
>
> [Friday, April 13]—Supp. in town with M.[argrethe] & E.[dward]—show
>
> [Saturday, April 14]—Stojana & Tina . . . out at studio—great great day—red tulips—night at house
>
> [Sunday, April 15]—T.[ina] M.[argrethe] E.[dward] & I walking at the tile factory . . . later all at Stojana—what a day!!! oh! T.[ina]—drunken with pictures, wine, rose petals—[33]

Hagemeyer also recorded their visit to the tile factory on film (see fig. 86). Lagging behind his three friends, he photographed them as they walked along, engrossed in conversation. In Hagemeyer's snapshot, Weston's box camera is slung over his shoulder and Mather and Modotti carry assorted pieces of photographic equipment. They appear to be walking along Los Feliz Boulevard, heading west toward the nearby tile factory grounds, where they would spend several hours photographing the geometrical forms of the factory's impressive kilns and chimneys. In casually snapping this candid of his three friends, Hagemeyer accidentally recorded a confluence of personalities that would never again occur.

Hagemeyer's diary continued:

> [Monday, April 16]—T.[ina] & I developing out with T.[ina]—met [Otto] Stade in Hollywood bookstore—there met Bengt Berg from Sweden (author)—together out for dinner—european style—wedding night—willow—confession
>
> [Tuesday, April 17]—rain hail thunder—T.[ina] not out—
>
> [Wednesday, April 18]—a night at Richard Bulig [sic] with Marg., Edw. and Billy Justema—young painter and poet—Bulig [sic] read "Waste Land" and other things—great night—walked till 2 am with Edward in rain to river
>
> [Thursday, April 19]—with Tina to Stojana—copying [—] walk through the hills—musterd [sic] path
>
> [Friday, April 20]—Stojana with Tina (copying) Helen Cole at studio and supper—
>
> [Saturday, April 21]—Brahms, Debussy, Strauss at Philharmonic (Rothwell splendid) last car home—(sailor hangout on 4th Street)

FIGURE 86. Attributed to Johan Hagemeyer (Dutch, 1884–1962), *Edward, Tina, and Margrethe: To the Tile Factory*, April 1923. Gelatin silver print, 9.4 × 7.2 cm (3⅝ × 2¾ in.). Rochester, N.Y., George Eastman House, International Museum of Photography and Film, 1974:0061:0144

[Sunday, April 22]—to Stojana in afternoon with E. (pipes) Margrethe out at studio at night for general discussion (2 am)[34]

Weston also kept an account of their time together, jotting down bits and pieces of their conversations about photography. After his meeting with Stieglitz, Weston was now convinced that all photographs should be sharply focused. Hagemeyer, however, defended his preference for a more interpretative approach, one that would take full advantage of diffuse lighting and a soft focus lens as a means of conveying a particular mood or creating a tangible atmospheric effect. Both men believed they were correct as they each advanced their own aesthetic precepts, and their discussions, which often extended into the early morning hours, were both exhaustive and exhausting:

> [Friday, April 20, 1923]…Johan is here—has been here for over a week—Days and nights of intensity—burning discourses on many topics—of course mostly photography!
>
> Johan brought new work—fine industrial things—nicely seen—but lacking in definition—an inexcusable fault when it comes to photographing modern architecture and machinery—even the "mood" could be better interpreted with sharp—clean lines.[35]

Back and forth they went, arguing and debating, with Hagemeyer insisting that in some instances a diffusion lens was useful, and Weston replying:

> Yes, it would aid you—to cloud and befog the real issue—and prevent you from telling the truth about the life towards which your lens is pointing—if you wish to "interpret" why not use a medium better suited to interpretation or subjective expression—or—let some one else do it—Photography is an objective means to an end—and as such is unequaled—It comes finally to the question: For what purpose should the camera be used?—and I believe you have misused it—along with many others—including myself![36]

The following day Hagemeyer said his good-byes and made his way north again. This time, however, he was not returning to San Francisco but to the small village of Carmel-by-the-Sea, where he had been residing since the previous November. Like his friend Weston, Hagemeyer was about to make a significant change in his life. He intended to build a studio in Carmel because he felt such a strong affinity for its wide, white beach of shifting sand dunes, a landscape he found strangely reminiscent of his native Holland, and although it had taken him five years to convince her, Lula Boyd Stephens had finally left her husband, and when the time was right she would be joining him in Carmel.

Weston greatly enjoyed the intensity of his dialogue with Hagemeyer, but was relieved to see his friend depart:

April 25 Quiet again—Johan beat his way north on Monday—I am glad to be alone—we love one another—but wear each other out—I really believe we would finally quarrel if thrown together too many succeeding days—I gave him a print of my "Stacks" [one of the ARMCO Steel images]—"I have never before demanded a print from you Edward—but I must have a copy of that"—He would return again and again to it—"It is a thing I wish I had made—but I'm glad you did it for me to enjoy—for I feel I could have done it."[37]

Weston also related details of their social activities of the previous week and one evening in particular that he had found memorably titillating:

Together or with Tina or Margrethe—sometimes all four of us—we spent many vivid hours—at [Gjura] Stojana's—the Philharmonic—once an evening with Buhlig listening to his reading of that amazing poem Waste Land by T. S. Eliot—and looking over Billy Justema's drawings—listening too—to his reading—That night it rained—and returning to the studio still keyed to adventure—we donned old hats and walked into the rain—I took him to the river—winding our way among the dripping willows—around us the silence of hours past midnight—Bedraggled and drenched we reached home—but thrilled with the beauty we had had....

Margrethe ever curious had heard of a Greek coffee house near Los Angeles Street where sailors gathered—there had been a murder committed there and fights were a nightly occurrence—So we went—and though not favored with a murder or fight had a sufficiently exciting night—yes a fascinating night—

A room full of sailors with here and there a collarless nondescript—but mostly those not in full uniform were that type of effeminate male who seek the husky sailor to complement their lacking vigour—One such fastidiously-dressed—unmistakable person—presented to us a most lascivious picture of impatient desire—his foot twitched continually—his whole body quivered—his lips fairly drooled—until finally with several others of his kind—a bunch of sailors were "dated up" and off they went in a limousine—Sailors danced together with biting of ears and open caresses—some sprawled over their tables down and out—every one had a bottle on the hip—while an officer of the law amiably overlooked his opportunity to enforce the 18th amendment—

A Negro droned on the saxaphone—or "sexaphone" as Margrethe calls it—another picked the banjo—the four or five waitresses watched their chance to pocket tips or pick the pockets of drunken "gobs"—one sailor prize fighter reeled to our table loudly confiding his troubles—the quarrel he had "with that 'gold digger' over there"—had us feel his muscles and related his life history—

Margrethe was the only girl in the place besides the waitresses—But we were too differently dressed—too conspicuous and I wonder we did not land in the street—I should like to go again under different circumstances.[38]

THE END IN SIGHT   On May 28 Weston wrote again to Stieglitz. He seemed to feel completely comfortable baring his soul to the older photographer, perhaps because Stieglitz had once faced similar quandaries. Weston was weary from his recent labors and disgusted with his own shortcomings, and Margrethe Mather was very much on his mind:

> This letter again comes from California—not Mexico City! However—the Gods willing and the winds and tides propitious—we sail June 21—This last month has been choas [sic] otherwise I should have written and thanked you for the fine letter you sent me—I have made sitting after sitting until my hand is exhausted and my nerves gone—for to satisfy something within I cannot help expending much energy upon the least of those who come to me—
>
> But the reaction comes from attempting too much and finding one's self going round in circles—and—knowing that I lie—lie about my subjects—lie to myself—I put in my work-room a card signed "E.W." which reads "I am a Liar"—this acknowledgment satisfies my ego—I get perverse joy in this mental lashing—admitting to myself that after all I know better!
>
> There is much sadness too on leaving—leaving a place where once one had dreams—and there is the poignant bitter-sweet of unfulfilled hopes—desires unattained—O yes the keenest regret of all is the realization that an association which should have reached a wonderful flowering has instead been always destined to frosting in the bud—...
>
> The manuscripts and Broom were greatly enjoyed—I should like if obtainable several copies of "Number Four"—for Margrethe Mather and myself—also a copy of Number One and Two for her—and if you can spare a catalogue of your late exhibit—I should like that for her too—John Tennant sent one to me—I wish that I might have seen it! Are catalogues of your first exhibit obtainiable [sic]? If so two copies—always "two" you see—Perhaps they are quite rare and I ask too much. I understand that Macdonald Wright has several of your photographs—I have never met him but am going to ask permission for Margrethe and myself to see them—I have talked with her about N.Y. and Alfred Stieglitz—don't worry I am not going to make a God of you—I know you do not wish that!
>
> So once more before I sail—best of wishes to you and Georgia O'Keefe [sic]—and "Good bye" until Mexico....I will send more money for my own subscription to mss. from Mexico—continue what you can from the enclosed to Margrethe Mather—above address[39]

Hagemeyer, assuming Weston was leaving in June, sent his final regards:

Six days from today you will sail—will start your expedition to a new country—the place of your dreams—

It seems difficult to believe yet—for me—strange to imagine you there—to think of you there.... But the day of realization will come—somehow—

My most-deeply felt affection will accompany you—How could I speak out what I feel for you—what my wishes are for you—! I could only transport it through my hand into yours—my eyes looking into yours—

I say merely—farewell!—best of luck!—and au revoir![40]

However, Hagemeyer's well wishes were premature, because once again Weston was forced to postpone his trip. In the middle of July Weston wrote one last letter to Stieglitz:

The catalogues—mss—your letter—all were a joy to me—quite the one worth while event—in a chaotic period—I do not underestimate the trouble you went to—They are in appreciative hands—

What you say re "pulling up roots" is true—it is ghastly for me!

To reconcile a certain side of one's life to another—to accept a situation without at the same time destroying another—to coordinate desires which pull first this way—then that—to know or try to know what is best for those one has brought into the world—and even knowing—to be able to do that "best" without satisfying oneself—looms as an almost hopeless problem—and makes one wonder the "why" of this whole mad life—

I feel myself in a critical period of readjustment—change—and yet through it all in the ever increasing urge to lose myself in work—I may have been overwhelmed at times—faltered—made mistakes—but I have never lost the desire to grasp that intangible something which haunts my ground-glass—It almost seems at times I must be cruel—or else give up my own desires—for there are those whom one has loved—still love—and though they stimulate—they also drag—hold back—involve—destroy a certain single-ness of purpose—clutter up the background—barricade the foreground—until I wonder if I am a weakling because I stand it or for the same reason very strong!...

I had to postpone again—the last time I assure you! Sail definitely July 23—E. W.

I enclose the orange-blossoms—thinking they grow not in N.Y.[41]

In spite of Weston's certainty, however, his departure date had to be rescheduled one more time. The delay allowed Weston to receive a letter from Betty Katz, bidding him farewell from her attic aerie:

It is not that I have seen so much of you in the last few years, but the fact that you were about where I could see you was comforting. I cannot get it thru my head that you are really going away to another country. My feeling for you has not been a transient whimsy....

Lovely as my moods have been with you, the memory of them is even lovelier and clearer—the present of any situation is always hampered by fever and passion and fear—

But the memory of beautiful hours, if we but keep our soul from scoffing at that which has been, (just because it is no more),—ah! there is a beauty about that which no actual reality has—it makes the thing removed from life and removed from death.—

Maybe we will meet again before death overtakes us, maybe not—a part of the best that is in me goes out to you.[42]

Weston's prolonged good-bye finally came to an end on the morning of July 29 as he and Modotti made their separate ways to the San Pedro harbor where they were scheduled to board the SS *Colima*, a rickety freighter bound for the Mexican port of Manzanillo. Joining them on their journey south would be thirteen-year-old Chandler Weston. Edward was convinced that his eldest son would benefit from the experience of a year in Mexico, and Flora had agreed to let him go, hoping that Chandler would serve as her eyes and ears. The other three boys would remain in Glendale with their mother, a decision that would haunt Weston for the duration of his stay in Mexico.

Modotti was delivered to San Pedro by Vocio and Marionne Richey and Marionne's beau, Emile Scolari, while Ramiel McGehee arrived via streetcar from Redondo Beach. Peter and Rose Krasnow motored down from Glendale, bringing Edward, Flora, and the four boys. As Krasnow maneuvered his way toward the harbor, his passengers could just make out the recently completed sign that announced in gigantic block letters the name of Harry Chandler's latest real estate venture—HOLLYWOODLAND—across the high ridge of hills above Beachwood Canyon.[43]

As the time of their departure approached, Edward, Tina, and Chandler boarded the ship, while the others assembled on the dock for group photographs. Flora even managed a pleasant smile as her husband snapped a few farewell mementos from the deck of the SS *Colima*. Neil, age six, and Cole, age four, fidgeted awkwardly, unsure exactly how to behave. As eleven-year-old Brett fought to keep his emotions in check, Ramiel McGehee sensed his dilemma and laid a steadying hand on Brett's shoulder.

Margrethe Mather, conspicuous in her absence, was there in spirit, nonetheless. Sitting alone in her Bunker Hill studio, she commemorated Weston's journey with a crestfallen bit of prose. Fraught with underlying meaning, her note contained a single sprig of delicate bamboo:

Sunday the 29th
one o'clock
you have gone—and I had wanted to give you this—
new leaves—from my garden—
there were no flowers.[44]

A few hours later, as the SS *Colima* plied the open waters of the Pacific Ocean, Weston suffered a sudden bout of melancholia, but his sadness soon gave way to relief as he began to realize that his difficult departure had finally been executed. In spite of himself he felt reborn:

At last we are Mexico bound, after months of preparation, after such endless delays that the proposed adventure seemed but a conceit of the imagination never actually to materialize. Each postponement became a joke to our friends and a source of mortification to us. But money had to be raised, and with rumors of my departure many last moment sittings came in, each one helping to secure our future. Nor was it easy to uproot oneself and part with friends and family—there were farewells which hurt like knife thrusts.

But I adapt myself to change—already Los Angeles seems part of a distant past. The uneventful days—the balmy air has relaxed me—my overstrained nerves are eased. I begin to feel the actuality of this voyage.[45]

It was the third time Weston had extricated himself from one life, only to plunge fearlessly ahead into another. There would be several more exits and entrances to come.

Painfully aware of the missed opportunities symbolized by her former colleague's departure, Mather composed another pensive requiem the following day:

Monday July 30
The studio misses you—And I do[46]

With that heartfelt haiku, Mather memorialized the conclusion of their ten-year collaboration and unresolved love affair, even as she struggled to relegate their languid Los Angeles days, spent together or in the company of their bohemian friends, to the province of the past.

Epilogue

A s Weston sailed away from California, he left in his wake the formative years of his photography career. At age thirty-seven his life was already half gone, but his greatest artistic achievements were yet to come. Weston's stay in Mexico lasted the better part of three years, with the exception of one eight-month hiatus spent almost entirely in San Francisco. During his Mexican sojourn he sorely missed his Los Angeles friends, but even as he was going through the darkest emotional periods and the most extreme poverty of his life, he refused to entertain thoughts of reestablishing himself in Southern California, and in spite of being jolted awake by guilty nightmares in which he imagined he could hear his sons pleading for his return, he would not surrender his freedom. As far as Weston was concerned his days as an Angeleno were over.

After Weston's departure Mather continued to operate the Glendale studio under her own name and, for a time, enjoyed a thriving business. A one-woman retrospective of her photographs was held in 1924 at the Cannell and Chaffin Gallery in Los Angeles,[1] and she occasionally served as a judge for exhibitions sponsored by the Shakudo Sha, or the Japanese Camera Club of Los Angeles (a loosely affiliated group of photographers who later became known as the Japanese Camera Pictorialists of California).[2] But not being cut from the same cloth as Weston, she gradually began to ignore her professional obligations in favor of other diversions—some harmlessly entertaining, others dangerously venturesome.

Consequently, Mather's relationship with Weston suffered to such an extent that in early 1925, when Flora Weston announced her intention to evict Mather from the studio, Edward made only a feeble attempt to dissuade her. However, he was well aware that Mather had greatly influenced his development, both as an artist and as a human being, and a few days after his wife served Mather with an eviction notice, he preserved Mather's farewell tribute to their collaborative years in his diary:

> At last the end has come for Margarethe, and my old studio passes into alien and vulgar hands. A letter from her, "Today—my last Sunday in the Studio—raining softly—like tears—for you and for me—and for the willowed river we never walked to—a terrific nostalgia envelops me."[3]

At the end of 1926 a wretchedly impoverished Weston finally gave up on Mexico and Tina Modotti. Swallowing his pride, he temporarily returned to work in his Glendale studio, but a few months later he migrated northward, first to San Francisco and then to

Carmel-by-the-Sea. There he stayed while his family remained in Los Angeles. As long as his boys were young and rambunctious Weston continued to love them best from afar, but as his four sons grew older, Weston discovered he could relate to them in much more satisfying ways. For short periods of time each of his boys came to stay with him in Carmel, and under his guidance three of them took up photography.

In 1939 Edward finalized his divorce from Flora, his wife of thirty years, so he could marry young Charis Wilson, and for the first time in his life he settled wholeheartedly into domesticity. By then Carmel had become his spiritual home, and it was there that he ultimately achieved his lifelong ambition to become a famous photographer. Today his work is widely collected, by both museums and individuals. (As of this writing, the highest price paid for a Weston photograph was achieved in 2008, when a print of an abstract nude study of Miriam Lerner, taken during Weston's brief stay in Los Angeles in 1925, sold at auction for $1,609,000[4]—a figure vastly exceeding the lifetime total of his earnings.)

Mather was not nearly as tenacious as Weston. After being evicted from the Glendale studio and stumbling her way down a path strewn with financial obstacles, ill health, and alcohol and opium addictions, Mather moved in with her old anarchist friend George Lipton, whose longtime companion, Marie Latter, had recently taken her own life. Over the years, Lipton had expanded his upholstery business to include the sale of Early American furniture and decorations, and Mather soon began to offer interior design advice to the Hollywood crowd. She also photographed chic Beverly Hills and Brentwood homes for shelter magazines, and occasionally—mostly out of habit—she made a portrait or two.

Then in the late 1920s, with encouragement from George Lipton and Billy Justema, Mather had one final burst of creativity that lasted about two years. During that time she produced some truly extraordinary images[5] and had a one-woman exhibition at the M. H. de Young Museum in San Francisco[6] before turning her back on photography altogether in the mid-1930s.

Although Mather's initial fascination with the camera had been little more than a diversion, as she allowed her talent to blossom it had become the thing that gave her purpose and direction. She was a self-taught artist whose inherently exquisite taste and rigorous eye gave her a substantial advantage over many of her colleagues in the photography world. As a personality she was generous, daring, capricious, rebellious, inquisitive, loyal, stubborn, irresponsible, and impulsive. In her work she was a perfectionist who honed her skills relentlessly, but she lacked Weston's self-discipline and his drive to succeed in the larger world, and left to her own devices she simply lost the will to compete and excel.

The City of the Angels, as Weston and Mather experienced it, was peopled by lively nonconformists who pursued their contiguous, often overlapping, lives with bravura and gusto. As these restless, inquisitive souls shuttled tirelessly back and forth across the country, communicating in long, descriptive letters and terse, witty telegrams, weaving meaningful connections with others like themselves, they often made mention of Mather and Weston. In recording the photographers' actions and interests and describing the rhythms of their lives, they revealed aspects of Weston's and Mather's personalities and substantiated the aphorism "you are who your friends are." Occasionally the tables would turn, and these peripatetic individuals would pause long enough in their headlong rush through life for Mather and Weston to record their presence, capturing and preserving their images like rare tropical butterflies, carefully mounted and displayed behind glass for posterity.

As the years went by, in spite of the damage inflicted by both parties, Weston and Mather gingerly repaired the rift that had grown between them and continued to share their work, albeit at a distance. They also stayed in touch with many of their bohemian colleagues, and often their lives interlaced in important and unexpected ways. A few of their colorful friends became famous, while others remained obscure. Some died tragically and prematurely, but many survived well into their eighth decade, their once photogenic flesh wrinkled, their perfect bodies corrupted by time. In the portraits made by their photographer friends, however, they remain vigorous and youthful, frozen by the camera in attitudes of grace, at the peak of their physical beauty.

During their decade-long association, Weston learned many things from Mather, not the least of which was the art of reinvention. That life lesson may have been what prompted him to burn the earliest pages of his journals in the spring of 1925, a few weeks after Flora Weston made good on her threat to evict Mather from the studio. Weston's symbolic self-immolation came during a period of utter frustration and despair, but a few months later he realized that his destructive act had been a shortsighted, ill-conceived attempt to lighten his load, to start afresh without the encumbrances of his own history to weigh him down. In December 1925 he wrote the words that inspired this book:

> I even regret destroying my day book prior to Mexico: if badly written, it recorded a vital period, all my life with M., the first important person in my life, and perhaps even now, though personal contact has gone, the most important. Can I ever write in retrospect? Or will there be someday a renewed contact? It was a mad but beautiful life and love![7]

Regrettably, Weston never wrote "in retrospect," and the historical record was never fleshed out. Weston's self-wrought conflagration eradicated virtually all autobiographical evidence of his relationship with Mather and the countless contributions she had made to his artistic development. Somewhere along the way he destroyed most of her correspondence as well.

From the mid-1930s through the mid-1940s, as Weston methodically went about the business of securing his own reputation, he persisted in denying all influences, and in doing so, prevented Mather from taking her rightful place in the history of photography. Although she must have felt some pangs of regret, she was in no position to protest. Her puzzling illness had grown worse. Her eyesight was failing, and she was gradually losing all sensation in her hands and feet.

For the remaining years of her life, she worked alongside George Lipton in his shop, taking whatever pleasure she could from the decorative objects and beautiful fabrics that surrounded her. In a cruel twist of fate, however, Lipton's antiques store stood only a stone's throw from the small, decrepit shack that had once been Weston's Glendale studio, so Mather was forced to confront the specter of her past every single day.

Struggling under the weight of her debilitating infirmities, at times confined to a wheelchair, Mather was unable to properly care for her trove of negatives and prints that were, in large part, stored in her rapidly deteriorating carriage-house studio on Bunker Hill. As that neighborhood continued its decline, vagrants broke into the vacant building and used the flammable paper and film they found there as tinder for the bonfires that kept them warm at night.[8] Considering Mather's political proclivities, perhaps she believed she was sacrificing her legacy to a worthwhile cause. In any case, she had already resigned herself to anonymity, knowing full well that if Weston did acknowledge her, it would be merely as model and muse.

In Mather's final, bittersweet letter to Weston, written a few months before her death on Christmas Day, 1952,[9] from what had finally been diagnosed as multiple sclerosis, she even went so far as to suggest "[it]...might be sensible just to forget me entirely—to pretend that I didn't exist."[10] As Mather was sure he would, Weston gratefully accepted her pragmatic advice at face value. By the time he (and others) had finished editing his *Daybooks* for publication, there remained only a few brief references to Mather, and even though Weston credited her with being the "first important person"[11] in his life, he offered no explanation as to why she deserved such a designation. As Mather's friend Billy Justema would later remark, "[Edward Weston]...was both a more kindly and more ruthless person than emerges from...[the *Daybooks*]."[12]

Instead, in those self-conscious, much-revised pages, Weston doggedly continued to dismiss his Los Angeles years, refusing to admit their importance to his ultimate success as an artist. With no substantive documentation to the contrary, Mather receded in memory until she became nothing more than an intriguing footnote to Weston's long and illustrious career. Given Mather's reticence, however, perhaps her greatest comfort came from the knowledge that in death, as in life, she would remain an enigma.

In the early morning hours of New Year's Day 1958, following a decade-long battle with Parkinson's disease, Weston left the world just as he had entered it—bathed in sunshine.[13] By that time Weston's past had been rewritten so convincingly that, in years to come, many historians of photography would take their cue from him and ignore his Southern California period altogether, discussing his career as though he had risen miraculously from the volcanic ash of Mexico, like the proverbial phoenix, when nothing could have been further from the truth.

Weston did not live the first half of his life in a vacuum. He was very much a product of his time, and with Mather's help he not only developed a keen awareness of what his contemporaries were doing and thinking, he was inspired to expand the boundaries of his world and populate it with some of the most gifted individuals of his day. While Mather challenged him to hone and refine his vision, he urged her to share her talent with the world. She was the yin to his yang, and together they achieved the highest level of symbiotic perfection.

In the parlance of their era, Weston and Mather enjoyed a relationship that was real and vivid. During the time the trajectory of their lives coincided, their pairing was so intense that even after their paths gradually, inevitably, arced up and away from each other, neither would ever find another colleague with whom they could mesh so effortlessly, and even though Weston and Mather would continue to add many intriguing chapters to their life stories—tales that have yet to be told—the chapter they wrote in tandem would never be surpassed in its poignancy or meaningfulness.

It is a cruel paradox that before something can be remembered it must first be forgotten. Weston and Mather's collaboration is a case in point, and remembering has not come easily. Both photographers have now been gone for more than half a century, and the Los Angeles of their day has all but vanished. Their studios, demolished in the 1950s, have long since been replaced by parking lots and freeway ramps, and most of their early letters and diaries are dust and ashes, destroyed either by intent or neglect. What *does* survive, however, are a few dozen photographs taken during their years together, offering irrefutable evidence of the creative spirit and formidable talent they shared in a time and place unlike any other. It is thanks to these visual aides-mémoire that the story of Edward Weston and Margrethe Mather's association can now become a part of photographic history.

Afterword

As of this writing, few physical traces remain of Weston and Mather's former haunts. The gabled house where Edward Weston was born still graces the city of Highland Park, Illinois, but his Drexel Boulevard home, on Chicago's South Side, has been demolished, and the surrounding area contains only tattered reminders of the neighborhood's former prosperity. Weston's much-despised grammar school is now a Catholic elementary school run by the Archdiocese of Chicago. The flagship Marshall Field's department store, where Weston might have elected to pursue a career in retail sales, recently became part of the Macy's chain. Remarkably, the tiny brick house where Mather spent her Salt Lake City adolescence is still occupied, although the area around it has become highly industrialized.

The luxurious Los Angeles Athletic Club at Seventh and Olive streets, where Chaplin and his cohorts cavorted, still welcomes members. The once-elegant Alexandria Hotel, where Mather plied her trade, also survives, although it no longer attracts the city's elite. After housing soldiers during World War II, and subsequently serving as a hotel for transients, it has recently been renovated into "affordable apartments." Los Angeles's original Chinatown was razed in the 1930s so that Union Station could take its place, and the Hancock Banning House on Fort Moore Hill, where Weston and Betty Katz trysted, was leveled in the early 1950s, during the construction of the Hollywood Freeway.

The small apartment building where Max Eastman and Florence Deshon heard "the lions roar" still sits on DeLongpre Avenue in Hollywood, although the meadow that once abutted it has long since disappeared. Chaplin's house on South Oxford Street, where Weston, Mather, and their friends played endless games of charades, has been demolished, and the lot where it once stood is occupied by a multistory parking structure in the area currently known as Koreatown.

Rudolph and Pauline Schindler's West Hollywood home on Kings Road and Aline Barnsdall's Hollyhock House have both been restored and are open to an admiring public. The Mack home, where Mather's "protector," Florence Reynolds, stayed when she visited Los Angeles, is gone, and a parking lot has taken its place. A few of the buildings where Mather and George Lipton resided and/or conducted their upholstery and antiques business still stand.

The thirty-acre parcel of land where Prince Hopkins built his second Boyland school remains intact, although all of the original school buildings have been torn down. Boyland's temporary reincarnation as a hotel called the Samarkand has lent its name to an entire Santa Barbara neighborhood and to a large retirement community that now occupies the former Boyland campus.

Lois Kellogg's Babylon was never completed. The half-finished structure eventually became an unsightly ruin, and in 1944 Kellogg sold her Palm Springs property for ten dollars. As of this writing, the site where Babylon once stood (the east side of Palm Canyon Drive between Baristo and Ramon roads) is occupied by a large office supply store and other retail businesses.

All of the beautiful Victorian houses and lush gardens that once covered Bunker Hill have been replaced by a dense cluster of high-rise office buildings. Because many of the Hill's nineteenth-century streets have been gouged away, resulting in a confusing, multilayered, urban labyrinth, the only way to comprehend the Hill's former grandeur and topography is to study historic photographs, as well as the WPA-era scale model of Bunker Hill on display at the Natural History Museum of Los Angeles County in Exposition Park. This Museum, formerly known as the Museum of History, Science, and Art, is where Weston, Mather, and the Camera Pictorialists held their 1916 salon, marking the first time photographs were exhibited in a museum setting in Los Angeles. Still holding pride-of-place in the center of the Museum's impressive rotunda is Julia Bracken Wendt's eleven-foot-high, bronze statue, *The Three Graces*, welcoming visitors just as it did when the Museum first opened its doors in 1913.

The Angels Flight funicular on Bunker Hill was dismantled and put into storage in 1969, restored and reopened in 1996, and closed again in 2001 after a rider was killed due to a faulty braking system. As of this writing, the funicular has just been reopened. All traces of Clay Street and Mather's Bunker Hill boarding house are gone, buried under the hulking Angelus Apartment complex, and the Bonaventure Hotel now looms over the former site of the Castle Tower Apartments.

In the autumn of 1952 Mather and George Lipton were evicted from her West Fourth Street studio after the Department of Water and Power condemned most of the properties on Bunker Hill, and a short time later the Hildreth house and Mather's carriage-house studio were demolished. A deep cut was subsequently made in the steep hillside between Hope and Flower streets to make room for the Fourth Street exit ramp of the Harbor Freeway. Surprisingly, the contour of the slope along the north side of the exit ramp (adjacent to the property currently known as the Bank of America Plaza) remains relatively unchanged. That is where the Hildreth house and Margrethe Mather's studio once stood.

The Westons' humble bungalow on Verdant Avenue is gone, and the lot it occupied is now surrounded by a cement-block wall. South of their vacant home site, fronting on Los Feliz Boulevard and extending east to the Metrolink train tracks, is a large shopping center that was built on the former site of the Gladding-McBean tile and ceramics factory (remembered by many Angelenos as the place where the widely popular Franciscan Ware was manufactured).

In 1931, at the height of the Depression, Flora Weston was finally forced to sell her husband's Glendale studio, and for a time the small building became a florist's shop, and then an office for a series of used car dealerships. In the early 1950s the building was whitewashed and moved further back on the property, but a few years later it, too, was torn down. As of this writing, the site where Weston and Mather created so many of their early photographs is a U-Haul parking lot.

Notes

ABBREVIATIONS USED IN NOTES

AAA	Archives of American Art, Smithsonian Institution, Washington, D.C.
AAP	*American Annual of Photography*
AP	*American Photography*
AS/GO Archive	Alfred Stieglitz/Georgia O'Keeffe Archive, Yale Collection of American Literature, Beinecke Rare Book and Manuscript Library, Yale University, New Haven
BK Papers	Betty Katz (Household, Brandner) Papers, Martin Lessow Collection, Breckenridge, Colorado
BN/NN Papers	Beaumont and Nancy Newhall Papers, Research Library, Getty Research Institute for the History of Art and the Humanities, Los Angeles
CC	*Camera Craft*
CS Papers	Carl Sandburg Papers—Connemara Collection, Rare Book and Manuscript Library, University of Illinois at Urbana-Champaign
EW Archive	Edward Weston Archive, Center for Creative Photography, University of Arizona, Tucson
EW/JH Collection	Edward Weston/Johan Hagemeyer Collection, Center for Creative Photography, University of Arizona, Tucson
FD MSS.	Florence Deshon MSS., Lilly Library, Indiana University, Bloomington
FD Papers	Floyd Dell Papers, Midwest Manuscript Collection, Newberry Library, Chicago
FMCS	Friday Morning Club Scrapbooks, Huntington Library, San Marino
FR Collection	Florence Reynolds Collection Related to Jane Heap and *The Little Review*, Special Collections, University of Delaware Library, Newark
GCC Papers	George Cram (Jig) Cook Papers, Henry W. and Albert A. Berg Collection of English and American Literature, New York Public Library
GPL	Glendale Public Library, Glendale, California
HF Papers	Hapgood Family Papers, Yale Collection of American Literature, Beinecke Rare Book and Manuscript Library, Yale University, New Haven
IC Papers	Imogen Cunningham Papers, Archives of American Art, Smithsonian Institution, Washington, D.C.
JH Collection	Johan Hagemeyer Collection, Center for Creative Photography, University of Arizona, Tucson
LAMHSAS	Los Angeles Museum of History, Science, and Art Scrapbooks, Museum Archives, Natural History Museum of Los Angeles County
LW/WG Archive	Lee Witkin/Witkin Gallery Archive, Center for Creative Photography, University of Arizona, Tucson
MA Papers	Merle Armitage Papers, Harry Ransom Humanities Research Center, University of Texas at Austin

MEG Papers	Maud Emily (Taylor) Glass Papers, Department of Special Collections, Charles E. Young Research Library, University of California, Los Angeles
ME	*Mother Earth* (magazine)
ME MSS.	Max Eastman MSS., Lilly Library, Indiana University, Bloomington
ML Papers	Miriam Lerner (Fisher) Papers, The Bancroft Library, University of California, Berkeley
MM Files	Margery Mann Files, Archives of American Art, Smithsonian Institution, Washington, D.C.
NARA	National Archives and Records Administration, Washington, D.C.
NMAH	National Museum of American History, Smithsonian Institution, Washington, D.C.
PE	*Photo-Era*
PJA	*Photographic Journal of America*
PK/RK Papers	Peter and Rose Krasnow Papers, Archives of American Art, Smithsonian Institution, Washington, D.C.
PP	*Platinum Print*
PY	*Photograms of the Year*
RR Papers	Roy Rosen Papers, Center for Southwest Research, University Libraries, University of New Mexico, Albuquerque
RSD Papers	Ruth St. Denis Papers, Department of Special Collections, Charles E. Young Research Library, University of California, Los Angeles.
RW Papers	Rob Wagner Papers, Department of Special Collections, Charles E. Young Research Library, University of California, Los Angeles
SC Records	Severance Club Records, Department of Special Collections, Charles E. Young Research Library, University of California, Los Angeles
SchF Collection	Schindler Family Collection
SH Papers	Sadakichi Hartmann Papers, Special Collections and Archives, Tómas Rivera Library, University of California, Riverside
TC	*The Camera*
TPG Papers	Dr. Theodore Perceval Gerson Papers, Department of Special Collections, Charles E. Young Research Library, University of California, Los Angeles
WC Papers	Will Connell Papers, Department of Special Collections, Charles E. Young Research Library, University of California, Los Angeles
WF Papers	Wilshire Family Papers, Department of Special Collections, Charles E. Young Research Library, University of California, Los Angeles
JZ Collection	Jake Zeitlin Collection, Department of Special Collections, Charles E. Young Research Library, University of California, Los Angeles

PROLOGUE

1. William Justema, "Margaret: A Memoir," in *Margrethe Mather*, Research Series, no. 11, Center for Creative Photography, Univ. of Arizona (Tucson, 1979), p. 10.
2. Edward Weston, *The Daybooks of Edward Weston*, vol. 1, *Mexico*, ed. Nancy Newhall (Millerton, N.Y., 1973), p. 145.

CHAPTER 1
EDWARD WESTON—A MIDWESTERN UPBRINGING, 1886–1905

1. Edward Weston, letter to Ramiel McGehee, March 28, 1929, EW Archive.
2. Another man by the name of Edward Payson Weston, often referred to as the Father of Modern Pedestrianism, became famous during the second half of the nineteenth century for walking long distances in record times. Because he and Edward Weston's grandfather had identical names, the two have often been confused.
3. Obituary of Edward P. Weston, *The Portland Transcript* (Maine), October 25, 1879, EW Archive. Lake Forest's Ferry Hall was located approximately 350 feet northwest of the intersection of Rosemary Avenue and Mayflower Avenue, in a house known locally as the Baxter Dickinson home.
4. Jay Pridmore, *Many Hearts and Many Hands: The History of Ferry Hall and Lake Forest Academy* (Lake Forest, Ill., 1994), p. 36.
5. Obituary of Edward P. Weston (note 3).
6. Pridmore, *Many Hearts* (note 4), pp. 36–37.
7. *The First Annual Catalogue of the Young Ladies' Seminary, at "Ferry Hall," Lake Forest, Ill., for The Collegiate Year 1869–70*, p. 7, EW Archive.
8. "A Brief History of Ferry Hall," *The University Stentor* (Lake Forest, Ill.), March 20, 1894, EW Archive.
9. *Register, Second Year, September '77–February '78, Highland Hall, Highland Park, Ill., A Preparatory and Collegiate Institution for Young Ladies*, student register, September 1877–February 1878, EW Archive; E. M. Haines, *Past and Present of Lake County, Illinois* (Chicago, 1877), p. 5; Marvyn Wittelle, *Pioneer to Commuter: The Story of Highland Park* (Highland Park, Ill., 1958), p. 57; *Highland Park, Illinois: A Bicentennial Community* (Highland Park, Ill., 1976), pp. 79, 108–9. Highland Park's Highland Hall was located on the southern half of the quadrangle of land bordered by St. Johns Avenue on the west, Ravine Avenue on the south, Linden Avenue on the east, and Hazel Avenue on the north. Built between 1869 and 1871, the Highland House Hotel was a large, three-story, Victorian-style wooden frame building. It was renamed Highland Hall in September 1875, when the building was converted to a school, with Professor Weston as superintendent. After Professor Weston's death in 1879, Highland Hall continued to operate as a school until 1887, when the building was purchased by Northwestern Military Academy. It was destroyed by fire the following year.
10. Ben Maddow, *Edward Weston: His Life* (New York, 1989), p. 48.
11. John W. Leonard, ed., *The Book of Chicagoans: A Biographical Dictionary of the Leading Men of the City of Chicago* (Chicago, 1905), p. 605.
12. Obituary of Edward P. Weston (note 3); Census and Mortality Schedule, Lake County, Illinois, 1880, s.v. "E. P. Weston."
13. Edward B. Weston, Martha E. Weston, and Mary E. Weston (heirs of Edward P. Weston, deceased) to highest bidder, Sarah H. Whitlock, Grantor Deed Record no. 49, filed with Recorder of Deeds, Lake County, Illinois, November 5, 1880.
14. As of this writing, the house in Highland Park where Edward Weston was born still stands; however, in the early 1950s the street address was changed from 286 to 304 Laurel Avenue. Built around 1875, the Queen Anne–style, Victorian-era house is located on the south side of Laurel Avenue, between Linden Avenue on the west and Dale Avenue on the east, approximately one block from Lake Michigan. In 1957 Edward Weston received a letter from a family friend, who described the former Weston home as "the loveliest old gabled house in town." (Sidney

D. Morris, letter to Edward Weston, November 23, 1957, EW Archive.) The house is featured briefly in a scene from the 1990 film *Home Alone*, in which actor Macaulay Culkin peers through one of the downstairs windows as he watches his neighbors celebrate Christmas.

15. It has been reported that Edward Weston was born in the observation tower of Highland Hall; see Maddow, *Edward Weston: His Life* (note 10), p. 48. However, according to May Weston Seaman, it was she who was born in Highland Hall, while Edward's birth took place in the Weston home on Laurel Avenue; see May Weston Seaman, letter to Edward Weston, May 17, 1946, EW Archive.

16. Wittelle, *Pioneer to Commuter* (note 9), p. 227.

17. *Dr. E. B. Weston, Highland Park, Lake Co., Ills, Breeder of Choicest Varieties of Thoroughbred Poultry*, advertising brochure, 1880s, EW Archive.

18. *Chicago City Directory*, 1887, s.v. "Edward Burbank Weston"; Glen E. Holt and Dominic A. Pacyga, *Chicago: A Historical Guide to the Neighborhoods, The Loop and South Side* (Chicago, 1979), pp. 48–57.

19. *Chicago City Directory*, 1891, s.v. "Edward Burbank Weston"; Holt and Pacyga, *Chicago* (note 18), pp. 58–65. The Weston home at 3975 Drexel Boulevard stood on the east side of the street, between Oakwood Boulevard on the north and Fortieth Street on the south. The house was demolished many years ago.

20. Mount Hope Cemetery, burial records, Chicago, Cook County, Illinois, July 1891, s.v. "Infant Weston."

21. Death certificate of Alice Jeannette Weston (b. ca. 1851, d. January 25, 1892), Chicago, Cook County, Illinois; Mount Hope Cemetery, burial records, Chicago, Cook County, Illinois, January 1892, s.v. "Alice Jeannette Weston."

22. Edward Weston, letter to Cole Weston, March 2, 1924, EW Archive.

23. May Weston Seaman, letter to Edward Weston, 1940s, quoted in Maddow, *Edward Weston: His Life* (note 10), p. 55.

24. Federal Census, Chicago, Cook County, Illinois, 1900, s.v. "Edward B. Weston."

25. Charis Wilson and Wendy Madar, *Through Another Lens: My Years with Edward Weston* (New York, 1998), p. 39.

26. "Weddings Past and to Come," announcement of Mary Jeannette (May) Weston's November 27, 1897, marriage to John Hancock Seaman, *Chicago Tribune*, November 28, 1897.

27. Federal Census (note 24).

28. Edward Henry Weston, letter to Edward Burbank Weston, August 20, 1902, EW Archive.

29. Amy Conger, *Edward Weston: Photographs from the Collection of the Center for Creative Photography* (Tucson, 1992), fig. 4/1906.

30. Edward Weston, *The Daybooks of Edward Weston*, vol. 2, *California*, ed. Nancy Newhall (Millerton, N.Y., 1973), p. 235.

31. Edward Weston, responses to questionnaire from Nancy Newhall [late 1940s], BN/NN Papers.

32. There are several extant photographs—including ones at the J. Paul Getty Museum and the Center for Creative Photography—that depict Edward Weston posing with his bow and arrow.

33. May Weston Seaman, letters to Edward Weston [ca. May–August 1905], EW Archive.

34. Wilson and Madar, *Through Another Lens* (note 25), p. 73; Weston, *Daybooks*, vol. 1 (prologue, note 2), p. xv.

CHAPTER 2
WESTON TAKES ON TROPICO, 1906–1912

1. Conger, *Edward Weston: Photographs* (chap. 1, note 29), p. 1.

2. A few of these early cyanotypes are now in the collection of the J. Paul Getty Museum.

3. Weston, *Daybooks*, vol. 1 (prologue, note 2), p. xvi.

4. John Calvin Sherer, *History of Glendale and Vicinity* (Glendale, Calif., 1922), pp. 321–22.

5. Robert Gottlieb and Irene Wolt, *Thinking Big: The Story of the Los Angeles Times, Its Publishers, and Their Influence on Southern California* (New York, 1977), pp. 32–52, 121–52; Kevin Starr, *Material Dreams: Southern California through the 1920s* (New York, 1996), pp. 102–3; Dennis McDougal, *Privileged Son: Otis Chandler and the Rise and Fall of the L.A. Times Dynasty* (Cambridge, Mass., 2001), pp. 16–166.

6. George Chandler, *The Chandler Family: The Descendants of William and Annis Chandler Who Settled in Roxbury, Mass., 1637* (Worcester, Mass., 1883); see p. 899 (s.v. Moses Knight Chandler, father of Harry Chandler and ninth-generation descendant of William Chandler) and p. 1011 (s.v. Jeremiah Chandler, father of Cornelius C. Chandler and ninth-generation descendant of William Chandler).

7. May Weston Seaman, letter to Edward Weston, April 7, 1906, EW Archive.

8. Mary Weston Seaman, letter to Edward Weston, April 14, 1905, EW Archive.

9. Maddow, *Edward Weston: His Life* (chap. 1, note 10), p. 67; Wilson and Madar, *Through Another Lens* (chap. 1, note 25), p. 41.

10. *Views and Press Notices*, illustrated brochure, Southern Oregon Historical Society, Jacksonville, cited in Amy Conger, "Edward Weston's Early Photography 1903–1926" (Ph.D. dissertation, University of New Mexico, Albuquerque, 1982), "Text," p. 163n24.

11. Lewis Horace Bissell may have been related to Rev. John H. Bissell, who served on the Highland Hall Board of Visitors; *Register, Second Year* (chap. 1, note 9).

12. Wilson and Madar, *Through Another Lens* (chap. 1, note 25), pp. 41–42.

13. In spite of his disagreement with Edward Weston, Lewis Horace Bissell was proud to claim Weston as a former student; see "With the Camera," AP, July 1913, p. 429; "Illinois College of Photography," CC, August 1913, p. 398; "With the Camera," AP, August 1914, p. 543; "Notes and News," AP, January 1915, p. 55; "Illinois College of Photography, CC, June 1916, p. 251; "Illinois College of Photography," CC, October 1916, p. 431; "Illinois College of Photography," CC, November 1919, p. 450.

14. *Los Angeles City Directory*, 1908, s.v. "George Steckel"; "Every Picture a Work of Art," advertisement for Steckel Studio, *Los Angeles Times*, February 16, 1913.

15. Maddow, *Edward Weston: His Life* (chap. 1, note 10), p. 68.

16. Weston is listed in the 1910 *Los Angeles City Directory* as working for A. L. Mojonier, 710 Auditorium Building, 427 West Fifth Street.

17. "Marriages," Edward H. Weston, 22, and Flora M. Chandler, 29, *Los Angeles Sunday Times*, January 31, 1909, EW Archive.

18. *Tropico City Directory*, 1913–14, s.v. "E. H. Weston."

19. California Death Index, s.v. "Chandler Weston" (b. April 26, 1910, d. November 27, 1995).

20. Sarah Lowe and Dody Weston Thompson, *Edward Weston Life Work: Photographs from the Collection of Judith G. Hochberg and Michael P. Mattis*, preface by Hochberg and Mattis (Revere, Pa., 2003), plate 3.

21. Social Security Death Index, s.v. "Theodore Brett Weston" (b. December 16, 1911, d. January 22, 1993).

22. Several of these family albums are now in the collection of the J. Paul Getty Museum.

23. *Tropico City Directory*, 1911–12, s.v. "E. H. Weston."

24. "Artist Wins Local Honor: Works of Local Photographer is Given Place in Permanent Salon by Association of America—To Demonstrate His Method in East," *Los Angeles Times*, August 6, 1916, in which Weston's studio is referred to as the "Little Studio."

25. *Glendale News*, November 3, 1911, newspaper clipping, Edward Weston biographical file, GPL, in which Weston's studio is referred to as "The Bungalow Studio"; Conger, "Edward Weston's Early Photography" (note 10), "Catalogue," p. 68, wherein an early Weston portrait is described as bearing the annotation "Bungalow Studio, Tropico, Cal., 1910."

26. "Camera Portraits by Weston," advertisement in *Glendale, The Jewel City*, promotional booklet, 1912, photocopy, Edward Weston biographical file, GPL.

27. Los Angeles County plat book, ownership history of 1315 South Brand Boulevard, Glendale, described therein as "Chandlers Replat of Blocks 1 & 2, Villa Del Tract, 1909, north 65 feet of lots 11, 12, and 13 located 110 feet north of corner of Los Feliz and Brand, total width 65 feet, total depth 160 feet."

28. The dimensions of Weston's studio are estimates based on the relative size of other objects depicted in exterior views of the structure.

29. "Camera Portraits" (note 26).

30. J. C. Thomas, "A David Grayson Kind of Man," *American Magazine*, August 1915, pp. 55–56, reprinted in Beaumont Newhall and Amy Conger, eds., *Edward Weston Omnibus* (Salt Lake City, Utah, 1984), pp. 4–6.

31. Conger, *Edward Weston: Photographs* (chap. 1, note 29), figs. 35–38/1919.

32. Myra C. K. Shuey, *Beautiful City of Tropico, Growing and Prosperous Community at the Gateway to the San Fernando Valley*, promotional booklet, ca. 1912, photocopy, Edward Weston biographical file, GPL.

33. May Weston Seaman, letter to Edward Weston [1940s], EW Archive.

34. "Tropico," *Los Angeles Times*, January 1, 1913; "Atwater Tract: 15 Minutes from 6th & Broadway," advertisement, *Los Angeles Times*, January 29, 1913.

35. Wilfred A. French, "Our Illustrations," PE, December 1911, p. 317.

36. Several examples of these early prints exist in various institutions, including the Center for Creative Photography and the J. Paul Getty Museum.

37. Nancy Newhall, notes from conversations with Edward Weston, typescript, n.d., Beaumont and Nancy Newhall Library, College of Santa Fe, Santa Fe, N.M.; Maddow, *Edward Weston: His Life* (chap. 1, note 10), p. 69.

38. PE, October 1912, pp. 192, 192ill., 201.

39. Edward H. Weston, "Photographing Children in the Studio," AP, February 1912, pp. 83–85.

40. AP, November 1912, p. 643ill.

41. Weston, "Photographing Children" (note 39), p. 85ill.

42. G. C. Henderson and Robert A. Oliver, *Tropico, the City Beautiful*, a promotional booklet published by the Tropico chapter of the Knights of Pythias, as an "Official Program and Souvenir of the Knights of Pythias Carnival" (Tropico 1914), reprinted by Michael Hargraves (Los Angeles 1986), in an edition of 100 photocopies.

43. Edward H. Weston, "Shall I Turn Professional?" AP, December 1912, pp. 620–23.

44. Arthur Wesley Dow was the former curator of Japanese prints at the Boston Museum of Fine Arts under his mentor, the renowned Japanophile, Ernest Fenellosa. Dow's book, *Composition: A Series of Exercises in Art Structure for the Use of Students and Teachers* (New York, 1899), became one of the standard texts included in the art curriculum of America's public schools between 1900 and the mid-1930s. In the spring of 1900, Dow lectured extensively in Chicago, so Weston might have become acquainted with Professor Dow's design philosophy even before he moved to California. Frederick C. Moffatt, *Arthur Wesley Dow* (Washington, D.C., 1977), pp. 7, 156–57.

CHAPTER 3
MARGRETHE MATHER—AN INAUSPICIOUS START, 1886–1912

1. Justema, "Margaret" (prologue, note 1), pp. 5–19, in which some of the information about Margrethe Mather's early life is incorrect.

2. *Los Angeles City Directory*, 1912.

3. Justema, "Margaret" (prologue, note 1), p. 6.

4. The Youngren name is spelled in several different ways in various historical documents (i.e., Youngren, Younggren, Youngreen, Younggreen, Jungren, Junggren, Jungreen, Junggreen). This inconsistent spelling was quite common in the nineteenth century, especially in cases where foreign immigrants did not speak or understand English. Names were often spelled phonetically, according to the way they sounded to the person recording the information. Other variations arose as the immigrants settled into their new environments and began altering the spelling of their names, sometimes shortening or Anglicizing them, so as to leave behind their ethnic roots and fit more seamlessly into their new community.

5. Youngren/Jungren family Bible, Collection of Myrna Chadwick, great-niece of Maren Sophie Kragh Youngren, Salt Lake City, Utah. The Youngrens noted birth and death dates of family members in their Bible prior to the time when such events were recorded in official documents, such as state-issued birth and death certificates. The pertinent dates were entered into the Bible by hand as each birth or death occurred.

6. Ellen Mable (Youngreen Hayward Watson) Layton, "Gabriel L. Jungreen or Youngreen" (unpublished family history compiled by the half-sister of Emma Caroline Youngren [aka Margrethe Mather], before 1993), Collection of Myrna Chadwick, great-niece of Maren Sophie Kragh Youngren.

7. Layton, "Gabriel L. Jungreen" (note 6).

8. Youngren/Jungren family Bible (note 5).

9. Obituary of Ane Sophie Junggren, *Deseret News* (Salt Lake City), March 23, 1889.

10. Layton, "Gabriel L. Jungreen" (note 6).

11. Sandra Pitts, discussions and correspondence with the author, 1997–98. Pitts is the great-granddaughter of Rasmine Laurentzen/Jensen/Mather. In the nineteenth century and well into the twentieth century, Danes were still using a patronymic naming system (i.e., they would take their father's first name and add the suffix "-sen" to form their own surname. Thus, Rasmine Laurentzen/Lorentzen sometimes used the name Rasmine Jensen, because her father's first name was Jens.

12. Horace E. Mather, *Lineage of Rev. Richard Mather* (Hartford, 1890), p. 254; Stephen Whitney Phoenix, *Whitney Family of Connecticut & Its Affiliations, Being an Attempt to Trace the Descendants, as Well in the Female as the Male Lines, of Henry Whitney, from 1649–1878* (New York, 1878), pp. 1593–94.

13. Mather, *Lineage* (note 12).

14. Mount Olivet Cemetery, burial records, Salt Lake City, Utah, s.v. "Clarissa Mather" (b. November 22, 1857, Chicago; d. December 10, 1883, Salt Lake City, Utah).

15. "The Late Judge Mather, Funeral Obsequies at the Second Presbyterian Church, Biographical Sketch of the Deceased by Dr. Patterson," *Chicago Tribune*, July 13, 1868.

16. Arthur Miller, "Lake Forest Country Places—XXXXI," *Lake Forest Journal*, July 1998, p. 2.

17. Phoenix, *Whitney Family* (note 12), p. 1594.

18. City Cemetery, burial records, Salt Lake City, Utah, s.v. "Clarissa Lewis Mather" (b. ca. 1835, London, England; d. April 5, 1875, Salt Lake City, Utah); Mather, *Lineage* (note 12); Phoenix, *Whitney Family* (note 12), p. 1594.

19. Mount Olivet Cemetery, burial records (note 14).

20. Justema, "Margaret" (prologue, note 1), p. 6.

21. Federal Census, Salt Lake City, Salt Lake County, Utah, 1900, s.v. "Joseph C. Mather."

22. Death certificate of Joseph Cole Mather (b. May 17, 1833, d. September 1, 1916), Salt Lake City, Salt Lake County, Utah.

23. *Salt Lake City Directory*, 1873, 1891, 1897, 1898, s.v. "J. C. Mather."

24. Layton, "Gabriel L. Jungreen" (note 6).

25. Bradley W. Richards, M.D., *The Savage View: Charles Savage, Pioneer Mormon Photographer* (Nevada City, Calif., 1995); see pp. 70, 87, and figs. 65, 81, for illustrations of Savage's Art Bazar at 12 and 14 Main Street, ca. 1881 and ca. 1885.

26. Pitts, discussions and correspondence (note 11).

27. Mather, *Lineage* (note 12).

28. Ellen Mable (Jungreen Hayward Watson) Layton, "History of Maren Sophie Craig [Kragh] Youngreen" (unpublished family history compiled by the half-sister of Emma Caroline Youngren [aka Margrethe Mather], before 1993), Collection of Myrna Chadwick, great-niece of Maren Sophie Kragh Youngren.

29. Federal Census, Salt Lake City, Salt Lake County, Utah, 1900, s.v.v. "Emma Youngren/Younggreen/Mather," "Minnie Laurentzen," and "Joseph C. Mather"; *Salt Lake City Directory*, 1900–6.

30. Salt Lake High School Records, 1900–5, s.v. "Emma Youngren/Younggreen."

31. "These Will Graduate," *Deseret Evening News* (Salt Lake City), May 24, 1904, p. 3; "High School and Its Graduates," *Deseret Evening News*, May 29, 1905, (page number illegible); "Graduates from the High School," *Deseret Evening News*, May 28, 1906, p. 5.

32. *Salt Lake City Directory*, 1903–6, s.v. "Emma Youngren/Younggreen/Mather."

33. *Salt Lake City Directory*, 1905, s.v. "Dr. Wm. H. Hanchett."

34. *Salt Lake City Directory*, 1907.

35. Several articles appeared in the April and May 1906 issues of the *Deseret News* asking Salt Lake City physicians to come to the San Francisco area to provide care for those who were injured or displaced by the recent earthquake.

36. *Salt Lake City Directory*, 1906, s.v. "Dr. Wm. H. Hanchett," which states that Dr. Hanchett "moved to Oakland, Cal."

37. Gordon Thomas and Max Morgan Witts, *The San Francisco Earthquake* (New York, 1971), p. 216.

38. The first listing for Charles H. Monroe's 56 West Second South Street photography studio appears in the 1906 *Salt Lake City Directory*.

39. According to the European Emigration Card Index at the Family History Center, Salt Lake City, Anna Margrethe (Pedersen) Laurentzen sailed from Liverpool, England, on June 25, 1881, and arrived in New York City on July 7. She continued her journey west by rail, arriving in Salt Lake City on July 15, 1881. She died on November 27, 1902, and is buried in Salt Lake City Cemetery, alongside other family members.

40. Emma Caroline Youngren always spelled her assumed name "Margrethe Mather," and she accommodated American ears by pronouncing her first name "Mär'-gret," rather than the traditional Danish way, with a rolled *r* in the second, emphasized syllable and a soft, enunciated "e" at the end, and she pronounced her surname with a short *a*, as in *math*. Although others would mistakenly and repeatedly spell her first name as "Margarethe" "Margaret," "Margret," "Margrete," or "Marguerite," and pronounce her surname with a long *a*, as in *lathe*, she did not; Pitts, discussions and correspondence (note 11).

41. Pitts, discussions and correspondence (note 11).

42. Federal Census, San Francisco, San Francisco County, California, 1910, s.v. "Margaret Mother" (her borrowed surname was misspelled when handwritten census rolls were transferred to index cards).

43. Jeanne Redman, "Los Angeles, Paradise of Bluestocking; San Francisco, Eden of Salamander: Men Dance with their Manicurists in the Northern City—Los Angeles Less Generous and Democratic—A Daring Analysis of the Social Ideals of the Two Cities," *Los Angeles Times*, February 13, 1916.

44. Thomas and Witts, *Earthquake* (note 37), pp. 171–73.

45. *San Francisco City Directory*, Apartment Buildings, 1908.

46. The St. Anna Apartment Building is visible in a photograph—taken at the intersection of Pine and Hyde streets looking east—in the collection of the California Historical Society, San Francisco. The St. Anna became a residential hotel soon after it was built, and around 1918 the building was torn down to make way for the St. Francis Hospital complex, which still occupies the site.

47. "Earth Shakes: Buildings Rock," *Los Angeles Times*, July 2, 1911.

48. *Los Angeles City Directory*, 1913, s.v. "Margrethe Mather." Although a "Marg. Mather" also appears in both the 1911 and 1912 directories, the earliest listing that can positively be linked to Margrethe Mather appears in 1913, firmly establishing her presence in Los Angeles by at least mid-1912, when the 1913 volume was compiled for publication.

49. *Los Angeles City Directory*, Apartments and Boarding Houses, 1913.

50. Virginia L. Comer, *Angels Flight: A History of Bunker Hill's Incline Railway* (Los Angeles, 1996), pp. 3–4; Arnold Hylen, *Bunker Hill: A Los Angeles Landmark Recorded in words and pictures* (Los Angeles, 1976), pp. 20–21.

51. Comer, *Angels Flight* (note 50), p. 4.

52. Comer, *Angels Flight* (note 50), p. 68.

CHAPTER 4
THE CITY OF THE ANGELS, 1850–1913

1. For a discussion of the role that Collis P. Huntington's Southern Pacific Railroad played in the development of late nineteenth-century Los Angeles, see Robert M. Fogelson, *The Fragmented Metropolis: Los Angeles, 1850–1930* (Los Angeles, 1993), pp. 43–62.

2. Hylen, *Bunker Hill* (chap. 3, note 50), p. xi.

3. Motley H. Flint, Postmaster, "Growth in Population of the City of Los Angeles," *Los Angeles Times*, January 1, 1910.

4. Federal Census, Salt Lake City, Salt Lake County, Utah, 1900.

5. Flint, "Growth in Population," (note 3); Fogelson, *Fragmented Metropolis* (note 1), p. 78, table 4.

6. Flint, "Growth in Population," (note 3).

7. "Beverly Hills," advertisement, *Los Angeles Times*, July 10, 1910.

8. "Griffith Park, Mass Meeting Held Last Night at East Hollywood, to Consider Plans for Improving Pleasure Ground Entrance," *Los Angeles Times*, March 19, 1911.

9. Hector Alliott, "Central Park Transformation, We Have Broiling Bricks in Place of Verdure and Cement Where Nature Once Reigned," *Los Angeles Times*, March 19, 1911.

10. "Sketches Made for Huge Hotel: Chicago Capital Behind Two-Million Dollar Project," *Los Angeles Times*, December 4, 1910.

11. "Scenic Bridge to Span Arroyo Seco, Funds for Splendid Structure Raised and New and Beautiful Highway from Los Angeles to Pasadena Assured—Miles of Asphalt," *Los Angeles Times*, May 15, 1910.

12. "Maud Allan Returns: Supreme Exponent of Visual Harmony," *Los Angeles Times*, April 10, 1910.

13. Julian Johnson, "Odd Nazimova," *Los Angeles Times*, November 20, 1910.

14. "Ruth St. Denis at the Mason: The Famous Dancer Will Give Oriental Numbers," *Los Angeles Times*, April 23, 1911.

15. "Blackbeard and His Blood Thirsty Crew—A Tragedy of the Sea," advertisement, *Los Angeles Times*, September 8, 1911.

16. Julian Johnson, "Behymer's Activities: Big Season and Double Course of Concerts," *Los Angeles Times*, September 17, 1911.

17. "Musician's Directory, California School of Artistic Whistling," advertisement, *Los Angeles Times*, January 7, 1912.

18. "Men's Association to Fight Equal Suffrage: Powerful Organization of Business and Professional Leaders, Centering about Executive Committee of Fifty, Now in the Field Against Votes for Women, Every City in Southern California Included," *Los Angeles Times*, September 8, 1911. Two members of the Committee of Fifty were George S. Patton, whose son would become the legendary World War II general, and H. W. O'Melveney, scion of the founding partner of the esteemed Los Angeles law firm, O'Melveney and Meyers, which today is headquartered in a Bunker Hill office building at 400 South Hope Street, overlooking the site where Margrethe Mather's studio once stood.

19. Harry Chandler, "Today's Editorial," *Los Angeles Times*, October 10, 1911.

20. "Suffrage Appears Lost—The Recall Carries: Close for Suffragists in South," *Los Angeles Times*, October 11, 1911.

21. "Woman's Suffrage Probably Wins, After All: Country Vote Piling Up in Favor of Suffragism," *Los Angeles Times*, October 12, 1911.

22. Willard Huntington Wright, "Hotbed of Soulful Culture, Vortex of Erotic Erudition: Carmel in California, Where Author and Artist Folk are Establishing the Most Amazing Colony on Earth," *Los Angeles Times*, May 22, 1910.

23. Gloria Rexford Martin and William H. Gerdts, *A Painter's Paradise: Artists and the California Landscape*, exh. cat. (Santa Barbara Museum of Art, 1996), pp. 33–35.

24. Antony Anderson, "Art and Artists," *Los Angeles Times*, January 22, 1910.

25. Antony Anderson, "Art and Artists," *Los Angeles Times*, September 25, 1910.

26. Antony Anderson, "Art and Artists," *Los Angeles Times*, September 4, 1910.

27. Paul DeLongpre died in Hollywood on June 29, 1911; Obituary of Paul DeLongpre, *New York Times*, July 1, 1911. Later that year his spacious home, surrounded by elaborate flower gardens, was opened to the public as an art gallery, and a street in Hollywood was named DeLongpre Avenue in his honor.

28. Antony Anderson, "Art and Artists," *Los Angeles Times*, June 19, 1910, February 18, 1912, March 3, 1912, March 10, 1912.

29. Antony Anderson, "Art and Artists," *Los Angeles Times*, February 5, 1911.

30. Antony Anderson, "Art and Artists," *Los Angeles Times*, September 18, 1910.

31. Nancy Dustin Wall Moure, *Dictionary of Art and Artists in Southern California Before 1930* (Los Angeles, 1978), p. 5; Antony Anderson, "Of Art and Artists," *Los Angeles Times*, May 18, 1924; Obituary of Antony Anderson, *New York Times*, March 13, 1939; Obituary of Antony Anderson, *Los Angeles Times*, March 15, 1939.

32. Antony Anderson, "Art and Artists," *Los Angeles Times*, December 10, 1911.

33. Anderson, "Art and Artists" (note 32); "Art and Artists," *Los Angeles Times*, December 17, 1911; January 28, 1912.

34. Carey McWilliams, *Southern California Country: An Island in the Land*, ed. Erskine Caldwell (New York, 1946), pp. 128–34.

35. Gottlieb and Wolt, *Thinking Big* (chap. 2, note 5), pp. 21–23.

36. McWilliams, *Southern California Country* (note 34), p. 161.

37. For more information about the creation of the harbor at San Pedro and the "free shop" movement in Los Angeles, see Fogelson, *Fragmented Metropolis* (note 1), pp. 108–34.

38. "Twenty-One Killed and More Injured in the Dynamited 'Times' Building: Bomb Exploded by the Enemies of Industrial Freedom and of This Paper Fearful in Deadliness and Destructiveness—Many Bodies Still in Ruins—Other Crimes Planned," *Los Angeles Times*, October 2, 1910.

39. "Twenty-One Killed" (note 38); "Bombs Burst, but 'The Times' Goes Marching On: Within Two Hours after Building Has Been Blown Up by Labor Union Assassins the Daily Issue Containing Vivid Report of Outrage and [illegible]," *Los Angeles Times*, October 2, 1910.

40. "Deadly Machine, Left at Editor's Home, Shows Plot," *Los Angeles Times*, October 2, 1910.

41. Gottlieb and Wolt, *Thinking Big* (chap. 2, note 5), pp. 89–101.

42. "Company Offers to Buy Normal Site for City," *Los Angeles Times*, February 4, 1912.

43. "City-County Library Plan is Laid Aside," *Los Angeles Times*, March 2, 1912.

44. "If Bunker Hill's to Go Now's Time to Do It," *Los Angeles Times*, October 20, 1912; "Proposed Reduction of Bunker Hill Live Issue on Los Angeles 'Roof': Heavy Property-owners Looking toward Removal of Great Business Obstruction; Strong, Favorable Force at Official Hearing Tomorrow Night," *Los Angeles Times*, October 27, 1912; "Razing Bunker Hill Figured in Detail: Full Report, Covering Several Plans, to Be Ready Next Saturday—Cost Probably Ten Millons and Estimated Increase in Value of Property Affected by Improvements Fifteen Millions," *Los Angeles Times*, November 24, 1912.

45. "Society Leader Sinks with the Titanic," *Los Angeles Times*, April 21, 1912.

46. "Fire Shots at Chief: Assassination Tried in San Diego," *Los Angeles Times*, May 26, 1912.

47. "Splendid Acropolis to House Treasure: Striking Buildings for Southwest Museum to Be Begun This Summer—Severe Type of Spanish Architecture and Patio Plan Adopted—To Extend Scope and Become a Dominant Factor in Educational Science," *Los Angeles Times*, June 16, 1912.

48. In 1910 there were already 20,000 cars registered in Los Angeles County; ten years later there would be five times that number; see Frederick Law Olmsted, Harland Bartholemew, and Charles H. Cheney, *A Major Traffic Street Plan for Los Angeles* (Los Angeles, 1924), quoted in Fogelson, *Fragmented Metropolis* (note 1), p. 92.

49. "The New Home of the Los Angeles Times," *Los Angeles Times*, January 1, 1913.

50. "Second Red-Car Line, Tropico–Glendale," *Los Angeles Times*, April 2, 1913.

51. "Beautiful Wilshire Home Price Only $17,000," advertisement, *Los Angeles Times*, May 11, 1913.

52. "Southern California the Most Famous Bungalow-land," *Los Angeles Times*, January 1, 1912.

53. "The New Ideal Winter Resort, Beverly Hills Hotel," advertisement, *Los Angeles Times*, January 1, 1913.

54. "Santa Barbara County Builds Great Highway: Rincon Road to Los Angeles," *Los Angeles Times*, January 1, 1912.

55. Fogelson, *Fragmented Metropolis* (note 1), p. 104.

56. "Magnificent Oak Knoll Hostelry, Opening Date for Which Has Been Set," *Los Angeles Times*, November 2, 1913.

57. Henry Huntington, quoted in McWilliams, *Southern California Country* (note 34), pp. 133–34.

58. "They Expect New Messiah: Theosophists Rear Temple for a Leader," *Los Angeles Times*, September 21, 1913.

59. "Druids to Initiate: New Grove to Be Formed Here and Large Class to Be Adopted into Membership," *Los Angeles Times*, October 26, 1913.

60. Antony Anderson, "Art and Artists," *Los Angeles Times*, December 15, 1912.

61. These murals are now in the collection of the California State Library, Sacramento. Anita Baldwin's home, Anoakia, eventually became the Anoakia School for Girls, but the school closed in the 1970s. After standing vacant for more than two decades, Anoakia was finally razed in 2000, and a development of thirty-one luxury homes, called Anoakia Estates, was built on the property.

62. Robert Rosenstone, *Romantic Revolutionary: A Biography of John Reed* (New York, 1975), pp. 150–51.

63. Gottlieb and Wolt, *Thinking Big* (chap. 2, note 5), pp. 165–80.

64. "Will Southern California Exhibit at San Francisco World's Fair? If Not What Shall We Tell the Million Tourists Who Will Ask Why? Way Still Open for Proper Showing at Exposition for Which South Is Paying Most," *Los Angeles Times*, October 26, 1913.

65. For a discussion of the events leading up to the opening of the Owens River aqueduct in 1913, see Fogelson, *Fragmented Metropolis* (note 1), pp. 95–102.

66. "Owens River Water to Come Dashing Down Sparkling Cascade Wednesday While Many Thousands of Its Owners Applaud: Exultant Celebration at Head of San Fernando Valley, on a Stage Set by Nature, Will Mark Culmination of Los Angeles' Glorious Enterprise in Bringing Limpid River through Mountains and Desert from High Sierras to Golden Plains and Wondrous City," *Los Angeles Times*, November 2, 1913.

67. "Glorious Mountain River Now Flows to Los Angeles' Gates: Silver Torrent Crowns the City's Mighty Achievement," *Los Angeles Times*, November 6, 1913.

68. T. R. Barrabee, "This City as a Center of Art: Exposition Park Display Attracts Attention," *Los Angeles Times*, November 7, 1913.

69. Antony Anderson, "Art and Artists," *Los Angeles Times*, November 24, 1912.

CHAPTER 5
GETTING ESTABLISHED, EARLY 1913

1. TC, October 1912, p. 466ill.

2. "The Monthly Competition," AP, April 1913, p. 219.

3. AP, October 1911, p. 611ill.

4. Edward Weston, "Shall I Turn Professional?" AP, November 1912, pp. 620, 622, 624.

5. Justema, "Margaret" (prologue, note 1), p. 7.

6. Justema, "Margaret" (prologue, note 1), pp. 9–10.

7. Margrethe Mather, letter to Edward Weston, October 4, 1950, EW Archive.

8. Dennis Reed and Michael G. Wilson, *Pictorialism in California: Photographs 1900–1940* (Los Angeles, 1994), p. 69.

9. For an illustration of the Wright-Callender building, see "The Noble Architecture of Modern Los Angeles," *Los Angeles Times*, January 1, 1910.

10. Helen L. Davie, "New Home of the Los Angeles [Camera] Club," CC, September 1900, pp. 238–39, reprinted in Peter Palmquist, ed., *Camera Fiends and Kodak Girls: 50 Selections by and about Women in Photography, 1840–1930* (New York, 1989), pp. 109–111.

11. R. L. Sleeth Jr., "The Ninth American Salon," AP, January 1913, p. 21ill.

12. William Butler Yeats, "The Song of the Happy Shepherd," *Crossways* (Dublin, 1889), reprinted in Richard J. Finneran, ed., *The Collected Poems of W. B. Yeats*, rev. 2nd ed. (New York, 1996), pp. 7–8.

13. One of the most popular books of the late nineteenth century was Edward Bellamy's *Looking Backward: 2000–1887* (Boston, 1888). Bellamy's novel promoted the concept of an idealized society based on socialist principles, and it inspired many of the utopian living experiments that came into existence around 1900.

14. "Portland Exhibition," AP, April 1913, p. 240; "Society News: Ninth American Salon," AP, May 1913, p. 303.

15. *Catalogue illustré du Salon international d'art photographique, Palais des beaux-arts*, exh. cat. (Ghent, Belgium, 1913), p. 51.

16. *Salt Lake City Directory*, 1891–92, s.v. "Elmer A. Ellsworth."

17. Richard Dearborn, discussion with the author, July 20, 1998. Dearborn is the nephew-in-law of Lucile Gilmer Ellsworth. Penny Gilmer, discussions and correspondence with the author, July–August 1998. Gilmer is the great-niece of Lucile Gilmer Ellsworth.

18. *Salt Lake City Directory*, 1896–97, s.v. "Elmer A. Ellsworth."

19. *Salt Lake City Directory*, 1900, s.v. "Elmer A. Ellsworth."

20. Mather, letter to Edward Weston (note 7).

21. *New York City Directory*, 1905–6, s.v. "Elmer A. Ellsworth."

22. *The Encyclopedia of New York City*, edited by Kenneth T. Jackson (New Haven, 1995), p. 277.

23. Federal Census, Los Angeles, Los Angeles County, California, 1910, s.v. "Elmer A. Ellsworth."

24. Mather, letter to Edward Weston (note 7).

25. Gilmer, discussions and correspondence (note 17).

26. "Emma Goldman: A Guide to her Life and Documentary Sources," compiled by Candace Falk; edited by Candace Falk, Stephen Cole, and Sally Thomas, online at http://sunsite.berkeley.edu/Goldman/Guide /chronology6900.html (1869–1900); http://sunsite.berkeley.edu/Goldman/Guide/chronology0119.html (1901–1919).

27. ME, June 1912, p. 128; June 1913, p. 110; August 1913, p. 173; Emma Goldman, "On the Trail," ME, August 1914, p. 205, wherein Margrethe Mather's name is misspelled as Margaret Mato.

28. "Gaylord Wilshire Dead," obituary, *New York Times*, September 8, 1927; Donald G. Davis Jr., "The Ionaco of Gaylord Wilshire," (masters thesis, WF Papers), pp. 426–28; Ralph Hancock, *Fabulous Boulevard* (New York, 1949), pp. 85–112; *National Cyclopedia of American Biography* (Clifton, N.J. 1958), vol. 42, p. 91; Kevin Roderick, *Wilshire Boulevard: Grand Concourse of Los Angeles*, researched by J. Eric Lynxwiler (Los Angeles, 2005), pp. 15–29.

29. Robert Laurence Moore, *European Socialists and the American Promised Land* (New York, 1970), p. 198; R. W. Sutters, "U.S. vs. Henry Gaylord Wilshire," *Clarion* (London), n.d., reprinted in *Wilshire's Magazine*, March 1902, p. 53, quoted in Elliott Shore, *Talkin' Socialism: J. A. Wayland and the Radical Press* (Kansas, 1988), p. 107.

30. Kevin Starr, *Inventing the Dream: California through the Progressive Era* (New York, 1985), p. 210.

31. *National Cyclopedia of American Biography* (note 28).

32. *Los Angeles City Directory*, 1916, s.v. "Gaylord Wilshire."

33. Roderick, *Wilshire Boulevard* (note 28), p. 27.

34. Harry Kelly, "Socialism and Fatalism," ME, May 1907, pp. 136–41.

35. *T. Perceval Gerson: A Memorial Tribute*, program published on the occasion of Gerson's memorial service at the Hollywood-Roosevelt Hotel on March 18, 1960, TPG Papers.

36. Sister Jean Martin, *An Interpretation of Dr. T. Perceval Gerson*, September 24, 1966, (master's thesis), TPG Papers.

37. Emma Goldman, letters to Dr. Perceval Gerson, 1913–16, TPG Papers.

38. Sarah Noble Ives, *Altadena* (Pasadena, 1938), pp. 119–20; "Mrs. Gartz Dies at Age of 84: Philanthropist, Liberal Leader Mourned by Many," *Pasadena Star News*, May 13, 1949, newspaper clipping, Pasadena biography notebooks, Pasadena Public Library; "Kate Crane Gartz," *Pasadena Community Book* (Pasadena, 1943), pp. 723–24.

39. William D. Haywood, *Bill Haywood's Book: The Autobiography of William D. Haywood* (New York, 1929); Peter Carlson, *Roughneck: The Life and Times of Big Bill Haywood* (New York, 1983).

40. Edward H. Weston, "A One-Man Studio," AP, March 1913, pp. 130–34.

41. Lowe and Thompson, *Edward Weston Life Work* (chap. 2, note 20), plate 5; PY: 1914, pp. 10, 17, and plate 27; PP, August 1914, p. 8ill., therein titled *Roses and Sunshine*; TC, September 1914, p. 552ill., therein titled *Study*; *Amateur Photographer and Photographic News*, September 21, 1914, p. 278ill..

42. Rae Davis Knight, letter to Edward Weston [ca. 1945], EW Archive.

43. James Russell Price, "Biography of James Russell Price," GCC Papers; *Dr. James Russell Price*, Lyceum Bureau brochure advertising Dr. Price's skills as a lecturer, ca. 1913, GCC Papers.

44. Douglas Clayton, *Floyd Dell: The Life and Times of an American Rebel* (Chicago, 1994), pp. 41–42.

45. Susan Glaspell, *The Road to the Temple* (New York, 1927); Clayton, *Dell* (note 44), pp. 25, 30, 37–42, 57–59, 61, 63, 81, 99, 116, 142–46, 155; Dale Kramer, *Chicago Renaissance: The Literary Life in the Midwest 1900–1930* (New York, 1966), pp. 19–23; *Dictionary of American Biography* (New York, 1929), vol. 4, pp. 372–73; *American National Biography* (New York, 1999), vol. 5, pp. 377–78.

46. Clayton, *Dell* (note 44), pp. 86–101.

47. Clayton, *Dell* (note 44), pp. 63–64.

48. *Los Angeles City Directory*, 1914, s.v. "Mollie Price Cook," wherein she is described as "Director and Principal, The Children's House, Kindergarten, A Montessori School, In and Out-of-Doors, 2319 Ocean View."

49. Mollie Price, letter to Mary McReynolds Wilshire, April 29, 1915, WF Papers.

50. Federal Census, Independent City of Lynchburg, Commonwealth of Virginia, 1900, s.v. "Maud E. Taylor."

51. Gordon Glass, interview by the author, January 6, 2000. Glass is the son of Maud Emily Taylor Glass (aka Emily Harvin).

52. Gaylord Wilshire's address book, s.v. "Mollie Price Cook," "Russell Coryell," "Margrethe Mather," and "Maud Emily Taylor," WF Papers.

53. Stanis Coryell, interview by the author, April 25, 1999. Stanis Coryell was the son of Russell Coryell.

54. Emma Goldman, *Living My Life* (New York, 1931), pp. 335–36; Douglas W. Churchill, "'Chaplin No. 6' Enters the Hollywood Lists; 'Earl of Chicago' Begins Production at Metro—Nick Carter Returns," *New York Times*, November 5, 1939.

55. John R. Coryell authored at least nine articles in *Mother Earth*, beginning with the inaugural issue in March 1906 and continuing through the June 1908 issue.

56. Paul Avrich, *The Modern School Movement: Anarchism and Education in the United States* (Princeton, 1980), pp. 76–77.

57. *Los Angeles City Directory*, 1912, s.v. "Russell Coryell."

58. Coryell, interview (note 53).

59. Russell Coryell, California scrapbooks, 1913–15, collection of Bea Coryell, daughter-in-law of Russell Coryell.

60. Coryell, California scrapbooks (note 59).

CHAPTER 6
GETTING ACQUAINTED, LATE 1913 TO 1914

1. Mather, letter to Edward Weston (chap. 5, note 7).

2. Mather, letter to Edward Weston (chap. 5, note 7).

3. Buffie Johnson, interview by the author, April 9, 1998. Johnson was photographed by Margrethe Mather in the early 1930s.

4. Margrethe Mather, letter to Edward Weston [ca. 1913], EW Archive.

5. Justema, "Margaret" (prologue, note 1), p. 11.

6. "Glorious Mountain River Now Flows" (chap. 4, note 67).

7. Margrethe Mather, letter to Edward Weston [ca. 1913], EW Archive.

8. Nancy Newhall, "One day there burst into his studio..." (typescript, 1940s), BN/NN Papers.

9. Will Connell, notes on the history of the Camera Pictorialists of Los Angeles, ca. 1931, WC Papers; Will Connell, "The Camera Pictorialists of Los Angeles," in *The Pictorialist: A Compilation of Photographs from the Fourteenth Annual International Salon of Pictorial Photography under the auspices of the Camera Pictorialists of Los Angeles* (Los Angeles, 1931), pp. 4–5.

10. Connell, notes on the history of the Camera Pictorialists (note 9).

11. "Photography at the Panama-Pacific," CC, March 1913, p. 133; April 1913, pp. 181–82; August 1913, pp. 381–82.

12. "Photography at the Panama-Pacific Exposition: A Protest," CC, April 1913, p. 183; "Pictorial Photography at Our Coming Exposition," CC, December 1913, pp. 578–79.

13. "Platinum Print," CC, November 1913, p. 545.

14. "How 'Platinum Print' Angered and Impressed," PP, December 1913, p. 13.

15. "Camera Pictorialists of Los Angeles," CC, May 1914, p. 250.

16. Connell, notes on the history of the Camera Pictorialists (note 9).

17. George Cram Cook, *Roderick Taliaferro: A Story of Maximilian's Empire* (London, 1903); Glaspell, *Road to the Temple* (chap. 5, note 45), p. 105.

18. AP, November 1916, p. 634.

19. "Society News," AP, July 1914, p. 473; "Toronto Camera Club," PE, July 1914, p. 47; "Edward H. Weston," *Glendale News* [autumn 1914], p. 41, newspaper clipping, Edward Weston biographical file, GPL.

20. "Notes from the Illinois College of Photography," CC, July 1914, p. 360; "With the Camera," AP, August 1914, p. 543; "Edward H. Weston" (note 19).

21. "Notes and News," AP, January 1915, p. 55; "Notes and Comment: Illinois College of Photography," CC, March 1915, p. 131.

22. Bertram Park, "A Symposium: Which Is the Best Picture at the London Salon? The Honorary Secretary Pronounces for a Series by Edward H. Weston," *Amateur Photographer and Cinematographer*, September 29, 1914, p. 250, reprinted in Newhall and Conger, eds., *Edward Weston Omnibus* (chap. 2, note 30), pp. 2–3.

23. *AAP*: 1916, p. 249ill.; Theodore E. Stebbins Jr., *Weston's Westons: Portraits and Nudes* (Boston, 1989), p. 10, fig. 1.

24. PY: 1914 (chap. 5, note 41); Lowe and Thompson, *Edward Weston Life Work* (chap. 2, note 20), plate 5.

25. "Edward H. Weston" (note 19).

26. The scrapbooks of the Friday Morning Club, now in the collection of the Huntington Library, San Marino, Calif., contain a large number of newspaper clippings detailing the club's involvement in the women's suffrage movement.

27. "Mr. Weston's Exhibit at Los Angeles Club," *Glendale News*, November 5, 1914; "Silva Paintings Now on Exhibit," *Los Angeles Examiner*, November 7, 1914; "Weston of Tropico Shows Art Prints," *Los Angeles Herald*, November 24, 1914 (newspaper clippings), FMCS, vol. 3, pp. 18, 19, 22.

28. Antony Anderson, "Art and Artists," *Los Angeles Times*, November 22, 1914.

29. Homer Croy, "Just a Bit of Fun with Los Angeles: American Humorist Going Around the World for 'Leslie's Weekly' Finds Us So Big on the Map He shows Us Happy Attention—Cafeterias, Wall Beds and Handy Apartments Impress Him," *Los Angeles Times*, April 12, 1914.

30. "Opium Released: Treasury Department Rules Chance Arrival of 'Dope' for Ensenada Does Not Warrant Seizure," *Los Angeles Times*, May 10, 1914.

31. "Reds Buying Rifles to Defy Authority: Los Angeles Labor-Union Temple to Be Armed Headquarters," *Los Angeles Times*, May 10, 1914.

32. "Drills Seek Mother Rock: Well Borers Blaze Way for Business Block," *Los Angeles Times*, September 20, 1914.

33. "To Make West Fifth Large Traffic Artery: Plans Drawn Provide for Widening from Olive to Grand and a Short Tunnel to Create Outlet-Inlet from Wilshire and Other Western Districts—Property Owners Directly Affected Will Be Organized," *Los Angeles Times*, July 12, 1914.

34. Jenifer Williams Angel, interview by the author, August 11, 1998. Angel is the daughter of Frayne Williams. Gilmer, discussions and correspondence (chap. 5, note 17); Jean Cooper, discussions with the author, July–August 1998. Cooper is a great-niece of Lucile Gilmer Ellsworth.

35. Angel, interview (note 34).

36. Joyce Milton, *Tramp: The Life of Charlie Chaplin* (New York, 1996), p. 55.

37. Charles Chaplin, *My Autobiography* (New York, 1964), pp. 142–43.

38. Milton, *Tramp* (note 36), p. 64.

39. Chaplin, *My Autobiography* (note 37), p. 140, wherein he incorrectly refers to the hotel as the Great Northern.

40. Milton, *Tramp* (note 36), pp. 77–78.

41. Emma Goldman's numerous West Coast visits are chronicled in detail in her magazine, *Mother Earth* (ME herein).

42. Emma Goldman, "The Power of the Ideal," ME, June 1912, p. 128; "The Ups and Downs in the Life of an Anarchist Agitator," ME, June 1913, p. 110; "The Ups and Downs of an Anarchist Propagandist," ME, August 1913, p. 173; Goldman, "On the Trail" (chap. 5, note 27).

43. Emma Goldman, "Appeal of the Rangel-Cline Defense Fund," ME, December 1913, pp. 306–7.

44. Alexander Berkman, "The Movement of the Unemployed," ME, April 1914, pp. 36–43.

45. Alexander Berkman, "The Lexington Explosion," ME, July 1914, pp. 130–58; "Intended for the Rockefellers: But the Bomb Makers Blew Themselves to Death," *Los Angeles Times*, February 27, 1915.

46. Berkman, "Lexington Explosion" (note 45), pp. 154–56.

47. Goldman, "On the Trail" (chap. 5, note 27).

48. Emma Goldman, "Observations and Comments," ME, October 1914, pp. 250–51.

49. Hutchins Hapgood, *A Victorian in the Modern World* (New York, 1939), p. 380.

50. Neil Baldwin, *Man Ray: American Artist* (New York, 1988), p. 33.

51. Nancy Newhall, "And then there was always Flora…" (typescript, ca. 1951), BN/NN Papers.

52. Charis Wilson, discussion with the author, November 4, 1997. Wilson was the second wife of Edward Weston.

CHAPTER 7
CHALLENGES, 1915

1. Milton, *Tramp* (chap. 6, note 36), pp. 79–85.
2. "Art as Camera Portrays It: Wonders of Photography in Local Exhibition," *Los Angeles Times*, February 26, 1915.
3. Prince (aka Prynce) Hopkins, *Both Hands Before the Fire* (Santa Barbara, 1962); Walker A. Tompkins, *Santa Barbara History Makers* (Santa Barbara, 1983), pp. 316–19; "History 101," Michael Redmon, *The Independent* (Santa Barbara), June 28, 1990, p. 70; Stella Haverland Rouse, "Olden Days: School for Boys," *Santa Barbara News Press*, June 1, 1975, and "Olden Days: The Story of Boyland's Rise, Fall," *Santa Barbara News Press*, June 8, 1975 (newspaper clippings), Prince Hopkins biographical file, Santa Barbara Historical Society.
4. Avrich, *Modern School* (chap. 5, note 56), p. 74.
5. Hopkins, *Both Hands* (note 3), pp. 44–45.
6. Rouse, "Boyland's Rise, Fall" (note 3).
7. Hopkins, *Both Hands* (note 3), pp. 46–48; E. C. Pentland, "Santa Barbara and Its Beautiful Homes: Beneficial Effects of Completed and Contemplated Good Roads—Where are Great Tourist Hotels. Seashore and Mountain are Near—Santa Cruz Island a Future Resort. Montecito and Its Millionaire Residents," *Los Angeles Times*, October 31, 1915.
8. Pentland, "Santa Barbara" (note 7).
9. Russell Coryell, letter to Maud Emily Taylor, January 21, 1915, MEG Papers.
10. Russell Coryell identified these two portraits as Margrethe Mather photographs in his scrapbook (see chap. 5, note 59); Beth Gates Warren, *Margrethe Mather and Edward Weston: A Passionate Collaboration* (New York, 2001), p. 18, fig. 4.
11. Moure, *Dictionary of Art* (chap. 4, note 31), p. 264; Antony Anderson, "Art and Artists," *Los Angeles Times*, May 15, 1910; January 29, 1911.
12. Frank Luther Mott, *A History of American Magazines* (Cambridge, Mass., 1938), vol. 4, p. 451.
13. Mott, *History* (note 12), vol. 4, p. 66.
14. Vital Records Office, death records, Santa Barbara County Courthouse, Santa Barbara, California, s.v. "Jessie Willis Wagner" (d. August 19, 1906).
15. *Santa Barbara City Directory*, 1909–10, s.v. "R. L. Wagner."
16. Antony Anderson, "Art and Artists," *Los Angeles Times*, November 12, 1911.
17. Antony Anderson, "Art and Artists," *Los Angeles Times*, January 23, 1910; February 6, 1910; April 10, 1910; May 15, 1910; June 19, 1910; July 3, 1910; September 4, 1910; October 23, 1910; November 6, 1910; January 29, 1911; November 12, 1911.
18. *Santa Barbara City Directory*, 1903–05, s.v. "James R. H. Wagner"; *Los Angeles City Directory*, 1906–17, s.v. "James R. H. Wagner."
19. *Who's Who in California*, ed. Justice B. Detwiler (Los Angeles, 1929), s.v. "James R. H. Wagner," p. 676.
20. "Art as Camera Portrays It" (note 2).
21. Ellen Katherine Cook was given the nickname Ma-Mie (or M'Amie) by the poet Rudyard Kipling while they were fellow passengers on a transatlantic voyage. See Emily Harvin (aka Maud Emily Taylor Glass), "The Most Unforgettable Character I've Met," n.d., MEG Papers.
22. Harvin, "The Most Unforgettable Character" (note 21); Emily Harvin, (aka Maud Emily Taylor Glass), "Ma-Mie," n.d., MEG Papers; Glaspell, *Road to the Temple* (chap. 5, note 45), pp. 16–19.
23. Eugene O'Neill would later base the character of Deborah Harford in his play *More Stately Mansions* (written between 1936 and 1939 but not produced until after his death) on Ellen "Ma-Mie" Cook, see Louis Sheaffer, *O'Neill: Son and Playwright* (Boston, 1968), p. 354.
24. Kevin Starr, *Americans and the California Dream 1850–1945* (New York, 1973), pp. 288–306; "San Francisco's Exposition Has World Wide Scope: Gladness and Color of San Francisco's Exposition" and "Novel Features of Fair to Astonish and Delight," *Los Angeles Times*, January 1, 1915; "Vivid Word Picture of San Francisco Exposition's Outburst: San Francisco's Emotion," *Los Angeles Times*, February 21, 1915.

25. *Pictorial Photography Catalogue*, exh. cat. (San Francisco: Panama-Pacific International Exposition, 1915).

26. "The Awards in the Pictorial Section, P.-P.I.E.," CC, October 1915, pp. 411–12.

27. "Edward H. Weston is Accorded Merited Article in Issue of 'Portrait,'" *Tropico Sentinel*, June 9, 1915, newspaper clipping, Edward Weston biographical file, GPL; AP, March 1915, p. 31; "The Awards in the Pictorial Section, P.-P.I.E.," CC, October 1915, p. 411; Conger, "Edward Weston's Early Photography" (chap. 2, note 10), fig. 14/9, therein titled "A Flower in the Land of Sunshine."

28. Edward Henry Weston, "Photography as a Means of Artistic Expression" (manuscript of lecture delivered to the College Woman's Club, Los Angeles, October 18, 1916), EW/JH Collection, reprinted in Peter Bunnell, *Edward Weston on Photography* (Salt Lake City, 1983), pp. 8–21.

29. Weston, "Photography as a Means" (note 28).

30. "Chronology of the War in Western Europe," *Los Angeles Times*, January 24, 1915.

31. "New Era of Gold Mining Activity in California: The Indispensable Cyanide," *Los Angeles Times*, January 1, 1915.

32. "To Stop Sale of Absinthe," *Los Angeles Times*, January 24, 1915.

33. James Thomson, "A Silver-Platinum Printing Paper," AP, November 1915, pp. 630–36.

34. Thomson, "Silver-Platinum" (note 33).

35. "Los Angeles: The Globe's Moving Picture Center," *Los Angeles Times*, January 1, 1915.

36. "The Jesse L. Lasky Feature Play Co. Announces the First Anniversary of Its Organization," advertisement, *Los Angeles Times*, January 1, 1915.

37. "Popular People in Film World," *Los Angeles Times*, January 1, 1915.

38. "Globe's Moving Picture Center" (note 35).

39. "Globe's Moving Picture Center" (note 35).

40. "The Selig Polyscope Company," *Los Angeles Times*, January 1, 1915.

41. "Oz Film Manufacturing Co.," *Los Angeles Times*, January 1, 1915.

42. "Laughlin Park," *Los Angeles Times*, January 1, 1915.

43. Starr, *Material Dreams* (chap. 2, note 5), p. 209.

44. "Borrowed from the Far East: Noted Importers Completing Unique House," *Los Angeles Times*, January 11, 1914; "Palatial Home is Finished: Crowns Hollywood Hill Like Shogun's Castle," *Los Angeles Times*, November 15, 1914. The Bernheimers' former home, now a Hollywood landmark, currently houses a restaurant called Yamashiro.

45. Antony Anderson, "Art and Artists," *Los Angeles Times*, October 31, 1915.

46. *AAP*: 1917, p. 79ill.

47. *AAP*: 1915, p. 193ill., therein titled *Gaunt, Driven Boughs in the Sweep of Open Wold*.

48. Anderson, "Art and Artists" (note 45).

49. George Hopkins became a highly respected Hollywood art director and set decorator. During his long career he was nominated for thirteen Academy Awards, and won the coveted Oscar four times—in 1951 for *A Streetcar Named Desire*, in 1964 for *My Fair Lady*, in 1966 for *Who's Afraid of Virginia Woolf?* and in 1969 for *Hello, Dolly!* Hopkins figures prominently in Sidney D. Kirkpatrick, *A Cast of Killers* (New York, 1986), because of his close relationship with director William Desmond Taylor.

50. Lowe and Thompson, *Edward Weston Life Work* (chap. 2, note 20), plate 10.

51. "Dancer Begins Her Tour Here: Mason to Have St. Denis with Large Troupe," *Los Angeles Times*, October 3, 1915.

52. Henry Christeen Warnack, "Maud Allan and the Dance: An Interesting Sketch of the Famous Lyric Terpsichorean Artist Who Is Visiting Here—Her Understanding of Esthetic Values and Her Vitality," *Los Angeles Times*, July 11, 1915.

53. "Unique Among Homes of America's Rich: Heiress to Half of 'Lucky' Baldwin's Millions Completes Dwelling of Charming Elegance on a Corner of Santa Anita Ranch—Giant Oaks, Rare Birds and Valuable Animals Complete Harmonious Setting," *Los Angeles Times*, September 21, 1913; "Southern California's Model Stock Farm and Its Prize Winners: The Santa Anita Rancho," *Los Angeles Times*, January 1, 1916; Sharon Palmer, "Anoakia, Anita Baldwin's Dream" (typescript, ca. 2003).

54. "An Artist-Photographer," TC, June 1916, cover ill., pp. 324, 327, 327ill.

55. AP, July 1918, p. 393ill.; Jennifer A. Watts, "Life-Work: Edward Weston's Guggenheim Gift," in Danly et al., *Edward Weston: A Legacy*, exh. cat. (San Marino, Calif., 2003), p. 11, fig. 3.

56. "An Artist-Photographer" (note 54); TC, November 1916, cover ill.

57. PY: 1915, p. 14 and plate 9.

58. Matthew Schmidt was arrested in New York City on February 13, 1915, shortly after leaving the Woodstock Hotel on West Forty-Third Street.

59. "David Caplan Caught on Bainbridge Island: Last of the McNamara Dynamiting Gang Held at Port Orchard," *Los Angeles Times*, February 19, 1915.

60. "Stolen Papers Lead to Chase: Detective Halted on Boat and Searched for Documents in Schmidt Case," *Los Angeles Times*, October 30, 1915; " 'Bad Faith' is State's Charge: Ulterior Motives Imputed to the Schmidt Defense," *Los Angeles Times*, November 3, 1915; " 'Old Man' The Storm Center: Tveitmoe may be Implicated in Dynamite Cases," *Los Angeles Times*, November 5, 1915.

61. "Schmidt is Found Guilty of Murder in the First Degree: Jury Fixes Penalty at Life Imprisonment After Three Ballots and Less than Half an Hour's Time Taken for Deliberation—Tveitmoe's Threat," *Los Angeles Times*, December 31, 1915.

CHAPTER 8
OUTSIDE INFLUENCES, 1916

1. Rosenstone, *Romantic Revolutionary* (chap. 4, note 62), pp. 242–43.

2. Alma Whitaker, "Pershing Memorial," *Los Angeles Times*, November 15, 1918; "Monument for Renamed Park: Victory Memorial to be Built in Pershing Square," *Los Angeles Times*, November 16, 1918.

3. "Friday Morning Club," January 11, 1916, and "Brahmin Priest to Speak to Women," n.d. (newspaper clippings), FMCS, vol. 4, p. 2; Dhan Gopal Mukerji, *Caste and Outcast* (New York, 1923), in which he refers to Terry Carlin as "Jerry."

4. Dorothy Willis, "Socialism's Aims Forcefully Told to Clubwomen," *Los Angeles Tribune*, February 19, 1916; and "Max Eastman as an Intellectual Force," *Los Angeles Graphic*, February 26, 1916 (newspaper clippings), FMCS, vol. 4, pp. 14–15.

5. "Tart Talk on Taboo Topic: Friday Morning Club is Told About Birth Control," *Los Angeles Times*, June 3, 1916 (newspaper clipping), FMCS, vol. 4, p. 69.

6. "Tagore Coming to Explain His Poems to L.A. Club Women: Indian Writer and Philosopher to Deliver Series of Lectures," *Los Angeles Herald*, September 13, 1916 (newspaper clipping), FMCS, vol. 4, p. 112.

7. "Pastor-Groom Holds 'Radical Woman' Ideal: New Husband of Mrs. Sarah Bixby Smith Outlines Views Before Friday Morning Club," *Los Angeles Examiner*, April 1, 1916 (newspaper clipping), FMCS, vol. 4, p. 26.

8. "Is It Yellow to Fight for Decency?" *Los Angeles Examiner*, April 6, 1916 (newspaper clipping), FMCS, vol. 4, p. 26.

9. "Trying Hard for an Alibi: Witnesses for David Caplan Tell Their Stories," *Los Angeles Times*, May 11, 1916.

10. "Emma Goldman in Chicago," ME, June 1906, pp. 11–12.

11. Hutchins Hapgood, *An Anarchist Woman* (New York, 1909).

12. Summarized testimony from respondent's brief, part 1, *People of State of California v. M. A. Schmidt*, Dist. Ct. App., 2d App. Dist., Los Angeles (October 1916), pp. 282–95

13. Although Emma Goldman never publicly accused Terry Carlin in the pages of *Mother Earth* (Emma Goldman, "Donald Vose: The Accursed," ME, January 1916, pp. 353–57), it was well known within the anarchist community that Goldman suspected Carlin of having collaborated with Vose in bringing about Schmidt's arrest. Several letters written by Carlin to Neith Boyce, wife of Hutchins Hapgood and close friend of Emma Goldman, document his anger over his anarchist friends' betrayal and his denial of any involvement in the events that led to Schmidt's capture (see Terry Carlin, letters to Neith Boyce [ca. 1914–15], HF Papers). When it came to the subject of the *Los Angeles Times*, Carlin knew he had a sympathetic ear in Neith Boyce. Her grandfather, Henry H. Boyce, had once co-owned the *Los Angeles Times* with Harrison Gray Otis, a partnership that had ended in much acrimony and multiple libel suits. Boyce subsequently invested in his own daily, the *Los Angeles Tribune*,

becoming Otis's archrival. After several years of cutthroat competition, Otis, with the help of his future son-in-law, Harry Chandler, finally forced Boyce and his newpaper into bankruptcy. Gottlieb and Wolt, *Thinking Big* (chap. 2, note 5), pp. 13, 20–21, 25, 28, 35, 122.

14. Sheaffer, *O'Neill* (chap. 7, note 23), pp. 335–38.

15. Federal Census, San Francisco, San Francisco County, California, 1910, s.v. "George Liberman."

16. *Los Angeles City Directory*, 1912–18, s.v. "George Lipton."

17. "'Bad Faith' Is State's Charge" (chap. 7, note 60).

18. Marie Latter, letter to Betty Katz [ca. 1917], BK Papers.

19. Latter, letter to Betty Katz (note 18).

20. Thomas, "A David Grayson," (chap. 2, note 30).

21. Antony Anderson, "Of Art and Artists," *Los Angeles Times*, February 6, 1916.

22. *First Annual Arts and Crafts Salon: Gallery of Fine and Applied Arts, Museum of History, Science and Art, Exposition Park, Los Angeles, California, February 4 to 27, 1916*, exh. brochure, EW Archive.

23. Antony Anderson, "Of Art and Artists," *Los Angeles Times*, February 18, 1916.

24. *Los Angeles Graphic*, February 19, 1916, newspaper clipping, LAMHSAS, vol. 3.

25. Anderson, "Of Art and Artists" (note 23).

26. AP, November 1916, p. 601ill.

27. "An Artist-Photographer" (chap. 7, note 54), cover ill., p. 327ill.

28. "An Artist-Photographer" (chap. 7, note 54), p. 335ill.

29. "An Artist-Photographer" (chap. 7, note 54), p. 336ill.

30. "An Artist-Photographer" (chap. 7, note 54), p. 331ill.

31. "An Artist-Photographer" (chap. 7, note 54), pp. 328ill, 332ill.

32. TC, July 1916, p. 387ill.

33. Conger, "Edward Weston's Early Photography" (chap. 2, note 10), "Catalogue," p. 191.

34. Antony Anderson, "Of Art and Artists," *Los Angeles Times*, June 11, 1916.

35. "Renaissance of the Dance Renews the Eldest of Arts: Lack of Exercise for the Legs and Relaxation of Religious Severity Fill Cafes with Dancers, Encourage Real Artists to Splendid Interpretations, Brings to Light an Old Masterpiece on the Technique of the Greeks and Brings a New Masterpiece from the Camera of Arnold Genthe—Brief Comment on the Vicissitudes of the Choregraphic [sic] Art," *Los Angeles Times*, September 3, 1916.

36. Cole Weston, discussion with the author, May 5, 1997. Cole Weston was the youngest son of Edward Weston.

37. *Los Angeles City Directory*, 1916, s.v. "Margrethe Mather."

38. Arnold Hylen, *Los Angeles Before the Freeways* (Los Angeles, 1981), pp. 52–53, pp. 149–50, plates 100–101.

39. *Los Angeles City Directory*, 1891, s.v. "Rev. Edward [sic] Hildreth."

40. Gebhard, David, Harriette von Breton, and Robert Winter, *Samuel and Joseph Cather Newsom: Victorian Imagery in California 1878–1908*, exh. cat. (University of California, Santa Barbara, 1979, pp. 16, 45, 83ill. The Hildreth house first appeared in the 1888 *Los Angeles City Directory*, listed at 245 South Hope Street. In 1891 the houses on Hope Street were renumbered, and the address of the Hildreth house was changed to 357 South Hope Street (*Los Angeles City Directory*, 1890–91).

41. Federal Census, Los Angeles, Los Angeles County, California, 1910, s.v. "George L. Haynes."

42. Hylen, *Los Angeles Before the Freeways* (note 38).

43. Justema, "Margaret" (prologue, note 1), p. 8.

44. *Los Angeles City Directory*, under heading "Photographers," 1916, s.v. "Margrethe Mather."

45. Justema, "Margaret" (prologue, note 1), p. 8.

46. Death certificate of Joseph Cole Mather (chap. 3, note 22); Mount Olivet Cemetery, burial records, Salt Lake City, Utah, September 1916, s.v. "Joseph Cole Mather"; "Called by Death," obituary, *Deseret Evening News*, September 2, 1916.

47. Marriage license of J.C. Mather and Minnie Jensen (aka Laurentzen), July 21, 1911, Salt Lake County Clerk, Salt Lake City, Salt Lake County, Utah.

48. Pitts, discussions and correspondence (chap. 3, note 11).

49. Death certificate of James Youngreen [Youngren], d. November 20, 1916, Salt Lake City, Salt Lake County, Utah; "Called by Death," obituary, *Deseret Evening News*, November 20, 1916.

50. Justema, "Margaret" (prologue, note 1), pp. 7–8.

51. Florence Treseder, audiotape interview by Jane Purse, February 1, 1976, FR Collection; Jane Purse, discussions and correspondence with the author, April–May, 1998. Treseder was the niece of Florence Reynolds.

52. Candace Falk, *Love, Anarchy, and Emma Goldman* (New York, 1984). In Emma Goldman's letters to Ben Reitman, also known as "king of the hobos," she frequently addresses him affectionately as "Hobo."

53. Ellen Katherine (Ma-Mie) Cook, letter to George Cram (Jig) Cook, postmarked January 17, 1916, GCC Papers.

54. Antony Anderson, "Art and Artists," *Los Angeles Times*, November 26, 1911.

55. Cook, letter to George Cram (Jig) Cook (note 53). Quotation courtesy of the Henry W. and Albert A. Berg Collection of English and American Literature, The New York Public Library, Astor, Lenox and Tilden Foundations.

56. Treseder, interview by Purse (note 51).

57. Treseder, interview by Purse (note 51).

58. Northwestern University, University Archives, University Library, Evanston, Illinois, Class of 1901, s.v. "Florence Reynolds."

59. Federal Census, Salt Lake City, Salt Lake County, Utah, 1900, s.v. "William Mack."

60. Various correspondents, letters to Florence Reynolds during her Salt Lake City visits, 1900–06, FR Collection.

61. Jane Heap, letters to Florence Reynolds, 1908–26, FR Collection.

62. Jane Heap and Florence Reynolds, *Dear Tiny Heart: The Letters of Jane Heap and Florence Reynolds*, ed. Holly Baggett (New York, 2000), pp. 23, 26, 29, 31.

63. Margaret Anderson, *My Thirty Years' War* (New York, 1930), pp. 103–16; Kramer, *Chicago Renaissance* (chap. 5, note 45), pp. 244–62; Purse, discussions and correspondence (note 51).

64. Goldman, *Living My Life* (chap. 5, note 54), pp. 530–32.

65. Goldman, *Living My Life* (chap. 5, note 54), p. 530.

66. Goldman, *Living My Life* (chap. 5, note 54), p. 531.

67. Anderson, *My Thirty Years' War* (note 63), pp. 69–75, 83–85.

68. Heap and Reynolds, *Dear Tiny Heart* (note 62), pp. 2–3; Heap, letters to Florence Reynolds (note 61).

69. Anderson, *My Thirty Years' War* (note 63), p. 107.

70. William Justema, letter to Lee Witkin, January 22, 1979, LW/WG Archive. Although Justema's chronology of events varies somewhat from historical fact, he gives further credence to the theory that Florence Reynolds was Mather's "Beau" when he writes, "Beau had been secretary to Emma Goldman the anarchist (& also a lesbian) before she joined Margaret Anderson (in Chicago) who had just founded the Little Review."

71. Addresses on correspondence in the FR Collection indicate that Florence Reynolds paid regular visits to the Macks, beginning around 1915 and continuing through 1942, at which time she moved permanently into their home at 1523 North Curson Avenue in West Hollywood.

72. *Los Angeles City Directory*, 1915–29, s.v. "Dr. William F. Mack."

73. O. C. Reiter and M. C. Rypinski, "The Sixth Pittsburgh Salon," PE, May 1919, p. 224–25.

74. Anderson, *My Thirty Years' War* (note 63), p. 111.

75. Lawrence Langner, *The Magic Curtain* (New York, 1951), pp. 83–84. Langner does not identify Aline Barnsdall by name, but rather refers to her as "Celeste."

76. "Nineteen Millions" is identified as Aline Barnsdall in Jackson Robert Bryer, "A Trial-Track for Racers—Margaret C. Anderson and The Little Review" (Ph.D. dissertation, University of Wisconsin, Madison, 1965), p. 201n73, wherein Bryer states that Margaret Anderson disclosed the identity of "Nineteen Millions" in a letter to him, dated February 28, 1964.

77. Anderson, *My Thirty Years' War* (note 63), pp. 111–112.

78. Anderson, *My Thirty Years' War* (note 63), p. 115.

79. "Disagreement is Indicated: No Verdict Near in Dynamite Case, Say Talesmen," *Los Angeles Times*, May 15, 1916.

80. "Dynamite Case to be Retried: Caplan Must Again Face Jury on Murder Charge," *Los Angeles Times*, May 17, 1916.

81. Alexander Berkman, "The Blast," ME, September 1915, pp. 369–70.

82. Alexander Berkman, "Planning Judicial Murder," ME, August 1916, pp. 597–603; Robert Minor, "The San Francisco Bomb," ME, August 1916, pp. 608–11; Emma Goldman, "Stray Thoughts," ME, August 1916, pp. 615–21.

83. Anderson, *My Thirty Years' War* (note 63), pp. 119–20.

84. Goldman, "Stray Thoughts" (note 82), p. 616.

85. "The Thirty-Sixth National Convention," CC, April 1916, p. 166; "Photographers' Association of America," PE, April 1916, p. 203; "The Thirty-Sixth Annual Convention Photographers' Association of America, Wigmore Coliseum, Cleveland, O., the Week of July 24," *Photography Journal of America*, May 1916, p. 224; "Photographers' Association of America, Cleveland, July 24 to 29," PE, June 1916, p. 306; Antony Anderson, "Of Art and Artists," *Los Angeles Times*, July 30, 1916; "Thirty-Sixth Annual Convention Photographers' Association of America, Wigmore Coliseum, Cleveland, Ohio, July 24 to 28, 1916," PE, September 1916, p. 143.

86. "Artist Wins Honor: Work of Local Photographer Is Given Place in Permanent Salon by Association of America—To Demonstrate His Method in East," *Los Angeles Times*, August 6, 1916.

87. Anderson, *My Thirty Years' War* (note 63), plate opp. p. 54.

88. Arthur Davison Ficke, "Rupert Brooke (A Memory)," poem accompanied by a tipped-in reproduction of Eugene Hutchinson's photograph of Brooke, *The Little Review*, June–July 1915, p. 33.

89. AP, July 1917, p. 383ill.

90. TC, April 1917, p. 179ill.; J. Addison Reid, "The Toronto Camera Club Salon," CC, November 1917, p. 460ill.; *Amateur Photographer and Photographic News*, October 22, 1917, p. 265ill; PY: 1917–1918, p. 12 and plate 23; Warren, *Passionate Collaboration* (chap. 7, note 10), p. 20, fig. 8.

91. Justema, "Margaret" (prologue, note 1), p. 8; Anderson, *My Thirty Years' War* (note 63), pp. 112, 133.

92. Elsie Whitaker Martinez, "San Francisco Bay Area Writers and Artists," interviews by Willa Klug Baum and Franklin D. Walker, September 10–13, December 18, 1962; May 8, July 9, 1963; Regional Oral History Office, The Bancroft Library, University of California, Berkeley, pp. 101–02

93. Antony Anderson, "Of Art and Artists," *Los Angeles Times*, May 20, 1917.

94. The July 1914 issue of *The Little Review* lists William Saphier as Circulation Manager; Kramer, *Chicago Renaissance* (chap. 5, note 45), p. 259; Mott, *History* (chap. 7, note 12), vol. 4, p. 438.

95. Alfred Kreymborg, *Troubadour: An Autobiography* (New York, 1925), pp. 260–61, 279–80, 290–91; "Alfred Kreymborg Is Dead at 82; Poet and Playwright in 'Village'; After Difficult Early Years, He Wrote 40 Books—Read Words to Music," obituary, *New York Times*, August 15, 1966.

96. Antony Anderson, "Of Art and Artists," *Los Angeles Times*, May 20, 1917.

97. William Saphier, "Margrethe," poem in *Others for 1919: An Anthology of the New Verse*, ed. Alfred Kreymborg (New York, 1920), p. 149.

98. Edward Henry Weston, "Notes on High Key Portraiture," AP, August 1916, p. 407–13.

99. Weston, "High Key Portraiture" (note 98), p. [411]ill.; Conger, "Edward Weston's Early Photography" (chap. 2, note 10), p. 128, fig. 15/10.

100. Weston, "High Key Portraiture" (note 98), p. [409]ill.; Conger, "Edward Weston's Early Photography" (chap. 2, note 10), p. 119, fig. 16/14.

101. Weston, "High Key Portraiture" (note 98), p. [413]ill.; Conger, "Edward Weston's Early Photography" (chap. 2, note 10), p. 97, fig. 14/10.

102. Weston, "High Key Portraiture" (note 98), p. [408]ill.; Conger, "Edward Weston's Early Photography" (chap. 2, note 10), p. 187, fig. 16/19.

103. AP, November 1916, pp. 589ill., p. 634.

104. AP (note 103), p. 601ill.

105. Milton, *Tramp* (chap. 6, note 36), pp. 99–101.

106. Milton, *Tramp* (chap. 6, note 36), pp. 99, 102–06.

107. Milton, *Tramp* (chap. 6, note 36), p. 102.

108. Milton, *Tramp* (chap. 6, note 36), pp. 111–12.

109. Milton, *Tramp* (chap. 6, note 36), pp. 126–27.

110. Severance Club Membership Ledger, p. 155, s.v. "Mr. and Mrs. Rob Wagner," SC Records.

111. "Los Angeles to Outdo World in Tribute to the Bard of Avon," *Los Angeles Times*, April 16, 1916; "Magnificent Reproduction of Old Rome in Hollywood Hills: Thirty-five Thousand Persons, Including Notables from Everywhere, Are to Witness Stupendous Open-Air Shakespearean Tercentenary," *Los Angeles Times*, April 16, 1916.

112. "Five Thousand Actors in Great Outdoor Play: Stage of Three Hundred and Sixty Acres for Presentation of 'Julius Caesar' in Beachwood Park—World Famous Actors in Leading Parts—Ancient Rome has been Reproduced for Actors' Fund Benefit," *Los Angeles Times*, May 14, 1916; "Forty Thousand See Rome's Mighty Tragedy Re-Enacted: Tremendous Outpouring Cheers Immense Cast in Spectacular Open-air Production of 'Julius Caesar' in Setting Copied from History on Hollywood Hills," *Los Angeles Times*, May 20, 1916.

113. Antony Anderson, "Art and Artists," *Los Angeles Times*, January 16, 1916.

114. Antony Anderson, "Art and Artists," *Los Angeles Times*, February 6, 1916.

115. "Hollywood Woman's Club," *Los Angeles Times*, September 17, 1916; "Women's Work, Women's Clubs: On Japan," *Los Angeles Times*, September 22, 1916.

116. "Child Prodigy Wins Plaudits: Eleven Years Old, Her Ambition is to be a Second Sarah Bernhardt—Is Special Student of Dramatics at the University of Southern California," *Los Angeles Times*, April 24, 1916.

117. Edwin Schallert, "Works of Beauty: Impressionistic Music," *Los Angeles Times*, April 16, 1916.

118. "Futuristic Genius," *Los Angeles Times*, August 8, 1915.

119. Jeanne Redman, "Modern Music Iconoclasts: The Boy Who Bangs the Piano with His Doubled Fist, The Mood of the Times Expressed in Music, War in Tones—How and When America May Hope to Have Art," *Los Angeles Times*, July 22, 1916.

120. "Shows Younger Men Duty of Citizen: Charles F. Lummis Aids in Enforcement of Law," *Los Angeles Times*, June 25, 1916.

121. "Rindge Estate Defines Stand: Dangers in Ungarded [sic] Travel Across Rancho Told," *Los Angeles Times*, May 14, 1916.

122. "Harvard Still Fastest Ship," *Los Angeles Times*, March 3, 1915.

123. "Steamships," advertisement for Yale and Harvard Steamship Line, *Los Angeles Times*, May 29, 1916.

124. "Plans Warmly Indorsed [sic] for a Union Terminal at Plaza: Council Unanimously Approves Viaduct Report Putting the Matter into Hands of Railroad Commission, and Chamber of Commerce Pledges Support," *Los Angeles Times*, May 17, 1916.

125. "Opium Joy-Ride Latest Fashion for Autoists," *Los Angeles Times*, August 3, 1916.

126. "Opium Cache to be Investigated: Santa Monica Officials Unearth Fence," *Los Angeles Times*, September 10, 1916.

127. Henry Christeen Warnack, "The Handmaid of Truth: A Passing Picture of the Higher Function of the Stage, in Connection with the Present Dramatic Revical [sic]—Two Local Dramatic Projects of Particular Excellence," *Los Angeles Times*, October 1, 1916.

128. Grace Kingsley, "Calcium and Camera: Director of Little Theater Company Arrives," *Los Angeles Times*, October 7, 1916; Grace Kingsley, "Calcium and Camera: Little Theater Opening Next Tuesday Night," *Los Angeles Times*, October 26, 1916; Henry Christeen Warnack, "Exactly Voices Idea: Staging of 'Nju' is Attuned to Author's Purpose," *Los Angeles Times*, November 2, 1916.

129. Norman M. Karasick and Dorothy K. Karasick, *The Oilman's Daughter: A Biography of Aline Barnsdall* (Encino, Calif., 1993), pp. 50–51.

130. "California Writer Passes Away Suddenly: Medical Aid Rushed from San Francisco, but Without Avail," *Los Angeles Times*, November 23, 1916.

131. The cause of Jack London's demise has long been a subject of controversy. Immediately after his death, rumors spread that he had committed suicide, in part because a half-empty bottle of morphine was found near his bed. However, London had suffered from kidney failure for at least three years prior to his death and was often in extreme pain, so it is very possible that he accidentally overdosed on the morphine he regularly used as a painkiller. According to his death certificate, he died of "uraemia following renal colic," with chronic interstitial nephritis listed as a contributing factor.

132. "Dancers are Coming: Famous Nijinsky Troupe is Due at Clune's Auditorium During Christmas Week—Will

Bring Many Big Colorful Attractions," *Los Angeles Times*, November 19, 1916, part 3; "Merrily Masculine: Easy to Pick Your Matinee Idol This Week," *Los Angeles Times*, December 24, 1916.

133. Jeanne Redman, "Futurist Dancing, Music, Art: Los Angeles Did Not Go Wild Over Russian Ballet, but Must Make Up Its Mind to Accept New Forms and Modes of Expression," *Los Angeles Times*, January 7, 1917.

134. Chaplin, *My Autobiography* (chap. 6, note 37), pp. 192–93.

135. "Charlie Chaplin's Artistic Bent," *Los Angeles Graphic*, June 16, 1917, newspaper clipping, LAMHSAS, vol. 4.

136. Milton, *Tramp* (chap. 6, note 36), p. 148; Chaplin, *My Autobiography* (chap. 6, note 37), pp. 190, 192.

137. Roy Rosen, letter to Lawrence Jasud, October 24, 1980, RR Papers.

138. Death certificate of L. Neil Weston (b. December 6, 1916, d. May 9, 1998), Waikoloa, Hawaii County, Hawaii.

139. Marriage license of Elmer Ellsworth and Lucile Gilmer, January 29, 1917, Salt Lake County Clerk, Salt Lake City, Salt Lake County, Utah.

140. Elmer Ellsworth and Lucile Gilmer lived at 814 West Twenty-Third Street, in the West Adams District of Los Angeles, from 1920 until at least 1930. Federal Census, Los Angeles, Los Angeles County, California, 1920, 1930, s.v. "Elmer Ellsworth."

CHAPTER 9
THE TIDE TURNS, 1917

1. *Photo=Graphic Art* (formerly PP), October 1917, p. 8ill.; CC, March 1919, p. 92ill.

2. Conger, "Edward Weston's Early Photography" (chap. 2, note 10), p. 218, fig. 17/2.

3. AAP: 1921 (New York, 1920), p. 263ill.

4. PY: 1917–1918, p. 16 and plate 59; see Warren, *Passionate Collaboration* (chap. 7, note 10), p. 46, plate 7.

5. "The John Wanamaker Exhibition," PE, April 1917, p. 206.

6. "1917 Spring Exhibitions," AP, May 1917, p. 310.

7. "1917 Spring Exhibitions" (note 6).

8. Maria Morris Hambourg, *Paul Strand: Circa 1916* (New York, 1998), plate 18.

9. *Twelfth Annual Exhibition, Photography, March 1st to 17th, John Wanamaker, Philadelphia*, exh. cat. (Philadelphia, 1917).

10. W. H. Porterfield, "The Pittsburg [*sic*] Salon, 1917," PJA, May 1917, p. 207.

11. Porterfield, "The Pittsburg Salon" (note 10), p. 184.

12. Antony Anderson, "Of Art and Artists," *Los Angeles Times*, March 11, 1917.

13. Alma Whitaker, "Women's Work, Women's Clubs," *Los Angeles Times*, April 28, 1917; Dorothy Willis, "Word Tumbling by Powys Stirs Women at Club," *Los Angeles Express*, April 27, 1917, and "Critic's View of Writers Stirs Club," *Los Angeles Examiner*, April 28, 1917 (newspaper clippings), FMCS, vol. 4, pp. 204–6.

14. Paul Jordan-Smith, *The Road I Came* (Caldwell, Idaho, 1960), pp. 329–30. Powys visited Los Angeles in both 1917 and 1918.

15. Jordan-Smith, *The Road I Came* (note 14), pp. 239–88; Kevin Starr, *Material Dreams* (chap. 2, note 5), pp. 315–319.

16. "The Literature of Individual Revolt: Six Lectures on American Writers by Paul Jordan-Smith," advertisement, *Los Angeles Times*, March 25, 1917.

17. Jordan-Smith, *The Road I Came* (note 14), pp. 314–20.

18. Rosenstone, *Romantic Revolutionary* (chap. 4, note 62), pp. 263.

19. Jordan-Smith, *The Road I Came* (note 14), pp. 321–22.

20. Jordan-Smith, *The Road I Came* (note 14), pp. 384–90.

21. J. Addison Reid, "The Toronto Camera Club Salon," CC, November 1917, p. 458.

22. "Club News and Notes: Southern California Camera Club," CC, July 1916, p. 293.

23. Antony Anderson, "Of Art and Artists," *Los Angeles Times*, May 13, 1917.

24. Antony Anderson, "Of Art and Artists," *Los Angeles Times*, May 20, 1917.

25. Kreymborg, *Troubadour* (chap. 8, note 95), p. 295–96; Alma Whitaker, "Women's Work, Women's Clubs," *Los Angeles Times*, July 2, 1917, n.p. (newspaper clipping), FMCS, vol. 4, p. 211.

26. Kreymborg, *Troubadour* (chap. 8, note 95), pp. 290–91. During Kreymborg's trip to California, his friend William Saphier took the reins at Kreymborg's literary journal, *Others*, editing the June and December 1917 issues and the February 1918 issue. After Kreymborg's return to New York City, Saphier stayed on as associate editor.

27. See "Exhibition Chronologies," 1917, herein, for titles of exhibited works.

28. "London Letter," PE, September 1917, p. 162; "E. H. Weston Honored," CC, September 1917, p. 388; "Our Workers at the London Salon," CC, November 1917, p. 516.

29. "Palladium in Place of Platinum," CC, September 1917, p. 358.

30. Weston, *Daybooks*, vol. 1 (prologue, note 2), p. 205; "Palladium in Place of Platinum" (note 29).

31. "New Community Theater of Hollywood to Open," *Los Angeles Times*, November 4, 1917; Henry Christeen Warnack, "Hollywood Discovers the Community Theater," *Los Angeles Times*, November 11, 1917.

32. Wilson and Madar, *Through Another Lens* (chap. 1, note 25), pp. 20–24.

33. "Inspirations of Author: Harry Leon Wilson's Two Greatest Prides," *Los Angeles Times*, September 23, 1917ill.

34. Angel, interview (chap. 6, note 34).

35. Karasick and Karasick, *Oilman's Daughter* (chap. 8, note 129), p. 52.

36. Karasick and Karasick, *Oilman's Daughter* (chap. 8, note 129), pp. 52, 54–55.

37. Angel, interview (chap. 6, note 34).

38. *Los Angeles City Directory*, 1921, s.v. "Frayne Williams."

39. *The Literary Theatre [A record] Formed for the purpose of presenting plays of Literary and Dramatic merit—without compromise to popular taste*, 1922, advertising brochure [ca. 1923]; *Dramatic Interpretation, Lectures and Studies, Frayne Williams, Director, Actor, and Dramatist*, advertising brochure, published under auspices of University of California, Extension Division, Los Angeles, 1920s; and *Dramatic Interpretation and Other Classes, Frayne Williams*, advertising brochure, published under auspices of University of California, Extension Division, Los Angeles, 1936, Collection of Jenifer Williams Angel.

40. Jordan-Smith, *The Road I Came* (note 14), p. 382.

41. Gordon Glass, interview by the author, January 6, 2000. Glass is the son of Maud Emily Taylor Glass (aka Emily Harvin).

42. Russell Coryell, letter to Maud Emily Taylor, May 2, 1917, MEG Papers.

43. Draft registration, July 3, 1917, World War I Draft Registration Cards, 1917–18, s.v. "Russell M. Coryell," NARA.

44. Coryell, letter to Maud Emily Taylor (note 42). Quotation by permission of Ben Coryell, Cold Spring Harbor, New York.

45. Andrée Ruellan, interview by the author, December 28, 1997. Ruellan was the widow of Jack Taylor.

46. Draft registration, September 12, 1918, World War I Draft Registration Cards, 1917–18, s.v. "John William Taylor," NARA.

47. Birth record of Thomas Gerald Joseph Mary McMurrough Kavanagh (b. August 12, 1879), City and County of Dublin, Republic of Ireland; "Actor's Injury Death Probed: Douglas Gerrard Discovered Unconscious," *Los Angeles Examiner*, June 6, 1950, section 1; "Injuries Fatal to Actor: Douglas Gerrard Was Found Unconscious in Los Angeles, *New York Times*, June 7, 1950; "Douglas Gerrard," *Variety*, June 7, 1950, p. 116; Death certificate of Douglas Gerrard, d. June 5, 1950, Los Angeles, Los Angeles County, California; Paul C. Spehr, with Gunnar Lundquist, *American Film Personnel and Company Credits, 1908–1920* (Jefferson, NC, 1996), pp. 227–28; Eugene Michael Vazzana, *Silent Film Necrology* (Jefferson, NC, 1995), p. 126.

48. Birth record of Charles Christopher McMurrough Kavanagh (b. December 20, 1883), City and County of Dublin, Republic of Ireland; Spehr, with Lundquist, *American Film Personnel* (note 47), p. 227; "An Irish Gentleman: Charles Gerrard Lends Strong Personality to His Roles," *Los Angeles Times*, September 2, 1917; Paul Hubert Conlon, "Among the Good Fellows of the Heidelberg Table," *Los Angeles Times*, December 30, 1917.

49. Obituary of Arthur MacMurrough Kavanagh, *The Irish Times* (Dublin), December 27, 1889, p. 7.

50. "Injuries Fatal to Actor" (note 47).

51. Warren, *Passionate Collaboration* (chap. 7, note 10), plate 34.

52. Emily W. Leider, *Dark Lover: The Life and Death of Rudolph Valentino* (New York, 2003), pp. 68–76; Irving Shulman, *Valentino* (New York, 1967), pp. 104–16.

53. "Boyland School at Beautiful Santa Barbara," *Los Angeles Times*, January 1, 1916.

54. Jordan-Smith, *The Road I Came* (note 14), pp. 321–22.

55. Patrick Renshaw, *The Wobblies: The Story of Syndicalism in the United States* (New York, 1967), p. 41.

56. Jordan-Smith, *The Road I Came* (note 14), pp. 322–23.

57. Renshaw, *The Wobblies* (note 55), pp. 43–47.

58. Marie Latter, letters to Betty Katz, 1916–19, BK Papers.

59. Harold Lee (formerly Lessow), essays based on conversations with Betty Katz, BK Papers; Lee was the nephew of Betty Katz. Martin Lessow, discussions with the author, October 8, 1998, and February 2, 1999; Lessow is the great-nephew of Betty Katz. Alex Rosen, interview by the author, July 21, 1998; Alex Rosen was the nephew of Betty Katz.

60. David von Drehle, *Triangle: The Fire That Changed America* (New York, 2003), p. 186.

61. Letters to and from Betty Katz, 1916–19, BK Papers.

62. *Los Angeles City Directory*, 1916–18; 1920–23, s.v. "Betty Katz," "Pauline Katz," and "Dora Katz."

63. Margrethe Mather, note to Betty Katz [ca. 1916], BK Papers.

64. Affidavit of birth for Betty Kopelanon, recorded May 17, 1926, City and County of San Francisco, California, BK Papers.

65. Justema, "Margaret" (prologue, note 1), p. [26]ill.

66. Federal Census, Manhattan Borough, New York City, New York, 1900, s.v. "Isidore [Roy] Rosen"; letters to and from Roy Rosen and various other documents, RR Papers.

67. Jack London, *The Road* (New York, 1907).

68. Richard Wormser, *Hoboes: Wandering in America, 1870–1940* (New York, 1994), p. 73.

69. Dr. Ben Reitman, quoted in Wormser, *Hoboes* (note 68), p. 11.

70. Admittance application of Isidore (Roy) Rosen to Executive Committee of the Jewish Consumptives' Relief Society (tuberculosis sanitarium), Denver, Colorado, November 29, 1912, Rocky Mountain Jewish Historical Society, Center for Judaic Studies, University of Denver. Rosen was admitted to the sanitarium on January 2, 1913, and discharged on July 8, 1914.

71. A photograph of the Hancock Banning House at 416 N. Broadway, taken by Al Greene & Associates, can be found in the Collection of the Seaver Center for Western History Research, Natural History Museum of Los Angeles County, Los Angeles.

72. Roy Rosen, letter to Betty Katz, December 9, 1980, BK Papers.

73. Roy Rosen, letter to Betty Katz, April 2, 1980, BK Papers.

74. Roy Rosen, memo to Beaumont Newhall, May 18, 1979, RR Papers.

75. Rosen, memo to Beaumont Newhall (note 74).

76. Roy Rosen, "Recollections of Conversations with Margrethe," typescript, early 1980s, RR Papers.

77. Roy Rosen, interview by Larry [?], Moira [?] and Big [?], June 24, 1982, transcript, RR Papers; Rosen, "Recollections" (note 76).

78. Roy Rosen, letter to Lawrence Jasud, October 24, 1980, RR Papers.

79. Rosen, letter to Lawrence Jasud (note 78).

80. Weston, *Daybooks*, vol. 1 (prologue, note 2), p. 159; Rosen, letter to Lawrence Jasud (note 78).

81. Marie Latter, letter to Betty Katz [ca. October–November 1917].

82. Sadakichi Hartmann, *The Valiant Knights of Daguerre* (Los Angeles, 1978), ed. Harry W. Lawton and George Knox, with the collaboration of Wistaria Hartmann Linton, pp. 6–28; see Gene Fowler, *Minutes of the Last Meeting* (New York, 1954).

83. Sadakichi Hartmann [Sidney Allan, pseud.], "Looking for the Good Points," *Bulletin of Photography*, November 1916, pp. 472–73, reprinted in *Edward Weston Omnibus* (chap. 2, note 30), pp. 9–10.

84. Conger, *Edward Weston: Photographs* (chap. 1, note 29), fig. 22/1917.

85. Sadakichi Hartmann, *The Whistler Book: A Monograph of the Life and Position in Art of James McNeill Whistler, together with a Careful Study of His More Important Works* (Boston, 1910).

86. Wistaria Hartmann Linton, discussion with the author, November 3, 1997. Linton was the daughter of Sadakichi Hartmann.

87. Alma Whitaker, "Women's Work, Women's Clubs," *Los Angeles Times*, November 10, 1917 (newspaper clipping), FMCS, vol. 4, p. 222.

88. John (Jack) Reed, *Ten Days that Shook the World* (New York, 1919).

89. "Need Photographers for Aviation Corps," *Los Angeles Times*, December 2, 1917.

90. Antony Anderson, "In the Realm of Art," *Los Angeles Times*, December 2, 1917.

91. *Camera Work*, no. 47 (January 1915).

92. Death certificate of Cornelius C. Chandler (b. July 13, 1837, d. November 28, 1917), Glendale, Los Angeles County, California; Sherer, *History of Glendale* (chap. 2, note 4), pp. 321–22; "Many at Funeral of C. C. Chandler: Late Civil War Veteran Was Charter Member of Glendale Masons," *Los Angeles Times*, December 2, 1917.

93. Antony Anderson, "In the Realm of Art," *Los Angeles Times*, December 23, 1917.

94. Toby Joysmith, "Atl: A Genius with a Volcanic Streak," *The News* (Mexico City), April 3, 1977.

95. "Hun Press Lauds Hearst, La Follette and I.W.W.: Three Credited with Being Chief Factors Antagonizing Our War Plans," *Los Angeles Times*, December 25, 1917; "Herr Hearst on Himself: 'Out of His Own Mouth He Shall Be Condemned,'" *Los Angeles Times*, December 27, 1917.

96. "German Is Abolished in the Los Angeles Public Schools: Unanimous Action by the Board of Education Makes This City First in United States to Free Boys and Girls from Medium for Insidious Propaganda," "Nation-Wide Interest in Anti-German Move," and "German Books Interned in the Public Library: Officials in Charge of City Institution Seal up Enemy Propaganda—Call the Spotts Case Closed," *Los Angeles Times*, December 27, 1917.

CHAPTER 10
WAR AND PESTILENCE, 1918

1. Antony Anderson, "In the Realm of Art" (chap. 9, note 90); Antony Anderson, "In the Realm of Art," *Los Angeles Times*, January 13, 20, 1918.

2. Johan Hagemeyer, diary, February 8, 1918, JH Collection.

3. Johan Hagemeyer, diary, February 9, 1918, JH Collection.

4. *Johan Hagemeyer*, Research Series, no. 16 (June 1982), Center for Creative Photography, Univ. of Arizona (Tucson, 1982); "Johan Hagemeyer, Photographer," interview by Corinne L. Gilb, transcript, May and July 1955, Regional Oral History Office, The Bancroft Library, University of California, Berkeley, p. 2; David and Jeanne Hagemeyer, interview by the author, July 10, 2004. David Hagemeyer is the nephew of Johan Hagemeyer.

5. Ellis Island Passenger Records, May 1, 1911, s.v. "Johan Hagemeyer."

6. Federal Census, Berkeley, Alameda County, California, 1920, s.v. "Edwin J. McCullagh."

7. "Hagemeyer, Photographer," interview (note 4), p. 28.

8. "Hagemeyer, Photographer," interview (note 4), p. 31.

9. Johan Hagemeyer, diary, April 19, 1918, JH Collection.

10. Edward Weston, letter to Johan Hagemeyer, May 12, 1918, EW/JH Collection.

11. "Hagemeyer, Photographer," interview (note 4), pp. 31–32.

12. Rosenstone, *Romantic Revolutionary* (chap. 4, note 62), p. 321.

13. Robert K. Murray, *Red Scare: A Study in National Hysteria, 1919–1920* (New York, 1964), pp. 13–14.

14. Ronald Kessler, *The Bureau: The Secret History of the FBI* (New York, 2002), pp. 13–16.

15. "Hagemeyer, Photographer," interview (note 4), pp. 29–30.

16. Goldman, *Living My Life* (chap. 5, note 54), p. 611.

17. Anderson, *My Thirty Years' War* (chap. 8, note 63), pp. 195–96.

18. Jane Heap, letter to Florence Reynolds, July 1917, FR Collection.

19. Hopkins, *Both Hands* (chap. 7, note 3), pp. 64–66; "Seven Caught in Wide Federal Dragnet: Greenfield and Three Others Arrested Here Under Espionage Act," *Santa Barbara Daily News and The Independent*, April 9, 1918; "Is It Treason?" *Santa Barbara Daily News and The Independent*, April 9, 1918; "Prince Hopkins Arrested under Espionage Act: Santa Barbara Man Locked Up in Los Angeles County Jail," April 9, 1918, *Santa Barbara Morning Press*; "Greenfield and Others Placed under Arrest: Prisoners Locked Up in Same Jail at Los Angeles with Prince Hopkins," April 10, 1918, *Santa Barbara Morning Press*; "Greenfield and Fellow Workers Arraigned Friday: Bunch of Men and Women Charged under Espionage Act Go South," April 18, 1918, *Santa Barbara Daily News*; "Millionaire Is Held as Disloyal to U.S.: Prince Hopkins' Bond Fixed at $25,000," April 19, 1918, *Santa Barbara Morning Press*; (newspaper clippings), Prince Hopkins biographical file, Santa Barbara Historical Society.

20. "'I'm Patriotic' Says Boyland Manager: Mrs. Mollie Price Cook Denies Disloyalty Charge of U.S.," *Santa Barbara Daily News and The Independent*, April 11, 1918, p.

21. Hopkins, *Both Hands* (chap. 7, note 3), p. 66.

22. Hopkins, *Both Hands* (chap. 7, note 3), p. 69.

23. Coincidentally, Mollie Price would later marry William Rapp, the journalist brother of Marie Rapp Boursault, secretary to Alfred Stieglitz at his 291 gallery.

24. Rob Wagner, letter to Mr. Keep, August 8, 1918, RW Papers. Quotation courtesy Department of Special Collections, Charles E. Young Research Library, University of California, Los Angeles.

25. Milton, *Tramp* (chap. 6, note 36), pp. 132–35.

26. Milton, *Tramp* (chap. 6, note 36), p. 133. Chaplin did, in fact, register for the draft in 1917. His registration card describes him as being of "medium" height, with a "slender" build. No other health issues are noted, so it seems unlikely that he would have been declared ineligible for service. Draft registration, June 5, 1917, World War I Draft Registration Cards, 1917–18, s.v. "Charles Spencer Chaplin," NARA.

27. Milton, *Tramp* (chap. 6, note 36), pp. 136–43.

28. "Hagemeyer, Photographer," interview (note 4), p. 29.

29. Hapgood, *A Victorian* (chap. 6, note 49), pp. 380, 385–87.

30. Birth record of Joseph Ely O'Carroll (b. January 17, 1888), City and County of Dublin, Republic of Ireland.

31. Various newspaper and journal clippings, Dr. Joseph O'Carroll biographical file, Library, Royal College of Physicians of Ireland (RCPI), Dublin. Dr. O'Carroll, who died in 1942, was a highly respected physician specializing in diseases of the heart and nervous system. He served for many years as president of the RCPI, and was also senior physician at the Richmond Hospital in Dublin and professor of medicine at University College, Dublin.

32. Patrick O'Mahony, discussion with the author, September 16, 2002. O'Mahony is the nephew of Joseph Ely O'Carroll.

33. Joseph O'Carroll's four-year-old brother, Morrogh (b. 1899), was drowned in Clew Bay near Westport, County Mayo, in August 1903, when the small boat he was sailing in capsized; see "A Child Drowned at Carraholly, Westport," *The Mayo News*, Westport, County Mayo, Ireland, August 15, 1903. The child's older brother, who remained unnamed in the newspaper account, was reportedly sailing only a short distance away, but by the time the older boy noticed his sibling's overturned boat, young Morrogh's body was floating lifeless in the Bay. Questions were raised about the circumstances surrounding the little boy's death, particularly because his drowning occurred in very shallow water. Morrogh's death certificate (d. August 8, 1903, Westport, County Mayo, Ireland) cryptically describes the cause of his demise as "Drowning, probably accidental." Whether Joseph O'Carroll was the older brother who failed to keep close watch over his younger sibling (or whether he played a more sinister role in his little brother's death) is not known, but it was not long after Morrogh's drowning that Joseph became estranged from his family. In September 1907 Joseph left Ireland on a ship bound for Canada, and the following year he crossed the border into the United States, where he remained for the rest of his life. Many years later, Joseph O'Carroll recalled his deceased younger brother and his memories of sailing on Clew Bay in a letter to his friend, Max Eastman. Joseph O'Carroll, letter to Max Eastman, August 23, 1947, ME MSS.

34. Joseph O'Carroll, "The Way of Victory," *Solidarity*, May 13, 1911, Archives of Labor and Urban Affairs, Wayne State University, Detroit.

35. "I.W.W. Army Riots in Cooper Union: Host of 300 Invades Socialist Symposium on Problem of the

Unemployed," *New York Times*, March 20, 1914; "O'Carroll in the Hospital: I.W.W. Leader Says His Illness Is Due to Police Clubbing," *New York Times*, May 11, 1914.

36. Marie Latter, letter to Betty Katz [1917–18?], BK Papers.

37. Moon Kwan was also known as Wenquing Guan, Guan Wenqing, Kwan Man Ching, and Man-ching Kwan. Ben Hecht, "Moon Quan," a short story reprinted in Florice White Kovan, *Rediscovering Ben Hecht: Selling the Celluloid Serpent* (Washington, D.C., 1999), pp. 20–25; www.hkcinemagic.com, s.v. "Kwan Man Ching."

38. Draft registration, June 5, 1918, World War I Draft Registration Cards, 1917–18, s.v. "Moon Kwan," NARA.

39. A.T. De Rome, "A Few Pictures Reviewed," CC, March 1919, p. 93ill.

40. Warren, *Passionate Collaboration* (chap. 7, note 10), p. 54, plate 15.

41. Warren, *Passionate Collaboration* (chap. 7, note 10), p. 55, plate 16; PJA, May 1919, p. 216ill.; *Pictorial Photography in America* 1920, p. 69ill.

42. AP, September 1919, p. 493ill.

43. Frank Roy Fraprie, "Our Illustrations," AP, September 1919, p. 547.

44. Antony Anderson, "Of Art and Artists," *Los Angeles Times*, May 5, 1918.

45. "Photographic Art Studies By Edward Henry Weston of Glendale," *Los Angeles Times*, June 23, 1918.

46. AP, July 1918, p. 393ill.

47. TC, September 1918, p. 460ill.

48. Sadakichi Hartmann, "Looking for the Good Points," TC, September 1918, pp. 460–62.

49. PY: 1917–1918 (chap. 9, note 4).

50. PY: 1917–1918 (chap. 8, note 90).

51. Antony Anderson, "Of Art and Artists," *Los Angeles Times*, December 2, 1917.

52. Antony Anderson, "Of Art and Artists," *Los Angeles Times*, April 1, 1917.

53. Ruellan, interview (chap. 9, note 45).

54. Warren, *Passionate Collaboration* (chap. 7, note 10), p. 51, plate 12.

55. Sadakichi Hartmann, letter to Wistaria Hartmann Linton, February 20, 1938, SH Papers.

56. Florence Reynolds's whereabouts between 1918 and the early 1920s can be loosely established based on her correspondence. In the early 1920s she accepted a position at the Weaver School for Girls, initially located in New York City and subsequently in Tarrytown, N.Y., FR Collection.

57. Federal Census, Manhattan Borough, New York City, New York County, New York, 1920, s.v. "George Lipton."

58. Marie Latter, letter to Betty Katz, 1918–19, BK Papers, signed, "Marie, 133 Macdougal St. c/o Christine." Much has been written about Christine Ell. She was a well-known personality in the Greenwich Village bohemian community, and during the months that she and Marie Latter were spending time together in New York City, Ell was having an affair with Jamie O'Neill, Eugene O'Neill's brother. Sheaffer, *O'Neill* (chap. 7, note 23), pp. 330–31, 401, 435, 439.

59. One of the cast members in the Provincetown Players production of *Moon of the Carribees* was a young woman named Berenice Abbott, who would later become well known as a photographer.

60. Several of Eugene O'Neill's numerous biographers have theorized that his character Anna Christie was based on Christine Ell, while others have stated that Anna Christie was inspired by Terry Carlin's stories about his former lover, Marie. (Arthur Gelb and Barbara Gelb, *O'Neill* [New York, 1962], pp. 290–91). However, none of O'Neill's biographers have known Marie's surname, nor have they been aware that O'Neill had an opportunity to observe Marie Latter firsthand. O'Neill's first version of the play, begun in January 1919, was titled *Chris Christopherson*, but he soon produced a second, much-revised version, which he titled *Anna Christie*. The play debuted on Broadway on November 2, 1921, garnering O'Neill the Pulitzer Prize for Drama in 1922.

61. "Liberty Fair Will Aid the State's War Work: Food and Other Great Industries of California to Be Shown—Displays will Be Educational," *Los Angeles Times*, July 14, 1918; Antony Anderson, "Of Art and Artists," *Los Angeles Times*, September 1, 1918; "Fair's Exhibits Doubled: Displays for Liberty Show Far Exceed Anticipations—Merritt is Orator," *Los Angeles Times*, October 6, 1918; "Liberty Fair Programme: Official Schedule of Daily Events at Our Great Exposition," *Los Angeles Times*, November 17, 1918.

62. L. E. Brackens, "Photography at the Liberty Fair," CC, November 1918, p. 431.

63. Anderson, "Of Art and Artists," (note 61).

64. Brackens, "Photography at the Liberty Fair," (note 62), pp. 431–32.

65. De Rome, "A Few Pictures" (note 39).

66. Death certificate of Edward Burbank Weston (b. July 31, 1846, d. September 14, 1918), Chicago, Cook County, Illinois; "Death Notices: Dr. Edward B. Weston," *Chicago Daily Tribune*, September 15, 1918; "Father of Modern Archery, Dr. E. B. Weston, Is Dead," *Chicago Daily Tribune*, September 16, 1918.

67. Cole Weston, discussion (chap. 8, note 36).

68. Lindsay Redican, "The Forgotten Killer," essay published online at www.haverford.edu/biology/edwards /disease/viral_essays/redicanvirus.htm.

69. "Plans for Fair Made," *Los Angeles Times*, October 27, 1918.

70. "Charlie's Wed Again: That's What Rumor Says but Chaplin Himself Modestly Declines to be Married," *Los Angeles Times*, November 9, 1918.

71. Milton, *Tramp* (chap. 6, note 36), pp. 145–49.

72. Redican, "The Forgotten Killer" (note 68).

73. "Fair to be Great Victory Fete: California Liberty Exposition Gains by Postponement," *Los Angeles Times*, November 17, 1918.

74. E. Caswell Perry, Shirley Catherine Berger, and Terri E. Jonisch, *Glendale: A Pictorial History* (Glendale, n.d.), p. 55.

75. *Glendale City Directory*, 1919, s.v. "Edward H. Weston."

CHAPTER 11
EXHILARATION, 1919

1. Antony Anderson, "The Photographic Salon," *Los Angeles Times*, January 12, 1919.

2. Birth certificate of [_____] Weston (b. January 30, 1919), Glendale, Los Angeles County, California. The first name *Cole* was later added to the birth record in a supplemental document dated March 16, 1940.

3. Death certificate of Ann Eliza Chandler (b. November 30, 1836, d. January 16, 1919), Glendale, Los Angeles County, California.

4. Los Angeles County plat books (chap. 2, note 27).

5. Federal Census, Glendale, Los Angeles County, California, 1920, s.v. "Frayne Weston."

6. Cole Weston, discussion (chap. 8, note 36). Although Cole Weston did not know why his parents changed his name from *Frayne* to *Cole*, he believed they finally settled on *Cole* because of their friendship with Helen Cole. However, according to information contained in the EW Archive, *Cole* was also a surname that appeared in the Weston family genealogy.

7. Johan Hagemeyer, diary, February 7, 21, 26, 1919, JH Collection.

8. Max Eastman, *Love and Revolution: My Journey through an Epoch* (New York, 1964), pp. 145–47.

9. Eastman, *Love and Revolution* (note 8), p. 146.

10. William L. O'Neill, *The Last Romantic: A Life of Max Eastman* (New York, 1978), p. 81.

11. Eastman, *Love and Revolution* (note 8), pp. 85–99.

12. Eastman, *Love and Revolution* (note 8), pp. 118–23.

13. Max Eastman was then working on his book *The Sense of Humor* (New York, 1921).

14. Max Eastman, *Enjoyment of Living* (New York, 1948), pp. 233–63.

15. Max Eastman, letter to Florence Deshon, July 29, 1919, FD MSS.

16. Eastman, *Enjoyment* (note 14), pp. 570–71, 583–86; Eastman, *Love and Revolution* (note 8), pp. 7–11, 39–44, 49–51, 56–57, 64–67, 80–82, 100–102, 108, 111–12, 119.

17. "Alhambra," review of the movie *Jaffery* at the Alhambra Theatre, *Los Angeles Times*, September 10, 1916.

18. Milton, *Tramp* (chap. 6, note 36), p. 154.

19. Eastman, *Love and Revolution* (note 8), pp. 143–44.

20. Johan Hagemeyer, diary, March 7, 1919, JH Collection.

21. Edward Weston, letter to Johan Hagemeyer, April 15, 1919, EW/JH Collection.

22. Weston, letter to Johan Hagemeyer (note 21). Louis LeGendre may have been a relative of Professor P.S. LeGendre, who taught French at Ferry Hall in Lake Forest while Edward Weston's grandfather was Principal there; *First Annual Catalogue* (chap. 1, note 7).

23. Severance Club Membership Ledger, 1919, p. 108, SC Records.

24. Severance Club Membership Ledger (note 23). Between 1910 and the mid-1940s, members of the Severance Club included, among others, John Bovingdon, Mr. and Mrs. Chauncey Clarke, Elmer and Lucile Ellsworth, Bertha Fiske, John Anson Ford, Dr. and Mrs. Perceval Gerson, Mrs. Kate Crane Gartz, Irwin Gill, John R. Haynes, Mr. and Mrs. Job Harriman, Richard Neutra, Mr. and Mrs. Paul Jordan-Smith, Mr. and Mrs. Rob Wagner, William Wendt, Mr. and Mrs. Jake Zeitlin, Llewelyn Bixby Smith, Mr. and Mrs. Reginald Pole, and Willard Huntington Wright.

25. Conger, *Edward Weston: Photographs* (chap. 1, note 29), fig. 51/1920.

26. Between 1904 and 1912 the Frenchman Romain Rolland authored ten books featuring the character Jean-Christophe. Strongly influenced by the Vedanta philosophy of Hinduism, Rolland was a lifelong pacifist who actively protested the Great War. He was awarded the Nobel Prize for Literature in 1916.

27. Conger, *Edward Weston: Photographs* (chap. 1, note 29), fig. 31/1919.

28. Edward Weston, letter to Johan Hagemeyer, May 8, 1919, JH Collection.

29. Antony Anderson, "Of Art and Artists," *Los Angeles Times*, June 1, 1919; Conger, "Edward Weston's Early Photography" (chap. 2, note 10), p. 286, fig. 19/13; AP, March 1921, p. 131ill.

30. Margrethe Mather, letter to Johan Hagemeyer, postmarked June 27, 1919, JH Collection.

31. Johan Hagemeyer, diary, June 24, 30, 1919, JH Collection.

32. Edward Weston, letter to Clarence Blocker (Ramiel) McGehee, July 11, 1919, EW Archive.

33. Cole Weston, discussion (chap. 8, note 36). The name *Ramiel* traditionally refers to one of the archangels in Judeo-Christian religions. The Hebrew translation of the name means "mercy of God" or "compassion of God," and the angel Ramiel is often described as a messenger of hope who escorts the souls of the faithful into Heaven.

34. Federal Census, Grayson, Grayson County, Texas, 1900, s.v. "Clarence McGee [*sic*]"; Federal Census, Redondo Beach, Los Angeles County, California, 1910, s.v. "Clarence B. McGehee"; Draft registration, September [date illegible], 1918, World War I Draft Registration Cards, 1917–18, s.v. "Clarence Blocker McGehee," NARA; Death certificate of Clarence McGehee (b. August 3, 1882, d. December 20, 1943), Redondo Beach, Los Angeles County, California.

35. Merle Armitage, "Early Notes on Edward Weston for Nancy Newhall," 1961, MA Papers. Quotation courtesy Harry Ransom Humanities Research Center, The University of Texas, Austin.

36. Armitage, "Early Notes" (note 35).

37. "Cherry Blossom Plays: Japanese Entertainment to be Staged Here Soon—Quaint Costumes, Settings and Acting Will Enhance Its Picturesqueness," *Los Angeles Times*, December 31, 1916.

38. Ruth St. Denis, autobiographical text (typescript), p. 203, RSD Papers. Quotation courtesy Department of Special Collections, Charles E. Young Research Library, University of California, Los Angeles.

39. Wilson and Madar, *Through Another Lens* (chap. 1, note 25), p. 43; Amy Conger, *Edward Weston: Photographs* (chap. 1, note 29), fig. 83/1922.

40. Wilson and Madar, *Through Another Lens* (chap. 1, note 25), p. 43.

41. Birth certificate of "Female [Florence] Danks" (b. July 19, 1893), Vital Statistics Section, Tacoma-Pierce County Health Department, Tacoma, Washington; Federal Census, Manhattan Borough, New York City, New York County, New York, 1900, s.v. "Florence Danks."

42. Eastman, *Love and Revolution* (note 8), pp. 64–65.

43. Eastman, *Love and Revolution* (note 8), p. 65.

44. Eastman, *Love and Revolution* (note 8), p. 211.

45. An Arnold Genthe photograph of Florence Deshon posing in the nude was sold at auction in 1977 (Sotheby's, New York, 19th and 20th Century Photographs, sale cat., October 4, 1977, lot 324). Deshon also mentions having

been photographed by Baron Adolph De Meyer. Florence Deshon, letter to Max Eastman, January 9, 1920, FD MSS.

46. Mildred Morris, "Greenwich Village As It Ain't!" *Photoplay*, December 1918, pp. 30–32.

47. Samuel Goldwyn, telegram to "Miss Deshaunt," June 1919, FD MSS.

48. Max Eastman, letter to Florence Deshon (note 15).

49. Florence Deshon, letter to Max Eastman, August 15, 1919, FD MSS.

50. Eastman, *Love and Revolution* (note 8), pp. 171–72.

51. Florence Deshon, letter to Max Eastman, September 6, 1919, FD MSS.

52. Antony Anderson, "Of Art and Artists," *Los Angeles Times*, June 22, 1919.

53. PY: 1919, p. 32 and plate 64; PE, August 1920, cover ill., frontispiece ill.; PE, November 1920, p. 231ill.; *Pictorial Photography in America 1920* (New York, 1920), p. 107ill.

54. Conger, *Edward Weston: Photographs* (chap. 1, note 29), fig. 50/1920.

55. Conger, *Edward Weston: Photographs* (chap. 1, note 29), fig. 30/1919.

56. Antony Anderson, "Of Art and Artists," *Los Angeles Times*, October 5, 1919.

57. Lady Jane, "Women's Work, Women's Clubs," *Los Angeles Times*, October 24, 1919; "Slav Program Given at Club," *Los Angeles Examiner*, October 25, 1919 (newspaper clippings), FMCS, vol. 5, pp. 187, 193.

58. Antony Anderson, "Of Art and Artists," *Los Angeles Times*, October 12, 1919.

59. Antony Anderson, "Of Art and Artists," *Los Angeles Times*, December 14, 28, 1919; *The Art of China and Japan: Descriptions of Paintings and Prints, including Examples of the Aristocractic [sic] Art and of the Democratic Art, from the Collection of Mr. and Mrs. T. R. Fleming of Long Beach, California*, exh. cat. (Los Angeles Museum of History, Science, and Art, misc. pub. no. 1, December, 1919).

60. Eastman, *Love and Revolution* (note 8), p. 171.

61. Milton, *Tramp* (chap. 6, note 36), pp. 149–52.

62. Milton, *Tramp* (chap. 6, note 36), p. 150.

63. Milton, *Tramp* (chap. 6, note 36), pp. 158–59.

64. Eastman, *Love and Revolution* (note 8), p. 172.

65. Eastman, *Love and Revolution* (note 8), p. 173.

66. Eastman, *Love and Revolution* (note 8), p. 172.

67. Eastman, *Love and Revolution* (note 8), p. 174.

68. Leider, *Dark Lover* (chap. 9, note 52), pp. 98–107.

69. "Club News and Notes: Boston Y.M.C.A.[sic] Camera Club," CC, November 1919, p. 447; "One Man Exhibits at the Boston Y.M.C. Union Camera Club," PJA, November 1919, p. 519; "Notes and News: Announcing a Series of Exhibits of Pictorial Photography 1919–1920," AP, December 1919, p. 746.

70. "Events of the Month: Shows by Arthur F. Kales and E. H. Weston," PE, June 1919, p. 323.

71. "Club News and Notes" (note 69).

72. Max Eastman, letter to Florence Deshon, December 21, 1919, FD MSS.

73. Edward Weston, letter to Johan Hagemeyer, December 11, 1919, EW/JH Collection.

74. Edward Weston, letter to Johan Hagemeyer, December 21, 1919, EW/JH Collection

75. Florence Deshon, letter to Max Eastman, December 15, 1919, FD MSS.

76. Florence Deshon, letter to Max Eastman, December (date illegible), 1919, FD MSS.

77. Florence Deshon, letter to Max Eastman, December 26, 1919, FD MSS.

78. Max Eastman, letter to Florence Deshon, December 26, 1919, FD MSS.

79. Florence Deshon, letter to Max Eastman, January 7, 1920, FD MSS.

80. Goldman, *Living My Life* (chap. 5, note 54), pp. 707–08.

81. Goldman, *Living My Life* (chap. 5, note 54), pp. 717–18.

82. Falk, *Love, Anarchy* (chap. 8, note 52), p. 298.

CHAPTER 12
SEEKING ACCLAIM, 1920

1. *Epilogue* and *Prologue to a Sad Spring* were exhibited together at the Society of Copenhagen Amateur Photographers 25th Anniversary Salon, August 25–September 10, 1920, and possibly on other occasions as well.

2. PY: 1919 (chap. 11, note 53), p. 32.

3. Edward Weston, letter to Johan Hagemeyer, April 13, 1920, EW/JH Collection.

4. Murray, *Red Scare* (chap. 10, note 13), pp. 191–222.

5. Murray, *Red Scare* (chap. 10, note 13), p. 193.

6. Florence Deshon, letter to Max Eastman, January 23, 1920, FD MSS.

7. Max Eastman, letter to Florence Deshon, January 17, 1920, FD MSS.

8. Florence Deshon, letter to Max Eastman, January 11, 1920, FD MSS.

9. Florence Deshon, letter to Max Eastman, January 15, 1920, FD MSS.

10. Florence Deshon, letter to Max Eastman (chap. 11, note 79).

11. Florence Deshon, letter to Max Eastman (note 6).

12. Max Eastman, letter to Florence Deshon, January 26, 1920, FD MSS.

13. Florence Deshon, letter to Max Eastman, February 26, 1920, FD MSS.

14. Max Eastman, letters to Florence Deshon, March 22, May 3, May 7, May 10, and May 13, 1920, FD MSS.

15. Florence Deshon, telegrams to Max Eastman, March 15, May 3, and May 6, 1920; Florence Deshon, letters to Max Eastman, March 29 and April 26, 1920, FD MSS.

16. "Seventh Annual Pittsburgh Salon," CC, March 1920, p. 99.

17. Warren, *Passionate Collaboration* (chap. 7, note 10), plate 22.

18. M.C. Rypinski, "The 1920 Pittsburgh Salon," PE, June 1920, p. 278.

19. Rypinski, "The 1920 Pittsburgh Salon" (note 18), p. 279.

20. "Notes and News," AP, July 1920, p. 440; "Events of the Month: Photo-Pictorialists Honored," PE, July 1920, p. 48.

21. Otto Matiesen, draft registration, September 12, 1918, World War I draft registration card, 1917–18, NARA; "Danish Actor Only Actor in His Family," *Los Angeles Times*, September 25, 1927; "Otto Matiesen Dies in Mishap: Actor Killed When His Car Plunges Off Highway," *Los Angeles Times*, February 20, 1932; "Hollywood Actor Instantly Killed on Highway: Car Failed to Make Turn West of Pima and Is Wrecked in Bar Pit—Traveling Companion Is Injured," *Graham County Guardian* [Safford, Ariz.], February 26, 1932; Fred W. Fox, "Otto Matiesen, the Total Actor," *Los Angeles Mirror*, September 6, 1960 (newspaper clipping), Otto Matiesen biographical file, Margaret Herrick Library, Academy of Motion Picture Arts and Sciences, Beverly Hills; Evelyn Mack Truitt, *Who Was Who on Screen* (New York, 1984); *New York Times Directory of the Film* (New York 1971), p. 821.

22. *Los Angeles City Directory*, 1921, s.v. "Otto Matiesen."

23. AP, September 1921, p. 471ill., p. 529; F.C. Tilney, "Pictorial Photography in 1921," PY: 1921, p. 17 and plate 28; Warren, *Passionate Collaboration* (chap. 7, note 10), plate 30.

24. Antony Anderson, "Of Art and Artists," *Los Angeles Times*, May 16, 1920.

25. Brainerd Family, biographical files, Evanston Historical Society, Evanston, Ill.; *Portrait and Biographical Record of the State of Colorado: Containing Portraits and Biographies of many well known Citizens of the Past and Present* (Chicago, 1899), pp. 305–08; "Former Army Man Claimed by Death: Col. Wesley Brainerd, Aged 77, Dies at Pt. Loma Home," *San Diego Union*, August 20, 1910; Federal Census, Evanston, Cook County, Ill., 1870, 1880, s.v. "Wesley Brainard" [sic]; Federal Census, Boulder County, Col., 1880, s.v. "Wesley Brainerd"; *San Diego City Directory*, 1907–10, s.v. "Wesley Brainerd"; Death certificate of Belle Phillipson (b. August 22, 1866, d. June 22, 1905), Omaha, Douglas County, Neb.; Lyman Gaylord, discussion with the author, April 20, 2000. Gaylord is the son of Marie Phillipson and her first husband, Vasia Anikeef, a Russian-born opera singer. They were later divorced, and around 1943 Sibyl married Dr. Simon Freed, an organic chemist who worked for the Atomic Energy Commission.

26. Emmett A. Greenwalt, *The Point Loma Community in California 1897–1942: A Theosophical Experiment* (Los Angeles, 1955).

27. Greenwalt, *Point Loma* (note 26), pp. 77–98.

28. "L. J. Gage Gets Nieces: By Court's Order Removes Phillipson Girls from Raja Yoga Academy," *New York Times*, December 3, 1910.

29. "Gage Studies Theosophy: His Interest Starts a Report That He Will Join the Tingley Colony," *New York Times*, July 8, 1906; "Gage's Theosophic Inquiry: Is Said to Have Had Vision of His Brother's Death," *New York Times*, July 9, 1906; "Not a Theosophist, Says Lyman J. Gage: He Likes the Society, but Has Not Been Invited to Join," *New York Times*, July 10, 1906.

30. *San Diego City Directory*, 1917–18, s.v. "Sibyl Brainard" [*sic*]. Sibyl consciously chose this unusual spelling of her first name, but her surname was misspelled in the directory listing; Gaylord, discussion (note 13).

31. Greenwalt, *Point Loma* (note 26).

32. Joseph E. Ross, *Krotona of Old Hollywood* (Montecito, Calif., 1989).

33. Robert V. Hine, *California's Utopian Colonies* (New Haven, 1966), pp. 54–57.

34. Severance Club Membership Ledger, p. 136, in which Hutchinson's address is given as "Krotona Institute, Hollywood," SC Records.

35. Antony Anderson, "Of Art and Artists," *Los Angeles Times*, June 13, 1920.

36. Frederic J. Haskin, "Large Thefts of Platinum: Becomes Extensive Business in United States," *Los Angeles Times*, August 8, 1920.

37. The J. Paul Getty Museum has conducted a number of spectrographic analyses of the Weston and Mather photographs in its collection. The Museum's findings show that around 1919 both photographers began using palladium paper almost exclusively, substituting it for the much costlier papers sensitized with platinum salts.

38. Shulman, *Valentino* (chap. 9, note 52), pp. 137–46.

39. C. Blythe Sherwood, "Enter Julio!," *Motion Picture Classic*, June 1920, quoted in Irving Shulman, *Valentino* (chap. 9, note 52), p. 141.

40. Edward Weston, letter to Johan Hagemeyer, May 19, 1920, EW/JH Collection.

41. A photograph titled *Anne of the Crooked Halo*, made by an unidentified photographer, is in the collection of the J. Paul Getty Museum. It depicts a costume party that very likely took place during Weston's 1920 visit to San Francisco. In addition to Weston, those pictured are Roi Partridge, Imogen Cunningham, Anne Brigman, Johan Hagemeyer, Roger Sturtevant, Dorothea Lange, and an unidentified man; Susan Ehrens, *A Poetic Vision: The Photographs of Anne Brigman*, exh. cat. (Santa Barbara Museum of Art, 1995), p. 83ill.

42. Conger, *Edward Weston: Photographs* (chap. 1, note 29), fig. 47/1920.

43. Conger, "Edward Weston's Early Photography" (chap. 2, note 10), p. 356, fig. 21/32, therein dated 1921.

44. Federal Census, Los Angeles County, Calif., 1920, s.v. "Clarence B. McGehee, Redondo Beach"; *Redondo Beach City Directory*, 1921–22, s.v. "Clarence McGehee."

45. The possible connection between Edward Weston's attic studies and the film *Cabinet of Dr. Caligari* was first pointed out by Ruth-Marion Baruch in her master's thesis, "Edward Weston: the Man, the Artist, and the Photographer" (University of Ohio at Athens, 1946), p. 19.

46. See "Edward Weston Exhibition Chronology," herein, under "1921."

47. Albert Edward Sutherland, "The Reminiscences of Albert Edward Sutherland," 1959 interview, transcript, pp. 44–45, Oral History Research Office, Columbia University, New York.

48. Florence Deshon, letter to Max Eastman, July 8, 1920, FD MSS.

49. Florence Deshon, letter to Max Eastman, August 7, 1920, FD MSS.

50. Imogen Cunningham (Partridge), letter to Edward Weston, July 27, 1920, EW Archive.

51. Many years later, Cunningham would agree to sell a group of her vintage prints to the Metropolitan Museum of Art only if the Museum would also accept one of the photographs she had received as a gift from Margrethe Mather. Curator John McKendry, unfamiliar with Mather's work, was apparently reluctant to admit the photograph into the museum's collection, but Cunningham finally succeeded in her campaign. Imogen Cunningham, letters to John McKendry, August 11, 1969; May 7, May 31, and Nov. 12, 1970; and Imogen Cunningham, letters

to Phyllis Massar, November 12, 1970, and February 22, 1971, IC Papers. In her letters Cunningham writes, "I also have a print by Margarethe Mather, who is THE person who had the greatest influence on the work of Edward Weston, having changed him from an expert retoucher to a realistic and poetic photographer" (Cunningham, letter to John McKendry, May 7, 1970); and "[Mather] may not have become well known but she was the first and the best influence on Edward Weston at a time when he was really a slick commercial photographer and expert retoucher. His historians seem to try to gloss over this fact and he himself in the Day Books gives little to Marguerite, but I feel that I have seen the whole thing" (Cunningham, letter to Phyllis Massar, November 12, 1970).

52. Edward Weston, letter to Johan Hagemeyer [July 1920], EW/JH Collection.

53. Edward Weston, letter to Johan Hagemeyer, July 30, 1920, EW/JH Collection.

54. "Women's Clubs," *Los Angeles Record*, April 16, 1920; "Ebell Club Luncheon," *Los Angeles Express*, April 14, 1920; "Marionettes on Friday Club Program," *Los Angeles Examiner*, May 2, 1920; "Modern Music at Friday Club," *Los Angeles Examiner*, May 23, 1920, newspaper clippings, FMCS, vol. 6, pp. 25, 28, 34, 41.

55. AP, October 1921, p. 547; Theodore E. Stebbins, Karen Quinn, and Leslie Furth, *Photography and Modernism*, exh. cat. (Museum of Fine Arts, Boston, 1999), plate 1, therein titled *Alfred Kreymborg—Poet*.

56. Alfred Kreymborg, "In a Dream," poem in *Mushrooms: A Book of Free Forms* (New York, 1916), pp. 39–40.

57. Kreymborg, *Troubadour* (chap. 8, note 95), pp. 354–55.

58. "Clubs Anticipate Irish Writer," *Los Angeles Express*, March 27, 1920 (newspaper clipping), FMCS, vol. 6, p. 19.

59. "British Writer Given Praise at Club," *Los Angeles Examiner*, December 12, 1920; "Los Angeles," *Riverside Press*, December 18, 1920; "Friday Club Hears Good Speakers," *Los Angeles Examiner*, December 11, 1920; "Paris Pastor Speaks to Club Women Here," *Los Angeles Times*, December 12, 1920; "Pasadena Members Attend Friday Club," *Pasadena Post*, December 10, 1920 (newspaper clippings), FMCS, vol. 6, pp. 94, 96, 97–98, 102–03.

60. "Friday Morning Club Has Fine Meeting," *Pasadena Post*, June 20, 1920 (newspaper clipping), FMCS, vol. 6, p. 59.

61. "Friday Morning Club New Home of Buhlig Lectures," *Los Angeles Record*, November 12, 1920 (newspaper clipping), FMCS, vol. 6, p. 88.

62. "To Slice Away Hill Barrier: As City Council Orders Widening of Fifth Street, Club Women File Protest" (unsourced newspaper clipping), FMCS, vol. 6, p. 40; "Club Joins in Plea for Hill: Asks Council to Go Slow on Normal Site Cut Plan," *Los Angeles Times*, February 5, 1921.

63. O. S. Barnum, "Support of Friday Morning Club," *Los Angeles Clubwoman*, April 1, 1920 (newsletter clipping), FMCS, vol. 6, p. 25.

64. Edward Weston, letter to Johan Hagemeyer, July 30, 1920 (note 53).

65. Weston, letter to Johan Hagemeyer (note 53).

66. Otto Matiesen's calling cards (3), JH Collection.

67. *Johan Hagemeyer* (chap. 10, note 4), plate 2.

68. *Johan Hagemeyer* (chap. 10, note 4), plates 4, 5.

69. Wilfred French, "Our Illustrations," PE, August 20, 1920, p. 96.

70. F. Billy Rubin, "Epilogue: Poem Suggested by Mr. Weston's Picture," PE, November 1920, p. 231, 231ill.

71. *International Exhibition of the London Salon of Photography*, exh. cat. (London, September 13–October 11, 1919).

72. *The Fourteenth Annual Exhibition of Photographs*, exh. cat. (Philadelphia: John Wanamaker Department Store, March 1–13, 1920).

73. *Copenhagen Photographic Amateur Club Exhibition 1920: American Section, collected under auspices of Pictorial Photographers of America*, exh. cat. (Copenhagen, August 25–September 10, 1920).

74. Edward Weston, letter to Johan Hagemeyer, August 30, 1920, EW/JH Collection.

75. Murray, *Red Scare* (chap. 10, note 13), pp. 257–59; Christopher Gray, *New York Streetscapes: Tales of Manhattan's Significant Buildings and Landmarks* (New York, 2003), research by Suzanne Braley, pp. 16–17.

76. Milton, *Tramp* (chap. 6, note 36), pp. 175–76.

77. "Chaplin Will Finish Big Film Here; Says Divorce Case is Due to Lawyers," *Deseret News* (Salt Lake City), August 11, 1920, p. 1; Gerith Von Ulm, *Charlie Chaplin: King of Tragedy* (Caldwell, Idaho, 1940), p. 122.

78. Florence Deshon, letter to Max Eastman, August 9, 1920, FD MSS.

79. Max Eastman, telegrams to Florence Deshon, August 13, 17, 1920, FD MSS.

80. Eastman, *Love and Revolution* (chap. 11, note 8), pp. 204–11.

81. Florence Deshon, letter to Max Eastman, October 10, 1920, FD MSS.

82. W. A. Swanberg, *Dreiser* (New York, 1965), pp. 243–45.

83. Theodore Dreiser, letter to Florence Deshon, October 29, 1920, FD MSS.

84. Theodore Dreiser, letter to Florence Deshon, November 23, 1920, FD MSS.

85. Theodore Dreiser, "Ernestine," *A Gallery of Women* (New York, 1929), vol. 2, pp. 527–64.

86. Florence Deshon, telegram to Max Eastman, October 27, 1920, FD MSS.

87. Max Eastman, letter to Florence Deshon, November 5, 1920, FD MSS.

88. Florence Deshon, telegram to Max Eastman, November 4, 1920, FD MSS.

89. Max Eastman, telegram to Florence Deshon, January 8, 1921, FD MSS.

90. John Paul Edwards, "The Eighth Pittsburgh Salon," PE, May 1921, plate opposite p. 221, pp. 227, 262.

91. Wilfred A. French, "Our Illustrations," PE, May 1921, p. 262.

92. Edward Weston, letter to Johan Hagemeyer, October 6, 1920, EW/JH Collection.

93. Edward Weston, letter to Johan Hagemeyer, October 25, 1920, EW/JH Collection.

94. Susan Danly and Weston Naef, *Edward Weston in Los Angeles* (Los Angeles, 1986), plate 2, therein titled *Betty Brandner*. Betty Katz married the architect, Alexander Brandner, on August 20, 1943.

95. Danly and Naef, *Edward Weston in Los Angeles* (note 94), plate 3, therein titled *Betty Brandner*.

96. Edward Weston, letters to Betty Katz [ca. late 1920], BK Papers.

97. Edward Weston, letter to Betty Katz [ca. late 1920], BK Papers.

98. Tilney, "Pictorial Photography" (note 23), p. 17 and plate 29.

99. Tilney, "Pictorial Photography" (note 23).

100. Tilney, "Pictorial Photography" (note 23).

101. Edward Weston, letter to Betty Katz [February 1921], BK Papers.

102. Edward Weston, letter to Betty Katz, December 9 [1920], BK Papers.

103. Johan Hagemeyer, diary, December 20, 1920, JH Collection.

CHAPTER 13
FAME AND ANGST, 1921

1. Max Eastman, letter to Florence Deshon, January 24, 1921, FD MSS.

2. Florence Deshon, telegram to Max Eastman, January 27, 1921, FD MSS.

3. Antony Anderson, "Of Art and Artists," *Los Angeles Times*, February 13, 1921.

4. Edward Weston, letter to Betty Katz [early February 1921], BK Papers.

5. Edward Weston, letter to Betty Katz, February 15, 1921, BK Papers.

6. Margaret Leslie Davis, *Dark Side of Fortune: Triumph and Scandal in the Life of Oil Tycoon Edward L. Doheny* (Los Angeles, 1998), pp. 21–33; MaryAnn Bonino, *The Doheny Mansion: A Biography of a Home* (Los Angeles, 2008), pp. 20–21.

7. Jake Zeitlin, interview by Joel Gardener, 1980, transcript, pp. 24–25, JZ Collection.

8. William C. Owen, "Viva Mexico," ME, April 1911, pp. 42–46; "Mexico's Hour of Need," June 1911, pp. 105–7; "Mexico and Socialism," September 1911, pp. 199–202; Emma Goldman, "Observations and Comments," ME, May 1913, pp. 72–73.

9. Goldman, "Appeal" (chap. 6, note 43).

10. Zeitlin, interview (note 7).

11. Goldman, *Living My Life* (chap. 5, note 54), p. vii; Miriam Lerner, letter to Betty Katz, June 29, 1929, BK Papers.

12. Davis, *Dark Side* (note 6), pp. 140–41.

13. Burl Noggle, *Teapot Dome: Oil and Politics in the 1920s* (New York, 1962); M. R. Werner and John Starr, *The Teapot Dome Scandal* (London, 1961).

14. Birth certificate of Miriam Lerner (b. September 24, 1896), Toronto, Middlesex County, Ontario, Canada.

15. Edward Weston, letter to Betty Katz (chap. 12, note 102).

16. Edward Weston, letter to Betty Katz (chap. 12, note 102).

17. Penelope Niven, *Carl Sandburg: A Biography* (New York, 1991), p. 363.

18. Niven, *Sandburg* (note 17), p. 230.

19. Col. Robert McCormick, quoted in Niven, *Sandburg* (note 17), p. 366. For more information about Chicago's role in the movie industry, see Arnie Bernstein, *Hollywood on Lake Michigan: 100 Years of Chicago and the Movies* (Chicago, 1998).

20. Carl Sandburg, review, *Chicago Daily News*, January 18–19, 1921, quoted in Niven, *Sandburg* (note 17), p. 375.

21. Carl Sandburg, review, *Chicago Daily News*, April 23, 1921, quoted in Niven, *Sandburg* (note 17), p. 375.

22. Carl Sandburg, review, *Chicago Daily News*, April 23, 1921, quoted in Niven, *Sandburg* (note 17), p. 375.

23. Bertha McCord Knisely, "Sandburg Poems Grip Hearers, *Los Angeles Record*, March 12, 1921 (newspaper clipping), FMCS, vol. 6, p. 132.

24. Edward Weston, letter to Carl Sandburg, May 21, 1921, CS Papers.

25. Conger, "Edward Weston's Early Photography" (chap. 2, note 10), p. 327, fig. 21/8.

26. The Monte Sano, or Glendale Boulevard, automobile/pedestrian bridge stood just north of, and parallel to, the Pacific Electric Railway bridge, which crossed the Los Angeles River between Los Angeles and Glendale. Damaged by a severe flood in February 1927, the wooden trestle bridge was replaced by a series of three concrete bridges, still in use today, which connect Hyperion Avenue and Glendale Boulevard on the west side of the Los Angeles River with Glendale Boulevard on the east side; Sally Shishmanian, conversations and on-site visit with the author, September–October 2005; Alan Fishel, Electric Railway Historical Association of Southern California, conversations with the author, January 2006.

27. Conger, "Edward Weston's Early Photography" (chap. 2, note 10), pp. 328, 330-32, figs. 21/9, 21/10, 21/11, 21/12.

28. "Photographic Exhibit at S. F. Camera Club Receives High Praise," *The Bulletin* [San Francisco], July 25, 1921, p. 3; *The Frederick & Nelson Second Annual Exhibition of Pictorial Photography*, exh. cat. (Seattle: Frederick & Nelson Department Store, November 1–12, 1921).

29. Eastman, *Love and Revolution* (chap. 11, note 8), p. 172.

30. Warren, *Passionate Collaboration* (chap. 7, note 10), plates 41, 42.

31. Grace Kingsley, "Pretty Dancers Will All Live Out of Doors," *Los Angeles Times*, May 26, 1918; "Marion Morgan in the Films: Noted Dance Instructor is to Supervise Effects," *Los Angeles Times*, July 25, 1920; "Mr. Martin Beck Presents Marion Morgan Dancers," Orpheum Theatre advertisement, *Los Angeles Times*, June 29, 1919.

32. Kingsley, "Pretty Dancers" (note 31).

33. *Theatre Magazine*, November 1922, contents page ill.; *Vogue*, February 1921, p. 60 ill.

34. Antony Anderson, "Of Art and Artists," *Los Angeles Times*, July 31, 1921; "Show L. A. Artist's Hawaiian Paintings," *Los Angeles Herald*, July 19, 1921 (newspaper clippings), LAMHSAS, vol. 7.

35. Federal Census, Honolulu, Hawaii Territory, 1920, s.v. "George Stanson," in which he is described as an "octoroon."

36. Warren, *Passionate Collaboration* (chap. 7, note 10), plate 43; for a variant, Conger, *Edward Weston: Photographs* (chap. 1, note 29), fig. 57/1921.

37. Conger, *Edward Weston: Photographs* (chap. 1, note 29), fig. 58/1921.

38. See Amy Stark, *The Letters from Tina Modotti to Edward Weston* (Tucson, 1981); Amy Conger, *Edward Weston in Mexico 1923–1926* (Albuquerque, 1983); Mildred Constantine, *Tina Modotti: A Fragile Life* (New York, 1983); Pino Cacucci, *Tina Modotti: A Life* (New York, 1991), trans. Patricia J. Duncan; Margaret Hooks, *Tina Modotti: Photographer and Revolutionary* (New York, 1993); Sarah M. Lowe, *Tina Modotti: Photographs* (New York, 1995); Pasquale Verdicchio and Pat Albers, *Dear Vocio: Photographs by Tina Modotti* (San Diego, 1997); Patricia Albers, *Shadows, Fire, Snow: The Life of Tina Modotti* (New York, 1999).

39. Robo de Richey spelled his fabricated name in several different ways; e.g., Robo deRichey, Robo DeRichey, Robo De Richey, Roubaix de Richey. For clarity's sake, the form used here is the one that most often appears in documents of the period.

40. Albers, *Shadows* (note 38), pp. 33–42.

41. Albers, *Shadows* (note 38), pp. 47–51.

42. Albers, *Shadows* (note 38), p. 23.

43. Albers, *Shadows* (note 38), p. 18.

44. *L'Italia*, September 5, 1917, quoted in Albers, *Shadows* (note 38), p. 30.

45. Lowe, *TM: Photographs* (note 38), p. 19, 19ill., figs. 7, 8.

46. Albers, *Shadows* (note 38), p. 57.

47. Edward Weston, letter to Johan Hagemeyer, April 18, 1921, EW/JH Collection.

48. Tina Modotti, letter to Edward Weston, excerpt copied by Weston in original *Daybooks* manuscript, April 25, 1921, quoted in Stark, *Letters from TM* (note 38), pp. 10–11.

49. Armitage, "Early Notes" (chap. 11, note 35). Quotation courtesy Harry Ransom Humanities Research Center, The University of Texas, Austin.

50. In the author's previous publication, *Margrethe Mather and Edward Weston: A Passionate Collaboration*, this image (p. 25, fig. 11) was dated 1920. Further research has shown that, while there is some reason to believe the photograph may have been taken in late 1920, the existing prints are all dated 1921.

51. Sotheby's, *Photographs*, sale cat. (New York, November 12, 1985, lot 372), therein titled *Attic*; Conger, "Edward Weston's Early Photography" (chap. 2, note 10), p. 317, fig. 21/2.

52. Conger, "Edward Weston's Early Photography" (chap. 2, note 10), p. 320, fig. 21/3.

53. Eastman, *Love and Revolution* (chap. 11, note 8), pp. 231–32.

54. Eastman, *Love and Revolution* (chap. 11, note 8), p. 243.

55. Eastman, *Love and Revolution* (chap. 11, note 8), p. iii with ill..

56. Florence Deshon, letter to Max Eastman, June 17, 1921, paraphrased in Eastman, *Love and Revolution* (chap. 11, note 8), p. 244.

57. Edwards, "Eighth Pittsburgh" (chap. 12, note 90), p. 227.

58. "Photographic Exhibit at S.F. Camera Club Receives High Praise," *The Bulletin* [San Francisco], July 25, 1921, p. 3.

59. Johan Hagemeyer, "Pictorial Interpretation," CC, August 1922, pp. 361, 361ill., 362–65; *Johan Hagemeyer* (chap. 10, note 4), plate 2.

60. Hagemeyer, "Pictorial Interpretation" (note 59), p. 362ill.; *Johan Hagemeyer* (chap. 10, note 4), plate 6.

61. Hagemeyer, "Pictorial Interpretation" (note 59), p. 363ill.; Edgar Felloes, "The Emporium (Second Annual) Photographic Exhibition," CC, October 1922, pp. 455–63; p. 461ill.

62. Hagemeyer, "Pictorial Interpretation," (note 59), p. 364ill.

63. Hagemeyer, "Pictorial Interpretation," (note 59), p. 365ill.

64. Edward Weston, letter to Johan Hagemeyer, July 11, 1921, EW/JH Collection.

65. Edward Weston, letter to Johan Hagemeyer, postmarked July 28, 1921, EW/JH Collection.

66. Laurie Pintar, "Behind the Scenes: Bronco Billy and the Realities of Work in Open Shop Hollywood," in *Metropolis in the Making: Los Angeles in the 1920s* (Los Angeles, 2001), ed. William Deverell and Tom Sitton, pp. 319–38.

67. Milton, *Tramp* (chap. 6, note 36), pp. 184–86.

68. L. Frank Baum's home, Ozcot, was located at 1749 North Cherokee Ave., one block north of Hollywood Blvd.; Starr, *Material Dreams* (chap. 2, note 5), pp. 67–68.

69. Hopkins, *Both Hands* (chap. 7, note 3), pp. 66–67; Stella Haverland Rouse, "Olden Days: The Story of Boyland's Rise, Fall," *Santa Barbara News Press*, June 8, 1975; Michael Redmon, "History 101," *The Independent* [Santa Barbara], June 28, 1990, p. 70 (newspaper clippings), Prince [Prynce] Hopkins's biographical file, Santa Barbara Historical Society.

70. Florence Deshon, letter to Max Eastman, July 2, 1921, FD MSS.

71. Sutherland, interview (chap. 12, note 47), pp. 44–45.

72. Florence Deshon, letter to Max Eastman, July 20, 1921, FD MSS.

73. Edward Weston, letter to Johan Hagemeyer, postmarked July 28, 1921, EW/JH Collection.

74. Edward Weston, letter to Johan Hagemeyer, September 16, 1921, EW/JH Collection.

75. The photographs Weston sent to the London Salon failed to arrive in time, due to insufficient postage (Edward Weston, letter to Betty Katz [late August/early September 1921]), BK Papers.

76. Edward Weston, letter to Johan Hagemeyer, August 13, 1921, EW/JH Collection.

77. Tina Modotti, letter to Johan Hagemeyer, September 17, 1921, JH Collection.

78. Modotti, letter to Johan Hagemeyer (note 77).

79. Weston, letter to Johan Hagemeyer (note 74).

80. Edward Weston, letter to Johan Hagemeyer, August 6, 1921, EW/JH Collection.

81. Weston, letter to Johan Hagemeyer (note 74).

82. *Photographic Salon, Municipal Art Gallery, Oakland, California*, exh. cat., October 30–November 26, 1921.

83. Edgar Felloes, "Oakland Photographic Salon," CC, November 1921, p. 361, 361ill.; Warren, *Passionate Collaboration* (chap. 7, note 10), plate 35. This photograph was also exhibited as *Portrait of a Lady*; see "Margrethe Mather Exhibition Chronology," herein, under "1921."

84. Danly and Naef, *Edward Weston in Los Angeles* (chap. 12, note 94), p. 25, fig. 25, therein titled *Nude Study*.

85. Conger, *Edward Weston: Photographs* (chap. 1, note 29), fig. 71/1921.

86. Albers, *Shadows* (note 38), pp. 62–63.

87. Ricardo Gómez Robelo, letter to Edward Weston, dated "Sunday 19" [June 19, 1921], EW Archive.

88. The phrase "lotus in the mud-pond," or some variant of it, often appears in Buddhist writings.

89. Ramiel McGehee, letter to Betty Katz [October–November 1921], BK Papers.

90. Shulman, *Valentino* (chap. 9, note 52), pp. 172–74.

91. Kenneth S. Lynn, *Charlie Chaplin and His Times* (New York, 1997), pp. 112–14.

92. Eastman, *Love and Revolution* (chap. 11, note 8), pp. 273–77.

93. Marie Howe was a former Presbyterian minister who had become well-known as a feminist. During the early 1920s she translated and edited the journals of the French author George Sand.

94. Florence Deshon, letter to Max Eastman [November 1921], FD MSS.

95. Albers, *Shadows* (note 38), pp. 71–78.

96. Albers, *Shadows*, (note 38), pp. 81–83.

97. *Fifth International Photographic Salon, Under the Auspices of the Camera Pictorialists of Los Angeles*, exh. cat. (Los Angeles Museum of History, Science, and Art, December 13, 1921–January 2, 1922).

98. Gilles Mora, *Forms of Passion* (New York, 1995), p. 46ill. This photograph was also exhibited as *The Source*.

99. Edward Weston, letter to Johan Hagemeyer, January 3, 1922, EW/JH Collection.

100. A.C. Clements, letter to Edward Weston, December 29, 1921, EW Archive.

101. The man behind the mask may have been the photographer T. K. Shindo. A variant of this image, in the collection of the Galleries of the Claremont Colleges, Claremont, Calif., bears the inscription *#1 Tatsujin/T. K. Shindo/1404 N. Los Angeles St./Los Angeles, Cal.*, on verso of the original mat; Conger, "Edward Weston's Early Photography" (chap. 2, note 10), p. 349, fig. 21/27.

CHAPTER 14
TRAGEDIES AND TRIUMPHS, 1922

1. Tina Modotti, letter to Edward Weston, January 27, 1922, EW Archive.

2. Edward Weston, letter to Johan Hagemeyer, January 12, 1922, EW/JH Collection.

3. Edward Weston, letter to Ramiel McGehee, postmarked January 12, 1922, EW Archive.

4. Kirkpatrick, *Cast of Killers* (chap. 7, note 49); Charles Higham, *A Murder in Hollywood: solving a silent screen mystery* (Madison, Wis., 2004).

5. Eastman, *Love and Revolution* (chap. 11, note 8), pp. 277–78.

6. Eastman, *Love and Revolution* (chap. 11, note 8), pp. 278–79.

7. "Actress Dies of Gas Poison: Found Unconscious in Her Apartment With Window Open," *New York Times*, February 5, 1922; "Eastman Denies Rift with Miss Deshon: Actress's Death Was Accidental, He Declares, and Her Friends and Medical Examiner Concur," *New York Times*, February 6, 1922; "Clews [*sic*] Sought in Death Case: Actress's Passing Causes Police Investigation," *Los Angeles Times*, February 6, 1922; "Miss Deshon Buried: Writer Vainly Gives Blood for Transfusion," *Los Angeles Times*, February 7, 1922; Death certificate of Florence Deshon (d. February 4, 1922), New York City, N.Y.

8. Marie Howe, letter to Max Eastman, February 6, 1922, FD MSS.

9. Betty Katz, letter to (Sophie) Pauline (Gibling) Schindler [ca. March 1922], SchF Collection.

10. Eastman, letter to Florence Deshon (chap. 11, note 72).

11. Robo de Richey, letter to Edward Weston, December 23, 1921, EW Archive.

12. de Richey, letter to Edward Weston (note 11).

13. Albers, *Shadows* (chap. 13, note 38), pp. 85–87.

14. Antony Anderson, "Of Art and Artists," *Los Angeles Times*, February 26, 1922, in which he mistakenly states that Robo de Richey's death took place on February 11, instead of February 9.

15. Edward Weston, letter to Johan Hagemeyer, February 13, 1922, EW/JH Collection.

16. Edward Weston, letter to Johan Hagemeyer, February 23, 1922, EW/JH Collection.

17. Johan Hagemeyer, letter to Edward Weston, March 23, 1922, EW/JH Collection.

18. Rafael Vera de Córdova, "Photographs as True Art," *El Universal Ilustrado* (Mexico City), March 23, 1922, pp. 30–31, 55, trans. Amy Conger, reprinted in *Edward Weston Omnibus* (chap. 2, note 30), pp. 13–16.

19. Albers, *Shadows* (chap. 13, note 38), p. 99.

20. Tina Modotti, letter to Johan Hagemeyer, April 7, 1922, EW/JH Collection.

21. Edward Weston, letter to Johan Hagemeyer, April 15, 1922, EW/JH Collection

22. Antony Anderson, "Of Art and Artists," *Los Angeles Times*, March 26, 1922.

23. Antony Anderson, "Of Art and Artists," *Los Angeles Times*, June 11, 1922.

24. R.W. Borough, "Art, Love and Death: Widow Must Sell Batiks," *Los Angeles Record* [ca. early May, 1922] (newspaper clipping), EW Archive.

25. Subtitle, final scene, *The Pilgrim*, a silent film starring Charlie Chaplin, released by First National Film Company on February 26, 1923.

26. According to Robert Sweeney, executive director of the Schindler House on Kings Road in West Hollywood, Schindler's surname was actually Schlesinger, as indicated by church records at St. Ägyd Catholic Church in Vienna, Austria. The Schlesinger family officially changed their surname to Schindler in 1904.

27. Robert Sweeney, "Life at Kings Road: As It Was 1920–1940," in *The Architecture of R. M. Schindler* (New York, 2001), with essays by Sweeney, Michael Darling, Kurt G. F. Helfrich, Elizabeth A. T. Smith, and Richard Guy Wilson; David Gebhard, *Schindler* (San Francisco, 1997), pp. 86–115; Kathryn Smith, *R. M. Schindler House 1921–22* (West Hollywood, 1987).

28. Charles Moore, Peter Becker, and Regula Campbell, *Los Angeles: The City Observed; A Guide to Its Architecture and Landscapes* (Santa Monica, 1998), p. 253.

29. Karasick and Karasick, *Oilman's Daughter* (chap. 8, note 129), pp. 69–81.

30. Sweeney, "Life at Kings Road," (note 27), p. 88.

31. Avrich, *The Modern School* (chap. 5, note 56), pp. 252–53. The Walt Whitman School operated from 1919 to 1924.

32. William Thurston Brown, letter to Edward Weston, April 17, 1920, EW Archive.

33. Sophie Pauline Gibling Schindler, letter to Mr. and Mrs. Edmund J. Gibling, July 16, 1922, SchF Papers. Quotation by permission of Margot Schindler-Ehrens.

34. Schallert, "Works of Beauty" (chap. 8, note 117); "Ruth Deardorff-Shaw: Tone colorist, who is to be heard in a piano recital Thursday evening at Trinity Auditorium," *Los Angeles Times*, April 9, 1916, ill.; "Musical Notes," *Los Angeles Times*, January 31, 1917; Jeanne Redman, "Piano and Song: Mrs. Shaw's Concert and Mr. Werrenrath Again," *Los Angeles Times*, February 11, 1918; "Art of Piano Center Here: Greatest Masters in Music City Residents," *Los Angeles Times*, December 24, 1922.

35. Aimée Brown Price, *Peter Krasnow (1887–1979)*, transcript of a lecture delivered on the occasion of Krasnow's retrospective exhibition at the Skirball Museum, Hebrew Union College, Los Angeles, 1978, PK/RK Papers; see also Howard Putzel, "Peter Krasnow—A Profile Sketch," *The Argus*, June 1928, p. 5; Arthur Millier, "Peter Krasnow," in *Peter Krasnow*, exh. cat. (Pasadena Art Institute, 1954); Peter Krasnow, "Peter Krasnow," in *Peter Krasnow: A Retrospective Exhibition*, Municipal Art Gallery, Barnsdall Park, Los Angeles, February 26–March 23, 1975, exh. brochure (Los Angeles, 1975); Peter Krasnow and Rose Krasnow, autobiographical manuscripts, PK/RK Papers.

36. *Exhibition of Paintings*, Whitney Studio Club, February 12–26 [1921–22], exh. cat. (New York [1921–22]), PK/RK Papers.

37. Edward Weston, letter to Johan Hagemeyer [July 1922], EW/JH Collection.

38. Antony Anderson, "Of Art and Artists," *Los Angeles Times*, July 23, 1922; Elizabeth Bingham, "Art Exhibits and Comments," *Saturday Night* (magazine clipping), LAMHSAS, vol. 8.

39. Antony Anderson, "Of Art and Artists," *Los Angeles Times*, September 17, 1922.

40. Antony Anderson, "Of Art and Artists," *Los Angeles Times*, October 15, 1922.

41. Warren, *Passionate Collaboration* (chap. 7, note 10), dust jacket, plate 62; Imogen Cunningham, interviews by Margery Mann, 1960–73, transcript, MM Files; interview by Louise Katzman and Paul Karlstrom, June 9, 1975, transcript, IC Papers.

42. Warren, *Passionate Collaboration* (chap. 7, note 10), plate 61.

43. Lowe and Thompson, *Edward Weston Life Work* (chap. 2, note 20), plate 12; Antony Anderson, "Of Art and Artists," *Los Angeles Times*, November 6 and November 19, 1922.

44. Antony Anderson, "Of Art and Artists," *Los Angeles Times*, August 13, 1922.

45. Antony Anderson, "Of Art and Artists," *Los Angeles Times*, July 23, July 30, and August 13, 1922.

46. Antony Anderson, "Of Art and Artists," *Los Angeles Times*, October 8, 1922.

47. Justema, "Margaret" (prologue, note 1), pp. 5–6.

48. Martinez, interview (chap. 8, note 92), transcript, pp. 101–2.

49. Weston, *Daybooks*, vol. 2 (chap. 1, note 30), p. 258.

50. Justema, "Margaret" (prologue, note 1), p. 5.

51. Chicago City Directory, 1905–8, s.v. "William Justema [Sr.]."

52. Los Angeles City Directory, 1915–18, 1920, 1923–24, s.v. "William Justema [Sr.]"; Los Angeles, Los Angeles County, Calif., Federal Census, 1910, 1920, s.v. "William Justema [Sr.]."

53. Justema, "Margaret" (prologue, note 1), pp. 12–15.

54. Justema, "Margaret" (prologue, note 1), p. [21]ill.

55. Justema, "Margaret" (prologue, note 1), pp. [4]ill., 13ill.

56. Charles Hopkins, "Richard Buhlig," in *The New Grove Dictionary of Music and Musicians*, 2nd ed. (London, 2001), ed. Stanley Sadie and John Tyrrell, vol. 4, p. 565.

57. "Friday Morning Club New Home of Buhlig Lectures," *Los Angeles Record*, November 12, 1920 (newspaper clipping), FMCS, vol. 6, p. 88.

58. Theodore Karp, *Dictionary of Music* (New York, 1973), s.v. "Henry Cowell," p. 118; Thomas Scherman, *The International Cyclopedia of Music and Musicians*, 11th ed. (New York, 1985), ed. Oscar Thompson and Bruce Bohle, s.v. "Henry Cowell," pp. 478–86; Theodore Baker, *Baker's Biographical Dictionary of Musicians*, 8th ed. (New York, 1992), rev. Nicolas Slonimsky, s.v. "Henry Cowell," pp. 367–69; David Nicholls, *The New Grove Dictionary of Music and Musicians*, 2nd ed., s.v. "Henry (Dixon) Cowell" (London, 2001), vol. 6, pp. 621–31.

59. Nicholls, *New Grove Dictionary* (note 58), p. 621.

60. Warren, *Passionate Collaboration* (chap. 7, note 10), plate 72.

61. Edward Weston, postcard to Johan Hagemeyer, October 7, 1922, EW/JH Collection.

62. Tina Modotti, letter to Edward Weston [ca. October 1922], quoted in Constantine, *A Fragile Life* (chap. 13, note 38), p. 55.

63. Weston, *Daybooks*, vol. 1 (prologue, note 2), p. 8.

64. Miriam Lerner, letter to Betty Katz [November 1922], BK Papers.

65. Hazel Jo Kellogg, acc. database, acc. no. H73.137.6, Oakland Museum of California; Hazel Jo Kellogg, letter to Edward Weston, November 20, 1922, EW Archive; Edward Weston, letter to Johan Hagemeyer, postmarked January 11, 1923.

66. Edward Payson Weston, biographical information and ephemera, EW Archive.

67. Gray, *New York Streetscapes* (chap. 12, note 75), pp. 12–13, 108–110; John Tauranac, *Essential New York: A Guide to the History and Architecture of Manhattan's Important Buildings, Parks, and Bridges* (New York, 1979), pp. 92, 126–27, 139–40, 144–45.

68. Weston, letter to Johan Hagemeyer (note 65).

69. Weston, letter to Johan Hagemeyer (note 65).

70. Edward Weston, letter to Johan Hagemeyer, postmarked November 5, 1922, EW/JH Collection.

71. Edward Weston, letter to Alfred Stieglitz, November 8, 1922, AS/GO Archive.

72. Alfred Stieglitz, letter to Edward Weston, November 9, 1922, AS/GO Archive. Quotation ©2010 Georgia O'Keefe Museum and by permission of the Artists Rights Society (ARS) New York City. Used courtesy Yale Collection of American Literature, Beinecke Rare Book and Manuscript Library, Yale University, New Haven.

73. Edward Weston, letter to Alfred Stieglitz, November 13, 1922, AS/GO Archive.

74. Edward Weston, letter to Johan Hagemeyer, November 18, 1922, EW/JH Collection.

75. Weston, letter to Johan Hagemeyer (note 65).

76. Weston, letter to Johan Hagemeyer (note 65).

77. Weston, *Daybooks*, vol. 1 (prologue, note 2), pp. 6–7.

78. Weston, *Daybooks*, vol. 1 (prologue, note 2), p. 7.

79. Hazel Jo Kellogg, letter to Edward Weston, November 20, 1922, EW Archive.

80. Weston, letter to Johan Hagemeyer (note 65).

81. Antony Anderson, "Of Art and Artists," *Los Angeles Times*, November 13, 1922.

82. Hooks, TM: *Photographer* (chap. 13, note 38), p. 62; Albers, *Shadows* (chap. 13, note 38), p. 108.

83. Antony Anderson, "Of Art and Artists," *Los Angeles Times*, December 17, 1922.

84. Elizabeth Bingham, "Pictorialists Annual Salon," *Saturday Night*, December 9, 1922 (magazine clipping), LAMHSAS, vol. 8.

85. William Deverell, "My America or Yours? Americanization and the Battle for the Youth of Los Angeles," in *Metropolis in the Making* (chap. 13, note 66), pp. 277–301.

86. Harry Haldeman was the grandfather of H. R. (Bob) Haldeman, who would become White House chief of staff under President Richard M. Nixon.

87. "Dr. Prynce Hopkins, Local Scholar, Dies," *Santa Barbara News Press*, August 17, 1970, pp. A1–A4.

88. Greg Hise, "Industry and Imaginative Geographies," in *Metropolis in the Making* (chap. 13, note 66), pp. 13–44.

89. Clark Davis, "The View from Spring Street," in *Metropolis in the Making* (chap. 13, note 66), p. 182.

90. Edward Weston, letter to Ramiel McGehee, December 28, 1922, EW Archive.

91. Margrethe Mather, letter to Ramiel McGehee [ca. December 1923], quoted in Weston, *Daybooks*, vol. 1 (prologue, note 2), p. 37.

CHAPTER 15
ENDINGS AND BEGINNINGS, 1923

1. Weston, letter to Johan Hagemeyer (chap. 14, note 65).

2. May Weston Seaman, fragment of a letter to Edward Weston [February 1923], EW Archive.

3. Edward Weston, letter to Ramiel McGehee, postmarked February 7, 1923, EW Archive.

4. Edward Weston, letter to A. J. Olmstead, August 12, 1921, acc. records, Photographic History Collection, NMAH.

5. Edward Weston, letter to A. J. Olmstead [ca. December 1922], acc. records, Photographic History Collection, NMAH.

6. Danly and Naef, *Edward Weston in Los Angeles* (chap. 12, note 94), p. 25, fig. 25, therein titled *Nude Study*.

7. Conger, *Edward Weston: Photographs* (chap. 1, note 29), fig. 72/1921.

8. Sotheby Parke Bernet, *Important Photographs*, sale cat. (New York, November 9, 1976, lot 352), therein titled *The Breast*; Mora, *Forms* (chap. 13, note 98), p. 46ill., therein titled *The Breast*; Conger, "Edward Weston's Early Photography" (chap. 2, note 10), p. 351, fig. 21/29.

9. Conger, *Edward Weston: Photographs* (chap. 1, note 29), fig. 69/1921.

10. Warren, *Passionate Collaboration* (chap. 7, note 10), plate 59; Dr. William F. Mack was the brother-in-law of Florence Reynolds. A roentgenologist is a physician who specializes in medical diagnosis and therapy through the use of X-rays. The term is derived from the surname of Wilhelm Konrad Roentgen, the German physicist who discovered X-rays in 1895.

11. A. J. Olmstead, letter to Edward Weston, February 8, 1923, acc. records, Photographic History Collection, NMAH. Quotation courtesy Museum of American History, Smithsonian Institution, Washington, D.C.

12. Edward Weston, letter to Alfred Stieglitz, February 21, 1923, AS/GO Archive.

13. Edward Weston, letter to Johan Hagemeyer, March 23, 1923, EW/JH Collection.

14. Lois Kellogg Isham (b. September 29, 1894), Second Presbyterian Church, Register of Baptisms, Chicago, Cook County, Illinois, p. 15; Helen Gerry, "Fool's Folly," *Palm Springs Villager Magazine*, November 1947, pp. 23, 33; Helen Gerry, "In Days Gone By," *Palm Springs Villager Magazine*, December 1947, pp. 9, 31, 33; Nell Murbarger, "Lois Kellogg of Fool's Folly: She Brought Glamour to Palm Springs," *Palm Springs Villager Magazine*, April 1954, reprinted in *Palm Springs Life*, October 1964, pp. 25–27; Shannon Star, "Wealthy desert eccentric led colorful life," *The Press-Enterprise* (Riverside, Calif.), July 15, 2002, p. B3; Mary Alice Molloy, Chicago architectural historian, conversations and correspondence with the author, August–September 1998; Professor Peter Wild, conversations and correspondence with the author, June 2007–January 2009.

15. Mary Alice Molloy, architectural historian, quoted in Avis Berman, "Blueprints from Points East," *New York Times*, July 12, 1998.

16. A.T. Andreas, *History of Chicago from the Earliest Period to the Present Time* (Chicago, 1886), vol. 3, pp. 296–97; "It's History is Told: Sketch by a Second Presbyterian Church Committee," *Chicago Tribune*, March 4, 1894; Moses Kirkland, *History of Chicago, Illinois* (Chicago, 1895), vol. 1, p. 722; "Four Blocks on Prairie Avenue Peopled by Widows and Widowers Whom Fortune Has Favored: Select Residence District Where Wealth Has Not Prevented Death from Visiting Many Houses," *Chicago Tribune*, January 9, 1898; Death certificate of Lois Kellogg (b. September 29, 1894, d. August 20, 1944), Arlemont, Nye County, Nevada; Molloy, conversations and correspondence (note 14).

17. Emma Lois Kellogg vs. Pierrepont Isham, case no. 199199, August 23, 1899, Clerk of the Cir. Ct. of Cook County, Ill.; "Death of Pierpont Isham," *The Keene Evening Sentinel* (New Hampshire), May 21, 1906, p. 5; "Lieut. Pierpont Isham," *The Keene Evening Sentinel*, May 22, 1906, p. 3; Wild, conversations and correspondence (note 14).

18. Harold Lee (formerly Lessow), essays (chap. 9, note 59); Martin Lessow, discussions (chap. 9, note 59).

19. Burial records of Emma Lois Kellogg (d. June 1, 1918), Forest Hill Cemetery, Utica, N.Y.

20. Kellogg might have named her desert oasis Babylon because of a poem reproduced in Emma Goldman's *Mother Earth*; see references to Babylon and its connotations (epilogue, note 3).

21. Gerry, "Fool's Folly" (note 14); Shannon Starr, "Friendship, Initiative Helped Keep Her Going," *The Press-Enterprise* [Riverside, Calif.], July 6, 2002, p. B3; Helen Gerry, "Portraits," *Palm Springs Villager Magazine*, n.d., pp. 28–36. See also *Los Angeles City Directory*, 1910–17, 1920, 1922–23, s.v. "Harold Bryant Cody"; World War I draft registration of Harold Bryant Cody, June 2, 1917, NARA; Death certificate of Harold B. Cody (b. January 3, 1887, d. July 8, 1924), Glendale, Los Angeles County, Calif.; Death certificate of Harriet Clark Dowie Cody (b. May 5, 1885, d. June 28, 1954), Palm Springs, Riverside County, Calif.

22. Barbara McCandless, "A Commitment to Beauty," in *New York to Hollywood: The Photography of Karl Struss*, introduction by William I. Homer, essays by McCandless, Bonnie Yochelson, and Richard Koszarski, afterword by John and Susan Edwards Harvith, exh. cat. (Ft. Worth: Amon Carter Museum, 1995), pp. 13–59.

23. Karl Struss, letter to Imogen Cunningham, January 25, 1919, IC Papers.

24. Warren, *Passionate Collaboration* (chap. 7, note 10), plate 60.

25. Mora, *Forms of Passion* (chap. 13, note 98), p. 53ill.; Conger, *Edward Weston: Photographs* (chap. 1, note 29), figs. 78–9/1922.

26. Edward Weston, letter to Johan Hagemeyer, April 9, 1923, EW/JH Collection.

27. Mora, *Forms of Passion* (chap. 13, note 98), p. 55ill.; Conger, *Edward Weston: Photographs* (chap. 1, note 29), figs. 90–1/1923.

28. Conger, *Edward Weston: Photographs* (chap. 1, note 29), fig. 93/1923.

29. Conger, *Edward Weston: Photographs* (chap. 1, note 29), fig. 94/1923.

30. Conger, *Edward Weston: Photographs* (chap. 1, note 29), fig. 95/1923.

31. Brett Abbott, *Edward Weston's Book of Nudes* (Los Angeles, 2007), plates 30–32; Watts, *Edward Weston: A Legacy* (chap. 7, note 55), pp. 30–31, figs. 19–21; Conger, *Edward Weston: Photographs* (chap. 1, note 29), figs. 924–929/1936.

32. Weston, *Daybooks*, vol. 1 (prologue, note 2), p. 27.

33. Johan Hagemeyer, diary, April 12–15, 1923, JH Collection.

34. Johan Hagemeyer, diary, April 16–22, 1923, JH Collection.

35. Weston, *Daybooks*, vol. 1 (prologue, note 2), p. 9.

36. Weston, *Daybooks*, vol. 1 (prologue, note 2), p. 9.

37. Weston, *Daybooks*, vol. 1 (prologue, note 2), pp. 9–10.

38. Weston, *Daybooks*, vol. 1 (prologue, note 2), p. 10.

39. Edward Weston, letter to Alfred Stieglitz, May 28, 1923, AS/GO Archive.

40. Johan Hagemeyer, letter to Edward Weston, June 15, 1923, EW/JH Collection.

41. Edward Weston, letter to Alfred Stieglitz, July 12, 1923, AS/GO Archive.

42. Betty Katz, letter to Edward Weston, July 26, 1923, EW Archive.

43. McDougal, *Privileged Son* (chap. 2, note 5), p. 98; Greg Williams, *The Story of Hollywoodland* (Los Angeles, 1992), pp. 14ill., 15ill.

44. Margrethe Mather, note to Edward Weston, July 29, 1923, EW Archive.

45. Weston, *Daybooks*, vol. 1 (prologue, note 2), p. 13.

46. Margrethe Mather, note to Edward Weston, July 30, 1923, EW Archive.

EPILOGUE

1. Antony Anderson, "Of Art and Artists," *Los Angeles Times*, May 18, 1924; Arthur Millier, "Of Art and Artists," *Los Angeles Times*, May 25, 1924.

2. *Artgram*, Los Angeles Japanese Camera Club (under the auspices of *Rafu Shimpo*, a Japanese-language newspaper published in Los Angeles), exh. cat. (Los Angeles, 1924); Dennis Reed, *Japanese Photography in America, 1920-1940*, exh. cat. (Japanese American Cultural & Community Center, Los Angeles, 1986), pp. 13, 33–53.

3. Weston, *Daybooks*, vol. 1 (prologue, note 2), p. 116. Mather's reference to the "willowed river we never walked to" relates to the poem "Revolution" by Ferdinand Freiligrath, the nineteenth-century German socialist poet. The poem became well known in America after it was translated and published in the March 1910 issue of *Mother Earth*. "Revolution" is based on Psalm 137, in which a group of exiled Jews refuse to play their harps for their conquerors and instead hang their instruments on willow trees along the riverbanks of Babylon. Because the poem carries a revolutionary message, its phrases became rallying cries for early-twentieth-century anarchists. Freiligrath's references to willow trees, which have long been symbols of death and lost love, would have had special meaning for Mather. Not only was she saddened by the imminent loss of her studio, she was also mourning the end of her decade-long relationship with Weston. Lois Kellogg intended to call her Palm Springs home "Babylon," which could also have been a reference to the poem, and Eugene O'Neill certainly found excerpts from the poem inspirational. In his play, *The Iceman Cometh*, which is replete with allusions to anarchism and revolution, the final scene features two lines borrowed from the poem: "The days grow hot, O Babylon! / 'Tis cool beneath thy willow trees." See Ferdinand Freiligrath, "Revolution," ME, frontispiece, March 1910; Winifred Frazer, *E.G. and E.G.O.: Emma Goldman and the Iceman Cometh* (Gainesville, Fla., 1974), pp. 73–75.

4. Sotheby's, *The Quillan Collection of Nineteenth and Twentieth Century Photographs* (New York, April 17, 2008, lot 19).

5. Warren, *Passionate Collaboration* (chap. 7, note 10), plates 83–89; *Margrethe Mather* (prologue, note 1), pp. 21–53ills.

6. "Opening of Museum Wing Nears," *San Francisco Chronicle*, July 12, 1931, p. 8D; "New Galleries at Museum to be Opened," *San Francisco Chronicle*, July 14, 1931, p. 3; "M. H. de Young Museum Again Opens Doors: Throngs View Display at Park Institution After Alterations to Building," *San Francisco Chronicle*, July 16, 1931, p. 5; Grace Hubbard, "New Wing Opens at De Young Museum," *The Wasp-Newsletter: A Weekly Journal of Illustration and*

Comment [San Francisco], July 18, 1931, p. 12; "Photography as Fine Art Is Demonstrated In Museum Exhibition," *San Francisco Chronicle*, July 26, 1931, p. 8D; Florence Wieben, "Art and Artists," *Oakland Tribune*, August 9, 1931, p. 6S.

7. Weston, *Daybooks*, vol. 1 (prologue, note 2), p. 145.

8. William Justema, letter to Lee Witkin, August 30, 1976, LW/WG Archive.

9. Death certificate of Margaret Lipton (b. March 4, 1886 [birth date incorrectly recorded as April 14, 1836], d. December 25, 1952), Los Angeles, Los Angeles County, California.

10. Mather, letter to Edward Weston (chap. 5, note 7).

11. Weston, *Daybooks*, vol. 1 (prologue, note 2), p. 145.

12. Justema, letter to Lee Witkin (note 8).

13. Ironically, Alfred Stieglitz was born on January 1.

Exhibition Chronologies

Following is a list of exhibitions in which Edward Weston and Margrethe Mather are known to have participated during the years they were active in Los Angeles. These listings include Weston's exhibitions of 1913–23 and Mather's of 1913–31. When titles of exhibited photographs are known, they are listed in italics. Sources of this information are cited in parentheses after each entry, and when the information is found in correspondence, the sender and recipient are noted. Titles of works are given here as they appear in the cited sources; they may not be consistent with one another or with the way they are shown elsewhere in this book. The following abbreviations are used:

AP	*American Photography*
BJP	*British Journal of Photography*
BK Papers	Betty Katz Papers, Martin Lessow Collection, Breckenridge, Colorado
CC	*Camera Craft*
CCP	Center for Creative Photography, University of Arizona, Tucson
CI	Carnegie Institute
CPLA	Camera Pictorialists of Los Angeles
CS	*California Southland*
EW Archive	Edward Weston Archive
EW/JH Collection	Edward Weston/Johan Hagemeyer Collection
FMCS	Friday Morning Club Scrapbooks
F&NDS	Frederick & Nelson Department Store
JWDS	John Wanamaker Department Store
LSP	London Salon of Photography
PE	*Photo-Era*
PJA	*Photographic Journal of America*
SN	*Saturday Night*
TC	*The Camera*

1913

EDWARD WESTON

April 28–May 3: Tenth Salon, 22nd Annual Exhibition, Toronto Camera Club (Amy Conger, *Edward Weston: Photographs from the Collection of the Center for Creative Photography* [Tucson, 1992], p. 59)

MARGRETHE MATHER

April–November: Salon International d'Art Photographique, Association Belge de Photographie, Palais des Beaux-Arts, Brussels: *Maid of Arcady* (Association Belge de Photographie, exh. cat.; CC, August 1912, p. 382)

November 1912–May: Ninth American Photographic Salon, shown at Carnegie Institute, Pittsburgh; L. D. M. Sweat Memorial Art Museum, Portland, Maine; Toledo Museum of Art; and Art Institute of Chicago: *Maid of Arcady* (CC, September 1912, p. 433; AP, September 1912, p. 545; AP, January, pp. 20–24; PE, March, p. 145; AP, April, p. 240; AP, May, p. 303; AP, July, p. 425)

1914

EDWARD WESTON

April 27–May 2: Eleventh Salon, 23rd Annual Exhibition, Toronto Camera Club: *Abandon* [bronze-medal award], *Bobbie, Flowers and Sunshine* [aka *Summer Sunshine*], *I Do Believe in Fairies,* and *Toxophilus: A Decorative Study* [bronze-medal award] (PE, July, p. 47; Amy Conger, "Edward Weston's Early Photography 1903–1926" [Ph.D. dissertation, University of New Mexico, Albuquerque, 1982], pp. 83, 89, 97, 110, 112)

June 15–June 20: Convention of the Photographers' Association of America, Atlanta: *Study* [aka *Summer Sunshine*] and possibly others [first-place award] (PE, August, pp. 101, 104; *Los Angeles Times,* October 31, 1915; Conger, "Edward Weston's Early Photography" [see above], p. 83)

September 5–October 17: International Exhibition of the London Salon of Photography, Galleries of the Royal Society of Painters in Water-Colours: *Abandon, Carlota, Child Study in Grey, Summer Sunshine,* and *Toxophilus: A Decorative Study* (LSP, exh. cat.; *Los Angeles Times,* October 31, 1915; PE, November, p. 236)

November: Solo exhibition, Friday Morning Club, Los Angeles: *Abandon, Carlota, Child Study in Gray, Summer Sunshine, Toxophilus: A Decorative Study,* and others (*Los Angeles Times,* November 22; FMCS, vol. 3, pp. 18–19, 22)

December: Northwest Photographers' Convention, Minneapolis: *Carlota* and others [grand-prize award] (AP, January 1915, p. 55; PE, February 1915, p. 102; CC, March 1915, p. 131; Conger, "Edward Weston's Early Photography" [see above], p. 91)

1915

EDWARD WESTON

February 20–December 4, 1915: Pictorial Photography Exhibition, Panama-Pacific International Exposition, Palace of Liberal Arts, San Francisco: *Carlota, Child Study in Grey* [bronze-medal award], and *Dolores* (Panama-Pacific International Exposition, exh. cat.; CC, October, pp. 411–12)

March: Solo exhibition, Shakespeare Club, Pasadena: *Abandon, Bobbie, Carlota, Chicago, Child Study in Gray, I Do Believe in Fairies, Portrait, Self-Portrait, Summer Sunshine, Toxophilus—A Decorative Study,* and *Valley of the Long Winds* (Conger, "Edward Weston's Early Photography" [see under 1914], pp. 84, 89, 92, 97, 99, 105–6, 110–12)

July 19–24: Convention of the Photographers' Association of America, Indianapolis: *Dolores* and others [first-place and certificate of merit awards] (CC, March, p. 131; PE, September, pp. 157–58; PJA, September, p. 452; *Los Angeles Times,* October 31; PE, October, p. 210; CC, November, p. 460)

September 18–October 16: International Exhibition of the London Salon of Photography, Galleries of the Royal Society of Painters in Water-Colours: *Maud Allan, Maud Allan—Character Study, Nude with Black Shawl,* and *Portrait of My Son* (LSP, exh. cat.; *Los Angeles Times,* October 31)

October–November: Solo exhibition, State Normal School, Los Angeles: *Carlota, Dolores, Margrethe, Maud Allan, Portrait of Master B., Ruth St. Denis, Summer Sunshine, Ted Shawn, Toxophilus, Valley of the Long Winds,* and others (*Los Angeles Times,* October 31)

MARGRETHE MATHER

February: Fifth Annual Exhibition, Los Angeles Camera Club (*Los Angeles Times,* February 26)

March 1–31: Second Annual Pittsburgh Salon of National Photographic Art, Academy of Science and Art, Carnegie Institute: *The Menace* (CI, exh. cat.; PJA, May, p. 218)

1916

EDWARD WESTON

February 4–27: Camera Pictorialists of Los Angeles, First Annual Arts and Crafts Salon, Los Angeles Museum of History, Science, and Art, Exposition Park: *Carlota* (CPLA, exh. cat.; AP, November, p. 589)

February 22–26: Wilkes-Barre Camera Club, Poli Building, Wilkes-Barre, Penn.: *Ruth St. Denis* [honorable-mention award] and possibly others (Wilkes-Barre Camera Club, exh. cat.)

March 1–17: Eleventh Annual Exhibition of Photographs, John Wanamaker [Department Store], Philadelphia: *Child Study in Gray* [honorable-mention award], *Dolores* [fifth-place award], *Maud Allan* [honorable-mention award], *Maud Allan—Character Study, Nude* [honorable-mention award], *Nude with Black Shawl, Portrait of My Son, Ruth St. Denis—Character Study, Ted Shawn as David,* and *Toxophilus—a Decorative Study* [fourth-place award] (JWDS, exh. cat.; AP, April, p. 220; PJA, May, p. 228)

April 27–May 21: Twenty-Sixth Annual Exhibition by the Department of Photography of the Brooklyn Institute of Arts and Sciences: *Dancing Nude, A Fleck of Sunshine—Ruth St. Denis,* and *Wake! For the Sun behind the Eastern height Has chased the Session of the Stars from night* (Brooklyn Institute of Arts and Sciences, exh. cat.)

May 15–27: Fifth International Photographic Salon of the California Camera Club, Fotocraft Society, Bangor, Maine: *A Flower from the Land of Sunshine* [aka *Child Study in Gray*] and possibly others (Conger, "Edward Weston's Early Photography" [see under 1914], p. 95)

July 24–26: Thirty-Sixth Annual Photographer's Association of America Convention, Wigmore Coliseum, Cleveland: *The Dancer, A Fleck of Sunshine—Ruth St. Denis,* and others. Weston was also one of the convention lecturers, advocating the use of a small portable camera to produce negatives that could then be enlarged and printed (PJA, May, p. 224; AP, June, p. 315; PE, June, pp. 306–7; *Los Angeles Times,* July 30; *Los Angeles Times,* August 6; PE, September, p. 143; PJA, September, pp. 391–92)

September 16–October 14: International Exhibition of the London Salon of Photography, Galleries of the Royal Society of Painters in Water-Colours: *Dancing Nude, A Fleck of Sunshine—Ruth St. Denis,* and *Wake! For the sun behind yon eastern height Has chased the Session of the Stars from night* (LSP, exh. cat.)

October 4–November 10: An Exhibition of Photography held under the auspices of the American Institute of Graphic Arts, National Arts Club, New York City: *A Fleck of Sunshine—Ruth St. Denis* and *Child Study in Grey* (National Arts Club, exh. cat.)

MARGRETHE MATHER

February 4–27: First Annual Arts and Crafts Salon, Camera Pictorialists of Los Angeles, Los Angeles Museum of History, Science, and Art, Exposition Park: *The Stairway* (CPLA, exh. cat.; AP, May, pp. 281, 342; AP, November, p. 601)

1917

EDWARD WESTON

March: Twenty-Seventh Annual Exhibition by the Department of Photography, Brooklyn Institute of Arts and Sciences (*Los Angeles Times*, March 11)

March 1–17: Twelfth Annual Exhibition of Photographs, John Wanamaker [Department Store], Philadelphia: *Eugene Hutchinson* [ninth-place award], *Miss Dextra Baldwin* [ninth-place award], and *The Plum Tree* [merit award] (JWDS, exh. cat.; *Los Angeles Times*, March 11; PE, April, p. 206; PJA, April, p. 163; TC, April, p. 179; AP, May, p. 310)

March 1–31: Fourth Annual Pittsburgh Salon of National Photographic Art, Academy of Science and Art, Carnegie Institute: *Antony Anderson, Eugene Hutchinson, Light Play—Margaret Loomis, The Plum Tree, Portrait Group,* and *Portrait of Miss Dextra Baldwin* (CI, exh. cat.; PJA, February, p. 70; *Los Angeles Times*, March 11; AP, May, p. 310; PJA, May, pp. 206–7)

March–April: Friday Morning Club, Los Angeles: *Eugene Hutchinson, Light Play, The Plum Tree, Portrait Group of a Mother and Two Children,* and *Portrait of Miss Dextra Baldwin* (*Los Angeles Times*, March 11 and May 20)

May 2–16: Fourteenth Salon, Twenty-Sixth Annual Exhibition, Toronto Camera Club, Art Museum of Toronto: *Miss Dextra Baldwin* [bronze-medal award] and other portraits employing unusual lighting effects (AP, March, p. 189; PJA, March, p. 121; CC, November, pp. 457–60)

May 17–26: First Annual Photographic Salon, Southern California Camera Club, Lyceum Building, Los Angeles: *Antony Anderson, Eugene Hutchinson, Light Play* (*Margaret Loomis*), *The Plum Tree, Portrait Group, Portrait of a Child,* and *Portrait of Miss Dextra Baldwin* (Southern California Camera Club, exh. cat.; *Los Angeles Times*, May 13 and 20)

September 1917–March 1918: An Exhibition of Pictorial Photography by American Artists, organized by the Pictorial Photographers of America, New York City, and shown at Minneapolis Institute of Arts; Milwaukee Art Society; Art Institute of Chicago; City Art Museum of St. Louis; Toledo Museum of Art; Newark Museum of Art; Detroit Museum of Art; and Cleveland Museum of Art: *Antony Anderson, Decoration, Eugene Hutchinson, Miss Dextra Baldwin, Portrait Group,* and *Violet Romer* (Pictorial Photographers of America, exh. cat.; Newark Museum, exh. cat.; PJA, August, p. 345)

September 15–October 13: London Salon of Photography, Galleries of the Royal Society of Painters in Water-Colours: two images titled *Eugene Hutchinson, The Fan* (*Margarethe Mather*), *Katharine Edson, Portrait Group, Portrait of Miss Dextra Baldwin,* and *Portrait of My Father* (LSP, exh. cat.; CC, September, p. 388; CC, November, p. 516). Weston was elected a member of the London Salon as a result of this exhibition.

MARGRETHE MATHER

March 1–31: Fourth Annual Pittsburgh Salon of Photography, Academy of Science and Art, Carnegie Institute: *A Lady* and *The Stairway* (CI, exh. cat.; PJA, May, pp. 184, 189)

May 2–16: Fourteenth Salon, Twenty-Sixth Annual Exhibition, Toronto Camera Club, The Art Museum of Toronto: *Portrait of a Lady* and *The Stairway* (Toronto Camera Club, exh. cat.)

May 17–26: First Annual Photographic Salon, Southern California Camera Club, Lyceum Building, Los Angeles: *The Lady*, *Portrait of H. Dean*, *Portrait of William Saphier*, *Poster Portrait*, and *The Stairway* (Southern California Camera Club, exh. cat.; *Los Angeles Times*, May 20)

September 15–October 13: International Exhibition of the London Salon of Photography, Galleries of the Royal Society of Painters in Water-Colours: *Edward Henry Weston and His Father*, *In Costume*, and *Miss Maud Emily* (LSP, exh. cat.)

1918

EDWARD WESTON

March 4–16: Thirteenth Annual Exhibition of Photographs, John Wanamaker [Department Store], Philadelphia: *Act 3, Scene 2*; *Black Gown and a Shadow*; *The Fan—"Margrethe Mather"*; *Katharine Edson*; and *Sadakichi Hartmann* (JWDS, exh. cat.; AP, January, p. 54)

March 4–31: Fifth Annual Pittsburgh Salon of Photography, Department of Fine Arts, Carnegie Institute: *Costume Study (Violet Romer)*, *The Fan (Margrethe Mather)*, *Kathrine Edson*, *Portrait of My Son*, *Sadakichi Hartmann*, and *Vaudeville* (CI, exh. cat.; AP, January, p. 54; PJA, May, pp. 201–2)

Spring: Solo exhibition, Portland Camera Club, Portland, Maine, spring 1918 (PJA, December 1917, p. 531)

September 14–October 12: London Salon of Photography, Galleries of the Royal Society of Painters in Water-Colours: *Act II, Scene III (Vera Vestow)*; *Ahna Z[aczek]*; *Costume Study of Violet Romer*; *Portrait of Mrs. C.*; *Triangulate Design of G. H.*; and *Vaudeville* (LSP, exh. cat.; PJA, September, p. 403)

September 23–October 26 (possibly postponed or interrupted due to citywide influenza quarantine): California Liberty Fair, The Bracks Shops Building and Pavilion of Fine Arts, Exposition Park, Los Angeles: *Antony Anderson*, *Costume Design by George Hopkins*, *Costume Study (Violet Romer)*, *Eugene Hutchinson*, *Katharine Edson*, *Miss Dextra Baldwin*, *Olga Grey*, *Portrait of My Son*, *Type Antique*, and *Vaudeville* (AP, July, p. 393; *Los Angeles Times*, September 1; AP, September, p. 552; CC, November, pp. 431–32; CC, March 1919, p. 92; Conger, "Edward Weston's Early Photography" [see under 1914], pp. 117, 145, 184, 206, 214, 216, 222–23, 254–55)

MARGRETHE MATHER

September 14–October 12: International Exhibition of the London Salon of Photography, Galleries of the Royal Society of Painters in Water-Colours: *Nude* (LSP, exh. cat.; PJA, September, p. 403)

September 23–October 26 (possibly postponed or interrupted due to citywide influenza quarantine): California Liberty Fair, The Bracks Shops Building and Pavilion of Fine Arts, Exposition Park, Los Angeles: *The Chinese Flute*, *Decoratif Chinois*, *Moon Kwan*, *Player on the Yit-Kun*, and three others [second-place award in portraiture category, honorable-mention award in genre category] (CC, November, pp. 431–32; CC, March 1919, p. 93; Conger, "Edward Weston's Early Photography" [see under 1914], p. 171n178)

1919

EDWARD WESTON

March 3–31: Sixth Annual Pittsburgh Salon of Photography, Department of Fine Arts, Carnegie Institute: *Alma Zacsek [Ahna Zaczek]*, *Figure in the Nude*, *John Cowper Powys*, *Karin Jansson*, *Paul Jordan Smith*, and *Portrait of a Lady* (CI, exh. cat.; CC, May, p. 183; PE, May, p. 226; PJA, May, pp. 207, 215; AP, October, pp. 563, 615)

May: Solo exhibition, Boston Young Men's Christian Union Camera Club, Boston (PE, November 1918, p. 273; AP, December 1918, p. 735; CC, December 1918, p. 502; PJA, December 1918, p. 554; PE, June, p. 323)

May–June: Solo exhibition, Friday Morning Club, Los Angeles: *Alfred Allen, Chandler Weston, Enrique, Girl Near Piano, John Cowper Powys, Lieut. Ryder, Lieut. Porter, Margrethe and Plum Blossoms, Mrs. Andrew Stewart Lobingier, Nude, Paul Jordan Smith in Profile, Portrait of a Lady, Spencer Kellogg Jr.,* and *W. A. Clark Jr.* (*Los Angeles Times,* May 25)

Summer: California State Fair, Sacramento [bronze-medal award in portraiture category] (PE, October, p. 275)

September 13–October 11: International Exhibition of the London Salon of Photography, Galleries of the Society of Painters in Water-Colours: *Bathing Pool, Enrique, Epilogue, Figure in the Nude, From a Japanese Dance* (Clarence McGehee), and *Paul Jordan-Smith* (LSP, exh. cat.; CC, June, p. 278; PJA, July, p. 331; BJP, September, pp. 544–46)

December 20–January 24, 1920: Twelfth Scottish National Photographic Salon, The People's Palace, Glasgow: *Enrique, Paul Jordan-Smith,* and possibly others (PJA, December, p. 571; CCP, acc. no. 76.5.33, and Charles E. Young Research Library, University of California, Los Angeles, coll. 98, box 1, folder XA, no. 1, inscriptions on mounts)

MARGRETHE MATHER

March 3–31: Sixth Annual Pittsburgh Salon of Photography, Department of Fine Arts, Carnegie Institute: *Ballerina, Chinese Poet, Nude with Cymbals, Portrait of Moon Kwan,* and *Study of a Chinese Poet* (CI, exh. cat.; AP, February, p. 120; PE, May, p. 225; PJA, May, pp. 206, 216; AP, June, p. 328; AP, September, pp. 493, 547)

Summer: California State Fair, Sacramento [silver-medal award in portraiture category] (PE, October, p. 275)

September 13–October 11: International Exhibition of the London Salon of Photography, Galleries of the Society of Painters in Water-Colours: *Acacia Seeds* and *Portrait of Edward Weston* (LSP, exh. cat.; CC, June, p. 278; BJP, September 19, pp. 544–46)

December: Solo exhibition, Boston Young Mens' Christian Union Camera Club—Twenty-five photographs (CC, November, p. 447; PJA, November, p. 519; AP, December, p. 746)

1920

EDWARD WESTON

March 1–13: Fourteenth Annual Exhibition of Photographs, John Wanamaker [Department Store], Philadelphia: *Epilogue* (CC, June 1919, p. 288; PJA, July 1919, p. 334; Conger, "Edward Weston's Early Photography" [see under 1914], pp. 268–69)

March 3–31: Seventh Annual Pittsburgh Salon of Photography, Department of Fine Arts, Carnegie Institute: *Magrethe Mather* and *Silhouette* (CI, exh. cat.)

May: Solo exhibition, State Normal School, Los Angeles: *Chandler Weston, Enrique, John Cowper Powys, Margrethe and Plum Blossoms, Nude, Paul Jordan-Smith, Prologue to a Sad Spring, Spencer Kellogg Jr., Sybil Brainerd,* and others (*Los Angeles Times,* May 16)

June: Solo exhibition, Los Angeles Museum of History, Science, and Art, Exposition Park (*Los Angeles Times,* June 13)

August 25–September 10: Society of Copenhagen Amateur Photographers, Fifth Anniversary Salon: *Bathing Pool, Epilogue, Margrethe Mather, Margrethe and Plum Blossoms, Prologue to a Sad Spring, Sun-Mask,* and *The White Peacock* (Society of Copenhagen Amateur Photographers, exh. cat.; PE, January 1921, p. 48)

November 1–13: The Frederick & Nelson [Department Store] Exhibition of Pictorial Photography, Seattle [third-place award] (CC, March, p. 140; CC, September, p. 309; *Seattle Post-Intelligencer,* November 7, part 6, p. 3)

MARGRETHE MATHER

March 1–13: Fourteenth Annual Exhibition of Photographs, John Wanamaker [Department Store], Philadelphia (CC, June 1919, p. 288; PJA, July 1919, p. 334)

March 3–31: Seventh Annual Pittsburgh Salon of Photography, Department of Fine Arts, Carnegie Institute: *Black Acacia*, *Claire*, *Evgenia Buyko*, and *Pointed Pines*. Mather was named a contributing member of the Pittsburgh Salon as a result of this exhibition. (CI, exh. cat.; AP, February, p. 126; PE, June, p. 278; AP, July, pp. 389, 439–40; PE, July, p. 48)

August 25–September 10: Copenhagen Photographic Amateur Club, 25th Anniversary Salon: *Black Acacia*, *Edward Weston*, *The Gray Vase*, *Pierrot's Death*, *Player on the Yit-Kim*, and *Portrait of Moon Kwan* (Copenhagen Photographic Amateur Club, exh. cat.; PE, January 1921, p. 48)

November 1–13: First Annual Frederick & Nelson [Department Store] Exhibition of Pictorial Photography, Seattle [third-place and honorable-mention awards] (CC, April, p. 140; CC, September, p. 309; *Seattle Post-Intelligencer*, November 7, part 6, p. 3)

1921

EDWARD WESTON

February: Joint exhibition with Margrethe Mather, Friday Morning Club, Los Angeles: *Alfred Kreymborg*, *The Donaldsons at Home*, *Polly*, *Prologue to a Sad Spring*, *Ramiel in His Attic*, and possibly *Betty in Her Attic* and others (*Los Angeles Times*, February 6 and 13; Edward Weston, letter to Betty Katz [February], BK Papers)

February 26–March 12: First Annual Exhibition of Pictorial Photographs, Kansas City Photo Supply Co.: *Alfred Kreymborg—Poet*, *Attic Arrangement* [special-mention award], *Costume Study*, *Prologue to a Sad Spring* [honorable-mention award], and *Ramiel in His Attic* (Kansas City Photo Supply, exh. cat.; Edward Weston, letter to Betty Katz [February], BK Papers)

February 28–April: First Annual Competition organized by *American Photography*, Boston, and shown at New York Camera Club and Pennsylvania State College: *Balloon Fantasy* [honorable-mention award], *Betty in Her Attic* and *Enrique* [honorable-mention award] (*American Photography* Annual Competition, exh. cat.; AP, April, p. 164; AP, October, p. 547; AP, November, p. 625; Edward Weston, letter to Betty Katz [February], BK Papers)

March 2–31: Eighth Annual Pittsburgh Salon of Photography, Department of Fine Arts, Carnegie Institute: *Alfred Kreymborg "Baloons"* [aka *Balloon Fantasy*], *Fantastique*, *The Hand of E. M.*, *Margrethe Mather*, *Ramiel in His Attic*, and *Scene-Shifter* (CI, exh. cat.; PJA, November 1920, p. 435; AP, May, p. 226; PE, May, p. 228)

March 7–26: Fifteenth Annual Exhibition of Photographs, John Wanamaker [Department Store], Philadelphia: *Fantastique* [fourth-prize award] and *Ramiel in His Attic* [merit award] (JWDS, exh. cat.; Edward Weston, letter to Betty Katz [February], BK Papers, in which he mentions also sending *Betty in Her Attic*)

July: Joint exhibition with Margrethe Mather, California Camera Club, 833 Market Street, San Francisco: *Carl Sandburg, Poet*; *Max Eastman, Poet*; and others (*The Bulletin* [San Francisco], July 25, p. 3)

September 19–October 29: Sixty-Sixth Annual Exhibition of the Royal Photographic Society of Great Britain, London: *Head of an Italian Girl* (Royal Photographic Society, exh. cat.). Note: Weston also sent six photographs to the 1921 London Salon of Photography, September 10–October 8, 1921, but his package was returned because of insufficient postage (AP, August, p. 468; Edward Weston, letter to Betty Katz [late August/early September], BK Papers)

October 8–early November: Joint exhibition with Margrethe Mather, Karl Struss, and Edward S. Curtis, The MacDowell Club of Allied Arts, Tajo Building, Los Angeles: *Prologue to a Sad Spring*, *Sybil*, and possibly others (MacDowell Club of Allied Arts, exh. brochure; *Los Angeles Times*, October 30)

October 30–November 26: The Annual Salon of Photography of the Oakland Municipal Art Gallery, Civic Auditorium: *The Batik Gown (Tina Modello)*, *Fragment of a Nude*, *Nude*, *Ramiel in his Attic*, *"Robo"—a Portrait of the Artist at Work*, and *Sr. Lic. Ricardo Gómez Robelo*. Weston could not compete for awards because he served as one of the judges, along with William H. Clapp, John Paul Edwards, J. Nilsen Laurvik, and Roi Partridge (Oakland Municipal Art Gallery, exh. cat.; CC, July, p. 243; PE, August, p. 103; CC, November, p. 360)

November 1–12: Second Annual Frederick & Nelson [Department Store] Exhibition of Pictorial Photography, Seattle: *The Ascent of Attic Angles*; *Girl in Canton Chair*; *The Lacquer Chest*; and in collaboration with Margrethe Mather, *Carl Sandburg, Poet*; *Floyd Dell, Novelist*; and *Max Eastman, Poet* (F&NDS, exh. cat.)

December 13–January 3, 1922: Fifth Annual International Photographic Salon under the auspices of the Camera Pictorialists of Los Angeles, Los Angeles Museum of History, Science, and Art, Exposition Park: *The Ascent of Attic Angles*, *The Breast*, *Head of an Italian Girl*, and *Poe-esque*. Weston could not compete for awards because he served as one of the judges, along with Dana Bartlett and Karl Struss (CPLA, exh. cat.; CC, February 1922, p. 62)

MARGRETHE MATHER

February: Joint exhibition with Edward Weston, Friday Morning Club, Los Angeles: *Claire*; *Edward Weston*; *Eugenia Buyko*; *The Gray Vase*; and *Moon Quan, Chinese Poet* (*Los Angeles Times*, February 6 and 13)

February 26–March 12: First Annual Prize Exhibition of Pictorial Photographs, Kansas City Photo Supply Co.: *Lady in Black* and *Player on the Yit-Kim* [honorable-mention award] (Kansas City Photo Supply, exh. cat.; Edward Weston, letter to Betty Katz [February], BK Papers)

February–April: First Annual Competition organized by *American Photography*, Boston, and shown at New York Camera Club and Pennsylvania State College: *Pierrot* [honorable-mention award] (*American Photography* Annual Competition, exh. cat.; AP, April, p. 164; AP, September, pp. 471, 529)

March 2–31: Eighth Annual Pittsburgh Salon of Photography, Department of Fine Arts, Carnegie Institute: *Edward Weston*, *Evgenia Buyko*, *Frayne Williams*, *Judith* [aka *Portrait of a Lady*], and *Pierrot (Otto Matiesen)* (CI, exh. cat.; PE, May, pp. 220, 227)

March–April: Group exhibition of Chinatown photographs with H. A. Hussey, James Doolittle, and G. H. F. Harding, Oakland Municipal Art Gallery (*Oakland Tribune*, April 3, p. 65)

April 15–May 15: First Annual Salon of Pictorial Photography, San Diego Museum Art Galleries: *Frayne Williams, Portrait*, *Otto Matiesen*, *Rex Ingram*, and *Robo de Richey—Painter* (San Diego Museum Art Galleries, exh. cat.)

July: Joint exhibition with Edward Weston, California Camera Club, San Francisco: *Carl Sandburg, Poet*; *Max Eastman, Poet*; and others (*The Bulletin* [San Francisco], July 25, p. 3)

September 19–October 29: The Sixty-Sixth Annual Exhibition of the Royal Photographic Society of Great Britain, London: *Edward Weston*, *The Hands of Robelo*, *Moon Kwan–Poet*, and *Portrait of a Lady* [aka *Judith*] (Royal Photographic Society, exh. cat.)

October 8–early November: Joint exhibition with Edward Weston, Karl Struss, and Edward S. Curtis, The MacDowell Club of Allied Arts, Tajo Building, Los Angeles: *Gray Vase*, *Portrait of Ricardo Robelo*, *Spring Dance*, and possibly others (MacDowell Club of Allied Arts, exh. brochure; *Los Angeles Times*, October 30)

October 30–November 26: The Annual Salon of Photography of the Oakland Municipal Art Gallery, under the auspices of The Oakland Art Association, Photographic Section, Civic Auditorium: *The Hands of Robelo*; *Portrait of Judith*; and *Robo de Richey, Painter* (Oakland Municipal Art Gallery, exh. cat.; CC, November, p. 360)

November 1–12: Second Annual Frederick & Nelson [Department Store] Exhibition of Pictorial Photography, Seattle: *Hands of Robelo*, and in collaboration with Edward Weston, *Carl Sandburg, Poet*; *Floyd Dell, Novelist*; and *Max Eastman, Poet* (F&NDS, exh. cat.)

December 13–January 3: Fifth Annual International Photographic Salon under the auspices of the Camera Pictorialists of Los Angeles, Los Angeles Museum of History, Science, and Art, Exposition Park: *Edward Weston*, *Hands of Robelo*, and *Roubaix de Richey* (CPLA, exh. cat.; CC, February 1922, p. 62)

1922

EDWARD WESTON

March: Group exhibition with photographers Margrethe Mather, Jane Reece, Arnold Schroeder, and Walter Frederick Seely, and painters Mahlon Blaine and J. W. Horwitz, Escuela Nacional de Bellas Artes, Mexico City: *Ricardo Gómez Robelo and Tina Modotti with Fan* (*El Universal gráfico* [Mexico City], March 9, p. 1; Rafael Vera de Córdova, *El Universal ilustrado* [Mexico City], March 23, pp. 30–31, 55)

March 19–April 14: Group exhibition with Margrethe Mather and painters Howard Russell Butler, Jean Mannheim, Clarence Hinkle, Henri De Kruif, John Hubbard Rich, John W. Cotton, Howell Brown, and Nellie Huntington Gere, MacDowell Club, Tajo Building, Los Angeles: *The Breast, Fragment of Nude, Gengo Rigos, Japanese Actor, The Lacquer Chest, Profile of H. J. K., Ruth Deardorff Shaw, Sybil, W. A. Clark Jr.*; and in collaboration with Margrethe Mather (who is not credited in newspaper reviews), *Carl Sandburg; Floyd Dell, Novelist*; and *George Stojana* (Weston, letter to Johan Hagemeyer, March 6, with exh. brochure enclosed, EW/JH Collection, CCP; *Los Angeles Times*, March 26; CS, April, p. 3)

April 17–May 15: Friday Morning Club, Los Angeles: *The Breast; Fragment of Nude; Gengo Rigos; Japanese Actor; The Lacquer Chest; Profile of H. J. K.; Ruth Deardorff Shaw; Sybil; W. A. Clark Jr.*; and in collaboration with Margrethe Mather (who is not credited in newspaper reviews), *Carl Sandburg; Floyd Dell, Novelist*; and *George Stojana* (Weston, letter to Johan Hagemeyer, March 6 [see March 19 entry above]; *Los Angeles Times*, April 23 and May 14)

May 20–June 18: First Annual International Exhibition of Pictorial Photography under Direction of the Pictorial Photographic Society of San Francisco, Palace of Fine Arts: *Girl in Canton Chair, Head of an Italian Girl, Maud Allan—Dancer, Nude*, and *Sunny Corner in an Attic* (Pictorial Photographic Society of San Francisco, exh. cat.; AP, September, p. 550; Conger, "Edward Weston's Early Photography" [see under 1914], pp. 315–16, 358)

June 8–18: Joint exhibition with Margrethe Mather and Johan Hagemeyer, Stedelijk Museum, Amsterdam: *Attic, Head of an Italian Girl, Johan Hagemeyer*, and others (Johan Hagemeyer, letter to Edward Weston, March 23, EW/JH Collection, CCP; George Eastman House, acc. no. 66:70:52, and CCP, acc. nos. 76:5:12 and 76:5:25, inscriptions on mounts)

MARGRETHE MATHER

March: Group exhibition with photographers Edward Weston, Jane Reece, Arnold Schroeder, and Walter Frederick Seely, and painters Mahlon Blaine and J. W. Horwitz, Escuela Nacional de Bellas Artes, Mexico City (*El Universal gráfico* [Mexico City], March 9, p. 1; Rafael Vera de Córdova, *El Universal ilustrado* [Mexico City], March 23, pp. 30–31, 55)

March 19–April 14: Group exhibition with Edward Weston and painters Howard Russell Butler, Jean Mannheim, Clarence Hinkle, Henri De Kruif, John Hubbard Rich, John W. Cotton, Howell Brown, and Nellie Huntington Gere, MacDowell Club, Tajo Building, Los Angeles: in collaboration with Edward Weston (although Mather is not credited in newspaper reviews), *Carl Sandburg; Floyd Dell, Novelist*; and *George Stojana* (Weston, letter to Johan Hagemeyer, March 6, [see above]; *Los Angeles Times*, March 26, CS, April, p. 3)

April 17–May 15: Friday Morning Club, Los Angeles: in collaboration with Edward Weston (although Mather is not credited in newspaper reviews): *Carl Sandburg, Floyd Dell, Novelist*; and *George Stojana*; (Weston, letter to Johan Hagemeyer, March 6 [see above]; *Los Angeles Times*, April 23 and May 14)

June 8–18: Joint exhibition with Edward Weston and Johan Hagemeyer, Stedelijk Museum, Amsterdam (Johan Hagemeyer, letter to Edward Weston, March 23, EW/JH Collection, CCP)

September 9–October 7: International Exhibition of the London Salon of Photography, Galleries of the Royal Society of Painters in Water-Colours: *Dr. William F. Mack* and *Finale* (LSP, exh. cat.; PE, August, p. 109; CC, November, p. 508)

November 20–December 11: Sixth International Salon of Photography, under the auspices of the Camera Pictorialists of Los Angeles, Los Angeles Museum of History, Science, and Art, Exposition Park: *Dr. William F. Mack, Roentgenologist; Mrs. Barbieri;* and *A Water Lily* (CPLA, exh. cat.; SN, December 9, p. 9)

1923

EDWARD WESTON

March: Group exhibition with painters Howard Russell Butler, Jean Mannheim, Clarence Hinkle, Henri de Kruif, John Hubbard Rich, John W. Cotton, Howell Brown, and Nellie Huntington Gere, MacDowell Club, Tajo Building, Los Angeles (*Los Angeles Times*, March 19)

April: Group exhibition with photographers Margrethe Mather, Karl Struss, Otis Williams, Oscar Maurer, Viroque Baker, Phil de Bois, and Marguerite Craig, Hollywood Woman's Club (*Los Angeles Times*, April 8)

May 3–31: International Salon of the Pictorial Photographers of America, The Art Center, New York City: *The Breast* and *Portrait of Alcock* (Pictorial Photographers of America, exh. cat.; AP, July, p. 394)

October 17–30 (extended through November 3): Solo exhibition, Aztec Land Gallery, Mexico City: At least six images of Margrethe Mather, including *The Gold Screen, Prologue to a Sad Spring,* and *Nude on Sand,* as well as *Gray Attic, Portrait of R. S., Romantic Mexico, Steel, Una Tehuana, Tehuana Costume,* and in collaboration with Margrethe Mather (who is not credited in newspaper reviews), *Marion Morgan Dancers; Max Eastman, Poet;* and possibly others (exh. guestbook and brochure, EW Archive, CCP; Edward Weston, *Daybooks,* vol. 1, p. 27; *El Automóvil en México* [Mexico City], November, pp. 15, 17)

MARGRETHE MATHER

April: Group exhibition with photographers Edward Weston, Karl Struss, Otis Williams, Oscar Maurer, Viroque Baker, Phil de Bois, and Marguerite Craig, Hollywood Woman's Club (*Los Angeles Times*, April 8)

October 17–30 (extended through November 3): Aztec Land Gallery, Mexico City: in collaboration with Edward Weston: *Marion Morgan Dancers, Max Eastman, Poet,* and possibly others (Mather is not credited in newspaper reviews) (exh. guestbook and brochure, EW Archive, CCP; Edward Weston, *Daybooks,* vol. 1, p. 27; *El Automóvil en México* [Mexico City], November, pp. 15, 17)

1924

MARGRETHE MATHER

May: Solo exhibition, Cannell & Chaffin Gallery, Los Angeles: *Ervin Nyiregyhazi; Eva Gauthier; Henry Cowell; Konrad Bercovici; Leon Bakst; Open Waterlily; Pablo Casals; Ramon Navarro; Rebecca West; Rex Ingram; Richard Buhlig; Rufus Spaulding, Esq.; Tropico Tile Works;* and *Walter Henry Rothwell* (*Los Angeles Times*, May 18)

October 14–November 3: Eighth International Salon of Photography, under the auspices of the Camera Pictorialists of Los Angeles, Los Angeles Museum of History, Science, and Art, Exposition Park: *Portrait of James Sadlier* and *Rex Ingram* (CPLA, exh. cat.)

Autumn: Los Angeles Japanese Camera Club Salon: *Billy Justema* and possibly others. Mather could not compete because she served as one of the judges, along with A. F. Kales and N. P. Moerdyke (*Artgram,* Los Angeles Japanese Camera Club [under the auspices of *Rafu Shimpo,* a Japanese-language newspaper published in Los Angeles], exh. cat.; CC, January 1925, p. 44)

1925

MARGRETHE MATHER

December 1–31: Fourth Annual Exhibition of Pictorial Photography, Southern California Camera Club, Southwest Museum, Los Angeles: *Eva Gauthier* and three untitled images described as a portrait of an Ethiopian woman, a study of hands, and an industrial study (Southern California Camera Club, exh. cat.; *Los Angeles Times*, December 13)

1927

MARGRETHE MATHER

September 4–30: Group exhibition, California Art Club, celebrating the opening of the club's new headquarters in Aline Barnsdall's Hollyhock House, Barnsdall Park, Los Angeles, including a selection of paintings, sculptures, etchings, and posters, and an exhibition of photographs chosen by Mather (Margrethe Mather, letter to Edward Weston, August, EW Archive, CCP; *Los Angeles Times*, September 1 and 12; CC, October, p. 502)

October 30–November 20: All American Photographic Salon—Sixth Year, Los Angeles Public Library (*Los Angeles Times*, October 23)

1931

MARGRETHE MATHER

July 15–late August: Solo exhibition, *Patterns by Photography*, M. H. de Young Memorial Museum, Golden Gate Park, San Francisco, one of the events surrounding the reorganization and reopening of the museum. Mather's display demonstrated ways in which photography could be used in fabric and decorative arts designs. Also on display was a group of Eugène Atget's Parisian street scenes (*San Francisco Chronicle*, July 12, p. 8D; *San Francisco Chronicle*, July 14, p. 3; *San Francisco Chronicle*, July 16, p. 5; *Wasp-Newsletter* [San Francisco], July 18, p. 12; *San Francisco Chronicle*, July 26, p. 8D; *Oakland Tribune*, August 9, p. 6S)

Publication Chronologies

The following list of publications includes articles in which Weston's and Mather's photographs are illustrated, their names are mentioned, or their likenesses appear. The publications cited that pertain to Weston are for the years 1906–23, and to Mather, 1906–31, the years that are the primary focus of this book. Titles of the published photographs follow the publication information. Titles of works are given here as they appear in the cited publications; they may not be consistent with one another or with the way they are shown elsewhere in this book. The following abbreviations are used:

AP	*American Photography*
APPN	*Amateur Photographer and Photographic News*
BJP	*British Journal of Photography*
BP	*Bulletin of Photography*
EW/JH Collection	Edward Weston/Johan Hagemeyer Collection
CC	*Camera Craft*
CCP	Center for Creative Photography, University of Arizona, Tucson
FMCS	Friday Morning Club Scrapbooks
LAMHSAS	Los Angeles Museum of History, Science, and Art Scrapbooks
PE	*Photo-Era*
PJA	*Photographic Journal of America*
PM	*Photo-Miniature*
TC	*The Camera*

1906

EDWARD WESTON

April: "Picture Criticism," *Camera and Dark Room*, pp. 132–33—*Spring*.

June: *American Amateur Photographer*, p. 290.

1908

EDWARD WESTON

March: "Our Portfolio," AP, p. 166—*Tropico, California*.

August: "Our Competition," AP, p. 461—*Priscilla*, p. 462.

1909

EDWARD WESTON

February: "Our Portfolio," AP, p. 103—*Helen*, p. 91.

May: "Editorial Comment," AP, pp. 292–93, 351—*In Reverie*, p. 293.

1910

EDWARD WESTON

May: TC, p. [192]—*Untitled* [Woman Standing with Head Bowed].

October: "Monthly Competition," PE, p. 206—*In Vacation Time*, p. 193.

November: "Our Monthly Competition," AP, p. 659.

1911

EDWARD WESTON

February: TC, p. [63]—*Let's Play Hookey*.

April: "Our Monthly Competition," AP, p. 232.

May: "Our Monthly Competitions," AP, p. 300.

July: "Our Monthly Competition," PE, p. 49—*An Interior*, p. 36.

August: "Our Monthly Competition," AP, p. 478—*Landscape with Figures*, p. 481.

October: "Our Competitions," AP, p. 612—*The Out-of-Doors Girl*, p. 611.

November: "Our Monthly Competition," AP, p. 671—*Joe*, p. 663.

"Our Monthly Competition," PE, p. 261—*Garden Vista, Early Morning*, p. 248.

TC, p. 480—*Chicago River*.

December: "Our Illustrations," PE, p. 317.

TC, p. [521]—*Study* [Portrait of a Child].

E. H. Weston, "Artistic Interiors," PE, pp. 298–300—*An Artistic Corner*, p. 299, and *An Artistic Interior*, p. 300.

1912

EDWARD WESTON

February: Wilfred A. French, ed., "Our Illustrations," PE, p. 85—*Artistic Interior*, p. 67.

Edward Weston, "Photographing Children in the Studio," AP, pp. 83–88—*The Far-Away, Dreamy Gaze into Some Distant Fairyland*, p. [85]; *Just Learning to Creep*, p. 86; and *In Everyday Play Clothes*, p. [87].

March: "Our Monthly Competition," AP, pp. 154, 159—*Portrait of Miss S.*, p. 157.

May: "Our Competition," AP, p. 282—*Ruth*, p. 271.

"Our Portfolio," AP, p. 284.

June: "Our Monthly Competition," AP, p. 342.

July: "Our Competition," AP, p. 402—*Almond Blossoms*, p. [391].

    TC, p. [361]—*What Shall I Say?*

September: "Our Monthly Competition," AP, p. 529.

October: "Our Monthly Competition," AP, p. [577]—*Atala*.

    "Our Monthly Competition," PE, p. 201—*Self-Portrait*, p. [192].

    TC, p. [466]—*Untitled* [Emily Ellias and Unidentified Girl on Settle Wearing 18th-Century Costumes].

November: "Our Competition," AP, p. 650—*Let's Play Hookey*, p. [643].

    "Our Monthly Competition," PE, p. 255—*View from Mt. Wilson*, p. 254.

    Edward H. Weston, "Shall I Turn Professional?," AP, pp. 620, 622, 624.

December: "Monthly Competition," AP, p. 709—*Decorative Study*.

1913

EDWARD WESTON

January: "Competition," TC, p. 44—*A Nude Study*, p. [30].

March: "The Monthly Competition," AP, p. 164.

    "Our Print Criticism Department," TC, p. 169—*Dorothy*.

    Edward H. Weston, "A One-Man Studio," AP, pp. 130, 132, 134.

April: "The Monthly Competition," AP, p. 219.

May: "Our Monthly Competition," PE, p. 253—*The Story-Hour*, p. 248.

June: "Our Monthly Competition," AP, p. 352.

July: "With the Camera," AP, p. 429.

August: "Illinois College of Photography," CC, p. 398.

September: TC, p. [526]—*Sunshine Girl*.

December: *American Annual of Photography: 1913* (New York)—*Atala*, p. [233], and *Child Portrait* [aka *Child Study in Gray*], p. [295].

    Wollensak Optical Company advertisement, AP, p. xxviii—*Ruth*.

    Wollensak Optical Company advertisement, *Wilson's Photographic Magazine*, advertising section, p. 10—*Ruth*.

MARGRETHE MATHER

January: R. L. Sleeth Jr., "The Ninth American Salon," AP, p. [21]—*Maid of Arcady*.

December: "How 'Platinum Print' Angered and Impressed," *Platinum Print*, p. 13.

1914

EDWARD WESTON

April: Edward H. Weston, "The Gummist," a poem, PE, p. 182.

May: "Camera Pictorialists of Los Angeles," CC, p. 250.

    "Of Importance to Pictorialists," *Platinum Print*, p. 12.

    "Society News," AP, p. 319.

July: "Notes from the Illinois College of Photography," CC, p. 360.

    "Society News," AP, p. 473.

    "Toronto Camera Club," PE, p. 47.

August: *Platinum Print*, p. [8]—*Roses and Sunshine* [aka *Summer Sunshine*].

    "The Official Picture-Exhibit," PE, p. 104.

    "With the Camera," AP, p. 543.

September: TC, p. [552]—*Study* [aka *Summer Sunshine*].

September 21: Antony Guest, "The Photographic Salon, 1914," APPN, p. 276—*Summer Sunshine*, p. 278.

September 29: Bertram Park, "A Symposium: Which Is the Best Picture at the London Salon? The Honorary Secretary Pronounces for a Series by Edward H. Weston," *American Photographer and Cinematographer*, p. 259.

November: *American Annual of Photography: 1914* (New York)—*Let's Play Hookey*, p. [61], and *Son*, p. 300.

Carine Cadby, "London Salon of Photography," *PE*, p. 236.

F.C. Tilney, "Observations on Some Pictures of the Year," *Photograms of the Year: 1914* (London), pp. 10, 17 —*Summer Sunshine*, plate 27.

November 2: *APPN*, p. 416—*A Flower from the Land of Sunshine* [aka *Child Study in Gray*].

November 5: "Mr. Weston's Exhibit at Los Angeles Club," *Glendale News* (newspaper clipping, FMCS, vol. 3, p. 18).

November 7: "Silva Paintings Now on Exhibit," *Los Angeles Examiner* (newspaper clipping, FMCS, vol. 3, p. 19).

November 16: *APPN*, p. 456—*Abandon*.

November 22: Antony Anderson, "Art and Artists," *Los Angeles Times*.

November 24: "Weston of Tropico Shows Art Prints," *Los Angeles Herald* (newspaper clipping, FMCS, vol. 3, p. 22).

Late 1914/early 1915: Arthur Hammond, Albert Kelly, et al., *Verito: The Lens That Improves on Acquaintance*, Wollensak Optical Company advertising brochure (Rochester, N.Y.)

Weston Studio advertising brochure (Tropico, Calif.)—*Carlota*, *A Flower from the Land of Sunshine* [aka *Child Study in Gray*], *Self-Portrait*, *Summer Sunshine*, and *Untitled* [Portrait of a Man].

MARGRETHE MATHER

May: "Camera Pictorialists of Los Angeles," *CC*, p. 250.

"Of Importance to Pictorialists," *Platinum Print*, p. 12.

"Society News," *AP*, p. 319.

Late 1914/early 1915: Weston Studio advertising brochure (Tropico, Calif.)—*Carlota*.

1915

EDWARD WESTON

January: "Notes and News," *AP*, p. 55.

February: "Edward H. Weston Wins a Grand Prize," *PE*, p. 102.

March: *AP*, p. [311]—*A [Child] Study in Gray*.

"Illinois College of Photography," *CC*, p. 131.

March 13: "Pasadena Art Notes," *Pasadena News*, p. 8.

May: *Portrait*, p. 15—*Portrait by Edward H. Weston* [aka *Child Study in Gray*].

July: *Studio Light*, p. 11—*Untitled* [Maud Allan].

August: "Our Competition," *AP*, p. 485.

J.C. Thomas, "A David Grayson Kind of Man," *American Magazine*, pp. 55–56.

September: "Notes and News," *PJA*, p. 452.

"Salon Honors," *PE*, p. 158.

September 24: F.C. Tilney, "London Salon of Photography," *BJP*, p. 620.

October: "Appreciation of Masterful Portraits," *PE*, p. 210.

"The Awards in the Pictorial Section, P.P.I.E." *CC*, p. 412.

TC, p. [592]—*Emily*.

October 4: Antony Guest, "The London Salon of Photography," *APPN*, p. 272.

October 31: Antony Anderson, "Of Art and Artists," *Los Angeles Times*.

November: "Illinois College of Photography," *CC*, p. 460.

L.B. Maynard, "Photography in Advertising," *AP*, p. 628—*Ambition* [mistakenly credited to both L.B. Maynard and Edward Weston], p. [627].

November 29: *APPN*, p. 437.

December : *American Annual of Photography: 1915* (New York)—*Atala*, p. [13], and *Gaunt, Driven Boughs in the Sweep of Open Wold* [aka *Valley of the Long Wind*], p. [193].

G. C. Henderson and Robert A. Oliver, *Tropico, the City Beautiful* (Tropico, Calif.)—Thirty photographs of Tropico and environs.

F. C. Tilney, "Observations on Some Pictures of the Year," *Photograms of the Year: 1915* (London), p. 14 —*Nude with Black Shawl*, plate 9.

December 22: "Dance Outdoors for Charity," *Los Angeles Evening Herald*—*Violet Romer*.

MARGRETHE MATHER

February 26: "Art as Camera Portrays It: Wonders of Photography in Local Exhibition," *Los Angeles Times*.

May: W. H. Porterfield, "The Pittsburg [*sic*] Salon," *PJA*, p. 218.

October 31: Antony Anderson, "Art and Artists," *Los Angeles Times*.

F. C. Tilney, "Observations on Some Pictures of the Year," *Photograms of the Year: 1915* (London), p. 14 —*Nude with Black Shawl*, plate 9.

1916

EDWARD WESTON

January 19: "Arts and Crafts Salon: California and Eastern Work to be Shown at Museum," *Los Angeles Times* (wherein Edward Weston is listed as Howard Weston).

January 29: Untitled article, *Los Angeles Graphic* (newspaper clipping, LAMHSAS, vol. 3, wherein Edward Weston is listed as Howard Weston).

February: "First Arts and Crafts Salon," *Out West* (magazine clipping, LAMHSAS, vol. 3, wherein Edward Weston is listed as Henry Weston).

February 5: Untitled article, *Los Angeles Graphic* (newspaper clipping, LAMHSAS, vol. 3, wherein Edward Weston is listed as Howard Weston).

February 11: Untitled article, *Los Angeles Examiner* (newspaper clipping, LAMHSAS, vol. 3).

February 11: Untitled article, *Los Angeles Tribune* (newspaper clipping, LAMHSAS, vol. 3).

February 13: Antony Anderson, "Of Art and Artists," *Los Angeles Times*.

February 19: Untitled article, *Los Angeles Graphic* (newspaper clipping, LAMHSAS, vol. 3).

April: Frank Roy Fraprie, "The Spring Exhibitions of 1916," *AP*, p. 220.

"Photographer's Association of America," *PE*, p. 203.

"The Thirty-Sixth National Convention," *CC*, p. 166.

May: "Awards at Eleventh Annual Exhibition John Wanamaker, March 1–17, 1916," *PJA*, p. 228.

"The Thirty-Sixth Annual Convention Photographers' Association of America, Wigmore Coliseum, Cleveland, O., the Week of July 24," *PJA*, p. 224.

June: *AP*, p. 315—*Ruth St. Denis*.

"An Artist Photographer," *TC*, pp. 343–44—*Violet Romer*, cover and p. [327]; *Violet Romer* (variant), p. [324]; *Enrica*, p. [328]; *Rae*, p. [331]; *Enrica*, p. [332]; *Ted Shawn*, p. [335]; and *Maud Allan*, p. [336].

"Illinois College of Photography," *CC*, p. 251.

"Photographers' Association of America, Cleveland, July 24 to 29," *PE*, p. 306—*Edward H. Weston*.

William H. Zerbe, "Brooklyn Institute of Arts and Sciences," *PE*, p. 303.

June 11: Antony Anderson, "Of Art and Artists," *Los Angeles Times*.

July: *Studio Light*—*Bobbie*, cover ; *Violet Romer*, frontispiece; *Ted Shawn as David in Field*, p. 2; *From an Artura Iris Print* [aka *Carlota*], p. 5; *From an Artura Iris Print* [aka *Violet Romer*], p. 7; *Portrait of a Painter*, p. 9; *Untitled* [*Maud Allan*], p. 11; *From an Artura Iris Print* [aka *Maud Allan*], p. 14; *A Fleck of Sunshine: Ruth St. Denis*, p. 15; *From an Artura Iris Print* [aka *Margrethe Mather*], p. 19; and *Man with Shaded Eyes*, p. 21.

"Southern California Camera Club," *CC*, p. 393.

TC, p. [387]—*Margrethe*.

July 30: Antony Anderson, "Of Art and Artists," *Los Angeles Times*.

August: "Photographing the Children," PM, pp. 329–60—*A Flower from the Land of Sunshine* [aka *Child Study in Gray*] and *Portrait of My Son*.

Edward Henry Weston, "Notes on High Key Portraiture," AP, pp. 407, 410, 412—*Portrait, Miss E.*, p. [408]; *Maud Allan*, p. [409]; *Ted Shawn as "David*," p. [411]; and *Bobbie*, p. [413];

August 6: "Artist Wins Honor: Work of Local Photographer Is Given Place in Permanent Salon by Association of America—To Demonstrate His Method in East," *Los Angeles Times*.

September: "The National Convention at Cleveland," PJA, p. 392.

"The South California Camera Club," PE, p. 152.

"Thirty-Sixth Annual Photographers Association of America, Wigmore Coliseum, Cleveland, Ohio, July 24 to 28, 1916," PE, pp. 143, 145.

September 22: "The London Salon of Photography: The Portraits," BJP, p. 517—*A Fleck of Sunshine: Ruth St. Denis*.

October: "A California Artist: Some of His Work Well Engraved," *Violet Romer*, frontispiece; *The Eternal Feminine* [aka *Violet Romer*], p. 152; and *The Pacific Printer—Another of His Creations* [aka *Carlota*], p. 152.

"Illinois College of Photography," CC, p. 431.

TC, p. [540]—*The Dancer*.

October 2: Antony Guest, "The London Salon of Photography," APPN, p. 272.

October 18: Edward Weston, "Photography as a Means of Artistic Expression," lecture delivered at the College Women's Club in Los Angeles, EW/JH Collection, CCP.

October 27: "New York Art Exhibition and Gallery News: Historical Photographic Exhibit," *Christian Science Monitor*, p. 6.

Edward Weston, "Notes on High Key Portraiture," BJP, pp. 582–83.

November: AP, p. 634—*Carlota*, p. 589.

Sadakichi Hartmann [Sidney Allan, pseud.], "Looking for the Good Points," BP, pp. 472–73—*Carlota*, p. 473.

"Notes and Comment," CC, p. 474.

"Notes and Comment: Reported by William Wolff," TC, p. 474.

TC—*Violet Romer*, cover.

December: *American Annual of Photography: 1916* (New York), p. [249]—*I Do Believe in Fairies*.

W. R. Bland, "Observations from Some Pictures of the Year," *Photograms of the Year: 1916* (London), p. 14—*Dancing Nude*, plate 59.

"The Man Who Made Tropico Famous," *Lensology and Shutterisms*, Wollensak Optical Company advertising brochure (Rochester, N.Y.), p. 10.

December 30: *The Californian*, p. 9—*Violet Romer*.

MARGRETHE MATHER

January 19: "Arts and Crafts Salon: California and Eastern Work to Be Shown at Museum," *Los Angeles Times*.

January 29: Untitled article, *Los Angeles Graphic* (newspaper clipping, LAMHSAS, vol. 3).

February 19: Untitled article, *Los Angeles Graphic* (newspaper clipping, LAMHSAS, vol. 3).

July: *Studio Light*, pp. 5, 19—*Carlota* and *Margrethe*.

TC, p. 387—*Margrethe*.

October: *The Pacific Printer*, p. 152—*Another of His Creations* [aka *Carlota*].

November: AP—*Carlota*, p. 589, and *The Stairway*, p. 601.

Sadakichi Hartmann [Sidney Allan, pseud.], "Looking for the Good Points," BP, p. 473—*Carlota*.

1917

EDWARD WESTON

January: TC, p. [28]—*Miss Reinecke.*
January 15: APPN, p. 40—*Wake!.*
February: "Edward H. Weston Enjoys a Pun," PE, p. 100.
February 15: APPN, p. 88—*A Fleck of Sunshine: Ruth St. Denis.*
March 11: Antony Anderson, "Of Art and Artists," *Los Angeles Times.*
April: "Awards John Wanamaker Twelfth Annual Exhibition of Photography March 1st to 17th," PJA, p. 163.
    TC—*Study* [Woman in White], p. [169], and *Miss Dextra Baldwin,* p. 179.
    "The John Wanamaker Exhibition" and "The Pittsburgh Salon," PE, p. 206.
May: "1917 Spring Exhibitions," AP, p. 310.
    W. H. Porterfield, "The Pittsburg [*sic*] Salon, 1917," PJA, p. 207—*Eugene Hutchinson,* p. 206.
May 13: Antony Anderson, "Of Art and Artists," *Los Angeles Times.*
May 20: Antony Anderson, "Of Art and Artists," *Los Angeles Times.*
June 6: "The Dance of a California Sunbeam," *Los Angeles Times—Violet Romer.*
June 22: J. H. Anderson, "The London Salon of Photography," BJP, p. 334.
July: AP, p. 383—*Eugene Hutchinson.*
September: "American Work at the London Salon, 1917," PM, p. 365.
    "E. H. Weston Honored," CC, p. 388.
    "London Letter," PE, p. 162.
    "Unconventional Portraiture: Weston's Methods," PM, pp. 337–56—*Baby Seated on a Wall*
        and *Lady in a Hoop Skirt.*
September 21: "The Portraits at the London Salon of Photography," BJP, p. 484.
October: *Photo═Graphic Art* (formerly Platinum Print), p. [8]—*Antony Anderson.*
October 8: Antony Guest, "American Work at the London Salon, 1917," APPN, p. 228.
October 22: APPN, p. 265—*Miss Dextra Baldwin.*
November: J. Addison Reid, "The Toronto Camera Club Salon," CC, pp. 458–59—*Miss Dextra Baldwin,* p. 460.
    "Our Workers at the London Salon," CC, p. 516.
December: *American Annual of Photography: 1917* (New York)—*Toxophilus* (A Decorative Study), p. 79,
        and *Violet Romer,* p. [201].
    "Exhibition of Pictorial Photography," PJA, p. 531.
December 14: "Unconventional Portraiture," BJP, p. 631—*Baby Seated on a Wall.*
Late 1917/1918: *Edward Henry Weston: Photographs,* advertising brochure (Tropico, Calif.)—*Baby Seated on
        Wall, Eugene Hutchinson, The Fan* (Margrethe Mather), and *A Fleck of Sunshine: Ruth St. Denis.*

MARGRETHE MATHER

May: W. H. Porterfield, "The Pittsburg [*sic*] Salon, 1917," PJA, p. 189—*A Lady,* p. 184.
May 20: Antony Anderson, "Of Art and Artists," *Los Angeles Times.*
Late 1917/early 1918: *Edward Henry Weston: Photographs,* advertising brochure (Tropico, Calif.)—*The Fan*
    (Margrethe Mather).

1918

EDWARD WESTON

April: W. G. Fitz, "A Few Thoughts on the Wanamaker Exhibition," TC, p. 207.
    "The Pittsburgh Salon," CC, p. 152.
    W. H. Rabe, "The Work of James N. Doolittle," CC, p. 150.
May: W. H. Porterfield, "The Pittsburg [*sic*] Salon, 1918," PJA, pp. 201–02.

June 23: "Photographic Art Studies by Edward Henry Weston of Glendale," *Los Angeles Times*—*Eugene Hutchinson*, *The Fan (Margrethe Mather)*, *Lieutenant M.*, *The Mirror (Violet Romer)*, *Portrait*, *Portrait of Miss Dextra Baldwin*, and *Vaudeville (Katherine Edson)*.

July: AP, p. 393—*Costume Study (Violet Romer)*.

August: "Book Reviews: Photograms of the Year," PE, p. 110.

September: Sadakichi Hartmann, "Looking for the Good Points," TC, pp. 461–62—*Portrait*, p. [460].

November: "B.Y.M.C.U. Camera Club," PE, p. 273.

L. E. Brackens, "Photography at the Liberty Fair," CC, p. 431.

December: W. R. Bland, "Observations on Some Pictures of the Year," *Photograms of the Year: 1917–18* (London), p. 12—*Miss Dextra Baldwin*, plate 23. Note: Due to the ongoing war, the 1917–18 issue did not appear until the late spring of 1918.

W. R. Bland, "Observations on Some Pictures of the Year," *Photograms of the Year: 1918* (London), p. 9—*Vaudeville*, plate 30.

"Boston Y.M.C.A. [*sic*] Camera Club," CC, p. 502.

"Boston Y.M.C.U. Camera Club One-Man Exhibitions," PJA, p. 554.

"Notes and News," AP, p. 735—*Sunbeams* [aka *Violet Romer*], p. 713.

MARGRETHE MATHER

May: W. H. Porterfield, "The Pittsburg [*sic*] Salon," PJA, p. 202—*In the Garden* [Margrethe Mather posing for a photograph by J. C. Carlton], p. 208.

June 23: "Photographic Art Studies by Edward Henry Weston of Glendale," *Los Angeles Times*—*The Fan (Margrethe Mather)*.

August: "Book Reviews: Photograms of the Year 1917–18," PE, p. 110.

November: W. R. Bland, "Observations on Some Pictures of the Year," *Photograms of the Year: 1917–18* (London), p. 16—*Miss Maud Emily*, plate 59.

L. E. Brackens, "Photography at the Liberty Fair," CC, pp. 431–32.

1919

EDWARD WESTON

February: AP, p. [62]—*Ted Shawn as "David."*

March: A. T. De Rome, "A Few Pictures Reviewed," CC, p. 93—*Anthony Anderson*, p. 92.

May: John Paul Edwards, "The Sixth Pittsburgh Salon," CC, p. 183—*Figure in the Nude*.

"The Pittsburg [*sic*] Salon, 1919," PJA, p. 207—*Figure in the Nude*, p. [215].

O. C. Reiter and M. C. Rypinski, "The Sixth Pittsburgh Salon," PE, p. 226.

"The Sixth Pittsburgh Salon," CC, p. 197.

May 25: Antony Anderson, "Of Art and Artists," *Los Angeles Times*.

May 28: "A Picture of the Week: Portrait of Mrs. C. by Edward Hy. Weston," *Amateur Photographer and Photography*, pp. 486–87—*Portrait of Mrs. C.*, p. 487.

June: Carine and Will Cadby, "London Letter," PE, p. 325.

Frank R. Fraprie, "Some Spring Exhibitions," AP, p. 328.

"Shows by Arthur F. Kales and E. H. Weston," PE, p. 323.

June 1: Antony Anderson, "Of Art and Artists," *Los Angeles Times*.

September 19: "London Salon of Photography: Portraits and Figure Work," BJP, p. 546.

October: "Awards at Sacramento State Fair," PE, p. 275.

"Our Illustrations," AP, p. 615—*Figure in the Nude*, p. 563.

November: "Illinois College of Photography," CC, p. 450.

November 16: Antony Anderson, "Of Art and Artists," *Los Angeles Times*.

December: F. C. Tilney, "Some Pictures of the Year: A Critical Causerie," *Photograms of the Year: 1919* (London), p. 32—*Epilogue*, plate 64.

December 15: Willard George Furs advertisement, *Vogue*, p. 78—*Margarita Fisher in Fur Coat*.

MARGRETHE MATHER

March: A. T. De Rome, "A Few Pictures Reviewed," CC, p. 93—*The Chinese Flute*.

May: "The Pittsburg [*sic*] Salon, 1919," PJA, p. 206—*Chinese Poet*, p. [216].

O. C. Reiter and M. C. Rypinski, "The Sixth Pittsburgh Salon," PE, pp. 225–26.

"The Sixth Pittsburgh Salon," CC, p. 197.

June: Frank R. Fraprie, "Some Spring Exhibitions," AP, p. 328.

June 1: Antony Anderson, "Of Art and Artists," *Los Angeles Times*.

September: Frank Roy Fraprie, "Our Illustrations," AP, p. 547—*Portrait of Moon Kwan*, p. 493.

September 19: "London Salon of Photography: Portraits and Figure Studies," BJP, p. 545.

October: "Awards at Sacramento State Fair," PE, p. 275.

November: "Boston Y.M.C.A. [*sic*] Camera Club," CC, p. 447.

"One-Man Exhibits at the Boston Y.M.C. Union Camera Club," PJA, p. 519.

December: "Announcing a Series of Exhibits of Pictorial Photography, 1919–1920," AP, p. 746.

F. C. Tilney, "Some Pictures of the Year," *Photograms of the Year: 1919* (London), p. 32—*Epilogue*, plate 64.

December 4: "Photographic Art Studies by the Southern California Camera Club," *Los Angeles Times*—*In the Garden (Posed by Margrethe Mather)*, photograph by J. C. Carlton.

1920

EDWARD WESTON

May 9: Antony Anderson, "Of Art and Artists," *Los Angeles Times*.

May 16: Antony Anderson, "Of Art and Artists," *Los Angeles Times*.

June: M. C. Rypinski, "The 1920 Pittsburgh Salon," PE, p. 279.

June 13: Antony Anderson, "Of Art and Artists," *Los Angeles Times*.

July: "Notes and News," AP, p. 440.

"Our Illustrations," AP, pp. 439–40—*Margrethe Mather*, p. 389.

August: Wilfred A. French, "Our Illustrations," PE, p. 96—*Epilogue*, cover, frontispiece.

September: "The Frederick & Nelson Exhibition," CC, p. 309.

November: Y. Billy Rubin, "Epilogue," a poem, PE, p. 231—*Epilogue*.

November 7: Madge Bailey, "Fine Art Notes," *Seattle Post-Intelligencer*, part 6, p. 3.

December: *American Annual of Photography: 1920* (New York), p. [57]—*Portrait* [Elderly Seated Woman].

"News and Reviews," PJA, p. 474.

Pictorial Photography in America (New York), p. 107—*Epilogue*.

Ted Shawn, *Ruth St. Denis: Pioneer and Prophet, Being a History of Her Cycle of Oriental Dance* (San Francisco), vol. 2, p. 51—*Ruth St. Denis at Denishawn in Teaching Costume*.

M. C. Williamson, from the Wollensak Optical Company, letter to editor, PJA, p. 475.

MARGRETHE MATHER

May 16: Antony Anderson, "Of Art and Artists," *Los Angeles Times*.

June: M. C. Rypinski, "The 1920 Pittsburgh Salon," PE, pp. 278–79.

July: "Notes and News," AP, p. 440.

"Our Illustrations," AP, pp. 439–40—*Margrethe Mather*, p. 389.

"Photo-Pictorialists Honored," PE, p. 48.

August: Wilfred A. French, "Our Illustrations," PE, p. 96—*Epilogue*, cover, frontispiece.

September: "The Frederick & Nelson Exhibition," CC, p. 309.

November: *Pictorial Photography in America* (New York)—*Player on the Yit-Kim*, p. 69, and *Epilogue*, p. 107.

Y. Billy Rubin, "Epilogue," a poem, PE, p. 231—*Epilogue*.

William Saphier, "Margrethe," a poem, in *Others for 1919* (New York), a poetry anthology edited by Alfred Kreymborg, p. 149.

November 7: Madge Bailey, "Fine Art Notes," *Seattle Post-Intelligencer*, part 6, p. 3.

1921

EDWARD WESTON

January: "Contents for January, 1921," CC, contents page—*Miss Dextra Baldwin*.

"The Copenhagen Salon," PE, p. 48.

February: *Vogue*, p. 60—*Marion Morgan Dancers*.

February 6: Antony Anderson, "Of Art and Artists," *Los Angeles Times*.

February 13: Antony Anderson, "Of Art and Artists," *Los Angeles Times*.

March: "Our Illustrations," AP, p. 157—*Margrethe and Plum Blossoms*, p. 131.

April: Frank Roy Fraprie, "Our First Annual Competition," AP, p. 164.

May: Charles K. Archer, "Pittsburgh Salon of 1921," AP, p. 226.

John Paul Edwards, "The Eighth Pittsburgh Salon," PE, p. 228.

July: "The Annual Salon of Photography, Oakland Municipal Art Gallery," CC, p. 243.

"The Year's Exhibitions," PM, p. 141—*Portrait of Alcock*.

July 25: "Photographic Exhibit at S.F. Camera Club Receives High Praise," *The Bulletin* (San Francisco), p. 3.

August: "Oakland Salon of Photography 1921," PE, p. 103.

October: "Our Illustrations," AP, p. 590—*Balloon Fantasy*, p. [547].

October 30: Antony Anderson, "Of Art and Artists," *Los Angeles Times*.

November: Edgar Felloes, "Oakland Photographic Salon," CC, pp. 356, 360.

"Our Illustrations," AP, p. 649—*Enrique*, p. [625].

December: *American Annual of Photography: 1921* (New York, 1920)—*The Plum Tree*, p. [136], and *Edward B. Weston, M.D.*, p. 263

Prize-Winning Prints in the First Annual Competition Organized by AP (Boston)—*Balloon Fantasy* and *Enrique*.

F. C. Tilney, "Pictorial Photography in 1921," *Photograms of the Year: 1921* (London), p. 17—*Betty in Her Attic*, plate 29.

December 10: "Photographers Will Exhibit Best Work," *Los Angeles Express* (newspaper clipping, LAMHSAS, vol. 7).

December 11: Henriette Boeckman, "World's Best Pictorial Artists Exhibit Here: Masters of Photography Will Show Finest Works in Salon Which Opens in Park Tomorrow," *Los Angeles Times*.

December 12: "Photographers Will Exhibit Best Work," *Los Angeles Express* (newspaper clipping, LAMHSAS, vol. 7).

"Photographic Salon of L.A. Opens Tomorrow," *Los Angeles Express* (newspaper clipping, LAMHSAS, vol. 7).

"Photographic Salon to Open Tomorrow," *Los Angeles Herald* (newspaper clipping, LAMHSAS, vol. 7).

December 18: Antony Anderson, "Of Art and Artists," *Los Angeles Times*.

December 19: R. W. Borough, "Thrills: Marguerite, Eucalypti, White Attics, Switzerland; Dream Stuff? No. It's L.A. Photographic Salon," *Los Angeles Record* (newspaper clipping, LAMHSAS, vol. 7).

December 23: "The Fifth International Photographic Salon," *Laguna Life* (magazine clipping, LAMHSAS, vols. 7–8).

"Go See Art Exhibit," *Los Angeles Record* (newspaper clipping, LAMHSAS, vol. 7)—*Poe-esque*.

December 24: Elizabeth Bingham, "Art Exhibits and Comment," *Saturday Night* (magazine clipping, LAMHSAS, vol. 7).

MARGRETHE MATHER

January: "The Copenhagen Salon," PE, p. 48.

February: *Vogue*, p. 60—*Marion Morgan Dancers*.

February 6: Antony Anderson, "Of Art and Artists," *Los Angeles Times*.

February 13: Antony Anderson, "Of Art and Artists," *Los Angeles Times*.

March: "Our Illustrations," AP, p. 157—*Margrethe and Plum Blossoms*, p. 131.

April: Frank Roy Fraprie, "Our First Annual Competition," AP, p. 164.

April 3: Laura Bride Powers, "Artists and Their Work," *Oakland Tribune*, p. 6S.

May: John Paul Edwards, "The Eighth Pittsburgh Salon," PE, p. 227—*Frayne Williams*, p. [220].

July 25: "Photographic Exhibit at S.F. Camera Club Receives High Praise," *The Bulletin* (San Francisco), p. 3.

September: Frank Roy Fraprie, "Our Illustrations," AP, p. 529—*Pierrot*, p. 471.

September 19–October 29: *The Sixty-Sixth Annual Exhibition of the Royal Photographic Society of Great Britain*, exh. cat.—*Portrait of a Woman* [aka Judith].

October 30: Antony Anderson, "Of Art and Artists," *Los Angeles Times*.

November: Edgar Felloes, "The Oakland Salon," CC, p. 360—*Portrait of Judith*, p. 361.

December: *Prize-Winning Prints in the First Annual Competition Organized by American Photography* (Boston)—*Pierrot*.

   F. C. Tilney, "Pictorial Photography in 1921," *Photograms of the Year: 1921* (London), p. 17—*Pierrot*, plate 28.

December 17: R. W. Borough, "Thrills: Marguerite, Eucalypti, White Attics, Switzerland; Dream Stuff? No. It's L.A. Photograph Salon," *Los Angeles Record* (newspaper clipping, LAMHSAS, vol. 7).

December 24: Elizabeth Bingham, "Art Exhibits and Comment," *Saturday Night* (magazine clipping, LAMHSAS, vol. 7).

1922

EDWARD WESTON

February: James N. Doolittle, "Fifth International Salon of The Camera Pictorialists of Los Angeles," CC, pp. 54, 62.

March: "Book-Reviews: Photograms of the Year 1921," PE, p. 178.

   California Southland, p. 17—*Costume Study, Violet Romer*.

March 9: "En la exposición de Bellas Artes," *El Universal gráfico* (Mexico City), p. 1.

March 23: Rafael Vera de Córdova, "Las Fotografías como verdadero arte," *El Universal ilustrado* (Mexico City), pp. 30–32, 55—*Tina Modotti with Fan*, p. 30.

March 26: Antony Anderson, "Of Art and Artists," *Los Angeles Times*.

April 16: Edward Weston, "Majesty of the Moment," letter to Antony Anderson, *Los Angeles Times*.

April 23: Antony Anderson, "Of Art and Artists," *Los Angeles Times*.

May 12: R. W. Borough, "Art, Love and Death; Widow Must Sell Batiks," *Los Angeles Examiner*—*Tina Modotti Profile*.

May 14: Antony Anderson, "Of Art and Artists," *Los Angeles Times*.

June: Edgar Felloes, "The Pictorial Photographic Exhibition of San Francisco," CC, p. 262.

   "A Treat for the Camerist," PE, p. 344.

   Edward Weston, "Random Notes on Photography," lecture delivered at the Southern California Camera Club, EW/JH Collection, CCP.

June 11: Antony Anderson, "Of Art and Artists," *Los Angeles Times*.

July 20: "Exhibit Prints," *Los Angeles Record* (newspaper clipping, LAMHSAS, vol. 8).

July 23: Antony Anderson, "Of Art and Artists," *Los Angeles Times*.

July 24: "Shows Unique Work in Art: Artist to Exhibit Examples of Woodblock Prints," *Los Angeles Times*.

July 29: Untitled article, *Saturday Night* (magazine clipping, LAMHSAS, vol. 8).

July 30: Antony Anderson, "Of Art and Artists," *Los Angeles Times.*

August: Edward Weston, "Correspondence," letter to editor, AP, pp. 533–34.

August 5: Elizabeth Bingham, "Art Exhibits and Comments," *Saturday Night* (magazine clipping, LAMHSAS, vol. 8).

August 19: Elizabeth Bingham, "Art Exhibits and Comment," *Saturday Night,* p. 9—*Blind.*

August 26: Advertisement for Violet Romer's dance school, *Saturday Night—Violet Romer.*

September: C. M. Harris, "The San Francisco Salon," AP, p. 550.

September 23: *Abel's Photographic Weekly,* p. 334—*Japanese Fencing Mask.*

November: Graf Optical Company advertising bulletin (Chicago)—*Japanese Fighting Mask* [aka *Japanese Fencing Mask*].

    Pictorial Photography in America (New York), p. 59—*Grey Attic.*

    Theatre Magazine, contents page—*Marion Morgan Dancers.*

    Wollensak Optical Company cat. (Rochester, N.Y.).

MARGRETHE MATHER

February: James N. Doolittle, "Fifth International Salon of the Camera Pictorialists of Los Angeles," CC, p. 62.

March 9: "En la exposición de Bellas Artes," *El Universal gráfico* (Mexico City), p. 1.

March 23: Rafael Vera de Cordóva, "Las Fotografías como verdadero arte," *El Universal ilustrado* (Mexico City), pp. 30–31, 55.

March 26: Antony Anderson, "Of Art and Artists," *Los Angeles Times.* Note: Although Mather is not credited in this review of Edward Weston's 1922 MacDowell Club exhibition, Anderson mentions three photographs that were Weston/Mather collaborations done in 1921: *Carl Sandburg; Floyd Dell, Novelist;* and *George Stojana.*

May 20: Penelope Ross, "Drama, Spoken and Silent," *Saturday Night,* p. 14—*Bertha Fiske in "Chinese Fan."*

July 29: Untitled article, *Saturday Night* (magazine clipping, LAMHSAS, vol. 8).

November: H. D'Arcy Power, M.D., "The London Salon 1922," CC, p. 508.

    Theatre Magazine, contents page—*Marion Morgan Dancers.*

December 9: Elizabeth Bingham, "Art Exhibits and Comments," *Saturday Night,* p. 9.

1923

EDWARD WESTON

March 19: Antony Anderson, "Of Art and Artists," *Los Angeles Times.*

April 8: Antony Anderson, "Of Art and Artists," *Los Angeles Times.*

May 23: Advertisement for Violet Romer's dance school, *Saturday Night,* p. 18—*Violet Romer.*

June: Floyd Vail, "Photographic Salon at New York," TC, p. 317.

July: John Wallace Gillies, "Impressions of the International Salon," AP, p. 394.

July 29: "Edward Weston Now in Mexico's Capitol," *Los Angeles Times.*

September 28: "Próxima exposición," *El Heraldo* (Mexico City).

October 11: "La Próxima exposición de Edwar [sic] Weston el original y vigoroso artista americano: un centenar de escogidísimas fotografías,—la delicada obra de Weston.—su admirable y su bella concepción de la vida moderna," *El Mundo* (Mexico City).

October 16: "La Exposición de Weston comprenderá todos los aspectos del artista: como ve Weston nuetro paisaje y nuestros tipos,—la exposición se abre el miercoles en 'The Aztec Land,'" *El Mundo* (Mexico City).

October 18: "Mr. Edward Weston," *El Universal ilustrado* (Mexico City), p. 21.

November: John Wallace Gillies, *Principles of Pictorial Photography* (New York), includes Edward Weston, letter to "Dear Gillies," pp. 28–32—*Japanese Fencing Mask,* p. 14.

    C. J. Ocampo, "Las Fotografías de Edward Weston," *El Automóvil en México* (Mexico City), p. 17— *Two Heads.*

MARGRETHE MATHER

April 8: Antony Anderson, "Of Art and Artists," *Los Angeles Times*.

July: "New Books in Brief Review," *Shadowland*, p. 68—Konrad Bercovici.

September 14–31: *Exhibition of Block Prints and Etchings by Frank Geritz*, exh. brochure, LAMHSAS, vol. 9.

September 23: Antony Anderson, "Of Art and Artists," *Los Angeles Times*.

September 28: "Próxima exposición," *El Heraldo* (Mexico City). Note: Although this article, as well as the following three starred (*) articles, do not credit Mather, at least two of the photographs exhibited by Edward Weston at his Aztec Land Gallery exhibition in October 1923 were Weston/Mather collaborations made in 1921. These were *Marion Morgan Dancers* and *Max Eastman, Poet*.

October 11: "La Próxima exposición de Edwar [sic] Weston el original y vigoroso artista americano: un centenar de escogidisimas fotografías,—la delicada obra de Weston.—su admirable y su bella concepción de la vida moderna," *El Mundo* (Mexico City).*

October 16: "La Exposición de Weston comprenderá todos los aspectos del artista: como ve Weston nuetro paisaje y nuestros tipos,—la exposición se abre el miercoles en 'The Aztec Land,'" *El Mundo* (Mexico City).*

November: C. J. Ocampo, "Las Fotografías de Edward Weston," *El Automóvil en México* (Mexico City), pp. 15, 17.*

1924

MARGRETHE MATHER

January 6: "An Oriental Motif," *Los Angeles Times*—"Moon Kwan," Chinese Poet.

May 18: Antony Anderson, "The Artistry of Margrethe Mather," *Los Angeles Times*.

May 25: Arthur Millier, "Of Art and Artists," *Los Angeles Times*.

Autumn: *Artgram*, Los Angeles Japanese Camera Club (under the auspices of *Rafu Shimpo*, a Japanese-language newspaper published in Los Angeles), exh. cat.—Billy Justema.

1925

MARGRETHE MATHER

January: "Los Angeles Japanese Camera Club," CC, p. 44.

December 13: Neeta Marquis, "Camera Folk Exhibit Work: Southland Club Shows Art in Annual Display," *Los Angeles Times*.

December 27: "Pictorial Photography," *Los Angeles Times*—*Untitled* [Industrial Study].

1926

MARGRETHE MATHER

June 1–30: *In the Print Rooms*, Los Angeles Museum, exh. cat. (Los Angeles), including works by printmakers Loren Barton, Grace M. Brown, Franz Geritz, and Francis W. Vreeland, LAMHSAS, vol. 12.

Summer: GRAF, Graf Lens Company cat. and instruction booklet—*Mr. Weston–Camera–Graf Variable*, p. [15].

July: "Notes and Comments: A New Graf Booklet," CC, p. 3.

1928

MARGRETHE MATHER

December: "Brentwood Heights Residence of Mr. and Mrs. William K. Howard," *Game & Gossip* (five photographs of the William K. Howard Residence, Brentwood Heights, Calif.).

1929

MARGRETHE MATHER

January: "Interior Decoration by H. W. Grieve," *The Architect and Engineer*—*Untitled* [Interior with Console and Mirror], p. 38.

1931

MARGRETHE MATHER

February: "Debut," *The San Franciscan*—*Dancing Slippers* and *Long Black Gloves*.

July 12: "Opening of Museum Wing Nears," *San Francisco Chronicle*, p. 8D.

July 14: "New Galleries at Museum to Be Opened," *San Francisco Chronicle*, p. 3.

July 18: "New Wing Opens at De Young Museum," *The Wasp–Newsletter: A Weekly Journal of Illustration and Comment* (San Francisco), p. 12.

July 26: "Photography as Fine Art Is Demonstrated in Museum Exhibition," *San Francisco Chronicle*, p. 8D.

August 9: Florence Wieben, "Art and Artists," *Oakland Tribune*, p. 6S.

The Pictorialist: A Compilation of Photographs from the Fourteenth Annual International Salon of Pictorial Photography under the auspices of the Camera Pictorialists of Los Angeles (Los Angeles), p. 5.

Acknowledgments

Writing a historical biography is a solitary pursuit, but conducting the necessary research and preparing the final manuscript for publication are entirely communal activities, and the "community" of people who made this book possible literally extends halfway around the world. Included in the mix are museum curators, private collectors, historians, librarians, editors, archivists, genealogists, photography dealers, designers, and relatives of the personalities whose stories appear in these pages. Without their assistance and generosity, this book would not exist.

For helping me better understand Edward Weston's early life and career, I am deeply grateful to Amy Rule and Leslie Calmes, the former and current director, respectively, of the Archives at the Center for Creative Photography in Tucson, Arizona, the repository for the extant papers of Edward Weston, Margrethe Mather, and Johan Hagemeyer. Thanks to their extensive knowledge of the Center's Archives, Amy and Leslie were able to point me down several paths that led to surprising discoveries. Cole Weston and Charis Wilson also provided important insights about Edward Weston's personal and professional history.

The true identity of the elusive Margrethe Mather was revealed, in large part, thanks to Myrna Chadwick and Sandra Pitts. The information they supplied about their distant relative Emma Caroline Youngren was invaluable in my search for the "real" Margrethe Mather.

The personalities of peripatetic Elmer Ellsworth and his wife Lucile Gilmer became clear to me during discussions with Jenifer Angel, Jean Cooper, Richard Dearborn, and Penny Gilmer. Jenifer also helped me more fully appreciate the genial personality and diverse talents of her father, actor Frayne Williams. Similarly, Russell Coryell's charms became obvious during a delightful afternoon spent in the company of his equally beguiling son, Stanis. Gordon and Mimi Glass related many anecdotes about his extraordinary mother, Maud Emily Taylor; and nonagenarian artist Andrée Ruellan gamely spent a wintry afternoon in her cozy home near Woodstock, New York, recounting stores about Jack Taylor, her late husband and Maud Emily's brother.

Yvette Eastman, widow of Max Eastman, permitted me to quote from the voluminous correspondence between her late husband and actress Florence Deshon. Their frequent exchanges filled in many details about early Hollywood and vividly brought to life the circle of friends they shared with Weston and Mather. Deshon even went so far as to make her haunting presence eerily felt when I gently shook open a softly bulging envelope, only to have a long coil of her chestnut brown hair unexpectedly tumble into my outstretched hand.

The belligerent Joseph Ely O'Carroll's complicated past was more easily understood following a visit to the stately, Georgian-era house on Merrion Square in the heart of downtown Dublin, Ireland, that had been his childhood home. His second cousins Patrick O'Mahoney and Moya Murray also helped by supplying information about the family dynamics of the O'Carroll clan. Other details of O'Carroll's life and those of his fellow countrymen Douglas and Charles Gerrard were sorted out under the exquisite domed ceiling in the Reading Room of the National Library of Ireland.

Otto Matiesen's dramatic talents were the topic of an enlightening discussion with Richard Renaldo, son of Matiesen's close friend, actor Duncan Renaldo. In addition, many details about Moon Kwan's multifaceted career as a poet and an advisor to the filmmaker D. W. Griffith were supplied during a conversation with Florice Whyte Kovan.

The importance of *The Little Review* circle—especially Margaret Anderson, Harriet Dean, Jane Heap, Florence Reynolds, and William Saphier—became evident during my conversations and subsequent correspondence with Jane Purse.

Valentina Cook assiduously answered all of my questions about her late husband's relatives Mollie Price Cook, George Cram (Jig) Cook, and Ellen Katherine (Ma-Mie) Cook. Details of writer Floyd Dell's life were shared by Dell's son Christopher. Also helpful were the talks I had many years ago with my maternal grandparents Carl and Della Hays, who were Floyd Dell's grammar school classmates. The aged Wistaria Hartmann Linton clearly recalled the comments her father Sadakichi Hartmann had made about Margrethe Mather; and over lunch at the historic Mission Inn in Riverside, California, writer Harry Lawton recounted his efforts to preserve Hartmann's papers and document his reputation as an important art critic.

The complexities of Johan Hagemeyer's personality became obvious during an afternoon spent with his nephew David Hagemeyer and his wife, Jeanne, in their wonderful adobe-block house in Carmel, California—a home handcrafted for them by two of Edward Weston's sons.

Many biographies have been written about the incomparable Charlie Chaplin, but my conversations with Joyce Milton, in particular, helped me interweave Chaplin's life with Weston's and Mather's activities. Mirel Bercovici spoke fondly of her memories of Chaplin's antic-filled visits with her father, the author Konrad Bercovici, a chronicler of Gypsy culture, and she also recalled the time her father sat for Mather's camera.

Painter Buffie Johnson recounted the story of how she, too, came to be photographed by Margrethe Mather while she was a fine arts student at UCLA. Although Buffie's memory was already beginning to fail at the time of our conversation, she recalled the portrait sitting in great detail, carefully describing the timbre of Mather's voice and the calm but authoritative manner with which she spoke.

Attorney Donnan Stephenson, executor of erstwhile hobo Isidore (Roy) Rosen's estate, provided astonishing insights about his client's posthumous generosity; professor Jeanne Abrams supplied documents related to Rosen's confinement and treatment for tuberculosis; and Kathlene Ferris furnished many photocopies of Rosen's writings about Weston and Mather.

Conversations with Professor Peter Wild and visits to the Palm Springs Historical Society enhanced my knowledge of Lois Kellogg, her childhood in Chicago, and her life in Palm Springs. Kellogg's relationship with Harold and Harriet Cody was explored in discussions with the Codys' granddaughter Shelby Gray and their great-granddaughter Sharon Saks Soboil.

Patricia Albers, Margaret Hooks, and Sarah Lowe have all written extensively on Tina Modotti's relationship with Edward Weston, but conversations with each of them further enlightened me about Modotti's Los Angeles years.

Rudolph and Pauline Schindler's son Mark; their granddaughter Margot Schindler-Ehrens, and Robert Sweeney, executive director of the Schindler House, graciously gave me access to Pauline Schindler's letters.

Many of America's anarchists found their way into this book thanks to Paul Avrich, Anne Diament, and Boris and Margo Kaufman. Emma Goldman's impact and influence on California's left-wing community became clear during my survey of her publication, *Mother Earth*, at the Newberry Library in Chicago.

Betty Katz's chameleon-like personality and her penchant for secrecy were clearly evident in the correspondence that her great-nephew Martin Lessow was kind enough to share with me. It was entirely due to those letters that I was able to confirm the ties that existed between the International Workers of the World, the anarchists of early twentieth-century America, and the lives of Katz and Margrethe Mather, as well as Elmer Ellsworth, Lois Kellogg, Marie Latter, Miriam Lerner, George Lipton, and Joseph O'Carroll. Katz's nephew Alex Rosen also supplied many anecdotes about his intriguing Aunt Betty, who changed her name almost as often as her place of residence.

The stories of Sibyl Brainerd's unusual childhood at Lomaland and her subsequent marriages to Vasia Anikeef and Simon Freed were conveyed to me by her son Lyman Gaylord; and Ramiel McGehee's austere existence became apparent when I was invited inside the tiny studio he had inhabited behind his sister's former home in Redondo Beach.

Several photography dealers were extraordinarily generous in sharing their reference libraries and research with me. Most notably, Paul Hertzmann and Susan Herzig allowed me to spend many hours perusing their collection of photography periodicals and overwhelming their photocopier. Additionally, they and their inveterate researcher Paula Freedman shared many details about Mather's career, which they unearthed during the course of their own scholarly efforts. Joseph Bellows, Keith Delellis, and Stephen White also gave me access to their treasured collections of photography salon catalogues. Denise Bethel and Chris Mahoney of Sotheby's New York Photographs Department helped me track down any number of people and images; and I owe an enormous debt to Michael Dawson, whose knowledge of early-twentieth-century Los Angeles is unparalleled and whose generous spirit has informed every aspect of this book.

Many have preceded me in studying and writing about Edward Weston's early life and career. First and foremost is Amy Conger, whose extensive research is frequently referenced in this book. Others include Nancy Newhall, who edited Weston's *Daybooks*; Ben Maddow, whose anecdotal biography makes for a highly entertaining read; and Charis Wilson, whose autobiography furnishes many insights into her former husband's personality and peccadilloes. Names of those who have made other valuable contributions to the Weston literature appear in the endnotes of this book.

By contrast, very few people have paid attention to the work of Margrethe Mather, although her friend William (Billy) Justema and her photographer colleague Imogen Cunningham would not allow her reputation to completely founder. In addition to Justema's brief memoir about his long-standing friendship with Mather, Lawrence Jasud authored an essay about her early work, Richard Lorenz intended to write about her but ran out of time, Lee Witkin of the Witkin Gallery mounted an exhibition of her work in 1979, and Jim Enyeart acquired Billy Justema's collection of Mather photographs for the Center for Creative Photography in Tucson long before other institutions were interested in her work.

I heartily thank all of those who allowed me to illustrate this book with photographs from their collections, as detailed in the figure captions. Others who deserve recognition and appreciation for a myriad of reasons include Jim Andrews, Kris Arnold, Anitra Balzer, Sid Berger, Hilda Bijur, MaryAnn Bonino, John Cahoon, Floramae Cates, Carolyn Cole, Lorraine Crouse, Gail Davies, Kirk Delman, Mary Dillwith, Steven Drew, Jacqueline Dugas, Susan Ehrens, Simon Elliott, Frank Finnegan, Alan Fishel, Ronda Frazier, Erin Garcia, Whitney Gaylord, Nora Goldsmith, Denise Gose, Jonathan Green, Tim Hafen, Kurt Helfrich, Kathleen Howe, Julia Johnas, Pia Johnson, Rich Johnson, Norman Karasick, Mead Kibbe, Robert Klein, Travis Kranz, Joel Kroin, Gary Kurutz, Harry Lawton, Mary MacNaughton, Ray Matthews, Peter McCoy, Sally McManus, Art Miller, Mike Mills, Doug Misner, Richard Moore, Gladys Murphy, Sharon Palmer, Dennis Reed, Michael Redmond, Leland Rice, Tania Rizzo, Diane Rochester, Richard Rudisill, Alan Rumrill, Janet Russek, Naomi Sawelson-Gorse, David Scheinbaum, Eileen Schwartz, Sally Shishmanian, Tom Sitton, Anne Smith, Catherine Smith, Stephanie Smith, Richard and Judy Smooke, Andrew and Marla Sobel, Gary Sokol, Rachel Stuhlman, Joe Struble, Thomas Tanselle, Dace Taube, Cathy Thomas, Melanie Ventilla, Carlos Vidali, Beth Werling, Maggi Weston, Laurie Whitcomb, Leon Wilson, Michael Wilson, and Emily Wolf.

Reference librarians—those unsung heroes and heroines—also provided much guidance and assistance. Particularly helpful were those people affiliated with the following institutions: Archives of American Art and the Museum of American History, Smithsonian Institution, Washington, D.C.; Beinecke Rare Book and Manuscript Library, Yale University, New Haven, Connecticut; California State Library, Sacramento; California State Railroad Museum, Sacramento; Charles Deering Library, Northwestern University, Evanston, Illinois; Charles E. Young Research Library, University of California, Los Angeles; Chicago Historical Society; Evanston

Historical Society; Family History Center, Salt Lake City; Family History Center, Wilmette, Illinois; George Eastman House Library, Rochester, New York; Special Collections, Glendale Public Library, Glendale, California; Golda Meir Library, University of Wisconsin, Milwaukee; H. Willard Marriott Library, Salt Lake City; Harry Ransom Humanities Research Center, University of Texas, Austin; Henry W. and Albert A. Berg Collection of English and American Literature, New York Public Library; Highland Park Public Library, Highland Park, Illinois; The Huntington Library, San Marino, California; Lilly Library, Indiana University, Bloomington; Los Angeles Public Library; Margaret Herrick Library, Academy of Motion Picture Arts and Sciences, Beverly Hills, California; Natural History Museum of Los Angeles County; Special Collections, National Library of Ireland, Dublin; Newberry Library, Chicago; New York Historical Society; Pasadena Historical Museum; Special Collections, Pasadena Public Library; The Getty Research Institute, Los Angeles; Ruth Chandler Williamson Gallery, Pomona College, Claremont, California; Santa Barbara Historical Society, Santa Barbara, California; Santa Barbara Public Library; Special Collections, Tamiment Institute Library, New York City; Tomás Rivera Library, University of California, Riverside; University Art Museum, University of California, Santa Barbara; University of Delaware Library, Newark; Rare Book and Manuscript Library, University of Illinois at Urbana-Champaign; Special Collections Department, General Library, University of New Mexico, Albuquerque; Utah State Archives, Salt Lake City; and Utah State History Center, Salt Lake City. I sincerely wish I could thank all of those wonderful librarians by name, but that list would fill several more pages. I extend my sincere gratitude to each one of them and to any institutions I may have neglected to mention.

A number of museum curators provided considerable help and encouragement along the way, including Keith Davis, Maria Morris Hambourg, Drew Johnson, Shannon Perich, Christian Peterson, Terence Pitts, Tim Wride, and especially Karen Sinsheimer, curator of photography at the Santa Barbara Museum of Art, who organized the traveling exhibition *Margrethe Mather and Edward Weston: A Passionate Collaboration* and whose recognition of the importance of Weston and Mather's collaborative years ultimately resulted in this volume.

Singular acknowledgment must go to Brett Abbott, curator of photography at the High Museum of Art in Atlanta, whose support for this book has spanned many years. Thanks are also due to Judith Keller, senior curator in the Department of Photographs at the J. Paul Getty Museum, who has been a stalwart advocate for the publication of this book; as well as Weston Naef, director emeritus and founder of that department, who in 1986 co-curated the exhibition *Edward Weston in Los Angeles*, the first serious examination of Edward Weston's early work.

A team of outstanding people at Getty Publications oversaw the intricacies of turning a lengthy and detailed manuscript into a completed volume. Dinah Berland, editor extraordinaire, managed every aspect of the process in collaboration with Jim Drobka, who is responsible for the book's elegant design, and Anita Keys, who supervised the book's production. Kimberly

Wilkinson, editorial staff assistant, also assisted with editorial production. Rachel Ross worked tirelessly to obtain copyright permissions for the photographs; Nomi Kleinmuntz did a superb job as copy editor, maintaining her sense of humor every step of the way; Jane Hyun edited the chronologies to exacting standards; and proofreader Mark Rhynsburger made sure the end result was as error free as humanly possible. Thanks are also due to Tricia Zigmund at the Getty's Imaging Services department for technical imaging of the Getty's prints.

I am especially grateful to friends and colleagues who took time out from their busy schedules to carefully read and thoughtfully comment on various aspects and versions of the manuscript. In addition to Brett Abbott, those readers included Lu Casto, Anne Horton, Amy Rule, Richard Smooke, Kate Ware, and Jennifer Watts, all of whom offered very helpful suggestions.

I also extend my deepest thanks to Scott Bernstein and Chris Imhoff, Nan Chisholm, Cynthia and Walter Flor, Susan and Scott Garrett, Carol and Rana Kamal, Mara Marsico, Rita Miranda, Beatrice Oshika, Barbara Schwartz, Jennifer Selino, Arlene Trinidad, and Peter Yelda for their friendship. And a special thank-you goes to the Ragdale Foundation in Lake Forest, Illinois, where the creative process is held in high regard.

Most of all I am grateful to my husband, Robert Boghosian, and my late mother, Bernadine Hays-Gates, for understanding that this book was an important and worthwhile endeavor and for believing that I was the person to write it.

Index

Credits

About the Author

Beth Gates Warren is an independent scholar and consultant in the field of fine art photography. Formerly the director of the Photographs Department at Sotheby's auction house, she writes and lectures widely on photography-related topics and is the author of *Margrethe Mather and Edward Weston: A Passionate Collaboration*, which accompanied an exhibition she curated on Weston and Mather's work for the Santa Barbara Museum of Art. She has also served on a number of advisory boards and taught photography connoisseurship courses at the International Center of Photography in New York.